Praise for Best Places

"Best Places *are the best regional restaurant and guide books in America.*"
—THE SEATTLE TIMES

"Best Places *covers must-see portions of the West Coast with style and authority. In-the-know locals offer thorough info on restaurants, lodgings, and the sights.*"
—NATIONAL GEOGRAPHIC TRAVELER

"*. . . travelers swear by the recommendations in the* Best Places *guidebooks . . .*"
—SUNSET MAGAZINE

"*For travel collections covering the Northwest, the* Best Places *series takes precedence over all similar guides.*"
—BOOKLIST

"Best Places Northwest *is the bible of discriminating travellers to BC, Washington and Oregon. It promises, and delivers, the best of everything in the region.*"
—THE VANCOUVER SUN

"*Not only the best travel guide in the region, but maybe one of the most definitive guides in the country, which many look forward to with the anticipation usually sparked by a best-selling novel. A browser's delight, the book* [Best Places Northwest] *should be chained to dashboards throughout the Northwest.*"
—THE OREGONIAN

"*Still the region's undisputed heavyweight champ of guidebooks.*"
—SEATTLE POST-INTELLIGENCER

"*Trusting the natives is usually good advice, so visitors to Washington, Oregon, and British Columbia would do well to pick up* Best Places Northwest *for an exhaustive review of food and lodging in the region. . . . An indispensable glove-compartment companion.*"
—TRAVEL AND LEISURE

"Best Places Southern California *is just about all the inspiration you need to start planning your next road trip or summer vacation with the kids.*"
—THE FRESNO BEE

"Best Places Alaska *is the one guide to recommend to anyone visiting Alaska for the first or one-hundredth time.*"
—KETCHIKAN DAILY NEWS

"Best Places Northern California *is great fun to read even if you're not going anywhere.*"
—SAN FRANCISCO CHRONICLE

TRUST THE LOCALS

The original insider's guides, written by local experts

COMPLETELY INDEPENDENT

- No advertisers
- No sponsors
- No favors

EVERY PLACE STAR-RATED & RECOMMENDED

★★★★   The very best in the region

★★★   Distinguished; many outstanding features

★★   Excellent; some wonderful qualities

★   A good place

NO STARS   Worth knowing about, if nearby

MONEY-BACK GUARANTEE

We're so sure you'll be satisfied, we guarantee it!

HELPFUL ICONS

Watch for these quick-reference symbols throughout the book:

 FAMILY FUN

 GOOD VALUE

 ROMANTIC

 UNIQUELY NORTHWEST

BEST PLACES®

NORTHWEST

Edited by
GISELLE SMITH

EDITION 13

SASQUATCH BOOKS
SEATTLE

Printed in the United States of America
Distributed in Canada by Raincoast Books Ltd.

Thirteenth edition
03 02 01 00   5 4 3 2 1

ISBN: 1-57061-250-1
ISSN: 1041-2484

Series editor: Kate Rogers
Cover and interior design: Nancy Gellos
Maps: GreenEye Design

SPECIAL SALES

BEST PLACES guidebooks are available at special discounts on bulk purchases for corporate, club, or organization sales promotions, premiums, and gifts. Special editions, including personalized covers, excerpts of existing guides, and corporate imprints, can be created in large quantities for specific needs. For more information, contact your local bookseller or Special Sales, BEST PLACES Guidebooks, 615 Second Avenue, Suite 260, Seattle, Washington 98104, 800/775-0817.

SASQUATCH BOOKS
615 Second Avenue
Seattle, WA 98104
206/467-4300
books@SasquatchBooks.com
www.SasquatchBooks.com

CONTENTS

Oregon

British Columbia

Contributors

LES CAMPBELL has written for the Vancouver, Washington, *Columbian* news-paper and frequently spends vacations exploring southwest Washington. On trips for this book, Les left his heart—and much of the original front end of his car—in the region.

A longtime fan of this book, **KIM CARLSON** wishes there were a Best Places guide to North America. She is editor of *Best Places Portland*, and is a freelance wordsmith and stay-home parent the rest of the time. She authored the Portland chapter in this edition.

JACK CHRISTIE is author of five regional outdoor recreation guides, including *Inside Out British Columbia*. He welcomes inquisitive guests to visit his home on the Internet: www.jackchristie.com.

Frequent Best Places contributor **RICHARD FENCSAK** is a food, fitness, and travel writer, and bike store owner in Astoria, Oregon. His "Mouth of the Columbia" restaurant column appears weekly in the *Daily Astorian* newspaper, and his "Day Tripper" column can be found in the Friday *Oregonian*.

Longtime Seattle freelance writer **NICK GALLO**, who wrote about the North Cascades for this edition, has covered the Northwest for *People* magazine and a variety of travel publications and Web sites.

JAN HALLIDAY is a regular contributor to Best Places, and the author of *Best Places Destinations: San Juan & Gulf Islands* and *Native Peoples of the Northwest*. She covered the south Oregon Coast, the valleys of Southern Oregon, and the length of Highway 97 for this edition.

SUSAN G. HAUSER regularly brags about the Northwest in the *Wall Street Journal* and the *New York Times*, so it was easy for her to pick out favorite spots in one of the most beautiful places on earth, the Columbia River Gorge–Mount Hood area.

Eugene writer and editor **BONNIE HENDERSON**, a Portland native, knows her Willamette Valley territory well. An editor and travel writer for *Sunset* magazine since 1984, she is also the author of Oregon hiking guidebooks.

MICHAEL HOOD is a Northwest native who uses his experience as a chef and restaurateur to write about Seattle restaurants. An NPR commentator and political writer, he writes restaurant reviews and a food column for the *Seattle Post-Intelligencer*.

At press time, **JUDY JEWELL** was exploring southeastern Oregon's camp-grounds for her forthcoming guide, *Camping! Oregon*. The Portland resident, who covered Eastern Oregon for this edition, has written and contributed to several books about the Pacific Northwest.

LESLIE KELLY grew up in the Seattle area, but now almost feels settled after living in Spokane for 16 years. She loves being The *Spokesman-Review*'s restau-rant critic and wine columnist nearly as much as she enjoys traveling around the region and the world with her husband and daughter.

Washington native and Northwest explorer **JENA MACPHERSON** wrote about the Central Cascades and Puget Sound, two of her favorite areas. A former staff editor and regular contributor to *Sunset* magazine, she also writes for *Journey*, has contributed to several guidebooks, and is the author of a travel book on the Northwest.

VANESSA MCGRADY grew up popping huckleberries and slurping clams near her grandmother's Lilliwaup home on Hood Canal. She is currently an editor at *Alaska Airlines Magazine* and a contributor to regional and national magazines. She wrote the Olympic Peninsula chapter for this edition.

SHANNON O'LEARY didn't have to stray far to write the Seattle chapter, and that's just the way she likes it. The University of Washington grad and lifelong Northwest resident has been writing about the people and places of the Puget Sound area for magazines and guidebooks, including *Best Places Seattle*, for a dozen years. She's currently managing editor of *Washington Law & Politics* magazine.

MELISSA O'NEIL grew up on the "wet side" of the Pacific Northwest, but gladly traded evergreens and rain for sunshine and sagebrush in the Tri-Cities, Washington, nine years ago. She works for the *Tri-City Herald*.

DAVID SARASOHN is an associate editor and a longtime restaurant reviewer at *The Oregonian*. He has contributed to *Best Places Northwest* since Ronald Reagan was president, and authored the section on Portland restaurants in this edition.

ALISA SMITH wrote about her stomping grounds of Vancouver Island and the Gulf Islands. Long a resident of Victoria, she recently relocated to Vancouver, where she freelances for publications including *Outside*, *Chatelaine*, *Western Living*, *Wahine*, and the *Vancouver Sun*.

KASEY WILSON is a freelance food and travel writer, editor of *Best Places Vancouver*, and author of several cookbooks. The Restaurant Association of BC awarded her the Media-Person of the Year for Outstanding Reporting in the field of Hospitality. She has been featured on CNN, PBS, and NBC, and co-hosts a popular weekly radio show called "The Best of Food and Wine" on CFUN 1410 AM.

Thanks also go to contributors Anne Aurand, Penny Rawson, and Emma Waverman, and to fact checkers Caroline Cummins, Elisabeth Root, and Stacy Wilson. In addition, the efforts of series editor Kate Rogers, assistant editor Laura Gronewold, and the eagle eyes of copy editor Kris Fulsaas and proofreader Amy Smith Bell were invaluable.

GISELLE SMITH is a freelance writer and editor whose work has appeared in regional, travel, and health magazines. She is the former editor of *Seattle* magazine and an instructor at the University of Washington's continuing education program. She is also the editor of *Best Places Seattle*.

About Best Places® Guidebooks

People trust us. BEST PLACES guidebooks, which have been published continuously since 1975, represent one of the most respected regional travel series in the country. Each guide is written completely independently: no advertisers, no sponsors, no favors. Our reviewers know their territory, work incognito, and seek out the very best a city or region has to offer. Because we accept no free meals, accommodations, or other complimentary services, we are able to provide tough, candid reports about places that have rested too long on their laurels, and to delight in new places that deserve recognition. We describe the true strengths, foibles, and unique characteristics of each establishment listed.

Best Places Northwest is written by and for locals, and is therefore coveted by travelers. It's written for people who live here and who enjoy exploring the region's bounty and its out-of-the-way places of high character and individualism. It is these very characteristics that make *Best Places Northwest* ideal for tourists, too. The best places in and around the region are the ones that denizens favor: independently owned establishments of good value, touched with local history, run by lively individuals, and graced with natural beauty. With this thirteenth edition of *Best Places Northwest*, travelers will find the information they need: where to go and when, what to order, which rooms to request (and which to avoid), where the best music, art, nightlife, shopping, and other attractions are, and how to find the region's hidden secrets.

We're so sure you'll be satisfied with our guide, we guarantee it.

NOTE: *The reviews in this edition are based on information available at press time and are subject to change. Readers are advised that places listed may have closed or changed management, and, thus, may no longer be recommended by this series. The editors welcome information conveyed by users of this book. A report form is provided at the end of the book, and feedback is also welcome via email: books@SasquatchBooks.com.*

How to Use This Book

This book is divided into twenty major regions, encompassing Washington, Oregon, and British Columbia. All evaluations are based on numerous reports from local and traveling inspectors. BEST PLACES reporters do not identify themselves when they review an establishment, and they accept no free meals, accommodations, or any other services. Final judgments are made by the editors. **EVERY PLACE FEATURED IN THIS BOOK IS RECOMMENDED.**

STAR RATINGS Restaurants and lodgings are rated on a scale of zero to four stars (with half stars in between), based on uniqueness, loyalty of local clientele, performance measured against the establishment's goals, excellence of cooking, cleanliness, value, and professionalism of service. Reviews are listed alphabetically.

★★★★ The very best in the region

★★★ Distinguished; many outstanding features

★★ Excellent; some wonderful qualities

★ A good place

NO STARS Worth knowing about, if nearby

(For more on how we rate places, see the BEST PLACES Star Ratings box below.)

PRICE RANGE Prices for restaurants are based primarily on dinner for two, including dessert, tax, and tip (no alcohol). Prices for lodgings are based on peak season rates for one night's lodging for two people (i.e., double occupancy). Peak season is typically Memorial Day to Labor Day; off-season rates vary but can sometimes be significantly less. Call ahead to verify, as all prices are subject to change.

$$$$ Very expensive (more than $100 for dinner for two; more than $200 for one night's lodging for two)

$$$ Expensive (between $65 and $100 for dinner for two; between $120 and $200 for one night's lodging for two)

$$ Moderate (between $35 and $65 for dinner for two; between $75 and $120 for one night's lodging for two)

$ Inexpensive (less than $35 for dinner for two; less than $75 for one night's lodging for two)

RESERVATIONS (for Restaurants only)
We used one of the following terms for our reservations policy: reservations required, reservations recommended, reservations not necessary, reservations not accepted.

BEST PLACES® STAR RATINGS

Any travel guide that rates establishments is inherently subjective—and BEST PLACES is no exception. We rely on our professional experience, yes, but also on a gut feeling. And, occasionally, we even give in to a soft spot for a favorite neighborhood hangout. Our star-rating system is not simply a AAA-checklist; it's judgmental, critical, sometimes fickle, and highly personal. And unlike most other travel guides, we pay our own way and accept no freebies: no free meals or accommodations, no advertisers, no sponsors, no favors.

For each new edition, we send local food and travel experts out to review restaurants and lodgings anonymously, and then to rate them on a scale of zero to four. That doesn't mean a one-star establishment isn't worth dining or sleeping at—far from it. When we say that *all* the places listed in our books are recommended, we mean it. That one-star pizza joint may be just the ticket for the end of a whirlwind day of shopping with the kids. But if you're planning something more special, the star ratings can help you choose an eatery or hotel that will wow your new clients or be a stunning, romantic place to celebrate an anniversary or impress a first date.

We award four-star ratings sparingly, reserving them for what we consider truly the best. And once an establishment has earned our highest rating, everyone's expectations seem to rise. Readers often write us letters specifically to point out the faults in four-star establishments. With changes in chefs, management, styles, and trends, it's always easier to get knocked off the pedestal than to ascend it. Three-star establishments, on the other hand, seem to generate healthy praise. They exhibit outstanding qualities, and we get lots of love letters about them. The difference between two and three stars can sometimes be a very fine line. Two-star establishments are doing a good, solid job and gaining attention, while one-star places are often dependable spots that have been around forever.

The restaurants and lodgings described in *Best Places Northwest* have earned their stars from hard work and good service (and good food). They're proud to be included in this book—look for our BEST PLACES sticker in their windows. And we're proud to honor them in this, the thirteenth edition of *Best Places Northwest*.

ACCESS AND INFORMATION At the beginning of each chapter, you'll find general guidelines about how to get to a particular region and what types of transportation are available, as well as basic sources for any additional tourist information you might need. Also check individual town listings for specifics about visiting those places.

THREE-DAY TOURS In every chapter, we've included a quick-reference, three-day itinerary designed for travelers with a short amount of time. Perfect for weekend getaways, these tours outline the highlights of a region or town.

ADDRESSES AND PHONE NUMBERS Every attempt has been made to provide accurate information on an establishment's location and phone number, but it's always a good idea to call ahead and confirm. If an establishment has two area locations, we list both at the top of the review. If there are three or more locations, we list only the main address and indicate "other branches."

CHECKS AND CREDIT CARDS Many establishments that accept checks also require a major credit card for identification. Note that some places accept only local checks. Credit cards are abbreviated in this book as follows: American Express (AE); Bravo (B); Carte Blanche (CB); Diners Club (DC); Discover (DIS); Enroute (E); Japanese credit card (JCB); MasterCard (MC); Visa (V).

EMAIL AND WEB SITE ADDRESSES Email and Web site addresses for establishments have been included where available. Please note that the World Wide Web is a fluid and evolving medium, and that Web pages are often "under construction" or, as with all time-sensitive information, may no longer be valid.

MAPS AND DIRECTIONS Each chapter in the book begins with a regional map that shows the general area being covered. Throughout the book, basic directions are provided with each entry. Whenever possible, call ahead to confirm hours and location.

HELPFUL ICONS Watch for these quick-reference symbols throughout the book:

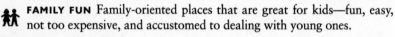 **FAMILY FUN** Family-oriented places that are great for kids—fun, easy, not too expensive, and accustomed to dealing with young ones.

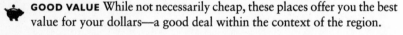 **GOOD VALUE** While not necessarily cheap, these places offer you the best value for your dollars—a good deal within the context of the region.

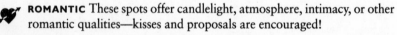 **ROMANTIC** These spots offer candlelight, atmosphere, intimacy, or other romantic qualities—kisses and proposals are encouraged!

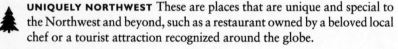 **UNIQUELY NORTHWEST** These are places that are unique and special to the Northwest and beyond, such as a restaurant owned by a beloved local chef or a tourist attraction recognized around the globe.

& Appears after listings for establishments that have wheelchair-accessible facilities.

INDEXES All restaurants, lodgings, town names, and major tourist attractions are listed alphabetically in the back of the book.

MONEY-BACK GUARANTEE Please see "We Stand by Our Reviews" at the end of this book.

READER REPORTS At the end of the book is a report form. We receive hundreds of reports from readers suggesting new places or agreeing or disagreeing with our assessments. They greatly help in our evaluations, and we encourage you to respond.

PORTLAND
AND ENVIRONS

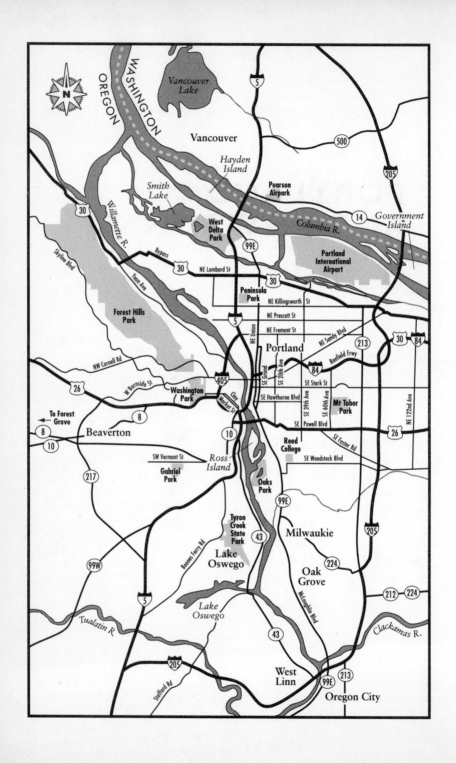

PORTLAND AND ENVIRONS

Portland has a stellar reputation among American cities. For years, people far and wide have taken its appeal for granted, whether they live here or not. But as the region's population continues to grow and shift, and we're in a new century, it seems a good time to ask, "Why?"

There are as many theories as there are theorists. Maybe it's Portland's nice size—not so big that it's an expedition to get downtown from the suburban or residential areas; not so small that there's nothing going on once you get there. Downtown Portland bustles with commerce and culture, and is an easy place to spend a few days—or a few years.

It could also be the people, a mix of lifelong Oregonians with strong opinions about such issues as salmon recovery, educational reform, and radical-minded newcomers; and newcomers, with their own strong opinions about salmon and schools—and about conservative old-timers. But what's heartening here is the way newcomers and old-timers—along with any lucky visitors who happen along—come together for classic events such as the Portland Rose Festival and the Mount Hood Festival of Jazz; nobody's a newcomer for long. Portlanders know how to throw a party when the occasion calls for it (a new millennium or a chance at the NBA championship, for instance), and they take seriously their civic responsibilities, as evidenced by the urban planning that's become a model for the country, a burgeoning arts scene, and an ever-expanding parks system.

Finally, Portland is undoubtedly enhanced by its location: it's a city with a river running through it; a pair of dramatic, volcanic mountains watching over it; and the lush and beautiful Willamette Valley spreading away from it to the south.

Of course, the City of Roses has detractors, and what many of them resent is the rain—buckets of it every year. True Oregonians don't mind, though; they just get out in the rain and play as hard as ever—or they curl up indoors with a book. Still, if you want to visit Portland when the weather is best, come in the late summer and early fall. The months of August, September, and October are usually glorious, but a few showers are needed to keep the place green all year.

ACCESS AND INFORMATION

PORTLAND INTERNATIONAL AIRPORT, or PDX (7000 NE Airport Wy; 503/460-4234; www.portlandairportpdx.com), is served by most major airlines, with excellent connections from points around the Pacific Northwest and beyond. But these days the airport is in a constant state of expansion, which can mean difficult parking and unexpected gate changes. Allow plenty of time, especially during rush hours, to get from airport to town—30 minutes at least—and the same on your return. All major **CAR RENTAL** companies operate from the airport. **TAXIS AND SHUTTLES** are readily available on the lower deck; expect to pay about $25 for the trip downtown. Another way to get from the airport to downtown (and back) is on the **GRAYLINE OF PORTLAND AIRPORT EXPRESS** (503/285-9845); cost is $12 one-way or $22 round trip, and buses leave every half hour. Two routes cover downtown hotels; check with the driver before you board to be sure you're on the right bus. The most economical ($1.15) trip into the city is via **TRI-MET** (503/238-7433). Catch bus number 12 outside the baggage claim area; the ride downtown takes about 45 minutes, along Sandy Boulevard. In 2001, the light rail system is expected to service the airport.

Most drivers reach Portland via either Interstate 5, which runs north-south, or Interstate 84 (east-west). US Highway 26 goes to Beaverton; Interstate 205 loops off Interstate 5 and passes near Lake Oswego, West Linn, Oregon City, and Milwaukie, among other towns. Rush hours in Portland can mean standstill traffic, but if you arrive midday (after 9am, but before 3pm) or after 7pm, you should have clear sailing into town.

AMTRAK (800/872-7245, 503/273-4866 locally) operates out of the lovely Union Station (800 NW 6th Ave) just north of downtown Portland. With its prominent tower, great curving entrance, and muscular features, this romantic structure memorializes the bygone era of the great railways. Trains come and go from points north, east, and south daily. The nearby **GREYHOUND** station (550 NW 6th Ave; 800/231-2222 or 503/243-2357) has a complete daily schedule of buses. Both train station and bus station are within walking distance (about 12 blocks) of downtown, where Tri-Met buses pick up passengers for trips to most suburbs in the metro area.

Portland

Portland has much to offer, and its increasing number of citizens make the most of it. The nationally noted light-rail service goes east to Gresham, west to Beaverton, and in fall 2001 will reach the airport. A cultural district downtown is home to a jewel of a performing arts center, a first-class art museum, and a historical center with an exhibit for every age, all located along a greenbelt called the **SOUTH PARK BLOCKS**, which run from Portland State University north to Salmon Street. In the lively downtown core, lunchtime concerts entertain summer weekday crowds at **PIONEER COURTHOUSE SQUARE** (at SW Broadway and SW Yamhill Sts), and a shopping complex stars Saks Fifth Avenue. Also here are a major convention center, a beautifully refurbished main library, and stunning digs for one of the city's favorite places: the **OREGON MUSEUM OF SCIENCE AND INDUSTRY** (see Major Attractions, below).

ACCESS AND INFORMATION

TRI-MET (503/238-7433) operates the city bus system and the sleek Metropolitan Area Express (MAX) light-rail trains; tickets for the two are interchangeable. Almost all bus lines run through the Portland Transit Mall (SW 5th and 6th Aves); MAX lines also pass through downtown. You can ride free downtown in "Fareless Square," a 300-block area; from the downtown to most outlying neighborhoods, you'll need a two-zone ticket ($1.15), which you can purchase on the bus (exact change only) or at MAX stops.

PORTLAND THREE-DAY TOUR

DAY ONE: Spend this first day exploring downtown Portland. King salmon hash at the **Heathman Restaurant and Bar** is a tasteful—and tasty—way to begin your day. If coffee and a pastry are all you need, head to **Pazzoria** (next to Pazzo). After breakfast, stretch your legs along the elm-lined **South Park Blocks.** Art lovers should then go to the **Portland Art Museum,** history buffs to the **Oregon History Center,** and shoppers to **Pioneer Place.** For lunch, stop for a sandwich at **Red Star Tavern & Roast House.** In the afternoon, catch an art film at the **Koin Cinemas** (SW 3rd Ave and SW Clay St; 503/225-5555 ext 4608 for recorded film schedules), but save time for **Powell's City of Books.** Make a dinner reservation at either **Higgins**—where local ingredients receive reverential treatment—or, if you're in the mood for top-drawer Mexican cuisine, **Cafe Azul.** Check in to the opulent **Heathman Hotel,** or the **5th Avenue Suites.**

DAY TWO: Excellent breakfasts are the norm at **Zell's: An American Cafe,** or for lighter fare have a cuppa joe and pastry at local coffee roastery **Coffee People** (737 SW Salmon; 503/227-1794). After breakfast, explore some of the parks in the city's pastoral West Hills: the views are dramatic from the **Washington Park International Rose Test Garden** or the **Japanese Garden.** For a bit more of a workout, hike through **Hoyt Arboretum** on the Wildwood Trail (start near the **Oregon Zoo**—itself an intriguing place to walk). Later, browse the boutiques and shops along **NW 23rd and 21st Avenues.** For outstanding Thai food, stop in for lunch at **Typhoon!** or make your way down NW 23rd Avenue for a salad and voluptuous dessert at **Papa Haydn.** Spend the afternoon in the **Pearl District**'s art galleries and shops. Reserve ahead for dinner at **Paley's Place** or **Wildwood.**

DAY THREE: Jump in the car; this is a day to see the outlying parts of the city. A late breakfast at the **Original Pancake House** is popular with everybody and will keep you going through the afternoon (expect to wait for a table, though service is snappy once you're seated). Then head to historic **Oregon City,** where you catch the multimedia presentation at the **End of the Oregon Trail Interpretive Center.** For dinner it's back to Portland to board a river cruise on the *Portland Spirit* from Tom McCall Waterfront Park. Late night, check out the eclectic music offerings at **Berbati's Pan** or the **Aladdin Theatre.**

MAJOR ATTRACTIONS

Portland is home to many small museums, but here are a couple of the larger ones: OMSI, the **OREGON MUSEUM OF SCIENCE AND INDUSTRY** (1945 SE Water; 503/797-4000), is an engaging place to take the whole family. There's a submarine moored in the Willamette to board, an IMAX theater, fascinating exhibits, even a toddler room. The **OREGON HISTORY CENTER** (1200 SW Park; 503/222-1741) pays tribute to our ancestors—Native Americans, white settlers, seafarers, and others. Its gift shop is first-rate. Not exactly a museum, but having an impressive (living) collection nonetheless, is the **OREGON ZOO** (4001 SW Canyon Rd; 503/225-1561), where myriad exhibits include many species common to the Pacific Northwest; ride MAX for an easy trip from downtown.

During the month of June, the city's roses—and its **ROSE FESTIVAL**—are in full bloom. Highlights of this monthlong extravaganza include three parades, the largest of which is the Grand Floral Parade; an air show; a carnival in Tom McCall Waterfront Park; the Festival of Flowers, for which Pioneer Courthouse Square is transformed with some 25,000 potted plants; and, of course, a world-class rose show.

TOM MCCALL WATERFRONT PARK, on the west side of the Willamette River, which flows right through town, is the perfect place for a run or stroll. The *Portland Spirit* (503/226-2517) docks here. **FOREST PARK**, northwest of the city, is a wilder option. And finally, the old warehouse district north of downtown (between NW 15th Ave and NW Broadway, and NW Lovejoy and NW Burnside) is now the **PEARL DISTRICT**, the gentrified home of art galleries, restaurants, and shops—as well as **POWELL'S CITY OF BOOKS**, the country's largest bookstore (see "City of Books" in this chapter).

GALLERIES AND MUSEUMS

Gallery walks once a month (on "First Thursdays") encourage visitors to expose themselves to art; galleries, clustered in the Pearl District or downtown, are among the hot showcases of both local and national work. The **PORTLAND ART MUSEUM** (1219 SW Park Ave; 503/226-2811) is the big name for exhibits of international acclaim; PAM has hosted many "blockbuster" shows, some of which require no small amount of political effort to bring to Portland—such as an exhibit on the tombs of China; work by Dale Chihuly; and Empire of the Sultans, Ottoman art from the Khalili Collection. Check out the smaller **CONTEMPORARY CRAFTS GALLERY** (3934 SW Corbett; 503/223-2654), an especially good place to purchase a unique gift of art, which might show chess sets by various artists, contemporary basketry, quilts, and affordable ceramics, as well as more costly sculpture.

The city is popping with public art, too; pick up the "Public Art: Walking Tour" booklet, free at the **REGIONAL ARTS & CULTURE COUNCIL** (620 SW Main, Ste 420; 503/823-5111) to hunt down these treasures. Pioneer Courthouse Square, at SW Broadway and SW Yamhill Streets, is a good place to begin, and the stunningly renovated **CENTRAL LIBRARY** (801 SW 10th Ave; 503/248-5123) is a great place to end.

PARKS AND GARDENS

Besides the sprawling and primitive **FOREST PARK** (see Sports and Recreation, below), there are nearly 150 other parks in the city, and **WASHINGTON PARK** (503/823-7529) is home to several of them. The **HOYT ARBORETUM** (503/228-8733), close to the Oregon Zoo (see Major Attractions, above), has an impressive collection of native and exotic flora and well-kept trails. More formal grounds are the **INTERNATIONAL ROSE TEST GARDEN** (503/823-3636), the **JAPANESE GARDEN** (503/223-1321), and, across town, the **CRYSTAL SPRINGS RHODODENDRON GARDEN** (503/823-3640). Also in Washington Park is the largest memorial of its kind in the nation, the **VIETNAM VETERANS' LIVING MEMORIAL**, an inspiring outdoor cathedral commemorating the Oregon victims of that conflict. It's possible for a person to walk from one of these parks to another, without really realizing it, so continuous is their reach of trails through Portland's West Hills. Although parts of Washington Park have a wild, overgrown feeling, much of it is well tended. Forest Park, on the other hand, is not a manicured park at all, but is rather a "wilderness" for the city.

SHOPPING

A few uniquely Portland shops not to miss: **POWELL'S CITY OF BOOKS** (1005 W Burnside; 503/228-4651), which is legendary for its number of volumes, both new and used; **TWIST** (30 NW 23rd Pl; 503/224-0334), where jewelry and folk art rise to new heights of function and form; **MADE IN OREGON** (10 NW 1st; 503/273-8354; and branches), where such names as Jantzen and Pendleton get top billing; and **KITCHEN KABOODLE** (NW 23rd and Flanders; 503/241-4040; and branches), where you can pick up anything from an egg timer to a chenille sofa.

Crafts—and a carnival atmosphere—can be found weekends at **SATURDAY MARKET** under the Burnside Bridge (closed Jan–Feb). Upscale specialty shops and eateries are found downtown, many in the area around Pioneer Courthouse Square, including the new, second phase of **PIONEER PLACE** (between SW Morrison and Yamhill, and SW 3rd and 5th). Across the river near the Convention Center is **LLOYD CENTER MALL** (between NE Halsey and Multnomah, and NE 9th and 15th), with its beloved ice-skating rink. Posh **NW 23RD AVENUE**, the arty **PEARL DISTRICT** (north of Burnside between 9th and 14th), and countercultural **SE HAWTHORNE BOULEVARD** (between 20th and 45th) are must-visits for shoppers. You may also want to check out **SELLWOOD**, southeast of downtown, across the Sellwood bridge; it's an entire neighborhood of antique stores.

PERFORMING ARTS

Portlanders pack the city's beloved **ARLENE SCHNITZER CONCERT HALL** (1000 SW Broadway) 52 weeks a year; contact the box office in the Portland Center for the Performing Arts (PCPA; 1111 SW Broadway; 503/796-9293) to see what's playing. A variety of performers—classical, jazz, and rock—play the "Schnitz" each season; the essential house "given" is the OREGON SYMPHONY ORCHESTRA (503/228-1353), under conductor James DePreist. Classical music fans should also know about CHAMBER MUSIC NORTHWEST (522 SW 5th Ave, Ste 725; 503/294-6400; www.cmnw.org), which presents a five-week summer festival spanning four centuries of music, with events throughout the season in various venues.

The PCPA's resident theater company, PORTLAND CENTER STAGE (1111 SW Broadway; 503/274-6588; www.pcs.org), offers excellent production values, whatever the play. You can always be assured of work by Shakespeare with productions by TYGRES HEART (503/288-8400), housed in the same facility. Plays by ARTISTS REPERTORY THEATRE (ART), staged at the new REIERSGAARD THEATRE (1516 SW Alder St; 503/241-1278), often garner critical praise, and many (though not all) would pick ART as their first choice for theater in Portland; the best actors work here and the season is usually thoughtfully put together.

The OREGON BALLET THEATER (Civic Auditorium, 222 SW Clay St; 503/222-5538) enlists youth and daring to serve the needs of Portland's ballet fans. Other companies schedule performances, but if the nonprofit WHITE BIRD organization in particular is promoting a performance, check it out (at various venues; call 503/245-1600 for information).

NIGHTLIFE

Check local newspapers' calendar listings for what's happening in the popular music world (*Willamette Week* is out each Wednesday; the *Oregonian's* Friday A&E section is also a good source). Rock fans get their licks at BERBATI'S PAN (10 SW 3rd; 503/248-4579) or LALUNA (215 SE 9th; 503/241-5862), while folkies hang at the ALADDIN THEATRE (3017 SE Milwaukie; 503/233-1994). If you feel like dancing, head to the refurbished CRYSTAL BALLROOM (1332 W Burnside; 503/778-5625), where the music—anything from reggae to ballroom—starts at 9pm. Check out the BRAZEN BEAN (2075 NW Glisan; 503/294-0636), where the posh ambience lends itself to something icy cold served up in an elegant glass; or JAKE'S FAMOUS CRAWFISH (401 SW 12th; 503/226-1419), where people have been bellying up to the bar for more than a century.

Some cities sport sports bars, but Portlanders love brewpubs. One longtime favorite is the BRIDGEPORT BREW PUB (1313 NW Marshall; 503/241-7179), where you can eat renowned pizza and hoist a classic Portland microbrew in a casual, noisy atmosphere.

SPORTS AND RECREATION

The town's big-league action can be found at the still shiny ROSE GARDEN ARENA (1 Center Ct), a huge dome easily visible from Interstate 5 and home of the NBA's PORTLAND TRAIL BLAZERS (Ticketmaster: 503/224-4400). The Trail Blazers usually make the playoffs, although they haven't won the championship since 1977. The **PORTLAND WINTER HAWKS** (503/238-6366), of the Western Hockey League, play at the Memorial Coliseum or Rose Garden Arena and hit the ice 36 times a season at home. Baseball fans are still waiting for the major league, but content themselves with the **PORTLAND ROCKIES** (503/223-2837)—who play to loyal crowds at **CIVIC STADIUM** (SW 20th Ave and SW Morrison St).

Individual sports thrive in the region: runners, hikers, and mountain bikers have access to more than 50 miles of trails in primitive 5,000-acre **FOREST PARK** (503/823-7529), easily accessed at points throughout the west hills. One easy access is on Leif Erikson Drive; park at the end of NW Thurman. A good map of Forest Park is a must; the **AUDUBON'S NATURE STORE** (5151 NW Cornell Rd; 503/292-9453) is a great resource for maps and information. Rowers are guaranteed miles of flat water on the Willamette; and cyclists make use of hundreds of miles of off- and on-street paved bike paths in the greater Portland area.

RESTAURANTS

Al-Amir / ★★

223 SW STARK ST, PORTLAND; 503/274-0010

The exterior decorations on the old Bishop's House may clash some with this restaurant's interior, which exudes Middle Eastern warmth, but the menu resolves everything. In Portland's most elaborate and satisfying Lebanese restaurant, the smoky, intense baba ghanouj and the creamy hummus are outstanding, but the kitchen's reach is extensive. It does a particularly savory job on meats. The shish kebab, lamb vibrant with spices and juices, highlights a menu that stretches to *kharouf muammar*, a huge pile of moist, faintly sweet lamb chunks, and *dujaj musahab*, a charcoal-grilled chicken breast in lemon and olive oil. Don't depart without trying the grape leaves. A little Lebanese beer makes the light through the bishop's stained-glass windows shine even more brightly. *$$; AE, MC, V; local checks only; lunch Mon–Fri, dinner every day; full bar; reservations recommended; between NW 3rd and 4th.* ♿

Alexis / ★★

215 W BURNSIDE, PORTLAND; 503/224-8577

This boisterous institution of a Greek restaurant is a family operation that makes every diner feel like a cousin: the welcome here is warmer than the flaming *saganaki* (Greek cheese ignited with ouzo). On their journey toward substantial, fork-tender lamb dishes and other entrees, diners are slowed by plump grape-leaf packets, terrific calamari, and the little pillows of phyllo and feta known as tiropetes. Be entertained by the appetizers, but don't fill up on them; moussaka and lamb souvlaki await, and you wouldn't want to miss them. Baskets of addictive warm house bread come with the meal—and if you like what you taste, take heart: Alexis sells it retail, along with other specialties. The food could even distract you from the belly dancers on weekends. *$$; AE, DC,*

MC, V; local checks only; lunch Mon–Fri, dinner every day; full bar; reservations not necessary; between NW 2nd and 3rd. &

Bread and Ink Cafe / ★★

3610 SE HAWTHORNE BLVD, PORTLAND; 503/239-4756

If a restaurant could survive just on the strength of its blintzes, the beloved Bread and Ink would be it. Sure, there are lots of other striking dishes in this homey, high-ceilinged bistro in the heart of the funky Hawthorne district— sizable sandwiches, impressive baked desserts including a legendary cassata, and a serious hamburger, with homemade condiments that do it justice. With intriguing framed line drawings on the walls, crayons on the table, and huge windows onto Hawthorne, the place has become a neighborhood landmark for good reason. But the blintzes, delicately crisped squares of dough enfolding cheese, are hallowed—especially with Bread and Ink's raspberry jam. Even after changes in kitchen and ownership, the restaurant has a powerful identity, especially at breakfast and lunch. Dinners, with serious efforts such as ancho-blackberry duck, also have fans. *$$; AE, MC, V; checks OK; breakfast, lunch, dinner Mon–Sat, brunch Sun; beer and wine; reservations recommended; at SE 36th.* &

Cafe Azul / ★★★

112 NW 9TH AVE, PORTLAND; 503/525-4422

Ever since Clair Archibald brought her skillful, strikingly authentic Mexican cuisine from McMinnville to the Pearl District, this restaurant has been rising in local estimation. Now the warm, high-ceilinged room draws a stream of diners eager for thick, rich moles; prawns rubbed with achiote and garlic paste; and corn-husk-wrapped tamales filled with wild mushrooms, or chicken and plantain. Choose from a range of different, carefully described tequilas, and accompany it with a handmade corn tortilla taco filled with Yucatan-style pork. Flavors are vivid and unexpected, with punchy chiles and unusual salsas. The creativity spreads buoyantly into dessert, with options such as a red banana ice cream sundae with chocolate crust, caramel, and candied peanuts. This is more than you're accustomed to spending for Mexican food, but you've probably never had Mexican food like this. If getting a reservation poses a problem, consider the diminutive bar, where the company is usually good. *$$$; DIS, MC, V; checks OK; dinner Tues–Sat; full bar; reservations recommended; between NW Couch and Davis.* &

Cafe des Amis / ★★★

1987 NW KEARNEY ST, PORTLAND; 503/295-6487

People often come to Dennis Baker's polished little restaurant knowing what they'll order before they sit down. Specialties are legendary: Dungeness crab cakes; fillet of beef in port garlic sauce; salmon in a sorrel sauce; duck in blackberry sauce. Diners are more likely to have a hunger for a favorite than to wonder what's new. They're also drawn by cobblers and fruit tarts that look like they've just been glazed in a Boulevard St. Germain patisserie. Specials, such as a melting lamb shank, can also warm the diner. For true bistro status, this cozy, intimate cafe tucked onto a northwest Portland residential street would need only outdoor tables—and a climate change, but not even Baker could cook up that. *$$–$$$; AE, MC, V; checks OK; dinner Mon–Sat; full bar; reservations recommended; at NW 20th.* ⅃

Caffe Mingo / ★★
807 NW 21ST AVE, PORTLAND; 503/226-4646
The dishes that made this tiny, exquisite trattoria an immediate smash when it opened a few years ago are still a draw. Diners eagerly wait in line for the spiedini with prawns and croutons, the Gorgonzola and walnut *raviolini*, and the Northwest mushrooms roasted in parchment. But Caffe Mingo has gotten a bit more ambitious, with items such as grilled rare tuna with tapenade, and spaghetti with hot pepper flakes and shrimp. (You can also now spend $100 on the reserve wine list.) Still, it remains a solid, inviting version of Italian cafe cuisine, and the somewhat expanded menu—and prices—still won't put a deep dent in your wallet. A seat in back gets you a close-up view of the kitchen preparing your dinner; a seat in front just lets you watch people waiting for your table. *$$; AE, MC, V; local checks only; dinner every day; beer and wine; reservations recommended for 6 or more; between NW Johnson and Kearney.* ⅃

Caprial's Bistro / ★★
7015 SE MILWAUKIE AVE, PORTLAND; 503/236-6457
In recent years Caprial Pence has expanded her reach in lots of different directions, from broadcast of her national public television cooking show to the publication of ever more cookbooks—to enlarging her restaurant. The original storefront is now a larger, warmer, more colorful space, with big soft chairs and walls as flashy as the cuisine. A night's offerings might include wok-steamed fish with a persimmon compound butter, or a pan-seared duck breast with a pomegranate glaze. There's still the Hot as Hell Chicken at lunch (grilled chicken with chile sauce over pungent peanut-sauced pasta) and creative sandwiches and salads. Mark Dowers has brought additional skills to the kitchen, and Melissa Carey is an impressive dessert chef; try the raspberry/blackberry linzertorte with caramel sauce. The menus shift but never stray far from the Northwest. The walls are lined with a sizable retail wine supply; a $2 corkage fee gets any bottle from the shelf to your table. *$$; MC, V; checks OK; lunch, dinner Tues–Sat; beer and wine; reservations recommended; in Westmoreland.* ⅃

Castagna / ★★
1752 SE HAWTHORNE BLVD, PORTLAND; 503/231-7373
The design of this precise new restaurant is spare and direct, but the cuisine is strikingly artful. Monique Siu, one of the founding troika of Zefiro, has devised a menu that uses flavors strongly and creates powerful but not overcomplicated

AN EMPIRE BUILT ON BEER

Most cities in the world have McDonald's; for that matter, Portland has McDonald's. But Portland also has **McMenamin's**, and when it comes to choosing a Big Mac, fries, and a Coke at the Golden Arches or choosing a Communication Breakdown Burger, fries, and a glass of Terminator Ale at the **Hillsdale Brewery and Pub** (1505 SW Sunset Blvd; 503/246-3938), there's no contest. McMenamin pubs—and there are dozens in the greater Portland area—are old-fashioned, art-filled hangouts, where you meet friends and linger long into the evening to the strains of the Grateful Dead, for instance, or take the family down the street for a quick dinner.

Brothers Brian and Mike McMenamin have been making handmade ales for a couple of decades now, but you won't find their brews in your grocer's cooler; they are sold only in the McMenamin pubs—and McMenamin hotels, movie theaters, and dance halls. McMenamins' diverse establishments are tied together by a comfortable, quirky, slightly mystic decorating scheme, including paintings created by artists who are members of the McMenamin's staff.

One of the special things these guys do, besides provide appealing, mostly non-smoking spots for Portlanders to get out of the rain, is refurbish old, dilapidated buildings. Several sites are on the National Register of Historic Places and have interesting histories. **Edgefield** (2126 SW Halsey, Troutdale; 503/669-8610), for example, a "destination resort" (20 minutes from downtown Portland) was a former poor farm; the **Kennedy School** (5736 NE 33rd Ave, Portland; 503/249-3983) in northeast Portland was a grade school; and the **Grand Lodge** (3505 Pacific Ave, Forest Grove; 503/992-9533) in Forest Grove was the former Masonic and Eastern Star Home.

You may not appreciate the ambience of every McMenamin establishment, but chances are great that if you're in Portland long enough, you'll find one you like well enough to visit again. Check out **www.mcmenamins.com** for more information, including menus, current movie offerings, and room rates. —*Kim Carlson*

effects. Sautéed quail filled with chanterelles and thyme is rich and pungent, the meat heightened and never overwhelmed. Grated fresh horseradish makes a potent impact on Alaskan salmon, but the fish is so deftly prepared that it stands up to it. Siu has created a comfortable restaurant, with the drama of the hottest new places but less of the overpowering noise level. Zefiro was a key player in the formation of NW 21st Avenue's restaurant row; Castagna may help elevate the heat along Hawthorne, but the exterior, like the rest of the Castagna experience, is understated. *$$$; AE, MC, V; no checks; dinner Tues–Sat; full bar; reservations recommended; at SE 17th.* &

Couvron / ★★★

1126 SW 18TH AVE, PORTLAND; 503/225-1844

This 32-seat, award-winning upper-upper-scale restaurant gets more and more elaborate, but Tony Demes's skills can keep up with it. Couvron now offers three seasonally changing, prix-fixe menus: vegetarian at $65, seven-course at $75, and nine-course Chef's Grand Menu at $95. Presentation is as elaborate as the menu—each dish is highly architectural, stacked into hillocks or condominiums—and the descriptions equally so. Diners might choose between "pan-roasted Maine diver scallops served with crème fraîche, melted leeks, hand-pressed herb pasta, and lobster glaze" or "cherrywood-smoked Oregon quail served with a salad of assorted autumn garden vegetables with summer truffles, Italian white truffle oil, and port sauce." Demes is particular about all of his ingredients, flying in seafood from Maine and selecting local organic vegetables. He makes it all work; a several-hour meal here is lovely and inviting, right down to the closing chocolate afterthoughts. It's also heartening to see a place with a cheese course. The dining rooms may feel a bit small and crowded, but the location is striking—Couvron is directly on the new west-side light-rail line, and really deserves its own station. *$$$; AE, MC, V; local checks only; dinner Tues–Sat; beer and wine; reservations required; between SW Salmon and Madison.*

Esparza's Tex-Mex Café / ★★★

2725 SE ANKENY ST, PORTLAND; 503/234-7909

People may wonder how a Tex-Mex restaurant has become a landmark in Portland—but the question doesn't survive the first visit, or the first smoked beef brisket taco. By then, new visitors have been educated by a restaurant resembling a San Antonio garage sale, with a stunning jukebox and a sweeping array of tequila bottles. It's a challenge deciding which tequila goes with the Cowboy Tacos, filled with thick slabs of smoked sirloin, barbecue sauce, guacamole, and *pico de gallo*, or the Uvalde, a smoked lamb enchilada, or some *nopalitos*—the best cactus appetizer around. The menu and specials have the reach of Texas—from red snapper to smoked pork loin stuffed with spiced buffalo and ostrich, to calves'-brains tacos. Watch the blackboard—and the faces of other diners—to catch the latest inspiration of Joe Esparza. Esparza's is so much fun, you might not appreciate how good it is—and so good, you might not realize how much fun you're having. *$$; AE, MC, V; no checks; lunch, dinner Tues–Sat; full bar; reservations recommended for large parties; at SE 28th.* &

Fong Chong / ★★

301 NW 4TH AVE, PORTLAND; 503/220-0235

In a three-block stretch of Portland's Chinatown, there are now enough dim sum places to cause serving-cart gridlock, but it's not just Fong Chong's historical reputation as the local shining dim sum star that should make you maneuver to this one. Along with vibrant humbao buns and addictive sticky rice in a lotus leaf, you might find something surprising, such as shallot dumplings—and implausible but heartwarming pork cookies. The much larger House of Louie, under the same ownership, is across the street. But whether it's the Chinese grocery next door, or because the place is crowded and loud, or because watching the carts maneuver through the tables is like watching the Super Mario Brothers, we like Fong Chong better. It's fun, inexpensive, and impressively tasty. At night, Fong Chong is transformed into a quiet Cantonese eatery, with average preparations and a few surprises. *$; MC, V; no checks; lunch, dinner every day; full bar; reservations not necessary; at NW Everett.* &

Genoa / ★★★★

2832 SE BELMONT ST, PORTLAND; 503/238-1464

Dinner here always begins with a reverent recitation, and just describing the dishes feels good in the mouth: maybe quail stuffed with pancetta, juniper berries, and sage, flamed with gin, and served on grilled bread spread with a chicken liver pâté. At Genoa, that would be the fifth course; a diner would already have enjoyed antipasto; bruschetta with mussels; a soup of deep fish stock; lasagne with artichoke hearts; and maybe a fish course of sautéed calamari. The elaborate, minuetlike seven-course meals (with a fewer-course option on weekdays) change every two weeks, and for almost 30 years Portlanders have been returning to see what's up next. Chef and co-owner Cathy Whims has been leading Genoa to ever new triumphs, including cooking a Columbus Day dinner at James Beard House in New York. It's a special-occasion restaurant; diners may have to spend some time training for the three-hour meal (with no choices except entree and dessert), and some time recovering from it. But at least once or twice in the meal, Genoa will stun you—often at the pasta course, which could be *ravioli di zucca*, thin sheets enfolding squash, sweet potato, and biscotti crumbs. Looking for highlights, it doesn't seem fair even to count the powerhouse dessert tray, with a double-digit range of choices from homemade pear ice cream with caramel to a creation that mixes fruit and chocolate into a result as intricate as a palazzo. The famously dark dining room has lightened a bit—although it's still Portland's immediate image of an intimate dinner. *$$$; AE, DC, MC, V; checks OK; dinner Mon–Sat; beer, wine, and apéritifs; reservations required; at SE 29th.* &

The Heathman Restaurant and Bar / ★★★★

1009 SW BROADWAY, PORTLAND; 503/241-4100

Philippe Boulot, who came to Portland by way of Paris and New York, has produced a consistently impressive kitchen to go with a dining room that continues to be the center of Portland power breakfasts and lunches.

After making strong statements about Northwest cuisine, such as a stirring salmon in pesto crust with a shard of crisp salmon skin planted on top, Boulot has returned to his Gallic roots. That means leg of lamb cooked for seven hours, and Alsatian stuffed veal breast. Also on the menu are Northwestern dishes such as roast venison wrapped in smoked bacon, or the consistently appearing—and appealing—crab cakes in a red curry butter sauce. King salmon hash prevails at breakfast, and lunch produces its own creations, including rich soups, pungent salads, and heartening stews. Evenings bring jazz, and brandy from upstairs and downstairs bars. All possible excuses should be sought for the dessert creations of Boulot's wife, Susan, precise and passionate patissier, such as a recent chocolate pear tart with pear brandy sauce and *dulce de leche* ice cream. Boulot regularly brings in friends, visiting chefs from France and New York. *$$$; AE, DC, MC, V; checks OK; breakfast, lunch, dinner every day; full bar; reservations recommended; at SW Salmon.* &

Higgins / ★★★

1239 SW BROADWAY, PORTLAND; 503/222-9070

Greg Higgins cooks with skill and principle, distilling dazzling dishes from the Northwest soil and seas. Dedicated to local producers and the idea of sustainability, he sets out deft, creative cuisine such as medallions of pork loin and foie gras, or crab and shrimp cakes with chipotle crème fraîche, or perhaps a saffron bourride of regional shellfish. Part of Higgins's policy is to maintain a vegetarian component on the menu, which can mean a forest mushroom tamale with hazelnut mole and tangerine salsa, or a black- and white-truffled risotto. In the bar is an inviting bistro menu, with offerings ranging from smoked goose to Higgins's signature sandwich, house-cured pastrami with white cheddar. Spectacular presentation endures, especially in desserts, which might be a roasted pear in phyllo or a chocolate-almond-apricot tart. And at lunch, this place dedicated to sustainability and authenticity produces a very good burger. *$$–$$$; AE, DC, MC, V; checks OK; lunch Mon–Fri, dinner every day; full bar; reservations recommended; corner of SW Jefferson.*

Il Piatto / ★★

2348 SE ANKENY, PORTLAND; 503/236-4997

This cozy, ever-inviting Italian neighborhood place almost qualifies as a secret; it takes a little finding, and the folks in the neighborhood aren't seeking competition for the tables. But chef Eugen Bingham has created a restaurant that draws widely, with nearly 20 pastas—notably a punchy puttanesca and deftly done risottos—and signature dishes such as pork saltimbocca, and wild mushroom crepes with a smoked pear crème fraîche. It's a particularly good place for midweek lunches. The attraction is heightened by decor resembling an overstuffed Venetian apartment, and a comfy sofa on which to wait for your table. *$$; DIS, MC, V; checks OK; lunch, Tues–Fri, dinner every day; beer and wine; reservations recommended; 1 block south of E Burnside.* &

Jake's Famous Crawfish / ★★

SW 12TH AVE, PORTLAND; 503/226-1419

This is the place that spawned an empire; owners Bill McCormick and Doug Schmick have almost as many restaurants as items on their fresh list. At the top of the menu, the list has seafood from Fiji to Maine to New Zealand. It might appear in a shiitake soy ginger glaze, or blackened with corn-pepper relish, or in a bouillabaisse. Jake's is strong on tradition, from the polished wooden fixtures to the waiters' white jackets, but the menu features constant experimentation. The combination of old tradition and new ideas applied to very fresh seafood could keep Jake's going for another 100 years. Those without reservations might wait an hour, knowing their patience will be rewarded with some of the better seafood in the city, and some of the best service anywhere. Lots of folks in the bar are in no hurry at all. Jake's was an early fan of Oregon wines, and it also has a powerful dessert tray: the three-berry cobbler endures, but the equally legendary chocolate truffle cake has been revised, and actually intensified. *$$; AE, DC, MC, V; checks OK; lunch Mon–Fri, dinner every day; full bar; reservations recommended; at SW Stark.* ፌ

L'Auberge / ★★

2601 NW VAUGHN ST, PORTLAND; 503/223-3302

This longtime establishment may no longer be among the city's hottest upscale restaurants, but it remains a solid, comfortable, deeply pleasant place to spend an evening. The casual bistro menu, served near the warm fireplace in the bar area—a softly lit den of upscale hipness—and on the outside deck in summer, is a powerful draw. Specialties include L'Auberge's classic pâté, steamed mussels and clams, and each evening's pasta. Downstairs in the dining room, dishes such as a richly moist and flavorful apple cider chicken breast can be warming; one attractive option of the new style is smaller bistro servings of restaurant entrees such as salmon pavé in a bacon cream or filet mignon. End with L'Auberge's dessert menu, including the hallowed poached lemon cheesecake—still dazzling—or the intense chocolate mousse. *$$–$$$; AE, DC, MC, V; local checks only; dinner every day (Sun, dinner in bar only); full bar; reservations recommended (dining room); at NW 26th.* ፌ

Le Bouchon / ★

517 NW 14TH AVE, PORTLAND; 503/248-2193

🐷 The phrase "bistro" is tossed around loosely in the present restaurant world, but this tiny, loud storefront in the Pearl District reminds you that it sounds best in a French accent. The menu is studded with French standards—onion soup, escargot, and pâté. The authenticity continues through entrees and desserts, from entrecote in red wine sauce through—*naturellement*—a potent chocolate mousse. There may be questions here about decibel level and the acrobatics needed to get around the closely packed tables, but that's part of the atmosphere. These folks know what they're doing—and it's worth it to listen to them discuss it. *$$; AE, DIS, MC, V; no checks; lunch Fri, dinner Tues–Sun; beer and wine; reservations recommended (dinner); between NW Glisan and Hoyt.*

Legin / ★★

8001 SE DIVISION ST, PORTLAND; 503/777-2828

At first glance, this huge, garish building among the fast-food architecture of SE 82nd Avenue looks like the chop suey palace of all time. It's only when you get inside, and see the huge Chinese menu and the multiple live seafood tanks, that you discover what may be the best Chinese restaurant in town. You'll find items here you just won't find anyplace else around—bamboo marrow? six kinds of shark fin soup?—and you can accompany them with live geoduck or a whole tilapia. Look for anything that's alive when you order it; try to find a place for the pepper and salt lobster; and take a shot at something you don't recognize—Cantonese ham, maybe. On Sundays, a giant, bustling dim sum scene seems to be dispensing all the chicken feet and shiu mai in the world. *$$; MC, V; no checks; lunch, dinner every day; full bar; reservations not necessary; at SE 82nd.* &

Lemongrass / ★★★

1705 NE COUCH ST, PORTLAND; 503/231-5780

There's big news at this exquisite Thai restaurant in an elegant old Portland Victorian house: the menu has added red curry. To understand why this is so exciting, you need to have tasted Shelley Siripatrapa's green curry and yellow curry. Tastes here are bright and sharp, sweet and hot and tangy, from emerald pools of green curry to snap-your-eyes-open shrimp with garlic and basil. Siripatrapa has a magical touch with seafood, such as shrimp snuggled into phad thai noodles or just floating in a clear-your-sinuses broth of lemongrass, Kaffir lime, and chile. She also produces a stunning peanut sauce, and in her new inspiration of prawn satay, the two specialties come together dramatically. There's a choice of heat intensity, but getting much past mild takes you into a place of pain. Reservations are not taken, and nothing is cooked ahead of time; you'll wait for a table, and then wait again at your table. But then you'll come back and wait again. *$$; no credit cards; checks OK; lunch Mon, Tues, Thurs, Fri, dinner Thurs–Tues; beer and wine; reservations not accepted; at NE 17th.*

McCormick & Schmick's Seafood Restaurant / ★★★

235 SW 1ST AVE, PORTLAND; 503/224-7522

This place is the template of the M&S Seafood Restaurant chain dotting the country. But you have to admire a restaurant where the fresh fish offerings include blue nose grouper from Gisborne, New Zealand, cashew-crusted and served with hot Jamaican vanilla-rum butter sauce—especially when the kitchen can carry it off, which is usually the case. McCormick & Schmick's has a vast range of both seafood and imagination, from blackened escolar from Fiji to pecan catfish with fried green tomatoes. The menu changes daily, but the place has its specialties, notably grilled alder-smoked salmon, crab cakes, and bouillabaisse. M&S is frequently jammed, offering a lively bar scene complete with a pianist and an extraordinary selection of single-malt Scotches. Reserve early for monthly Cigar Nights, when they could smoke a salmon in the dining room. *$$; AE, DC, MC, V; checks OK; lunch Mon–Fri, dinner every day; full bar; reservations recommended; at SW Oak.* ⑆

Oba / ★★

555 NW 12TH AVE, PORTLAND; 503/228-6161

Even for the ultrahip Pearl District, this place has created the buzz of all buzzes. With its flashy red walls and star-hung ceiling, and its sizzling bar scene, it's won awards for design. Diners have also given thumping approval to its cuisine, but nothing could be as hot as the ambience here. Chef Scott Newman's style is called Nuevo Latino, and the menu extends across everything Latin, from Brazilian feijoada to Cuban flank steak to fish Veracruz-style, and from sangría to Brazilian sugar-cane liquor. There are big fans of the ribs with guava-habanero barbecue sauce, and others who prefer putting together arrays of openers such as crispy shrimp tostadas and shiitake mushroom rellenos. Try to be beautiful, or very cool. *$$; AE, DC, MC, V; checks OK; dinner every day; full bar; reservations recommended; at NW Hoyt.* ⑆

The Original Pancake House / ★★

8600 SW BARBUR BLVD, PORTLAND; 503/246-9007

Show some respect the next time you come here for Swedish or banana or simply perfect pancakes. In 1999 the Original Pancake House was designated by the James Beard Foundation as a regional landmark restaurant, a thick-battered legend. The question is whether, when the New York foundation folks came to present the award, they had to wait in line—the way people have been here since it opened in 1955. This place hums from the time it opens at 7am until it closes in midafternoon. The sourdough flapjacks—from wine-spiked cherry to wheat germ to a behemoth apple pancake with a sticky cinnamon glaze—are made from scratch. A good bet is the egg-rich Dutch baby, which arrives looking like a huge, sunken birthday cake, dusted with powdered sugar and served with fresh lemon. Omelets big enough for two (made from a half-dozen eggs) arrive with a short stack. The name may mention only pancakes, but this is a place that knows how to handle eggs. Service is cheerful and efficient; after all, people are waiting for your table. *$; no credit cards; checks OK; breakfast, lunch Wed–Sun; no alcohol; reservations not accepted; at SW 24th.* ⑆

Paley's Place / ★★★

1204 NW 21ST AVE, PORTLAND; 503/243-2403

It's been a few years now since Vitaly and Kimberly Paley waltzed into Portland from New York and swept diners off their feet, but the Paleys' restaurant continues to dazzle, warm, and thrill—and Portlanders love it.

Kimberly Paley circles the intimate, thoughtfully designed dining room, closely watching everything that her husband sends out from the kitchen, maintaining an atmosphere as artful as the food. In winter their seasonal menu might offer crispy veal sweetbreads with herbed spaetzle and chestnuts, or a mixed grill of bacon-wrapped pork tenderloin, venison sausage, and duck confit. You might warm up with tuna tartare, or with the Belgian mussels with mustard aioli that have become a local addiction. Other seasons might bring a bisque of spring asparagus, broccoli, or steelhead set off by a smoked seafood sausage. Menus change with the harvests, but the dessert tray is consistently impressive. *$$$; AE, MC, V; local checks only; dinner Tues–Sat; beer and wine; reservations recommended; www.teleport.com/~paleys; at NW Northrup.*

Papa Haydn / ★★★

701 NW 23RD AVE, PORTLAND; 503/228-7317
5829 SE MILWAUKIE AVE, PORTLAND; 503/232-9440

Portland's dessert headquarters trails waiting diners out of its doors the way it trails chocolate sauce across its cakes. The northwest Portland outpost now extends across most of a block, incorporating Jo's Bar (the grill has different entrees but the same desserts). Dozens of choices include huge architectural cakes such as Autumn Meringue (layers of chocolate mousse and meringue, festooned with chocolate slabs), boccone dolce (a mountain of whipped cream, chocolate, meringue, and fresh berries), cookies, house-made sorbets, and ice creams. Before dessert, Papa Haydn offers salads and sandwiches at lunch (try the chicken club with avocado and sun-dried tomato mayonnaise), and daily changing dinner choices, such as pasta with scallops and Gorgonzola cream, and filet mignon bresaola. The Sellwood location is more low-key with a less ambitious menu, but don't think that's a way to avoid the lines—it has most of the same desserts, and regulars know it. *$$; AE, MC, V; local checks only; lunch, dinner Tues–Sat, brunch Sun; full bar (NW 23rd Ave), beer and wine (SE Milwaukie Ave); reservations not accepted Fri–Sat nights; at NW Irving St (in NW Portland) and between SE Bybee and Holgate (in Sellwood).*

Pazzo Ristorante / ★★

627 SW WASHINGTON ST, PORTLAND; 503/228-1515

After some kitchen upheaval, and a little while finding his home on the range, Kenny Giambalvo has remade Pazzo into an exciting place to eat once again. This flashy hotel restaurant—in the posh Vintage Plaza Hotel—with a dining room perfumed by the wood grill, a lively bar, and wine cellar seating now produces Northern Italian cuisine that's steadily interesting and not steadily predictable. Spaghetti wild with mushrooms, chunks of pancetta bacon, and garlic cloves is wonderful, and slices of rare Muscovy duck breast find a homey nest atop unexpected bitter greens. Warm up for it with an expansive antipasto and crisp grilled calamari. For breakfast and lunch, Pazzoria Cafe next door sets out pastries, panini, and pasta. *$$; AE, DC, MC, V; checks OK; breakfast every day, lunch Mon–Sat, dinner every day; full bar; reservations recommended; www.pazzo.com; at SW Broadway.* &

Red Star Tavern & Roast House / ★★

503 SW ALDER, PORTLAND; 503/222-0005

In this towering-ceilinged restaurant of the 5th Avenue Suites hotel, Rob Pando describes his cooking as regional American cuisine, from seared Nantucket scallops to Kansas City baby back ribs. He covers the continent impressively, using the huge wood-burning grill and rotisserie at the center of the restaurant, as well as the kind of sauté skill that produces splendid crab-and-smoked-salmon cakes, or raviolis of winter squash and goat cheese. Also on the menu are longtime favorites, including a moist skillet of corn bread and a tangy barbecued pork and wild mushroom sandwich at lunch. The range is considerable, portions are sizable, the atmosphere is entertaining—the tone reflects giant workingman murals of the restaurant's bounty—and you couldn't be closer to the middle of downtown. A great place for breakfasts too. *$$; AE, DC, MC, V; local checks only; breakfast, lunch, dinner every day; full bar; reservations recommended; at SW 5th.* &

Restaurant Murata / ★★★

200 SW MARKET ST, PORTLAND; 503/227-0080

Murata has had a small but significant breakthrough: Portland's best Japanese restaurant is now actually open on Saturday nights. For years it was closed then, on the assumption that its core clientele was on the Delta nonstop back to Tokyo—a calculation that told you everything you needed to know about Murata. At the tiny sushi bar, specials are listed in Japanese, with a "translation" underneath: Japanese names spelled out in English. But once someone has translated the specials, they're often worth the culinary gamble: crisp grilled sardines, mackerel necks, layers of deep purple tuna. Murata has a particular affinity for fish, displayed in terrific sushi, great grilled fish, and the nabe—huge bowls of stewlike soups, thick with seafood. The elaborate, prearranged Japanese multicourse banquet, *kaiseki*, runs as high as your wallet allows; it's the ideal way to celebrate your software company going public. *$$–$$$; AE, DC, MC, V; no checks; lunch Mon–Fri, dinner Mon–Sat; beer and wine; reservations recommended (except at sushi bar); murata@teleport.com; between SW 2nd and 3rd.*

The Ringside / ★★

2165 W BURNSIDE, PORTLAND; 503/223-1513

🌲 Some national organization calls the Ringside one of the Top 10 independent steak houses in the country, but nobody needed to tell Portlanders that. For 50 years, the restaurant has staked out the territory here, and the only real question for most fans of the Ringside is which cut—the New York, the filet mignon, or the prime rib? People come here for beef, and that's what they get—in large, juicy slabs. The steaks appear at the table on black cast-iron platters, preceded by the sound of sizzling. Against the designer starches of the newer steak houses, the Ringside holds to the standards—and doesn't charge extra for them. Starring on the side are the plump, light, slightly salty onion rings, made with Walla Walla sweets, that single-handedly made the Ringside famous. For those with an aversion to beef, there is a well-reputed fried chicken and something to be said for the seafood Caesar. The dignified black-jacketed and bow-tied waiters are eminently professional, and the wine list is substantial—especially if you're looking for something to go with beef. *$$; AE, DC, MC, V; checks OK; dinner every day; full bar; reservations recommended; at NW 21st Ave.* &

Saucebox / ★★

214 SW BROADWAY, PORTLAND; 503/241-3393

This ultrahip, pan-Asian shoebox of a restaurant has kept to the same basic, lively food presentations since opening in the mid-1990s, but there is something new to notice: a substantial, witty meditation on the History of Sex all over the wall. You can read it while waiting for your Javanese salmon fillet crisped in soy, garlic, and ginger, a wait that might otherwise seem intolerable. The menu here may be limited, but it's remarkably creative and satisfying. Think dumplings, curries, and noodles, and some stirring (and changing) entrees. Lunchtimes, people come for the inspiring Chinese roast pork sandwich. The bar scene is hot and crowded, especially after 10pm, when a disc jockey gets rolling. But the food jumps all day. *$$; AE, MC, V; local checks only; lunch Tues–Fri, dinner Tues–Sat; full bar; reservations recommended; across from the Benson Hotel.* &

Southpark / ★★

901 SW SALMON, PORTLAND; 503/326-1300

This Heathman Hotel offshoot, just behind the hotel and across the South Park Blocks, has not only been reformatted under chef Paul Ornstein, it's been totally remodeled from its days as B. Moloch's. What had been a brewpub now opens into a sophisticated wine bar, and what was a deli-counter atmosphere is now polished wood and earth-toned columns. Overall, the general level of elegance has been raised considerably. The general food level has been raised too, as Ornstein has produced a Mediterranean seafood menu, from a rich paella to a powerful southern French fish soup. The day's catch drives innovation, and the wine treatment is equally creative, with wines grouped according to style rather than geography and a wine bar that offers flights of several treatments of one kind of varietal. *$$; AE, DC, MC, V; no checks; lunch Mon–Sat, dinner every day, brunch Sun; full bar; reservations recommended; on SW Park.* &

Swagat / ★★

2074 NW LOVEJOY AVE, PORTLAND; 503/227-4300
4325 SW 109TH AVE, BEAVERTON; 503/626-3000

Neither of the two locations of this fragrant, accomplished Indian restaurant—the suburban house-and-garage in Beaverton, nor the expansive restaurant-bar space in Northwest Portland—are big on atmosphere. But if you close your eyes and breathe deeply, you can get closer

21

to the spicy tandoori dishes and vindaloo stews that make Swagat so inviting. The range here is substantial, from curries and *samosas* to South Indian specialties such as the oversize rice pancake *dosas*. Nothing will cost much, especially the mandatory Indian restaurant lunch buffet. Swagat is also a fine place for vegetarians—unless atmosphere is a requirement. *$; AE, DIS, MC, V; local checks only; lunch, dinner every day; full bar (in Portland), beer and wine (in Beaverton); reservations not necessary; at NW 21st (in Portland), a few blocks off Beaverton-Hillsdale Hwy (in Beaverton).* &

Sweetwater's Jam House / ★★
3350 SE MORRISON, PORTLAND; 503/233-0333
Out back of the renovated Belmont Dairy, Sweetwater's is sending up some serious heat in a damp climate. In a flashy version of Caribbean cuisine (and mood), the restaurant puts out peppered shrimp and goat curry that could cauterize your taste buds—better grab quickly for your bottle of Red Stripe beer or your lethal Rum Runner. Sweetwater's has an extensive list of Caribbean rums, and does wicked things with them; it's a thumping bar scene. Barbecued ribs, jerk chicken, and stunning dark, molasses-infused corn bread are also highlights, along with spicy Caribbean vegetable options such as not-for-Thanksgiving curried pumpkin. And on warm days, outside tables bring you just slightly closer to Jamaica plain. In 2000, Sweetwater's plans to expand again—maybe to a Creole beat. *$; AE, MC, V; no checks; dinner every day, brunch Sun; full bar; reservations not necessary; 1 block west of Belmont.* &

Tapeo / ★★
2764 NW THURMAN ST, PORTLAND; 503/226-0409
To a deceptively modest storefront on a quiet northwest Portland street, Ricardo Segura has brought the flavors of his native Spain—notably the flavors of serrano ham, salmon cured with manzanilla sherry, and boneless quail with bittersweet chocolate sauce. Thirty different tapas—small plates designed for casual munching—and a list of 20 sherries have captivated Portlanders accustomed to big entrees and pinot noir. In a place of powerful relaxation and an almost Iberian lack of hurry, diners might start by combining a few cold tapas—some marinated trout, or ham and cheese on thick toasted bread—with some hot items, such as a white bean stew or a *zarzuelita*, seafood in brandy, almonds, and cinnamon. Then after some sipping and some conversation, and some wiping off the empty plates with crusty bread, retrieve the menu and explore a bit further. As in a sushi bar, the bill can mount up, but it will record some striking flavors. Come summer, tables outside make NW Thurman seem even more Southwest European. *$$; MC, V; local checks only; dinner Tues–Sat; beer and wine; reservations not accepted; between NW 27th and 28th.* &

3 Doors Down / ★★★

1429 SE 37TH AVE, PORTLAND; 503/236-6886

The people out on the street in front of this modest storefront aren't grabbing a smoke. They're waiting patiently—well, maybe not always patiently—for a table at this unpretentious, no-reservations Italian/seafood restaurant. The menu changes, but it always lists the bountiful seafood Fra Diavolo, penne with vodka sauce and Italian sausage, and clams baked with a hint of parmesan. The kitchen also does skillful things with salmon—maybe roasting it with pancetta in a red-wine port sauce—and other fish, and provides heartening pastas in substantial portions. Desserts are splendid, and the service particularly warm. If the wait is long, head up to Hawthorne and window-shop the boulevard until your table is ready. *$$; AE, DC, MC, V; checks OK; dinner Tues–Sat; beer and wine; reservations not accepted; north of SE Hawthorne.*

Typhoon! / ★★

2310 NW EVERETT, PORTLAND; 503/243-7557

400 SW BROADWAY (THE IMPERIAL HOTEL), PORTLAND; 503/224-8285

Typhoon! is blowing into a small empire. The original northwest Portland space—where the atmosphere is a bit more upscale than much of the Thai competition in town—has been joined by a larger downtown location in the Imperial Hotel (called Typhoon! on Broadway), and it's entered the Seattle-area market too. Notice in national food magazines can do that, and besides, Bo Kline is a deeply gifted chef. From openers of *miang kum* (spinach leaves to be filled with a half-dozen ingredients) and mouth-filling soups, the menu moves into a kaleidoscope of curries, inspired seafood dishes, and multiple pungent Thai noodle dishes. Try the King's Noodles, and know why it's good to be king. Scored into a checkerboard grid, a fried fish blossoms into a pinecone, and dishes with names such as Fish on Fire and Superwild Shrimp turn out to be named right. Typhoon! also offers 150 different teas—including one that goes for $65 a pot. *$–$$; AE, DC, DIS, MC, V; no checks; lunch Mon–Sat, dinner every day; beer and wine; reservations recommended; at NW 23rd Ave (in NW Portland), between SW Stark and Washington (downtown).* &

Wildwood / ★★★

1221 NW 21ST AVE, PORTLAND; 503/248-9663

Emanating from the busy, modern restaurant at the north end of NW 21st Avenue's restaurant row, the fragrance from Cory Schreiber's wood oven has become the signature aroma of Portland's new Northwest cuisine. In 1998, Schreiber was named the James Beard top chef in the Northwest, but Portlanders had already grown to appreciate his dazzling touch, especially with local seafood. Among the standards on a changing menu are skillet-roasted mussels in tomato, garlic, and saffron, and crispy pizzas that might hold bacon, Bosc pear, and sweet onion. Schreiber does steadily interesting things with salmon, such as give it a mushroom and thyme crust, and with Muscovy duck breast. You also might see a mesquite-roasted pork loin chop with corn bread and bacon stuffing. The bar is rousing—the noise level hums all around the restaurant—and offers some more casual menu choices. Try the highly hospitable brunch, and don't miss the basket of breads. In its open, boisterous style, Wildwood feels a bit like San Francisco, but tastes like the best of Oregon. *$$$; AE, MC, V; checks OK; lunch, dinner every day, brunch Sun; full bar; reservations recommended; cory@wildwoodpdx.com; www.wildwoodpdx.com; at NW Overton.* &

Zell's: An American Cafe / ★★

1300 SE MORRISON ST, PORTLAND; 503/239-0196

Sure, lots of places pride themselves on their seasonally changing menu, but how many offer a seasonally changing breakfast? At Zell's that can mean pumpkin pancakes or a fresh nectarine waffle—all skillfully produced. This is a place that will dare a German pancake with rhubarb. Zell's serves one of the best breakfasts in this time zone: a range of waffles and pancakes (try ginger if they're available) and inspired eggs. The trademark chorizo-and-peppers omelet has been joined by a Brie-and-tomato effort and, if you're lucky, scrambled eggs with smoked salmon, Gruyère, and green onions. Lunch means a whole other set of specialties, from meat loaf and vegetarian sandwiches to clam cakes. The catch, especially on weekend mornings, is the wait for a table. *$; AE, MC, V; checks OK; breakfast, lunch every day; beer and wine; reservations not accepted; at SE 13th.* &

LODGINGS

The Benson Hotel / ★★★

309 SW BROADWAY, PORTLAND; 503/228-2000 OR 800/426-0670

The Benson is the grand dame of Portland hotels; since the early part of the past century, it has been a frequent host of significant goings-on in this city. Many locals who want to spend the night downtown opt for the Benson—as at many luxury hotels, special rates abound—and it is still the first choice for politicos and film stars; with 287 rooms, there's space for everyone. The palatial lobby—a fine place to linger over a drink—features a stamped-tin ceiling, mammoth chandeliers, stately columns, and a generous fireplace, surrounded by panels of carved Circassian walnut imported from Russia. The guest rooms, though comfortable, lack the grandeur of the public areas, with modern furnishings in shades of black and beige. Characterized by service that's completely competent, though sometimes impersonal, the Benson is, literally and figuratively, quite corporate (it's run by WestCoast Hotels), but the place is well loved nonetheless. The London Grill, with its white linens, upholstered chairs, tableside steak Diane, and formal service, caters to an old-fashioned dining crowd. *$$$$; AE, DC, DIS, JCB, MC, V; checks OK; www.bensonhotel.com; between SW Oak and Stark.* &

Embassy Suites Downtown Portland / ★★

319 SW PINE, PORTLAND; 503/279-9000

 The most interesting thing about this newish (opened in 1997) hotel on the edge of the downtown center is its pedigree: it's in the former Multnomah Hotel building, a lavish hostelry that hosted U.S. presidents and royalty, plus practically any Hollywood star who passed through town, until its closure in 1965. For the next 30 years, the place led a sort of Orwellian existence as home to a large number of boxy federal offices until the Embassy Suites chain bought and remodeled it in an effort to restore it to its original grandeur. Best known for predictable hotels dotting the banks of freeways, Embassy Suites is not the chain one would expect to have an interest in the Multnomah Hotel— but as it turns out, they've done a reasonable job in the refurbishment. The spacious lobby is probably the finest room, with its gilt-touched columns and player grand piano (pounding out carols during December), but the Arcadian Gardens, where both a complimentary happy hour and a complimentary full breakfast are served, has a hollow, unfinished feeling. Guest rooms are relatively large with average furnishings but lots of nice touches—ample glassware, basic kitchen facilities, his and her television sets, and a coffee-table book describing the building's history. The hourglass-shaped pool, sunk beneath the ground in what was for years a parking lot, is great for the Pokemon set; there's an exercise room and sauna as well as a pair of spa pools. *$$$; AE, DC, DIS, MC, V; no checks; www.embassy-suites.com; between 2nd and 3rd.* &

5th Avenue Suites / ★★★

506 SW WASHINGTON, PORTLAND; 503/222-0001 OR 800/711-2971

A truly pleasant stay in the city—for business travelers, yes, but excellent for families too. Most of the 221 rooms are spacious suites, but even those that are not have a sense of grandeur (and plenty of room for a crib, if requested). Two sets of French doors open automatically, ushering guests in, and yellow-and-white striped wallpaper makes the rooms look like well-wrapped presents. Each suite has three phones (with personalized voice mail and data ports), a couple TVs, and its own fax machine, plus traveler details such as pull-down ironing boards and irons, plush cotton robes, and hair dryers. The staff is gracious and bellhops are extremely attentive—and like its sister inn, the Hotel Vintage Plaza, 5th Avenue Suites welcomes the occasional dog or lizard. The Kimpton Group has covered its bases: everything from indoor parking with an unloading area to protect you from the rain to the stunning but welcoming lobby with its large corner fireplace, where you'll find complimentary coffee and newspapers in the morning, and wine-tastings come evening. The Red Star Tavern & Roast House (see review) is a very good open-spaced bistro, and there's an Aveda spa on the ground floor. *$$$; AE, DC, DIS, JCB, MC, V; checks OK; www.5thavenuesuites.com; at 5th Ave.* &

The Governor Hotel / ★★★

611 SW 10TH AVE, PORTLAND; 503/224-3400 OR 800/554-3456

🌲 On the northwestern edge of the downtown core—and an easy walk from Powell's City of Books and the rest of the Pearl District—sits the handsome Governor. The hotel's lobby is the first thing that impresses you; a dramatic mural depicting scenes from the Lewis and Clark Expedition spans one wall, and Arts and Crafts–style furnishings, yards of mahogany, and a true wood-burning fireplace give the place a clubby feel. Alas, the rooms are less dramatic: done in Northwest earth-tone pastels with a faint oak-leaf pattern wallpaper, they feature standard hotel furnishings; some have whirlpool tubs, and suites feature gas-burning fireplaces, wet bars, and balconies. Most rooms have big windows, but the upper-floor rooms on the northeast corner of the adjacent Princeton Building sport the best city views (guest rooms 5013 and 6013 are the only standard rooms with private balconies). The list of amenities is long, and includes 24-hour maid service, access to the business center, and use of the adults-only Princeton Athletic Club ($8 fee)—or call Studio Adrienne for an invigorating Pilates workout (it's under the same roof). The restaurant downstairs, Jake's Grill, also provides better-than-average room service fare. *$$$–$$$$; AE, DC, DIS, JCB, MC, V; checks OK; www.govhotel.com; at SW Alder.* ♿

The Heathman Hotel / ★★★★

1001 SW BROADWAY, PORTLAND; 503/241-4100 OR 800/551-0011

🌲 A 1998 refurbishment of all guest rooms has helped the intimate, elegant Heathman keep pace with the competition—of which there is plenty these days. While its appeal is broad—excellent business services, a central downtown location, and fine artistic details—guests especially appreciate the meticulously courteous staff, who provide exceptional but low-key service from check-in to check-out. (Those not accustomed to the rain will appreciate the umbrella service, for instance.) Common rooms are handsomely appointed with Burmese teak paneling, and the elegant lobby lounge is a great place to enjoy afternoon tea or evening jazz performances. Among the guest rooms, the Symphony Suites, with a sofa and king bed, are our favorite. Depending on your interests, you might be impressed by the video collection, the library (with author-signed volumes), or the fitness suite (personal trainer available). A strong supporter of the arts, the hotel itself features an impressive display of original artwork, from Andy Warhol prints to the fanciful Henk Pander mural on the east wall of the Arlene Schnitzer Concert Hall (many guest rooms have a view onto the details of the room-brightening work). And, finally, you're just steps (or room service) away from one of the city's finest restaurants (Heathman Restaurant and Bar; see review). *$$$–$$$$; AE, DC, DIS, JCB, MC, V; checks OK; www.heathmanhotel.com; at SW Salmon.* ♿

CITY OF BOOKS

Other cities might have bragging rights to majestic cathedrals or towering monuments, but Portland has Powell's. Since 1971, **Powell's City of Books** (1005 W Burnside; 503/228-4651) has wielded a huge influence on the intellectual life of this city—not only in terms of its inventory, but also with readings, a cafe (aka the Anne Hughes Coffee Room), and its sponsorship of literary events. The shelves in its half-dozen outlets cater to a reader's every whim. If you're the bookish type—or even if you're not, but want to be impressed—check out the downtown store with its full city block of new and used books, or visit the **travel store** (SW 6th Ave and SW Yamhill St; 503/228-1108) in Pioneer Courthouse Square or **Powell's Books for Cooks and Gardeners** (3747 SE Hawthorne Blvd; 503/235-3802). While you're shopping, here's a list of titles you might look for that will get you just a little closer to Portland's essence.

Ramona the Pest lives in northeast Portland, like her author, Beverly Cleary, once did. Any of the Ramona books are almost sure hits with children (and their grown-ups); check out the Ramona statues in Grant Park.

Local publisher Timber Press recently published William Hawkins and William Winnigham's *Classic Houses of Portland, Oregon: 1850–1950* (1999). Complete with black-and-white photos, this book tells stories of many local residences. *One City's Wilderness: Portland's Forest Park* (Oregon Historical Society, 1996), by Marcy Cottrell Houle, includes an excellent map of the 5,000-acre park, plus trail descriptions.

Author and cooking teacher extraordinaire James Beard grew up in Portland during the early part of the 20th century. His book *Delights and Prejudices* contains lavish passages about Portland markets, the city's social life, the summer trip to the Oregon Coast on the train—and other aspects of life in Portland 100 years ago. *The Solace of Food: A Life of James Beard*, by Robert Clark, affords a broader view of Beard's world than Beard himself would offer.

A hard-to-find book that's worth a look is *The Portland Bridge Book* (Oregon Historical Society Press, 1994), by Sharon Wood. With complete descriptions of Portland's many varied bridges, this book is a treasure for visitors and residents alike.

Oregon's beloved poet William Stafford taught for years at Portland's Lewis and Clark College, and contributed much to the literary life of his adopted city until his death in 1993. *The Way It Is: New and Selected Poems* (Graywolf Press, 1998) is an invaluable collection of Stafford's work.

Finally, *Best Places Portland* (Sasquatch Books, 2001) is *Best Places Northwest*'s city companion. With some 200 restaurant reviews, plus the city's best shopping, arts, recreation, and top attractions, it lays Portland bare. *Portland Cheap Eats* (Sasquatch Books, 1999) gives you 200 ideas about where to eat for the best value.   —*Kim Carlson*

Heron Haus B&B / ★★

2545 NW WESTOVER RD, PORTLAND; 503/274-1846

Although Heron Haus is just blocks away from NW 23rd Avenue, with some of Portland's best-known restaurants and hippest boutiques, its location at the base of the West Hills has a residential feel. The common areas in this 10,000-square-foot English Tudor home include a bright living room with a cushy sectional sofa, a mahogany-paneled library punctuated by an inviting window seat, and a cozy sunroom. Six guest rooms, each with a fireplace and private bath (one bathroom has a seven-nozzle shower), are comfortably furnished in pastels, with large brass beds, sitting areas, telephones, and TVs. The extraordinary bath in the Kulia Room features an elevated spa tub with a city view and all the deluxe bathing accoutrements one could want—from his-and-her robes to a rubber ducky. Innkeeper Julie Keppeler caters to the business crowd, with a reduced corporate rate, phone hookups, and no-frills continental breakfast served at individual tables in the dining room. *$$$; MC, V; checks OK; www. innbook.com/heron.html; near NW 25th and Johnson.*

Hotel Vintage Plaza / ★★★

422 SW BROADWAY, PORTLAND; 503/228-1212 OR 800/243-0555

 In a city that's becoming crowded with luxury hotels, the Vintage still shines, mostly because of what it offers, for what you pay. Weekend rates are competitive, making this an ideal destination for out-of-town shoppers who want to be in the city center—and feel like they're staying somewhere special. Just blocks from Nordstrom and Pioneer Courthouse Square, Vintage Plaza is run by the Kimpton Group, and like other Kimpton hotels, its decor is elegant but not opulent. We appreciate the intimate scale of the place (107 rooms), the inviting lobby, and the gracious staff—including perfectly attentive bellhops. In the early evening, complimentary Northwest wines are served in the lobby (most rooms are named for local wineries), with classical piano music. Even pets get royal treatment here; just inquire well in advance. Best rooms are the top-floor starlight rooms with greenhouse-style windows (ask for one of the larger corner rooms) or the spacious bi-level suites (one of which is the Michael Jordan suite—his when he comes to Portland). All rooms come with two phone lines, complimentary shoe shine, nightly turndown service, morning coffee and baked goods in the lobby, and the newspaper delivered to your door. Pazzo Ristorante on the main floor serves excellent Northern Italian cuisine in a variety of settings (see review). Pazzoria Cafe, next door to the restaurant, sells pastries, crusty Italian breads, and panini sandwiches to take out or eat in. *$$–$$$; AE, DC, DIS, JCB, MC, V; checks OK; www. vintageplaza.com; at SW Washington.* &

The Lion and the Rose / ★★★

1810 NE 15TH AVE, PORTLAND; 503/287-9245 OR 800/955-1647

 Housed in a 1906 Queen Anne mansion in the Irvington District (not far from Lloyd Center), the Lion and the Rose maintains its status as one of

Portland's more elegant B&Bs. The two hosts let few details go unchecked—from the candles in the baths to beverages in the refrigerator to the extra blankets upon request. The best rooms are the Joseph's (rich colors contrast with ample natural light) and the Lavonna (done in lavender and white, it boasts a spacious bay window reading nook); the place is indisputably well decorated, with rich drapery, fine rugs, and antiques. Breakfast is lavish (available in the formal dining room or your room), and tea is offered to guests from 4 until 6pm. Those set on relaxing appreciate the porch swing—roofed to guard against rain—but businesspeople find plenty of phone lines and other amenities. *$$; AE, MC, V; checks OK; www.lionrose.com; north of NE Broadway.*

Mallory Motor Hotel / ★

729 SW 15TH AVE, PORTLAND; 503/223-6311 OR 800/228-8657

 Some things never change; look no farther than the Mallory for evidence. Located just west of downtown, a 15-minute stroll from Pioneer Courthouse Square, the beloved Mallory remains the favorite lodging of many regular visitors to the City of Roses—and has been since they were kids. It's an older establishment in every sense, from the massive hunks of ornate wooden lobby furniture to the senior staff. It's also one of the best bargains in town, starting at $80 for a spotless double and topping out at $140 for a suite—so it's a good idea to reserve a room far in advance. The Mallory sits in a quiet area of town where its new four-story garage makes parking a breeze. Have breakfast in the restaurant—simple, charming touches and almost motherly service—and dinner downtown. The quirky cocktail lounge draws denizens from both the older and retro crowds for the reasonably priced well drinks and bowls of cheesy popcorn. *$$; AE, DC, DIS, JCB, MC, V; checks OK; at SW Yamhill.* ♿

Marriott Residence Inn/Lloyd Center / ★

1710 NE MULTNOMAH ST, PORTLAND; 503/288-1400 OR 800/331-3131

This hotel near Lloyd Center has 168 rooms that you might mistake, from the outside at least, for apartments. It's geared toward longer stays (four to seven days) and rates drop accordingly. Each suite has a full kitchen, as well as a sitting area with a couch and a desk, and most have wood-burning fireplaces. Extra conveniences include weekday dry cleaning and complimentary grocery-shopping services. The hotel doesn't have much of a view or a restaurant, but a continental breakfast and afternoon hors d'oeuvres are served in the lobby. Three Jacuzzis and a heated outdoor pool are on premises for guest use. An extra $5 a day gains you access to the Lloyd Center Athletic Club seven blocks away. *$$; AE, DC, DIS, JCB, MC, V; no checks; www.marriott.com; 2 blocks east of Lloyd Center.* ♿

Portland's White House / ★★

1914 NE 22ND AVE, PORTLAND; 503/287-7131

Owners Lanning Blanks and Steve Holden hired a historian to help with the restoration of this stately old home, built in 1911 of solid Honduras mahogany by local timber baron Robert F. Lytle. Now the exquisite interior replicates the original. On the outside, Portland's White House looks a bit like its Washington, D.C., namesake, complete with fountains, a circular driveway, and a carriage house with newly converted guest rooms and baths. In the house are more guest rooms, also with private baths. The Canopy Room is especially inviting, with its large canopied bed and bright bath. The Garden Room's private terrace is nice in summer, and if you like, you can have your breakfast here (full gourmet breakfast is served every day). Evenings, wander down to the formal parlor for a glass of sherry or a game of chess. *$$; DIS, MC, V; checks OK; www.portlands whitehouse.com; 2 blocks north of NE Broadway.*

RiverPlace Hotel / ★★★

1510 SW HARBOR WY, PORTLAND; 503/228-3233 OR 800/227-1333

If you're looking for a room with a view, look no further than RiverPlace. The only downtown luxury hotel that fronts the busy Willamette River—and the boat show that comes with it—the European-style RiverPlace (run by the same hoteliers who run the Benson) is lovely to look at and glorious to look out from. The better rooms among the 84—doubles, suites, and condominiums—face the water or look north across park lawns to the downtown cityscape. Inside are plush furnishings, TVs concealed in armoires, and generously sized bathrooms. Complimentary continental breakfast can be brought to your room, along with your requested newspaper; massage and spa treatments are available by appointment. Use of the adjacent RiverPlace Athletic Club is complimentary, but on nice days there's plenty of opportunity for exercise outside: wide, paved paths lead from the hotel through the fountains and monuments of Tom McCall Waterfront Park. Downstairs, the Esplanade restaurant makes a stunning location for a meal. *$$$; AE, DC, MC, V; checks OK; www. riverplacehotel.com; south end of Tom McCall Waterfront Park.* &

Sheraton Portland Airport Hotel / ★★

8235 NE AIRPORT WY, PORTLAND; 503/281-2500 OR 800/325-3535

For the traveling businessperson, the airport's Sheraton tops the list. For one thing, it's located—literally—on the airport grounds (FedEx planes load up next door, and some arrival and departure times are broadcast at the hotel's main entrance). Inside, amenities abound: everything from meeting rooms and a small but complete, complimentary business center (with a computer, printer, fax machine, and secretarial service) to an indoor swimming pool, sauna, and workout room. The mini-suites consider the personal needs of the businessperson, providing two phones, sitting areas, jacks for computer hookup, and pullout makeup mirrors in the bathrooms. Mount Hood stands tall to the east, but you'd never know it from the airport-facing rooms. *$$; AE, DC, JCB, MC, V; corporate checks OK; www.sheraton.com; on your right as you approach terminal.*

The Westin Portland / ★★★
750 SW ALDER, PORTLAND; 503/294-9000 OR 800/937-8461

Downtown Portland is blessed with a healthy offering of distinctive upscale hotels. So the challenge for the new Westin was to create a big (205 rooms), new (opened in August 1999) hotel that didn't feel like another cookie-cutter chain offering that left guests wondering if this was Atlanta or Cincinnati. By almost every measure, they got it right. The ground-floor lobby and desk have an intimate feel; a sitting room with a fireplace is comfortably separate from the bustle of guests checking in and out. The knowledgeable and professional staff are pleasant and helpful. And it's a handsome place; the architectural style suggests both modern and traditional (with lots of tile, even on elevator floors). Rooms house tasteful modern furniture, big televisions, fax machines (some rooms), phones with data ports and voice mail, clock/radio/CD players, and uncommonly luxurious beds with down comforters and tons of pillows. But the bathroom is worth the price of admission: a separate, spacious glass shower stall, nice deep tub, tile floor, and a big slab of marble for the counter. No pool, but a workout room has an array of weight and aerobic machines. Diners considering pretty Oritalia downstairs should have a cocktail here, then move on to one of the better restaurants nearby. *$$$; AE, CB, DC, DIS, JCB, MC, V; checks OK; www.westin.com; at SW Park.* &

Forest Grove

Pacific University is why most people come here, and the towering firs on the small campus do justice to the town's name. But there's also quite a collection of local wineries, making the area worth exploring, perhaps on your way to the ocean. South of town on Highway 47 is the huge **MONTINORE VINEYARDS** (3663 SW Dilley Rd, Forest Grove; 503/359-5012), with a fancy tasting room and wines that improve with each vintage. In nearby Gaston, **ELK COVE VINEYARDS** (27751 NW Olson Rd, Gaston; 503/985-7760) has a spectacular site for a tasting room perched on a forested ridge, and **KRAMER VINEYARDS** (26830 NW Olson Rd, Gaston; 503/662-4545) is a tiny place in the woods with tasty pinot noir and excellent raspberry wine. West of Forest Grove on Highway 8, on the site of a historic Oregon winery, **LAUREL RIDGE WINERY** (46350 NW David Hill Rd, Forest Grove; 503/359-5436) specializes in sparkling wines and makes good sauvignon blanc. **SHAFER VINEYARDS** (6200 NW Gales Creek Rd, Forest Grove; 503/357-6604) has produced some fine, ageable chardonnays, and **TUALATIN ESTATE VINEYARDS** (10850 NW Seavey Rd, Forest Grove; 503/357-5005) produces exquisite chardonnay, as well as an excellent Müller Thurgau. Finally, just outside of town you can sample sake from **MOMOKAWA SAKE** (820 Elm, Forest Grove; 503/357-7056), where quality sakes are brewed on-site.

RESTAURANTS

El Torero / ★

2009 MAIN, FOREST GROVE; 503/359-8471

You may have a tough time getting past the terrific light, crisp chips, but if you do, you'll probably end up devouring all your excellent *frijoles refritos*. For the main course, stick with specialty beef items—the massive serving of *carnitas de res* is super. The decor is college hangout, but service is friendly and English (authentically) limited. *$; MC, V; checks OK; lunch, dinner every day; full bar; reservations not accepted; just off Hwy 8.* &

Lake Oswego, West Linn, and Oregon City

South of Portland, these three towns have differing characters and qualities, but taken together make a nice excursion. You might start with a walk in Lake Oswego's 645-acre **TRYON CREEK STATE PARK** (11321 SW Terwilliger Blvd, Lake Oswego; 503/636-9886), where you'll see, if you're lucky enough to be there in early spring, the trillium light up the hiking trails. The scenic campus of **LEWIS AND CLARK COLLEGE** is near here, as is the lake itself, though swimming and boating access is private.

Next, drive south on Highway 43 to Interstate 205 and go east to historic Oregon City. Visit the **END OF THE OREGON TRAIL INTERPRETIVE CENTER** (1726 Washington St, Oregon City; 503/657-9336), with its easy-to-spot covered-wagon architecture. See what it was like coming to Oregon 150 years ago—but call ahead for show times. You won't be allowed in to the multimedia presentation unless you're on the tour, except to see a few exhibits and the well-stocked museum store.

End your day in West Linn, at **BUGATTI'S RISTORANTE** (see review).

RESTAURANTS

Bugatti's Ristorante / ★★

18740 WILLAMETTE DR, WEST LINN; 503/636-9555

Lydia Bugatti and John Cress's endearing Italian neighborhood restaurant features seasonal foods and a menu that changes every few weeks. Keep watch for rigatoni carbonara and spaghetti frutti di mare. There's a nice olive oil spiked with garlic for bread-dipping, but save room for dazzling desserts such as the cloudlike tiramisù. The atmosphere is comfortably elegant—but not fussy. *$$; MC, V; local checks only; dinner Tues–Sun; beer and wine; reservations recommended; south of Lake Oswego on Hwy 43.*

COLUMBIA RIVER GORGE AND MOUNT HOOD

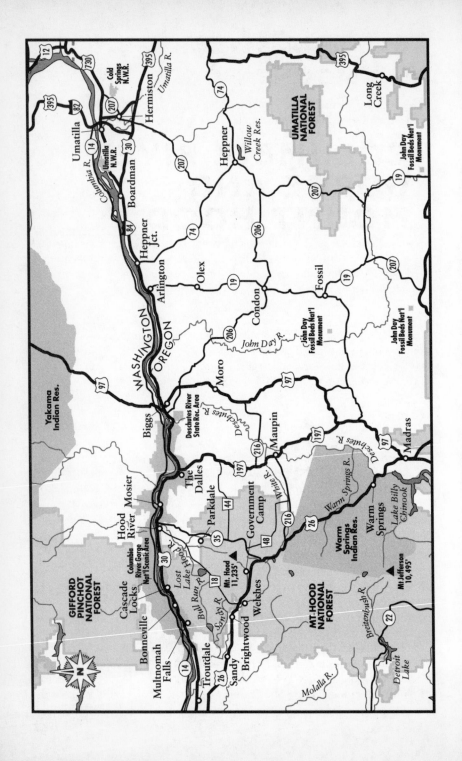

COLUMBIA RIVER GORGE AND MOUNT HOOD

The Columbia River Gorge, a National Scenic Area since 1986, was carved by cataclysmic ice-age floods about 15,000 years ago, leaving cliffs as high as 4,000 feet. Streams flowing seaward suddenly plunged to the newly created river, becoming the more than 70 waterfalls that still grace the craggy walls of the gorge. But until the Columbia River Highway opened in 1915, views of the gorge were enjoyed by few, mainly Native Americans, who for centuries netted salmon from thundering falls, and pioneers, who reached the end of the Oregon Trail via the river or across the flanks of Mount Hood. Intended as a means to share the beauty of the gorge without marring it, the highway was an engineering marvel of its day, featuring intricate stonework, dry-masonry rock walls, arched bridges, viaducts, tunnels, and lookout points. For a memorable excursion, drive along the few stretches of the old highway that remain, and along parallel Interstate 84 to Oregon's number one tourist attraction, 620-foot Multnomah Falls.

Don't miss the Columbia Gorge Discovery Center, opened in The Dalles in 1997, offering a fascinating look at the gorge from prehistory to the present, from the Bonneville and The Dalles Dams to the "board heads" who ply the river on colorful sailboards all summer. Hood River may be the sailboard capital of the gorge, but the town is also renowned for its thriving fruit industry. A drive on Highway 35 takes you past acres of apple, pear, peach, and cherry orchards, and eventually to the snowy slopes of Mount Hood.

The mountain's crown jewel, Timberline Lodge, is worth a visit in any season. President Franklin D. Roosevelt personally dedicated it in 1937, praising the masons, craftsmen, and artists who made this mountain lodge an enduring classic. High above the lodge is Palmer Snowfield, now a year-round ski area. In 1845 Joel Palmer stood here to scout what would become the last leg of the Oregon Trail, Barlow Road. At several places westward along US Highway 26, you can still see wagon ruts cut into the ground, indelible traces of the first white settlers.

ACCESS AND INFORMATION

The Columbia River Gorge and Mount Hood are most commonly approached from Portland, via **INTERSTATE 84** east; follow the freeway through the gorge to Hood River and The Dalles. Another option is exiting at Troutdale to follow the **HISTORIC COLUMBIA RIVER HIGHWAY**, or cutting over to **HIGHWAY 26** and heading southeast to Mount Hood.

In winter, usually after mid-November, traction devices are required on Mount Hood. Call the Oregon Department of Transportation (800/977-6368 inside Oregon or 503/588-2941 outside Oregon) to see if roads are snowy or icy on Mount Hood. The on-line Travel Advisor (www.tripcheck.com) has the latest and most complete information on road conditions. Also, an Oregon Department of Transportation **WINTER SNO-PARK PERMIT** is required if you plan to stop. Permits are sold at Timberline Lodge (see review), as well as service stations, Department of Motor Vehicle offices, and sporting goods stores in the gorge and on the mountain: $3.50 for one day; $7.50 for two days; $15.50 for the season.

GREYHOUND (503/243-2357 or 800/231-2222) has daily bus service up the Columbia River Gorge from Portland, stopping at Hood River and The Dalles, as well as service from Portland to Government Camp on Mount Hood.

The **COLUMBIA RIVER GORGE VISITORS ASSOCIATION** (404 W 2nd St, The Dalles; 800/984-6743; www.gorge.net/crva) and **MOUNT HOOD INFOR-MATION CENTER** (65000 E Hwy 26, Welches; 503/622-4822 or 888/622-4822; www.mthood.org) provide tourist information.

Columbia River Gorge National Scenic Area

The Columbia River Gorge National Scenic Area was created by an act of Congress in 1986 to shield the river corridor from rapacious development, while also fostering and guiding industry in designated urban areas. It begins near the mouth of the Sandy River, near Troutdale, and ends at the Deschutes River, east of The Dalles. It encompasses 292,500 acres in Oregon and Washington.

Troutdale

Named for the town founder's trout ponds, Troutdale was a welcome sight to Oregon Trail pioneers who rafted their covered wagons here from about 40 miles up the Columbia River. From the freeway, these days Troutdale looks like a jarring assortment of truck stops, factory outlets, and fast-food joints. But behind all the neon you'll find the town's heart, a quaint street of antique shops, galleries, and cafes that marks the beginning of the **HISTORIC COLUMBIA RIVER HIGHWAY**, built in 1913–15. Until it merges with Interstate 84, 5 miles east of Multnomah Falls, the highway winds along 22 miles of breathtaking views and awesome waterfalls. **THE VISTA HOUSE** (40700 E Historic Columbia River Hwy; 503/695-2230) at Crown Point, constructed in 1916–18 as a rest stop, sits atop a 733-foot-high cliff. Built of stone, its interior features a marble floor, stairs, and wainscoting; ornate carvings, stained glass, and other decorative elements. It's open May 1 through October 15, and has historic displays, a gift shop, and rest rooms. For more information contact the **TROUTDALE CHAMBER OF COMMERCE** (338 E Historic Columbia River Hwy; 503/669-7473).

RESTAURANTS

Multnomah Falls Lodge

53000 HISTORIC COLUMBIA RIVER HWY 30 E, BRIDAL VEIL; 503/695-2376

Designed by Portland's renowned architect A. E. Doyle, this rustic lodge was built in 1925 with every type of stone found in the gorge. A gift shop and naturalists and visitors center is on the ground floor; the restaurant and lounge are upstairs. Ask to sit in the rear of the restaurant, where your view is of the falls. Sandwiches and fish-and-chips are offered for lunch; prime rib and salmon are featured on the dinner menu. *$$; AE, DIS, MC, V; no checks; breakfast, lunch, dinner every day, brunch Sun; full bar; reservations not required; exit 31 from I-84.* &

Tad's Chicken 'n' Dumplings

1325 E HISTORIC COLUMBIA RIVER HWY, TROUTDALE; 503/666-5337

Overlooking the Sandy River, this steady favorite started out in the late '20s as a hot dog and beer stand, then evolved into an honest to gosh restaurant where chicken 'n' dumplings has been a menu staple for more than half a century. *$; AE, MC, V; checks OK; dinner every day; full bar; reservations not accepted; just south of the east end of Sandy River bridge.* &

LODGINGS

McMenamin's Edgefield / ★

2126 SW HALSEY ST, TROUTDALE; 503/669-8610 OR 800/669-8610

This place was built in 1911 as the county poor farm, but was transformed by local microbrew barons Mike and Brian McMenamin into a sprawling complex of lodging, libations, eateries, golf, and a cinema. About 100 rooms, with shared bathrooms, no telephones or TVs, and sparsely furnished with antiques, are brightened by colorful murals and paintings. Edgefield is most inviting in spring and summer, when gardens on the 38-acre estate are in bloom. The murals and paintings on doors and walls lend an air of whimsy, and there's plenty to do, from golfing on the 18-hole par-3 course to catching a recent release at the Power Station Movie Theater. Choose from several bars—with much of the beer, wine, and spirits produced on the premises—for lunches and dinners. Complimentary breakfast is served in the Black Rabbit Restaurant. *$$; AE, MC, V; checks OK; edge@mcmenaminspubs.com; www.mcmenamins. com; Wood Village exit off I-84, south to Halsey, turn left, drive ½ mile to Edgefield sign on right.* &

Cascade Locks

The cascades (rapids) here were once so treacherous that boats had to be portaged overland. Navigational locks built in 1896 solved the problem, but when Bonneville Dam was built in 1937 and the river behind it rose by 60 feet, the locks, for which this town was named, were submerged. Now a museum is in what used to be the home of the lock tender, next door to the ticket office for the **STERN-WHEELER COLUMBIA GORGE** (Cascade Locks Marina Park, 355 Wa-Na-Pa St; 541/374-8427; www.sternwheeler.com). It's a 600-passenger replica of turn-of-the-century paddle-wheel riverboats that used to churn their way east from Portland. In winter, the boat moves from the Columbia to make excursions along the Willamette River in Portland. When it returns to Cascade Locks in June, it's celebrated with the annual **STERNWHEELER DAYS** (541/374-8619), featuring boat rides, a salmon feed, and an arts-and-crafts show. Mid-June to early October, the *Columbia Gorge* makes three two-hour narrated excursions daily, as well as brunch and dinner cruises.

Just west of town is **BONNEVILLE DAM** (exit 40 from I-84 or Hwy 14; 541/374-8820), built in 1937, and the 1909 **BONNEVILLE FISH HATCHERY** (541/374-8393). At the fish hatchery are more than 60 salmon-rearing and - holding ponds, plus areas for viewing rainbow trout and sturgeon. Two dam visitors centers are on Bradford Island and the Washington shore, at the second powerhouse, built in 1981. At the navigational locks, built in 1993, watch barges and boats moving up- or downriver.

A perfect spot for watching river traffic is **CHARBURGER** (714 SW Wa-Na-Pa; 541/374-8477), a cafeteria-style restaurant with great burgers and home-made pie. From a booth next to the large windows, you can admire the river and the beautiful **BRIDGE OF THE GODS**, a graceful silver cantilever toll bridge built in 1926 to link Oregon and Washington. The bridge is also part of the 2,000-mile Pacific Crest National Scenic Trail, which runs from Mexico to Canada.

For more information contact the **CASCADE LOCKS VISITORS CENTER** (Cascade Locks Marina Park; 541/374-8619).

Hood River

Once known simply for the glorious fruit orchards in the neighboring hills, Hood River has broadened its appeal. The vibrant town owes its renaissance to the adventurers who come from all points of the globe to launch sailboards from **COLUMBIA GORGE SAILPARK** at Port Marina Park, taking advantage of the excellent windsurfing conditions on the Columbia River. The closest of Mount Hood's five ski areas is just 27 miles away; a multitude of hiking and biking trails are similarly close. What better location for July's annual **GORGE GAMES** (541/386-7774), with windsurfing, mountain biking, paragliding, kayaking, and other sports. Rent gear or sign up for lessons at **GORGE SURF HOUSE** (13 Oak St; 541/386-1699; www.gorgesurfhouse.com).

But this is still one of the world's premier fruit-growing regions. The first fruit trees were planted here in 1854 and the first commercial orchard was started in 1876. The fertile volcanic soil, produced by ancient eruptions of Mount Hood, proved to be ideal, particularly for pears, which make up 75 per-cent of the fruit grown here. Pick your own fruit, or buy from roadside stands along Highway 35 south of town. For more information, contact **HOOD RIVER**

COLUMBIA RIVER GORGE THREE-DAY TOUR

DAY ONE: Begin in **Troutdale** after spending the night at **McMenamin's Edgefield**; enjoy your complimentary breakfast, then spend the morning browsing through the town's antique shops and factory stores. Then head east on a 22-mile stretch of the **Historic Columbia River Highway**, across the Sandy River and into the hills above the Columbia River Gorge. Follow the highway to Multnomah Falls and stop for lunch at **Multnomah Falls Lodge**. Get on Interstate 84 and drive to the little town of **Cascade Locks;** tour the **Bonneville Dam** visitors center and watch fish swim up the fish ladder. Get a closer look at salmon, trout, and sturgeon at the **Bonneville Fish Hatchery**. At **Mosier**, exit the freeway and follow another 9-mile stretch of the historic highway to **Rowena Crest Viewpoint** and the **Tom McCall Preserve**, taking in a spectacular view and acres of wildflowers and native plants. At **The Dalles**, check in to the **Columbia House Bed & Breakfast**, then enjoy a relaxed dinner at **Bailey's Place**.

DAY TWO: Eat breakfast in the shade of the apple tree on the B&B's deck, while taking in the hilltop view of the Columbia River. Plan to spend a couple of hours going through the **Columbia Gorge Discovery Center** and adjoining **Wasco County Historical Museum**. Return west to Hood River and enjoy a tasty pasta lunch at **Sixth Street Bistro & Loft**. Then it's decision time: either catch the afternoon **Mount Hood Railroad** spring excursion by orchards of apple, pear, apricot, and cherry trees; or continue west to **Cascade Locks** and ride the **Stern-Wheeler Columbia Gorge** on its summer afternoon river cruise. No matter how you spend the afternoon, in the evening enjoy an early dinner at the casually elegant **Stonehedge Inn** in Hood River. Then head 15 miles south on Highway 35 to the **Mount Hood Hamlet Bed & Breakfast** for the night.

DAY THREE: When you open your eyes and look out your bedroom window, you'll think Mount Hood is close enough to touch. Take your time; you're almost there. After a leisurely breakfast, have a soak in the outdoor spa with its heated deck. Drive south and then west over Bennett and Barlow Passes to Government Camp. Have a late lunch here, perhaps a gourmet personal pizza, at **The Brew Pub at Mount Hood Brewing Co.** Spend the afternoon hiking and exploring the mountain. You'll work up an appetite for dinner at the **Cascade Dining Room** at **Timberline Lodge**, and be ready to sink into bed while the snowy peak of Mount Hood shimmers in moonlight.

COUNTY CHAMBER OF COMMERCE (405 Portway Ave; 541/386-2000 or 800/366-3530; www.gorge.net/fruitloop). Trees are most beautiful in spring, when they blossom. The area celebrates with food and music for the entire growing cycle, from the **HOOD RIVER VALLEY BLOSSOM FESTIVAL** in April to the **HOOD RIVER VALLEY HARVEST FESTIVAL** in October.

The Fruit Blossom Special, a spring rail excursion through the orchards, is one of many annual special-occasion trips on the **MOUNT HOOD RAILROAD** (110 Railroad Ave; 541/386-3556 or 800/872-4661; www.mthoodrr.com). Some trips feature brunch or dinner (Mar–mid-Dec). The restored train, built in 1906, follows its original route through the valley, past packing plants, lumber mills, and orchards. The 1911 depot is a designated National Historic Site.

The town is a comfortable mix of old and new. **FRANZ HARDWARE** (116 Oak St; 541/386-1141) has been owned and operated by the same family since 1909, and still sells nails and bolts individually, as well as household goods. Just up the street, the goods are a bit more yuppified at **ANNZPANZ** (311 Oak St; 541/387-2654), where you'll find upscale cookware while sipping an espresso and nibbling a gourmet lunch. Across the street is **WAUCOMA BOOKS** (212 Oak St; 541/386-5353), which offers books for every taste and age, as well as pottery by a local artist. At **FULL SAIL BREWERY AND PUB** (506 Columbia; 541/386-2247), take a tour, then sit down to a bowl of chili and some of the best microbrews in Oregon.

RESTAURANTS

Big City Chicks / ★

1302 13TH ST, HOOD RIVER; 541/387-3811

You may think you've known a few Big City Chicks, but here the phrase means chicken dishes from various points on the globe. Try your chicken curried, blackened, jerked, herb-crusted, stir-fried, with dijon mustard, in enchiladas, or in phad thai. Also try the extensive vegetarian and seafood offerings, the kids' menu, and even some red meat options. The restaurant's in a big old house surrounded by a picket fence. Inside, art deco decor adds to the fun. *$$; MC, V; local checks only; dinner every day; full bar; reservations not necessary; at B St.* &

North Oak Brasserie / ★★

113 3RD ST, HOOD RIVER; 541/387-2310

The adventure begins when you descend a stairway from the sidewalk to the basement level. Inside, according to the street-level sign, the cozy bistro serves "extremely comfortable Italian food." Owners Mike and Shawna Caldwell planned their restaurant like a novel (in fact, they've done that too, collaborating on Mike's 1998 novel about wine and food, *Varietal Tendencies*). The former cellarmaster at Flerchinger Vineyards, Mike selected about 150 wines for a list that complements the food. Shawna, a former art teacher, decorated the place with her own art and added her touch to the sophisticated menu selections. A shiitake mushroom ravioli whets your appetite for one of the delectable entrees, such as a pork chop stuffed with Italian sausage and mushrooms, served with Calvados sauce, Hood River pears, and garlic potatoes. Kids are welcome. *$$; MC, V; checks OK; lunch Tues–Fri, dinner Tues–Sun; full bar; reservations recommended; northoak@gorge.net; downtown, at Oak St.*

Pasquale's Ristorante / ★

102 OAK ST (HOOD RIVER HOTEL), HOOD RIVER; 541/386-1900 OR 800/386-1859

Airy and bright, with large windows looking out on Oak Street, here everything's Italian—even the beer. Even steak and seafood dishes have an Italian touch. Start with antipasti, crostini, or a spinach Rosso salad, made with sautéed Italian bacon and portobello mushrooms in a warm balsamic vinaigrette and topped with Gorgonzola. Pastas include capellini *vongole*, made with fresh clams, and smoked-salmon ravioli with pesto sauce. Main dishes might feature chicken saltimbocca, and duck *boscaiola* with sautéed shiitake mushrooms and cranberries. This is a hometown favorite with consistent quality. Enjoy your espresso or after-dinner drink in the cozy fireplace lounge (which doubles as the hotel's lobby) or at an outside table. *$$; AE, DIS, MC, V; checks OK; breakfast, lunch, dinner every day; full bar; reservations recommended; hrhotel@gorge.net; www.hoodriverhotel.com; at 1st Ave.* &

Sixth Street Bistro & Loft / ★

509 CASCADE ST, HOOD RIVER; 541/386-5737

Upstairs are a pool table, nine microbrews on tap, a tandem bike hanging from the ceiling, and clever art reproductions painted right on the walls. Pastas and sandwiches satisfy the lunch crowd. Downstairs, tables are set with white linen. That's where dinner—perhaps T-bone steak with garlic mashed potatoes and sautéed kale; salmon; seared halibut with couscous and vegetables; or linguine with scallops and shrimp—is served, along with the restaurant's "famous Loft bread," a popular herb bread baked fresh daily. On summer nights, sit under the maple tree on the patio. *$$; MC, V; local checks only; breakfast, lunch, dinner daily; full bar; reservations recommended in summer; at 6th.* &

Stonehedge Inn / ★

3405 CASCADE DR, HOOD RIVER; 541/386-3940

After driving up a winding gravel road, you'll find this historic house built in 1908 as a summer residence for a prominent Portland family. New owners in 1976 converted it to a dinner house, naming it after the hand-built stone hedges that are part of the landscaping. Since 1986, Jean Harmon has been the hospitable owner, welcoming guests in her warm and inviting home. You'll be seated in one of four rooms—the bar room, main room with fireplace, library, or porch room. Start with an appetizer, such as sautéed mushroom crepes with Fontina cheese, then feast on dishes such as grilled salmon, roast Long Island duckling, or veal chanterelle. *$$; AE, DIS, MC, V; checks OK; dinner Wed–Sun; full bar; reservations recommended; exit 62 off I-84, look for sign on south side of Cascade Dr, follow gravel road for ¼ mile.*

LODGINGS

Columbia Gorge Hotel / ★

4000 WESTCLIFF DR, HOOD RIVER; 541/386-5566 OR 800/345-1921

Lumber baron Simon Benson built his luxury hotel in 1921 to accommodate motorists on the new Columbia River Highway. This Spanish-style, golden stucco beauty with green shutters and red-tile roof has been restored to its former grandeur and is on the National Register of Historic Places. The common areas are elegant and roomy, but by comparison the rooms may seem a tad cozy. Some larger suites have fireplaces; the most unique rooms have polished brass or canopy beds. Ask for a room with a river view. Enjoy acres of beautiful gardens, stone bridges, and a 208-foot waterfall cascading to the Columbia. The hotel features nightly entertainment, and evening turndown service includes a rose and chocolate. Included in the room rate is the five-course "World Famous Farm Breakfast," which includes eggs, pancakes, fresh fruit, and oatmeal. *$$$; AE, DIS, MC, V; checks OK; cghotel@gorge.net; www.columbiagorgehotel.com; 1 mile west of Hood River, exit 62 off I-84.* &

Hood River Hotel / ★★

102 OAK AVE, HOOD RIVER; 541/386-1900 OR 800/386-1859

This brick structure, built in 1912 as the annex to the long-gone Mount Hood Hotel, is fully restored and on the National Register of Historic Places. The lobby, with inviting chairs and a fireplace, greets visitors, and comfortable, spacious rooms extend the welcome. Each of the 32 rooms and 9 kitchen suites is individually furnished with antique reproductions, including four-poster, sleigh, or brass beds. Ask for a room with a river view. Meals (not included in room rate) are available at Pasquale's, the hotel's restaurant (see review). *$$; AE, DIS, MC, V; checks OK; hrhotel@gorge.net; www.hoodriverhotel.com; at 1st Ave.* &

Vagabond Lodge /

4070 WESTCLIFF DR, HOOD RIVER; 541/386-2992

 This motor lodge wins no beauty prizes, but if you ask for a riverfront suite you'll get a winner of a view at a good price. Forty-two rooms include five suites that overlook the river, all with fireplaces and one with a kitchen. Two newer suites don't have river views, but have separate Jacuzzi rooms. The lodge is on 4½ acres in a parklike setting with a playground. *$; AE, DC, DIS, MC, V; no checks; jcranmer@gorge.net; www.vagabondlodge.com; go west on Westcliff Dr past Columbia Gorge Hotel.*

Mosier

This sleepy little town of 260 was a bit more lively when orchards, lumber mills, and sawmills were operating, and motorists taking their Model Ts out on the highway stopped for refreshment. Since interest in the Historic Columbia River Highway has revived, Mosier is a popular stop again. From here, follow a 9-mile stretch of the old highway east to The Dalles, ascending to **ROWENA CREST**, a high bluff overlooking the gorge, and the **TOM MCCALL PRESERVE**, a

WATERFALL TOUR

More than 70 waterfalls line the Oregon shore of the Columbia River Gorge. Driving Interstate 84, you can look up and see many of the falls cascading (or trickling) down craggy, moss-covered cliffs that tower hundreds of feet above the freeway. For more information contact the **Troutdale Chamber of Commerce** (338 E Historic Columbia River Hwy, 503/669-7473).

For a better view, start at the **Vista House at Crown Point** (40700 E Historic Columbia River Hwy, Corbett; 503/695-2230). From that breathtaking viewpoint, 733 feet above the river, you'll wind down the scenic Columbia River Highway until it parallels the freeway. Hugging the hillside, the old road comes so close to a series of dramatic waterfalls that you may even have to switch on your windshield wipers to clear away the mist. Most roadside falls have parking lots, picnic tables, and hiking trails; some have rest rooms.

You'll see **Latourell Falls** as you cross a lovely bridge that arches over the water rushing to the Columbia. A short distance away is **Shepperd's Dell**, named for the family that once owned the property.

Like a blushing bride, **Bridal Veil Falls** hides from motorists. It can be seen by taking a ⅔-mile round-trip hike from the parking lot.

Wahkeena Falls is part of the property that lumber baron Simon Benson donated to the City of Portland, along with its famous neighbor to the east, Multnomah Falls. A ¼-mile trail leads to a bridge over the 242-foot falls' lower tier. Wahkeena, a Yakama Indian word meaning "most beautiful," is just a warmup for what's to come: 642-foot **Multnomah Falls**, the nation's second-largest year-round waterfall. A trail leads to the bridge overlooking the lower falls.

Oneonta Gorge, just beyond Multnomah Falls, is for the truly adventurous. The falls at the end can be reached only by hiking the riverbed upstream. The wildflowers and rare plants growing along the narrow gorge make drenching your sneakers worthwhile.

Finally, before the old highway joins Interstate 84 at Ainsworth State Park, **Horsetail Falls** practically swishes you in the face, it's so close to the road. Hiking trails lead to various points along the 176-foot falls, as well as to an upper cascade called Pony Tail Falls. —*Susan Hauser*

230-acre Nature Conservancy refuge for native plants and rare and endangered wildflowers. Trailhead parking is just beyond mile 6 on Highway 30. A 1-mile trail leads along the plateau, and a 3-mile trail gains 1,000 feet in elevation and is open only May through November.

About a half mile west of town, along Rock Creek Road, is the **HISTORIC COLUMBIA RIVER HIGHWAY STATE TRAIL**, a 4½-mile hiking, biking, and wheelchair-accessible trail along the old highway to the **MOSIER TWIN TUNNELS**. The tunnels, which took highway engineers two years to complete in 1921, were deemed too narrow for modern cars and closed to automobile traffic in the 1950s. (You can still hike or bike through the tunnel, however.)

LODGINGS

Mosier House Bed & Breakfast / ★

704 3RD AVE, MOSIER; 541/478-3640

This beautiful 1904 Queen Anne home was built by Jefferson Newton Mosier, son of the town's founder, Jonah H. Mosier, who settled here in 1854. But it was Jefferson who platted the town and became a civic leader. Sitting on a knoll overlooking the river, his lovingly restored home is on the National Register of Historic Places. Up the wooden staircase are four rooms with shared baths; the master guest room has a private bath (with a claw-footed tub and shower) and a private entrance and porch. An abundant breakfast is served in the dining room, which overlooks the gardens, creek, and ponds. *$$; MC, V; checks OK; innkeeper@mosierhouse.com; www.mosierhouse.com; turn up Washington St and go left on 3rd.*

The Dalles

French traders and voyageurs dubbed this point on the river *Le Dalle*, meaning "the trough." It referred to dangerous rapids that flowed through a narrow channel, now covered by the reservoir behind The Dalles Dam. Lewis and Clark came through those rapids in large canoes, then camped at Rock Fort, just west of what is now downtown The Dalles, on a high bank overlooking the river. About 40 years later, The Dalles became the decision point for Oregon Trail pioneers. From here they either hired rafts to float their wagons downriver, or continued on a land route southwest across Mount Hood's foothills via the Barlow Road. Samuel Barlow blazed the trail in 1845, then charged a toll for wagons and livestock. Although travelers on the Barlow Road avoided an arduous river journey, their trip was just as difficult and dangerous.

Be sure to spend several hours at the **COLUMBIA GORGE DISCOVERY CENTER** and the adjoining **WASCO COUNTY HISTORICAL MUSEUM** (5000 Discovery Dr; 541/296-8600), which overlooks the river 3 miles west of town. You'll learn about the origins of the Columbia River Gorge and the history of the area, including Native Americans, Lewis and Clark, and the Oregon Trail. Interactive exhibits bring you up to date, even offering a simulated ride on a sailboard. **FORT DALLES MUSEUM** (15th and Garrison; 541/296-4547), housed in the fort's 1857 surgeon's quarters, has its own collection of memorabilia from pioneer days. **ST. PETER'S LANDMARK** (3rd and Lincoln; 541/296-5686), an 1898 gothic revival church, was built of local red brick and adorned with stained-glass windows made by Portland's famed Povey Brothers. The spire is adorned with a 6-foot rooster.

At **THE DALLES DAM** (2 miles east of The Dalles, off I-84; 541/296-9778), the visitors center has informative displays on Lewis and Clark and the fishing industry. A free tour train departs from the center and makes stops at the dam, powerhouse, fish ladders, and a picnic area.

Seventeen miles east of The Dalles is **DESCHUTES STATE PARK** (just off I-84) on the Deschutes River, renowned for steelhead and trout fishing, and white-water rafting. The park has a campground with RV hookups, hiking trails, fishing, and swimming. In Dufur, 13 miles south on Highway 197, steam-driven and horse-drawn harvesting equipment go to work each August at the **DUFUR THRESHING BEE** (541/296-2231 or 800/255-3385).

RESTAURANTS

Bailey's Place / ★

515 LIBERTY ST, THE DALLES; 541/296-6708

This is a reincarnation of the beloved but humble Ole's Supper Club, which literally fell down around itself in 1998. But it has returned to life in a much more glamorous form, an 1865 Victorian home that's on the National Register of Historic Places. Ross and Laura Bailey, who also owned Ole's, decided to name this one after themselves. It does them proud, with quiet tables and white linen tablecloths, high Italianate windows with lace curtains, and soft jazz playing in the background. Prime rib is the most requested item on the menu; seafood items, including oysters, prawns, halibut, lobster, and salmon, are also very popular. The huckleberry duck is tender and moist. The extensive, reasonably priced wine list has a reputation all its own and reflects the Baileys' expertise. Ross Bailey also offers wine classes. A full bar—and a view—are in the upstairs lounge. *$$; AE, MC, V; checks OK; dinner Mon–Sat; full bar; reservations recommended; at 4th.* &

Baldwin Saloon / ★

205 COURT ST, THE DALLES; 541/296-5666

After stints as a steamboat office, a warehouse, a coffin storage site, an employment office, and a saddlery, the 1876 Baldwin Saloon has returned to its roots, right down to the original brick walls and fir floor. Gracing those walls and flanking the antique mahogany bar is an impressive collection of turn-of-the-century Northwest landscape oil paintings. Chef/owner Mark Linebarger specializes in seafood. Start with steamed mussels, then try Pork Roberto—sautéed medallions of pork tenderloin with a creamy Dijon brown sauce—or Salmon Rockefeller with Parmesan sauce, one of the chef's favorites (he also serves the Rockefeller sauce, made with spinach and licorice liqueur, on oysters). The long list of homemade desserts includes a Snickers-like mousse. *$; MC, V; checks OK; lunch, dinner Mon–Sat; full bar; reservations recommended for 6 or more; at 1st Ave.* &

LODGINGS

The Columbia House Bed & Breakfast / ★

525 E 7TH ST, THE DALLES; 541/298-4686 OR 800/807-2668

This 13-room house was built in the late '30s, and owner Mazie Starnes has decorated from that era. The four guest rooms, all with private baths, have movie themes. The *Gone With the Wind* room has a scarlet bathroom (get it?). Admiring the river view from the living room is wonderful; better yet is stepping onto the multitiered deck, perhaps to enjoy breakfast sitting under the apple tree. A basement rec room has a pool table and full bar. *$$; AE, DIS, MC, V; checks OK; south on Washington St and east on 7th.*

Mount Hood

With an elevation of 11,245 feet, Mount Hood is Oregon's highest point. Dotted with lakes, campgrounds, and areas for hiking and biking, the mountain has a year-round recreation season. Every winter, its five ski areas attract thousands of skiers and snowboarders of all levels, from beginners to pros, who are drawn by the mountain's fantastic runs.

From the east via Hood River, drive 27 miles south on Highway 35 and you'll first encounter **COOPER SPUR** (11000 Cloud Cap Rd; 541/352-7803; www.cooperspur.com), elevation 4,500 feet, on the north side of the mountain. It's a day- and night-ski area popular with beginners, with a T-bar and rope tow. Next you'll come to **MOUNT HOOD MEADOWS** (2 miles north of Hwy 35 on Forest Rd 3555; 503/337-2222; www.skihood.com). At 7,300 feet elevation, it's the largest area on the mountain, with 87 runs, four high-speed quads, six chairlifts, and a full-service Nordic center with groomed tracks, instructors, and rentals. Many of the lodgings in the Hood River–Mount Hood area offer Meadows ski packages with reduced lift-ticket prices.

From the west via Portland, drive 53 miles east on Highway 26 and the first ski area you'll reach is on the mountain's south side in the town of **GOVERN-MENT CAMP**, so named because a contingent of U.S. Army Rifles (mounted riflemen) wintered here in 1849. **SUMMIT** (54 miles east of Portland on Hwy 26, near rest area at east end of Government Camp; 503/272-0256), at 4,306 feet, is for beginners, or families who want to slide on inner tubes; ski and tube rentals are available. Just a mile ahead is **MOUNT HOOD SKIBOWL** (87000 E Hwy 26; 503/272-3206; www.skibowl.com); at 5,026 feet, America's largest night-ski area offers 34 lighted runs, four double chairlifts, and a tubing hill. At 6,000 feet, **TIMBERLINE** (4 miles north of Hwy 26, just east of Government Camp; 503/622-7979; www.timberlinelodge.com) has six chairlifts, including Palmer Lift, which takes skiers up to Palmer Snowfield for year-round skiing.

Mount Hood is understandably popular with people who never want to put their skis away. It's even the summer training ground for the U.S. Ski Team, among others. But the mountain's also a playground for people in shorts and sneakers.

There's hiking, biking, horseback riding, golf, and other sports. In addition, the **MOUNT HOOD SKIBOWL SUMMER ACTION PARK** (87000 E Hwy 26; 503/222-2695; www.skibowl.com; open 11am–6pm weekdays and 10am–7pm weekends) offers more than 25 activities. SkiBowl is transformed in summer to an adventureland with a half-mile dual alpine slide, Indy karts, miniature golf, croquet, bungee jumping, a mountain bike park with 40 miles of trails, horseback and pony rides, batting cages, volleyball, horseshoes, and other attractions. Get an all-day pass or pay for individual activities.

Climbers who want to scale the mountain's 11,235 feet must register and obtain a free mandatory wilderness permit in the 24-hour climbing room of Timberline's Wy'east Day Lodge. Guided climbs are available through **TIMBERLINE MOUNTAIN GUIDES** (541/312-9242). Recreation on the south side of Mount Hood (the safest climbing route) is managed by the **ZIGZAG RANGER DISTRICT** (503/622-3191).

TIMBERLINE LODGE is another popular stop for summer visitors. From here, the Palmer Snowfield is accessible even to nonskiers. It takes just 6 minutes to travel the **MAGIC MILE SUPER EXPRESS** chairlift 1,000 vertical feet to Palmer Junction. Lunch is available here or a few hundred feet away at Silcox Hut, the restored 1939 warming station for skiers and mountaineers. The Magic Mile Interpretive Trail leads back to Timberline Lodge.

RESTAURANTS

The Brew Pub at Mount Hood Brewing Co.

87304 E GOVERNMENT CAMP LOOP HWY, GOVERNMENT CAMP; 503/272-3724

Ask for a sampler of all eight beers and you'll get a dandy placemat identifying the contents of each glass, from Ice Axe India Pale Ale to Pittock Wee Heavy Ale. Then move on to the food: options include ribs, pasta, tamales, bratwurst, or pizza—their specialty. Try the Renegade, a Tuscan-style white pizza with garlic dressing, spinach, red onion, zucchini, asparagus, red peppers, oregano, and a three-cheese blend. The kids' menu features quesadillas, fish-and-chips, burgers, pizza, and grilled cheese sandwiches. You can look out over the snowy scene from the warm, inviting restaurant, where the focal point is a circle of comfortable chairs for après-ski schmoozing. For dessert, have mountain blackberry cobbler with chilled vanilla cream. *$; AE, DIS, MC, V; checks OK; lunch, dinner every day; beer and wine; reservations not necessary; www.mthoodbrewingco.com; west end of Government Camp, next to Mount Hood Inn.* &

Cascade Dining Room / ★★★

TIMBERLINE LODGE, TIMBERLINE; 503/622-0700

Beyond the hand-forged iron gate on the lodge's second level is the Cascade Dining Room, renowned for 20 years for the award-winning cuisine of executive chef Leif Eric Benson. Don't let the rustic setting fool you; the food here is very sophisticated, with a wine list to match. Although the chef is Swiss, he loves to showcase foods of the Northwest, particularly salmon, steelhead, chanterelle mushrooms, and huckleberries. Swiss specialties, such as raclette fondue, may appear on the menu, but you're more likely to find Oregon duck with huckleberries, roasted salmon fillet with raspberry chipotle glaze, or even Thai pork dumpling and seared sea scallops. The fine food and service are two reasons many Portlanders make the drive here for special occasions. *$$$; AE, MC, V; checks OK; breakfast, lunch, dinner every day; full bar; reservations recommended; sales@timberlinelodge.com; www.timberlinelodge.com; 60 miles east of Portland off Hwy 26.* &

LODGINGS

Falcon's Crest Inn / ★★

87287 GOVERNMENT CAMP LOOP HWY, GOVERNMENT CAMP; 541/272-3403 OR 800/624-7384

A two-story picture window offers an alpine view as you relax in a comfortable armchair on the main or second level. The five rooms in this spacious chalet are elegant and roomy, from the Safari Room, overlooking the deck, to the romantic Mexicalli Suite, complete with a Jacuzzi for two. With advance notice, Bob and Melody Johnson will prepare a six-course dinner, with select wines, and set the table with fine linens, crystal, and china. *$$$; AE, DIS, MC, V; checks OK; falconscrest@earthlink.net; www.falconscrest.com; just off loop road, on north side.*

Mount Hood Hamlet Bed & Breakfast / ★★

6741 HWY 35, MOUNT HOOD; 541/352-3574 OR 800/407-0570

The newly built 18th-century-style New England colonial sits on a hill overlooking the farm where owner Paul Romans was raised. After careers as schoolteachers, he and his wife, Diane, returned and built this gorgeous house, inspired by the family's ancestral home in Rhode Island. Three second-floor guest rooms have private baths and TVs, one with a fireplace and Jacuzzi; all have views. Ample common areas include a warm, inviting library, which shares a fireplace with the Great Room, where guests can read or enjoy the view of Mount Hood. Full breakfasts are served family style in the dining room or on the 44-foot-long patio and feature fruits of the valley or berries from the Romans' own garden, and homemade jams and jellies. Breakfast offerings may be a Belgian waffle with fruit topping or an omelet soufflé. The outdoor spa can be used year-round, and has a heated deck and an extraordinary view of Mounts Hood and Adams. *$$$; AE, DIS, MC, V; checks OK; hoodhamlet@gorge.net; www.mthoodhamlet.com; 20 miles north of Mount Hood Meadows on Hwy 35.* &

Old Parkdale Inn / ★★

4932 BASELINE RD, PARKDALE; 541/352-5551

Colorful gardens surround the 1911 Craftsman house, and the three themed rooms reflect owner Heidi Shuford's passion for art. Named

NATIVE AMERICAN FISHING

For centuries the shores of the Columbia River were a meeting ground for Native Americans who came from hundreds—even thousands—of miles away to trade. The commodity that local tribes traded was like gold—red gold. It was the flavorful and nourishing red meat, either fresh or dried, of the wild salmon. You can still see Native Americans from the Umatilla, Nez Perce, Warm Springs, or Yakama tribes fishing with dip nets from the river's shore, often from wooden platforms.

Celilo Falls, flooded and filled when The Dalles Dam was built in 1957, was a vital fishing area for about 10,000 years. Petroglyphs and pictographs preserved near The Dalles attest to the Indians' ancient presence. The touring train at the dam (see The Dalles) takes you to **Petroglyph Wall**, where pictures of faces, animals, figures, spirals, spirits, and symbols are displayed. The famous petroglyph Tsagaglalal—"She Who Watches"—is on the Washington shore at Horsethief State Park. It and other petroglyphs there may be seen only on ranger-guided tours (509/767-1159; 10am, Fri–Sat, Apr–Oct); reservations are required.

To get an idea of how powerful and magnificent Celilo Falls were, visit the **Wasco County Historical Museum** at the **Columbia Gorge Discovery Center** in The Dalles (5000 Discovery Dr; 541/296-8600). You'll see documentary film footage dating from 1910 to 1950, when the roar of the falls was deafening. Also at the museum is a 33-foot-long model of the Columbia River that shows its before- and after-dam appearance. As the water recedes, the extraordinary rock formations and falls appear, as well as Memaloose Island, which was the largest Indian burial island on the river and now is only partially above water.

Local Indians still mourn the loss of the falls but continue to celebrate the arrival of the first spring chinook salmon at Celilo Village. The village longhouses are open to the public for the **Celilo Salmon Feed** on the second weekend of April; contact The Dalles Convention & Visitors Bureau (404 2nd St; 541/296-6616 or 800/255-3385).

—*Susan Hauser*

Monet, Gauguin, and Georgia O'Keeffe, each of the rooms has a distinctive decor, art, and quotes from the artist written on the door. "I perhaps owe having become a painter to flowers" is attributed to Monet. Two of the suites have complete kitchens and can sleep up to four people. Heidi delivers award-winning breakfasts (perhaps baked apples and coffee cake) to your room, at whatever time you request. She's also a master gardener, and the grounds are lovely for a stroll. *$$; MC, V; checks OK; parkdaleinn@gorge.net; www.gorge.net/lodging/parkdaleinn; take Hwy 35 north from Mount Hood, take turnoff to Parkdale, and look for sign on right.*

Timberline Lodge / ★★

TIMBERLINE SKI AREA, TIMBERLINE; 503/622-7979 OR 800/547-1406

Built at the 6,000-foot level on Mount Hood as a Civilian Conservation Corps project during the Depression, this rustic stone-and-timber lodge was dedicated by President Roosevelt in 1937, and is now a National Historic Landmark. A central, walk-in stone fireplace, the focal point of both levels, is surrounded by handmade furnishings and artwork, including wonderful examples of wood- and ironworking, rug weaving, mosaics, and painting. The 70 rooms range from bunkrooms to the Timberline Fireplace Room. Many of the upholsteries, draperies, rugs, and bedspreads in the public and guest rooms have been re-created in their original patterns—in some cases with the help of the original craftspeople. The best rooms are those with fireplaces. Taking a dip in the outdoor heated pool in the middle of winter is a bracing experience. A sauna is also available, and in summer Timberline offers hiking, picnicking, and guided nature tours. For dining, visit the award-winning Cascade Dining Room (see review), the Blue Ox Bar, or the Ram's Head Bar. *$$$; AE, MC, V; checks OK; sales@timberlinelodge.com; www.timberlinelodge.com; 60 miles east of Portland off Hwy 26.* &

Welches

Continuing west from Mount Hood, you reach Welches, south of Highway 26 along the Salmon River. The town takes its name from Samuel Welch, who welcomed travelers at the hotel (now the Old Welches Inn) he built in 1890. These days you'll find a warm welcome at **MOUNT HOOD COFFEE ROASTERS** (67441 E Hwy 26; 541/622-5153 or 888/661-2326), which recently expanded from beans to brew. Owner Serene Elliott-Graber just happens to be married to the brewmaster at Mount Hood Brewery, so she has three of his creations ("brewed just 15 miles away") on tap. Along with coffee, she serves soup, chili, sausages, appetizers, and fresh pastries, and offers live acoustic music most weekend evenings.

RESTAURANTS

The Rendezvous Grill and Tap Room / ★★★

67149 E HWY 26, WELCHES; 503/622-6837

Since it opened in 1995, this place's reputation for wonderful, innovative food has been growing. Although her emphasis is on seasonal, local products, including chanterelle mushrooms and huckleberries, chef/co-owner Kathryn Bliss incorporates new influences, such as those from her recent trip to China. Diners drive all the way from Portland to see what she's serving, which might be rigatoni with alder-smoked chicken in a champagne cream sauce with toasted hazelnuts, dried cranberries, and fresh spinach; fresh halibut cheeks with a lime-ginger sauce; or panfried Quinault razor clams lightly breaded with sesame seeds and served with an aioli sauce. The regularly changing wine list features

Northwest varietals, but might also include wines from California, Spain, Italy, and Australia. Choosing a bottle is easy with succinct reviews written by co-owner Tom Anderson such as, "Wonderful wine, lightly spiced, love it." *$$; AE, DIS, MC, V; checks OK; lunch, dinner every day; full bar; reservations recommended; rndzvgrill@aol.com; on north side of Hwy 26, just west of traffic light.*

LODGINGS

Old Welches Inn / ★

26401 E WELCHES RD, WELCHES; 503/622-3754

You'd never guess this charming blue-roofed white house behind a picket fence was more than a century old. Built in 1890, it was the first hotel and summer resort on Mount Hood; the Welch family converted it into their private home in the 1930s. The four cozy guest rooms in the main house are named after wildflowers. Three of the rooms are on the second floor, while the Forget-Me-Not Room is tucked away atop two flights of stairs. Whole families, and their pets, are welcome at the cottage next door. It's a bit more modern—built in 1901—with two bedrooms, bath, kitchen, and a fireplace in the living room. The lush lawn extends all the way to the shore of the Salmon River. *$$; AE, MC, V; checks OK; oldwelchesinn@bbdirectory.com; www. lodging-mthood.com; 1 mile south of Hwy 26.*

The Resort at the Mountain / ★★

68010 E FAIRWAY AVE, WELCHES; 503/622-3101 OR 800/669-7666

Clan crests decorate the lobby walls, the Scottish Shoppe sells all manner of Scottish collectibles and gifts, and the Highlands Dining Room and Tartans Inn are your source for food and drink here. The highly visible Scottish theme is a clue that, just as in Scotland, golf is a big deal here. Though it has a 27-hole golf course, this is a resort for all seasons, with tennis, croquet, lawn bowling, volleyball, badminton, swimming, hiking, biking, fishing, and, of course, skiing just up the road. Many of the 160 spacious, modern guest rooms have fireplaces, and the grounds, not unlike the surrounding forests, seem to go on forever. Condos and suites face the fairway; other rooms face the wooded courtyard and pool area. *$$$; AE, MC, V; checks OK; www.theresort.com; 1 mile south of Hwy 26.*

Sandy and Brightwood

This little town really comes to life in the winter when carloads of skiers and snowboarders clog the highway on their way to and from Mount Hood. En route, folks may stop here for rentals at **CASCADE SKI & SNOWBOARD** (36785 Hwy 26; 503/668-9218). On the way back, casual restaurants beckon.

On a clear day, turn off Highway 26 at Bluff Road and go 1 mile north to **JONSRUD VIEWPOINT**, named for a pioneer family who settled near here in 1877. Their son built the big white house across the road in 1922, and his son in 1984 donated the viewpoint to the city. It's a spectacular lookout over the Sandy

River and the forested foothills of Mount Hood to the east. Interpretive signs help you find where the last leg of the Oregon Trail came down the mountainside.

About 5 miles east of Sandy, stop at the **OREGON CANDY FARM** (48620 SE Hwy 26; 503/668-5066) for handmade caramels, marshmallows, assorted candies, and chocolates. In business since 1933, and located in Sandy since 1972, the owners use traditional candy-making methods, which you can observe through large glass windows behind the retail room. Bavarian truffles are the specialty.

RESTAURANTS

The Elusive Trout Pub

39333 PROCTOR BLVD, SANDY; 503/668-7884

The row of decorative German beer steins gives a clue as to what is prized here: 19 Northwest microbrews are on tap. An upside-down canoe and wagonwheel chandeliers complete the Northwest touch. Owners Jim and Kim Simonek specialize in burgers, as well as Mexican and vegetarian fare. *$; MC, V; checks OK; lunch, dinner Tues–Sun; beer and wine; reservations not necessary; on westbound Hwy 26 at Hoffman Ave.* &

LODGINGS

Brookside Bed & Breakfast / ★

45232 SE PAHA LOOP, SANDY; 503/668-4766

Back when Jack and Barbara Brooks were vacationing with six kids, it was always a problem finding places to stay. When they bought their spacious farmhouse in 1988, they decided to help other traveling families with kids, who love this place. It may have something to do with the goats, chickens, geese, peacocks, llamas, and Rascal the dog. The great view of Mount Hood is a plus, not to mention the five spacious rooms. The upstairs area, for example, can accommodate a family of seven with a private entrance, full kitchen, sitting room, and balcony. A basement game room and hearty breakfasts are other pluses. *$; no credit cards; checks OK; brooksidesandy@hotmail. com; www.brooksidebandb.com; east of Sandy, turn south off Hwy 26 at Paha Loop.*

Maple-River Bed & Breakfast / ★★

20525 E MOUNTAIN COUNTRY LN, BRIGHTWOOD; 503/622-6273

The lower level of Jim and Barbara Dybvig's lovely, secluded home has two luxurious suites with private entrances. The Suite, with a queen bed and two futons, a game table, and a fireplace, is filled with antiques. The Northwoods Room has hunting/fishing decor, with a queen bed and rustic furniture. Visit with other guests in the elegantly furnished great room upstairs. The deck, with hot tub and fireplace, overlooks the Salmon River. *$$; MC, V; checks OK; www.valley tomthoodbnbs.com/maple.html; from Hwy 26 take first Brightwood exit onto Brightwood Loop Rd, cross bridge over Salmon River, and turn right at E Mountain Country Ln, then take first right into driveway.*

WILLAMETTE
VALLEY

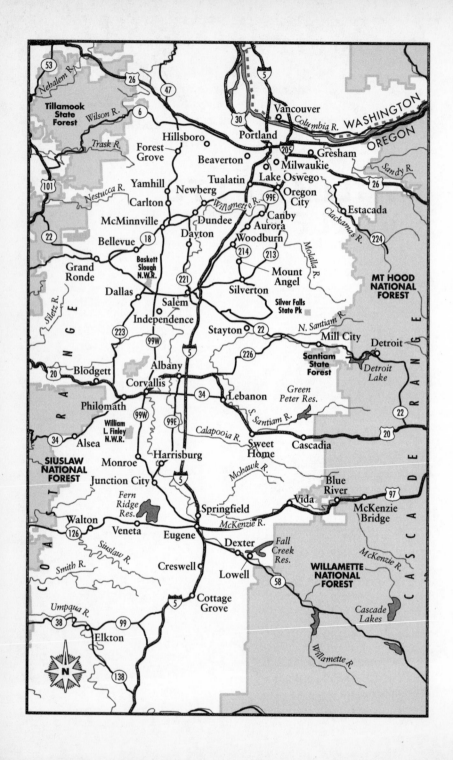

WILLAMETTE VALLEY

Lush and green, temperate of climate, a long river valley edged by mountains and dotted with farms and small towns, often rainy in winter but rarely snowy. Sound quintessentially like Oregon? In fact, most of the state is in mountains or high desert. But it's the Willamette Valley that most people picture when they think of this state. And it's here that nine out of ten Oregonians live. In that sense, the Willamette Valley *is* Oregon.

The Willamette River defines the valley. Its forks wind their way out of the Central Cascade mountains to merge southeast of Eugene, where—a substantial river now—it heads north to meet the Columbia River at Portland. The valley, barely 10 miles wide near Eugene but broadening to more than 30 miles near Salem, is defined by mountains: the Coast Range to the west, the Cascades to the east, and—south of Eugene—the uniquely east-west range, the Siskiyous. That broad, flat valley and the uncrowded rural roads that traverse it are inviting to cyclists, as are extensive networks of paved bicycle paths, especially in Eugene and Corvallis. Venture into the foothills of those ranges for some memorable hiking—past waterfalls, through wild bird refuges, to the summits of modest peaks.

When the pioneers pushed west with covered wagons in the mid-1800s, they were lured by promises of an agricultural paradise. What they found, and what you'll find today, isn't too far off the mark. Wherever you live in the United States, there's a good chance your Christmas tree, dahlias, and irises, the berries in your berry pie, the hazelnuts in your biscotti, even your front lawn was grown in the Willamette Valley. Thank the climate, and Oregon's tough land-use laws. Driving from Portland to Eugene along Highway 99W west of the Willamette River, and along lesser routes, you'll still find roadside stands with fresh produce, flowers, honey, and jams, spring through fall; some are open year-round. On weekends, farmers markets bloom in many town centers.

The wine at your table may also have come from here, especially if you favor fine reds; pinot noir has emerged as the Willamette Valley's star varietal. First came the vines, some 30 years ago, and then came the wineries. Happily for travelers, fine dining was the next step. Exceptional wine-country accommodations are still scarce, but more are in the wind.

So what about that rain? There's plenty, but not more than in a lot of places: around 45 inches a year. Here it tends to fall bit by bit. True Willamette Valley locals don't wait for the sun to shine to get out hiking, nursery browsing, or touring wine country; the showers tend to go as quickly as they come. Less well known is the valley's summer surprise: sunny and hot, with low humidity, from about July 5 into September and sometimes through October.

ACCESS AND INFORMATION

Commuter airlines America West, Horizon Air, United, and United Express serve the **EUGENE AIRPORT** (north of town, off Hwy 99; 541/682-5544). The greatest choice of flights are to and from Portland, Seattle, San Francisco, and Denver. **CAR RENTALS** are available at the airport and in town.

Most travelers arrive by car via **INTERSTATE 5**, its four lanes (at Eugene) widening to six around Salem. This is the express route; figure less than two hours from Eugene to Portland. More leisurely north-south travelers prefer scenic old **US HIGHWAY 99W**, parallel to Interstate 5 west of the Willamette. At the north end it's known as the "wine road," where it passes through the wine-country hubs of Newberg, Dundee, and McMinnville; unobtrusive blue signs point the way to wineries. For road conditions, contact the Department of Transportation (800/977-6368 or 503/588-2941 outside of Oregon; www.odot. state.or.us/travel/).

AMTRAK (800/USA-RAIL) from Seattle and Portland stops at Salem, Albany, and Eugene; the Coast Starlight continues south to Los Angeles. Service and schedule improvements have made the train more attractive for getting in and out of the Willamette Valley; Spanish-made Talgo trains have a little less leg room and no white-linen dinner service, but they're faster, with contemporary amenities such as plug-ins for laptops (and a snack bar). If you want to go by train, make sure that's what you're getting when you make reservations: Amtrak uses motor coaches on some links.

The **ALBANY VISITORS CENTER** (541/928-0911 or 800/526-2256) is a good source for information on the Willamette Valley.

Wine Country

Wine is a growth industry in Oregon: acres of grapes and numbers of wineries both have nearly doubled in the past decade. The greatest concentration of wineries is in Yamhill County, mostly between Newberg and McMinnville. Here among rolling oak-covered hills are increasing numbers of vineyards and enough wineries (more than 50 in the North Willamette Valley appellation) to keep touring wine lovers tipsy for a week. The wine country stretches south past Salem and Eugene, west of the Willamette; wineries down this way are more widely scattered but well worth visiting.

So many of Oregon's pinot noirs have achieved international renown that many of the better-known bottlings are quite pricey. But ardent wine explorers can still find up-and-coming producers cheerfully selling fabulous wine at reasonable prices out the winery's front door. Summer weekends, as well as Memorial Day and Thanksgiving weekends, can be busy, but are good times to visit, because some wineries are only open then. Most are open year-round, at least on weekends (though a few are not open to visitors at all). Many are small family operations well off the beaten track, and visitors are rare enough that they receive hearty welcomes. Tasting is free most places; some charge a small fee to try a sampling of wines, or just for "premium pours"—worth paying,

WILLAMETTE VALLEY THREE-DAY TOUR

DAY ONE: Start at the valley's north end, epicenter of the wine country. Spend the day touring wineries, stopping for lunch at **Dundee Bistro**. Take a break from tasting with antiques-prowling in Lafayette and Carlton or a little browsing in downtown **McMinnville**. You might stop for a microbrew at **Hotel Oregon**—try the Terminator Stout. Then drive out to **Youngberg Hill Vineyards & Inn**, where your room awaits. Take a walk on one of the old roads in the vicinity, but don't be late for your dinner reservations at **Joel Palmer House** in Dayton.

DAY TWO: Enjoy the view as you breakfast in the dining room at Youngberg Hill, then mosey southwest on Highway 18, stopping at another winery or two, before reaching the **Lawrence Gallery** and **Fire's Eye** in **Bellevue**. By now it's lunchtime, or at least brunchtime; take yours at the **Fresh Palate Café**. Well fortified, hop back in the car and, with help from your detailed state map, follow farm roads east, crossing the Willamette River on the tiny **Wheatland Ferry**. Continue east to hook up with Highway 214, taking you to **Silver Falls State Park**, where you ogle the eye-popping waterfalls as you hike as far as your energy and interest carry you. Allow 1 ½ hours to take Highway 214 west and Interstate 5 south to **Eugene** and the **Campbell House**, where a short soak in the Jacuzzi revives you for dinner at **Chanterelle**, two blocks away. If you forgot to make reservations, never mind; **Zenon Cafe** is just a few blocks farther, and the food's grand.

DAY THREE: What's your pleasure? The **beach** is just an hour west, and fishing and rafting on the **McKenzie River** is even closer. Alternately, wander down to **Fifth Street Public Market** for local color and fun shopping, following your nose west down Fifth for more shops and cafes, or over to Eighth and Oak Streets if the **Saturday Market**'s in swing; food booths at either spot can provide lunch. Spend the afternoon driving the rolling farmland southwest of Eugene, stopping at some secluded wineries, and wind up at **Mount Pisgah**, south of Springfield, for a late-afternoon hike along the river or up to the summit to take in the valley from on high. Try to arrive at **McKenzie View Bed & Breakfast** while you can still enjoy the view in the daylight, and make your dinner reservations: perhaps fireside at **Adam's Place**.

since visitors are fewer at these spots and you tend to get more time to converse with your host. (The fee may be applied toward any wine you purchase.)

The best advice is to arm yourself with a map (it's easy to get lost on the backroads) and the winery guide from the **OREGON WINE ADVISORY BOARD** (1200 NW Naito Pkwy, Ste 400, Portland, OR 97209; 800/242-2363; www. oregonwine.org), or from any member winery. Use it to seek out your favorites: a particular varietal, sparkling wines, or boutique wineries. When you come across a wine you especially like, ask the vintner (or whoever's pouring) to suggest other wineries in that vein to visit. In fine weather, take along a picnic; many wineries have tables outside, and some sell chilled wine and lunch supplies.

Wine experts suggest touring with a chilled ice chest in the trunk, to avoid overheating wines you buy. Consider designating a driver so the rest of you can taste with abandon. In any case, remember that this is tasting; there's no shame in tossing out the rest after a sip or two.

Dundee

Not much more than a wide spot in the road a generation ago, Dundee has become the culinary capital of Northern Oregon's wine country. Highway 99W—the wine road—runs right through town, and crossing it on foot is a challenge on weekends; but it's one worth taking, to hop from Dundee Bistro (see review) to the sparkling wines awaiting your palate at **ARGYLE WINERY** (691 Hwy 99W; 503/538-8520). A handful of stellar restaurants now lines the highway's west side; any one is worth a visit. Some say Dundee is a bit like Napa 20 years ago—a farming town still rough around the edges, with touches of refinement. Visit now so you can say you knew it when.

RESTAURANTS

Dundee Bistro / ★★★

100-A SW 7TH ST, DUNDEE; 503/554-1650
The latest addition to Dundee's restaurant row is a smart, bustling bistro-pizzeria-bakery-bar built by the Ponzi family, respected local wine makers. The large windows, walls and floor in tones of sage and pumpkin, and courtyard arrangement lend it a Tuscan air, but the food is inventively, seasonally Northwestern. A fall dinner might start with garnet yam flan with smoked salmon, or roasted butternut squash soup with comice pear. The half-dozen entree choices could include mesquite-roasted chicken with apples and fig vinaigrette, or locally grown pork loin with hedgehog mushrooms and applesauce. Pizza appears as an appetizer choice at dinner or as an entree at lunch, topped with such unusual combinations as air-dried sausage, cremini mushrooms, roasted onion, and Gorgonzola. The same care is evidenced in the handful of desserts and the eclectic wine list: not long, but well chosen, with a dozen available by the glass. Next door is the Ponzi Wine Bar, where you can taste Ponzi and other premium Oregon wines. *$$; AE, MC, V; local checks only; lunch, dinner Tues–Sat, brunch Sun; full bar; reservations recommended; on Hwy 99W at 7th St.* &

Red Hills Provincial Dining / ★★☆

276 HWY 99W, DUNDEE; 503/538-8224
You'll be warmly received in this 1912 Craftsman-style house-turned-restaurant. The simple European-country dinner menu changes often, and the

choices are all intriguing: veal osso buco with creamy polenta, perhaps, or fricassee of game hen with chanterelles and black trumpet mushrooms, or a classic coquilles St.-Jacques. All the details are just right, whether it's bread dusted with fresh rosemary or a crisp mesclun salad, or poached pears with caramel sauce and chocolate ganache. Add to this an award-winning wine list with a huge selection from all over the world. A private dining room seats up to 12. *$$; MC, V; checks OK; lunch Tues–Fri, dinner Tues–Sun; full bar; reservations recommended; redhills@teleport.com; www.redhills.citysearch.com; north edge of town.*

Tina's / ★★★
760 HWY 99W, DUNDEE; 503/538-8880

This jewel box of a restaurant resides in a small, unassuming house on the side of the highway. Inside it's stylish and pretty, bright with white walls and warmed by a fireplace. Chef/proprietors Tina and David Bergen take culinary cues from Italian, French, Northwest, and even Asian cuisines to create inventive dinner entrees such as roasted duck breast with corn soufflé and ginger-fig sauce, or seared yellowfin tuna with olive tapenade and grilled polenta. Lunch choices range from Burgundian lamb stew with olives and green lentils, to flavorful eggplant Parmesan with chicken Italian sausage. The green salad is perfectly fresh; the herbs flavoring your entree are more likely than not homegrown. The dessert menu offers custard, ice cream, tarts, and other house-made specialties. *$$; AE, DIS, MC, V; checks OK; lunch Tues–Fri, dinner every day; full bar; reservations recommended; center of town, across from fire station.* &

Dayton

RESTAURANTS

Joel Palmer House / ★★★★
600 FERRY ST, DAYTON; 503/864-2995

For anyone with an adventurous palate, a trip to Oregon's wine country is no longer complete without a pilgrimage to Joel Palmer House. Chef Jack Czarnecki is a renowned authority on cooking with mushrooms, and rare is the dish that emerges from his kitchen without some variety of fungus in either a starring or supporting role. Not a mushroom fan? There's still plenty to like. Czarnecki is influenced by a variety of world cuisines, but his sensibilities are primarily European. Appetizers include Heidi's Three Mushroom Tart (Heidi being Czarnecki's wife, partner, and fellow mushroom hunter) and escargot with black chanterelles. The rack of lamb comes with pinot noir–hazelnut sauce, and the coq au vin may come with chanterelles or a more exotic mushroom. If you're ready to get serious, consider Jack's Mushroom Madness, a prix-fixe multicourse dinner including your choice of entree and Jack's choice of three appetizers. Service is formal and attentive, and the setting—a white Southern Revival home built in the 1850s by Dayton co-founder Gen. Joel Palmer—

59

heightens the romance. The extensive wine list is overwhelmingly a gushing ode to Oregon pinot noir; don't even mention merlot. *$$; AE, DIS, MC, V; checks OK; lunch Tues–Fri, dinner Tues–Sat; full bar; reservations recommended; joel palmerhouse@onlinemac.com; www.joelpalmerhouse.com; downtown.* &

LODGINGS

Wine Country Farm / ★

6855 BREYMAN ORCHARDS RD, DAYTON; 503/864-3446 OR 800/261-3446

In the "red hills of Dundee" (the soil really is red), just past the unmarked entrance to Domaine Drouhin (makers of some of the country's finest pinot noir—no visitors), surrounded by vineyards, you'll find the Wine Country Farm. From the hilltop watch clouds (or Oregon's trademark rain squalls) drift across the valley, for the setting and view are the draw here. Guest rooms in the white stucco 1910 house are unexceptionally furnished, but all seven have private baths and two have fireplaces. The farm also has a commercial winery, Wine Country Farm Cellars, with a public tasting room next door to the main inn; a spacious two-room suite occupies the second floor and is also available to guests. A sauna and hot tub are recent additions. In warm weather guests can enjoy the hearty farm breakfast on the sun-washed deck. Owners of the 13-acre farm also raise Arabian horses; guided trail rides to nearby wineries and horse-drawn buggy rides are available. *$$; MC, V; checks OK; www.wine country.com; right onto McDougal just past Sokol Blosser Winery, then right to Breyman Orchards Rd.*

Yamhill

LODGINGS

Flying M Ranch / ★★

23029 NW FLYING M RD, YAMHILL; 503/662-3222

The terrific setting is what draws people. It's literally at the end of the road in the Coast Range, with nothing around but mountains and forest. Ponds for swimming and fishing, tennis courts, and miles of hiking and horse trails (you can actually follow trails all the way to the coast) should keep anyone busy. Motel-style rooms are pretty ordinary; savvy visitors rent one of the cabins (one of which has 10 beds) that have their own kitchens and are plenty rustic, with no phones or TVs. For a really large group (up to 20), check out the small lodge on Trask Mountain—one of the highest peaks in the Coast Range—or camp (considerably cheaper, of course) along the little creek. You can even fly in to the airstrip. For a fee, local cowboys take you trail riding on one of the Flying M's horses and maybe even grill you a steak along the way. The massive log lodge has a western-style lounge (with a bar made from 6-ton logs) and a restaurant that serves standards, but experiments with more exotic fare. *$–$$; AE, DIS, MC, V; checks OK; flyingm@bigplanet.com; www.flying-m-ranch. com; 10 miles west of Yamhill, call for directions.* &

Carlton

RESTAURANTS

Caffe Bisbo / ★★

214 MAIN ST, CARLTON; 503/852-7248

When Claudio and Joanne Bisbocci opened their trattoria in little Carlton, fourth-generation restaurateur Claudio could barely speak English. But communication has never been a problem; this Italian speaks volumes with his food and is enthusiastic about everything. Celebrating a birthday? Count on Claudio to emerge from the kitchen to boom out "Buon Compleanno." The food is straight-ahead, traditional northern Italian, the likes of rice torta redolent with extra-virgin olive oil and basil, Genoa shrimp with garlic and marsala, and fresh cannelloni. Minestrone is thick and basily, salad dressed simply in the Italian manner—much as you would expect somewhere along the Cinque Terre, Claudio's home turf. The tiramisù's presentation, in a dessert dish looking like pudding, is unspectacular, but it's the real thing. Some dishes disappoint a bit (the prosciutto with melon wasn't as tender, thin, or flavorful as one hopes) and the interior, with its travel posters and artificial flora, is indistinguishable from many small-town American cafes. Come to enjoy the food and a small-town Italian welcome. *$$; MC, V; local checks only; dinner Wed–Sun; beer and wine; reservations not necessary; downtown.* &

McMinnville

McMinnville is growing up; the feed stores are still here, now cheek by jowl with stores supplying the burgeoning wine industry. Driving through town, turn off the highway onto Third Street to reach the gracious old tree-shaded city center sporting a growing collection of wine shops, cafes, and boutiques. Its central location makes this town a good headquarters for wine touring; pick up information at the **MCMINNVILLE CHAMBER OF COMMERCE** (417 N Adams St; 503/472-6196; www.mcminnville.org). Serious wine lovers can OD on great wine and food while hobnobbing with wine celebrities (including some of France's hot young wine makers) at the three-day **INTERNATIONAL PINOT NOIR CELEBRATION** (503/472-8964 or 800/775-4762) in late July or early August on the campus of Linfield College; tickets tend to sell out well in advance. Need a break from vino? Try a pint at **GOLDEN VALLEY BREWPUB AND RESTAURANT** (984 E 4th St; 503/472-2739), housed in a recycled bottling plant.

RESTAURANTS

Kame / ★

228 N EVANS, MCMINNVILLE; 503/434-4326

A tiny downtown storefront, Kame is a local favorite for simple, savory Japanese food served beautifully (or made to go). White walls, plain wooden tables and chairs, and a few artfully placed decorations set the tone. Owner Mieko Nordin learned to cook family style from her mother. A basic (and satisfying) meal might include tasty miso soup, a small salad of pickled cabbage, and chicken or pork with vegetables on a bed of steaming rice. Tempura and teriyaki are available as well. *$; MC, V; local checks only; dinner Tues–Sat; beer and wine; reservations recommended; kame@onlinemac.com; at 3rd.*

Nick's Italian Café / ★★★

521 E 3RD ST, MCMINNVILLE; 503/434-4471

Long before Dundee's restaurant row emerged, Nick's in McMinnville was the culinary headquarters of Oregon's wine country. Other local restaurants have more atmosphere, but Nick's is still the one to beat when it comes to exciting cooking. Owner Nick Peirano sticks to the Northern Italian cooking he learned at his mother's knee. The fixed-price five-course meal includes a second-course tureen of his grandmother's heavenly, rich, garlicky minestrone, followed by a simply dressed green salad and chewy French bread. Seasonal antipasto might include shellfish in winter, or melon with prosciutto in summer. The fourth course is always delicious pasta. Entrees could include perfectly grilled swordfish steak, or top sirloin marinated in garlic and rosemary. Dessert choices include crème brûlée, truffles, and tiramisù. Guests are welcome to order à la carte. The setting, a former luncheonette, is far from fancy. But the food and a fabulous, well-priced wine list keep them coming. *$$$; AE, MC, V; checks OK; dinner Tues–Sun; beer and wine; reservations recommended; nicks cafe@onlinemac.com; next door to Hotel Oregon.* &

LODGINGS

Hotel Oregon / ★★

310 NE EVANS ST, MCMINNVILLE; 503/472-8427 OR 888/472-8427

Oregon's ubiquitous microbrew *meisters*, the McMenamin brothers, have revitalized a 1905 hotel in the center of McMinnville, contributing to the town's downtown renaissance and giving adventurous wine-country tourers a rather spartan but lively new lodging option. Ceilings are high, beds firm, furnishings predominately antique, and decor a bit brooding (including original artwork). Only a handful of the 42 rooms have private baths; the rest either share a bath with an adjoining room or utilize one down the hall (terry-cloth robes provided). All have phones, but no TVs. Late-night street noise can be a bit much, due in part to the hotel's own pub downstairs. As at other McMenamin accommodations, a featured activity is drinking, with a large main-floor pub as well as diminutive basement and rooftop bars starring the brothers' formidable brews and wines from their Edgefield winery. Breakfast, lunch, and dinner—tasty tavern fare—are served in the pub. Breakfast vouchers provided to overnighters cover most options, from steel-cut oats with all the trimmings to creative variations on eggs Benedict. *$$; AE, DIS, MC, V; checks OK; reserve@hoteloregon.mcmenamins.com; www.mcmenamins. com; at 3rd St.* &

Steiger Haus Inn / ★
360 WILSON ST, MCMINNVILLE; 503/472-0821

Tucked in a neighborhood of older homes on the edge of the Linfield College campus, Steiger Haus is a peaceful oasis. The contemporary cedar-shingled house has a comfortable Northwest feel, with lots of light. Predecessors of current hosts Susan and Dale DuRette designed the inn as a B&B, so downstairs rooms have private decks, offering guests the opportunity to sip coffee outside and enjoy the large, woodsy backyard. All five rooms and suites (three downstairs, two up) have private baths; one downstairs has a fireplace; and the upstairs suite has a soaking tub and bay window. A conference room is available. Full breakfast might include fresh poached pears, raisin muffins, and German pancakes; the DuRettes have their coffee roasted specially for them. *$$; DIS, MC, V; checks OK; steigerhaus@onlinemac.com; www.steigerhaus.com; ¼ mile east of Linfield College entrance.*

Youngberg Hill Vineyards & Inn / ★★★
10660 YOUNGBERG HILL RD, MCMINNVILLE; 503/472-2727 OR 888/657-8668

In 1997, Kevin and Tasha Byrd took over Youngberg Hill—a gracious inn and 12-acre vineyard in a stupendous setting—and have only improved it. The setting can't be beat: from the crest of a 700-foot hill you have views that stretch 180 degrees across the Willamette Valley. Even in winter, guests may want to take their coffee and sit on the wraparound porch. The inn's vineyard skirts the house, and the Byrds offer tastings of their stellar pinot noir as well as other local wines. All seven spacious rooms and suites (three with fireplaces) in the rambling contemporary house have private baths, fabulous views, and comfortable furnishings. Common areas, including a cozy music room and gracious living room, double as gallery space for local artists. The three-course breakfast in the bright dining room includes as many fresh, local ingredients as possible: a fruit course, homemade bread or muffins, perhaps apple French toast with an herbed poached egg, or eggs and crab in pastry. The quiet of the place is deeply refreshing, and guests can walk for miles on old logging roads. *$$$; MC, V; checks OK; youngberg@netscape.net; www.youngberghill.com; 12 miles southwest of McMinnville off Youngberg Hill Rd, call for directions.* &

Bellevue

A crossroads 8 miles southwest of McMinnville on Highway 18, this wide spot in the road from Portland to the beach at Lincoln City is a destination in itself, mainly for the **LAWRENCE GALLERY** (19706 SW Hwy 18; 503/843-3633), Oregon's largest—and some say finest—art gallery; don't miss the water-and-sculpture garden outside. The attached **OREGON WINE TASTING ROOM** (19700 SW Hwy 18; 503/843-3787) lets you sample offerings from some two dozen Oregon wineries. Across the street, a second gallery—**FIRE'S EYE** (19915 SW Muddy Valley Rd; 503/843-9797)—features clay artists.

RESTAURANTS

Fresh Palate Café / ★

19708 SW HWY 18, BELLEVUE; 503/843-4400

Break up a drive to the beach with breakfast or lunch at this pleasant atelier cafe. The informal, airy space feels like an extension of the Lawrence Gallery it overlooks on one side, with original art on the walls; to the west, windows look toward forest and farmland, and the door opens onto a broad deck (for summer supping). The menu isn't prone to surprises, but everything is freshly made, from salad dressings to bread and desserts. Breakfast choices range from hotcakes and eggs to alder-smoked salmon with scrambled eggs and tender fried red potatoes. Sandwiches are mostly standards but done well, with good bread and condiments. Soups, salads, and several pasta dishes are also on the menu, along with a smoked-salmon platter with homemade garlic crostini. Bring a bottle from your day's travels in the wine country or from the Oregon Wine Tasting Room downstairs, and they'll pour it for a $5 corkage fee. *$; MC, V; checks OK; breakfast, lunch every day, dinner every day in summer (usually July–Oct); full bar; reservations recommended (weekends); 7 miles southwest of McMinnville.*

Grande Ronde

This small valley community serves as hub for the Confederated Tribes of Grande Ronde, on the upswing economically thanks largely to the success of **SPIRIT MOUNTAIN CASINO** (27100 SW Salmon River Hwy, Willamina; 800/760-7977). The public is also welcome at the tribes' annual powwow in August, and at the **SPIRIT MOUNTAIN STAMPEDE** rodeo in June.

LODGINGS

Spirit Mountain Lodge / ★

27100 SW SALMON RIVER HWY, GRANDE RONDE; 888/668-7366

One of Oregon's biggest tourist attractions is not an ocean or a waterfall: it's Spirit Mountain Casino, the state's largest gaming facility. Surprisingly, the attached five-story, 100-room lodge completed in 1998 is understated, stylish, and comfy—a refreshing contrast with the casino's glare and glitz. Pendleton blankets drape every bed; quiet touches of Native American art adorn the walls. Colors are muted and earthy, and solid sound-proofing keeps the slots out of earshot. It's everything you'd expect of a modern resort hotel in a remote location—except there's not much to do but gamble: no pool, no spa, no stationary bicycles, not even a walking trail. There is a play area for kids and a video arcade for teens. And food—nothing surprising, but well prepared and reasonably priced—in the Legends Restaurant and Coyote Buffet, as well as in two 24-hour cafes, Rock Creek (light meals and snack foods) and Spirit Mountain Café (espresso and pastries). Don't miss the multimedia Hall of Legends, with its animal murals and atmospheric sound effects, between the

hotel and casino. *$$; AE, DIS, MC, V; no checks; www.spirit-mountain.com;
¼ mile west of Valley Junction.* &

Salem and Vicinity

What was once a staid state capitol surrounded by sleepy farmland is now
growing like crazy, as Portlanders' notion of an acceptable commute
broadens. Look beyond the interstate and its malls, though; you'll still find
the upper valley's rural heart in small towns and fields of tulips and irises, bril-
liant in spring.

Aurora

Antique hunters find a fertile field in this well-preserved historic village. In 1856
Dr. William Keil brought a group of Pennsylvania Germans called the Har-
monites to establish a communal settlement. After the death of its founder, the
commune faded away; today most visitors are drawn to the town, on the
National Register of Historic Places, to comb through **ANTIQUE STORES** occu-
pying the many clapboard and Victorian houses along US Highway 99E. A
former ox barn is now the **OLD AURORA COLONY MUSEUM** (212 2nd St NE;
503/678-5754), with unusual and well-displayed artifacts.

History-minded visitors also enjoy nearby **CHAMPOEG STATE PARK** (off
Hwy 99W, 7 miles east of Newberg; 503/678-1251), site of a historic meeting
in 1843 to create the first provisional government by Americans on the Pacific;
it's now a fine place to picnic. Rose lovers wander a few miles farther up the
river (west on Champoeg Rd and across Hwy 219) to **HEIRLOOM OLD GARDEN
ROSES** (503/538-1576), one of the country's premier commercial growers of old
garden roses.

Mount Angel

Visit **MOUNT ANGEL ABBEY** (1 Abbey Dr, St. Benedict; 503/845-3030), a cen-
tury-old Benedictine seminary, on a foggy morning when its celestial setting atop
a butte sacred to local Indians makes it seem as if it's floating in the clouds. The
seminary's library (503/845-3303) is a gem by the internationally celebrated
Finnish architect Alvar Aalto. The town is best known for its pull-out-the-stops
OKTOBERFEST (503/845-9440) in mid-September; the rest of the year, try the
home brew and hearty fare at cavernous **MOUNT ANGEL BREWING COMPANY**
(210 Monroe St; 503/845-9624).

Silverton

The historic downtown is pretty in summer, with hanging baskets overflowing
with flowers and interesting shops to browse. Nearby is lush, dramatic **SILVER
FALLS STATE PARK** (off Hwy 214, 26 miles east of Salem; 503/873-8681) with
its awesome concentration of waterfalls, plus camping and hiking, biking, and

horse trails. Iris farmers cultivate acres of fields around of town, creating a brilliant palette in late May; that's also the time to wander **COOLEY'S IRIS DISPLAY GARDENS** (11553 Silverton Rd NE; 503/873-5463). The big show is at the **OREGON GARDEN** (503/874-8100), about 2 miles southwest of town off Highway 213, which opened in May 2000; its 240 landscaped acres should make this a world-class attraction as plantings mature.

RESTAURANTS

Silver Grille Café & Wines / ★★★

206 E MAIN ST, SILVERTON; 503/873-4035

Donna Mattson and Kim Reierson left a comfortable niche in Portland's restaurant scene to open a wine shop and bistro in Silverton's historic downtown in 1996. Portland's loss is the mid–Willamette Valley's gain. Inside, it's as elegant as a lacquered Chinese box, dimly lit with dark wood wainscoting below dark red grass-paper walls. The menu, chalked on a blackboard, changes weekly. You may find Asian influences in the food as well: in the Indonesian peanut sauce with the lime prawns appetizer, or in the Thai lime dressing—one of three original options—on your salad. Start with bruschetta and your choice of three toppings, then choose among five entrees: vegetarian (say, penne with fresh asparagus purée), fish, chicken, and two grilled meat choices (perhaps tenderloins of beef with potato pancakes and porcini sauce). Wind up the evening with a luscious Russian cream with cardamom apricots; Mattson's inventive menus take inspiration from many quarters. Reierson's hand-picked wine selection is displayed just inside the front door, convenient for retail customers; diners choose here, too, then add a modest corkage fee. *$$; DIS, MC, V; checks OK; dinner Wed–Sun (closed for a week in late Sept); full bar; reservations recommended; at 1st St.* &

Salem

Handsome parks flank Oregon's 1938 **CAPITOL BUILDING** (900 Court St NE; 503/986-1388), topped by a pioneer sheathed in gold; take in the Depression-era murals in the rotunda, on your own or on a free tour, offered daily in summer. Just behind is **WILLAMETTE UNIVERSITY** (900 State St; 503/370-6300), the oldest university in the West. The campus is a happy blend of old and new brick buildings, with Mill Creek nicely incorporated into the landscape. It's a pleasant place to stroll, and plant lovers should visit the small but well-tended botanical gardens. The university's **HALLIE FORD MUSEUM OF ART** (700 State St; 503/370-6855) is the second largest in the state, with some 3,000 pieces of art from around the globe.

Across the road from Willamette University is **HISTORIC MISSION MILL VILLAGE** (1313 Mill St SE; 503/585-7012; tours 10am–4:30pm, Tues–Sat). The impressive 42-acre cluster of restored buildings from the 1800s includes a woolen mill, a parsonage, a Presbyterian church, and several homes. The mill, which drew its power from Mill Creek, now houses a museum that literally makes the sounds of the factory come alive. **JASON LEE HOUSE**, dating from 1841, is the Northwest's oldest remaining frame house; picnic along the stream and feed the ducks. The **SALEM VISITOR INFORMATION CENTER** (503/581-4325 or 800/874-7012) is part of the complex.

BUSH HOUSE (600 Mission St SE; 503/363-4714) is a Victorian home built in 1877 by pioneer newspaper publisher Aashal Bush. It sits in a large park complete with conservatory, rose gardens, hiking paths, and barn turned art gallery. Tours are available.

GILBERT HOUSE CHILDREN'S MUSEUM (116 Marion St NE; 503/371-3631) on the downtown riverfront between the bridges is a delightful hands-on learning and play center for young children. Kids also appreciate **ENCHANTED FOREST** (8462 Enchanted Wy SE, Turner; 503/371-4242), a nicely wooded storybook park with picnic space.

WILLAMETTE VALLEY VINEYARDS (8800 Enchanted Wy SE, Turner; 503/588-9463), a big investor-owned winery offering a broad range of wines, commands a spectacular view just south of town. Follow Highway 221 northwest of town to visit several smaller, noteworthy wineries including Stangeland, Witness Tree, Cristom, and Bethel Heights.

If you're in the area during the 10 days of the **OREGON STATE FAIR** (503/378-3247), held around Labor Day, don't miss it—it's one of the biggest in the Northwest.

RESTAURANTS

Alessandro's 120 / ★★
120 COMMERCIAL ST, SALEM; 503/370-9951
This upscale Italian restaurant—the most elegant place in Salem—has moved into new quarters in the downtown business district. Owner Alessandro Fasani characterizes the cuisine as Roman, with a menu that emphasizes elegant pasta and seafood dishes. Nothing is particularly original, but classics are done with flair: perfectly cooked veal piccata, rich meat-stuffed tortellini in light cream sauce. In addition to the regular menu, a multicourse dinner is offered; the staff asks only if there's a particular dish you don't like, and they surprise you with the rest. Service is quiet and professional. *$$; AE, DIS, MC, V; local checks only; lunch Mon–Fri, dinner Mon–Sat; full bar; reservations recommended; sandros@teleport.com; near Court St.* &

The Arbor Café / ★★
380 HIGH ST NE, SALEM; 503/588-2353
The Arbor Café feels a bit out of place—an informal, airy garden cafe camped in a steel-and-concrete "plaza" at the foot of a downtown office tower. It's not the most elegant spot, but plenty of locals think the food is Salem's best. Stop for continental breakfast—great house-made pastries and espresso. Midday, try a muffuletta panini, some homemade soup, maybe honey-mustard chicken salad. At dinner, you can go simple with soup and a sandwich, but entrees are

compelling: Sichuan stir-fry is lightly spicy and comes with beef or prawns, and cashew chicken is sauced with ginger, lime, and chile. Provençal meat loaf dresses up this old chestnut with a savory roasted-shallot brown gravy. A number of microbrews are joined by a small selection of Oregon and Italian wines. Desserts perform solidly, particularly the dense, flavorful cakes. *$$; MC, V; local checks only; breakfast, lunch Mon–Sat, dinner Tues–Sat; beer and wine; reservations recommended (weekends); between Center and Chemeketa.* &

Morton's Bistro Northwest / ★
1128 EDGEWATER, SALEM; 503/585-1113

A clever design puts the diner below roadway level, looking out on an attractive courtyard backed by an ivy-covered wall that screens a busy highway. The interior is intimate, with dark wood beams and soft lighting. The menu is an appealing mix of Northwest cuisine with hints of international influences, featuring fresh seafood and veal, and a short list of pastas. Salmon fillet might be accompanied by a potato-pumpkin mash with basil and balsamic braised tomatoes; vegetarian lasagne combines roasted red peppers, mushrooms, goat cheese, and spinach. Service is expert and pleasant, and the selection of reasonably priced Northwest wines is good. *$$; MC, V; checks OK; dinner Tues–Sat; full bar; reservations recommended; between Gerth and McNary Aves in West Salem.* &

LODGINGS

Mill Creek Inn
3125 RYAN DR SE, SALEM; 503/585-3332 OR 800/346-9659

In a town dominated by chain lodgings, this well-kept motel is the nicest of the lot. The 109 spacious guest rooms all have microwaves, minifridges, data ports, even irons and ironing boards. Amenities include an indoor pool, Jacuzzi, and fitness room. It's just off Interstate 5, but close enough to the city center to be convenient for business or pleasure travelers. *$; AE, DC, DIS, MC, V; no checks; bwmci@open.org; www.bestwestern.com/millcreekinn; exit 253 off I-5.* &

Independence

The riverside town looks pretty untouched by modern times, and if you want to remind yourself (or learn) what an old-fashioned fountain was like, visit **TAYLOR'S FOUNTAIN AND GIFT** (296 Main St; 503/838-1124), on Main and Monmouth. Marge Taylor, her daughter, and two granddaughters have been serving burgers, shakes, and malts, as well as breakfasts, pretty much the same way for more than 50 years.

Albany and Corvallis

Time and the interstate have bypassed Albany, which is probably a blessing. Once you get off the freeway (ignore the smell of the nearby pulp mill), you'll discover a fine representative of the small-town Oregon of an earlier era, with broad, quiet streets; neat houses; and a slow pace. Corvallis is a pleasant mix of old river town and funky university burg. In 1998 Corvallis was the first city in Oregon to ban all smoking in restaurants, bars, and taverns, and it's ideal for biking and running; most streets include wide bike lanes, and routes follow both the Willamette and Marys Rivers.

Albany

Once an important transportation hub in the Willamette Valley, Albany has an unequaled selection of historic homes and buildings in a wide variety of styles; many of them have been lovingly restored. You can see 13 distinct architectural styles in the 50-block, 368-building **MONTEITH HISTORIC DISTRICT**. Then there are the **HACKLEMAN** (28 blocks, 210 buildings) and **DOWNTOWN** (9 1/2 blocks, 80 buildings) **HISTORIC DISTRICTS**. Many buildings are open for inspection on annual tours—the last Saturday in July and the Sunday evening before Christmas Eve. A handy, free guide, "Seems Like Old Times," is available from the Albany Convention and Visitors Center (300 SW 2nd; 800/526-2256; www.albanyvisitors.com).

Wander First Avenue, where it all began: have a cup at **BOCCHERINI'S COFFEE AND TEA HOUSE** (208 1st Ave SW; 541/926-6703), a pint at **WYATT'S EATERY & BREWHOUSE** (211 1st Ave NW; 541/917-3727), or a memorable meal at Capriccio Ristorante (see review). In summer enjoy an outdoor concert at **MONTEITH RIVERPARK** (Water Ave and Washington St; 541/917-7772).

The **COVERED BRIDGES** that were so characteristic of this area in the mid-1900s are disappearing; from 300 throughout Oregon, their number has dwindled to less than 50. But that's still more than in any state west of the Mississippi. Most remaining bridges are in the Willamette Valley counties of Lane and Linn and, to the west, Lincoln. Best starting points for easy-to-follow circuits of the bridges are Albany, Eugene, and Cottage Grove. Six bridges lie within an 8-mile radius of Scio, northeast of Albany; for a map, contact the Albany Convention and Visitors Center. In addition, many handsome bridges dot the woods of Oregon's Coast Range. For other tours, send an SASE with two first-class stamps to the **COVERED BRIDGE SOCIETY OF OREGON** (PO Box 1804, Newport, OR 97365; 541/265-2934).

RESTAURANTS

Capriccio Ristorante / ★★★

442 W IST ST, ALBANY; 541/924-9932

Longtime Albany restaurateurs Matt and Marcia Morse have created an elegant, unpretentious trattoria in one of Albany's oldest commercial buildings. They kept the exposed brick and big windows, added more windows and a big English-style wood-burning fireplace, and topped it off with constellations of tiny lights in the high ceiling to create the feel of a starry night, even when weather prohibits dining on the *terrazza*. Matt has put his Italian travels to use in this menu that ranges all over the boot and changes seasonally. Starters might include baked, sliced polenta gnocchi with a light Gorgonzola sauce, or Venetian-style scallops. Pasta is mostly Capriccio-made; Matt's rightfully proud of his Uncle Luke's braised short rib sauce served with the tenderest wide noodles. Go light on starters if you order Ligurian seafood stew, a feast for the eyes and palate. Two dozen well-chosen, moderately priced wines from Italy and Oregon are described on the back of the menu; a list of 100-odd reserve wines is also available for more serious wine drinkers. *$$; AE, DC, DIS, MC, V; checks OK; dinner Tues–Sat; beer and wine; reservations recommended (weekends); farecapriccio@aol.com; at Washington St.* &

Corvallis

The Willamette River lines small, lively downtown Corvallis, with the 19th-century **BENTON COUNTY COURTHOUSE** (120 NW 4th St) lending a nostalgic charm. Get touring information downtown at the **CONVENTION AND VISITORS BUREAU** (420 NW 2nd; 541/757-1544 or 800/334-8118; www.visitcorvallis. com). Poke around interesting shops, and stop for pastry and coffee at **NEW MORNING BAKERY** (219 SW 2nd; 541/754-0181) or **THE BEANERY** (500 SW 2nd; 541/753-7442).

The **OREGON STATE UNIVERSITY** (15th and Jefferson Sts; 541/737-0123) campus is typical of big Northwest universities, with a gracious core of old buildings, magnificent trees, and lots of open space, surrounded by a maze of boxlike classroom and residential buildings with less character. Corvallis has a thriving art scene; visit the **CORVALLIS ART CENTER** (700 SW Madison; 541/754-1551), in a renovated 1889 Episcopal church off Central Park.

AVERY PARK (15th St and Hwy 20) offers a labyrinth of wooded trails as well as prime picnic sites and a rose garden. Tree lovers may also enjoy **MCDONALD STATE FOREST** (off Hwy 99W, 6 miles north of Corvallis), with its 10 miles of biking, horseback riding, and hiking trails, including one among the native and exotic plants of **PEAVY ARBORETUM**. For a bigger outing, head west on Highway 34 to **MARYS PEAK**, at 4,097 feet the tallest point in the Coast Range; stroll the last mile to the summit, or try any of several interconnecting forest paths. Waldport Ranger District (541/563-3211) has details. Look for dusky Canada geese from trails in **FINLEY NATIONAL WILDLIFE REFUGE** (541/757-7236), 10 miles south of town on Highway 99W.

LATINO WOODBURN

When the highway bypassed historic Woodburn's city center, the town's fate seemed sealed, finished off by construction of a huge outlet mall along Interstate 5 in 1999. But a transformation has since taken place here, as local Latinos have reclaimed the 100-year-old brick-and-stone buildings for cafes, shops, and tortillerias reminiscent of their roots in Mexico and Central America.

Take the Woodburn exit (exit 271) from Interstate 5, head east 1½ miles, then follow signs right (Settlemeier Ave) and left (Garfield St) to the city center, minutes from the freeway. Most Latino businesses are clustered within a block or two of First and Hayes Streets.

Your first stop should be **Salvador's Bakery** (405 N 1st St; 503/982-4513) for fresh-baked sugar cookies or *bolillos*, or traditional Mexican deli items such as *carnitas* or *queso cotija*. Stop in at **La Morenita Tortilleria** (270 Grant St; 503/982-8221) for tortillas fresh off the griddle or for masa to make your own.

You'll find several fast and inexpensive taquerias, with flavors more familiar in Michoacán than middle America. These aren't the fish tacos they serve at the upscale restaurants back home; **Taqueria El Rey** (966 N Pacific Hwy; 503/982-1303), for instance, lists *cabeza* (head), *tripa* (tripe), and *lengua* (tongue) on its taco menu, but no *pescado* (fish).

Lupita's Restaurant (311 N Front St; 503/982-0483) is a good choice for a sit-down meal; the English-Spanish menu includes offerings from several regional cuisines. **Mexico Lindo** (430 N 1st St; 503/982-1832) is one of the oldest Latino restaurants in Woodburn and has an attached import shop. There and at **Su Casa Imports** (297 S Front St; 503/981-7361), you can find piñatas, religious statuary, and other staples of Latin American culture. —*Bonnie Henderson*

RESTAURANTS
Big River / ★★★
101 NW JACKSON ST, CORVALLIS; 541/757-0694

Arty, jazzy, noisy—Big River brought big flavors to Corvallis and became a big hit. Against an industrial-strength background (high ceilings with exposed beams and ductwork), Big River has added lots of bold original art, full of color and whimsy. Food is bold as well, and solidly, eclecticly Northwest, with a taste of Sichuan here, a bit of curry there, and lots of fresh (often organic) local produce. Salad niçoise uses smoked albacore tuna and roasted red peppers; sautéed calamari comes with fresh ginger, grilled eggplant, tomatoes, Kaffir lime, and cilantro. Appetizers are equally intriguing: grilled homemade bread with kalamata olive tapenade and local herbed goat cheese, or garlicky steamed

Manila clams. You'll find a dozen or so seafood and meat entrees, and a half-dozen vegetarian options on the menu, which changes weekly. Pizza is baked in a wood-fired oven and topped with interesting combinations. Desserts are equally original and good. Order off the menu in the Bow Truss Bar as well; perch at a high table or burrow into an upholstered chair to enjoy live jazz and a glass of wine or a shot from a long menu of Kentucky bourbons and single-malt Scotches. A private dining room seats up to 100. *$$; AE, MC, V; checks OK; lunch Mon–Fri, dinner Mon–Sat, brunch Sun; full bar; reservations recommended for 8 or more; www.bigriverrest.com; at 1st St.* &

Bombs Away Cafe / ★

2527 NW MONROE, CORVALLIS; 541/757-7221

This is a taqueria with an attitude. You'll find several Tex-Mex favorites—with a wholesome twist: heaps of herb-flavored brown rice and black beans and hardly any fat. Check this out: flautas stuffed with duck confit. How about a goat cheese and black bean quesadilla? Recent additions include top sirloin steak with a tasty tomatillo chipotle sauce, pollo con mole, and a smoked tofu, shiitake, peppers, and zucchini chimichanga. The menu is loaded with vegetarian options, and has a short list of simple, inexpensive kids' meals. Order at the counter in the front room; the ambience is basic college campus casual, but the help is friendly and service speedy. The bar in back offers an impressive variety of tequilas. *$; MC, V; checks OK; lunch Mon–Fri, dinner every day; full bar; reservations recommended for 6 or more; www.bombsawaycafe.com; at 25th.* &

Le Bistro / ★★★

150 SW MADISON, CORVALLIS; 541/754-6680

The name is misleading: This is a fine French restaurant, a modest chef d'oeuvre of French chef Robert Merlet, who arrived in Corvallis via Paris, Bordeaux, and the Bay Area. Ignore the sponge-painted walls and acoustic-tile ceiling and enjoy the quiet, intimate atmosphere and lovingly prepared food. The menu is classic French—no fireworks—and everything is cooked just right. Roast duckling might come with fresh rhubarb and a French sweet-and-sour demi-glace; grilled fish choices are lightly sauced. Cheese tortellini comes with fresh diced vegetables and a roasted-garlic pesto. Not all restaurants get risotto right, but Le Bistro does. You know it's French when the menu includes escargots, sweetbreads, and the simplicity of sliced tomatoes with a bit of anchovy and feta, and when dessert choices include profiteroles, a fresh fruit tartlet, and melt-in-your-mouth mousse. *$$; MC, V; local checks only; dinner Tues–Sat; full bar; reservations recommended; www.lebistro.com; downtown near 1st.*

LODGINGS

Hanson Country Inn / ★★

795 SW HANSON ST, CORVALLIS; 541/752-2919

The inn is just a few minutes from town, but you'll feel you're in the country as you drive up to this wood-and-brick 1928 farmhouse. Formerly a prosperous poultry ranch, it's now a registered historic home, thanks to extensive renovation by former San Franciscan Patricia Covey. The gleaming living room (with piano and fireplace), sunroom, and library are often used for weddings. Step outside to a formal lawn and garden. Upstairs are three guest suites, luxuriously wallpapered and linened, each with its own sitting room and private bath; two have decks overlooking the garden or valley to the north. After breakfasting on crepes with blackberries, or a fresh frittata, explore the grounds and the original egg house. If you're traveling with kids, the two-bedroom cottage behind the main house with fully equipped kitchen, private bath, and living area is perfect. *$$–$$$; AE, DC, DIS, MC, V; checks OK; hcibb@aol.com; 5 minutes west of town.*

Harrison House Bed and Breakfast / ★

2310 NW HARRISON BLVD, CORVALLIS; 541/752-6248 OR 800/233-6248

Three blocks from the Oregon State University campus, Harrison House makes a homey base camp for a Corvallis stay—nothing innovative in the way of decor, but nicely appointed and immaculate. The restored 1939 Dutch Colonial is in a neighborhood of older homes, and owners Maria and Charlie Tomlinson are gracious and accommodating. Four large rooms are furnished with a mix of antiques and reproductions, and all have private baths. The English Garden Cottage comes with kitchenette and sitting area; it's available when the hosts' sons are out of town. Enjoy a microbrew or a glass of wine when you arrive, and let Maria know your breakfast preferences for the next morning: just fruit with scones or muffins, or a full meal with the likes of eggs Benedict or stuffed crepes. *$$; AE, DC, DIS, JCB, MC,V; checks OK; stay@corvallis-lodging. com; www.corvallis-lodging.com; at 23rd St.*

Eugene

Although it's the state's second-largest urban area, Eugene is still Portland's laid-back sister to the south. There's no skyline here—unless you count the grain elevator and 12-story Hilton—and a Eugenean's idea of a traffic jam is when it takes more than five minutes to traverse downtown. There's always parking, people smile at you on the street, and even in its downtown core—recent urban renewal projects notwithstanding—Eugene is more treed than paved.

Still, this overgrown small town has a sophisticated indigenous culture, from its own symphony to homegrown ballet, opera, and theater companies. There are more speakers and events, courtesy of the **UNIVERSITY OF OREGON**

(13th Ave and University St; 541/346-3111), the state's flagship institution, than one could possibly attend. The university also features a natural history museum, several historic landmark buildings, a lovely art museum expected to reopen in summer 2002 after a $12 million expansion, and a good bookstore (541/346-4331). There are other good bookstores in town—don't miss SMITH FAMILY BOOKSTORE (768 E 13th Ave; 541/345-1651 or 541/343-4714)—as well as the requisite number of coffeehouses, fabulous bakeries, and trendy brew pubs. Try STEELHEAD (188 E 5th Ave; 541/686-2739), in the Fifth Avenue historic district, or the WILD DUCK (169 W 6th Ave; 541/485-3825). Two serious chocolatiers set up shop here: EUPHORIA (6 W 17th; 541/345-1990) and FENTON & LEE (35 E 8th Ave; 541/343-7629). Finally, there's enough local color—from persevering hippies to backcountry loggers—to make life interesting.

The WILLAMETTE RIVER and the MCKENZIE RIVER run through or near town and provide opportunities for canoeists and rafters. Hikers find miles of forest trails just outside the city limits. Runners love the city's several groomed, packed running trails. Run along the banks of the Willamette through ALTON BAKER PARK (off Centennial Blvd) on the groomed PREFONTAINE TRAIL. Solo runners may feel safer on the sloughside circuit that borders AMAZON PARK (off Amazon Pkwy), site of spirited outdoor concerts in summer. HENDRICKS PARK (follow signs from Fairmont Blvd), the city's oldest, features an outstanding 10-acre rhododendron garden (best blooms in May and early June).

Whatever else you do in Eugene, hike the 1½-mile trail up SPENCER'S BUTTE (off S Willamette St), the landmark just south of town, for a spectacular view of the city, valley, and its two rivers. Spend a morning at SATURDAY MARKET (High St at Broadway; 541/686-8885; spring through fall), the state's oldest outdoor crafts fair; shop and eat your way through the FIFTH AVENUE PUBLIC MARKET (5th Ave and High St) one afternoon; and attend the HULT CENTER FOR THE PERFORMING ARTS (7th Ave and Willamette St; 541/342-5746), the city's world-class concert facility, with two architecturally striking halls. In early July, don't miss the area's oldest and wildest countercultural celebration, the OREGON COUNTRY FAIR (541/484-1314). WISTEC (2300 Leo Harris Pkwy; 541/687-3619), a small but nicely conceived hands-on science and technology museum (with accompanying laser light-show planetarium), is the place to take kids on rainy afternoons.

RESTAURANTS

Adam's Place / ★★★

30 E BROADWAY, EUGENE; 541/344-6948

This is Eugene's most elegant restaurant. Adam Bernstein, a third-generation restaurateur who trained at the Culinary Institute of America, has tastefully decorated this intimate downtown spot by adding mahogany wainscoting, arches, pillars, sconces, and a lovely fireplace. The result is quietly sophisticated, unpretentious yet classy—think San Francisco. Service is attentive, presentation exquisite, and the cuisine inventive, with a menu that changes weekly. Catch the salmon and dill potato pancake with dill crème fraîche and salsa appetizer; or the grilled eggplant, tomato, and warm duck salad. For an entree, consider salmon—perfectly undercooked—topped with a sweet, tangy, chutneylike orange glaze; or sesame-encrusted ahi with pickled ginger and wasabi. Vegetarian options are always interesting. Desserts are stunning—such as a caramelly, buttery bread pudding. An award-winning wine list, with many by the glass, adds to the experience. The pretty lounge offers a lighter pub menu with tapas and oyster shots, live jazz most nights, and a large collection of single-malt Scotches. *$$–$$$; AE, MC, V; checks OK; dinner Tues–Sat; full bar; reservations recommended; on the downtown mall.* &

Ambrosia / ★

174 E BROADWAY, EUGENE; 541/342-4141

Pizzas are wonderful here: small, crisp pies topped with rich plum tomato sauce and trendy ingredients (sun-dried tomatoes, artichoke hearts, roasted eggplant), baked in a huge wood-burning oven. But Ambrosia is much more than a designer pizzeria: take the ravioli San Remo, homemade and stuffed with veal, chicken, and ricotta; or the dill-sauced crepes filled with smoked salmon, spinach, and ricotta. Low lighting creates a warm, intimate atmosphere in this cavernous restaurant, where tables are tucked into "rooms" on the ground floor or scattered on an airy mezzanine; sit at the gorgeous wooden bar to take in the chefs' oven action. End the evening with a cool bowl of home-made gelato. *$$; MC, V; checks OK; lunch Mon–Sat, dinner every day; full bar; reservations recommended for 6 or more; at Pearl St.* &

Beppe and Gianni's Trattoria / ★★★

1646 E 19TH AVE, EUGENE; 541/683-6661

Italian native Beppe Macchi teamed up with John Barofsky in 1998 to create a neighborhood trattoria with the spirit and flavor of Beppe's homeland—with great success. The old house it occupies retained most of its interior walls, cre-ating nice nooks for intimate dining, though there's a family feel to the place, with Beppe shouting greetings to friends and customers, and tables jammed with a town-and-gown crowd. The menu offers mainly Italian standards, perfectly executed. Antipasto choices include bruschetta, and melon with prosciutto di Parma. Salads include a lovely fresh orange-and-grapefruit arrangement with a light Sicilian vinaigrette. *Primi* dishes—mostly imported or homemade pasta with lovely, light sauces and accompaniments—are generous enough to serve as the main course, including melt-in-your-mouth ravioli of the day, and excellent seasonal risottos (chanterelles and shiitakes in the fall). *Secondi* entrees are simple, classical presentations of, for example, grilled fish, sautéed chicken breast (with wild mushrooms in a marsala sauce), or rosemary-perfumed lamb chops. Choose a glass or bottle of wine from a short, modestly priced list. *Bam-bini* have several simple, inexpensive menu choices. Desserts, most made on the premises, don't disappoint. *$$; MC, V; checks OK; dinner every day; beer and wine; reservations not accepted; east of Agate St.* &

Café Navarro / ★★

454 WILLAMETTE ST, EUGENE; 541/344-0943

Like the world beat music that plays on the sound system, Jorge Navarro's restaurant is a rich cross-cultural experience, with dishes ranging from Africa and Spain to Cuba and the Caribbean. A partnership between Navarro and new chef John Davila is adding interest, as Davila brings his Latin roots and culinary apprenticeship in Hawaii to the extensive menu. The two freely fuse cuisines, often arriving at extraordinary results. Start with a bowl of chips accompanied by three inventive salsas, including pumpkin seed–habanero, or with *souscaille*—mango marinated in hot peppers, garlic, and lime. Chicken may come in a Caribbean jerk sauce, or slow-smoked in a beer bath, Cajun-style; lamb is simmered with mangos and an aromatic herb-and-chile mixture Africando. Vegetarian options range from the simplicity of red bean quesadillas to a hominy stew with three kinds of chiles. On the brunch menu, several egg dishes and a world tour of pancakes appear alongside dinner favorites. *$$; DIS, MC, V; checks OK; dinner Tues–Sun, brunch Sat–Sun; beer and wine; reservations recommended; navarro@efn.org; www.cafenavarro.uswestdex.com; by the train station.* &

Café Soriah / ★★

384 W 13TH AVE, EUGENE; 541/342-4410

In this jewel box of a neighborhood restaurant, chef and owner Ibrahim Hamide has wrapped an adventurous Mediterranean and Middle Eastern menu in an elegant little package, comfortable enough for everyday dining but deserving of special occasions. Squeeze past the tiny bar—a work of art in wood—to reach the pretty, well-appointed dining room, airy and smart with original art and fine woodworking; the atmosphere is intimate but not claustrophobic. In good weather, dine outdoors in the leafy, stylish walled terrace. Hamide's roots are revealed in the menu, starting with a stellar appetizer plate of hummus, baba ghanouj, and stuffed grape leaves sized for two or more. The menu changes regularly and might include roasted salmon with a coconut-curry sauce, or marlin Gaza-style (spicy); count on such favorites as lamb tagine and moussaka. Memorable desserts range from wonderful amalgams of sponge cake and buttercream to a subtly exotic cardamom-scented flan. *$$; AE, MC, V; checks OK; lunch Mon–Fri, dinner every day; full bar; reservations recommended; www. clickoregon.com/menus/soriah; at Lawrence St.* &

Chanterelle / ★★☆

207 E 5TH ST, EUGENE; 541/484-4065

Understated, sophisticated, and unfailingly wonderful, chef Ralf Schmidt's intimate restaurant offers the very freshest of every season, cooked with respect and restrained imagination. The small menu reflects Schmidt's classical French culinary sensibilities. You'll find escargots bourguignonne and oysters Rockefeller among a handful of appetizers; traditional baked French onion soup is deeply satisfying. A dozen entree choices, from delicate coquilles St.-Jacques to richly sauced tournedos of beef, are supplemented by a wide selection of specials—whatever is fresh and appeals to the chef's sense of adventure. In spring, it's chinook salmon and local lamb. You'll find a respectable wine list and extraordinary desserts. *$$$; AE, DC, MC, V; checks OK; dinner Tues–Sat; full bar; reservations recommended; www.clickoregon.com/chanterelle; across from public market.* &

The LocoMotive Restaurant / ★★

291 E 5TH AVE, EUGENE; 541/465-4754

Owners Lee and Eitan Zucker came to Eugene via Israel, the Caribbean, and Manhattan, and they bring sophistication and subtlety to vegetarian cooking in their friendly restaurant backed against the railroad tracks in the lively Fifth Street Public Market district. The menu is 100 percent vegetarian (vegan on request), ingredients 100 percent organic, and results 100 percent delicious. The Zuckers know the world's variety of legumes and grains, and enjoy playing with them. With your bread, you're served an "appetizer mix" of nicely seasoned beans. The menu changes weekly but always includes a variety of wonderful soups (try the *shorba al hummus*, a hearty, peppery chick-pea and vegetable mix). Musts include portobello mushrooms in reduced red wine sauce with garlicky mashed potatoes, and thick and richly flavored Ottoman stew. Don't miss the Oregon Snow—creamy white sorbet with flavors of lime and coconut. With the bill come three perfectly roasted hazelnuts, a concise summary of the place: fresh, light, regional—just right. *$$; MC, V; checks OK; dinner Wed–Sat (closed 2 weeks in Jan and July); beer and wine; reservations recommended; www. thelocomotive.com; across from public market.* &

Marché / ★★★

296 E 5TH AVE, EUGENE; 541/342-3612

Stephanie Pearl Kimmel, Eugene's first lady of cuisine, again raised the bar on local restaurants with the opening of Marché, on the ground floor of the Fifth Street Public Market. The day's menu lists well-crafted combinations of fresh and often organically grown local foodstuffs; the interior is elegantly hip with dark gleaming wood and wry artwork. The menu is an ode to the Northwest's bounty, with a nod to France, and is as reliable an indicator of the seasons as any calendar. In fall, locally raised pork chops come with an autumn fruit and onion confit, and the sage-infused roasted leg of venison is accompanied by sweet potato purée, baked apple, and huckleberry sauce. Lunch is a lighter version of dinner, with the addition of a few *pizzettas* (picture pancetta, *delicata* squash, sage, and romano cheese) and sandwiches (consider portobello mushroom with sun-dried tomato relish and smoked mozzarella on homemade flatbread). The wine list and dessert menu reflect the same regional leanings and attention to detail. In a hurry? Stop at either of two Kimmel creations upstairs: Café Marche, or Chow Fun with its pan-Asian offerings. *$$–$$$; AE, DC, DIS, MC, V; checks OK; lunch Mon–Sat, dinner every day,* *brunch Sun; full bar; reservations recommended; www.marcherestaurant. com; in public market.* &

Oregon Electric Station / ★

27 E 5TH, EUGENE; 541/485-4444

The Electric Station narrows the culinary generation gap between the prime-rib-and-baked-potatoes crowd and the yellowfin-tuna-in-roasted-pepper-butter folks. While nothing is spectacular about the diverse menu—no great risks taken—it also has few failures. Seafood is never overcooked; steak is invariably juicy. You eat in converted railroad cars parked behind the lovely brick station that gives the restaurant its name. The historical station building with its 30-foot ceilings and arched windows houses a lively bar with live jazz on weekends. The extensive wine list (more than 300 choices) leans toward California vintages; some 15 are available by the glass. *$$; AE, DIS, MC, V; local checks only; lunch Mon–Fri, dinner every day; full bar; reservations recommended; at Willamette St.* &

Ring of Fire / ★★

1099 CHAMBERS, EUGENE; 541/344-6475

Pull open the heavy entry door, inhale the exotic fragrances from the kitchen, and allow Ring of Fire's elegant, tranquil ambience to transport you far from busy, strip-malled W Eleventh Street. The menu claims inspiration from many Pacific Rim cuisines, mainly Thai and Indonesian. Start with a Korean-style vegetable tempura served with Japanese *tagaragi* spice, or a taste of beef satay with black bean–ginger sauce. Curries are coconut-based, Thai style, and noodle dishes include the reliable phad thai as well as *phad se yu*, with sweet wheat noodles and broccoli. Crispy ginger red snapper comes with roasted garlic and vegetables. Many dishes offer meat, tofu, or tempeh options. Takeout is available until midnight. The smoke-free Lava Lounge may be the most stylish little bar in town; try a "My Thai" or another original tropical drink. *$$; MC, V; no checks; lunch, dinner every day; full bar; reservations recommended; off W 11th.* &

Zenon Cafe / ★★★

898 PEARL ST, EUGENE; 541/343-3005

A compelling combination of culinary imagination and consistency has made Zenon one of Eugene's best restaurants. Urbane, noisy, crowded, and invariably interesting, Zenon offers an ever-changing international menu featuring, on any given night, Italian, Greek, Middle Eastern, Cajun, Caribbean, Thai, and Northwest cuisines. Nothing disappoints, from Chinese "Hot as Hell" skewered pork tenderloin with cucumber relish and daikon-carrot salad, to sautéed duck breast with raspberry Gibier sauce, sautéed shiitake mushrooms, and wild rice. Vegetarian dishes range from a lovely eggplant-based dish named "The Priest Fainted" to Southwest-inspired black bean and posole chili. For a light meal, you can't miss with a bowl of the day's soup and a basket of fresh breads. A good selection of regional wines by the glass (and bottle) is available; Zenon's own complex sangría, juicy with fresh seasonal fruits, is a reliable local harbinger of summer. Leave room for dessert: Zenon's list is the city's largest and, perhaps, best. In the spirit of lively European restaurants, this is a good place for kids; order them plates of plain fettuccine and Italian sodas, which they can mix themselves. *$$; MC, V; checks OK; breakfast, lunch, dinner every day; beer and wine; reservations not accepted; corner of E Broadway.* &

LODGINGS

Campbell House / ★★★

252 PEARL ST, EUGENE; 541/343-1119 OR 800/264-2519

Built in 1892 and restored as a grand bed-and-breakfast inn, Campbell House has everything: a location that's quiet (an acre of beautifully landscaped grounds) yet convenient (two blocks from Fifth Street Public Market); elegant, light-filled rooms with old-world charm (four-poster beds, high ceilings, dormer windows) and modern amenities (TVs and VCRs tastefully hidden, phones with data ports, stocked minirefrigerators); and smart, attentive service. Each of the inn's 18 rooms has a private bath, several have gas fireplaces, and one, the Dr. Eva Johnson Room, has a luxurious bathroom alcove with jetted tub. The inn is designated nonsmoking, but the Cogswell Room offers a private entrance that opens onto a pretty patio for those who must light up. If you like the personalized service of a B&B but don't like to feel hovered over, if you love country-cottage decor but lament the day Laura Ashley was born, this is your kind of place. Coffee and tea delivered to your room in the morning are followed by a full breakfast featuring waffles, homemade granola, and a special egg dish. *$$$–$$$$; AE, DIS, MC, V; no checks; campbellhouse@campbellhouse.com; www.campbellhouse.com; 2 blocks north of public market.* &

Eugene Hilton / ★

66 E 6TH AVE, EUGENE; 541/342-2000 OR 800/937-6660

For convenience to downtown, the Hilton fills the bill, and extensive renovations completed in 1999 nicely spiffed up common areas and guest rooms. It's attached to the Eugene Conference Center, across a brick courtyard from the Hult Center for the Performing Arts, a block from the downtown mall, and within easy strolling distance of most of Eugene's best restaurants. Rooms are predictable, but have nice city views from south-facing rooms and quiet views of Skinner Butte to the north. Amenities include a (very small) indoor pool along with sauna, Jacuzzi, and fitness room. *$$$; AE, DC, DIS, MC, V; checks OK; www.hilton.com; exit 194B off I-5.* &

Excelsior Inn / ★★
754 E 13TH AVE, EUGENE; 541/342-6963 OR 800/321-6963

This European-style inn sits atop the Excelsior restaurant, two blocks from the University of Oregon. Each of the 14 rooms is named for a composer and is charmingly decorated, featuring hardwood floors, arched windows, vaulted ceilings, and marble-and-tile baths with fluffy towels. All rooms have TVs, VCRs, and computer hookups; two have Jacuzzi tubs. The Bach Room, with its king-size sleigh bed, pretty sitting area, and Jacuzzi, is a favorite. The downside: most rooms are small, some with a view of a blank wall, and we've found the reception at the inn's alley entrance to be uncertain; you may have to chase down an innkeeper at the attached restaurant. The upside: old-world ambience, good soundproofing, and amenities that cover the bases. An excellent complimentary breakfast is served in the restaurant, where guests order from the regular menu. *$$$; AE, DC, MC, V; checks OK; excelinn@pacinfo.com; www. excelsiorinn.com; across from Sacred Heart Medical Center.* &

Secret Garden / ★★
1910 UNIVERSITY ST, EUGENE; 541/484-6755 OR 888/464-6755

Originally a 1910 farmhouse, this is now an airy, enchanting 10-room inn on a hilltop just south of the UO campus. Thoughtfully chosen art and antiques give this inn a refined feeling reminiscent of the Edwardian era from which the novel of the same name sprung. Each room is individually decorated, taking cues from the garden, from the rusticity of the Barn Owl to the refinement of the Scented Garden. All rooms have private baths as well as TV/VCRs, minifridges, and phones. Fix yourself a cup of tea in the second-story sitting room, or lounge in the great room downstairs, where you may meet Mack (the house dog) or a guest playing the baby grand piano. Breakfasts are inventive and generous. Depending upon the season, the street noise in this university neighborhood can be a bit much. *$$$–$$$$; AE, DIS, MC, V; checks OK; gardenbb@efn.org; www.secretgardenbbinn.com; 1 block south of campus.* &

Valley River Inn / ★★
1000 VALLEY RIVER WY, EUGENE; 541/687-0123 OR 800/543-8266

This elegant, low-profile hotel is neighbor to a regional shopping mall with acres of parking lots, but the hotel itself looks toward the Willamette River for its ambience. With pretty inner courtyards, lovely plantings, and an inviting pool, this sprawling complex effectively creates a world of its own. The 257 rooms are oversize and well decorated, with the best ones facing the river. Guests can use a workout room, sauna, Jacuzzi, and outdoor pool, or rent bicycles for a spin on the paved riverside path just out the door. The inn's Sweetwaters restaurant has an outdoor dining area overlooking the river that's wonderful for drinks and hors d'oeuvres. *$$–$$$; AE, DC, DIS, MC, V; checks OK; reserve@valleyriverinn.com; www.valleyriverinn.com; exit 194B off I-5.* &

Springfield

"Gateway" is the catchword for Springfield, Eugene's smaller neighbor to the east. The town promotes itself as the gateway to the **MCKENZIE RIVER**, wild with white water upstream but placid and sweet where it flows by town. And the Gateway district along Interstate 5, centered on **GATEWAY MALL** (3000 Gateway St; 541/747-3123), is fast becoming the de facto town center. Here you'll find chain motels, fast food, and a respectable microbrewery, **SPENCER'S RESTAURANT AND BREWHOUSE** (980 Kruse Wy; 541/726-1726).

The old downtown isn't much to look at these days, but second-hand and collectibles shops occasionally yield a gem. Lively **PARK SWIM CENTER** (6100 Thurston Rd; 541/736-4244), the state's first wave pool, is a kid magnet at the east end of town. Down by the river, wander the old orchards and riverside paths of **DORRIS RANCH LIVING HISTORY FARM** (2nd St S and Dorris St; 541/747-5552), birthplace of the state's hazelnut industry (they're still called filberts here).

RESTAURANTS

Kuraya's / ★

1410 MOHAWK BLVD, SPRINGFIELD; 541/746-2951

Its location is off the beaten path, but Kuraya's remains a popular spot with local Thai-food fanciers. The casual atmosphere, friendly service, and large, inventive menu keep people coming back. So do the seafood basket—shrimp and scallops in a hot, coconutty sauce—and the Bangkok prawns, charcoal broiled and served with a crabmeat-and-peanut dipping sauce. *$; DC, MC, V; checks OK; lunch Mon–Sat, dinner every day; beer and wine; reservations recommended for 7 or more; at Market.* &

Mookie's Place / ★

1507 CENTENNIAL BLVD, SPRINGFIELD; 541/746-8298

Housed in a former drive-in, Mookie's is a local favorite for come-as-you-are, sit-down dinners or ready-to-eat takeout. It's not nouvelle cuisine, but chef Randy Hollister's menu is playful and surprising, like spicy Cajun chicken Alfredo, honey-marinated grilled salmon, and hot artichoke dip with garbanzo beans. Slow-roasted prime rib is offered Friday and Saturday nights. Eat in, ensconced in plush orange banquettes at teal-and-pink-tiled tables, or order anything to go, from an entire meal to just your favorite sauce or salad dressing. Expect to take something home, in either case; portions are generous. There's a decent selection of microbrews, several West Coast wines, and an extensive children's menu. *$$; MC, V; checks OK; lunch Mon–Fri, dinner Mon–Sat; beer and wine; reservations not accepted; mook1507@aol.com; at Mohawk Blvd.* &

Spring Garden / ★

215 MAIN ST, SPRINGFIELD; 541/747-0338

This resolutely uncharming spot on Springfield's decaying Main Street serves some of the best Chinese food south of Portland. Although tables have a panoramic view of a Goodwill Industries outlet, you feast on truly inspired sizzling rice soup, egg rolls that are simultaneously crunchy and eggy, and a variety of fresh, flavorful entrees. Seafood lovers make a beeline for stuffed garlic prawns or pan-fried shrimp, two of the menu's best items. David Tofu, chicken or vegetarian, is divine. Do not be influenced by those around you ordering combination plates. *$; AE, MC, V; local checks only; lunch Sun–Fri, dinner every day; full bar; reservations not necessary; downtown at Pioneer Pkwy W.*

LODGINGS

McKenzie View Bed & Breakfast / ★★★

34922 MCKENZIE VIEW DR, SPRINGFIELD; 541/726-3887 OR 888/625-8439

Roberta and Scott Bolling's large, contemporary country home is 15 minutes—and a world away—from downtown Eugene. There's nothing between your room and the wide, placid lower McKenzie River but a broad back porch, immaculate gardens, lawns dotted with hammocks, and a maple-shaded deck hanging over the river's edge. The four rooms have private baths and range from good-sized to spacious; three overlook the river through large picture windows, and two have gas fireplaces. Rooms have no TVs or VCRs, phones, or data ports, but guests can get their fix in the common areas if need be. Roberta's full breakfasts are inventive and satisfying, and you are welcome to raid a well-stocked minifridge and cookie jar in the kitchen. The recently (1996) transplanted Midwesterners have furnished the house with antiques and quality reproductions, giving it a conservative feel by Oregon standards, but one freshened by the Bollings' enthusiasm for innkeeping and for their adopted home. Don't be put off by the Christian fish symbol subtly incorporated in the brochure logo; it's part of the package, but they're not pushy. *$$$–$$$$; AE, MC, V; checks OK; mckenzieview@worldnet.att.net; www. mckenzie-view.com; exit 199 off I-5.* ♿

NORTHERN
OREGON COAST

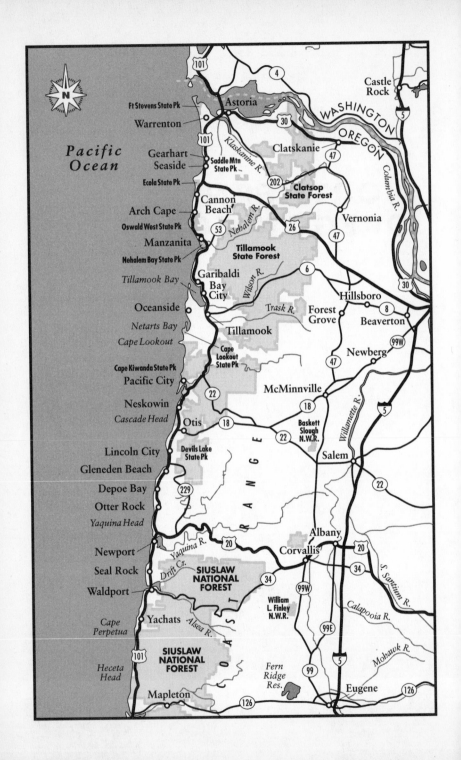

NORTHERN OREGON COAST

Residents will tell you that living is easy along Oregon's north coast. Almost everyone's friendly, the climate is mild year-round, pollution is almost nonexistent, and the scenic splendor is second to none.

But the place is changing: urban folks are relocating here in record numbers, and in many locales (such as Cannon Beach, Oceanside, and Pacific City), new houses are sprouting fast as fall mushrooms in a coastal rain forest. Everyone comes to escape the big city, but aspects of urban life are already part of the north coast landscape. Fast-food franchises, big-box retailers, even outlet malls now line sections of Highway 101. And summer traffic through Seaside, or between Lincoln City and Newport, can be stifling.

Fortunately, commercial progress hasn't undermined the area's breathtaking geography. From Astoria to Yachats—the mouth of the Columbia River to Cape Perpetua—this rugged coastline is embossed with a series of spectacular headlands holding out against Neptune's fury, separated intermittently by broad expanses of sand. Some of these coastal capes, such as Tillamook Head and Cape Foulweather, are forested with conifers, including humongous old-growth spruce, cedar, and hemlock trees. Stark sandstone cliffs sculpted by weather and waves distinguish other headlands, such as Cape Kiwanda, purportedly the coast's most photographed landmark. The promontories feature hiking trails leading to vistas with miles of view. Many stretches of coastline remain pristine, preserved as state parks, and Oregon's "beach bill" (unique in the United States) guarantees public access to the state's beaches.

The Oregon Coast Trail begins at the South Jetty of the Columbia River (within Warrenton's Fort Stevens State Park), then traverses beaches and headlands to the California border. Surfers will tell you The Point in Seaside boasts the best waves north of Santa Cruz, and that the north coast's windsurfing conditions are second only to the Columbia River Gorge. Thousands of cyclists pedal Highway 101 every summer, and like numbers mountain bike the logging roads and trails that crisscross the Coast Range mountains.

It's no surprise that tourism now surpasses commercial fishing and logging as the region's foremost economic activity. Tiny hamlets of a few hundred people—Manzanita, in Tillamook County, for example—showcase upscale lodgings and galleries. Once a culinary wasteland, this area is now loaded with top-drawer restaurants. Even those quintessential Northwest urban establishments, brewpubs, are thriving in Astoria, Cannon Beach, Pacific City, Lincoln City, and Newport.

Certainly it rains—55 to 80 inches a year; that's why the landscape is forever green. Winter storms that carry much of the moisture—sou'westers, they call them—afford one of nature's greatest spectacles: rain falls in horizontal sheets, beach sands swirl, and the Pacific becomes a frothing cauldron. What the locals keep to themselves is that come summer, days are sunny, temperatures almost never go below 55 or above 80, and a refreshing breeze blows daily.

ACCESS AND INFORMATION

Driving is your best bet to and from the Northern Oregon Coast. From Portland or Seattle, take Interstate 5 to Longview, Washington, cross the interstate bridge, and follow US Highway 30 west to Astoria. From downtown Portland, take US Highway 26 west (the road traverses the Coast Range mountains and can be dangerous in winter) to its intersection with Highway 101 at the Cannon Beach Junction. **HIGHWAY 101** (also known as the Coast Highway) is the only highway along Oregon's coast. The **STATE WELCOME CENTER** (111 W Marine Dr, Astoria; 503/325-6311 or 800/875-6807) or the **SEASIDE VISITORS BUREAU** (7 N Roosevelt, Seaside; 503/738-3097 or 888/306-2326) are good starting points.

Limited alternatives include bus and air transportation. **PACIFIC TRAILS** (888/483-1111) offers one bus daily from Portland to Astoria, and as far south as Cannon Beach. **HARBOR AIR** (800/359-3220) flies daily between Portland and Newport.

WEATHER on the north coast is rainy in winter and dry in summer (which generally begins around the beginning of July and lasts through September). After Labor Day, crowds diminish considerably, warm east winds blow, and days are gorgeous.

Astoria

The oldest American city west of the Rockies features a bustling waterfront (with a river walkway and a year-round trolley), neighborhoods dotted with Victorian homes (many now bed-and-breakfasts), and numerous historic attractions. The **COLUMBIA RIVER MARITIME MUSEUM** (1792 Marine Dr; 503/325-2323) displays restored fishing and lifesaving vessels and two periscopes from a WWII submarine that extend through the roof in its Great Hall. Seven thematic galleries depict different aspects of the region's maritime history, and the lightship *Columbia*, the last of its kind on the Pacific coast, is moored outside and open to visitors. Named for a prominent 19th-century businessman and one of the first Columbia River bar pilots, **CAPTAIN GEORGE FLAVEL HOUSE** (8th and Duane Sts; 503/325-2563) is the city's best example of ornate Queen Anne architecture. Both the Flavel House and the restored **HERITAGE MUSEUM** (1618 Exchange St; 503/325-2203), 8 blocks away, feature local history. Six miles southwest of Astoria, off Highway 101, the Lewis and Clark Expedition's 1805–06 winter encampment is re-created at **FORT CLATSOP NATIONAL MEMORIAL** (92343 Fort Clatsop Rd; 503/861-2471). You can watch videos and view period artifacts in the visitor center and, during the summer, watch living-history demonstrations, such as musket-firing and candle-making, inside the reconstructed fort.

For a breathtaking panorama of the Columbia River estuary, the Pacific Ocean, and more, climb the 160 steps of the **ASTORIA COLUMN** (drive to the top of 16th St and follow the signs), which sits atop Coxcomb Hill, Astoria's highest point.

NORTHERN OREGON COAST THREE-DAY TOUR

DAY ONE: Drive up to the **Astoria Column**, soak in the superb view, and get the lay of the land. Meander back down the hill along Franklin and Grand Avenues (between 16th and 17th Sts) for a look at some of the restored Victorian homes. At the foot of 17th, tour the **Columbia River Maritime Museum** (and the lightship *Columbia*), then stroll the riverfront walkway to 14th Street. Retire to the **Home Spirit Bakery Cafe** for lunch; save room for Key lime pie and buy some raisin-nut scones or a baguette for later. Check in at the **Rose River Inn Bed & Breakfast**, and schedule an evening massage with proprietor Kati Tuominen. Next, drive south to **Fort Stevens State Park**, where you can frolic on the beach, inspect the remains of the *Peter Iredale*, and climb the South Jetty viewing tower. In summer, you can rent a boat or bicycle here too. Detour back to Astoria via **Fort Clatsop National Memorial**. Have dinner at the funky but fun **Columbian Cafe**, then take a riverfront walk to the 6th Street viewing tower, where you can watch seals, sea lions, and river traffic.

DAY TWO: Following a sumptuous breakfast at the Rose River Inn, head south to Cannon Beach and browse the shops and galleries along **Hemlock Street** (public parking lots are in downtown and midtown, with free bus service between the two). The salt air will make you hungry, so stop at the **Midtown Cafe** for lunch and a fruit smoothie. From here, walk to the beach and majestic **Haystack Rock**. Or drive north into **Ecola State Park**, south of Seaside, where a cliffside trail affords wondrous vistas. Then head south on to **Manzanita** and check in at **The Inn at Manzanita**. Drop off your bags and drive north again to the **Neahkahnie Mountain** trailhead (look for a green sign on the highway's east side). The trail to the summit is steep, but you'll be rewarded with the north coast's finest panorama. Return to Manzanita, take a quick spa, and dine at the fusion-food-oriented **Blue Sky Cafe**. The beach is a couple of blocks away and ideal for an evening stroll, especially at low tide.

DAY THREE: Take a bracing morning walk or jog on the beach, enjoy a hearty breakfast at Manzanita's **Big Wave Cafe** (822 Hwy 101; 503/368-9283), and head south on Highway 101. In Tillamook, detour to **Three Capes Scenic Drive**, a route that rejoins Highway 101 just south of Pacific City. Continue on to Lincoln City and a Mediterranean-inspired lunch at the quirky **Chameleon Cafe**. Afternoon entertainment comes courtesy of the finny, feathery, and furry critters at the **Oregon Coast Aquarium** in Newport. Check in to the literary-inclined **Sylvia Beach Hotel** for a restful night.

FORT STEVENS STATE PARK (off Ridge Rd, Hammond; 503/861-1671), 20 minutes northwest of Astoria off Highway 101, is a 3,500-acre outdoor wonderland of forest trails, paved bike paths, a freshwater lake, and uncrowded beaches—including the permanent resting place of the *Peter Iredale*, a sailing vessel wrecked in 1906. The **SOUTH JETTY** lookout tower, perched at Oregon's northwesternmost point, is a supreme storm-watching spot and a good place to spy whales in calmer weather. It also marks the start of the **OREGON COAST TRAIL**, which traverses sandy beaches and forested headlands all the way to the California border. With 517 campsites, 15 yurts, and 4 group camps, Fort Stevens is Oregon's largest publicly owned campground.

The **JEWELL MEADOWS WILDLIFE AREA** (26 miles east of Astoria on Hwy 202; 503/755-2264) is a 3,000-acre refuge at times populated by hundreds of elk. Fishing and river-viewing trips leave from the West End mooring basin, just west of the interstate bridge.

RESTAURANTS

Cannery Cafe / ★

1 6TH ST, ASTORIA; 503/325-8642

The setting couldn't be better at this aptly named eatery, housed in a century-old former cannery building perched on pilings over the Columbia River. Every table offers a superb view of ship traffic and the finned and feathered critters cavorting outside. Clam chowder is credible, and the panini du jour is built around thick focaccia slices. More substantial fare includes seafood cakes concocted with crab and shrimp, piquant lime prawns, and grilled salmon garnished with a Swedish dill sauce and seasonal fruit chutney. After your meal, stroll to the end of the 6th Street pier (or to the top of an adjacent viewing tower) for an even better Columbia River panorama. *$$; DIS, MC, V; checks OK; lunch Mon–Sat, dinner Tues–Sat; full bar; reservations recommended; on 6th St pier.* &

Columbian Cafe / ★★

1114 MARINE DR, ASTORIA; 503/325-2233

What began as a diminutive, trend-setting cafe (the coast's first espresso outlet, for example) is now Astoria's best-known eatery, earning raves from as far afield as the *New York Times*. Customers crowd the wooden booths and the adjacent dining area next door for veggie-oriented crepes and burritos and fabulous seafood-pasta preparations. Look for halibut cheeks slathered with mole verde, or smoked salmon tossed with artichoke hearts and sun-dried tomatoes. From borscht to vegetable bisque, soups are satisfying and arrive with hearty slabs of grilled garlic bread. The wilted spinach salad (with walnuts, tomatoes, and blue cheese) is a cafe mainstay. Chef Uriah Hulsey presides over the place like a prince in his palace, showcasing his culinary talents while bantering with counter customers. If you're feeling frisky, order his Chef's Mercy, a surprise potpourri of the day's best fixings. *$$; no credit cards; checks OK; breakfast, lunch, dinner Mon–Sat; beer and wine; reservations not accepted; at 11th St.* &

Home Spirit Bakery Cafe / ★★

1585 EXCHANGE ST, ASTORIA; 503/325-6846

The bread and baked goods sold in this gorgeously restored 1885 Victorian home are the Oregon Coast's finest, and reasonably priced to boot. For about the same price as supermarket bread, you can savor any of the five different artisan loaves baked daily (don't miss the Columbia sourdough or the olive and feta). Beyond breads, baked goods include delicately flaky yeast-dough croissants, scones drizzled with fruits and raisins, and sweet mounds of puffy perfection called Gateway cinnamon rolls. Noontime fare might include smoked salmon and Greek salads, chanterelle-and-shrimp quiche, beefy chili, or a croissant sandwich stuffed with Black Forest ham. Comforting soups—carrot-cilantro, seafood chowder, even chicken noodle—are Astoria's finest. Prix-fixe dinners, offering entrees such as house-made pasta tossed with wild mushrooms, and duck bathed in a cranberry–pinot noir reduction, are on tap. *$; no credit cards; checks OK; breakfast, lunch Tues–Sat, dinner Thurs–Sat; beer and wine; reservations recommended (dinner); corner of 16th.* &

Rio Cafe / ★

125 9TH ST, ASTORIA; 503/325-2409

Instead of the usual taco-and-burrito Tex-Mex fare, authentic south-of-the-border chow (the chef hails from Mexico) is purveyed by this gaily decorated cantina. Begin with an order of *totopos*, oversize white-corn tortilla chips served with spicy black-bean dip, guacamole, and a trio of fresh salsas. The *puerco en salsa verde* features pork stewed tender with onions, chiles, and tomatillos, while the grilled beef slices in the carne asada are flavored with green peppers, tomatoes, and jalapeños. Heat-craving diners opt for *camarones ala diabla* (prawns sautéed with chiles and garlic), or the *pescado rojo*, fresh, lightly breaded sole grilled with a fiery red-chile-and-garlic sauce. *$; MC, V; checks OK; lunch Mon–Sat, dinner Thurs–Sat; beer and wine; reservations not necessary; 1 block south of the Columbia.* &

LODGINGS

Benjamin Young Inn / ★★

3652 DUANE ST, ASTORIA; 503/325-6172 OR 800/201-1286

Painted in antique gold, bedecked with scalloped shingles, and ornamented with an impressive turret, this 20-room mansion was built in 1888 on Astoria's east side for Benjamin Young, a Swedish immigrant and pioneer salmon packer. Wrought-iron gates lead to a roomy front porch outfitted with wicker furniture; the eaves above are trimmed with gingerbread. Stained-glass panels adorn inner doors leading to a living room with gold wallpaper, elegant drapes, red-velvet settees, and a huge white-brick fireplace. Five guest rooms (one downstairs, four on the second floor) are lavishly decorated. The Honeymoon Suite has antique Eastlake furnishings and stellar Columbia River vistas from a circular sitting room in the turret. Exotic plants (a Chilean monkey puzzle tree near the entrance, for example) flourish on the expansive grounds, and a carriage house graces the backyard. *$$–$$$; AE, DIS, MC, V; checks OK; benyoung@willapabay.org; benjaminyounginn.com; 1 block above Marine Dr.*

Clementine's Bed and Breakfast / ★

847 EXCHANGE ST, ASTORIA; 503/325-2005 OR 800/521-6801

This stylish Italianate Victorian built in 1888 is across the street from the Flavel House (the town's most recognized Victorian) and on the edge of downtown. Innkeepers Judith and Cliff Taylor possess a wealth of talent, experience, and local knowledge (she was a professional singer, the director of the Nevada Symphony, and a restaurant owner and chef; he's a former Colorado River guide). Their B&B has a lived-in look, with a baby grand piano and a crystal chandelier in the living room and a bevy of antiques throughout. Upstairs rooms feature private balconies and captivating river vistas. Next door are two suites equipped with kitchens, fireplaces, and two bedrooms apiece (ideal for families). Judith also serves one of Astoria's finest breakfasts: Dutch babies, eggs baked with tomatoes and three cheeses, and a stunning array of sweet treats. *$$; AE, DIS, MC, V; checks OK; jtaylor@clementines-bb.com; www.clementines-bb.com; across 8th from Flavel House.* &

Rosebriar Hotel / ★★

636 14TH ST, ASTORIA; 503/325-7427 OR 800/487-0224

Small, intimate hotels are becoming popular on the Oregon Coast, even in Astoria, a town with a dozen B&Bs. The 11-unit Rosebriar is situated in a residential area three blocks above the waterfront. A porch (supported by stately columns) and front-yard benches afford river views; in the lush side yard, a shrine made of stones and seashells is a reminder that this was formerly a convent. Inside, a homey lobby is furnished with comfy chairs and a fireplace. Guest quarters (all with private baths) range from cozy rooms trimmed with richly stained fir to more spacious view units featuring fireplaces and spas. A separate carriage house—built in 1885, it predates the main building by 17 years—has all that, plus a kitchen. The included full breakfast might feature Finnish pancakes and salmon-and-egg dishes. *$$; AE, DIS, MC, V; checks OK; rosebriar@oregoncoastlodgings.com; www.oregoncoastlodgings.com; corner of Franklin.* &

Rose River Inn Bed & Breakfast / ★★

1510 FRANKLIN AVE, ASTORIA; 503/325-7175 OR 888-876-0028

With a blush-pink exterior and lush gardens teeming with flowering shrubs, evergreens, and climbing rosebushes, the Rose River Inn is easy to spot. From Finland, proprietors Kati and Jaakko Touminen lend European flair to their lodging (four guest rooms; no children or pets), which exemplifies American four-square architecture. He's a former Finnish Olympic hurdler; Kati is a licensed therapist who offers massages ($40 an hour). Reserve the River

Suite and sweat away your worries in a Finnish sauna paneled in Alaskan yellow cedar, soak in the claw-footed tub, or gaze at the Columbia River from a private sun porch. Afterward, relax with a warm beverage in the glow of the parlor fireplace. *$$; DIS, MC, V; checks OK; jaska@pacifier.com; 3 blocks up from waterfront.*

Gearhart and Seaside

Seaside, the Oregon Coast's oldest resort town, sprawls north and south along Highway 101, but most of the fun remains downtown. Visitors stroll Broadway, eyeing the entertainment parlors, bumper cars, and sweet-treat concessions, then emerge at **THE PROM**, the 2-mile cement walkway that parallels the beach. Duck into **PACIFIC BENTO** (111 Broadway, Ste 12; 503/738-2079) for espresso or nutritious fast food—try charbroiled chicken over *yakisoba* noodles. At the Prom's south end, browse **TILLAMOOK HEAD BOOKS** (150 Ave U; 503/717-1477).

Surf fishing is popular in the Cove area (along Sunset Boulevard). Steelhead and salmon can be taken (in season) from the **NECANICUM RIVER**, which flows through town. **QUATAT MARINE PARK** is a relaxing picnic spot and the setting for summer concerts (downtown Seaside, along Necanicum River). Sunset Empire Park & Recreation District headquartered at **SUNSET POOL** (1140 E Broadway; 503/738-3311) has water slides, lap swims, and a covered skateboard park. Across the highway, **BUTTERFLIES FOREVER** (910 Broadway; 503/738-3180; admission charged) is an enclosed butterfly "garden" with as many as 300 free-flying butterflies, open in summer.

On Seaside's south end, a 7-mile trail begins at the end of Sunset Boulevard, winds over **TILLAMOOK HEAD**—a rock promontory that's part of **ECOLA STATE PARK** (primitive camping only)—and ends at Indian Beach.

RESTAURANTS

Corpeny's / ★

2281 BEACH DR, SEASIDE; 503/738-7353

This delightful corner cafe is known for enticing baked goods, sumptuous soups du jour, and extraordinary sandwiches. A bright, airy interior features a rock fireplace and porcelain tile floor, while each wooden table showcases an under-glass collage of old coins, fishing flies, and such. French apple tarts, raspberry streusel muffins, and lemon–poppy seed scones are a few of baker/owner Suzanne Ziegler's oven-fresh treats. For lunch, try a tamale pie or a dazzling chicken salad sandwich, a melange of fixings held together with an apricot mayonnaise. Beef eaters should consider the "WOW" burger, a grilled half-pound of ground chuck layered with melted blue cheese, sautéed spinach, red peppers, and a couple rashers of crispy bacon. *$; no credit cards; checks OK; breakfast, lunch Thurs–Sun; no alcohol; reservations not necessary; corpenys@pacifier. com; at Ave U, 1 block from beach.* &

North Star Restaurant and Lounge / ★★★

1200 N MARION AVE, GEARHART; 503-738-3370

Appropriate that a restaurant with a celestial name should serve heavenly food. Nestled in the dunes above the Gearhart beach, this eatery with a picture-postcard ocean view purveys a tantalizing mix of Mediterranean- and Caribbean-influenced dishes and creative comfort food. North Star is a three-woman operation, run by former Portlanders Merianne Meyers, Gretchen Day, and Britta Nelson. But the soft-spoken Nelson, former pastry chef at Portland's acclaimed Zefiro restaurant (and head chef at Gearhart's Pacific Way Cafe), sets the tone in the kitchen. She takes salmon into uncharted territory with a fillet rubbed with chipotle peppers, then grilled in corn husks. A lightly crusted rack of lamb is drizzled with pungent mint vinaigrette, and perfectly moist meat loaf comes sided with buttery mashed potatoes. Noontime sustenance ranges from Dungeness crab cakes to a fabulous eggplant sandwich slathered with melted chèvre. Sweet-potato pie ringed with a cinnamon-tinged granola crust, chocolate mousse spiked with Grand Marnier, and seasonal berry crisps highlight a revolving dessert tray. Service is as good as it gets at the coast. *$$; AE, DC, DIS, MC, V; checks OK; breakfast Sat–Sun, lunch, dinner every day; full bar; reservations recommended; n.star@pacifier.com; oceanfront and 13th.*

Vista Sea Cafe

150 BROADWAY, SEASIDE; 503/738-8108

At Seaside's busiest intersection, Vista Sea offers a welcome respite from the street-side frenzy. Step inside for a spinach salad tossed with bacon, a bevy of veggies, sliced egg, and raspberry vinaigrette, or a Greek-pasta version served with beer bread. A slab of hot meat loaf stuffed into a doughy house-made bun highlights sandwich selections, while spanakopitta and veggie lasagne are other enticing options. Soft-crusted, hand-spun pizzas have just the right amount of olive oil, cheeses, and tangy sauce. The well-seasoned Vista Veggie Blue is a winner. *$; AE, DIS, MC, V; checks OK; lunch, dinner every day (Fri–Tues in winter); beer and wine; reservations not accepted; at Columbia.* ♿

LODGINGS

Gilbert Inn / ★★

341 BEACH DR, SEASIDE; 503/738-9770 OR 800/410-9770

Sure, Seaside is crowded and ofttimes noisy. But this Queen Anne–style Victorian, built in 1892, is the city's finest lodging and an oasis of comfort just a block off the Prom, on the edge of downtown. All 10 guest rooms within the light-yellow structure are appointed with period furnishings and include private baths. Richly finished tongue-and-groove fir covers the walls and ceilings throughout the inn, and a large fireplace dominates the downstairs parlor, decorated with lush green carpeting and cushy couches. The original Gilbert cottage, which predates the house, is now a main-floor suite. Upstairs, the Turret Room has a four-poster bed and an ocean-view turret window. The Garret, a third-floor suite with three hand-hewn fir beds, is ideal for families. Breakfasts, served in summer on the side porch, are superior. *$$; AE, DIS, MC, V; checks OK; closed Jan; gilbert@west-connect.com; www.clatsop.com/gilbertinn; at Ave G.*

Cannon Beach

Often called the Carmel of the Northwest, Cannon Beach is a hip, artsy community showcasing aesthetically pleasing structures constructed with cedar and weathered wood (no neon signs are allowed). Come summer (and most winter weekends as well), the town explodes with tourists, who come to browse the galleries, craft shops, and boutiques along bustling Hemlock Street.

Still, the main draw is the wide-open white-sand beach, dominated by **HAYSTACK ROCK**, one of the world's largest coastal monoliths and approachable at low tide. In summer, interpreters with the **HAYSTACK ROCK AWARENESS PROGRAM** (on the beach; 503/436-1581) explain the geology and marine life. Less crowded stretches of sand are located at Chapman Point, at the north end of town (limited parking) and at Tolovana Beach Wayside, at the south end. A natural gas–powered free shuttle travels the length of the town (along Hemlock) year-round.

Art reigns in many coastal communities, but Cannon Beach counts some of the best galleries; most are clustered along Hemlock Street. Not to be missed are the **WHITE BIRD** (251 N Hemlock; 503/436-2681), with an eclectic collection on two levels; the **BRONZE COAST GALLERY** (224 N Hemlock, Ste 2; 503/436-1055 or 800/430-1055), with dramatic bronze sculptures of wildlife and landscapes; and the **PACIFIC RIM GALLERY** (131 W 2nd; 503/436-1253), displaying wood and copper sculptures, ceramics, and jewelry. Watch two glass blowers working in tandem at **ICEFIRE GLASSWORKS** (116 Gower; 503/436-2359).

CANNON BEACH BOOK COMPANY (132 N Hemlock; 503/436-1301) has a surprisingly extensive selection. Quick eats and picnic fixings can be found at **OSBURN'S ICE CREAMERY & DELI** (240 N Hemlock; 503/436-2234) and **ECOLA SEAFOOD MARKET** (208 N Spruce; 503/436-9130). **PIZZA 'A FETTA** (231 N Hemlock; 503/436-0333) offers pizza by the slice. **HANE'S BAKERIE** (1064 S Hemlock; 503/436-0120) purveys the town's best breads, muffins, and croissants. Quaff a handcrafted beer at **BILL'S TAVERN & BREWHOUSE** (188 N Hemlock; 503/436-2202).

ECOLA STATE PARK (on the town's north end) offers fabulous vistas, quiet picnic areas, and fantastic hiking trails. A mile offshore is the former **TILLAMOOK ROCK LIGHTHOUSE**, built more than a century ago and decommissioned in 1957 (today it's a columbarium, a repository for cremated remains).

TOLOVANA PARK, as the locals call the south side of Cannon Beach, has a laid-back, residential feel. Leave your vehicle at the **TOLOVANA BEACH WAYSIDE** (at Hemlock and Warren Wy), with parking and rest rooms, and stroll a quiet beach, especially in the off season. At low tide you can walk all the way to Arch Cape, some 5 miles south (check your tide book, so the ocean doesn't block your return).

RESTAURANTS

The Bistro / ★

263 N HEMLOCK ST, CANNON BEACH; 503/436-2661

Cannon Beach may be ultratouristy, but some folks actually grew up here. After graduating from the California Culinary Institute in San Francisco, homeboy Matt Dueber returned to his roots and opened the Bistro 15 years ago, when Cannon Beach was lacking quality restaurants. Over the years, this charming establishment tucked away in a row of shops has won a following for its unpretentious seafood dinners. Top-drawer entrees include garlicky and perfectly prepared prawns tossed with linguine, grilled halibut coated with avocado butter, and seafood du jour served with saffron risotto. Beef eaters enjoy tenderloin bathed in port and slathered with portobellos. For lighter fare, adjourn to the pint-sized bar (a local hangout) for grilled crab cakes, pasta plates, and occasional live acoustic music. *$$; MC, V; local checks only; dinner every day (Wed–Mon in winter; closed most of Jan); full bar; reservations recommended; opposite Spruce downtown.*

Kalypso / ★★

140 N HEMLOCK ST, CANNON BEACH; 503/436-1585

Apropos for an oceanfront community such as Cannon Beach, Kalypso is named after a sea nymph. Formerly a nondescript breakfast and lunch hangout, this downtown eatery is now an understated but elegant dinner house decorated with wired vine sculptures, dried flower arrangements, and watercolors adorning the stucco walls. Mediterranean-inspired meals (Kalypso tempted the Greek king Odysseus on his long journey home from the Trojan War) highlight chef John Nelson's eclectic menu. Soups are blended with palate-pleasing flavors: a concoction fused with carrots, ginger, lemongrass, and oranges is splendid hot or cold. Smoked-salmon curry and a pine nut–shiitake bisque are other enticing possibilities. Beachcomber stew replete with shrimp, whitefish, oysters, and prawns is Nelson's take on cioppino. Lightly grilled calamari is stuffed with prosciutto and mushrooms, while land-based meals might include baked quail or a tender braised veal shank. Sweet ricotta pie and coconut cake drizzled with caramel sauce are standouts on the dessert tray. *$$; MC, V; checks OK; dinner Thurs–Tues; beer and wine; reservations recommended; downtown, at W 2nd St.* &

Midtown Cafe / ★★

1235 S HEMLOCK, CANNON BEACH; 503/436-1016

Locals like to hang here, and no wonder: This diminutive and lively cafe serves Cannon Beach's best breakfasts, and creative lunches. Banana waffles, salami and eggs, and blueberry-cornmeal pancakes are sumptuous morning choices. Midday at the Midtown means imaginative specials: hippie soup thick with tofu, tahini, myriad veggies, and a dollop of peanut butter, for example. Lentil burgers, seafood stews, and lots of Tex-Mex fare (pork burritos, tuna tacos) are other possibilities. Desserts might include applejack coffee cake, butterscotch cream pie, or Cowboy cookies. Just about everything's handmade; the owners even grind their own flour. *$; no credit cards; checks OK; breakfast, lunch Wed–Mon; no alcohol; reservations not necessary; midtown, at Coolidge.* &

LODGINGS

The Argonauta Inn / ★

188 W 2ND, CANNON BEACH; 503/436-2601 OR 800/822-2468

Visitors, particularly first timers, are ofttimes flustered by the numerous lodging choices in and around downtown Cannon Beach. The Argonauta, not really an inn but a cluster of distinctive lodgings, is just off the beach and within easy walking distance of galleries, restaurants, and the Coaster Theater. The Light House has two suites, both with fireplaces and a sundeck or private courtyard. Built in 1906 and one of Cannon Beach's oldest residences, the two-story Town House (with two bedrooms and bathrooms, kitchen, oceanview deck, and stone fireplace) accommodates five guests. Families should consider the cozy Chartroom, with one large bedroom, a living room (with fireplace), and kitchen. Most expensive is the Beach House, an oceanfront home (three bedrooms, two baths) that sleeps 10. If the Argonauta is full, inquire about The Waves or the White Heron Lodge nearby, under the same management. *$$$; DIS, MC, V; checks OK; 3-night min in summer; the waves @seasurf.com; www.thewavesmotel.com; corner of Larch.*

Cannon Beach Hotel / ★

1116 S HEMLOCK ST, CANNON BEACH; 503/436-1392 OR 800/238-4107

Located a block from the beach in view of sprawling resort motels, this century-old former boardinghouse feels like a tidy European inn. A comfy-cozy lobby is appointed with a fireplace, flowers, and a huge bowl of fresh fruit. Nine guest rooms upstairs vary from a nicely appointed one-bedroom arrangement to a suite with gas fireplace, spa, and ocean views. A light breakfast (juice, baked goods, fruit, hot beverages, and a newspaper) is brought to your door in a French market basket. Sharing the same building, the bistro-casual JP's serves superb seafood fettuccine, a Black Forest salad garnished with garlicky chicken and lamb, and chunky seafood chowder. *$$; AE, DC, DIS, MC, V; checks OK; cbh@oregoncoastlodgings.com; www.oregoncoastlodgings.com/ cannonbeach/cbh; corner of Gower.*

Sea Sprite Guest Lodgings / ★

280 NEBESNA ST, TOLOVANA PARK; 503/436-2266

This cute and clean oceanfront motel is a good choice for families (no pets, though) and for couples who want to sleep a few steps from the broad Tolovana beach. All six units have kitchens, color TV/VCRs, decks, and ocean views. Many enjoy glass-front wood stoves. Studio 1B is the best choice for couples. Families can rent a two-bedroom cottage (that sleeps eight); the

SEE THE WHALES

Those darn **gray whales**. They migrate past Oregon's coastline (they winter in Baja California, Mexico, and spend the summer in Arctic waters) during some of the worst weather of the year. Not to worry; the north coast affords a few sheltered spots to spy these magnificent creatures, sometimes close enough to eye the barnacles attached to their backsides. Spotting them usually isn't difficult: adults measure 45 feet and weigh 35 tons, and more than 22,000 whales of all sizes take part in the two annual migrations—typically late December and late March. Here's a specialized, north-to-south guide for intrepid whale watchers hoping to sight a spout or witness a breach. During **Whale Watch Week** (last weeks of Dec and Mar; call 541/563-2002 for information), volunteers are on hand at the following sites (and numerous others) to answer questions.

Fort Stevens State Park (northwest of Astoria, off Ridge Rd): The South Jetty parking area has a covered viewing platform for watching storms, whales, and ship traffic. **Ecola State Park** (2 miles north of Cannon Beach, off Hwy 101): A short walk from a parking area is a spacious, covered picnic shelter with cliffside vistas of—hopefully—spouting whales. Lincoln City's **Inn at Spanish Head** (4009 SW Hwy 101; 541/996-2161 or 800/452-8127): The inn's 10th-floor viewing lounge is open for whale watchers. The **Cape Perpetua Interpretive Center** (south of Yachats on Hwy 101): Good looks can be had from inside the center, or outside on a covered deck.

Want a closer look? Get eye to eye with gray whales from the safety of a chartered boat. The leviathans travel less than 5 mph during their migrations, and sometimes surface almost alongside the boat. Weather permitting, many **charter operators** throughout the Northern Oregon Coast offer tours. In **Garibaldi**, try Linda Sue III Charters (304 Moving Basin Rd; 503/322-3666 or 800/232-4849) or Garibaldi/D&D Ocean Charters (607 Garibaldi Ave; 503/322-0007 or 800/900-4665). **Depoe Bay**'s offerings include Tradewinds (Hwy 101 at north end of bridge; 541/765-2345 or 800/445-8730; www.tradewindscharters.com) and Dockside Charters (270 Coast Guard Pl; 541/765-2545 or 800/733-8915). In the **Newport** area, Bayfront Charters (1000 SE Bay Blvd, Newport; 541/265-7558 or 800/828-8777) and Marine Discovery Tours (345 SW Bay Blvd, Newport; 541/265-6200 or 800/903-2628) are two reputable operations. —*Richard Fencsak*

living room features a stellar vista. Guests can use the washer and dryer and an outdoor grill. Beach towels and blankets are provided on request. Also available is Hemlock House, a fully furnished home a block from the beach (with backyard deck and hot tub) that accommodates eight and has minimum-stay requirements year-round. $$; MC, V; *checks OK; www.10kvacationrentals. com/seasprite; on the oceanfront.*

Stephanie Inn / ★★★

2740 S PACIFIC ST, TOLOVANA PARK; 503/436-2221 OR 800/633-3466

Perhaps the most attractive lodging on the north coast, this gorgeous oceanfront getaway radiates the elegance of a New England country inn. A large one, too: 46 spacious rooms are luxuriously appointed with gas fireplaces, spas, wet bars, and exquisite furnishings. Most rooms (some are two-bedroom suites) have outdoor balconies or patio decks with ocean or mountain scenes. The oceanfront Dormer Rooms on the third floor offer the most privacy; a newer-addition Carriage House (with four suites) is a separate facility. Every afternoon, Northwest wines are served in the chart room, outfitted with a wall of windows overlooking the ocean. Grab a book and sink into an overstuffed chair, tickle the piano keys, or eye migrating whales through a tripod-mounted spotting scope. A masseuse is on call, and a shuttle transports you downtown. A complimentary breakfast buffet is served in the second-floor dining room, decorated with ruffly valances and scores of fresh flowers. Dinners are elegant prix-fixe affairs (reservations required). Look for beautifully plated Northwest cuisine, such as gingered seafood cakes, spinach and venison salad, a jumbo prawn risotto, maybe even passion fruit cheesecake for two. *$$$$; AE, DC, DIS, MC, V; checks OK; 2-night min stay Sats and Aug; stephin@transport. com; www.stephanie-inn.com; oceanfront at Matanuska.* &

Webb's Scenic Surf

255 N LARCH, CANNON BEACH; 503/436-2706 OR 800/374-9322

There's no such thing as inexpensive oceanfront lodgings in Cannon Beach, but this place offers good value and a homey atmosphere right downtown. All 14 units front the beach and some include fireplaces and kitchens. Three top-deck minisuites (9, 10, 11), ideal for couples, feature gas fireplaces, private balconies, and gorgeous views. Ground-level suites (1, 3) have fireplaces, full kitchens, and private oceanfront decks and can sleep four (kids are welcome). *$$; MC, V; checks OK; webbsurf@seasurf.com; www.at-e.com/ webbsurf; on the oceanfront.*

Arch Cape

Stretching from Hug Point south to Arch Cape (a rock formation you can walk through at extreme low tides), this is a quiet community of shoreside residences. The Oregon Coast Trail winds up and over Arch Cape (beginning at east end of Hwy 101, just north of tunnel; ask for directions at post office, 79330 Hwy 101) and into **OSWALD WEST STATE PARK** (4 miles south of Arch Cape along Hwy 101; 800/551-6949), where you walk a half mile from a parking lot to tent sites (wheelbarrows are available to carry your gear) among old-growth trees. The ocean, with a protected cove and tide pools, is just beyond. Surfing and kayaking are favorite year-round activities. No reservations are taken, and the place gets packed in summer.

LODGINGS

St. Bernards / ★

3 E OCEAN RD, ARCH CAPE; 503/436-2800 OR 800/436-2848

This palatial-looking wooden lodging—lighted evenings with white lights—is perched at forest's edge on a 1.5-acre estate on the east side of Highway 101. The interior is no less impressive, decorated with tiled floors, elegant tapestries, French Provincial furnishings, and winding castlelike stairways. All seven rooms have spacious private baths, gas fireplaces, TV/VCRs, and refrigerators. Hand-painted wallpaper and a carved armoire grace the Victorian Room; the Provence suite features a spa and French doors leading to a private patio. The best views can be had from the top-floor Tower. A multicourse breakfast—salmon soufflé, maple-glazed pears, sour-cream coffee cake, for example—is served in the Conservatory overlooking the gardens. Guests can enjoy a sauna and workout room. Outside is a sizable deck and a windless courtyard. No children younger than 12. *$$$; AE, MC, V; checks OK; bernards@ pacifier.com; www.st-bernards.com; across from post office.*

Manzanita

This growing community (lots of Willamette Valleyites retire here) rests mostly on a sandy peninsula covered with beach grass, Scotch broom, shore pine, and manzanita shrubs. Still uncrowded, the town is a popular destination for Portland day trippers and windsurfers, who flock to the always-breezy oceanfront and nearby Nehalem Bay. Overlooking town is **NEAHKAHNIE MOUNTAIN** (1 mile north of Manzanita, along Hwy 101), with a steep, switchbacked trail leading to its 1,600-foot summit, the best panorama on the Northern Oregon Coast.

Three miles south of Manzanita, **NEHALEM BAY STATE PARK** (off Hwy 101; 503/368-5154) offers hiking and paved biking trails as well as miles of little-used beaches. At the mouth of the Nehalem River (on the park's south end), resident Steller's sea lions bask in the sand.

For sweet treats and espresso, visit **MANZANITA NEWS AND ESPRESSO** (500 Laneda Ave; 503/368-7450). Takeout burritos are special at **LEFT COAST SIESTA** (288 Laneda Ave; 503/368-7997). Boats and tackle to explore or fish Nehalem Bay can be rented at **WHEELER MARINA** (278 Marine Dr, Wheeler; 503/368-5780); rent kayaks at **WHEELER ON THE BAY LODGE** (580 Marine Dr, Wheeler; 503/368-5858).

RESTAURANTS

Blue Sky Cafe / ★★★

154 LANEDA AVE, MANZANITA; 503/368-5712

Trendy cooking is always on the front burner at the Blue Sky Cafe, where recipes are as wild as winter sou'westers and culinary rules are made to be broken. Fusion food may be on the outs in urban areas, but Blue Sky's chef, Julie Barker, believes in mixing and matching. Witness her Thai-curry pork ribs, salmon baked in mustard-seed vinaigrette, lemon mascarpone polenta, and smoked-duck quesadillas. Barker garnishes her salmon with caramelized apples and onions, and coats her chicken in a Thai peanut sauce. Even desserts, such as fruit crisps slathered with cinnamon ice cream, and chocolate bread pudding garnished with raspberry sauce and a dollop of orange whipped cream, enter unfamiliar, but tasty, territory. Avant-garde decor—every table sports a conversation-starting pair of cutesy salt 'n' pepper shakers, and the walls showcase provocative artwork—keeps the hip clientele occupied between courses. Service is coastal-casual but efficient, and the wine list is superior. *$$; no credit cards; checks OK; dinner every day (Fri–Sat in winter); full bar; reservations recommended; at 2nd.* &

Cassandra's / ★★

60 LANEDA AVE, MANZANITA; 503/368-5593

Vintage surfboards, saltwater paraphernalia, and imprints of ocean creatures decorate the walls, a "longboard" surfs (er, serves) as a counter for myriad wave 'zines, and the waitstaff is knowledgeable about north coast waves and weather. Cassandra's is not only a shrine to ocean play; this beachy eatery is the coast's best pizzeria, too. Meats and flours without preservatives, organic produce—only the finest and freshest fixings find their way into transplanted New Yorker Fawn deTurk's kitchen. Her golden-crusted creations sport surfer names, such as Off the Lip (with sweet Italian sausage, artichokes, olives, and feta) and Back Door (a garlic, herb, and olive oil pie). Luscious lasagne and an array of salads (try the Neapolitan) are other options. Order house-baked focaccia to go; it's flavorful enough to double as a dessert. *$; no credit cards; checks OK; dinner every day (closed Jan); beer and wine; reservations not necessary; last restaurant on left side before beach.* &

Jarboe's / ★★★

137 LANEDA AVE, MANZANITA; 503/368-5113

The only complaint folks have with Jarboe's is that it's hard to find a seat in this diminutive beach bungalow transformed by husband-and-wife owners Klaus Monberg and Suzanne Lange into an outstanding dining venue. Inside, the decor is unassuming, with unobtrusive lighting and eight tables dressed with crisp white linens and small clumps of flowers. The Danish-born, classically trained Monberg (he cooks; she oversees the operation) purveys a limited, prix-fixe menu (with a few à la carte options) that changes daily. Starters might feature a warm Reggiano-Parmigiano tart kissed with basil, or poached oysters bathed in a distinctly green parsley bouillon. Many meats and fishes are mesquite-grilled, such as a rib-eye steak (with roasted peppers and chèvre), pork sausage matched with duck confit, and silver salmon delicately garnished with crab, artichokes, and cherry tomatoes. Desserts—vanilla pot de crème, ricotta cheesecake laced with currants—are equally stellar. Service is impeccable, and the wine list is exceptional. *$$$; MC, V; checks OK; dinner Thurs–Sun; beer and wine; reservations required; at Carmel.*

LODGINGS

The Inn at Manzanita / ★★

67 LANEDA AVE, MANZANITA; 503/368-6754

A block from soul-soothing sand and surf, this tranquil retreat occupies a multilevel, woodsy setting similar to a Japanese garden. Each of 13 spacious, nonsmoking units is finished in pine or cedar and decorated with stained glass. Every room has a gas fireplace, a good-size spa, TV/VCR, and (except for the Hummingbird unit) a treetop ocean view. The larger Cottage and Laneda units (the latter sleeps four) are equipped with full kitchens and separate bedrooms. Extra touches include terry cloth robes, fresh flowers daily, and the morning paper delivered. *$$$; MC, V; checks OK; 2-night min in summer; dromano@nehalemtel.net; www.neahkahnie.net; 1 block from beach.*

Ocean Inn / ★★

32 LANEDA AVE, MANZANITA; 503/368-6797 OR 800/579-9801

You're so close to the beach here, the tide practically laps at your bedpost. Four cottagelike units (1 is the nicest, with beachfront living room, wood stove, and sheltered deck) are nestled on a grassy bluff a seagull's flight from the surf. All have knotty pine interiors and good-size kitchens (with microwaves and dishwashers). Six newer units (9 is our favorite) boast vaulted ceilings with stained-glass chandeliers and gorgeous fir woodwork. Most have full kitchens and wood heaters set in brick alcoves. Number 10 is fully equipped for persons with disabilities, and 2 and 4 allow pets. Covered parking is provided. *$$$; MC, V; checks OK; 1-week min July–Aug (except units 5 and 10); mrc@nehalemtel.net; www.manzanitarentals.com; at the beach.* &

Garibaldi, Bay City, and Tillamook

TILLAMOOK BAY is a mecca for salmon fishermen, and these burgs along Highway 101 are good places for fresh seafood. Drive out on the pier at Bay City's **PACIFIC OYSTER COMPANY** (5150 Oyster Dr, Bay City; 503/377-2323) for 'sters and a view. In Garibaldi, ask what's fresh at **MILLER'S SEAFOOD MARKET AND RESTAURANT** (1007 Hwy 101, Garibaldi; 503/322-0355); the adjoining restaurant serves outstanding Dungeness crab cakes. Out back is a viewing deck with interpretive signs, and a walkway along the bay and marina. Numerous charter boats operate from here and are good for whale-watching as well as fishing; see "See the Whales" in this chapter for more information. Or try your luck in the bay or nearby rivers. Anglers routinely haul in 30-pound chinook from the Ghost's Hole section of Tillamook Bay, and area rivers are well-regarded salmon and steelhead streams.

Best known as dairy country, the town of Tillamook is in a broad, flat expanse of bottomland formed by the confluence of three rivers, the Tillamook, Trask, and Wilson (which often overflow their banks during winter and temporarily close Highway 101). On the north end of town sits the home of world-renowned Tillamook Cheese, the **TILLAMOOK COUNTY CREAMERY**

ASSOCIATION plant and always-crowded visitor center (4175 Hwy 101 N, Tillamook; 503/842-4481 or 800/542-7290). The tour is self-guided but interesting, especially for children. Afterward, buy a scoop of Tillamook ice cream—31 flavors range from Brown Cow to vanilla bean. **MUNSON FALLS NATURAL SITE**, Oregon's newest state park, is 7 miles south of Tillamook (turn off Hwy 101 to Munson Creek Rd) and features a 319-foot waterfall—Oregon's second tallest.

Oceanside

A quaint seaside hamlet, Oceanside lies 8 miles west of Tillamook along the 22-mile **THREE CAPES SCENIC DRIVE**. Tracing one of Oregon's most magnificent stretches of coastline, the narrow, winding road skirts the outline of Tillamook Bay and climbs over Cape Meares. At **CAPE MEARES STATE PARK** (just north of Oceanside), you can walk up to and inside **CAPE MEARES LIGHTHOUSE** (503/842-2244) and inspect an oddly shaped Sitka spruce known as the Octopus Tree. The Three Capes route winds along Netarts Bay before reaching **CAPE LOOKOUT STATE PARK** (1300 Whiskey Creek Rd; 503/842-3182), with 250 campsites (and yurts), as well as headland-hugging trails and a huge stretch of little-used beach. After scaling Cape Lookout, the westernmost headland on the Northern Oregon Coast, the scenic drive traverses a desertlike landscape of sandy dunes. The road to Pacific City and the route's third cape, Kiwanda, runs though lush, green dairy country.

RESTAURANTS

Roseanna's Oceanside Cafe / ★★

1490 PACIFIC ST, OCEANSIDE; 503/842-7351

With the exception of some new homes on Maxwell Mountain, Oceanside hasn't changed much over the years. Except that Roseanna's, the town's lone restaurant, keeps getting better. Outside's pretty much the same: a converted grocery store fronted by wooden walkways and a weathered facade. But inside, Roseanna's has evolved from a funky fern bar to an elegantly understated setting. Dining-room views of the ocean and offshore Three Arch Rocks make meals more memorable and, best of all, the food is sublime. Seafood, especially, is afforded almost reverential treatment. Smoked salmon is baked in puff pastry, then finished with a chive vinaigrette. Halibut might arrive bathed in a creamy pesto sauce or an apricot-ginger glaze. Petite oysters can be panfried or poached (in wine and herbs), then baked with a Parmesan coating. Try the penne in sherried-Gorgonzola sauce, or umpteen other pasta preparations. If you're not hungry enough for a full meal, order a bowl of excellent clam chowder, followed by a warm slice of Toll House pie topped with Tillamook ice cream, a Roseanna's favorite. *$$; MC, V; checks OK; lunch, dinner every day; full bar; reservations not accepted; on main drag.* &

LODGINGS

House on the Hill

1816 MAXWELL MOUNTAIN RD, OCEANSIDE; 503/842-6030

You couldn't pick a more perfect setting, 250 feet up Maxwell Mountain overlooking Three Arch Rocks. The "house" is actually a collection of buildings, with 16 units. Some are cozy sleeping rooms, others have kitchens, and all enjoy fabulous ocean views. Choose a kitchen unit and stock up on groceries in Tillamook (the pickings in tiny Oceanside are slim). The Rock Room, with binoculars to spy on the wildlife and scan the horizon for whales, is open to all guests. Kids are fine for some units. *$$; DIS, MC, V; no checks; www.house onthehillmotel.com; halfway up Maxwell Mountain Rd.*

Pacific City

A tidy river and ocean community, Pacific City is home to the **DORY FLEET**, Oregon's classic fishing boats. The vessels are launched from the beach in the lee of **CAPE KIWANDA** (a brilliantly colored sandstone headland), sometimes competing with sea lions, surfers, and kayakers for water space. Up above, hang gliders swoop off the sandy slopes of the cape and land on the beach below. The region's second **HAYSTACK ROCK** sits a half mile offshore (Cannon Beach has the other). **ROBERT STRAUB STATE PARK** (at south end of town; 800/551-6949) occupies most of the Nestucca beach sand spit. The Nestucca and Little Nestucca Rivers are topnotch salmon and steelhead streams.

RESTAURANTS

Grateful Bread Bakery / ★

34805 BROOTEN RD, PACIFIC CITY; 503/965-7337

 Transplanted New Yorkers Gary and Laura Seide found their way to tiny Pacific City and opened a bakery with a catchy name, a cheery interior, robust breads (don't miss the spinach-garlic loaf), and a scrumptious array of cakes, buns, and muffins. Gingerbread pancakes, a black bean chili omelet, garlic-potato soup, and a Hangtown Fry bursting with oysters highlight the extensive breakfast and lunch menus. Vegetarian plates include a cheese and nut loaf sandwich; dilled shrimp salad and New York–style pizza are other options. A spacious deck allows alfresco dining. Purchase picnic goodies here for forays to Cape Kiwanda. *$; MC, V; checks OK; breakfast, lunch Thurs–Tues (closed Jan and Wed–Thurs in winter); no alcohol; reservations not necessary; on Pacific City loop road.* &

LODGINGS

Eagle's View Bed & Breakfast / ★

37975 BROOTEN RD, PACIFIC CITY; 503/965-7600 OR 888/846-3292

Perched on a steep hill backdropped by forest, this secluded B&B enjoys a bird's-eye view of Nestucca Bay and adjacent dairy lands. Built in 1995, the attractive two-story country cottage set on 4 acres (with walking trails and a fish pond) features a covered porch, wraparound deck, vaulted pine ceilings, rocking chairs, and comfy-country decor throughout. Five guest rooms, all with private baths, have TV/VCRs, CD players (there's a video and CD library), and cheery quilts and dolls crafted by innkeeper Kathy Lewis (who runs the B&B with her husband, Mike). Three rooms feature spas, and one is wheelchair-accessible. Full breakfasts (Nestucca farm eggs with smoked salmon, for example) are served in the downstairs dining area or out on the deck. *$$; DC, DIS, MC, V; checks OK; eagle@wcn.net; www.moriah.com/eaglesview/; ½ mile east of Hwy 101.* &

Neskowin

A mostly residential hamlet lying in the lee of Cascade Head—a steeply sloped and forested promontory—Neskowin is the final port of refuge before the touristy "20 miracle miles" (as the stretch from Lincoln City south to Newport used to be called). The beach here is narrower but less crowded than other locales. Proposal Rock, an offshore island, can be reached at very low tides.

CASCADE HEAD has miles of little-used hiking trails that traverse rain forests and meadows; begin your hike at a marked trailhead about 2 miles south of Neskowin (visible from Highway 101). The OLD NESKOWIN ROAD (turn east off Hwy 101, 1 mile south of Neskowin), a narrow route that winds through horse farms and past old-growth groves, is an enchanting side trip.

HAWK CREEK GALLERY (48460 Hwy 101; 503/392-3879; closed in winter) offers an interesting browse, and HAWK CREEK CAFE (4505 Salem; 503/392-3838) is a good bet for sandwiches, pizza, and baked goods.

LODGINGS

The Chelan / ★
48750 BREAKERS BLVD, NESKOWIN; 503/392-3270

You could get temporarily lost looking for this place nestled in the trees in narrow-laned Neskowin. Of course, that's part of the charm; even though it's near private homes, the Chelan feels like a getaway retreat. A manicured front lawn and lush gardens add to the seclusion. The nine condominium units each have two bedrooms, well-equipped kitchens, and large living rooms with picture windows and fireplaces. Ground-floor units have a private entrance to a tiny backyard, with the ocean just beyond. Upstairs accommodations (off-limits to children) enjoy private balconies. *$$; MC, V; checks OK; just off Salem Blvd.*

Lincoln City

Welcome to coastal congestion. There is no off season here, and every weekend (every day in summer) traffic creeps from one end of town to the other, past miles of strip development. A gaming casino complex and a slew of factory outlet stores further complicate the gridlock. Still, Lincoln City's restaurant scene is vibrant, and 7 miles of broad, sandy beaches stretch from

Road's End (north end of town) to the peaceful shores of Siletz Bay (first-rate beachcombing).

Amid the chaos on Lincoln City's north end, retire to **LIGHTHOUSE BREWPUB** (4157 N Hwy 101; 541/994-7238) for handcrafted ales and good grub. **BARNACLE BILL'S SEAFOOD MARKET** (2174 NE Hwy 101; 541/994-3022) has fresh and smoked seafood galore. **CATCH THE WIND KITE SHOP** (266 SE Hwy 101; 541/994-9500) is headquarters for a kite manufacturing company, with eight coastal outlets from Seaside to Florence. Kite festivals are held throughout the year at **D RIVER BEACH WAYSIDE** (milepost 115, halfway through town). Walk among rhododendrons, azaleas, irises, and other flowers and plants that thrive in a coastal climate at the **CONNIE HANSEN GARDEN** (1931 NW 33rd St; 541/994-6338).

The arts flourish here. North of town, the quarter-century-old **RYAN GALLERY** (4270 N Hwy 101; 541/994-5391) has 3,000 square feet filled with the work of Northwest artists. **AMERICAN SHADOWS** (825 NW Hwy 101; 541/996-6887) displays a variety of Native American art. On the south side of Lincoln City, the **FREED GALLERY** (6119 SW Hwy 101; 541/994-5600) exhibits functional and decorative glass, furniture, and sculptures, as well as paintings. A little farther south, **MOSSY CREEK POTTERY** in Kernville (½ mile up Immonen Rd; 541/996-2415) sells finely crafted high-fired stoneware and porcelain.

RESTAURANTS

Bay House / ★★★

5911 SW HWY 101, LINCOLN CITY; 541/996-3222

Located just out of reach of Lincoln City's glitzy tourist trade, the Bay House is spectacularly situated on Siletz Bay, with the ocean looming beyond. Inside, the ambience is traditional—crisp tablecloths, richly finished wood and brass, and seasoned service personnel garbed in black and white. Chef Greg Meixner's seasonal menu showcases Pacific Rim–inspired cuisine, highlighted by creative seafood dishes. Dungeness crab and Asian vegetables fill delicately crafted wontons, while oysters are breaded and fried crisp, then bathed in an Asian broth redolent of lemon grass and ginger. Salmon might come poached in a tomato-herb vinaigrette or pan-seared and coated with hazelnut crust (with a curried pear sauce), and grilled Columbia River sturgeon is topped with seasonal mushrooms. Creamy onion soup garnished with bay shrimp is renowned as the coast's finest rendition, and regulars claim Meixner's Dungeness ravioli is otherworldly. Carnivores can feast on pecan-crusted rack of lamb, a grilled pork chop stuffed with andouille sausage, or chicken roulade served with a curry-apricot sauce. Lemon-almond cheesecake and ginger crème brûlée are legendary. Time your reservations with sunset and savor the solace of Siletz Bay. *$$$; AE, DIS, MC, V; checks OK; dinner every day (Wed–Sun in winter); full bar; reservations recommended; south end of town.* &

COASTAL CELEBRATIONS

Want variety? Oregon coastal festivals highlight everything from berries and craft beers to kites and quilts. Some of the best center around food. Eat, drink, and be merry with thousands of revelers at February's **Seafood & Wine Festival** (800/262-7844) in Newport, the coast's original (and, many say, still the best) seafood bash. Not to be outdone, the Astoria-Warrenton area hosts a **Dungeness Crab and Seafood Festival** (800/875-6807) in April, featuring 140 vendors clustered under a big top of tents. Seaside (visitors bureau: 888/306-2326) holds a **Coffee & Chocolate Lovers Festival** in February, and a **Chowder Cook-Off** in March, an event geared to clam (both New England– and Manhattan-style) and fish chowder aficionados. Another well-regarded gathering is September's **Chowder, Brews & Blues** gala in Florence (Chamber of Commerce: 800/524-4864), where visitors taste myriad chowders, sip handcrafted ales, and listen to live music.

Some of the world's finest kite flyers gravitate to Lincoln City for May's **Spring Kite Festival** (541/994-3070) and the even more grandiose **Fall International Kite Festival** (800/452-2151) held in October. With good reason: Lincoln City, situated on the 45th parallel, halfway between the equator and the North Pole, is considered one of America's premier kite-flying venues, and lack of wind is rarely a concern. Probably the coast's best-known festival is Cannon Beach's annual **Sandcastle Day** (800/546-6100), a contest that attracts national attention until the tide comes in and washes away the magnificent sculptures.

Other possibilities include Newport's classically oriented July **Ernest Bloch Music Festival** (541/265-2787) and August's **Tillamook County Fair** (503/842-2272)—don't miss the pig 'n' Ford races, where drivers share vintage Model Ts with squealing porkers. The **Bandon Cranberry Festival** (541/347-9619), in September, has been going on for more than a half-century; Depoe Bay's **Indian Salmon Bake** (800/452-2151) is a sumptuous September feast. Cannon Beach's appropriately named November **Stormy Weather Arts Festival** (800/546-6100) features music, theater, and gallery hopping, while the **Holiday Lights & Open House at Shore Acres** (541/269-0215), west of Coos Bay, showcases a dazzling display of more than 200,000 holiday lights.   —*Richard Fencsak*

Blackfish Cafe / ★★

2733 NW HWY 101, LINCOLN CITY; 541/996-1007

More than anyplace on the coast, Lincoln City is experiencing a rash of new restaurants, some operated by chefs who formerly cooked in other area establishments. Rob Pounding, past head honcho in Salishan's kitchen, has opened an attractive cafe exuding an industrial-chic look, accentuated by exposed pipes, dark gray walls and ceilings, and a bustling open kitchen. Offerings—such as a white-Cheddar flatbread spiked with chanterelles, seared ahi in a citrus risotto, and gingered crab pudding—exemplify Pounding's sophisticated culinary background. But his varied menu (which changes weekly) also includes skillet-roasted salmon, fried-cornmeal oysters (or beer-battered rockfish-and-chips), and a petite New York steak sandwiched in a garlic baguette. Clam chowder is exemplary, and the crab or shrimp cocktails come with a sauce made with tequila, tomatoes, and horseradish. Chocolate fanciers save room for the Blackfish ding dong, an ultrarich fudge cake oozing creamy innards. *$$; AE, DIS, MC, V; checks OK; lunch, dinner Wed–Mon; beer and wine; reservations recommended; west side of Hwy 101.* &

Chameleon Cafe / ★

2185 NW HWY 101, LINCOLN CITY; 541/994-8422

Occupying a small, innocuous storefront decorated with provocative artwork, this trendy cafe packs one heck of a culinary punch, with plenty of variety. An international theme permeates the intriguing lunch and dinner menus. For starters, try a smoked-salmon pita pizza, Asian vegetable egg rolls, or the coast's best hummus, an ultrasmooth, garlicky concoction sided with pita crisps. Brazilian black bean soup, spicy fish tacos, and spinach cakes (with toasted-walnut sauce) are noontime possibilities. Evening grub ranges from Mediterranean-inspired fare (such as prawns dressed with feta-cream sauce, or spanakopitta) to penne tossed with a choice of myriad ingredients (don't miss the citrus-chile sauce). Even salads are unusual: a plate of wild greens graced with roasted yams, feta, and toasted walnuts with a maple vinaigrette, for example. On Fridays, the Chameleon goes Thai. *$; DIS, MC, V; checks OK; lunch, dinner Tues–Sat; beer and wine; reservations not necessary; west side of Hwy 101.* &

LODGINGS

Brey House Bed & Breakfast Inn

3725 NW KEEL AVE, LINCOLN CITY; 541/994-7123

Most Lincoln City overnighters are content with high-rise motels propped somewhere on the west side of Highway 101, so B&Bs have never thrived here. The Brey House (named for owners Milt and Shirley Brey) is a modest but roomy, 60-year-old Cape Cod–style home a block from the beach on the north side of town. Four guest rooms (with private baths and private entrances) occupy three floors of the house. Three rooms have ocean views (the first-floor Cascade Room does not). On the third level, the knotty-pine Admiral's Room enjoys the choicest vistas, along with a fireplace and a skylight above the bed. In usually frantic Lincoln City, staying here is like sleeping over at a friend's house. A full breakfast adds to the homey feeling. *$$; DIS, MC, V; checks OK; www.moriah.com/breyhouse; off Hwy 101.*

O'dysius Hotel / ★

120 NW INLET CT, LINCOLN CITY; 541/994-4121 OR 800/869-8069

Nondescript oceanfront motels rule Lincoln City's shoreline, backed by still more uninspiring lodgings along Highway 101. Fortunately, the O'dysius offers an alternative. This upscale, oceanfront hotel (too big to be termed an inn) contains 30 sizable units outfitted with attractive furnishings, fireplaces, whirlpool baths, down comforters, and TV/VCRs (and a selection of videos). All units enjoy private decks or balconies looking seaward, and suites have full kitchens. Slippers and terry cloth robes are provided for lounging. Wine is served afternoons in the lobby sitting room, which also houses a well-stocked library. Continental breakfast and the newspaper arrive at your doorstep in the morning. *$$$; AE, DIS, MC, V; checks OK; odysius@harborside.com; www.odysius. com; just north of D River Beach Wayside.* &

Gleneden Beach

Across the highway from the famous Salishan resort, a cluster of shops includes the **GALLERY AT SALISHAN** (7760 N Hwy 101; 541/764-2318), which sells wood carvings, wool tapestry, pottery, paintings, even furniture. **EDEN HALL** (6675 Gleneden Beach Loop Rd; 541/764-3825) stages local and regional music and theater.

RESTAURANTS

Chez Jeannette / ★★

7150 OLD HWY 101, GLENEDEN BEACH; 541/764-3434

The Gleneden Beach intelligentsia usually opt to eat here rather than Salishan (although some now patronize the Side Door Cafe; see review). Windows with flower boxes, whitewashed brick walls, and an intimate woodsy setting lend the appearance of a French country inn. The food and prices, however, are decidedly uptown, and the kitchen isn't as French-oriented as it used to be. Oh, you'll still find salmon stuffed with Dungeness crab, awash in a wine-and-dill beurre blanc; but the menu might also offer pan-seared ahi coated with sesame seeds and served with pickled ginger and wasabi. Carnivores can rejoice in the favorable meat-to-seafood ratio: oven-roasted rack of lamb, duck, chicken with mushrooms, apple wood–smoked pork loin, and filet mignon finished with Armagnac and a Gorgonzola demi-glace—and venison is often a possibility. The coast's finest escargots are a mainstay, desserts are sinfully excessive, and the wine list is topped only by Salishan. *$$$; AE, DIS, MC, V; checks OK; dinner every day; full bar; reservations recommended; ¼ mile south of Salishan.* &

Side Door Cafe / ★★

6675 GLENEDEN BEACH LOOP RD, GLENEDEN BEACH; 541/764-3825

 Many restaurants feature live entertainment and most theaters have snack bars, but there's nothing like the Side Door Cafe anywhere on the

Oregon Coast. This open, airy eatery exudes a bistro feel, but shares a dramatic setting with Eden Hall, arguably the Northwest's coziest entertainment venue. The cafe occupies a large, stylized room sporting an exquisite wood-and-marble fireplace, colorful backdrops from theatrical presentations, and a high ceiling with exposed rafters. Numerous skylights allow greenery to thrive inside. The food draws as many raves as the shows next door. A fire-roasted quail appetizer—served on a bed of wild greens and chanterelles, then drizzled with a blackberry vinaigrette—tastes fresh from the surrounding coastal forest. Alder-roasted salmon accompanied by pumpkin polenta and cranberry-orange chutney, and broiled lamb finished with minted marionberry coulis afford a cornucopia of colors and flavors. Bread pudding and caramel-hazelnut cheesecake are the stars on the dessert tray. *$$; MC, V; local checks only; lunch, dinner Wed–Mon; full bar; reservations recommended; www.sidedoorcafe.com; on old highway.* &

LODGINGS

The Westin Salishan / ★★★

7760 N HWY 101, GLENEDEN BEACH; 541/764-2371 OR 888/SALISHAN
Hard to believe, but Salishan has been around since 1965. For its first 20 or so years, this sprawling resort enjoyed a well-deserved reputation as the Oregon Coast's finest lodging. More recently, some travelers called it staid, pretentious, and not as friendly. When the place was sold in 1996, Salishan aficionados held their collective breath to see what the new owners would do. We're happy to report that the resort's many amenities remain intact, and a spirit of excellence, once so pervasive here, has returned. Dispersed over a lush, 350-acre landscape, Salishan includes 205 guest units, arranged in eight-plexes that occupy a hillside rising from the main entrance. Golfers like the 18-hole (par 72) course, driving range, 18-hole putting course, pro shop, and resident PGA professional. You can swim in a covered pool, play indoor or outdoor tennis, exercise in the sizable fitness center, sweat in a sauna, soak in a hot tub, or jog and hike the forested trails. Kids have their own game room and can partake in "Camp Salishan," an on-site activity center, three days a week. All guest accommodations come with gas fireplaces and decks or balconies. The best deals are standard rooms—about the size of a typical motel room, only nicer. Premier accommodations (such as Estuary house) enjoy Jacuzzi tubs, vaulted ceilings, and Siletz Bay vistas. Each of three Suites can easily accommodate four. The massive wooden lodge houses restaurants, a nightclub, a library, meeting rooms, and a gift shop. In the main dining room, a gorgeous venue with lovely views, prices continue to rise, while quality fluctuates. Wine lovers appreciate Salishan's 10,000-bottle cellar. Service personnel throughout the resort are well informed and eager to please. *$$$–$$$$; AE, DC, DIS, MC, V; checks OK; salishan@salishan.com; www.salishan.com; east side of Hwy 101.* &

Depoe Bay

Coastal sprawl has intensified between Lincoln City and Newport, and Depoe Bay sits squarely in the middle of the commercial blitz. Fortunately, parts of this still-charming community remain intact, including its picturesque and tiny harbor (billed as the smallest anywhere). **WHALE-WATCHING** is big here, and during the gray whale migratory season (Dec–Apr), the leviathans may cruise within hailing distance of headlands, sometimes rubbing against offshore rock formations to rid themselves of troublesome barnacles; see "See the Whales" in this chapter. The **CHANNEL BOOKSTORE** (243 S Hwy 101; 541/765-2352) is a used book–browsers' paradise. Metal art, ceramics, and unusual indoor fountains can be seen at **DANCING COYOTE GALLERY** (34 NE Hwy 101; 541/765-3366).

RESTAURANTS

Tidal Raves / ★
279 NW HWY 101, DEPOE BAY; 541/765-2995

Diners are drawn to this classy, cliffside eatery for the fabulous views (from every table) of swirling surf crashing on shoreside rocks and partially submerged reefs (plus a spouting whale or two during migrating season). But they return for the food, an enticing and extensive array of surf-and-turf preparations. Appealing appetizers include pungent black bean and snapper soup, smoked-salmon chowder, and Dungeness crab cakes. A charbroiled chicken breast is infused with lemon and rosemary with cranberry relish, and Pacific snapper is crusted in cornmeal. Thai barbecue prawns, a panfried New York pepper steak in a brandy-onion sauce, and an unusual crab casserole baked with white Cheddar in a white wine sauce are other stalwart entrees. *$$; DIS, MC, V; checks OK; lunch, dinner every day; beer and wine; reservations recommended; west side of Hwy 101.*

LODGINGS

Channel House / ★
35 ELLINGSON ST, DEPOE BAY; 541/765-2140 OR 800/447-2140

Spectacularly situated on a cliff above the Depoe Bay channel and the Pacific, this attractive inn has 12 units, all with private baths and ocean views. A rocky shoreline—not beach—lies below, so surf crashes right outside your room. Ten units are truly special, outfitted with private decks, gas fireplaces, and spas (the seven roomier, and spendier, suites feature oceanfront spas on private decks). Two additional (and similarly appointed) units are located in the owner's house a few doors away. Come morning, guests enjoy a continental buffet breakfast in an oceanside dining area that sports a nautical motif. Don't forget binoculars, especially during whale-watching season. No children. *$$$; AE, DIS, MC, V; checks OK; cfinseth@newportnet.com; www.channelhouse.com; end of Ellingson St.*

Inn at Otter Crest / ★

301 OTTER CREST LOOP, OTTER ROCK; 541/765-2111 OR 800/452-2101

It's not as luxurious as Salishan (a few miles north), but the Inn at Otter Crest occupies an even better location, on the lower slopes of Cape Foulweather looking out over the ocean. Upon arrival, leave your vehicle and hop a shuttle van to your room, where traffic noise is nonexistent. Breathtaking views abound, and many of the 280 units (some privately owned and not for rent) have fireplaces, full kitchens, and ocean vistas; all have private decks and refrigerators. Other amenities include an outdoor pool (with sauna and spa) and tennis courts. An isolated low-tide beach awaits 50 or so feet below, and nature trails lead to nearby Devil's Punch Bowl and additional beach access. Better dining options are available (in Gleneden Beach and Newport) than the on-premises restaurant, but the Flying Dutchman Winery adjacent to the restaurant, which produces pinot noir, pinot gris, and chardonnay wines, is worth a visit. Grapes are grown in the Willamette Valley, then crushed in the fall at the winery (open daily; free tastings). *$$$; AE, DC, DIS, MC, V; no checks; rooms@otterrock.com; www.otterrock.com; 2 miles south of Depoe Bay.* &

Newport

Keiko (the *Free Willy* killer whale) is gone from the Oregon Coast Aquarium, but Newport continues to draw crowds by offering more activities and attractions than any other coastal destination. To discover what the town has to offer, steer away from Highway 101's commercial chaos. First turn east on Canyon Way off Highway 101, and head for the **YAQUINA BAY** front, a working harbor going full tilt where all types of fishing boats berth year-round. Many charter boat companies offer fishing trips, whale-watching excursions, and eco trips. After watching the cetaceans at play, quaff a native beer at **ROGUE ALES PUBLIC HOUSE** (748 SW Bay Blvd; 541/265-3188), with upstairs "bed & beer" rooms; or head for the brewpub, called **BREWERS ON THE BAY** (2320 OSU Dr; 541/867-3664), located directly underneath the Yaquina Bay Bridge. **SHARK'S SEAFOOD BAR & STEAMER CO.** (852 SW Bay Blvd; 541/574-0590) serves fresh fish and fine chowder. Just up the hill, the supposedly haunted **YAQUINA BAY LIGHTHOUSE** (536 Bay Front St; 541/265-5679) is open for tours.

Art reigns at numerous Newport galleries. **OCEANIC ARTS CENTER** (444 SW Bay Blvd; 541/265-5963) displays jewelry, paintings, pottery, and sculpture. The **WOOD GALLERY** (818 SW Bay Blvd; 541/265-6843) exhibits woodwork, pottery, and weaving. Watch glass blowing at **PYROMANIA GLASS STUDIO** (3101 Ferry Slip Rd; 541/867-4650 or 888/743-4116). **FORNISH GALLERY** (856 SW Bay Blvd; 541/265-8483) has land- and seascape photography.

The **NYE BEACH AREA**, on the ocean side of the highway, has a funky arts-community feel and an easily accessible beach. Here the **NEWPORT PER-FORMING ARTS CENTER** (777 S Olive; 541-265-ARTS) hosts music, theater, and other events, some national caliber. For a bird's-eye perspective of boats, bay, and ocean, take a drive through **YAQUINA BAY STATE PARK** (under Yaquina Bay Bridge), which wraps around the south end of town.

On the southeast side of the Yaquina Bay Bridge, Oregon State University's **HATFIELD MARINE SCIENCE CENTER** (2030 S Marine Science Dr; 541/867-0100) has an octopus tank (and a touch tank with other marine animals), interactive video displays, ecology classes, and nature walks. Nearby, the **OREGON COAST AQUARIUM** (2820 SE Ferry Slip Rd; 541/867-3474) features furry, finny, and feathery critters cavorting in re-created tide pools, cliffs, and caves. A couple of miles farther south is the area's best and most extensive camping site (including yurts), **SOUTH BEACH STATE PARK** (off Hwy 101; 541/867-4715). Along the way, stop at **LIGHTHOUSE FISH MARKET & DELI** (3640 Hwy 101; 541/867-6800) for topnotch fish-and-chips.

North of town, above Agate Beach, **YAQUINA HEAD OUTSTANDING NATURAL AREA** (off Hwy 101; 541/574-3100) includes the restored Yaquina Head Lighthouse (circa 1873; open to the public), an interpretive center, hiking trails, and fantastic cliffside panoramas. Visit the intertidal area for viewing marine organisms ranging from seaweeds to shore crabs; it's accessible for people with disabilities and safe for kids.

RESTAURANTS

April's / ★

749 NW 3RD, NEWPORT; 541/265-6855

Beach cabins, cafes, bookstores, and boutiques crowd each other for space in Nye Beach, Newport's original oceanfront resort. April's is shoehorned into a funky-looking corner building, pressed up against the sidewalk, that houses the Sea Cliff Bed and Breakfast. April's intimate interior is nonetheless warm and charming, although it can feel claustrophobic when crowded. The imaginative, Italian-influenced food shines. Salmon is pan-seared and served with barley risotto; *zuppa di pesce* is bathed in a zesty tomato-herb broth; and steamed clams are prepared with peppers and spicy sausage. Polenta might arrive crispy with melted Gorgonzola, while portobello mushrooms see duty in a four-cheese (provolone, Parmesan, ricotta, and mozzarella) cannelloni. Upward of 15 wines are sold by the glass at reasonable prices. *$$; AE, DIS, MC, V; checks OK; dinner Tues–Sun (closed Jan); beer and wine; reservations recommended; aprils@newportnet.com; across from Sylvia Beach Hotel.* &

Canyon Way Restaurant and Bookstore / ★★

1216 SW CANYON WY, NEWPORT; 541/265-8319

Where else but the Northwest would you find a bookstore, gift shop, deli, and restaurant under the same roof? Canyon Way feels as much like an emporium as an eatery, and you could easily get sidetracked on the way to your table. Do find the restaurant, however, where a pleasingly diverse menu awaits. King Neptune's cocktail built with poached prawns, sea scallops, shrimp, and a crab claw—all in an orange-dill aioli—is a delightful primer on coastal bounty.

Swordfish tacos and Southwestern oysters Rockefeller baked with spinach, ham, and ancho chiles are other unusual concoctions. Or play it safe with an order of Dungeness crab cakes, sautéed Yaquina Bay oysters, or prime rib (Friday only) sided with garlic mashed potatoes. Pasta plates include a piquant Cajun seafood fettuccine and linguine tossed with mussels and linguiça. Lower-priced "early entrees" are served before 6pm, and the deli, which offers everything from massive subs to pb&j sandwiches, is a good bet for picnic grub. *$$; AE, DIS, MC, V; checks OK; lunch, dinner Tues–Sat (bookstore and deli open every day); full bar; reservations recommended; between Hurbert and Bay.* &

Whale's Tale / ★

452 SW BAY BLVD, NEWPORT; 541/265-8660

It's been around for almost a quarter century, but this whale isn't stale yet. Open the wooden door and step into a cavelike interior decorated with whale paraphernalia and frequented by a diverse clientele (who long ago realized this place was superior to better-known Mo's, down the block). The person at the next table might be a commercial fisher folk, a suit from "uptown" Newport, or an adventuresome tourist. Huevos rancheros, stacks of outstanding poppy-seed pancakes, and plates piled with fried red potatoes, onions, and chiles smothered in cheese are morning favorites. At noon, the shrimp Louis sandwich and a lusty fisherman's stew draw raves. Panfried tiger prawns, grilled Yaquina oysters, and sausage or veggie lasagne are top-drawer evening choices. Service is coastal-casual. *$$; AE, DC, DIS, MC, V; checks OK; breakfast, lunch, dinner every day; beer and wine; reservations not necessary; bayfront at Hurbert.*

LODGINGS

Nye Beach Hotel & Cafe / ★

219 NW CLIFF ST, NEWPORT; 541/265-3334

Historic Nye Beach has been welcoming vacationers for more than a century, and some of the weathered beach cottages look like they've been around that long. Built in 1992, the Nye Beach Hotel & Cafe is a newcomer, but this '50s-looking oceanfront lodging fits right in. Green metal railings lead to second and third floors with narrow carpeted hallways sporting wildly shaped mirrors and myriad greenery. All 18 tidy guest rooms have private baths, fireplaces, willow love seats, balconies, and ocean views (a half-dozen units have spas). A piano and a tiny bar grace the hotel's lobby. Steps lead down to a bistro-like setting where meals (ranging from chicken satays to oyster stew) are available. Outside is an expansive heated deck for oceanfront dining. *$$; AE, DIS, MC, V; checks OK; nyebeach@teleport.com; www.nyebeach.com; just south of Sylvia Beach Hotel.* &

Sylvia Beach Hotel / ★★☆

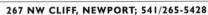

267 NW CLIFF, NEWPORT; 541/265-5428

What a concept: a bed-and-breakfast for book lovers. Owners Goody Cable and Sally Ford have dedicated each of the 20 guest rooms in their rambling, pleasantly funky bluff-top hotel to a renowned author. The spendiest rooms are the "classics," such as the Agatha Christie Suite, decorated in lush green chitz, with tiled fireplace, large deck overlooking the ocean, and numerous mysterious "clues" (shoes poking out from beneath a curtain, bottles labeled "poison" in the medicine cabinet). The "best sellers" (views) and the "novels" (no views) are smaller and not as impressive, but are equally imaginative (a mechanized pendulum swings over the Edgar Allan Poe bed, for example). Books are everywhere, especially in the oceanfront upstairs library, where complimentary hot wine is served at 10pm. Breakfast is included in the price of the room and is served family-style in the downstairs Tables of Content restaurant, where interaction among diners is encouraged. The emphasis is on local seafoods at the prix-fixe, reservation-only dinners. As at breakfast, the food is noteworthy, but meals take a back seat to the conversation. No phones, TVs, or radios. $$–$$$; AE, MC, V; checks OK; www.sylviabeachhotel.com; on the oceanfront. &

Waldport

In terms of visitor amenities and scenic splendor, Waldport has much to offer. Yet this town has become renowned for a runaway shipwreck (the *New Carissa*, which inadvertently beached south of here in 1999). On Waldport's north end, the **ALSEA BAY BRIDGE**, built in 1937 and rebuilt in 1991 (on Hwy 101), is the coast's most picturesque span, and protected walkways stretch its length. At the south end, an interpretive center has photos and historic transportation displays.

Waldport's city center is unspoiled by tourism. Buy and fly a kite from **PACIFIC MOTION** (205 SW Hwy 101; 541/563-5575). Nearby, **GRAND CENTRAL PIZZA** (235 Hwy 101; 541/563-3232) offers massive "grinder" sandwiches, pizza, and second-deck dining overlooking Alsea Bay. In the Old Town section, **DOCK OF THE BAY MARINA** (1245 Mill; 541/563-2003) sells angling equipment and rents boats and crab rings. Buy some bait, then try your luck from the Port of Alsea pier (Port St and the bayfront).

Two miles north of town, the distinctive-looking **TRIAD GALLERY** (5667 Hwy 101; 541/563-5442) exhibits watercolors, jewelry, wearable art, and provocative metal figures (including an outdoor neon horse).

LODGINGS

Cliff House Bed and Breakfast / ★★

1450 ADAHI RD, WALDPORT; 541/563-2506

Waldport's finest views can be enjoyed from the aptly named Cliff House, a romantic retreat geared to cuddling couples (leave kids at home). Watch

113

frolicking seals, sea lions, and migrating gray whales, and savor memorable sunsets from this bright blue lodging perched above the Alsea River's mouth. Four rooms, all with ocean views, are appointed with antiques and TV/VCRs; three have balconies. Guests can sip afternoon tea, warm to a roaring fire, or tickle the keys on a grand piano in the ocean-facing Great Room. Out back, a spacious, ocean-view deck is surrounded by glass and outfitted with a hot tub and sauna. Massages ($50 per hour) are administered in the cliff-top gazebo. Continental breakfasts are served during the week; full breakfast are the norm Saturday and Sunday. Perhaps the coast's most opulent accommodation, the Bridal Suite includes a tufted-velvet sleigh bed with canopy, a turn-of-the-century parlor stove, and a mirrored bath with spa. Though the Cliff House has elicited both rants and raves over the years, our experiences have been mostly positive. *$$$; DIS, MC, V; checks OK; clifhos@pioneer.net; www.virtualcities.com; 1 block west of Hwy 101.*

Edgewater Cottages / ★

3978 SW PACIFIC COAST HWY, WALDPORT; 541/563-2240

The owners live on the premises, contributing to the homey atmosphere at these shaked, shingled, and very popular (full all summer) lodgings situated on a bluff above the beach. All eight units have ocean views, fireplaces, well-equipped kitchens, and sundecks, but no TVs or phones (guests can use the office phone). The pint-sized Wheel House (with a queen bed and skylights) is strictly a two-person affair, while the commodious Beachcomber can accommodate as many as 15. Children are welcome; even pets can stay with prior approval. Out back, a short trail leads to an uncrowded stretch of sand. *$$; no credit cards; checks OK; min stay requirements; 2½ miles south of Waldport.*

Yachats

Eight miles down the road from Waldport, Yachats (pronounced "YA-hots") hosts a mix of aging countercultural types, yuppies, and tourists, and exudes a hip, artsy ambience. Called the "gem of the Oregon Coast," this resort village of 600-plus residents counts numerous galleries, such as **EARTHWORKS GALLERY** (2222 N Hwy 101; 541/547-4300), a remodeled myrtlewood factory specializing in ceramics, hand-blown glass, and metal and wood sculptures. **BACKPORCH GALLERY** (4th and Hwy 101; 541/547-4500) sells basketry, jewelry, handcrafted dolls, and soft-hued seascapes.

Yachats is a coastal Native American word meaning "dark waters at the foot of the mountain," and just a few blocks west of Highway 101, tide pools teem with marine life. The Yachats River intersects downtown and empties into the Pacific, providing a playground for seabirds, seals, and sea lions. Yachats is also known for runs of silver smelt, savory sardinelike fish that congregate near shore in bunches, May through September (call the Yachats Visitor Center for info on July's annual smelt fry; 541/547-3530). A likely location to view the fish is **SMELT SANDS STATE RECREATION AREA** (off Hwy 101), a small day-use area on the north side of town. This is also the beginning of Yachats 804 oceanfront trail, a wheelchair-accessible, paved path that meanders north almost a mile above driftwood-strewn coves.

A 2,700-acre rain forest boasting twice the botanical mass, per square acre, of the Amazon jungle, the **CAPE PERPETUA SCENIC AREA** is just south of town. To get oriented, head for the **CAPE PERPETUA INTERPRETIVE CENTER** (2400 Hwy 101, 3 miles south of Yachats; 541/547-3289), which features please-touch exhibits, and family environmental programs, such as tide-pool explorations, on spring and summer weekends. On a clear day, the West Shelter (above the Interpretive Center; accessible by road or trail) affords the coast's finest view, a 150-mile, north-to-south panorama from Cape Foulweather to Cape Blanco and 40 miles out to sea.

RESTAURANTS

La Serre / ★

160 W 2ND, YACHATS; 541/547-3420

The sole fine-dining option between Seal Rock and Florence, La Serre ("the greenhouse") houses the largest plant collection this side of Cafe Perpetua's rain forest. An expansive dining area with overhead skylights and a beamed ceiling is sided by a cozy lounge with comfy couches and fireplace. Though the kitchen offers French-inspired dishes such as clams baked in puff pastry and an elaborate filet mignon wrapped in bacon, topped with prawns, and bathed in a cream sauce, simply prepared seafood is your best bet. Shrimp or crab cocktails, fishermen's stew, lightly breaded Umpqua oysters, Dungeness crab cakes, and grilled salmon are all keepers. Or have it all in the seafood extravaganza, a cornucopia of saltwater bounty. La Serre is also one of the coast's only purveyors of Manhattan-style clam chowder. Daily vegetarian specials, too. *$$; AE, MC, V; local checks only; dinner Wed–Mon (closed Jan); full bar; reservations recommended; at Beach, downtown.*

LODGINGS

The Kittiwake / ★

95368 HWY 101, YACHATS; 541/547-4470

Built in 1993 on a couple of sandy acres covered with salal, shore pine, and blackberry bushes (deer and elk often spend the night in the bunchgrass), the Kittiwake is a more contemporary structure than its neighboring B&Bs. The cheery interior is outfitted with overstuffed furniture, cushy window seats overlooking the Pacific, and a sizable collection of reading material. All three guest rooms (two have spas) are on the main floor and enjoy ocean views and private beach access via an outside deck, where breakfast is served on sunny mornings. *$$$; AE, DIS, MC, V; checks OK; holidays@kittiwakebandb.com; www.kittiwakebandb.com; 6½ miles south of Yachats.*

Sea Quest Bed & Breakfast / ★★★

95354 HWY 101, YACHATS; 541/547-3782 OR 800/341-4878

Three neighboring B&Bs hug the shoreline south of Yachats; they are among the coast's finest offerings. At Sea Quest, the choice pick, you spend the night in a luxurious, estatelike cedar structure perched on a sandy knoll right above the Pacific. Four of five guest rooms have bathtub spas, private entrances, and ocean views. In the commodious and inviting living room, guests can scan the horizon with a spyglass, or plunk down with a good book in one of the plush chairs. Elaine Ireland, who runs the place with her husband, George Rozsa, is renowned for her breakfast buffet: fresh pastries, blintzes topped with Oregon blueberries, Sea Quest puffs (Dutch babies) sided with bananas Foster, and a Chilean casserole blended with eggs, black beans, and assorted chiles. *$$$; DIS, MC, V; checks OK; seaquest@newportnet.com; www.seaq.com; 6½ miles south of Yachats.*

Shamrock Lodgettes

105 HWY 101 S, YACHATS; 541/547-3312 OR 800/845-5028

This cluster of affordable lodgings occupies a parklike, oceanfront setting on 4 acres along the Yachats River. Don't let the quaint name dissuade you: these 19 units (6 are log cabins) are comfortable and not at all schlocky. All units have fireplaces, and some include small kitchens. Rooms 8–15 and Apartment 7 are the best deals. Cabin 6 (with two bedrooms and baths) is family friendly. Guests receive a morning newspaper, have use of a sauna and hot tub, and can arrange for a personal massage ($40 per hour). Pets are welcome in the cabins. *$$; AE, DIS, MC, V; checks OK; shamrock@actionnet.net; www. beachesbeaches.com/shamrock.html; just south of Yachats River bridge.*

Ziggurat Bed & Breakfast / ★★

95330 HWY 101, YACHATS; 541/547-3925

A four-story, glass-and-wood structure that takes its name from the ancient Sumerian word for "terraced pyramid," this is surely the coast's most visually stunning B&B. The location is equally dramatic, on a sandy knoll just back from the ocean and beside the gurgling waters of Tenmile Creek. Inside, views from all 40 windows (including glass-enclosed decks) enthrall guests, especially during storms. Two 800-square-foot suites are available: the east suite faces the Coast Range mountains and boasts a sauna and an additional bed; the west suite enjoys a round, glass-block shower and stellar views enhanced by 27-foot-long windows. A wood stove and a baby grand piano highlight the expansive living quarters. No children younger than 14. *$$$; No credit cards; checks OK; 6½ miles south of Yachats.*

SOUTHERN
OREGON COAST

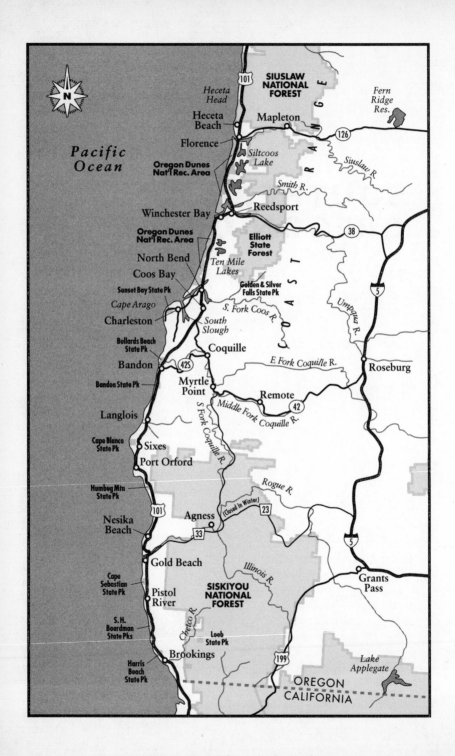

SOUTHERN OREGON COAST

Oregon's spectacular south coast is distinct from the north coast in several ways. About five hours south of metro Portland and eight hours north of San Francisco, the south coast is sparsely populated and has far fewer visitors. Six major towns, most with populations well under 10,000, are ports situated near or at the mouths of rivers: Florence, on the Siuslaw; Reedsport, on the Umpqua; Coos Bay on the Coos; Bandon, on the Coquille; Gold Beach, on the Rogue; and Brookings, on the Chetco. The largest "city" is Coos Bay (formerly named Marshfield), combined with the adjacent communities of North Bend and Empire, as well as the little fishing village of Charleston.

In addition, the south coast has much more sand, including Sahara-sized dunes. Rocky slopes are covered with myrtlewood trees, waxy-leafed cousins to California bay laurel trees; cinnamon-barked arbutus (a.k.a. madrona), typically found on nearly bare-rock volcanic outcroppings; prolific wild azaleas and rhododendrons; aromatic Port Orford cedars and yews; and magnificent, towering redwoods, at their northern limit on Oregon's south coast.

Coos Bay is the largest natural bay north of San Francisco, and for years has been the Southern Oregon Coast's center of resource extraction—gold and coal in the 1800s, then fish and shellfish. Since the early 1900s, it was the major timber and finished-lumber exporter on the Pacific Coast—until timber crashed and the mills pulled out in the 1980s. The city of Coos Bay is less charming than its considerable surrounding natural beauty. A virtually untouched estuary here is habitat for thousands of migrating waterfowl as well as the newly arrived colony of white egrets that roost in fir trees above North Bend's museum; from lookouts on the rugged cliffs of Cape Arago, you can see the Pacific, and offshore rocks with hundreds of barking sea lions.

Two developments promise tourism as the economic savior of the south coast: the Coquille Indian Tribe has transformed a huge plywood mill on the Coos Bay waterfront into a thriving casino/hotel resort complex, which anchors a waterfront development plan; and near Bandon, sand dunes are being developed to build back-to-back golf courses, reminiscent of Scotland's St. Andrews and California's Pebble Beach.

ACCESS AND INFORMATION

HIGHWAY 101 follows the Pacific coastline from Washington to Southern California, and links most of the towns along the Southern Oregon Coast. From Interstate 5, four two-lane paved roads follow rivers west to the south coast: From Eugene, HIGHWAY 126 follows the Siuslaw River to Florence; from Drain, HIGHWAY 38 follows the Umpqua River to Reedsport; from Roseburg, HIGHWAY 42 follows the Coquille River to Bandon and Coos Bay; and from Grants Pass, US HIGHWAY 199 follows the Smith River, then cuts through the redwoods and dips into Northern California near the Oregon border and

Brookings. All are scenic routes; most appealing are Highways 38 and 199, but none will disappoint.

Air service between Portland and North Bend is offered several times daily on **HORIZON AIR** (800/547-9308); **GREYHOUND** (800/231-2222) offers regular daily bus service.

Florence

Florence, intersected by the deep, green Siuslaw River, is surrounded by the beauty of the **OREGON DUNES NATIONAL RECREATION AREA**. The geography here—and for 50 miles south—is devoid of the trademark rugged Oregon Coast headlands. Instead, expansive, wind-sculpted sand dunes, some of them hundreds of feet high, dominate the landscape. The recreation area extends more than 50 miles from Heceta Beach to Coos Bay—32,000 acres of mountainous dunes. Orient yourself to this intriguing ecosystem by exploring **SOUTH JETTY ROAD**, just south of the bridge across the Siuslaw River, or the **OREGON DUNES OVERLOOK**, 11 miles south on Highway 101. The dunes, some of which reach 600 feet high, hide excellent swimming lakes. Just east of the dunes, several large freshwater lakes and many lily-pad-studded ponds are circled by pines and, in spring and summer, bright pink and red rhododendrons.

Florence has transformed itself from a sleepy fishing village to a tourist mecca, but the local catch can still be had at **WEBER'S FISH MARKET** (802 Hwy 101; 541/997-8886). The revitalized **OLD TOWN**, a continually upgraded few blocks of 60 shops, restaurants, bed-and-breakfasts, and some of the town's oldest structures, has become visitor-oriented without selling out to schlock. The best coffee is at **SIUSLAW RIVER COFFEE ROASTERS** (1240 Bay St; 541/997-3443), with a river view from the deck and a paperback book library. A small sternwheeler, **WESTWARD HO!** (Maple and Bay Sts; 541/997-9691), offers half-hour and dinner river cruises from Old Town. If you want a closer view, launch a kayak from **CENTRAL COAST WATERSPORTS** (1560 2nd St; 541/997-1812). Check out Florence's early history, including a film on shipwrecks, at the **SIUSLAW PIONEER MUSEUM** (85192 S Hwy 101; 541/997-7884), 1 mile south of the 1930s-era bridge crossing the Siuslaw.

DARLINGTONIA BOTANICAL WAYSIDE (5 miles north of Florence on the east side of Hwy 101) is a bog featuring cobra lilies. The unusual burgundy flowers of these insect-eating plants bloom in May. Another 6 miles north, on the breathtaking cliffs of **HECETA HEAD**, are the **SEA LION CAVES** (91560 Hwy 101; 541/547-3111; www.sealioncaves.com)—far less kitschy than the advance hype might suggest. You descend 21 stories to a peephole in a natural, surf-swept cavern, where hundreds of golden brown Steller's sea lions frolic or doze on the rocks. During spring, peer over the cliffs with binoculars to watch cormorants' ritual mating displays. **HECETA HEAD LIGHTHOUSE** is the Oregon Coast's most powerful beacon and perhaps the most photographed lighthouse on the coast. Perched on the 1,000-foot headland, just off Highway 101, the

SOUTHERN OREGON COAST THREE-DAY TOUR

DAY ONE: Breakfast in Florence's Old Town at **Bridgewater**, then head north to Heceta Head and the **Sea Lion Caves**, to see the spectacular view and take the elevator from the top of the cliff into a natural ocean cave. Back in Florence, stop for coffee and check out the waterfront shops in **Old Town**. Then take the one-hour lunch cruise aboard the **Westward Ho!** stern-wheeler on the Siuslaw River, or pack a picnic and hike through the sand dunes at **Honeyman State Park** south of town. Head back to Florence for high tea at **Lovejoy's English Tea Room** or have a beer in **Lovejoy's pub**; both overlook the river. Drive south to Reedsport and check out the **Umpqua Discovery Center Museum**, then watch elk grazing in fenced wetlands at the **Dean Creek Elk Reserve**. Have dinner at **Cafe Francais** in Winchester Bay, and watch the sunset from the overlook at the **Umpqua Lighthouse**. Drive south about 20 miles to Coos Bay and check in to a "corner suite" (second floor, Jacuzzi at the window) at the **Mill Resort & Casino**'s hotel. Try your luck at the casino or sack out early.

DAY TWO: Breakfast at the **Pancake Mill**, then drive west on a side road about 8 miles and spend a half day exploring the trails, gardens, and overlooks at **Shore Acres State Park**. Return to the **Charleston boat basin** for fresh fried oysters or fish-and-chips (in summer get them to go, then sit on the jetty and watch brown pelicans scoop up fish). Take a quick visit to the interpretive center at **South Slough National Estuarine Research Center Reserve**, then drive on south on the side road—through heavy clear-cuts here—to Highway 101 southbound. If you've arranged a tee-time for **Bandon Dunes golf course**, play 18 holes; if you haven't, check out the lodge (a sunny lounge with a full-service bar—and espresso—overlooks the first course). If you don't golf, go directly to **Bandon Cheese factory** for samples of cheddars (try the smoked), and a huge Umpqua ice cream cone, then cross the street to **Old Town** for cranberry fudge. Follow the Coquille River to the jetty at its mouth and hike the spectacular beach past enormous haystack rocks. Grab dinner at **Harp's**, overlooking the river and the historic lighthouse. Some of the best accommodations on the south coast are at Bandon's **Sunset Motel**. Watch the sun and moon set from your oceanfront room; all units have coffeemakers and microwaves, so stock up for an early breakfast.

DAY THREE: Rise at the crack of dawn, thermos of coffee in hand, and drive 40 scenic miles to **Gold Beach**; try to resist the charms of Cape Blanco and Humbug Mountain State Parks (near Port Orford) so you can go on a daylong **jet-boat trip** up the Rogue River (make arrangements in advance)—a stop is made for lunch on the way upriver. Stay overnight at **Tu Tu'Tun Lodge** overlooking the Rogue, and have dinner in the lodge's pretty dining room. Request a room with a hot tub on your deck, then have a soak, wrap up in a robe, and relax in front of your private fireplace.

56-foot-high lighthouse isn't open to the public, but the grounds, with a trail to Heceta Head Lighthouse State Viewpoint, are yours for a $3 day-use fee.

RESTAURANTS

Bridgewater / ★

1297 BAY ST, FLORENCE; 541/997-9405

The barn-sized first floor of Florence's oldest clapboard building (the Kyle building) in Old Town serves a bodacious breakfast: stacks of hazelnut pancakes with sweet blackberry butter, or eggs Benedict topped with heaps of fresh crab. Coffee is good and strong. We favor seats in the old general store's front windows that warm with morning sun. Lunches feature fish-and-chips and burgers; dinners favor seafood pasta dishes. *$; MC, V; local checks only; breakfast, lunch, dinner every day (breakfast Sat–Sun in winter); beer and wine; reservations not necessary; in Old Town.*

Lovejoy's / ★★★

85625 HWY 101, FLORENCE; 541/902-0502

Named after the fictional antique dealer in Jonathan Gash mysteries, Lovejoy's is, hands down, one of the best places to eat on the coast. Popular with Canadians—drawn by British flags whipping in the wind and the 1963 Austin taxicab out front—the British-style pub, English Tea Room, and fine-dining room are co-owned by London-born Martin Spicknell and his Dutch-Indonesian wife, Marianne. In the California antique business for years, they have filled the place with antiques and oddities. Expect generous entrees—perfectly prepared rack of New Zealand lamb, veal chops, steaks, seafood, wild boar, or kangaroo—with shrimp cocktail, soup or salad, crisp vegetables, mashed red potatoes, and bread pudding with rum sauce included in the price. There's a view from every table and live piano music on weekend nights. In the tea room (2–4pm every day), choose between cream tea, light tea, or high tea, or order from a menu of traditional English sandwiches, and crumpets or scones. The pub features cod-and-chips, meat pies, Scottish kippers, bangers, or a ploughman's lunch. Martin oversees the full bar, with beers on tap and in bottles from England and Australia. Its move from Old Town across the river to the circa 1970 Best Western Pier Point Inn has increased the 57-riverside-room hotel's business. Travelers who stop for a meal often change their itinerary and stay overnight (riverfront rooms, two Jacuzzi spas, sauna, and indoor pool). *$$; AE, DIS, MC, V; checks OK; lunch, dinner every day, brunch Sun; full bar; reservations recommended; martin@restaurants-5560.com; south side of Siuslaw River bridge.* &

LODGINGS

Edwin K Bed & Breakfast / ★

1155 BAY ST, FLORENCE; 541/997-8360 OR 800/8EDWINK

Built in 1914 by one of Florence's founders, the Edwin K sits in a quiet residential neighborhood beyond the bustle of Old Town. Inside the place looks formal, but feels warm and homey. Ivory wall-to-wall carpeting contrasts nicely with aged and swarthy Douglas fir woodwork. All six spacious guest rooms (named for seasons) are fitted with private baths and adorned with antiques. New owners Inez and Victor West serve a five-course breakfast in the exquisitely appointed dining room. Out back are a private courtyard and water-fall. *$$; DIS, MC, V; checks OK; west edge of Old Town.*

The Johnson House Bed & Breakfast / ★★

216 MAPLE ST, FLORENCE; 541/997-8000 OR 800/768-9488

We're thankful for the wit, curiosity, and lofty aesthetic standards Jayne and Ron Fraese bring to their perennially popular B&B. Reflecting the Fraeses' interests (he's a political science prof, she's an English teacher), the library is strong on local history, natural history, politics, and collections of essays, letters, cartoons, and poetry. One of six guest rooms is a cute garden cottage; two have claw-footed tubs. Stellar breakfasts include fresh garden fruit and produce (grown out back) and home-baked bread. The Fraeses live next door, and also own Moonset, an extraordinary, couples-only lodging north of town (2 miles south of Sea Lion Caves). This spendy retreat includes a CD library, full kitchen (stocked with staples plus complimentary Oregon wine), sauna, and a sizable, ocean-view spa. *$$$$; MC, V; checks OK; fraese@presys.com; www. touroregon.com/thejohnsonhouse; www.moonsetromance.com; 1 block north of river.*

The Landmark Inn / ★

1551 4TH ST, FLORENCE; 541/997-9030

Those who can't bear one more cookie-cutter motel room—or facing other guests around the B&B table—find privacy and comfort in this new 10-room, nonsmoking inn, perched on a rhododendron- and fir-covered sand hill overlooking the Coast Range, dunes, and Old Town. The luxury honey-moon suite is in the quiet east wing, with a private deck and hot tub; some suites have kitchens with seating areas, and separate bedrooms. Kitchen units are dis-counted for longer stays. Local contractor Eugene Bukowski (no relation to author Charles) designed and built the inn, and except for a formidable driveway, it's Florence's best "motel." All guests have access (by appointment and for a $15 fee) to a private spa facing the woods, with a Finnish cedar sauna and large, chlorine-free spa tub scrubbed and refilled for every use. *$$; AE, MC, V; checks OK; north side of river.* &

Reedsport and Winchester Bay

Reedsport is a port town on the Umpqua River a few miles inland, and Win-chester Bay sits at the river's mouth. The former Antarctic research vessel *Hero* is moored on the riverfront at Reedsport and is open to the public in summer. On a large adjacent public wharf, with a cafe on either side, is the **UMPQUA DIS-COVERY CENTER MUSEUM** (409 Riverfront Wy, Reedsport; 541/271-4816), which features a weather station and exhibits on Kuuich tribal history and culture, marine life, ocean beaches, and logging. Jet boats leave the center dock daily for **NARRATED TOURS OF THE UMPQUA**; book at the Schooner Inn Cafe (423 Riverfront Wy, Reedsport; 541/271-5694). Observe wild elk grazing on protected salt marsh and meadow, and watch for new calves in June, at the **DEAN CREEK ELK RESERVE**, 4 miles east on Highway 38.

Winchester Bay's 700-slip **SALMON HARBOR MARINA** (100 Ork Rock Rd, Winchester Bay; 541/271-0287) was once filled with commercial and charter fishing boats, but is now geared to the RV crowd, with bayside or ocean-view sites. Tours of the **UMPQUA LIGHTHOUSE** (1020 Lighthouse Wy, Winchester Bay; 541/271-4631) are available Wednesday through Sunday in summer; an adjacent museum in the former Coast Guard administration building displays photographs and pioneer history. The lighthouse and **COASTAL VISITOR CENTER** are perched atop a headland overlooking the dunes, Winchester Bay, and the river's mouth. (That "triangle" visible between jetties is the only long-line oyster-growing farm in the Northwest.)

RESTAURANTS

Cafe Francais / ★★

HWY 101, WINCHESTER BAY; 541/271-9270

 Chef Francois Pere transformed a former seafood market into a French dining room right on Highway 101 in Winchester Bay—proof again that if you build it, they will come. The dining room is charming, with fresh flowers, French wines, and some of the best country-French cooking outside of France (escargot, traditional French onion soup for starters). Diners order from a simple nine-item menu, or from the chef's selections of the day, scribbled on a blackboard. Entrees include chateaubriand in cream sherry with soft green peppercorns, tiny scallops in a garlic butter sauce, and *filet mignon flambé au Cognac*. Dinners come with salad, fresh bread, and perfectly cooked vegetables. All ingredients, such as Oregon lamb, are fresh; sometimes the chef tells diners that the catch of the day is determined when the boat docks. *$$; MC, V; checks OK; dinner Wed–Sun; beer and wine; reservations recommended; on Hwy 101.*

North Bend and Coos Bay

Side by side on the finest natural harbor between San Francisco and Seattle, the twin port cities of North Bend and Coos Bay, formerly the world's foremost wood-products exporters, have been undercut by a sagging timber industry and the political struggle to control Northwest forests. The cities are making a slow transition to a service-oriented economy from one based on natural resource extraction, which began with gold and coal in the 1860s.

The Coquille Indian Tribe, now the area's third-largest employer, in 1995 transformed a former Weyerhaeuser plywood mill into the **MILL RESORT & CASINO** (3201 Tremont Ave, North Bend; 541/756-8800), with a restaurant overlooking the waterfront. The three-story hotel opened in spring 2000 and is

MYRTLEWOOD

Oregon's myrtlewood tree, a symmetrical beauty with shiny green leaves, related to the California bay, grows only within 90 square miles on the Southern Oregon Coast—between Coos Bay and the California border.

The **House of Myrtlewood** (1125 S 1st, Coos Bay; 541-267-7804; www.oregon connection.com or www.houseofmyrtlewood.com), has been churning out bowls, plates, salt shakers, and clocks (among other doodads) since 1929. Thousands of visitors, many of them on bus trips, tour the factory annually, and bowls are their favorite purchase. Trees used in production are usually about 100 years old, about 4 feet in diameter, and grow as tall as 150 feet. Cut trees regrow from undisturbed roots.

Unlike other hardwoods that have characteristic blond or dark wood, myrtlewood is blond, red, gold, and a deep chocolate brown—stressed trees produce the prettiest "fiddleback" grain. The aromatic leaves can be used in soups and stews; nuts are dried and drilled for jewelry. Coastal Indians knew all about myrtlewood—they husked newly fallen nuts and roasted them slowly in earth ovens. If harvested correctly, the nuts are slightly sweet, like chestnuts. If not, they're as bitter as bile. The Natives also used the dried nut for adornment.   —*Jan Halliday*

furnished in rustic-lodge style, including Pendleton wool blankets on the beds. Most rooms have sunrise views of the bay, river, and Coast Range mountains. Eventually hotel and casino will be part of a boardwalk that begins on the Coos Bay waterfront and follows the river several miles north and east to North Bend.

Park downtown and cross the railroad tracks to see fishing boats, tugs, and historic photographs on the **COOS BAY WATERFRONT**. Board the *Rendezvous* (541/267-5661) here for 1½-hour tours of the river, or a dinner cruise.

The local arts scene includes the **COOS ART MUSEUM** (235 Anderson, Coos Bay; 541/267-3901), with many big-city-quality exhibits; **SOUTHWESTERN OREGON COMMUNITY COLLEGE** (1988 Newmark, Coos Bay; 541/888-2525), which schedules art shows and musical performances; and July's two-week **OREGON COAST MUSIC FESTIVAL** (541/267-0938), which features classical, jazz, and world music up and down the coast.

Score newspapers, magazines, coffee drinks, and fresh-baked pastries at **BOOKS BY THE BAY'S GROUNDS CAFE** (1875 Sherman Ave, North Bend; 541/751-1114); get Oregon wines and Bandon cheese from **OREGON WINE CELLARS ETC.** (155 S Broadway, Coos Bay; 541/267-0300), and picnic fixings from **DICK AND MARGIE'S FARMERS MARKET** (1434 Virginia Ave, North Bend; 541/756-0109). **THE HOP** drive-in (1122 Barry St, Coos Bay; 541/269-9668), south of the town of Coos Bay, serves burgers, floats, and banana splits at your car.

RESTAURANTS

Bank Brewing Restaurant & Brew Pub / ★

201 CENTRAL AVE, COOS BAY; 541/267-0963

This bank-turned-inviting-microbrewery features a spacious main floor, high ceilings, huge windows, and architectural details—creating a congenial, upscale atmosphere. The restored, late-19th-century ornate bar originally came 'round the Horn to North Bend's Anchor Tavern. Sweet Wheat or Gold Coast Golden Ale top the craft-beer list; pub grub includes stuffed (with cheddar) jalapeños; burgers; thin-crust, hand-tossed pizzas; fresh fish; steak; and pasta. *$; MC, V; checks OK; lunch, dinner every day; beer and wine; reservations not necessary; corner of 2nd.* &

Kum-Yon's / ★

835 S BROADWAY, COOS BAY; 541/269-2662

 Kum-Yon is a showcase of South Korean cuisine. Some Japanese (sushi, sashimi) and Chinese (eggflower soup, fried rice, chow mein) dishes are offered, but what makes this place special is unknown territory for many diners. Try spicy *chap chae* (transparent noodles panfried with veggies and beef), *bul ko ki* (thinly sliced sirloin marinated in honey and spices), or yakitori (Japanese-style shish kebab). Arrive early on weekends. *$; AE, MC, V; local checks only; lunch, dinner every day; beer and wine; reservations not necessary; south end of main drag.* &

Pancake Mill / ★

2390 TREMONT, NORTH BEND; 541/756-2751

 The unassuming Pancake Mill, orphaned on Highway 101 after the mills pulled out, started in 1949 as The Top Hat drive-in, but over the years has been closed in so customers don't feel the chilly morning breeze of the oft-opened front door. This is the hot spot for breakfast. Whatever you want, you can probably get here: croissant French toast, blintzes and crepes, corn and potato pancakes, nut-filled waffles, and real oatmeal served with half-and-half, brown sugar, and pecans. Big appetites order the "Tortilla de Patata," a monster omelet filled with potatoes, zucchini, ham, cheese, and onions on a hot tortilla. It's served with a friendly, down-home attitude you'd expect with the wood-paneled decor. Locals buy pies here, including a heart-stopping coffee toffee pie, dark pecan pie, or cheese pie—less than $3 a slice. *$; AE, DC, MC, V; local checks only; breakfast, lunch every day; no alcohol; reservations not necessary; on Hwy 101.* &

LODGINGS

Coos Bay Manor Bed & Breakfast / ★

955 S 5TH ST, COOS BAY; 541/269-1224 OR 800/269-1224

Up the hill from the commercial glitz of Highway 101 are beautifully restored homes among deciduous and coniferous trees and flowering shrubs. Coos Bay Manor, a grand Colonial-style structure with large rooms and high ceilings, is such a place, on a quiet residential street overlooking the water-front. Five guest rooms (three with private baths) are distinctively decorated—the Baron's Room has a four-poster canopy bed in brocade and tapestry; the Victorian features lots of lace and ruffles. On mellow summer mornings, Patricia Williams serves breakfast on the upstairs open-air balcony patio. Mannerly children over 4, and dogs who tolerate cats, are welcome. *$$; DIS, MC, V; checks OK; 4 blocks above waterfront.*

The Old Tower House / ★★
476 NEWMARK AVE, COOS BAY; 541/888-6058

One of few historic houses remaining in the former bustling Empire district of Coos Bay, this lovely Victorian built by Dr. C. W. Tower in 1872 overlooks passing ships on the bay. It was saved from the wrecking ball and beautifully restored by owners Don and Julia Spangler, who wallpapered and filled the place with unusual antiques. The private garden includes the original apple orchard and dozens of whimsical birdhouses. Three nicely appointed guest rooms with two large baths are in the main house. Separate, more private quarters are on the back side of the garden: the "Ivy Cottage," done in green and white; and the carriage house, with its own kitchen. Full breakfast is served on white linens in a cozy sunroom. *$$; DIS, MC, V; checks OK; donspanl@gte.net; take Charleston exit from downtown.*

Charleston

Charleston's docks moor Coos Bay's commercial fishing fleet. Fresh fish is inexpensive here, the pace is slow, and there's lots to do, even if it's just watching brown pelicans or seals.

Visit **CHUCK'S SEAFOOD** (5055 Boat Basin Dr; 541/888-5525) for fish, and **QUALMAN OYSTER FARMS** (4898 Crown Point Rd; 541/888-3145) for oysters. Locals favor the **SEA BASKET** (63502 Kingfisher Rd; 541/888-5711), overlooking the boat basin, for deep-fried seafood. Hikers, canoeists, and kayakers (no motorboaters) explore the **SOUTH SLOUGH NATIONAL ESTUARINE RESEARCH CENTER RESERVE** (61907 Seven Devils Rd; 541/888-5558), 4 miles south of Charleston.

Southwest of town on the Cape Arago Highway, **SUNSET BAY STATE PARK** (12 miles southwest of Coos Bay; 541/888-3778), with year-round camping (including yurts), has a bowl-shaped cove with 50-foot cliffs on either side—good for a swim, because the water is perpetually calm, though cold. Farther down the road at **SHORE ACRES STATE PARK** (13 miles southwest of Coos Bay; 541/888-3732), a cliffside botanical garden contains a restored caretaker's house (impressively lit at Christmas) and an impeccably maintained display of native and exotic plants. Watch winter storms—or whales—from an enclosed shelter here. Farther south, **CAPE ARAGO STATE PARK** (541/888-3778) overlooks the **OREGON ISLANDS NATIONAL WILDLIFE REFUGE** (541/867-4550), home to seabirds, seals, and sea lions. The **OREGON COAST TRAIL** winds through all three parks. For more information, contact the Oregon Parks and Recreation Department (503/378-6305); for camping reservations, call 800/452-5687.

RESTAURANTS

Portside / ★

8001 KINGFISHER RD, CHARLESTON; 541/888-5544

It's dark and cavernous inside, so you'll notice the lighted glass tanks containing live crabs and lobsters—a good sign that the kitchen uses fresh ingredients. From your table, you can watch fishing gear being repaired and vessels coming and going in the Charleston boat basin. Naturally, fresh seafood simply prepared is the specialty. Try the "cucumber boat," a medley of shrimp, crab, and smoked salmon with cucumber dressing. Fridays, a sumptuous Chinese seafood buffet includes everything but the anchor. *$$; AE, DC, MC, V; local checks only; lunch, dinner every day; full bar; reservations not necessary; in boat basin.*

Bandon

Some locals believe Bandon sits on a "ley line," an underground crystalline structure reputed to be the focus of powerful cosmic energies; others know it lies close to the point where the Juan de Fuca plate is diving under the North American continent. Or maybe it's the grandeur of the scenery—huge haystack and monolithic offshore rocks—that inspires.

Begin in **OLD TOWN** on the Coquille River waterfront, where galleries include the **SECOND STREET GALLERY** (210 2nd; 541/347-4133), the **CLOCK TOWER GALLERY** (198 2nd; 541/347-4721), and **BANDON GLASS ART STUDIO** (240 Hwy 101; 541/347-4723). Buy fish-and-chips at **BANDON FISHERIES** (250 1st SW; 541/347-4282) and nosh at the public pier. For another treat, try the *New York Times*–touted candies (and generous free samples) at **CRANBERRY SWEETS** (1st and Chicago; 541/347-9475). At **BREWMASTER'S** (375 2nd; 541/347-1195), taste a handful of beers—five on tap—from among the repertoire of 100 recipes. Sample the famous cheddar cheeses (especially squeaky cheese curds) at **BANDON CHEESE** (680 2nd; 541/347-2456). Select a wine from the outstanding selection at **TIFFANY'S DRUG** (44 Michigan Ave NE; 541/347-4438), and get picnic fixings from **MOTHER'S NATURAL GROCERY** (975 Hwy 101; 541/347-4086). **THE CROW'S NEST LOUNGE** (125 Chicago Ave; 541/347-9331), with cozy seating areas, fireplace, and bar overlooking the Coquille, is Bandon's most charming bar.

The best beach access is from the south jetty in town or from Face Rock Viewpoint on **BEACH LOOP ROAD** (west of Bandon). This route parallels the ocean in view of weather-sculpted rock formations, and is a good alternative (especially by bicycle) to Highway 101. Meet the last true beachcomber at **NEPTUNE'S NOVELTIES** (1605 Beach Loop Rd; 541/347-3058); owner Hazel Colgrove has been picking the beach (shells, fossils, agates, bottles, and more) for over 30 years.

Two miles north of Bandon, **BULLARDS BEACH STATE PARK** (541/347-2209) occupies an expansive area crisscrossed with hiking and biking trails leading to uncrowded, driftwood-and-kelp-cluttered beaches. The campground, with yurts near the entrance, is nestled in the pines. Built in 1896, the **COQUILLE RIVER LIGHTHOUSE** (open to the public) is at the end of the park's main road. Good windsurfing is on the river side of the park's spit. Tour the gently flowing Coquille River before the afternoon winds kick up, and poke around the edges of **BANDON MARSH NATIONAL WILDLIFE REFUGE** (look for osprey, harriers, and egrets) in a kayak from **ADVENTURE KAYAK** (315 1st St; 541/347-3480; www.adventurekayak.com).

Bandon's cranberry bogs make it one of the nation's largest producers. Call **FABER FARMS** (541/347-1166) for directions to its tasting room (harvest tours begin in October). Buy 30 varieties of homemade fruit jellies and jams (including cranberry) from the Keller family's large roadside stand, called Misty Meadows (888/795-1719; www.oregonjam.com), 5 miles south of Bandon on Highway 101. Seven miles south of Bandon on Highway 101, you can view lions, tigers, elk, and more at the **WEST COAST GAME PARK SAFARI** (541/347-3106).

RESTAURANTS

Harp's / ★★

480 1ST ST SW, BANDON; 541/347-9057

In 1998 new owner Robert James, a baker and remodeler, bought the name and the recipes and moved Harp's from its Old Town location to this spectacular riverfront spot across from Bandon's lighthouse. Harp's is one of only three buildings in town to survive over time devastating gorse fires and floods; built in 1911, it's been everything from a Coast Guard station to a concrete company. James installed a bar on ground level and a lounge on the third floor with views of the ocean and river mouth. The menu is much the same as the old Harp's. Look for wonderful halibut with hot pistachio sauce, grilled snapper, pasta with prawns and a hot pepper and lemon sauce, and charbroiled filet mignon marinated in garlic and teriyaki. Salads, a simple enticing mix of homegrown greens, come with a garlicky balsamic house dressing. Sweet onion soup made with beef broth and vermouth is still on the menu. The wine list is excellent. *$$; AE, DC, MC, V; checks OK; dinner every day (Tues–Sat in winter); full bar; reservations recommended; across from lighthouse.* &

Keefer's Old Town Cafe / ★

160 BALTIMORE AVE, BANDON; 541/347-1133

New owner Elizabeth French, a former Hawaii resident, bought Andrea's Old Town Cafe and transformed it with antiques, polished wood floors, and more wooden booths, then stamped the place with her own additions (live Hawaiian music, and Hawaiian fish). Breakfast here is still first-rate, and unusual: Hawaiian blue marlin Benedict with cilantro lime hollandaise, for example, along with the usual omelets, crepes, and blintzes. Show up early for Sunday brunch or expect to wait. Lunch includes substantial sandwiches, with a deliciously garlic caesar salad. For dinner choose from veal, beef, chicken, and four or five fish specials daily, such as mahi mahi with fresh mango salsa. *$$; MC, V; checks OK; breakfast, lunch Mon–Sat, dinner every day, brunch Sun; full bar; reservations not necessary; www.bandonbythesea.com; in Old Town.* &

Lord Bennett's / ★★

1695 BEACH LOOP DR, BANDON; 541/347-3663

Occasionally an oceanfront eatery with a great view serves worthwhile food. Lord Bennett's, named for Bandon's founder, doubly-damned for bringing invasive Scotch broom and prickly gorse with him from Scotland, is across Beach Loop Drive from Bandon's oceanside cliffs, but the view is stunning. Shellfish selections are sautéed and broiled. Oysters are baked with spinach and bacon, and finished with Pernod; snapper is breaded in cornmeal, grilled, and served with hazelnut butter. Herb-marinated chicken is charbroiled with port-cranberry-pomegranate sauce, or stuffed with spinach and pancetta, grilled in sesame seeds, and served with ginger-lime butter. Check out the Sunday brunch: crab enchiladas, shrimp-topped eggs Benedict, and lemon soufflé pancakes. *$$; AE, DIS, MC, V; checks OK; lunch, dinner every day, brunch Sun; full bar; reservations recommended; next to Sunset Motel.*

LODGINGS

Bandon Beach House / ★★★

2866 BEACH LOOP DR, BANDON; 541/347-1196

A private wing in this new two-story Craftsman-style house on the beach has just two luxurious guest rooms: one upstairs, one down, and both separated from the rest of the house by a large living room. Each has its own wood-burning stone (quarried from Smith River) fireplace and large private bath. Furnishings are spare, expensive, and tasteful, with comfortable king-size four-poster beds and big chairs in front of mullioned windows overlooking the ocean. If you don't want to leave the tranquility of your room for breakfast (fruit, soufflés, fresh scones), innkeepers Adrienne and Steve Casey deliver it. No pets, children, or smoking. *$$$; cash only; 2-night min; www.bandonbeach.com; south of town.* &

Bandon Dunes / ★★★

ROUND LAKE DR, BANDON; 541/347-4380 OR 888/345-6008

Bandon Dunes' monastic clubhouse is a favorite place to stay for golfers. The largest suite has four master bedrooms and a card room; all suites and guest rooms are luxuriously but simply furnished. The focus here is on the walking Scottish links course, designed by Scot architect David McLay Kidd, which is already winning kudos from golf magazines. The resort, paid for in cash by millionaire Michael Keiser, who made his fortune selling greeting cards printed on recycled paper, has no ubiquitous housing development or real-estate

OREGON DUNES NATIONAL RECREATION AREA

Often overlooked, the Oregon Dunes National Recreation Area, 32,000 acres of open sand sculpted into magnificent hills and valleys by the wind, is one of the state's greatest natural wonders—the largest expanse of coastal dunes in the world. But they're actually only the remaining visible tip of a giant sand dune sheet that stretches from Northern Oregon to Southern California. The rest of the dune sheet is blanketed with vegetation and forest. This giant sheet was formed over millions of years of glacial erosion, carried down rivers, dumped into the ocean, and then washed back to shore. Geologists have fancy names for visible sand dune formations: fore dunes, hummocks, deflation plains, transverse dunes, oblique dunes, parabola dunes. All kinds of things are buried under the shifting sand: Indian villages, shipwrecks, and conifer forests. When the wind blows across the dunes, sometimes at 100 miles per hour, it doesn't take long to be engulfed with sand.

There are 13 campgrounds (in forest) and 14 hiking trails through the dunes, which front the Pacific Ocean from Florence south to North Bend; many pullouts and access points are along Highway 101. The central **Oregon Dunes Visitor Center** (855 Hwy 101, Reedsport; 541/271-3611) has more information.   —Jan Halliday

hustle around it; the attitude demonstrated here (play fast, enjoy your friends, score isn't the point) may change how golf is played in the United States. The two-story, light-filled public clubhouse, with four monolithic spires of columnar basalt in the lobby, understated rooms, and subtle Celtic symbols, is on the cutting edge of new-millennium design. It's uplifting architecture that encourages contemplation and the gathering of friends. Guest rooms are on the second floor of the clubhouse overlooking the course, or in four 12-room cottages surrounding a lily-pad-covered pond. Breakfast, lunch, and dinner are served in the dining room (with full bar) every day. Children, especially young golfers, are welcome. $$$; AE, DC, DIS, MC, V; no checks; www.bandondunesgolf.com; north end of Coquille River bridge. &

Beach Street B&B / ★★
200 BEACH ST, BANDON; 541/347-5124
A homey, romantic place (floral bedspreads on king-size beds, dried flowers, and a huge vaulted-ceiling living room with comfy chairs and a massive fireplace), Beach Street is perfect for small wedding parties and honeymooners. Some of the six guest rooms have gas fireplaces and private balconies, all have unobstructed westerly ocean views; five have two-person spa tubs (our favorites are the Windsor and Oak Rooms). Breakfasts are served buffet-style in the living/dining room; guests can request a favorite Benedict or crepe, and co-owner Sharon McLean will add it to the morning repast. No children (unless

you rent all the rooms) or pets. *$$; AE, DIS, MC, V; checks OK; across from riding stable.*

Lighthouse B&B / ★★

650 JETTY RD, BANDON; 541/347-9316

Spacious and appealing (though the groundskeeping remains uninspired), this contemporary home has windows opening toward the mouth of the Coquille River, its lighthouse, and the ocean, a short walk away. Guests can watch fishing boats, windsurfers, seals, and seabirds. Five guest rooms (four enjoy ocean or river vistas) are roomy and wonderfully appointed. The Gray Whale Room, on the third floor, is a stunner, with a king-size bed, wood-burning stove, TV, and whirlpool tub for two in a view alcove. Breakfasts are topnotch, prepared by amiable hostess Shirley Chalupa. No children or pets. *$$; MC, V; checks OK; www.lighthouselodging.com; at 1st St.*

Sunset Motel / ★

1755 BEACH LOOP DR, BANDON; 541/347-2453 OR 800/842-2407

This complex of ocean-cliff motel rooms, cabins, and triplex houses gets our rave for spectacular views of Bandon's haystack rocks, especially Face Rock (it looks like a woman, head back, mouth open in reverie). For the most romantic view, ask for a room with a corner fireplace in the Vern Brown unit—a great spot for cuddling to watch storms and sunsets. All units have balconies and are equipped with coffeemakers and microwaves; several rooms have kitchens and fireplaces. Best of the beach cabins is 1930s-era number 410 (sleeps eight), tucked into a niche in the cliff, and finished with aged knotty pine and a massive stone fireplace. All guests have use of the spa, pool, and laundry facilities. Stairs lead to the beach. *$$; AE, DIS, MC, V; no checks; www.sunset motel.com; across from Lord Bennett's.* &

Langlois

With sheep farms, cranberry bogs, and blueberry fields, Langlois is also the source of many organic vegetables served in local restaurants or sold at local markets—odd little pinecone-shaped potatoes, flower petals, and salad greens. You can pick flowers, strawberries, elephant garlic, peas, beets, beans, and other organic produce—as well as bunk in their 1886 farmhouse—at **MARSH HAVEN FARM** (47815 Floras Lake Loop; 541/348-2564).

BOICE-COPE COUNTY PARK (north of Langlois off Hwy 101; 541/247-7011) is the site of freshwater **FLORAS LAKE**, popular with boaters, anglers, and board sailors. The area has the coast's best (and little-used) trail system, perfect for hiking, running, horseback riding, and mountain biking. Snowy plover nesting grounds in the dunes are marked and off-limits. The largest town in Curry County in the early 1800s thrived briefly on the shores of Floras Lake. Developers promised to build a canal from the lake to the ocean to create a bustling port city. A three-story hotel was built before developers discovered the lake was higher than the ocean and scrapped their plans.

LODGINGS

Floras Lake House by the Sea / ★

92870 BOICE COPE RD, LANGLOIS; 541/348-2573

If the summer sun beckons you to cool swims in a freshwater lake, choose Floras. This modern two-story house offers four spacious rooms, each with a bath and deck access; two have fireplaces. Most elegant are the North and South Rooms, but you can see Floras Lake and the ocean beyond from all four. Full breakfast, buffet style, is served by owner Liz Brady. Husband Will runs a windsurfing rental and instruction school on the lake. *$$; DIS, MC, V; checks OK; www.floraslake.com; from Hwy 101, turn west on Floras Lake Loop.* &

Port Orford

Port Orford is Southern Oregon's oldest town. In the early 1850s, Indians at Port Orford, attempting to protect their plank-house settlements, were overcome and forced to walk to the Coast Reservation (near Newport) along with families from the Sixes, Elk, Pistol, Rogue River, Coquille, Coos, and Umpqua River villages. It's a shameful period of history, which up until the 1960s Port Orford celebrated by throwing an Indian effigy off Battle Rock on the anniversary of Capt. William Tichenor's cannon-fire victory. Interpretive signs at **BATTLE ROCK** (in town, on beach on Hwy 101) begin to tell both sides of the story.

Gold mining here was short-lived, and little of the original town remains. Check out the **PORT ORFORD HEADS LIFESAVING STATION** (edge of town, on 9th St; 541/332-2352; open summer only), built in 1934, one of the best remaining examples of period architecture. You can catch a movie at the newly restored **SAVOY THEATRE** (811 Hwy 101; 541/332-3105). Have lunch at **SEAWEED NATURAL GROCERY & CAFE** (832 Hwy 101; 541/332-3640). The only gourmet food store on the South Coast is **PORT ORFORD BREADWORKS** (1160 Idaho St; 541/332-4022), with fresh daily European-style (heavy, hand-formed) country French, Kalamata olive, and herb and cheese loaves; fine imported cheeses and meats (real French roquefort, mascarpone, gavianella, finocchiona salami, slabs of prosciutto), wild capers in sea salt; 30-year-old Portuguese vinegar; and black truffle oil.

Locals here are sheep ranchers, cranberry farmers, sea urchin divers, fishermen, and retirees; a seasonal proliferation of surfers and board sailors heads for Battle Rock and Hubbard's Creek beaches and the windy waters of nearby Floras Lake. **FISHING** fanatics visit the Elk and Sixes Rivers for salmon and steelhead. Port Orford marks the beginning of Oregon's coastal "banana belt," which stretches to the California border and means warmer winter temperatures, an earlier spring, and more sunshine. One warning: From here south, poison oak grows close to the ocean. Watch for it at Battle Rock. **CAPE BLANCO LIGHTHOUSE** (541/332-2207) in **CAPE BLANCO STATE PARK** (10 miles north of Port Orford 6 miles west of Hwy 101; 541/332-6774) is the oldest (1870) and most westerly lighthouse in the Lower 48 states—and the windiest station on the coast. The lighthouse, 245 feet above the ocean, and small interpretive center are open seasonally to the public. West of the light station, a path leads to the end of the cape. On the way to Cape Blanco, check out historic **HUGHES HOUSE** (open Thurs–Mon, Apr–Oct) overlooking Sixes River, part of the state park. Built by the English-born Hughes family, the area's first settlers, the house has been lovingly restored. Walk the south bank of the river to the ocean on a trail through the salt marsh.

HUMBUG MOUNTAIN STATE PARK (541/332-6774), 5 miles south of Port Orford off Hwy 101, features a steep switchbacked trail to a top-of-the-world panorama at the summit.

LODGINGS

The Cape Coddler / ★
1136 WASHINGTON ST, PORT ORFORD; 541/332-4304

This new and sunny yellow Cape Cod–style house has no ocean view, but offers two nicely furnished, roomy guest quarters upstairs with queen-size beds and private baths. Early risers get homemade sticky buns and fresh hot coffee; a full breakfast is delivered to your room or served in the dining room. Several blocks from Highway 101, the inn offers a restful night's sleep and good food served by congenial, knowledgeable hostess Barbara Rush Breuer. No pets or children under 12. *$; MC, V; checks OK; open Mar–Oct; www.thecapecoddler.com; across from elementary school playground.*

Home by the Sea B&B / ★
444 JACKSON ST, PORT ORFORD; 541/332-2855

You can see the south-facing ocean view from both guest rooms in this modest, homey B&B atop a bluff near Battle Rock. Beach access is easy, and guests have the run of a large, pleasantly cluttered dining/living room with a view. Quiche, waffles, omelets, and fresh strawberries are morning mainstays. Surf the Internet with chatty Alan Mitchell, a friendly whirlwind of information and a Mac enthusiast. *$$; MC, V; checks OK; www.homebythesea.com; 1 block west of Hwy 101.*

Gold Beach

Named for the gold found here in the 19th century, Gold Beach is famous as the town at the ocean end of the **ROGUE RIVER**, a favorite with whitewater enthusiasts. It's also a supply town for hikers heading up the Rogue into the remote **KALMIOPSIS WILDERNESS AREA**. The Rogue enjoys fabulous salmon and steelhead runs; catch angling tips, or rent clam shovels and fishing gear at the **ROGUE OUTDOOR STORE** (29865 Ellensburg Ave; 541/247-7142). Pick up maps and hiking or rafting information from the **U.S. FOREST SERVICE** (1225 S Ellensburg; 541/247-3600).

JET-BOAT TRIPS are a popular way to explore the backcountry. Guides discuss the area's natural history and stop to observe wildlife (otter, beaver, blue herons, bald eagles, and deer) on these thrilling forays (64–104 miles) up the Rogue. Boats dock at lodges along the way for lunch and sometimes dinner. (Prepare for sun exposure, because most boats are open.) Outfits include **JERRY'S ROGUE RIVER JET BOAT TRIPS** (800/451-3645 or 541/247-4571) and **MAIL BOAT HYDRO-JETS** (800/458-3511 or 541/247-7033). Call **ROGUE RIVER RESERVATIONS** (800/525-2161 or 541/247-6504) for information and bookings on Rogue River outings, jet-boat trips, or overnight stays in the wilderness (including backcountry lodges).

The little-used **OREGON COAST TRAIL** (800/525-2334) traverses headlands and skirts untraveled beaches between Gold Beach and Brookings. A portion of trail winds up and over **CAPE SEBASTIAN**, 3 miles south of town off Highway 101. Take the steep drive to the top of the cape for breathtaking vistas.

RESTAURANTS

The Captain's Table / ★

1295 S ELLENSBURG AVE, GOLD BEACH; 541/247-6308

This funky-looking structure overlooking the highway (with nice ocean views) is Gold Beach's old favorite. Nothing is breaded or deep-fried, so broiled salmon or halibut is a good choice (although doneness is not always consistent). Corn-fed beef from Kansas City is meat you can't often get on the coast. Scallop and beef kebabs (with bacon, bell peppers, and onions) are interesting choices. The dining area, furnished with antiques, is moderately small, and can get smoky from the popular bar. Staff is courteous, enthusiastic, and speedy. *$$; MC, V; local checks only; dinner every day; full bar; reservations not necessary; south end of town.* &

LODGINGS

Gold Beach Resort

29232 ELLENSBURG AVE, GOLD BEACH; 541/247-7066 OR 800/541-0947

This sprawling in-town beachfront complex is close enough to the ocean that roaring surf drowns out highway noise. All rooms and condos have private decks and ocean views. There's an indoor pool and spa, and a private, beach-access trail leads over the dunes to the ocean. Roomy condos come with fireplaces and kitchens. *$$; AE, DC, MC, V; no checks; gbresort@harborside. com; www.gbresort.com; south end of town.*

Inn at Nesika Beach / ★★★

33026 NESIKA RD, GOLD BEACH; 541/247-6434

Many visitors to this three-story neo-Victorian (built in 1992) think the secluded inn in residential Nesika Beach is the Oregon Coast's finest B&B. A jewel of a structure occupying a bluff overlooking the ocean, it boasts lovely landscaping, a relaxing wraparound porch, and an enclosed oceanfront deck. The expansive interior, with hardwood floors and attractive area rugs, is grandly decorated. Four large guest rooms are upstairs, and all enjoy fabulous ocean views, uncommonly comfortable (and large) feather beds, and private baths with deep whirlpool tubs. On the third floor, a suite-size room has a fireplace and private deck overlooking the Pacific. Wine and nibbles are offered evenings in the "fireside room" and living room. Hostess Ann Arsenault serves a full breakfast (in a dining room facing the ocean) that might include crepes, scones, gingerbread pancakes, myriad egg dishes, and muffins. No small children or pets. *$$$; no credit cards; checks OK; 5 miles north of Gold Beach.*

Tu Tu'Tun Lodge / ★★★★

96550 NORTH BANK ROGUE, GOLD BEACH; 541/247-6664 OR 800/864-6357

The lodge complex, named after a local Indian tribe, is one of the loveliest in the Pacific Northwest, though it's 7 miles inland from the ocean. Tall, mist-cloudy trees line the north shore of the Rogue River, and hosts Dirk and Laurie Van Zante will help you get a line in for salmon, steelhead, or trout. The main building is handsomely designed, with lots of windows, fireplaces, private porches overlooking the river, racks for fishing gear, and stylish decor. The two-story main building holds 16 units, and the adjacent lodge has two larger kitchen suites, all with river views. In the apple orchard is the lovely Garden House, which sleeps six and features a large stone fireplace. The nearby two-bedroom and two-bath River House, open in summer, is the spendiest and most luxurious, with a cedar-vaulted living room, outdoor spa, satellite TV, and washer/dryer. Guests can swim in the heated lap pool, use the four-hole pitch-and-putt course, play horseshoes, relax around the mammoth rock fireplace in the main lodge, hike, or fish. A madrona-wood fire is lit every evening on the terrace, and you might spot two resident bald eagles. Breakfast, hors d'oeuvres, and a prix-fixe dinner are served (for an additional fee). The four-course evening meal might include your own fish, or perhaps chicken breasts with a champagne sauce, or prime rib. Outside guests can dine here also (by putting their names on a mailing list). *$$$; MC, V; checks OK; tututun@harborside.com; www.tututun.com; 7 miles up from Rogue River bridge.*

Brookings

Situated 6 miles north of the California line, Brookings enjoys the state's mildest winter temperatures. To the north lie **SAMUEL H. BOARDMAN** and **HARRIS BEACH STATE PARKS** (800/452-5687 or 541/469-0224). To the east are the verdant Siskiyou Mountains, deeply cut by the Chetco and Winchuck Rivers, and the ancient redwood groves lie to the south. Most of the **EASTER LILIES** sold in North America are grown in this favorable clime. Brookings also boasts the Oregon Coast's safest harbor—so it's busy. Retirees have inundated the area: the hills hum with new housing, the real-estate market is red hot, and chains such as Fred Meyer are building megastores.

At **AZALEA CITY PARK** (just east of Hwy 101 at the south end of town; 541/469-3181) fragrant western azaleas bloom in May, alongside wild strawberries, fruit trees, and violets; picnic amid the splendor on hand-hewn myrtlewood tables. **MYRTLEWOOD** (which grows only on the Southern Oregon Coast and in Palestine) can be seen in groves in **LOEB PARK** (8 miles east of town on North Bank River Rd; 541/469-2021). Drive 4 miles up curvy Carpenterville Road from N Highway 101 to visit the tasting room at **BRANDY PEAK DIS-TILLERY** (18526 Tetley Rd; 541/469-0194), a family-owned microdistillery producing fruit brandies, grappa, and eau-de-vie.

The **REDWOOD NATURE TRAIL** in Siskiyou National Forest winds through one of the few remaining groves of old-growth coastal redwoods in Oregon. See where a Japanese pilot dropped a bomb during World War II—the only place in the contiguous United States bombed by a foreign power—on **"BOMBSITE TRAIL,"** a pretty walk through the redwoods. The bomber pilot later honored the city with his samurai sword, on display at the local library. Check with the U.S. Forest Service (555 5th St; 541/469-2196) for directions to trails.

FISHING is renowned here. The fleet operates from the south end of town. Stop in at **SPORTHAVEN MARINA** (16372 Lower Harbor Rd; 541/469-3301) for supplies and info, or at nearby **TIDEWIND CHARTERS** (16368 Lower Harbor Rd; 541/469-0337) for oceangoing fishing adventures. Soak up the harbor ambience, and scarf an order of halibut-and-chips, at **CHETCO SEAFOOD CO** (16182 Lower Harbor Rd; 541/469-9251). Purchase canned and smoked salmon and tuna from **DICK & CASEY'S GOURMET SEAFOOD** (16372-A Lower Harbor Rd; 541/469-9494; www.gourmetseafood.com).

RESTAURANTS

Chives / ★★

1025 CHETCO AVE, BROOKINGS; 541/469-4121

This place has had the town talking for five years: a top-drawer eatery unceremoniously stuck into the rear of a Highway 101 retail building. Disregard the setting; inside, the mood's casual but upscale—with 30 seats. Richard Jackson, chef and co-owner (with wife, Carla), was formerly with San Francisco's Sheraton Palace Hotel and Four Seasons. Lunch and dinner menus offer variety, including preparations previously unknown on the south coast. Everything is cooked to order. Veal is as rare in Brookings as a winter freeze, but Chives purveys a classic osso buco, although it's often served with garlic mashed potatoes (a local preference) rather than traditional risotto (by request). Creamy wild-mushroom risotto accompanies roast duck, and a rock-shrimp risotto appetizer can be had. Exotic fresh fish, such as Gulf Coast soft-shell crab, monkfish from the Mediterranean, Dover sole, and Hawaiian Hebi, is overnighted from all over the world and prepared in a variety of ways, such as rolled in sesame seeds and served with hot-peppered noodles. Fresh pasta is cut and rolled to order. Out front is Jackson's Pasta Pasta (summer only)—line up for fast Italian food and choose among eight kinds of noodles and sauces (such as pesto cream, traditional marinara) for $4.99 a pound; top it with your choice of eight meats or shellfish for an additional charge. *$$; MC, V; checks OK; dinner Wed–Sun (closed Jan); full bar; reservations recommended; north end of town.*

LODGINGS

Chetco River Inn B&B / ★★

21202 HIGH PRAIRIE RD, BROOKINGS; 541/670-1645 OR 800/327-2688

Expect a culture shock: this secluded, alternative-energy retreat/farm planted with lavender sits on 35 forested acres of a peninsula formed by a sharp bend in the turquoise Chetco River, 17 mostly paved miles east of Brookings. Solitude is blissful; the five newly furnished bedrooms and cottage have no phones, and cell phone service is iffy at best. But you can read by safety propane lights and in the cottage watch TV via satellite (there's also a VCR). The large, open main floor—done in lovely, deep-green marble—offers views of the river, myrtlewood groves, and wildlife. Full breakfast is included, and you can make special arrangements for a deluxe sack lunch or an exemplary five-course dinner. Guests who want it bring their own alcohol. Anglers and crack-of-dawn hikers (the Kalmiopsis Wilderness is close by) are served early-riser breakfasts. *$$; MC, V; checks OK; www.chetcoriverinn.com; off North Bank Rd, call for directions.*

South Coast Inn / ★★

516 REDWOOD ST, BROOKINGS; 541/469-5557 OR 800/525-9273

Twin gargoyles guard this handsome, 4,000-square-foot, Craftsman-style home designed in 1917 by renowned San Francisco architect Bernard Maybeck. It's two blocks above downtown, so traffic noise is audible, but it's surrounded by soundproofing trees and shrubs. Some of them flower all year in the mild climate. A spacious, partially covered deck, lighted in evening, extends around most of the house. Four luxurious guest rooms (two with ocean views and one with gas fireplace) are appointed with antiques. The downstairs parlor sports a stone fireplace and grand piano, while a workout room includes weight machine, sauna, and hot tub. An unattached cottage (with kitchen) is outfitted with rustic log furniture. Innkeepers Ken Raith and Keith Popper will pick you up at the nearby Crescent City (California) airport. No children under 12; no pets. *$$; AE, DIS, MC, V; checks OK; scoastin@wave.net; www. scoastinn.com; 2 blocks above Hwy 101.*

SOUTHERN OREGON AND THE CASCADES

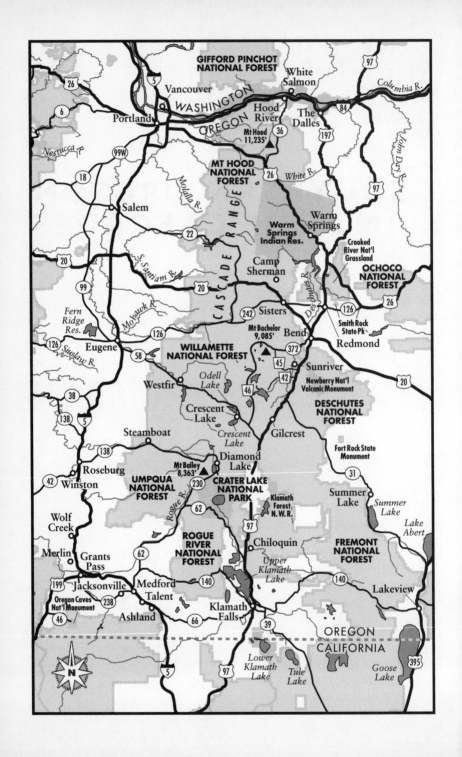

SOUTHERN OREGON
AND THE CASCADES

Like a hastily dotted exclamation point, Southern Oregon sits at the end of the Cascade range, a series of narrow valleys, forming a unique ecological zone, through which Interstate 5 winds to California. Surrounding hills shelter each valley from the prodigious rains that flood the more wide open Willamette Valley in the north, and make these pockets both warmer and drier than the rest of Western Oregon.

Just east of the Cascades, at 4,000-feet elevation, Oregon's "high desert" is less arid than deserts of the American Southwest and offers another unique ecological niche. Anchored at the north and south ends by Indian reservations, about 200 miles apart, the high desert is cut with deep canyons of running and dry rivers; it's scabbed with hardened lava flows and riddled with underground lava caves created by violent volcanic eruptions. Resplendent with stands of red-barked ponderosa pine, soft green juniper trees spackled with blue-gray berries, and an understory of manzanita bushes and sage, it looks and smells good.

Towering above this desert floor only a few miles from US Highway 97, the Cascade range stands like a curtain, featuring the snowcapped peaks of Mounts Jefferson, Washington, and Bachelor, as well as the Three Sisters and Broken Top. The crown jewel in this setting is Crater Lake National Park, at the southernmost end.

ACCESS AND INFORMATION

A major north/south highway travels down each side of the Cascade Mountains: Interstate 5 on the west, and Highway 97 on the east. US Highway 26, the main route between Portland and the desert, crosses Mount Hood southeast into the scenic Warm Springs Indian Reservation, where it soon connects with Highway 97. Routes to Bend, the largest town on the east side, depart from Salem on Highway 22, and from Albany on US Highway 20; from Eugene on Highway 126 (McKenzie Pass). From Eugene follow Highway 28 (Willamette Pass) to Highway 97 at the halfway point between Bend and Klamath Falls. The most scenic route to the east side of the mountains, open only in summer, is the narrow Old McKenzie Highway (Hwy 242) from Eugene. Farther south, Crater Lake is accessible from Roseburg on Highway 138 and from Medford on Highway 62. The most southerly routes are from Medford on Highway 140 and Ashland to Klamath Falls on Highway 66.

Jet service between Portland and Bend/Klamath Falls is offered several times daily on **HORIZON AIR** (800/221-1212) and other carriers. **AMTRAK** (800/872-7245), bound for California from Portland, crosses Willamette Pass into Klamath Falls, bypassing most of Southern Oregon.

Roseburg and the Umpqua Valley

The Willamette Valley and Interstate 5 corridor south of Eugene leads to Roseburg and the Umpqua River Valley. The wild-and-scenic North Umpqua River is famed worldwide among serious fly-fishers. This has also become a wine-growing area.

Roseburg

In the former timber town of Roseburg, you'll find **DOUGLAS COUNTY MUSEUM OF HISTORY AND NATURAL HISTORY** (off I-5 at fairgrounds, exit 123; 541/957-7007; www.co.douglas.or.us/museum), which imaginatively displays the area's logging, fur-trapping, and pioneer history in a handsome contemporary structure.

Find picnic fixings at **KRUSE FARMS** (532 Melrose Rd; 541/672-5697), a family farm dating to 1923. Berries and tomatoes, Dillard cantaloupes, 45 varieties of veggies, and cherry, peach, prune, apple, pear, and walnut orchards keep the produce stand filled.

The Roseburg area now has seven wineries: **CALLAHAN RIDGE** (340 Busenbark Ln; 541/673-7901; www.callahanridge.com); **GIRARDET** (895 Reston Rd; 541/679-7252; www.sales@shoporegon.com); **HENRY ESTATE WINERY** (Hwy 9, Umpqua; 541/459-5120; www.henryest.com); **HILLCREST** (240 Vineyard Ln; 541/673-3709); **LA GARZA CELLARS & GOURMET KITCHEN** (491 Winery Ln; 541/679-9654); **LOOKINGGLASS** (6561 Lookingglass Rd, 541/679-8198); and **UMPQUA RIVER VINEYARDS** (451 Hess Ln; 541/673-1975). Henry Estate and HillCrest are open for tours and tastings all year; the others have limited hours in winter. La Garza also has a tasting-room restaurant, the first in the region.

WILDLIFE SAFARI (Hwy 99, 4 miles west of I-5, exit 119; 541/679-6761; www.wildlifesafari.org) lets you drive through rolling country to see a quasi-natural wildlife preserve, with predators discreetly fenced from their prey.

The **SEVEN FEATHERS HOTEL AND CASINO RESORT** (146 Chief Milwaleta Ln, Canyonville; 800/548-8461), owned by the Cow Creek Band of Umpqua Indians, is located about 25 miles south of Roseburg, and is the most luxurious hotel on Oregon's Interstate 5 corridor. Funded by hundreds of slots and gaming tables, the four-story, 156-room hotel (with pretty indoor swimming pool and spa) is one of the better bargains too, especially on weekdays. Golf packages include a room, breakfast for two, morning paper, and a round of golf for two (and cart rental) at the Myrtle Creek championship course. The dramatic crystal-chandeliered Camas Room offers fine dining (fresh tuna steaks, lobster bisque, chicken breasts stuffed with goat cheese).

OREGON CASCADES THREE-DAY TOUR

DAY ONE: Having overnighted at **Ka-Nee-Ta Lodge**, take an early-morning soak in the swimming pool and spas heated with natural hot spring water (nonsulfurous), then have your coffee and a roll before visiting the award-winning **Museum at Warm Springs** on the Warm Springs Indian Reservation. Head south to Bend, where you catch a huge lunch at the **Alpenglow Cafe**. Take Century Drive as it climbs out of Bend through the Three Sisters, Broken Top, and Mount Bachelor peaks, then returns to earth near Sunriver. Take a hike on any of the marked trails along the road, or if it's winter, ski **Mount Bachelor**'s downhill or groomed Nordic trails. Check in to **Sunriver Lodge** and have dinner on-site at the Meadows restaurant, then enjoy a hot soak in your tub.

DAY TWO: Rise early and breakfast at the **Trout House** at the Sunriver Marina (57235 River Rd; 541/593-8880), then buy picnic fixings at the local grocery store. Visit the **High Desert Museum** a few miles north of Sunriver before driving to the nearby **Lava Lands Visitor Center**. There, walk into **Lava River Cave**, a mile-long natural tube underground. Head south on Hwy 97 a short way to **Newberry Crater National Volcanic Monument** and picnic at Paulina or East Lake. Continue south on Highway 97 to either Highway 138 in summer for the north entrance to Crater Lake, or to Highway 62 just north of Klamath Falls in winter to the south entrance, and proceed on the 33-mile Rim Drive (closed in winter) in **Crater Lake National Park**. Check in to **Crater Lake Lodge** (book months in advance) and make your dinner reservations for the dining room, then take a short hike or boat ride out to Wizard Island.

DAY THREE: After breakfast at the lodge, drive west on Highway 62 to **Medford** and detour east to **Jacksonville**. Stroll **California Street** and visit the **Jacksonville Museum**, then continue the gold rush nostalgia with lunch at century-old **Bella Union**. Head south on Interstate 5 to Ashland, take a short walk in **Lithia Park**, then check in to the romantic **Romeo Inn** and enjoy afternoon refreshments. Slip into your glad rags, have a leisurely dinner at **Cucina Biazzi**, and take in a play at the **Oregon Shakespeare Festival**. If you still have energy, have an after-theater drink at **Chateaulin**, or soak in the hot tub before bed.

RESTAURANTS

Roseburg Station Pub & Brewery / ★

700 SHERIDAN ST, ROSEBURG; 541/672-1934

The Brothers McMenamin's familiar stamp of pub antiquities and peculiar art, which eerily reflects the past of whatever historic building they've "pubicized," is repeated in this restoration of Roseburg's 87-year-old train depot. But we aren't complaining. The cozy bar and dining room look out onto the tracks over which the Southern Pacific Railroad's "Shasta Route" once ran. The brick depot's vaulted, 16-foot-high ceiling, tongue-and-groove fir wainscoting, and marble molding have been shined up and the roof replaced. The usual McMenamins' beer (Hammerhead, Terminator Stout, and Ruby, infused with raspberry juice) is as good as ever, and the hearty menu is the same as in other McMs' pubs: Captain Neon and Communication Breakdown burgers, grilled smoked bratwurst with mashed potatoes, red wine beef stew, and baked porter and onion soup. *$; AE, DIS, MC, V; local checks only; lunch, dinner every day; full bar; reservations not necessary; www.mcmenamins.com; across from Village Bistro.* &

Village Bistro & Bakery / ★

500 SE CASS, ROSEBURG; 541/677-3450

This is the sunniest spot in Roseburg, with a wide-open floor plan, and patio seating under umbrellas on the warmest days. Generous portions of down-to-earth bistro food are served here. The short breakfast menu includes home fries and biscuits and gravy. For lunch, try seared salmon and fresh spinach salad, topped with miso-ginger dressing. Comfort food is on the menu too: chicken potpie, meat loaf with garlic mashed potatoes, pork medallions, and tenderloin. Vegetarians order falafel, veggie foccacia, lasagne, and yogurt smoothies. *$; AE, MC, V; checks OK; breakfast, lunch, dinner every day; beer and wine; reservations not necessary; village@rosenet.net; south of downtown.* &

LODGINGS

Steamboat Inn / ★★

42705 N HWY 138, STEAMBOAT; 541/498-2230 OR 800/840-8825

On the banks of a fly-only fishing stream is this plain-seeming lodge run for many years by Jim and Sharon Van Loan. Linked by a long veranda paralleling the North Umpqua River are eight small cabins, remodeled in 1997; rooms have knotty pine walls and just enough space, with Jacuzzi tubs in the rooms (adults only). Five secluded cottages in the woods have living rooms and kitchens, suitable for small families; two suites are by the river. Remarkably good family-style dinners are served in the main building each night a half hour after dark, by reservation ($35 per person, including premium Oregon wines). The inn also serves breakfast and lunch every day, and is now entirely nonsmoking. No pets; enjoy the Van Loan's instead. *$$$; MC, V; checks OK; closed Jan–Feb, weekends only Nov–Dec, Mar–Apr; www.the steamboatinn.com; 38 miles east of Roseburg.*

Wolf Creek Inn / ★

100 RAILROAD AVE, WOLF CREEK; 541/866-2474

An 1880s stagecoach stop and the oldest inn in Oregon, this two-story clapboard inn was purchased by the state, restored in 1979, and recently refurbished to what it reportedly looked like in 1925. This charming historic spot could be one of the "Taverns" out of Virginia's Colonial Williamsburg (sans candles and costumed servants). Eight nicely furnished guest rooms, including one suite, have comfortable antique beds. All have private, basic baths. Downstairs is an attractive parlor, and a cozy dining room with hearty fare such as a thick steak soup and homemade bread. Children OK; no pets. *$; MC, V; local checks only; www.rogueweb.com/riverloop/wolfcreek; 25 miles north of Grants Pass, exit 76 off I-5.* &

The Rogue River Valley

The Rogue River is one of Oregon's most beautiful rivers. Running west from the Cascades, it's chiseled into the coastal mountains, protected by the million-acre Siskiyou National Forest, flecked with abandoned gold-mining sites, and inhabited by splendid steelhead. Many rustic lodges along the river cater specifically to fly-fishers and rafters, and are often only accessible via water. Grants Pass, along the upper reaches of the Rogue, offers the best access for fishing and rafting.

Grants Pass

Two companies offer jet-boat tours of the Rogue River. **HELLGATE JETBOAT EXCURSIONS** (966 SW 6th St; 541/479-7204) departs from the Riverside Inn in Grants Pass. **JET BOAT RIVER EXCURSIONS** (8896 Rogue River Hwy; 541/582-0800) leaves from the city of Rogue River, 8 miles upstream (south on I-5). Guide services such as **ORANGE TORPEDO TRIPS** (209 Merlin Rd, Merlin; 541/479-5061) conduct popular, though sometimes wild and daring, white-water trips.

RESTAURANTS

Hamilton River House / ★

1936 ROGUE RIVER HWY/HWY 99, GRANTS PASS; 541/479-3938

Chef/owner Doug Hamilton moved his restaurant from his childhood home to a new riverside location, and it's built for a crowd. Casual and colorful (bright yellow, green, and coral), with tiered seating inside and out, the restaurant still serves the same good food. Count on moist and exquisite salmon, and rich, creamy Jamaican jerk chicken over angel hair pasta. A daily fresh sheet might feature lingcod, snapper, and halibut—and steaks. Grants Pass is noted for inexpensive dining, and Hamilton River House fits the mold. Lunches include Milano-style wood-fired pizza, smoked-salmon ravioli, and great burgers.

Jazz plays on weekends. *$; AE, DIS, MC, V; checks OK; lunch, dinner every day; full bar; reservations recommended; Grants Pass exit off I-5.* &

Matsukaze

1675 NE 7TH ST, GRANTS PASS; 541/479-2961

This small Japanese restaurant offers fresh preparations in a calm setting, just off the interstate. There are fish, vegetable, and meat teriyakis; tempura; sukiyaki; king crab and Oregon lox sushi (of course); and plate lunches served with salad, rice, vegetables, and hot tea. Or try mahimahi in a light egg wash, sautéed. Finish up with refreshing green tea ice cream. *$; DIS, MC, V; no checks; lunch Mon–Fri, dinner Mon–Sat; beer and wine; reservations not necessary; corner of Hillcrest.*

Summer Jo's / ★

2315 UPPER RIVER RD LOOP, GRANTS PASS; 541/476-6882

This bright garden room, owned by two retired *MacWorld* editors, sits on 6½ acres of flower, vegetable, and herb gardens and 100-year-old fruit trees. The gardens are lovely, with more than 200 varieties of roses, many of them climbing a series of trellises. The restaurant, overseen by Philip Accetta, who trained at the Hyde Park Culinary Institute, offers hearty sandwiches such as Mediterranean braised lamb with cucumbers, red onion, and minted yogurt; smoked rosemary chicken with wilted greens, artichokes, and feta; and roasted portobello mushroom with smoked-tomato relish and white cheddar. All are served with soup or salad. Afternoons (Tues–Sat), have tea with scones served with Devonshire cream, lemon curd, brown-sugar shortbread, fruit, and tea sandwiches. For sale in the adjoining pantry are fresh vegetables, herbal vinegars and oils, tinctures, dilled beans, honey, lemon curd, and potted herb starts. *$; MC, V; local checks only; lunch Tues–Sat (closed mid-Dec–mid-Feb); beer and wine; reservations recommended; www.summerjo.com; exit 58 off I-5.* &

LODGINGS

Flery Manor / ★★

2000 JUMPOFF JOE CREEK RD, GRANTS PASS; 541/476-3591 OR 541/471-2303

This classy two-story, 5,000-square-foot 1990s rural home on 7 acres of wooded mountainside became a B&B in 1996. Owners John and Marla Vidrinskas did much of the finishing work themselves. The showpiece is the Moonlight Suite, favored by honeymooners and second-honeymooners. Its king-size canopied bed sits in front of a fireplace. French doors open to a private balcony. The bath has a double vanity, double Jacuzzi, and glassed-in shower. A second suite, added in 2000, offers the same luxury with a private first-floor patio. There are three additional guest rooms; two have private baths and the third can be connected to make a two-bedroom suite. Marla serves a three-course breakfast in a formal dining room, with baked goods, quiches, and frittatas (featured in several gourmet magazines). No pets, but children over 10 are OK. *$$;*

MC, V, checks OK; flery@flerymanor.com; www.flerymanor.com; 10 miles north of Grants Pass, Hugo exit 66 off I-5. &

Morrison's Rogue River Lodge / ★

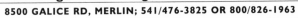

8500 GALICE RD, MERLIN; 541/476-3825 OR 800/826-1963

Start your Rogue River rafting adventures here and you'll follow in the footsteps of George Bush and Jimmy Carter. This is the best of the Rogue River lodges favored by anglers and river-runners. It is also easiest to reach. While others are accessible only by boat or plane, Morrison's is accessed via a paved road. The lodge, dating to the 1940s, has four guest rooms and nine river-view cottages (most guests prefer the latter, with fireplaces, private decks, and covered parking). One- or two-bedroom cottages and lodge rooms have private baths. Rates include a four-course dinner and breakfast. Dinners—by reservation—taste best on the deck, and may feature cucumber soup, osso buco, grilled lamb, and apple-walnut torte or bread pudding with lemon curd; the dining room is also open to nonguests. *$$–$$$; DIS, MC, V; checks OK; closed Dec–Apr; info@morrisonslodge.com; www. morrisonslodge.com; 12 miles west of I-5.*

Weasku Inn / ★★

5560 ROGUE RIVER HWY/HWY 99, GRANTS PASS; 541/476-6873 OR 800-493-2758

This 1924 log lodge where Hollywood actors once retreated to fish was resuscitated in 1999. Weasku Inn (pronounced "we-ask-you"), with its river-rock fireplace and broad lawn among giant trees, is an idyllic place to stay on the banks of the Rogue River. Better yet, book one of nine luxurious river cabins. Any potential traffic noise is drowned out by the rush of water over Savage Rapids Dam. A short trail from the cabins to the rocky shore below the dam brings you to a fabulous bird-watching spot for mergansers, mallards, osprey, and herons. River cabins have gas fireplaces, lodge-style furnishings, large baths that are well appointed, and decks for morning sun. Whirlpool tubs are in some cabins as well as in several lodge rooms. Continental breakfast is served in the lodge dining room, and evening wine and cheese next to the fireplace. *$$; AE, DIS, MC, V; no checks; www.weasku.com; exit 48 off I-5.*

Oregon Caves National Monument

Cave Junction is 28 miles southwest of Grants Pass on US Highway 199. The Cave Junction area is home to two of Oregon's better wineries: **FORIS** (654 Kendall Rd, Cave Junction; 541/592-3752) and **BRIDGEVIEW** (4210 Holland Loop Rd, Cave Junction; 541/592-4688). Both have tasting rooms open daily.

About 20 miles east of Cave Junction, on Highway 46, is **OREGON CAVES NATIONAL MONUMENT** (20000 Caves Hwy; 541/592-3400), a group of intriguing formations of marble and limestone set among redwoods. Tours leave periodically year-round. They are a bit strenuous, and the caves remain a chilly 41°F; the tight spaces can get awfully packed with tourists. After a

1997 renovation, part of the caves walkway is now wheelchair-accessible. Children under six are allowed if they meet the height requirement; babysitting service is available. Arrive early in summer, or you may have a long wait.

OREGON CAVES LODGE (541/592-3400; www.oregoncaves.com; open May–Oct) is nothing fancy, but a restful old wooden lodge with 22 rooms and a down-home dining room.

Medford

Southern Oregon's largest city may not win any contests for prettiness, but it is the center of things in this part of the world. It's well known across the nation due to the marketing efforts of Harry and David's, a mail-order giant purveying pears, other fruit, and condiments. **HARRY AND DAVID'S COUNTRY VILLAGE** (1314 Center Dr; 541/776-2277; www.harry-david.com) offers "seconds" from gift packs and numerous other items, as well as tours of the complex, also home to **JACKSON & PERKINS** (www.jackson-perkins.com), the world's largest rose growers.

The **CRATERIAN GINGER ROGERS THEATER** (39 S Central Ave; 541/779-3000) is Medford's showpiece, a downtown performing arts center with a 742-seat theater that opened in 1997. (The former Craterian movie theater dated back to the 1920s.) Why Ginger Rogers? The actress owned a ranch on the nearby Rogue River for many years, once danced on the Craterian stage, and in the last couple of years before her death helped raise money for the theater's $5.3 million renovation.

Locals like lunch and dinner at **SAMOVAR** (101 E Main St; 541/779-4967), a Russian cafe; for Thai food they flock to **ALI'S THAI KITCHEN** (2392 N Pacific Hwy; 541/770-3104), a humble spot north of town with good, inexpensive fare.

LODGINGS

Under the Greenwood Tree / ★★★½

3045 BELLINGER LN, MEDFORD; 541/776-0000

Innkeeper Renate Ellam—a Cordon Bleu chef and former interior designer—will have you relaxing in the lap of luxury amid green lawns and 300-year-old trees on her 10-acre farm with an orchard, beautiful rose gardens and gazebo, and antique farm buildings. The 1862 home has five guest rooms, each with private bath, Persian rugs, elegant linens, fresh flowers, and amenities such as terry cloth robes and hair dryers. Guests who arrive early are greeted by such things as lemon pound cake, hot scones with orange butter, or ice-cold watermelon; Ellam's elaborate three-course breakfasts include dishes such as vanilla-poached pears with Chantilly cream. Turndown service includes truffles. Popular for weddings, the B&B has a dance floor under the stars. *$$; no credit cards; checks OK; grwdtree@cdsnet.net; www.greenwoodtree.com; exit 27 off I-5.* &

Jacksonville

The town, a few miles west of Medford on Highway 238, started with a boom when gold was discovered in Rich Gulch in 1851. Then the railroad bypassed it, and the tidy little city struggled to avoid becoming a ghost town. Much of the 19th-century city has been restored; Jacksonville now boasts more than 85 historic homes and buildings, some open to the public. The strip of authentic Gold Rush–era shops, hotels, and saloons along **CALIFORNIA STREET** has become a popular stage set for films, including the TV-movie version of *Inherit the Wind*. Jacksonville is also renowned for **ANTIQUE SHOPS**.

JACKSONVILLE MUSEUM (206 N 5th St; 541/773-6536), housed in the stately 1883 courthouse, follows the history of the Rogue River Valley with photos and artifacts, and displays works by Peter Britt (see below). The adjacent **CHILDREN'S MUSEUM** lets kids walk through various miniaturized pioneer settings (jail, tepee, schoolhouse). Walking trails thread around old gold diggings in the hills; the longest (3 miles) is **RICH GULCH HISTORIC TRAIL** (trailhead off 1st and Fir St), an easy climb to a panoramic view. Also stroll through the 1875 "country gothic" **BEEKMAN HOUSE** and gardens (on east end of California St; 541/773-6536).

VALLEY VIEW WINERY (1000 Applegate Rd; 541/899-8468), the area's oldest, is at Ruch, 6 miles southwest of here on Highway 238. The winery maintains another tasting room in town, in **ANNA MARIA'S** (130 W California St; 541/899-1001).

The **BRITT FESTIVAL** (541/773-6077 or 800/882-7488; www.brittfest.org; late June–Sept), an outdoor music-and-arts series, is held on the hillside field where Peter Britt, a famous local photographer and horticulturist, lived. Listeners gather on benches or blankets to enjoy music ranging from jazz and bluegrass to folk, country, and classical, as well as musical theater and dance. Performance quality varies, but the series includes big-name artists. Begun in 1963, the festival now draws some 70,000 visitors each summer.

RESTAURANTS

Bella Union / ★

170 W CALIFORNIA ST, JACKSONVILLE; 541/899-1770

This restaurant, in the original century-old Bella Union Saloon (half of which was reconstructed when *The Great Northfield, Minnesota Raid* was filmed in Jacksonville in 1969), has everything from pizza and pasta to elegant dinners, to summer picnic baskets. The fresh sheet is usually good, with choices such as salmon with chile butter, bass with lime salsa, sole with Romano fettuccine, and ahi tuna. The garden out back is pleasant in warm weather. Proprietor Jerry Hayes, a wine fancier, pours 35 labels by the glass as well as the bottle. *$$; AE, DIS, MC, V; checks OK; lunch, dinner every day, brunch Sun; full bar; reservations recommended; downtown.*

Jacksonville Inn / ★★

175 E CALIFORNIA ST, JACKSONVILLE; 541/899-1900

Ask a native to name the area's best, and the answer is often the Jacksonville Inn. The staff is considerate, and the antique-furnished dining room, housed in the original 1863 building, is elegant and intimate. The inn's restaurant features steak, seafood, pasta—plus health-minded low-cholesterol fare and an expanded variety of vegetarian entrees. Dinners can be ordered as leisurely seven-course feasts or à la carte. Desserts are lovely European creations. Jerry Evans maintains one of the best-stocked wine cellars in Oregon, with more than 1,500 domestic and imported labels. Upstairs, eight rooms are decorated with 19th-century details: antique beds, patchwork quilts, and original brickwork on the walls. Modern amenities include private baths and air conditioning (a boon on 100-degree summer days). The inn has three honeymoon cottages nearby, all with king-size canopied beds and two-person Jacuzzis. Guests enjoy a full breakfast. Reserve in advance, especially during the Britt Festival. *$$; AE, DC, DIS, MC, V; checks OK; breakfast, dinner every day, lunch Tues–Sat, brunch Sun; full bar; reservations recommended; jvinn@ mind.net; www.jacksonvilleinn.com; on main thoroughfare.*

McCully House Inn / ★★

240 E CALIFORNIA ST, JACKSONVILLE; 541/899-1942 OR 800/367-1942

McCully House, an elegant Gothic Revival mansion, was built in 1860 for Jacksonville's first doctor—and later housed the first private school in Southern Oregon. Inside, three intimate dining rooms draw raves for ambience and food. Executive chef Anthony Mouyious, who grew up in Jacksonville and learned to cook side-by-side with chefs in local kitchens, offers succulent dishes such as rack of lamb accompanied by Italian *torta*, and pork tenderloin stuffed with garlic Gorgonzola and served with pear and apple chutney. The bistro menu includes lighter dishes (angel hair pasta with fresh vegetables topped with Asiago cheese, or tarragon prawn skewers). One of the first six homes in the city, the house has hardwood floors, lace curtains, antiques, and lovely grounds. Best of the three guest rooms flaunts a fireplace, huge clawfooted pedestal tub, and the original black-walnut furnishings that traveled round the Horn with J. W. McCully. Children welcome; no pets. *$$; AE, DC, DIS, MC, V; checks OK; dinner every day, brunch Sun; full bar; reservations required; mccully@wave.net; www.mccullyhouseinn.com; downtown.* &

LODGINGS

TouVelle House / ★★

455 N OREGON ST, JACKSONVILLE; 541/899-8938 OR 800/846-8422

This stately mansion, one of Jacksonville's first, was built in 1855. Frank TouVelle and his bride remodeled and added to the three-story Craftsman-style house after moving to Oregon from Ohio. Today it's a Jacksonville landmark, which Steven Harris and Nick Williamson run as a six-room B&B. New period wallpapers flatter the extensive wood paneling and square-beamed ceilings. Two suites are large enough to accommodate three or four; the owners have added a new garden, pond, and historic garden with old-fashioned roses, hedging, and pergolas. A modern swimming pool with a gazebo is out back. Breakfast is a gourmet, three-course affair. Corporate rates available. *$$; AE, DIS, MC, V; checks OK; touvelle@waves.net; www.touvellehouse.com; downtown.*

Talent

RESTAURANTS

New Sammy's Cowboy Bistro / ★★★
2210 S PACIFIC HWY/HWY 99, TALENT; 541/535-2779

Proprietors Vernon and Charleen Rollins rely entirely on word-of-mouth advertising, and appear amused when you find them. There's no sign other than a flashing light at night, and the outside looks barely a cut above a shack. Inside, though, is as charming a dinner house as you're likely to find in Southern Oregon. With just six tables, reservations are a must, and you may have to wait a couple of weeks. The French-inspired menu usually lists a handful of entrees, like duck breast with spinach, chicken with spicy couscous, and salmon with dill sauce and vegetables (perfectly cooked). The wines include 40 choices from Oregon, California, and France. *$$; no credit cards; checks OK; dinner Thurs–Sun (Fri–Sat in midwinter); beer and wine; reservations required; halfway between Talent and Ashland.*

Ashland

The remarkable success of the **OREGON SHAKESPEARE FESTIVAL** (see "Shakespeare Festival Tips" in this chapter), now well over 50 years old, has transformed this sleepy town into one with, per capita, the region's best tourist amenities. The festival draws some 350,000 people through the nine-month season, filling its theaters to an extraordinary 97 percent capacity. Visitors pour into this town of 18,000, and fine shops, restaurants, and bed-and-breakfasts spring up in anticipation. Amazingly, the town still has its soul: for the most part, it seems a happy little college town, set amid lovely ranch country, that just happens to house one of the largest theater companies.

Designed by the creator of San Francisco's Golden Gate Park, **LITHIA PARK**, Ashland's central park, runs for 100 acres behind the outdoor theater, with duck ponds, Japanese gardens, grassy lawns, playgrounds, and groomed or dirt trails for hikes and jogging. There's even an ice-skating rink in winter. **SCHNEIDER MUSEUM OF ART** (1250 Siskiyou Blvd; 541/552-6245) at the south end of the Southern Oregon State College campus is the best art gallery in town.

WEISINGER ASHLAND WINERY (Hwy 99 just south of Ashland; 541/488-5989; ysingers@oregonwine.org; www.weisingers.com) and **ASHLAND VINEYARDS** (near Hwy 66 exit from I-5; 541/488-0088; www.winenet.com) offer opportunities to sample Ashland vintages.

SHAKESPEARE FESTIVAL TIPS

The **Oregon Shakespeare Festival** mounts plays in three theaters. In the outdoor Elizabethan Theater, which seats 1,200, famous and authentic nighttime productions of Shakespeare are staged (three each summer). The outdoor theater was remodeled in the early 1990s to improve acoustics. The season for two indoor theaters (Feb–Oct) includes comedies, contemporary fare, and some experimental works. Visit the **Exhibit Center**, where you can clown around in costumes from plays past. There are also lectures and concerts at noon, excellent backstage tours each morning, and Renaissance music and dance nightly in the courtyard.

The best way to get current **information and tickets** (last-minute tickets in summer are rare) is through a comprehensive agency: Southern Oregon Reservation Center (541/488-1011 or 800/547-8052; www.sorc.com; Mon–Fri), or the festival box office (15 S Pioneer, Ashland; 541/482-4331; www.orshakes.org).

Ashland is also home to a growing number of smaller theater groups—often called **Off Shakespeare** or Off Bardway—and worth watching. Festival actors often join in these small companies to have a bit of fun. Oregon Cabaret Theater (1st and Hargadine; 541/488-2902; www.oregoncabaret.com), for example, presents musicals and comedies through much of the year, with dinners, hors d'oeuvres, and desserts for theater patrons.

—Jan Halliday

Nearby daytime attractions include river rafting, picnicking, and historical touring. The **ROGUE RIVER RECREATION AREA** has fine swimming on sizzling summer days, as does the lovely Applegate River. **HOWARD PRAIRIE LAKE RESORT** (3249 Hyatt Prairie Rd; 541/482-1979) is 22 scenic miles southeast of Ashland up Dead Indian Memorial Road. **SKI ASHLAND** (1745 Hwy 66; 541/482-2897), on nearby Mount Ashland 18 miles south of town, offers 22 runs for all classes of skiers, usually Thanksgiving to mid-April.

RESTAURANTS

Chateaulin / ★★★

50 E MAIN ST, ASHLAND; 541/482-2264

Less than a block from the theaters is a romantic cafe reminiscent of New York's upper West Side. During Shakespeare season, the place bustles with before- and after-theater crowds gathered for fine French cuisine or drinks at the bar. House specialties are pâtés and veal dishes, but seafood and poultry are also impressive; watch the specials: delicate butterflied shrimp in a subtle sauce of sherry, cream, tomato, and brandy are delicious. Chef David Taub and co-owner Michael Donovan change the menu seasonally. The cafe menu is a favorite of the after-show crowd: baked goat cheese in puff pastry with sun-dried tomatoes served on mesclun green salad with raspberry vinaigrette gets raves, as does an outrageously delicious onion soup; coffee and specialty drinks round out the menu. Service is polished and smooth even during the rush. *$$; AE, DIS, MC, V; checks OK; dinner every day (closed Mon–Tues in winter); full bar; reservations recommended; chateau@jeffnet.org; www.chateaulin.com; down walkway from Angus Bowmer Theater.*

Cucina Biazzi / ★★
568 E MAIN ST, ASHLAND; 541/488-3739

Chef April Morehouse and proprietor Beasy McMillan have turned this pretty little house into a traditional Tuscan trattoria with a wisteria-covered patio. Four-course dinners are served on white linen in the former living room. Don't fill up on the delicious antipasto course alone (though it's tempting): Asiago cheese, imported olives, marinated mushrooms, over-roasted vegetables, and bean salad, with plenty of warm bread. Pasta portions, made with fresh pasta and creamy cheeses, are filling, followed by a full plate of fish or meat entree such as osso buco. Dinner finishes with a perfectly dressed green salad. Desserts might be lemon tarts or rich chocolate cake. *$$; MC, V; checks OK; dinner every day; full bar; reservations recommended; near fire station on E Main.*

Firefly / ★★
23 N MAIN, ASHLAND; 541/488-3212

Prepare for a visual feast as well as unusual fare at this dining room, the entire third floor (with elevator access) of Ashland's historic Masonic Temple. The room is simple, rich, and beautiful: plum and grape, hand-carved walnut, and two fireplaces. Chef/owners Tim and Dana Keller's entrees may include banana-wrapped swordfish with coconut rice and green sauce, or pork tenderloin rubbed with anise and curry, served with lentils and applesauce. A spicy satay may be decorated with circular slices of vegetables resembling paints on an artist's palette. Portions tend to be ample; leave room for dessert. *$$; MC, V; local checks only; lunch, dinner every day; full bar; reservations recommended (dinner); on plaza.*

Monet / ★★★
36 S 2ND ST, ASHLAND; 541/482-1339

Pierre and Dale Verger have created a gentrified French restaurant that is the talk of Ashland (and even gets mentioned in Portland). Favorite dishes in this gracious house include shrimp sautéed in white wine and Pernod, and veal with wild mushrooms and Madeira. Pierre Verger goes out of his way to make interesting vegetarian choices—sautéed artichoke hearts with sun-dried tomatoes, olives, mushrooms, garlic, shallots, feta, and Parmesan over pasta, as well as a simple French-country dish called *la crique Ardechoise*, a kind of gourmet potato pancake with garlic and parsley. The wine list is extensive. Dine outdoors in summer. *$$; MC, V; local checks only; dinner every day (Tues–Sat off season); full bar; reservations recommended; ½ block from Main St.*

LODGINGS

Chanticleer Inn / ★★★

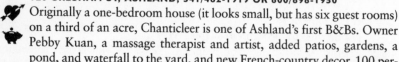

120 GRESHAM ST, ASHLAND; 541/482-1919 OR 800/898-1950

Originally a one-bedroom house (it looks small, but has six guest rooms) on a third of an acre, Chanticleer is one of Ashland's first B&Bs. Owner Pebby Kuan, a massage therapist and artist, added patios, gardens, a pond, and waterfall to the yard, and new French-country decor, 100 percent cotton linens, and original watercolors to the rooms. Three of them have extra beds; others have queen beds. The largest has a gas fireplace; all have private baths and cotton robes for the trek to the Jacuzzi out back. You might read scripts of all the plays running at the Shakespeare festival (four blocks from the inn) in front of the gas fireplace in the cozy common area. A gourmet breakfast is served in the dining room, and complimentary afternoon wine, sherry, port, and homemade cookies are available. On-site massage is offered in your room. A gift shop on premises offers Oregon-made gourmet foods, robes, and bath products. Children over 12 OK; no pets. *$$; AE, MC, V; checks OK; innkeeper@ ashland-bed-breakfast.com; www.ashland-bed-breakfast.com; 2 blocks from library, off Main St.*

Country Willows Inn / ★★★

1313 CLAY ST, ASHLAND; 541/488-1590 OR 800/945-5697

Set on 5 acres of farmland seven minutes from downtown, this rebuilt 1896 country home offers peace and quiet and a lovely view of the hills. Dan Durant and David Newton offer five rooms, three suites, and a separate cottage, with air conditioning and private baths, plus a swimming pool and a hot tub on the large back deck. The best room is in the barn: the Pine Ridge Suite has a bed/living room with lodgepole pine king-size bed, and a bath bigger than most bedrooms. Breakfast is organic juices and egg dishes, pumpkin pancakes or waffles, presented on a pretty sun porch. The grounds offer running and hiking trails into the adjacent foothills; the owners keep a small flock of ducks, a gaggle of geese, and even a couple of goats. Children over 12 OK; no pets. *$$; MC, V; checks OK; www.willowsinn.com; 4 blocks south of Siskiyou Blvd.* &

Cowslip's Belle / ★★

159 N MAIN ST, ASHLAND; 541/488-2901 OR 800/888-6819

Named after a flower mentioned in *A Midsummer Night's Dream* and *The Tempest*, the home has a cheery charm, with its swing chair on the front porch, vintage furniture, and fresh flowers inside. A huge deck with redwood arbor overlooks a koi pond and lagoon. Two lovely bedrooms (one a suite) are in the main house—a 1913 Craftsman bungalow—and two more in a romantic carriage house in back. Jon and Carmen Reinhardt, owners for 16 years, provide turndown service (with chocolate truffles) and full breakfasts such as cheese blintzes, walnut wheat-germ pancakes, and Jon's brioche, scones, and other baked goods (his wholesale bakery is on premises, so the inn always smells heavenly). Children 10 or over OK; no pets. *$$; no credit cards; checks OK; stay@cowslip.com; www.cowslip.com; 3 blocks north of theaters.* &

Mount Ashland Inn / ★★★

550 MOUNT ASHLAND RD, ASHLAND; 541/482-8707 OR 800/830-8707

Wind your way up Mount Ashland Road and you discover a huge, custom-made two-story log cabin, built in 1987, using some 275 cedar trees cut from the 160-acre property in the Siskiyous. Examples of the original owner's handiwork are seen throughout: stained-glass windows, a spiral cedar staircase with madrona railing. Chuck and Laurel Biegert have owned the inn for five years and recently reconfigured it into five suites, each with gas fireplace and jetted or soaking tub, as well as microwave, fridge, and wet bar. Spectacular views of Mount Shasta and Mount McLoughlin are visible from the dining room (where a three-course breakfast is served). An outdoor spa, cross-country skis, snowshoes, and mountain bikes are available for guests' use. The golden aromatic-cedar logs, high-beamed ceilings, large windows, and huge stone fireplace make this the perfect après-ski spot. Expect snow November through April. Children 10 and over OK; no pets. *$$$; DIS, MC, V; checks OK; www. mtashlandinn.com; follow signs to Mount Ashland Ski Area.*

Peerless Hotel / ★★

243 4TH ST, ASHLAND; 541/488-1082 OR 800/460-8758

Originally a hotel in Ashland's now-historic railroad district in 1900, the building fell into disrepair, but was saved by Chrissy Barnett. She merged hotel rooms into six new B&B units (two of them suites), and filled them with antiques collected from places as disparate as New Orleans and Hawaii. High ceilings and oversize bathrooms are trademarks. Suite 3 features a bath with his-and-her claw-footed tubs and a glassed-in shower. Several have Jacuzzis. Breakfast is cooked for guests in the adjoining restaurant (open to the public for dinner), across the garden; you can walk to the theaters. Children over 14 OK. *$$$; AE, DIS, MC, V; checks OK; www.peerlesshotel.com; between A and B Sts.* &

Romeo Inn / ★★★

295 IDAHO ST, ASHLAND; 541/488-0884 OR 800/915-8899

This imposing 1932 Cape Cod home has four plush guest rooms and two suites, some decorated in English country with antiques, some neoclassical. Spacious rooms have king-size beds, phones, and private baths. The Stratford Suite is a separate structure with its own bedroom, bath, and kitchen; it features a vaulted ceiling with skylight, marble-tiled wood fireplace, and raised whirlpool tub for two. The second suite, the Cambridge, has a fireplace, patio, and private entrance. Heated pool and hot tub on the large back deck are open year-round. Innkeepers Don and Deana Politis serve freshly squeezed orange juice, melon with blueberry sauce, eggs Florentine, sausage, and baked goods—plus afternoon refreshments and bedtime chocolate. Children over 12 OK; no pets. *$$$; MC, V; checks OK; romeo@mind. net; www.romeoinn.com; downtown.*

Klamath Falls

This city of 17,000 people, the largest for 70 miles around, is so isolated that it once led a movement to secede from Oregon and become the state of Jefferson. Now residents happily welcome tourists, bird-watchers, and sports enthusiasts from Oregon and California (25 miles south). Seemingly dormant for years, the geothermally heated town has bubbled to life in the past few years with a flurry of construction, including chain hotels and the $250 million **RUNNING Y RANCH RESORT** (5500 Running Y Rd; 888/850-0275), with its 85-room hotel, Arnold Palmer 18-hole golf course, restaurant, and condo development on 9,000 acres on Klamath Lake, 10 miles out of town. The Klamath Indian Tribe, a confederation of the Klamath, Modoc, and Yahooskin Natives who have occupied the region for thousands of years, opened their **KLA-MO-YA CASINO** (541/783-7529) on Highway 97 at Chiloquin, just a few miles north of the Klamath Falls Airport.

The **FAVELL MUSEUM OF WESTERN ART AND INDIAN ARTIFACTS** (125 W Main St; 541/882-9996) is a true western museum, with arrowheads, Native artifacts, and the works of more than 300 western artists. **KLAMATH COUNTY MUSEUM** (1451 Main St; 541/883-4208) exhibits the volcanic geology of the region, Indian artifacts from all over Oregon, and relics of the tragic Modoc wars. The **BALDWIN HOTEL MUSEUM** (31 Main St; 541/883-4207; open June–Sept), in a spooky 1906 hotel, retains many fixtures of the era. **ROSS RAGLAND THEATER** (218 N 7th St; 541/884-0651; www.rrtheater.org; Sept–May), a onetime art deco movie theater, now presents stage plays, concerts, and the like 130 nights a year.

UPPER KLAMATH LAKE, 143 square miles, lies on the remains of a larger ancient lake system and is the largest lake in Oregon; it's fine for fishing and serves as the nesting grounds for many birds, including white pelicans. The Williamson River, which flows into the lake, yields plenty of trout.

RESTAURANTS

Fiorella's / ★★

6139 SIMMERS AVE, KLAMATH FALLS; 541/882-1878

Fiorella and Renato Durighellois came here from a town near Venice, Italy, and 13 years ago opened one of the town's best restaurants. They've done their best to re-create rustic Italian ambience in a former residence with white tablecloths, fresh flowers, plastered walls, wooden-beamed ceilings, and a copper polenta pot nestled in the fireplace. Best is the restaurant's quarter-acre garden, which produces arugula, radicchio, and tender lettuces, along with vegetables and herbs—all finding their way onto your plate. Specials may include beef roll stuffed with sausage and served with grilled polenta, or osso buco. Homemade egg pastas are delicious, including ravioli stuffed with wild mushrooms. $$; AE, MC, V; local checks only; dinner Tues–Sat; full bar; reservations not necessary; S 6th St to Simmers.

Lakeview

At nearly 4,300-feet elevation, Lakeview calls itself "Oregon's Tallest Town." It's better known for its geyser, **OLD PERPETUAL**—which doesn't exactly rival Old Faithful but is Oregon's only geyser. The geyser goes off once every 30 seconds or so, shooting 75 feet into the air for 3 to 5 seconds. It's been erupting regularly for some 60 years, apparently unleashed by someone trying to drill a well. It's located in a pond at **HUNTER'S HOT SPRINGS** (on west side of Hwy 395, 2 miles north of town; 541/947-4142), a 47-acre property dotted by hot-spring pools. Built in the 1920s, the resort now includes a 19-unit motel.

Abert Lake, 20 miles north of Lakeview on Highway 395, is a stark, shallow body of water over which looms **ABERT RIM**, a massive fault scarp. One of the highest exposed geologic faults in North America, the rim towers 2,000 feet above the lake.

Summer Lake

From Summer Lake, continue north on Highway 31 and you'll pass **FORT ROCK STATE MONUMENT** (541/388-6055), where Klamath Indians found refuge when Mount Mazama exploded 6,800 years ago. Woven sandals found in one of Fort Rock's caves were carbon-dated to 9,000 years ago; archaeological studies have found Klamath-style artifacts that date back 13,000 years in the prehistoric lakebed. Summers, the mom-and-pop grocery store, and the small pioneer museum nearby are usually open.

LODGINGS

Summer Lake Bed & Breakfast Inn / ★★
31501 HWY 31, SUMMER LAKE; 541/943-3983 OR 800/261-2778

If you are looking for luxury in a remote setting, this is it—about 160 miles northeast of Klamath Falls on the edge of one of Oregon's largest bird refuges, Summer Lake Wildlife Refuge. From the inn's hot tub on the wide deck you can see 40 unmarred miles in all directions and, at night, more stars than you can count. Stay in one of three upstairs rooms in the rustic main house, or one of three cabin-style condos with kitchens, Jacuzzis, decks, music, and VCRs. All are equally attractive. Owners Darrell Seven and Jean Sage serve a big breakfast, and will cook dinner (Thurs–Sun) with advance notice (there's no grocery store or restaurant for miles). The area has considerable natural charms, which you'll have mostly to yourself—hiking in the Gearhart Mountain Wilderness Area to the south, fly-fishing, snowmobiling, and cross-country skiing. Ask advice from Seven about his guided three-day camping trips into the high desert. *$$; AE, MC, V; checks OK; between mileposts 81 and 82.*

Crater Lake National Park

Heading north from Klamath Falls on Highway 97, then west on Highway 62, you'll reach the south entrance to Crater Lake National Park. Some 7,700 years ago, 10,000- to 12,000-foot Mount Mazama became the Mount St. Helens of its day. It blew up and left behind a 4,000-foot-deep crater—now a lake filled by rainwater and snowmelt. With the water plunging to 1,932 feet, it's the deepest lake in the United States. A prospector searching for gold found this treasure in 1853; it was designated a national park in 1902, the only one in Oregon.

Crater Lake National Park is extraordinary: the impossibly blue lake, eerie volcanic formations, a vast geological wonderland. The **STEEL INFORMATION CENTER** (near the south entrance at park headquarters; 541/594-2211; www.nps.gov/crla/) offers an information desk, books, and an interpretive video; in summer, a second visitors center operates in **RIM VILLAGE**. Visitors can camp at Mazama Campground or other designated areas. The 33-mile **RIM DRIVE** along the top of the caldera offers many vistas; or take the two-hour boat ride from Cleetwood Cove out to Wizard Island and around the lake. There are dozens of trails and climbs to magnificent lookouts. In winter, when the crowds thin out, only the south and west entrance roads are open. Then, cross-country skiing and snowshoe walks are popular.

LODGINGS

Crater Lake Lodge / ★★

RIM DR, CRATER LAKE NATIONAL PARK; 541/830-8700

Originally built in 1909, the historic wood-and-stone building, perched at 7,000 feet on the rim of the caldera, was weakened considerably by decades of heavy snowfall. The four-story summer lodge was restored in the mid-'90s with a $15 million taxpayer-funded makeover, and features 71 rooms. Although only 26 rooms face the lake, all have great views of one of the world's indisputable wonders. Best are eight with claw-footed bathtubs in window alcoves. You won't find TVs or in-room phones here. The dining-room motif is 1930s lodge decor, but the menu (breakfast, lunch, dinner) is contemporary. The small (71-seat) dining room serves guests who reserve on check-in; nonguests must reserve months in advance. If the dining room is full, choose between two less-than-grand restaurants at Rim Village, 500 feet from the lodge. *$$$; MC, V; checks OK; open mid-May–Oct; via Hwy 138 (north) or Hwy 62.*

Diamond Lake and Mount Bailey

MOUNT BAILEY ALPINE SKI TOURS (off Hwy 138, just north of Crater Lake; 541/793-3348 or 800/446-4555; www.mountbailey.com) offers true back-country skiing, with snow-cats instead of helicopters to take you to the top of this 8,363-foot ancient volcano, and experienced, safety-conscious guides. **DIAMOND LAKE RESORT** (800/733-7593) is headquarters for the guide service. Also popular in winter: snowmobiling, cross-country skiing, inner-tube and snowboard hills, and ice-skating. When the snow melts, the operation turns to mountain bike tours, boating, swimming, and hiking.

Cascade Lakes Area

The 100-mile scenic **CASCADE LAKES HIGHWAY** (Hwy 58) tour needs several hours and a picnic lunch for full appreciation; stunning mountain views and a number of lakes and rustic fishing resorts are tucked along the way. Odell and Davis Lakes, near Willamette Pass on Highway 58, mark the southern end of the tour that winds its way north, eventually following the Deschutes River on Century Drive to Bend. Contact the Bend Chamber of Commerce (63085 N Hwy 97; 541/382-3221; www.bendchamber.org) for a booklet called "Cascade Lakes Discovery Tour."

Odell Lake

LODGINGS

Odell Lake Lodge and Resort

E ODELL LAKE ACCESS OFF HWY, CRESCENT LAKE; 541/433-2540
This resort on the shore of Odell Lake is ideal for the fisher, hiker, and skier in all of us. The lake's a bit alpine for swimming; instead, cast for Mackinaw trout, rainbow, or kokanee. (Most sports equipment—fishing rods to snowshoes—is rentable here.) The small library is perfect for sinking into an overstuffed chair in front of the fireplace. Request a lakeside room, one of seven in the hotel (Room 3, specifically, is a corner suite warmed with knotty pine paneling and lake and stream views). If you'd prefer a cabin, the few additional dollars required to get one lakeside are well spent. Newer, well-lit Cabin 10 is best (and the only wheelchair-accessible one). Or try Cabins 6 or 7. Cabin 12 sleeps a crowd of 16. Second-tier cabins are significantly smaller (no views). Pets OK in cabins. The restaurant is open year-round for three squares a day. *$$; DIS, MC, V; checks OK; 2-night min stay winter weekends; iyp.uswestdex. com/odelllakeresort; from Oakridge on Hwy 58, head east for 30 miles, take E Odell Lake exit.* &

Westfir

This former logging town flanks the North Fork of the Middle Fork of the Willamette River, excellent for rainbow trout fishing. The **AUFDERHEIDE NATIONAL SCENIC BYWAY** winds west from the Cascade Lakes out to Westfir, meandering along the river, and is popular with bicyclists, although heavy snowfall closes the route November through early April.

LODGINGS

Westfir Lodge / ★★

47365 1ST ST, WESTFIR; 541/782-3103
Westfir Lodge has long anchored the tiny community of Westfir. For many years it housed the former lumber company offices, then Gerry Chamberlain and Ken Symons converted the two-story building into a very pleasant eight-room inn. The bedrooms ring the first floor; in the center are a living area, kitchen, and formal dining room where guests are served a full English breakfast (English bangers and fried potatoes, eggs, broiled tomato topped with cheese, and scones). Cottage gardens outside and a plethora of antiques inside lend an English country ambience. The longest covered bridge in Oregon—the 180-foot Office Bridge (1944)—is just across the road. *$$; no credit cards; checks OK; 3 miles east of Hwy 58 near Oakridge.* &

Bend and Mount Bachelor

Bend was a quiet, undiscovered high-desert paradise until a push in the 1960s to develop recreation and tourism tamed Bachelor Butte (later renamed Mount Bachelor) into an alpine playground. Then came golf courses, an airstrip, bike trails, river-rafting companies, hikers, tennis players, rockhounds, and skiers. Bend's popularity and its population (now more than 50,000) have been on a steady increase ever since.

Heading north from Summer Lake on Highway 31 or Klamath Falls on Highway 97, the road to Bend passes through **NEWBERRY NATIONAL VOLCANIC MONUMENT** (between La Pine and Bend on both sides of Hwy 97; 541/593-2421 or 541/388-5664), a 56,000-acre monument in the Deschutes National Forest that showcases geologic attractions tens of thousands of years old. **NEWBERRY CRATER**, 13 miles east of Highway 97 on Forest Road 21, is the heart of the monument. Major attractions also include Paulina Peak, the Big Obsidian Flow, Paulina Falls, and East and Paulina Lakes, each with a small resort. Tour **LAVA RIVER CAVE**, a mile-long lava tube on Highway 97 (13 miles south of Bend). As you descend into the dark and surprisingly eerie depths, you'll need a warm sweater. **LAVA LANDS VISITOR CENTER** at the base of Lava Butte (12 miles south of Bend) is the interpretive center for the miles of lava beds. Drive or—when cars are barred—take the shuttle up Lava Butte, formed by a volcanic fissure, for a sweeping, dramatic view of the moonlike landscape.

Seasons for Newberry attractions vary, depending on snow, but generally run May through October.

Bend

The main thoroughfare through Bend, Highway 97's 10 miles of uninspired strip development, bypasses the historic town center, which thrives just to the west. **DESCHUTES HISTORICAL CENTER** (NW Idaho and Wall Sts; 541/389-1813) features regional history and interesting pioneer paraphernalia. Want to check your e-mail? Use the computers at **CAFE INTERNET** (133 SW Century Dr; 541/318-8802), Bend's original cybercafe.

The **HIGH DESERT MUSEUM** (59800 S Hwy 97; 541/382-4754) is an outstanding nonprofit center for natural and cultural history, 4 miles south of Bend. A "Desertarium" exhibits desert animals, including live owls, lizards, and Lahontan cutthroat trout. Twenty acres of natural trails and outdoor exhibits offer replicas of covered wagons, a sheepherder's camp, a settlers' cabin, and an old sawmill; and support three resident river otters, three porcupines, and about a half-dozen raptors (animal presentations daily). A new curatorial center and two new wings (one featuring an extensive collection of Columbia Plateau Indian artifacts, and the other focusing on birds of prey) are all just part of a $15 million expansion taking place over the next few years.

Part of Bend's charm comes from the blindingly blue sky and pine-scented air. The other part is its proximity to outdoor attractions. Mountain bike or hike for 9 miles along the **DESCHUTES RIVER TRAIL**, from downtown Bend past the Inn of the Seventh Mountain, taking in a series of waterfalls. **PILOT BUTTE STATE PARK** (541/388-6055 ext 23), just east of town on US Highway 20, is a red-cinder-cone park with a mile-long road to the top. It offers a knockout panorama of the city and the mountains beyond; look out for pedestrians on the road. Have a shake and a burger at the **PILOT BUTTE DRIVE-IN** (at Pilot Butte's base; 541/382-2972).

RESTAURANTS

Alpenglow Cafe

1040 NW BOND ST, BEND; 541/383-7676

The alpenglow they're referring to is probably the warm feeling you'll have after eating their mountain of breakfast (served all day). Orange juice is fresh squeezed and full of pulp, bacon and ham are locally smoked (salmon is brined and smoked in-house), and breads (even lunchtime hamburger buns) are homemade. Chunky potato pancakes, made with cheddar and bacon, are served with homemade applesauce or sour cream. The salmon eggs Benedict is huge—two eggs on two English muffin halves, topped with smoked king salmon, fresh basil, tomatoes, and a rich, lemony hollandaise. Even the huevos rancheros have the Alpenglow touch—a generous dollop of cilantro pesto and fresh salsa on top. Entrees come with a pile of home fries and coffee cake or fresh fruit. *$; AE, DIS, MC, V; local checks only; breakfast, lunch every day; beer only; reservations not accepted; next to Deschutes Brewery.* &

Broken Top Club / ★★
61999 BROKEN TOP DR, BEND; 541/383-8210

The 25,000-square-foot clubhouse of the Broken Top golf course captures an exceptional view of the Cascades with the golf course and lake gracing the foreground. Make your reservation for a half hour before sundown, and if Mother Nature is accommodating, you'll see a spectacular sunset over the jagged Broken Top and Three Sisters. The food is equally sensational and consistent, in spite of staff turnover. You might start with shrimp quesadilla with guacamole and tomato, and move to mixed seafood and spinach lasagne with fresh pesto cream and roasted pine nuts, or grilled salmon with wild rice and sweet pepper relish on tarragon-pecan sauce. This is central Oregon elegance. *$$; MC, V; local checks only; lunch Tues–Fri, dinner Tues–Sat; full bar; reservations recommended; www.brokentop.com/pages/restaurant.html; just off Mount Washington Dr from Century Dr.* &

Cafe Rosemary / ★★★
222 NW IRVING, BEND; 541/317-0276

Appreciative diners have been known to stand and applaud the food and chef Bob Brown at this simple bistro. The bright room has a fireplace and Oriental carpets to complement white-tablecloth fine dining. Lunches include savory thick-crusted pizzette, salads of field greens, and specials such as roasted-vegetable ravioli. Dinners are pure magic—especially when served prix fixe for, say, Valentine's Day—and might feature caviar on heart-shaped blini; prawns on rosemary skewers; consommé with truffles; smoked duck breast with jalapeño polenta; salads with fresh pears, Gorgonzola, and sweet roasted nuts; peppered chateaubriand; and chocolate marquise to finish. Tuesday nights feature a changing prix-fixe worldly regional menu. All food can be prepared to go. *$$; AE, MC, V; checks OK; lunch Mon–Fri, dinner Tues–Sun; beer and wine; reservations not necessary; call for directions.* &

Hans / ★★
915 NW WALL ST, BEND; 541/389-9700

This long-established Bend centerpiece has recently expanded to keep up with demand. A casual, bright cafe with hardwood floors and big windows, Hans offers a fine selection of salads and interesting daily specials. Service is sometimes brisk, but the bustle is hospitable. Lunch menus have mix-and-match sandwiches with all kinds of breads, cheeses, and other ingredients. Dinner brings finer dining, ranging from grilled portobello appetizers, unique pizzas, and seafood pasta, to salmon in a lemon herb beurre blanc, and tenderloin, all with creative yet simple sauces and flavors. A case full of pastries and sweets tempts. *$; MC, V; checks OK; lunch Mon–Sat, dinner Thurs–Sat in winter* *(summer hours expand); beer and wine; reservations recommended; near breezeway.* &

Marz Planetary Bistro / ★★

163 MINNESOTA AVE, BEND; 541/389-2025

This lively, loud, and colorful bistro is a welcome change from standard central Oregon cuisine. An interesting but limited ethnic-fusion menu matches the bright decor, disco ball, and funky artwork. Often backed by jazz or blues, closely set tables create a metropolitan ambience. A wide selection of wines and microbrews accompany everything from Argentinian marinated skirt steak or Asian-style rice paper–wrapped fresh fish. Three young couples own the restaurant and are knowledgeable yet unpretentious. *$–$$; DIS, MC, V; checks OK; lunch (summer only), dinner every day; beer and wine; reservations not necessary; between NW Bond and NW Wall Sts.* &

Pine Tavern Restaurant / ★★

967 NW BROOKS, BEND; 541/382-5581

Buttonhole three out of four Bend citizens and tell them you're ready for a fancy night out, with good food, service, atmosphere, and a decent value for your dollar—they'll recommend the Pine Tavern. This establishment has 50 years of history and a reputation for quality. Request a table by the window (overlooking placid Mirror Pond) in the main dining room and marvel at the tree growing through the floor. The prime rib petite cut is ample even for a hungry diner, but prime rib is the restaurant's forte. Don't miss the great apple butter for the soft rolls. *$$; AE, DIS, MC, V; checks OK; lunch Mon–Sat, dinner every day; full bar; reservations not necessary; www.pinetavern.com; foot of Oregon Ave downtown.*

LODGINGS

Inn of the Seventh Mountain / ★★

18575 SW CENTURY DR, BEND; 541/382-8711 OR 800/452-6810

The Inn offers the closest accommodations to Mount Bachelor and is popular with families, no doubt due to the vast menu of activities built into the multicondominium facility and the reasonable prices. It has the biggest ice rink around (though not full-size), which converts to a roller rink in April; a coed sauna large enough for a dozen friends; three bubbling hot tubs; and two heated swimming pools. In summer the pools are the center of activity—there's a whole layout complete with water slide and wading pool. An activities roster for the week gives the rundown on tennis, horseback riding, biking, skating, rafting, snowmobiling, skiing, aerobics, Frisbee golf—you name it. Josiah's restaurant offers fine dining, as well as breakfast and lunch, in the spacious lounge downstairs. *$$–$$$; AE, DIS, MC, V; checks OK; www.innofthe7thmountain.com; 7 miles west of downtown.* &

Mount Bachelor Village / ★★

19717 MOUNT BACHELOR DR, BEND; 541/389-5900 OR 800/452-9846

What this development has over some of its more famous neighbors is spacious rooms. Every unit (130 in all) has a furnished kitchen, wood-burning fireplace, and private deck. We prefer the newer units, where the color scheme is modern and light, and soundproofing helps mute the thud of ski boots. Some units look out to the busy mountain road, but the River Ridge addition looks out over the Deschutes River. Amenities include two outdoor Jacuzzis, seasonal outdoor heated pool, six tennis courts, and a 2⅕ mile nature trail. *$$$; AE, DIS, MC, V; checks OK; www.mtbachelorvillage.com; toward Mount Bachelor on Century Dr.* &

The Phoenix Inn / ★

300 NW FRANKLIN AVE, BEND; 541/317-9292 OR 888/291-4764

Huge, spotless minisuites with leather couches, microwaves, refrigerators, coffeemakers, and other amenities make you feel at home in this new 85-room establishment. Request a room with a mountain view. The staff is informative and friendly. There's a pool, Jacuzzi, and fitness center. Best is this inn's downtown location. And local calls are free. The continental breakfast buffet in a comfortable dining room includes fresh pastries, fruit, and newspapers. *$$–$$$; AE, DC, DIS, MC, V; checks OK; at Lava St.*

Pine Ridge Inn / ★★★

1200 SW CENTURY DR, BEND; 541/389-6137 OR 800/600-4095

Perched on the edge of the river canyon on Century Drive, this 20-suite inn is smaller than neighboring resorts but big on privacy, luxury, and south-facing bird's-eye views of the Deschutes River. Suites have step-down living rooms with antique and reproduction furniture, and gas-log fireplaces, private porches, and roomy, well-stocked baths. The second-floor Hyde Suite is best, with luxurious king bedroom, living/dining room, Jacuzzi tub, adjoining powder room, and several decks. Complimentary full breakfasts are served in a small gathering room or delivered to your door. Afternoons, nibble crostini with salmon or smoky cheddar spreads with a glass of wine or local beer. Well-behaved children are welcome; they can choose from a well-stocked library of videos, munch popcorn in their room, and get a special turndown treat of hot chocolate and cookies before bed (grown-ups get tea, cookies, and fruit). It's good for corporate retreats too; each room has a big desk and data ports. Budget tip: six rooms facing the parking lot are less expensive. *$$$; AE, DC, DIS, MC, V; checks OK; pineridge@empnet.com; www.pineridgeinn.com; just before Mount Bachelor Village.* &

Rock Springs Guest Ranch / ★★

64201 TYLER RD, BEND; 541/382-1957

From late June through late August and at Thanksgiving, the emphasis here is on family vacations. (The rest of the year, it's a topnotch conference center.) Counselors take care of kids in daylong special programs while adults hit the trail, laze in the pool, play tennis, or meet for evening hors d'oeuvres on the deck. Digs are comfy knotty pine two- and three-room cottages with fireplaces. Only 50 guests stay at the ranch at one time, so it's easy to get to know everyone, particularly since you eat family style in the lodge. The setting, amid ponderosa pines and junipers alongside a small lake, is secluded and lovely. The main activity here is riding, with nine wranglers and a stable of 70 horses. Summer season is booked by the week ($1,760 per person—kids for less, children under 2 free), which includes virtually everything. Look for lighted tennis courts, a free-form whirlpool with a 15-foot waterfall, a sand volleyball court under the tall pines, and fishing in the ranch pond. It's ideal for weddings or reunions. *$$$; AE, MC, V; checks OK; info@rocksprings.com; www.rocksprings.com; 7 miles from Bend and 20 miles from Sisters.* ♿

Sunriver Lodge / ★★★

SUNRIVER; 541/593-1000 OR 800/547-3922

More than a resort, Sunriver is an organized community with its own post office, chamber of commerce, realty offices, outdoor mall, grocery store, and more than 1,500 residents. The unincorporated town sprawls over 3,300 acres, and its own paved runway for private air commuting does brisk business. Sunriver's specialty is big-time escapist vacationing, and the resort has all the facilities to keep families, couples, or groups busy all week long, year-round. Summer months offer golf (three 18-hole courses), tennis (28 courts), rafting, canoeing, fishing, swimming (three pools, two complexes of hot tubs), biking (30 miles of paved trails), and horseback riding. In winter the resort is home base for skiing (Nordic and alpine), ice-skating, snowmobiling, and indoor racquetball. For the best bargain, deal through the lodge reservation service, request one of the large contemporary homes (often with hot tubs, barbecues, and decks), and split expenses with another family. If you want access to the pool and hot tub facility, request a house that has a pass. Even the bedroom units in the lodge village have a small deck and a fireplace and come with privileges such as discounted recreation, depending on the season. Recent additions are the resort's four River Lodges, which hold 33 luxury rooms with balconies overlooking the Meadows golf course, slate-floored bathrooms with soaker tubs and separate showers, and fireplaces. Lodge dining includes the Meadows, a much-acclaimed showplace for lunch, dinner, and Sunday brunch. Elsewhere in the town of Sunriver, choose anything from Chinese to pizza. We like breakfast at the Trout House at the Sunriver Marina, too. *$$; AE, DIS, MC, V; checks OK; www.sunriver_resort.com; 15 miles south of Bend.*

Mount Bachelor

MOUNT BACHELOR SKI AREA (22 miles southwest of Bend, on Century Dr; 800/829-2442 or 541/382-7888, ski report; www.mtbachelor.com), one of the largest ski area in the Pacific Northwest, has seven high-speed lifts (13 lifts in all) feeding skiers onto 3,100 vertical feet of dry and groomed skiing. The **SKIER'S PALATE** (at midmountain Pine Marten Lodge) serves excellent lunches; **SCAPOLO'S** (on lodge's lower level) features Italian cuisine. The 9,065-foot elevation at the summit makes for late-season skiing (open until July 4). High-season amenities include ski school, racing, day care, rentals, and an entire Nordic program and trails.

Elk Lake

LODGINGS

Elk Lake Resort

CENTURY DR, BEND; 541/480-7228

This remote fishing lodge—reached by snow-cat or 10 miles of cross-country skiing in the winter (or by car in summer)—consists of a dozen self-contained cabins, most with fireplace, kitchen, bathroom, and sleeping quarters for two to eight, and a small store. It's nothing grand, but the place is favored by Bend dwellers and the scenery is wonderful. New owners are remodeling the cabins and adding some primitive units. The dining room is also in for improvement, with changing daily specials. Reserve in advance for cabins or dining, and bring bug juice in summer—mosquitoes can be ravenous. *$$; MC, V; no checks; www.elklakeresort.com; look for signs to Elk Lake.*

Sisters and the Deschutes River Area

From Bend, Highway 20 heads northwest to Sisters, and from Sisters, Highway 126 goes east to Redmond; together with Highway 97 they form a triangle in an area rich with rivers and parks. North from Madras on Highway 26 is the Warm Springs Indian Reservation. And through it all runs the Deschutes River, designated a scenic waterway north of Warm Springs.

Redmond

Often overlooked in favor of its big sister to the south (Bend), Redmond offers a nice alternative base for exploring the Sisters region. About 6 miles north of Redmond, east of Terrebonne, some of the finest rock climbers gather to test their skills on the red-rock cliffs of **SMITH ROCK STATE PARK** (off of Hwy 97; 541/548-7501). Year-round camping is available.

The **CROOKED RIVER DINNER TRAIN** (4075 NE O'Neil Rd; 541/548-8630; dintrain@coinet.com) ambles up the 38-mile Crooked River Valley between Redmond and Prineville with three-hour scenic excursions and white-tablecloth dinner service. Special events and theme rides are offered, from murder-mystery tours to champagne brunches to western hoedowns. Reservations required.

LODGINGS

Inn at Eagle's Crest / ★★

1522 CLINE FALLS HWY, REDMOND; 541/923-2453 OR 800/MUCH-SUN

Sisters has Black Butte, Bend has Sunriver, and Redmond has Eagle's Crest. The private homes at this full resort rim the 18-hole golf course, and visitors choose one of the 75 rooms in the hotel (best ones have decks facing the course) or a condominium. Condos are a better deal, especially if you come with four to eight people. They've got kitchens and access to the recreation center (an additional $5 per day fee to those who stay in the main building) with its indoor tennis, squash, and racquetball courts, workout room, masseuse, tanning salon, heated outdoor pool, and tennis courts. The resort also has miles of biking and jogging trails, an equestrian center, and playfields. The food at the resort's formal Canyon Club is predictable for such a clubby atmosphere, with rancher-size portions for breakfast, lunch, and dinner; service can be slow. The three-tiered deck outside provides a good view. *$$; AE, MC, V; checks OK; 5 miles west of Redmond.*

Sisters

Named after the three mountain peaks (Faith, Hope, and Charity) that dominate the horizon, this little community is becoming a mecca for tired urbanites looking for a taste of cowboy escapism. On a clear day (about 250 a year here), Sisters is exquisitely beautiful. Surrounded by mountains, trout streams, and pine and cedar forests, this little town capitalizes on the influx of winter skiers and summer camping and fishing enthusiasts.

There's mixed sentiment about the pseudo-western storefronts that thematically organize the town's commerce, but then again, Sisters hosts 56,000 visitors for each of four shows during the annual June **SISTERS RODEO**. It also has the world's largest outdoor quilt show, the **SISTERS OUTDOOR QUILT SHOW**, in July, with 800 quilts hanging from balconies and storefronts. Call the visitor center (541/549-0251) for information on both events.

In the early 1970s, Sisters developed the western theme, but it's grown much more sophisticated. The town, built on about 30 feet of pumice dust spewed over centuries from the nearby volcanoes, has added mini-mall shopping clusters with courtyards and sidewalks to eliminate blowing dust. There are several large art galleries, good bakeries, an excellent fly-fishing shop, **THE FLY FISHER'S PLACE** (151 W Main; 541/549-3474), and even freshly roasted coffee at **SISTERS COFFEE COMPANY** (273 W Hood Ave; 541/549-0527). Although the town itself is about 1,000, more than 7,500 live in the surrounding area on miniranches.

RESTAURANTS

Hotel Sisters Restaurant and Bronco Billy's Saloon / ★

190 E CASCADE ST, SISTERS; 541/549-RIBS

The social centerpiece of western-themed Sisters, this bar and eatery serves ranch cooking—good burgers and some Mexican fare. Seafood is fresh, filet mignon grilled perfectly, chicken and ribs succulent. The waitstaff is friendly and diligent. Owners John Keenan, Bill Reed, and John Tehan have succeeded in turning old friendships into a going business consortium, re-creating the look of a first-class 1900 hotel. The upstairs hotel rooms are now private dining rooms. The deck is a good place for drinks. *$$; MC, V; checks OK; lunch, dinner every day (lunch Sat–Sun only in winter); full bar; reservations recommended; at Fir St.* &

Royal Thai Cafe / ★★

291 E CASCADE, SISTERS; 541/549-3025

It doesn't look like much from the outside but the small, dark downtown establishment serves unbeatable traditional Thai cuisine. Run by Sineenat Spofford, from Thailand, and Mark Spofford, who ran a restaurant in Thailand where he met his wife, the restaurant generally attracts a full house with good food and warm, efficient service. Start with seafood soup, full of prawns, mussels, calamari, and mushrooms, in a ginger, lemon-lime coconut milk broth, then try one of the curries. The small, casual room is intimate enough to suit a date or feed a festive family. *$; MC, V; checks OK; lunch Mon–Thurs and Sun, dinner every day; beer and wine; reservations recommended (weekends); at Spruce St.*

LODGINGS

Black Butte Ranch / ★★★

HWY 20, BLACK BUTTE RANCH; 541/595-6211

With 1,800 acres, this vacation and recreation wonderland remains the darling of Northwest resorts. Rimmed by the Three Sisters mountains and scented by a plain of ponderosa pines, these rental condos and private homes draw families year-round to swim, ski, fish, golf, bike, boat, ride horses (summer only), and play tennis. The best way to make a reservation is to state the size of your party and whether you want a home (most are large and contemporary) or simply a good-sized bed and bath (lodge condominiums suffice, though some are dark and dated, with too much orange Formica and brown furniture). The main lodge is handsome but not overwhelming, and serves as dining headquarters (breakfast, lunch, dinner). Tables at the Restaurant at the Lodge are tiered so everyone can appreciate the meadow panorama beyond. *$$$; AE, DIS, MC, V; checks OK; info@blackbutteranch.com; www.black butteranch.com; 8 miles west of Sisters.* &

Conklin's Guest House / ★★

69013 CAMP POLK RD, SISTERS; 541/549-0123

An expensive remodel of an old farmhouse makes this one of the best B&Bs in central Oregon. Each of five large rooms is wallpapered and well appointed, with a big, private bath (claw-footed porcelain tub and separate shower). Rooms have no phones or TV—just peace. The Forget-Me-Not, on the first floor, has a gas fireplace, sunset view, and deck. The second-floor Morning Glory Suite has a stunning view of the pond and gardens, pastures, and mountains. One room under the eaves has been remodeled into the Heather room, with one queen bed and two singles. Large farm breakfasts are served with espresso on the glass-enclosed sun porch, or next to the outdoor heated pool. Guests are welcome to use laundry facilities, fish for trout from two ponds, and make themselves at home next to the stone fireplace. The pretty grounds are a perfect wedding backdrop. *$$; no credit cards; checks OK; www.conklinsguesthouse.com; across from Sisters airport.* &

Rags to Walkers Bed and Breakfast / ★★★

17045 FARTHING LN, SISTERS; 541-548-7000 OR 800-422-5622

This new, exquisitely clean five-room B&B is a big ranch house, complete with antiques and claw-footed tubs, in the middle of 125 acres of farmland just outside Sisters. Miles of trails meander around the property's pasture and trees, gardens, ponds, and waterfalls. Unwind in the hot tub after a day of horseback riding or fishing. All suites have fireplaces and most have Cascade mountain views; request them when you make reservations, preferably weeks in advance. After their own children moved out, Bonnie Jacobs and Neal Halousek turned their big house into a B&B and they welcome all guests, including children. Bonnie cooks quiches, muffins, fruit, and meats for breakfast and accommodates special requests. The property also has guest houses for rent, each on about 50 acres for ultimate rural luxury. *$$$; DIS, MC, V; checks OK; off Cloverdale Rd.*

Camp Sherman

This little settlement is on a road north of Highway 20, about halfway between Sisters and Santiam Pass. Try **KOKANEE CAFE** (25545 SW Forest Service Rd 1419; 541/595-6420; late May–Oct) for a quick bite.

LODGINGS

House on the Metolius / ★★

FOREST SERVICE RD 1420, CAMP SHERMAN; 541/595-6620

This private fly-fishing resort on 200 acres of gorgeous scenery, with exclusive access to a half-mile of the majestic Metolius River, is open only in summer. Lodgings are limited to seven cabins, each with kitchenette, microwave, gas barbecue, fireplace, and king-size bed. Units 1 and 2 have ovens. Don't forget your fly rod. *$$$; MC, V; checks OK; 2½ miles north of Camp Sherman.*

Metolius River Resort / ★★

**25551 SW FOREST SERVICE RD 1419, CAMP SHERMAN; 541/595-6281
OR 800/81-TROUT**

Not to be confused with the lower-priced, worn and well-loved, circa-1923 Metolius River Lodges across the bridge, these 11 gracious cabins on the west bank are wood-shake with large decks and river-rock fireplaces. All have river views, master bedrooms and lofts, furnished kitchens, and French doors leading to large river-facing decks. Because the cabins are privately owned, interiors differ; most have CD players and TV/VCR with satellite dish. *$$$; MC, V; checks OK; reservations@metolius-river-resort.com; www. metolius-river-resort.com; 5 miles north of Hwy 20.*

Warm Springs

Many travelers pass through the Warm Springs Indian Reservation on their way south to Bend or north to Mount Hood. If you're not spending a night at the Kah-Nee-Ta Resort (see review), at least be sure to stop and visit the incredible **MUSEUM AT WARM SPRINGS** (541/553-3331; open daily). The award-winning museum includes a stunning exhibit of a Wasco wedding ceremony, a contemporary art gallery, and a gift shop.

LODGINGS

Kah-Nee-Ta Resort and Village / ★★

100 MAIN ST, WARM SPRINGS; 541/553-1112 OR 800/554-4786

The spring water bubbling from the ground near the Warm Springs River is hot, sweet water—no sulphur—and the basis for Kah-Nee-Ta Resort and Village on the Warm Springs Indian Reservation. Owned by the Confederated Tribes of Warm Springs, the resort was completely revamped in 1997. The 139-room lodge perches on the canyon wall, with sweeping southerly views, above the river where there's a huge new pool complex, spa, and tepee encampment (kid-heaven). The resort also includes 50 RV spaces, a 30-room motel, gift shop, tennis courts, and 18-hole golf course. Popular Indian-style salmon bakes, sometimes with dance performances, are held Saturdays during summer. Fillets are skewered on alder sticks and baked around an alderwood fire. The resort is a peaceful getaway 11 miles from Highway 26. *$$; AE, DC, DIS, MC, V; checks OK; 11 miles north of Warm Springs on Hwy 3.* &

EASTERN OREGON

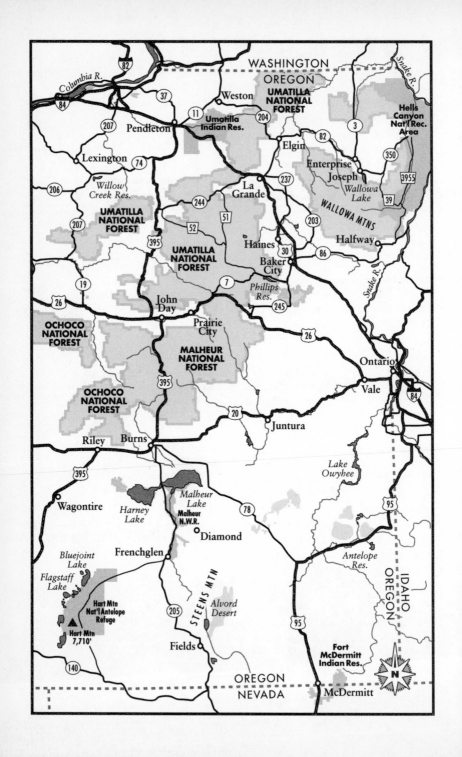

EASTERN OREGON

Eastern Oregon is as different from Western Oregon as it is from, say, Kansas, and it's commonly misrepresented by Western Oregonians, who refer to it as a "desert." Sure, some areas here are pretty dry, with about a million pick-up loads' worth of sagebrush, but Eastern Oregon also has mountains galore, where winter snows pile up and springtime snowmelt feeds streams and wetlands. Lava flows and glaciers formed much of the landscape, including Steens Mountain, the world's largest fault block. The Wallowa Mountains, in the northeast corner of the state, are classic examples of glacial action—their crags and cirques and gemlike lakes were all formed by ice-age glaciers.

Oregon Trail pioneers got across this land as quickly as they could, but some returned here after a short stay in Western Oregon. Here they became gold miners and cattle ranchers. Today, though the bulk of the gold has been grabbed, this is still cattle country, where a rugged western spirit prevails.

ACCESS AND INFORMATION

Interstate 84 is the main route across Eastern Oregon, connecting Pendleton, La Grande, and Baker City with Portland to the west and Boise, Idaho, to the east. The other east-west routes are US Highway 26 through Prineville, John Day, and Prairie City, and US Highway 20, the route from Bend to Burns and Ontario. US Highway 395 is the main north-south route, with Pendleton, John Day, and Burns along its route. Between Pendleton and La Grande, Interstate 84 crosses the Blue Mountains at 4,193 feet; this pass often closes down for a day or so after a heavy snow. For road conditions throughout the state, check in with the **OREGON DEPARTMENT OF TRANSPORTATION** (503/976-7277; www.tripcheck.com).

HORIZON AIRLINES (800/547-9308) flies to Pendleton and Redmond from Portland. And even though you may not want to hear about it (we didn't, until our car broke down in La Grande), buses are another option out here. **GREYHOUND** (800/231-2222; www.greyhound.com) runs along Interstate 84 and stops in towns such as La Grande and Pendleton; **PEOPLE MOVERS** (541/575-2370 or 800/527-2370) travels between Prairie City and Bend; **WALLOWA VALLEY STAGE LINES** (541/569-2284) makes the trip between Wallowa Lake and La Grande.

Pendleton

Looking for the Wild West? Stop by Pendleton in mid-September, when the whole town puts on a party hat (the Stetson kind) for the **PENDLETON ROUND-UP** (1205 SW Court St; 800/457-6336 tickets and information). The event features a dandy rodeo and a crazy street scene.

HAMLEY'S AND COMPANY (30 SE Court St; 541/276-2321) has been selling Western clothing, boots, hats, tack items, and custom-made saddles since

1883. It's a kind of shrine, like the L. L. Bean of the West. **PENDLETON WOOLEN MILLS** (1307 SE Court Pl; 541/276-6911; www.pendleton-usa.com; tours Mon–Fri) sells woolen yardage and imperfect versions of its famous blankets at reduced prices. **PENDLETON UNDERGROUND TOURS** (37 SW Emigrant Ave; 541/276-0730) offers a 90-minute walk through Pendleton's subterranean history to view the remains of businesses that date back to the turn of the century: bordellos, opium dens, and Chinese jails. Reservations are necessary and should be made at least 24 hours in advance; $10 per adult.

The Umatilla tribe's **TAMUSTALIK** (say "ta-MUST-ah-luck") **CULTURAL INSTITUTE** (72789 Hwy 331; 541/966-9748), on 640 acres behind the Wildhorse Gaming Resort (which has a golf course and a spendy bare-bones hotel), tells the story of Oregon from the Native point of view.

LODGINGS

Parker House Bed and Breakfast / ★★

311 N MAIN ST, PENDLETON; 541/276-8581 OR 800/700-8581

In 1917 this magnificent 6,000-square-foot home was more than just a place to live for the prominent L. L. Rogers family; it was a testament to the success of their ranch and their standing in Pendleton society, what with imported Chinese silk wallpaper, a formal ballroom draped in elegance, and a grand porch overlooking an English garden. It all seems out of place in the wheat fields of Eastern Oregon, but somehow the clash is welcome. Of the five rooms, Gwendolyn is the grandest, with a fireplace and French doors. All rooms are brightened with fresh flowers and enhanced with thick robes (you never want to get dressed). This is one of the classier stays this side of the Cascades. *$$; MC, V; checks OK; www.parkerhousebnb.com; north on Hwy 11, follow City Center signs to downtown, head north on Main, cross Umatilla River to N Main.*

The Working Girl's Hotel

17 SW EMIGRANT AVE, PENDLETON; 541/276-0730 OR 800/226-6398

Here's the first nonprofit hotel we've ever seen. Its mission? To bring tourism to Pendleton—and at these prices, you'll come back, round-up or no. The hotel gets its name from its former incarnation as a bordello. The girls are gone, but the five spacious rooms (one long flight up) in this pretty brick building are just as welcoming. Each has 18-foot ceilings and antique furnishings (even the television is cleverly hidden in a vintage radio cabinet). The plumbing's still the original stuff, so you'll need to cross a hall to the bath—but that's a small price to pay for such a fun night's stay. Continental breakfast is served, and if you stay longer, the kitchen is available for your preparations. Young children are discouraged. *$; MC, V; checks OK; between Main and SW 1st.*

NORTHEASTERN OREGON THREE-DAY TOUR

DAY ONE: Start the day in **La Grande** with breakfast at **Foley Station**. Wander around downtown and stop in for a while at **Sunflower Books** (1114 Washington Ave; 541/963-8057), which has a tiny, cozy cafe; a friendly staff; and a wide selection of books. Then hop in the car and head east along Highway 82. Several antique stores make up the whole of small-town **Elgin**, and it's a nice place to get out of the car. By the time you get to **Enterprise**, the Wallowa Mountains dominate the scenery, and you may be tempted to head toward **Hurricane Creek** for a hike. Stop by the huge **Wallowa Mountain Visitors Center**, on the bluff as you enter Enterprise, for information on hiking, mountain biking, or cross-country skiing. From Enterprise, it's just 6 miles to Joseph, where the **Wildflour Bakery** is a good lunch spot (pick up some baked goods there for tomorrow's breakfast). Spend the afternoon browsing the galleries and shops along Main Street. Head out toward **Wallowa Lake State Park** and check into the **Wallowa Lake Lodge;** you can grab dinner at the lodge restaurant and spend the evening playing gin rummy in the lobby.

DAY TWO: Sleep in if you must, but an early start will make for the best **hike** or **horseback ride**; **Eagle Cap Wilderness Pack Station** can set you up with a horse and guide. For an easy ride to mountaintop views, hitch a ride on the **Wallowa Lake Tramway**. Try to finish by lunch, when you'll want to eat a giant "breakfast burrito" at the **Old Town Café**. Head east out of town, then turn south onto Forest Road 39, a paved road that takes you high above **Hells Canyon** (be sure to take the short side road to the scenic overlook) to link up to Highway 86. Head west on Highway 86 into Halfway. Even though it's only 65 miles between Joseph and Halfway, allow at least two hours for the drive, and remember: this is remote country, with no restaurants, stores, or gas stations. (Forest Road 39 is closed in the winter.) In Halfway, stay and eat at **Pine Valley Lodge and Restaurant**.

DAY THREE: After breakfast at Pine Valley Lodge, backtrack east along Highway 86 to the **Snake River**. Choose a noisy **jet-boat ride** or a quiet **hike**. If you opt for the latter, drive north from Oxbow Dam until the long, dusty dirt road ends. Park and walk. For lunch, you'll want to be back in Halfway, grabbing a bite at the Pine Valley Lodge bakery. Then take Highway 86 west to the **Oregon Trail Interpretive Center** in Baker City for both the indoor exhibits and the trail to the wagon ruts. By late afternoon, leave the dusty trail behind and check into the **Geiser Grand Hotel** for a little rest before dinner at the **Phone Company Restaurant**.

Weston

RESTAURANTS

Tollgate Mountain Chalet

60477 HWY 204, WESTON; 541/566-2123

👫 Walla Walla folks often drive 50 miles south through lovely, waving wheat fields to eat at this rustic place in the Blue Mountains forest. Locals order chili, the prime-rib sandwich on homemade bread, a hamburger, a Reuben, or a reasonable steak; the pies are homemade and change daily. It's a particularly good spot for breakfast before a day of hiking or mushroom hunting. *$; MC, V; local checks only; lunch, dinner Tues–Sun, breakfast Fri–Sun; full bar; reservations not necessary; 16 miles east of Weston on Tollgate Mountain Hwy.*

The Wallowas and Hells Canyon

This is the fabled land of the Wallowas, ancestral home of Chief Joseph, from where he fled with a band of Nez Perce to his last stand near the Canadian border. Although Chief Joseph's remains are interred far from his beloved land of the winding water, he saw to it that his father, Old Chief Joseph, would be buried here, on the north shore of Wallowa Lake (see also "The Wallowas' First Residents" in this chapter). **HELLS CANYON NATIONAL RECREATION AREA** (35 miles east of Joseph) encompasses the continent's deepest gorge, an awesome trench cut by the Snake River through sheer lava walls.

La Grande

RESTAURANTS

Foley Station / ★★

1011 ADAMS, LA GRANDE; 541/963-7473

🌲 If you want to hang with the happening folks in La Grande, show up at Foley Station at 7am. That's when the doors open to Eastern Oregon's most sophisticated breakfast joint. Settle into a big wood booth or perch at the marble bar and get down to the formidable task of deciding what to eat. Try the light huckleberry cornmeal johnnycakes, or the sausage, pear, and goat cheese frittata, and wash it all down with good coffee or a giant French press thermos filled with delicious tea. Foley's does dinner too, with a menu that changes monthly and shows off chef/owner Merlyn Baker's culinary pedigree (he was chef at Jake's in Portland before opening Foley's in 1997). The focus is on locally grown, seasonal produce and local meats (providing an outlet for Eastern Oregon emu ranchers) prepared in a Northwest style, with Mediterranean influences. A nice touch is the attention to side dishes; pan-roasted duck breast is accompanied by spaghetti squash sautéed with fennel and tomatoes, for example. *$$; MC, V; checks OK; breakfast, lunch Wed–Sun, dinner Thurs–Sat; beer and wine; dinner reservations recommended; between 4th and Chestnut.* &

Mamacita's

110 DEPOT ST, LA GRANDE; 541/963-6223

The menu here is pretty much standard Mexican fare, but well prepared and offered up in a friendly, easygoing way. House specials such as the Full Meal Steal (yummy corn soup, a salad, and a cheese quesadilla) for less than $6 at dinner are usually the best things out of the kitchen. In winter, try to catch Mamacita's on International Night (once a month) for a multicourse meal featuring foods of another nation; it sounds crazy, coming to a Mexican restaurant for Swiss food, but owner Sandy Sorrels makes it into a fun local event. *$; no credit cards; checks OK; lunch Tues–Fri, dinner Tues–Sun; full bar; reservations not necessary; just west of Adams.* &

Ten Depot Street

10 DEPOT ST, LA GRANDE; 541/963-8766

Sandy Sorrels (who also owns Mamacita's a block away) has been wining and dining La Grande for well over a decade. Ten Depot has had its up and downs, but it's still popular with locals and is a good place to get a feeling for this friendly town. The dining room, in an old brick building with antique furnishings, is nice but it's more fun to eat dinner in the bar, with its beautiful carved-wood back bar. Bargain hunters look for the blue-plate special—less than $10 all week. Dinners range from a two-fisted (half-pound) burger to chicken and pesto pasta, to prime rib (the house specialty). Lunch features superior salads (try the caesar with halibut) and meaty sandwiches. *$$; AE, MC, V; checks OK; lunch, dinner Mon–Sat; full bar; reservations recommended; 2 blocks west of Adams.* &

LODGINGS

Stang Manor Inn / ★

1612 WALNUT ST, LA GRANDE; 541/963-2400 OR 888/286-9463

This restored timber baron's house on the hill behind town lends a touch of elegance to homey La Grande. It's a huge place, with four bedrooms at the top of a sweeping staircase. The master suite is best, but even if you opt for the former maid's quarters, you won't have to lift a finger. The owners, Marjorie and Pat McClure, are warm and good-natured, and enjoy getting to know their guests (many of whom are business travelers). They welcome kids over the age of 10. Breakfasts (way too rich for the hosts to eat themselves, they confess) are always served on china and crystal. One note: the McClures have put the B&B on the market, and even though it won't necessarily sell quickly, it will eventually change hands. *$$; MC, V; checks OK; innkeeper@stangmanor.com; www.stang manor.com; at Spring St.*

Joseph

Joseph has become something of an art colony. **MANUEL MUSEUM AND STUDIO** (400 N Main St; 541/432-7235) features the work of David Manuel; **VALLEY BRONZE OF OREGON** (307 W Alder; 541/432-7551) has a foundry, a showroom, and weekday tours.

WALLOWA LAKE STATE PARK (just south of Joseph on the edge of the lake) is full of campers and camper-friendly deer all summer, but it's near trailheads

THE WALLOWAS' FIRST RESIDENTS

The beautiful Wallowa Valley is the homeland of the Nez Perce tribe. Outside town and off the main roads, little has changed since they wintered in the canyon bottoms, dug camas on the prairies, and hunted at the base of the Wallowa Mountains.

Lewis and Clark's Corps of Discovery were the first whites encountered by the Nez Perce. They had an exceptionally good relationship, and relations with whites remained good even as pioneers began to settle the valley. In 1877, the government ordered the Nez Perce to a reservation in north-central Idaho. The Wallowa Valley bands were reluctantly ready to comply, when a few young men lashed out by killing white settlers. Their band feared retribution and thus began one of history's great and tragic treks, as more than 800 Indians sought safety in Canada, east of the Continental Divide. The U.S. Army pursued the Nez Perce and suffered some defeats, but ultimately wore them down, killing not only warriors but women and children as well. The Nez Perce finally surrendered in northern Montana, where Chief Joseph gained his fame as an orator.

Surviving Nez Perce were sent to Oklahoma, then eventually back to the Northwest, where they were split between reservations in Idaho and Colville, Washington. Chief Joseph is buried on the Colville reservation; his father, Old Chief Joseph, is buried at the northern end of Wallowa Lake. From Chief Joseph's surrender speech:

It is cold and we have no blankets.
The little children are freezing to death.
My people, some of them, have run away to the hills,
and have no blankets, no food;
no one knows where they are—perhaps freezing to death.
I want to have time to look for my children
and see how many I can find.
Maybe I shall find them among the dead.
Hear me my chiefs.
I am tired;
My heart is sick and sad.
From where the sun now stands,
I will fight no more forever.

—Judy Jewell

that lead into the **EAGLE CAP WILDERNESS AREA**, a rugged, remote, and generally uncrowded mountain wilderness that looks more Alpine than Oregonian. (This resemblance isn't lost on the Joseph tourist board; an Alpenfest with music, dancing, and Bavarian feasts occurs in September.)

It's not considered cheating to get to the top of 8,200-foot Mount Howard via the **WALLOWA LAKE TRAMWAY** (59919 Wallowa Lake Hwy; 541/432-5331), a four-person summer gondola that shimmies you up to spectacular overlooks and 2 miles of hiking trails. The best view of Hells Canyon National Recreation Area is from **HAT POINT** near Imnaha, though McGraw Lookout is more accessible if you don't have four-wheel drive. Maps of the region's roads and trails, and information on conditions, are available at the **WALLOWA MOUNTAINS VISITOR CENTER** (88401 Hwy 82, Enterprise; 541/426-5546).

As you hike down into Hells Canyon or up to the lake-laden Eagle Cap Wilderness, let a llama lug your gear with **HURRICANE CREEK LLAMAS** (541/432-4455 or 800/528-9609; www.hcltrek.com; June–Aug). A day's hike takes you 4–8 miles (some trips are easier than others), and hearty meals are included; reserve in advance. Sign up for a morning horseback ride or an extended pack trip into the wilderness at the **EAGLE CAP WILDERNESS PACK STATION** (59761 Wallowa Lake Hwy; 541/432-4145 or 800/681-6222; www. neoregon.net/ wildernesspackstation).

Don't let winter stop you from exploring the Wallowas—get ambitious and head into the backcountry for a few days of guided telemark skiing with **WING RIDGE SKI TOURS** (541/426-4322 or 800/6466-9050; www.wingski.com). Experienced backcountry ski guides lead you to accommodations in a rustic cabin or wood-floored tent shelters (conveniently located next to a wood-fired sauna tent).

RESTAURANTS

Old Town Café

8 S MAIN ST, JOSEPH; 541/432-9898

Even in the off season, this place is packed at lunchtime—it's a favorite with the locals who come for breakfast burritos (eat 'em any time of day, smothered in homemade salsa) and artery-plugging desserts. *$; MC, V; checks OK; breakfast, lunch Fri–Wed, dinner Fri–Sat; beer and wine; reservations not accepted; downtown.*

Wildflour Bakery / ★

600 N MAIN, JOSEPH; 541/432-7225

It's easy to cruise right by this glorified double-wide on the north side of downtown Joseph, but if you keep your eyes open, you'll see a bunch of happy noshers out on the front deck. Inside, the Wildflour Bakery is light and airy, staffed by friendly folks who are proud of their organic, slowly risen breads. If a loaf of bread isn't proper hiking fuel for you, grab a marionberry turnover from the pastry case. Good sandwiches appear at lunch, and it's as easy to go vegetarian here as it is to cave in and order the delicious grilled sausage sandwich (the sausages are from Enterprise's Blue Willow Sausage Company). *$; no credit cards; checks OK; breakfast, lunch Wed–Mon; no alcohol; reservations not accepted; north end of town.* &

LODGINGS

Wallowa Lake Lodge / ★

60060 WALLOWA LAKE HWY, JOSEPH; 541/432-9821
If you're a fan of great national park lodges, you'll want to at least visit the lobby here. It's like Glacier Park Lodge's little sister—not as grand perhaps, but rustic and cozy. Many of the guest rooms are quite small, but that shouldn't matter; you're here to hike the trails, knock around downtown Joseph, and try for the perfect photo of Wallowa Lake. That said, the lake-view rooms with balconies have a little more space, and evenings are best spent sprawled in front of the big stone fireplace in the lobby. If you plan to stay longer than a night, the lakeside cabins, each with a living room, fireplace, and kitchen, allow for a bit more flexibility. Neither lodge rooms nor cabins have television or phones, which contributes to the quiet appeal. The lodge and its restaurant are open only on weekends and holidays from mid-October through Memorial Day, but cabins are available year-round. *$$; DC, MC, V; checks OK; info@wallowalake.com; www.wallowalake.com; near Wallowa Lake State Park.*

Halfway

Once just a midway stop between two bustling mining towns, Halfway is now the quiet but quirky centerpiece of Pine Valley—stashed between the fruitful southern slopes of the Wallowa Mountains and the steep cliffs of Hells Canyon.

The continent's deepest gorge, **HELLS CANYON**, begins at **OXBOW DAM**, 16 miles east of Halfway. For spectacular views of the **SNAKE RIVER**, drive from Oxbow to Joseph (take Hwy 86 to Forest Rd 39; summers only). Maps of the region's roads and trails are available from the U.S. Forest Service ranger station in Pine (541/742-7511) 1½ miles outside Halfway. The folks at **WALLOWA LLAMAS** (36678 Allstead Ln; 541/742-2961; wallama@Pinetel.com; www.neoregon.com/wallowallamas.html) lead three- to seven-day trips into the pristine Eagle Cap Wilderness high in the Wallowas, while their surefooted beasts lug your gear and plenty of food. For those who would rather experience the raging river up close, **HELLS CANYON ADVENTURES** (4200 Hells Canyon Dam Rd; 541/785-3352) in Oxbow arranges jet-boat tours or combination excursions leaving from Hells Canyon Dam.

LODGINGS

Pine Valley Lodge and Restaurant / ★★

N MAIN ST, HALFWAY; 541/742-2027
A wacky good spirit came to Halfway with Babette and Dale Beatty. They've put together an eccentric complex of lodgings on one side of

Main Street, and a restaurant and bakery across the street. Rent a room in the main lodge or the Blue Dog house—it sleeps up to 10 in four charming bedrooms. Try the blue room with a handpainted headboard, and lounge in the sitting room. And take the time to chat with Babette. Upstairs from the bakery, look for the inaugural *Sports Illustrated* swimsuit issue from 1963, where you'll recognize Babette on the cover. Next to '60s fashion magazine covers, you'll see her extensive cookbook collection, and nearby is the art studio where she paints (mostly on silk) and Dale builds giant whimsical fishing rods and lures. If you visit on a weekend, dine at the Halfway Supper Club (part of the Pine Valley operation). On days when the restaurant is closed, Babette will make you dinner anyway, if you request it when you make room reservations. *$$; no credit cards; checks OK; www.neoregon.net/pinevalleylodge; downtown.*

Baker City and Haines

Baker City is still a cow town, albeit a sophisticated one. For proof, just stay over on a Saturday night when the streets (and bars) fill with hats, boots, and big belt buckles. Located in the valley between the Wallowas and the Elkhorns, it makes a good base camp for forays into the nearby mountain Gold Rush towns. The **NATIONAL HISTORIC OREGON TRAIL INTERPRETIVE CENTER** at Flagstaff Hill (Hwy 86, Baker City; 541/523-1843), 4 miles east of Interstate 84, is worth a detour. The multimedia walk-through brings the Oregon Trail experience to life. Open every day; admission is $5 per adult or $10 per carload; one day a month it's free.

The Elkhorn Mountains, west of Baker City, contain most of the old **MINING GHOST TOWNS**, which you can tour on a 100-mile loop from Baker City (some on unpaved roads). The loop begins on Highway 7, then leads through the deserted towns of Bourne, Granite, Bonanza, and Whitney. A restored narrow-gauge steam train, the **SUMPTER VALLEY RAILWAY** (541/894-2268; www.svry.com), in the now revitalized ghost town of Sumpter, runs from Memorial Day through September. **ANTHONY LAKES SKI AREA** (20 miles west of North Powder on Forest Rd 73; 541/856-3277) has good powder snow, one chairlift, cross-country trails, and snow-cat skiing.

RESTAURANTS

Haines Steak House / ★

910 FRONT ST, HAINES; 541/856-3639

There's no mistaking that you're in cattle country, Pilgrim, so get ready to chow down on a giant steak. Some say this is the state's best steak house, and there's no doubt that it's popular with Eastern Oregonians. Teenage boys in cowboy hats try to act suave at the salad bar to impress their dates, but the minute the meat is served, it's all eyes on the plate. Don't stray from beef here—it's well selected, well cut, and well cooked (rare, natch). *$$; AE, DC, MC, V; checks OK; lunch Sun, dinner Wed–Mon; full bar; reservations recommended; on old Hwy 30.* &

The Phone Company Restaurant / ★

1926 1ST ST, BAKER CITY; 541/523-7997

The Phone Company was going strong even before Roger and Shirley Ivie, erstwhile owners of the Tollgate Mountain Chalet, took it over in 1997, and they have kept to the high standards that earned the restaurant a place in Baker City's pantheon of fine dining. Locals know it as one of the few places in town that makes everything from scratch—nothing canned or bottled. The menu is small but has a few nice surprises, such as apple-hazelnut chicken breasts, alongside Eastern Oregon favorites like prime rib cooked very slowly over apple and hickory wood. And if you think you can pass up dessert, you haven't had the fresh berry cobbler. The classic 1910 building once housed the telephone company—check out some of the old black-and-white photos on the wall. *$$; MC, V; checks OK; lunch Mon–Fri, dinner Mon–Sat (closed Mon in winter); full bar; reservations recommended; at Washington.*

LODGINGS

Geiser Grand Hotel / ★★

1996 MAIN ST, BAKER CITY; 541/523-1889 OR 888/434-7374

A $7 million restoration to this landmark downtown hotel made all of Oregon look up and pay attention to Baker City. A highlight of the restoration is the Palm Court, a dining area that rises three stories to a huge stained-glass skylight. If the biggest stained glass in the Pacific Northwest doesn't shed enough light, check out the bejeweled chandeliers—they're probably not what you would choose for your own house, but they fit right into this 1889 Italianate Renaissance Revival hotel. The rooms are large and comfortable—the cupola suites are a bit of a splurge, but have great views of the mountains and downtown Baker City. Some slips indicate that Dwight and Barbara Sidway, who shepherded the Geiser Grand from an eyesore to a beauty, need to devote more attention to routine hotel management. The staff could be more consistently helpful, the lobby carpeting could stand a good shampooing, and the restaurant menu is more appealing than the food, but in all, this place makes a trip to Baker City something special. And oh, yes, it's nice to be able to bring your dog to a fancy downtown hotel. *$$; AE, DIS, MC, V; checks OK; downtown at Washington.* &

John Day

Sure, it looks like just another cow town, but John Day's surroundings are loaded with history. It's just off the Oregon Trail, and before the 1860s, the whole region was packed tight with gold (in 1862, $26 million in gold was mined in the neighboring town of Canyon City). **KAM WAH CHUNG MUSEUM** (250 NW Canton; 541/575-0028; open May–Oct, closed Fri), next to the John Day city park, was the stone-walled home of two Chinese herbalists at the turn of the 20th century. A tour makes for an interesting glimpse of the Chinese settlement in the West: opium-stained walls, shrines, and herbal medicines are on display, as well as a small general store.

JOHN DAY FOSSIL BEDS NATIONAL MONUMENT lies 40 to 120 miles west, in three distinct groupings: the colorfully banded hillsides of the Painted Hills Unit, an ancient fossilized forest at the Clarno Unit, and fascinating geological layers at the Sheep Rock Unit. Stop by the visitor center and museum near the Sheep Rock Unit (on Hwy 19 10 miles northwest of Dayville; 541/987-2333; open daily, 9am–5pm) for a look at the choicest fossils.

LODGINGS

The Ponderosa Guest Ranch / ★★★

PO BOX 190, SENECA; 541/542-2403 OR 800/331-1012

Been fantasizing about trading in your Nikes for pointy-toed boots? Checking out the cowboy Web sites? (Yup, they're out there.) Well, pardner, must be time for the Ponderosa. This isn't some big-shot developer's fluffed-up idea of a ranch—it's a real working cattle ranch, with all the buckaroos to prove it. Guests help staff cowboys manage 2,500 to 4,000 head of cattle—this can mean assisting with a bovine Caesarean section, branding, or driving cattle to mountain pastures—all the little things that go into that nice steak dinner you're gonna get at the end of a long day's work. But nobody here is going to make you get on a horse. You can grab a field guide and go rustle up some wildflowers, or look for antelope, bear, ground hogs, eagles, sandhill cranes, cinnamon ducks, and sage hens. The eight log guest cabins have three double units each (request Jump Creek, with its unobstructed view), and the massive main lodge has a spacious dining room, a bar, and plenty of areas for relaxing. Hearty ranch fare (included in the price) is served family style, and there's plenty of it, starting with eggs and biscuits with sausage gravy and ending with a full steak dinner. Guest operations are scaled back in winter. Groups of 15 or more can rent the ranch as a cross-country skiing lodge, but the horses stay put in their corrals. Ages 18 and up only. *$$$; MC, V; checks OK; 2-night min Nov–Apr, 3-night min May–Oct; seeyou@ ponderosaguestranch.com; www.ponderosaguestranch.com; on Hwy 395 halfway between Burns and John Day.*

Prairie City

LODGINGS

Strawberry Mountain Inn

E HWY 26, PRAIRIE CITY; 541/820-4522 OR 800/545-6913

Anyone in Prairie City will tell you what a nice woman Linda Harrington is, and what a classy bed-and-breakfast she runs. Even though it's perched right above the highway, the highway runs through Prairie City, so traffic's not likely to keep you awake. And it's a prime spot for views of the Strawberry

Mountains, rising from the horse pasture across the road. Ask for one of the two rooms with mountain views—the backyard is nice, with a little orchard and a garden, but it's the mountains that give Prairie City its life. In addition to the requisite B&B reading room, there's a hot tub and a pool table here at the Strawberry Mountain Inn, and plenty of videos and CDs. Unlike many B&B hosts, Linda and Bill Harrington welcome kids, and have a play area in the yard. Breakfasts fuel you for a hike into the Strawberry Mountain Wilderness Area. *$$; AE, MC, V; checks OK; strawberry@moriah.com; www.moriah.com/ strawberry; just east of downtown.*

Southeast High Desert

MALHEUR NATIONAL WILDLIFE REFUGE (37 miles south of Burns on Hwy 205; 541/493-2612) is one of the country's major bird refuges—184,000 acres of wetlands and lakes. See "Birds of the Malheur" in this chapter.

Burns

The town of Burns, once the center of impressive cattle kingdoms ruled by legendary figures Peter French and William Hanley, is still a market town, but a pretty quiet one. Walking downtown, you can hear a luff as a flock of quail take flight from a parking lot.

    CRYSTAL CRANE HOT SPRINGS (25 miles southeast of Burns on Hwy 78, Crane; 541/493-2312) is a good place to take a break from driving and swim in the hot springs pond, or soak in a water trough–turned–hot tub.

RESTAURANTS

Pine Room Café / ★

543 W MONROE, BURNS; 541/573-6631

This may be Burns's fanciest restaurant, but that doesn't mean you have to take your cowboy hat off at the dinner table. It's a good-natured, chummy spot where locals call out to each other and comment, sotto voce, on who's dining with whom. But it's not cliquish, and the staff is eager to make out-of-towners feel like hanging around the bar after dinner. Besides the expected array of steaks, popular entrees include the Chicken Artichoke and fish dishes (though don't count on your halibut being flown in fresh). The bread is homemade, and the steaks hand-cut in the kitchen. *$$; MC, V; local checks only; dinner Tues–Sat; full bar; reservations recommended; at Egan.* &

LODGINGS

Sage Country Inn / ★

351½ W MONROE, BURNS; 541/573-7243

Set well back from the main drag through Burns, the Sage Country Inn is the project of three longtime friends who rotate hostess duties. They're all ranch women, so they're friendly and welcoming without a lot of fuss. Likewise, the rooms in this 1907 Georgian-Colonial house are comfortable, but not cloying—they're filled with antiques and stacks of books on local history and ranchers' witticisms. Read up, and save your questions for breakfast—Carole, Georgia, and Susan can tell you all about life present and past in southeastern Oregon. *$; MC, V; checks OK; pstick@centurytel.net; at S Court.*

Diamond

LODGINGS

Hotel Diamond

12 MILES EAST OF HWY 205, DIAMOND; 541/493-1898

When you drive into Diamond, the first thing you see are dilapidated stone buildings tucked under giant old poplar trees. Buzz by and you might mistake Diamond for a ghost town; however, its handful of residents keep the looming ghosts at bay. Judy and Jerry Santillie cater to those exploring Malheur territory. The Diamond now doubles as hotel and general store (watch the pickups pull in at 5pm for the evening sixpack). The small five bedrooms upstairs share two baths and a sitting area; three larger rooms off the front porch have private baths. Dinners are available for hotel guests (a big family-style meal if the house is full; smaller, simpler dinners if only a couple of guests are staying) and that's a good thing—the food is delicious, and there sure isn't anyplace else to grab a meal in Diamond. *$; MC, V; checks OK; closed Nov 15–Mar 15; 12 miles east of Hwy 205.*

Frenchglen

This beautiful little town (population 15) 60 miles south of Burns is a favorite stopover for those visiting the Malheur National Wildlife Refuge (see "Birds of the Malheur" in this chapter) or **STEENS MOUNTAIN**. Steens rises gently from the west to an elevation of 9,670 feet and then drops sharply to the Alvord Desert in the east. A road goes all the way to the ridge top (summers only), and another skirts this massive escarpment—an adventurous day trip by the vast borax wastelands of the former Alvord Lake, numerous hot springs, and fishing lakes near the northeastern end of the route. Contact the Bureau of Land Management (Hwy 20 W, Hines; 541/573-4400) just southwest of Burns for information about Steens Mountain.

It's a rough but scenic ride from Frenchglen to the 275,000-acre **HART MOUNTAIN NATIONAL ANTELOPE REFUGE** (509/947-3315). Turn west off Highway 205 and follow Rock Creek Road to the visitor center, where you can learn what wildlife has been spotted recently. Pronghorn, of course, are frequently noted, and bighorn sheep live east of the headquarters on the steep cliffs that form the western boundary of fault-block Hart Mountain. No visit here is really complete without a prolonged dip in the local hot spring. It's south of the visitor center in the campground—very rustic and absolutely free.

BIRDS OF THE MALHEUR

Malheur National Wildlife Refuge is ground zero for Eastern Oregon birding— it is located on the Pacific Flyway and has 120,000 acres of wetlands, making it a hospitable stop for migrating birds. Spring is the best time to see birds; more than 130 species nest on the refuge, and many more make rest stops. Sandhill cranes (with 8-foot wingspans) and tundra swans may show up as early as February, followed by waterfowl in March, shorebirds in April, and songbirds late in May, when other birds are beginning to fly off. During the hot summer months, trumpeter swans swim the refuge ponds. Sandhill cranes, ducks, and geese return in the fall, then fly on to California, leaving the winter to eagles and hawks.

Start your trip to Malheur with a visit to the **refuge headquarters** (32 miles southeast of Burns on south side of Malheur Lake; 541/493-2612), where you can pick up maps and brochures, visit the **George Benson Memorial Museum** (chock full of mounted birds), and spy on birds in the pond and in the trees around headquarters. From there, drive south on Central Patrol Road, a good gravel road that passes a number of ponds before ending at P Ranch, right near the Frenchglen Hotel. In order to protect the wildlife, most areas are closed to hiking, but if you need to burn off some energy, it's okay to mountain bike along Central Patrol Road. *—Judy Jewell*

LODGINGS

Frenchglen Hotel / ★

FRENCHGLEN; 541/493-2825

One of the handful of historic hotels owned by the Oregon State Parks system, the Frenchglen is a small, white frame building that dates back to 1916. It has eight small, plain bedrooms upstairs with shared baths. Room 2 is the largest and nicest, and the only one with a view of Steens Mountain. Nothing's very square or level here, and that's part of the charm. Downstairs are a large screened-in front porch and the dining room, where guests mingle and compare travel notes. Many of the guests are birders, and the lobby is well stocked with field guides. The hotel managers, John and Stacey Ross, cook up good, simple meals for guests and drop-by visitors. Ranch-style dinner is one seating only (6:30pm sharp) and reservations are a must. But if you miss dinner, the Rosses won't let you go hungry (this is ranch country). *$; MC, V; checks OK; closed mid-Nov–mid-Mar; fghotel@ptinet.net; on Hwy 205, 60 miles south of Burns.*

SEATTLE
AND ENVIRONS

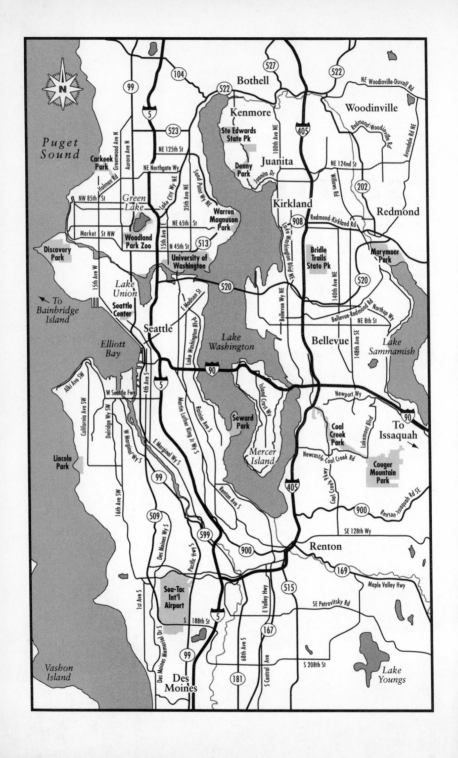

SEATTLE AND ENVIRONS

You know a city has achieved world-class status when it has its own shorthand. Seattle need only flash one of several symbols to be internationally recognized: Microsoft, Boeing, Amazon.com, Starbucks.

Of course, Seattle is more than the sum of its slick corporate logos. (Though, except for L.A., it's hard to imagine a city with a more Nike-wearing, Starbucks-drinking, SUV-driving citizenry.) It's also a city of disarming optimism—fueled by hot technology and cool culture—and rapidly increasing confidence. A place where gray days far outnumber sunny ones, but sunglasses and sunroofs are big sellers nonetheless.

The area's geography matches its expansive mood. A diverse obstacle course of bookend mountain ranges (Olympics on the west, Cascades on the east) and around-the-compass waterways (Elliott Bay, Lake Washington, Lake Union, and Lake Sammamish) make an exhilarating outdoor playground. And when the sun does shake its cover, the resulting Technicolor perfection makes it hard not to hum "the bluest skies you've ever seen are in Seattle" as you run, bike, kayak, sail, windsurf, or skate on your way. The lush landscape also creates a sense of expectation with something compelling—mountains, skyscrapers, water, floatplanes, boats, bridges—always visible in the near distance. This yin-yang pattern is repeated in the urban grid: historic Pike Place Market on First Avenue gives way to the swanky retail on Fifth and Sixth Avenues, and Fremont, Capitol Hill, and Belltown each claim a distinctive corner of the city's hip neighborhood triangle. Seattle's sibling suburbs are a study in divergent personalities: the mini-metropolis glam of Bellevue, corporate sprawl of Redmond, charming waterfront style of Kirkland and Bainbridge Island, and the wannabe-village quaintness of Issaquah.

And, as it turns out, those once deeply resented newcomers (to avoid driveby sneers, Californians at one time traded in their license plates faster than their fluorescent wardrobes) have added an edge to the native low-key style. With the swell in population—and inflated traffic and housing prices—has come a welcome cultural spike, with hip hotels, restaurants, shops, and nightclubs springing up like so many dot-coms.

Even the city's longtime architectural conservatism has begun to bend. The newly opened Frank Gehry–designed, Paul Allen–owned Experience Music Project museum threatens to eclipse the adjacent Space Needle in sheer attitude if not altitude. Its lumpy psychedelic exterior drew mews of dislike, but now the downtown public library has revealed a similarly ambitious blueprint for its new building. And when a city's *library* is cutting new architectural ground, a corner undeniably has been turned.

Seattle hasn't completely abandoned its cautious side. (The city canceled its millennial celebrations because of terrorist concerns.) And sometimes optimism isn't enough. (The high-profile hosting of the World Trade Organization in 1999 devolved into a street spectacle of protesters and police—tagged the "Battle in Seattle" by the national press.) But Seattle is just hitting its 21st-century stride.

ACCESS AND INFORMATION

The nightmare traffic story has become something of a competitive sport in Seattle. It doesn't require dramatic license: a recent national study pegged Seattle as having the third-worst traffic jams in the nation (behind Los Angeles and Washington, D.C.). And though a light rail system should alleviate some of the carbon-monoxide crush, it's not set to go on-line until 2006.

In the meantime, the best defense is a sense of humor and street smarts. The road basics are as follows: Interstate 5 is the main north-south arterial; two east-west arterials connect it to Eastside communities (such as Bellevue) via two floating bridges—Interstate 90 (south of downtown) and Highway 520 (north of downtown); the major north-south highway on the Eastside is Interstate 405. Downtown Seattle is divided into "avenues" (starting with First near the water-front) running north-south, and "streets" running west-east. Watch out: many are one-way.

Fortunately, getting to downtown from the **SEATTLE-TACOMA INTERNA-TIONAL AIRPORT** (206/431-4444) is a 35-minute straight shot north on Interstate 5 (avoid peak rush hours 7–9:30am and 4:30–7pm). **GRAY LINE AIRPORT EXPRESS** (206/626-6088) runs airport passengers to and from major downtown hotels for about $8.50 one-way. **TAXIS** from the airport cost $30–$35. Thanks to a new law, however, taxis to the airport from downtown Seattle charge a flat fee of $25 (though some cabbies might need reminding). Large **CAR RENTAL** agencies, such as Budget (800/527-0700) and Enterprise (800/736-8222), have locations near the airport, in downtown Seattle, and in the outlying suburbs.

AMTRAK (3rd Ave S and S Jackson St; 800/872-7245) trains arrive at and depart from King Street Station, and **GREYHOUND** (811 Stewart St; 800/231-2222) also serves the city.

The **SEATTLE-KING COUNTY CONVENTION AND VISITORS BUREAU** (800 Convention Pl, Galleria level; 206/461-5840; www.seeseattle.org) is a good source for information and maps. In summer, visit the outdoor kiosks at Seattle Center and Pioneer Square.

Seattle

Traditionalists yearn for Seattle's small-town *Pleasantville* past. Those care-free—and, by comparison, car-free—days before our clothes, musicians, and hot beverages were hijacked as fashion statements, and the only jet set we knew built planes at Boeing. Such nostalgia is understandable, of course—particularly since Seattle's sheltering location in the far corner of the national map afforded a blissfully long childhood. But though it may have lost some innocence, the city has gained some of the more intriguing complications and entertaining perks of adulthood.

SEATTLE THREE-DAY TOUR

DAY ONE: You'll find it's easy being car-less in Seattle. Don't bother with a sit-down breakfast on your first morning, either; there are plenty of walk-by attractions to nibble on, such as an apple fritter at **Three Girls Bakery** (1514 Pike Pl; 206/622-1045), as you meander through the bustling **Pike Place Market**. After lunch at the charming "hole-in-the-alley" trattoria the **Pink Door**, take a stroll through the **Seattle Art Museum**. (On your way to SAM, swing by **Ticket/Ticket** in the Market to pick up half-price day-of-show tickets for that evening's entertainment). Back in your waterfront room at the **Inn at the Market** (hip but moderately priced rooms can be had at the nearby **Ace Hotel**), you'll have plenty of time for a shower and wardrobe change before dinner at downstairs **Campagne**. Then it's a leisurely walk to **Benaroya Hall** and an evening of music courtesy of the **Seattle Symphony**. Cab it back for a nightcap at the romantic **Chez Shea** lounge in the Market before tucking in for the night.

DAY TWO: Rise early, but indulge in a room-service breakfast from **Bacco** before descending the Pike Place Hillclimb to hop the vintage **waterfront trolley** for historic **Pioneer Square**. After the Underground Tour of old Seattle, resurface to peruse the Square's collection of galleries and the **Elliott Bay Book Co.**, then take a seat at the **Painted Table** in the Alexis Hotel for a gourmet lunch. Cross the nearby pedestrian overpass to the **ferry dock** at Pier 52 and a 35-minute ride on a jumbo ferry to **Bainbridge Island**. After plumbing the antiques shops of quaint Winslow, settle in for dinner at **Cafe Nola**. No need to rush dessert: ferries to the city run late—and if you're lucky, a moonlit Seattle skyline will be your closing scene.

DAY THREE: Wake up like a local with a latte and pastry (or bowl of fresh fruit) at Belltown's **Macrina Bakery and Café**. Then it's off for some serious shopping and people-watching at the splashy **Pacific Place** mall and flagship **Nordstrom**. (Kids should be directed to the high-end GameWorks video arcade.) Grab a bite to eat at the Place's **Gordon Biersch Brewery Restaurant** (4th floor; 206/405-4205). Or, if it's Sunday and the Mariners are in town, baseball fans can catch a bus to the new open-air **Safeco Field**—pre-game activities should include partaking of a mess of ribs at **Pecos's Pit BBQ** (2260 1st Ave S; 206/623-0629). If not, walk to Westlake Center, where the **Monorail** will whisk you to Seattle Center for an afternoon of high-tech musical exploration at the brand-new rock-and-roll museum, **Experience Music Project**. Before winding up your day and your stay with dinner at Belltown's **Flying Fish**, say goodbye to the city from atop the landmark **Space Needle**.

ACCESS AND INFORMATION

Take advantage of the city's **METRO** buses (206/553-3000; transit.metrokc.gov), free until 7pm in the downtown core, between the waterfront and Interstate 5, Jackson Street to the south, and Bell Street to the north. You can use Metro Transit to get to the Eastside; it also connects with buses from greater Puget Sound to the north and south. The **WATERFRONT STREETCAR** (part of Metro Transit) makes stops along the waterfront, Pioneer Square, and the International District. For off-road transport, ride the space-age **MONORAIL** (also part of Metro Transit), which glides between downtown's Westlake Center (Pine St and 4th Ave, 3rd floor) and the Seattle Center in 90 seconds, or catch a **WASHINGTON STATE FERRY** (206/464-6400 or 800/84-FERRY; www.wsdot.wa.gov/ferries/) at Pier 52 to nearby islands, including Bainbridge.

Check the free weeklies, *Seattle Weekly* or *The Stranger*, for timely event listings. Most theater and event tickets are sold through **TICKETMASTER** (206-292-ARTS); **TICKET/TICKET** (401 Broadway E and Pike Place Information Booth, 1st and Pike; 206/324-2744) sells half-price, day-of-show tickets.

MAJOR ATTRACTIONS

Even first-timers can probably rattle off the big must-sees in Seattle: **PIKE PLACE MARKET** (Pike St and 1st Ave), **PIONEER SQUARE** (1st Ave and James St), the **SPACE NEEDLE**. The Needle actually anchors a corner of another major attraction, the **SEATTLE CENTER** (between Denny Wy and Broad St; 206/684-8582). Born out of the 1962 World's Fair, the 74-acre park is home to arts and athletics venues—such as the **OPERA HOUSE** and **KEYARENA**—as well as the **PACIFIC SCIENCE CENTER** (200 2nd Ave N; 206/443-2880), home to cool hands-on science exhibits and an IMAX theater.

Water-based exhibits are the focus of the **ODYSSEY DISCOVERY MARITIME CENTER** (2205 Alaskan Wy, Pier 66; 206/374-4000) and the **SEATTLE AQUARIUM** (1483 Alaskan Wy, Pier 59; 206/386-4320), which boasts a 400,000-gallon Underwater Dome. And visitors and animals come breathtakingly close in the **WOODLAND PARK ZOO**'s (5500 Phinney Ave N; 206/684-4800) animal-friendly natural habitats.

In **PIONEER SQUARE**, the hokey-but-fun **UNDERGROUND TOUR** (610 1st Ave; 206/682-4646) takes in the sights—and some of the smells—of old Seattle, preserved from the 1889 great fire that leveled much of the city.

MUSEUMS

The striking street-corner *Hammering Man* sculpture directs patrons into the **SEATTLE ART MUSEUM** (100 University St; 206/654-3100), home to impressive Asian, African, and Northwest Native art collections, as well as national traveling exhibits. The **HENRY ART GALLERY** (15th Ave NE and NE 41st St; 206/543-2280), on the UW campus, is known for its photography collection and more experimental shows, particularly video installations. First Hill's once frumpy **FRYE ART MUSEUM** (704 Terry Ave; 206/622-9250) has been redesigned inside and out, adding imaginative exhibits and music and film events. Downtown **GALLERIES** open new shows for the popular monthly **FIRST THURSDAY** art walk.

The **CHILDREN'S MUSEUM** (Seattle Center; 206/441-1768) encourages exploration of other cultures with hands-on activities and inventive exhibits, such as a global village featuring child-size dwellings from Japan, Ghana, and the Philippines. The **WING LUKE ASIAN MUSEUM** (407 7th Ave S; 206/623-5124) examines the Asian-American experience in the Northwest, including an exhibit concerning the internment of Japanese-Americans during World War II. Bankrolled by Microsoft co-founder Paul Allen, the new eye-and-ear popping **EXPERIENCE MUSIC PROJECT** (Seattle Center; 206/770-2700; www.emplive.com) at Seattle Center celebrates rock 'n' roll and its roots with high-tech installations. The **BURKE MUSEUM OF NATURAL HISTORY AND CULTURE** (17th Ave NE and NE 45th St; 206/543-5590) on the UW campus harbors the Pacific Northwest's only dinosaurs (snap a shot of Junior sitting on the 5-foot-tall sauropod thigh bone). Twenty full-size airplanes are suspended in midair at the **MUSEUM OF FLIGHT** (9404 E Marginal Wy S; 206/764-5720).

PARKS AND GARDENS

Throw a rock, hit a park. Local favorites include **DISCOVERY PARK** (3801 W Government Wy; 206/386-4236), with 534 wild and woodsy acres, miles of trails, and cliff views of the Sound. **WASHINGTON PARK ARBORETUM** (2300 Arboretum Dr E; 206/543-8800) has 200 wooded acres, walking and running trails, a Japanese garden, and Graham Visitors Center. **VOLUNTEER PARK** (1247 15th Ave E; 206/684-4075) features a 1912 conservatory full of hothouse plants and a popular view from the top of the water tower; it's also home to the **SEATTLE ASIAN ART MUSEUM** (206/654-3100). **GAS WORKS PARK** (N Northlake Wy; 206/684-4075) is where Seattleites go to fly a kite.

SHOPPING

NORDSTROM's downtown flagship store (500 Pine St; 206/628-2111) includes a spa and five floors of clothes and accessories. Connected to Nordies via a glass skybridge is **PACIFIC PLACE** (600 Pine St; 206/405-2655), a splashy four-level commercial cathedral stocked with name retailers, restaurants, and a cinema. Other downtown malls include **WESTLAKE CENTER** (400 Pine St; 206/467-1600) and **CITY CENTRE** (1420 5th Ave; 206/624-8800).

Neighborhoods are where to find unusual or handmade goods, from funky jewelry and artwork at Fremont's **FRANK AND DUNYA** (3418 Fremont Ave N; 206/547-6760) to cool products made from recycled materials at Capitol Hill's **PORTAGE BAY GOODS** (1121 Pike St; 206/622-3212) to retro office objects at Belltown's **MINT** (91 Wall St; 206/956-8270). **PIONEER SQUARE** has cutting-edge galleries and old-fashioned shops such as **WOOD SHOP TOYS** (320 1st Ave S; 206/624-1763), while the **PIKE PLACE MARKET** is justly famous for its fresh fruit, flower, and fish stalls and authentic crafts, including **MILAGROS MEXICAN FOLK ART** (1530 Post Alley; 206/464-0490).

PERFORMING ARTS

THEATER/DANCE. The big three playhouses are **A CONTEMPORARY THEATRE** (700 Union St; 206/292-7676), **INTIMAN THEATRE** (Seattle Center; 206/269-1900), and **SEATTLE REPERTORY THEATRE** (Seattle Center; 206/443-2222). The toasts of Broadway land at the **5TH AVENUE THEATRE** (1308 5th Ave; 206/625-1900) and **PARAMOUNT THEATRE** (911 Pine St; 206/443-1744), while wonderfully imaginative, and surprisingly sophisticated, productions play out at **SEATTLE CHILDREN'S THEATRE** (Seattle Center; 206/441-3322). Classics are at the core of the city's premiere dance company, the **PACIFIC NORTHWEST BALLET** (Seattle Center; 206/292-2787). An annual holiday favorite, *The Nutcracker*, features spectacular Maurice Sendak sets.

MUSIC. Grunge long ago earned a place on the "get over it" list (along with Seattle's coffee habits) locals would like to e-mail to the mass media. Music of all genres—from alternative rock and reggae to chamber and classical—is amply represented here. The **SEATTLE SYMPHONY** (200 University St; 206/215-4747), under the baton of Gerard Schwarz, has an elegant new downtown home, Benaroya Hall. In 2001, the **SEATTLE OPERA** (Seattle Center; 206/389-7676), guided by Speight Jenkins, mounts its world-renowned production of Wagner's *Ring* cycle for its last season in the Opera House. (The Opera will perform at the Mercer Arena—better known for booking pop acts than divas—until 2003, when its refurbished home reopens.) First-rate jazz clubs include classy **DIMITRIOU'S JAZZ ALLEY** (2033 6th Ave; 206/441-9729) and cozy **TULA'S** (2214 2nd Ave; 206/443-4221).

Some of the city's most anticipated festivals revolve around music. The **NORTHWEST FOLKLIFE FESTIVAL** (Seattle Center; 206/684-7300) showcases a melting pot of talent—from African marimba players to American fiddlers—on Memorial Day weekend. **BUMBERSHOOT** (Seattle Center; 206/281-8111), on Labor Day weekend, hosts headliner acts ranging from Beck to Tony Bennett. And jazz artists, from beboppers to swing, make the rounds of local clubs for the **EARSHOT JAZZ FESTIVAL** (various venues; 206/547-9787) in October.

LITERATURE/FILM. Seattle's reputation for being well-read is reinforced by the daily author readings at the **ELLIOTT BAY BOOK CO.** (101 S Main St; 206/624-6600) in Pioneer Square and the heavily attended annual **NORTHWEST BOOKFEST** (206/378-1883), which celebrates all things bookish—from authors to small presses—every October.

The **SEATTLE INTERNATIONAL FILM FESTIVAL** (various theaters; 206/324-9996) brings together world premieres, stars, filmmakers, and film buffs for a staggering three-plus weeks starting in late May.

NIGHTLIFE

It's still not a party-all-night kind of city, but Seattle's urban neighborhoods have definitely put more snap in the nighttime. Some of the best see-and-be-seen nightspots are on Capitol Hill and in Belltown. In fact, they compete for the hippest head count. Hot spots on the Hill, a favorite with Seattle's lesbian and gay population, range from in-your-face cool—**ARO.SPACE** (925 E Pike St; 206/320-0424) dance club/cafeteria and **MANRAY** (514 E Pine St; 206/568-0750) video bar—to retro chic like the **BALTIC ROOM** (1207 Pine St; 206/625-4444). Belltown counters with the cultured **AXIS** (2214 1st Ave; 206/441-9600) and funky hybrids like the live-music club/cafe **CROCODILE CAFÉ** (2200 2nd Ave; 206/441-5611) and the live-music club/cafe/laundromat **SIT & SPIN** (2219 4th Ave; 206/441-9484).

In Queen Anne, classy lounges—**PARAGON** (2125 Queen Anne Ave N; 206/283-4548) and **TINI BIGS** (100 Denny Wy; 206/284-0931)—easily coexist with colorfully cheesy hangouts such as **PESO'S TACO LOUNGE** (605 Queen Anne Ave N; 206/283-9353) and **ROMPER ROOM** (106 1st Ave N; 206/284-5003).

SPORTS AND RECREATION

So what if star slugger Ken Griffey Jr. took a powder to Cincinnati, and the squabbling continues between the **SEATTLE MARINERS** (206/622-HITS) and the city over millions in cost overruns. Open-air **SAFECO FIELD** (between Royal Brougham Wy and S Atlantic St; 206/346-4003) is popular even with nonbaseball fans (public tours Tues–Sun, 12:30pm and 2:30pm). The Paul Allen–owned **SEATTLE SEAHAWKS** (206/682-2800) football team shares the lakefront gridiron of the **UNIVERSITY OF WASHINGTON HUSKIES** (Husky Stadium, 3800 Montlake Blvd NE; 206/543-2200) until a new stadium opens atop the rubble of the Kingdome in 2002. Seattle's new pro women's basketball team, the WNBA **SEATTLE STORM** (206/283-DUNK), tips off in the KeyArena (305 N Harrison St) in summer; the **SEATTLE SUPERSONICS** (206/283-DUNK) dominate the Key from November through April.

There are plenty of outlets for amateur athletes. In-line skaters and bikers work up a sweat on the **BURKE-GILMAN TRAIL**, a stretch of blacktop running from north Lake Union to the Eastside. **GREGG'S GREENLAKE CYCLE** (7007 Woodlawn Ave NE; 206/523-1822) rents bikes and skates. For a map of Seattle bike routes, call the City of Seattle Bicycle and Pedestrian program (206/684-7583). Kayakers, rowers, and canoeists ply the waters of Lake Union and Lake Washington. **MOSS BAY ROWING AND KAYAK CENTER** (1001 Fairview Ave N; 206/682-2031) gives lessons and rents kayaks and rowboats. Outdoor enthusiasts of all stripes flock to the two-level flagship **REI** (222 Yale Ave N; 206/223-1944), which, along with an abundance of equipment, houses an indoor climbing wall, an outdoor mountain bike/hiking test trail, and the U.S. Forest Service's Outdoor Recreation Information Center (206/470-4060) for trip planning.

RESTAURANTS

Andaluca / ★★☆

407 OLIVE WY (MAYFLOWER PARK HOTEL), SEATTLE; 206/382-6999

The hotel's once stodgy dining room has been transformed into a romantic place that's intimate and informal, with rosewood booths, fresh flowers, and textured walls. Chef Wayne Johnson's lively seasonal menu's emphasis is Mediterranean conversant with Northwest seafood and produce. Especially inviting is the shareables menu—little dishes of roasted mussels, artichoke and roasted pepper tartlets, mushrooms à la *grecque*, or spicy calamari. Crisp duck cakes are golden brown and served with apricot chutney and cucumber yogurt sauce. The vegetable meze is a plate crammed with pistachioed asparagus, roasted wild mushroom relish, white bean salad, beets in an orange–star anise dressing, and artichokes. Try the *fideua* Andaluca, a paella-like dish loaded with prawns, clams, mussels, chicken, and chorizo, in a saffron broth. Don't miss the *cabrales*-crusted beef tenderloin with a marsala glaze and grilled pears. Service is competent and lighthearted, and the wine list is great. *$$$; AE, DC, DIS, MC, V; checks OK; breakfast, dinner every day, lunch Mon–Sat; full bar; reservations recommended; andaluca@andaluca.com; www. mayflowerpark.com/frames.html; downtown.* &

Anthony's Pier 66 / ★★★
Bell Street Diner / ★★

2201 ALASKAN WY (AT PIER 66), SEATTLE; 206/448-6688

Ever since this upscale/midscale, upstairs/downstairs, sprawling restaurant complex opened downtown, seafood with a view hasn't been the same. Upstairs at Anthony's Pier 66 you might drink a bracing ginger-infused martini at the bar while you hold out for a snug booth in the graceful arc of the handsome koa wood–accented dining room. Thrill to such appetizers as the Poke Trio—a Hawaiian-style starter that elevates ahi to new heights—or the Potlatch—a feast of local shellfish, known to cause a swoon—and then make your way through a menu heavy with more seafood (don't miss the crab cakes). Presentation points are well earned here, and service deserves a nod, as it does downstairs at the decidedly more casual Bell Street Diner. Sit at the *santée* counter (where stools flank a gleaming stainless-steel counter), in the bar (with seating both indoors and out), or in the bustling dining room, and order the justly popular mahimahi tacos or the excellent tempura-fried seafood. For quick-stop cheap eats, there's Anthony's Fish Bar, an adjoining walk-up window on the promenade. *$$$, $$; AE, DC, DIS, MC, V; local checks only; dinner every day (Anthony's Pier 66), lunch, dinner every day (Bell Street Diner); full bar; reservations required (Pier 66), reservations recommended (Bell Street); www.anthonysrestaurants.com; on waterfront.* &

Assaggio Ristorante / ★★

2010 4TH AVE (CLAREMONT HOTEL), SEATTLE; 206/441-1399

There's an air of festivity at Assaggio, either because the high-ceilinged two-room trattoria is always packed (making for an agreeable din), or because owner Mauro Golmarvi shakes hands with, hugs, and/or kisses everyone who enters. Whatever it is, Assaggio brings Roman ambience to this downtown hotel space, especially when the weather's warm and sidewalk seats are filled. Chef Don Curtiss brings untraditional ideas (baby bok choy with the lamb shank) to what had been a traditional menu, though many classics remain. Fusilli with currants and pine nuts in a saffron-tinted cream sauce proves he's on the right track. To wind up, choose the tiramisù. *$$; AE, DC, DIS, MC, V; checks OK; lunch Mon–Fri, dinner Mon–Sat; full bar; reservations recommended; www. assaggioseattle.com; downtown.* ⅃

Brasa / ★★★
2107 3RD AVE, SEATTLE; 206/728-4220

Owners Tamara Murphy and Brian Hill (chef and manager) have created one of the loveliest and most inviting spaces in town. Large at 170 seats, it's understated in dark wood, a gorgeous iron gate, walls in warm pinks and oranges. Murphy and her co-chef, Holly Smith, are creating some of the most imaginative food and lively menus in the region. Dark-meated guinea hen is served with Yukon gold potatoes mashed with walnut oil, alongside a braising of radicchio, wispy French wing beans, green peppercorn jus, and a hint of orange. Fresh scallops surround a browned creamy chive potato cake with a fried quail's egg on top, served with sautéed leeks in a butter sauce and fat slices of house-cured bacon. Chocolate lovers swoon for pastry chef Valerie Mudry's Valrhona chocolate torte with pistachio ice cream and dried cherries. *$$$; AE, MC, V; checks OK; dinner every day; full bar; reservations recommended; Belltown.* ⅃

Cafe Lago / ★★★
2305 24TH AVE E, SEATTLE; 206/329-8005

This warm, bustling gem near the Montlake Bridge is filled nightly by locals who have come to expect consistently wonderful and unpresuming Italian fare from owners Jordi Viladas and Carla Leonardi (chef and pastry chef, respectively). Start with the antipasto plate (also available meatless), stacked with eggplant, bruschetta with *olivata*, goat cheese, roasted peppers, mozzarella, roasted garlic, prosciutto, and Asiago. Also fine is the caponata, a tart compote of eggplant, olives, capers, and garlic, served with grilled bruschetta. The lasagne is so popular, it's suggested you order it before 8pm to make sure it isn't already gone. It's made with thin, tender pasta sheets layered with ricotta and bechamel so light it's like a soufflé. Try a thin-crusted wood-fired pizza. Viladas's wood-fired grill turns out New York steak marinated in *balsamico* and herbs, covered with Gorgonzola, grilled onions, and radicchio. Finish with a slice of Carla's incredibly light chocolate truffle in a puddle of espresso *crema inglese. $$; AE, DC, MC, V; checks OK; dinner Tues–Sun; full bar; reservations recommended; Montlake.* ⅃

Campagne / ★★★★
Cafe Campagne / ★★★

86 PINE ST, SEATTLE; 206/728-2800
1600 POST ALLEY, SEATTLE; 206/728-2233

Linen tablecloths, tiny vases of flowers, and wall space dedicated to wine bottles set the French-countryside mood in this very urban setting. In a courtyard off Pike Place Market, Campagne takes its cue from the cuisine of southern France. Owner Peter Lewis (one of the city's most gracious hosts) and some of Seattle's finest servers ensure you dine with gusto. An oxtail tart braised with orange peel with black olive purée is amazing, as is cold lobster salad with apples and Belgian endive on kasha, tart with an apple cider reduction. Next choose fillet of monkfish wrapped in bacon on stewed flageolet beans with dandelion greens, flavored with salt cod. Other nightly specials reflect the day's catch, the season's offerings, and the inspirations of chef James Drohman. Campagne's famous cassoulet—white beans crammed with lamb, pork, duck confit, and garlic sausage—is deliciously rich. The inspired, carefully wrought wine list is not the least among many successes here. A wonderful late-night menu is served in the bar—smoky but romantic—not unlike France.

Lewis's Cafe Campagne, which opened in 1994 just below its stylish sibling, is a small, casual bistro-cum-charcuterie. Wherever you sit (at a cherry-wood table or the elegant counter), be sure to utter the most important words spoken here: garlic mashed potatoes. *$$$, $$; AE, DC, MC, V; no checks; breakfast, lunch, dinner Mon–Sat, brunch Sun (Cafe Campagne), dinner every day (Campagne); full bar; reservations recommended; Pike Place Market.* &

Canlis / ★★★

2576 AURORA AVE N, SEATTLE; 206/283-3313

This old establishment steak house was literally and spiritually aloof from the Seattle restaurant scene for decades. Cantilevered above Lake Union, it has the best views of the lakes and Cascades of any non-revolving joint in town. A generation passed it by before Chris and Alice Canlis updated the restaurant with a $1.5 million revamp and a new chef. Greg Atkinson has gradually transformed Canlis into an exciting regional restaurant, drawing national acclaim in the process. He keeps older clientele happy by retaining 80 percent of the old menu, while attracting a new bunch by reworking and seasonally enhancing classic pan-Asian Canlis fare. Salads are wonderful, such as oil-free Mrs. C. Salad with greens, strawberries, and fresh basil. The famous copper broiler yields salmon broiled, ahi seared rare, and a spectrum of grilled meats like fork-tender New York cuts of Wasyugyu Kobe–style beef. Sommelier Rob Bigelow's massive and much-lauded wine list ranges from $30 to $1,000. Expect to be treated like royalty and pay accordingly. *$$$$; AE, DC, DIS, MC, V; checks OK; dinner Mon–Sat; full bar; reservations required; canlis@canlis.com; www.canlis.com; south end of Aurora Bridge, call for directions.* &

Carmelita / ★★☆

7314 GREENWOOD AVE N, SEATTLE; 206/706-7703

In their first restaurant venture, owners and interior designers Kathryn Newmann and Michael Hughes transformed a dilapidated retail space into a theatrically lit, art-filled haven of color and texture. Neighbors from Greenwood and Phinney Ridge embraced Carmelita from the beginning, and the sophisticated, seasonal vegetarian menu remains enticing, despite chef changes. Start with bruschetta sprinkled with luscious aged balsamic vinegar; favored entrees include dramatically plated, caponata-stuffed, marinated tofu coated with cornmeal, and panfried, leek-wrapped portobello stuffed with asparagus, roasted peppers, and caramelized onion. The wine list is short, with nothing over $30; teas, tisanes, juices, and refreshing tamarind-ginger lemonade round out beverage options. In summer, there's a charming, plant-filled deck. *$$; MC, V; local checks only; dinner Tues–Sun; beer and wine; reservations recommended; carmaveggy@earthlink.net; www.carmelita.net; Greenwood.* &

Cascadia / ★★★

2328 1ST AVE, SEATTLE; 206/448-8884

Eat with French flatware off Limoges china and sip out of handblown glassware in this spare but luxurious elegant setting. An etched-glass wall separating dining room from kitchen has water sluicing through it like rain against a window. Chef/owner Kerry Sears celebrates "Cascadia," the region between our mountains and the Pacific, by using only indigenous foods and flavors. Prepare to spend a bundle on innovative and unusual dishes like Oregon fallow venison loin and Dungeness crab steak; white truffled partridge baked in hay; or wild King salmon on cedar fronds. The menu gives four or five choices of seven-coursed tasting menus including cheese and dessert; items can also be ordered à la carte. While the food can be quite exciting, presentation can border on precious. The stiffness and impersonality of the seamless service gives this beautiful place a cold feel. A surprisingly fairly priced wine list features bottlings from Cascadia. *$$$$; AE, DC, MC, V; no checks; dinner Mon–Sat; full bar; reservations recommended; Belltown.* &

Chez Shea / ★★★
Shea's Lounge / ★★

94 PIKE ST, 3RD FLOOR, SEATTLE; 206/467-9990

You might walk through Pike Place Market 100 times and not know Sandy Shea's tiny, romantic hideaway, Chez Shea, is perched just above, looking out over Puget Sound. Dinner here is prix fixe, with four courses reflecting the bounty of the seasons and ingredients fresh from Market stalls. A winter meal might begin with asparagus soufflé with yellow pear tomato vinaigrette, followed by gingered soup. Main-course choices might include sautéed halibut moistened by lemon-sorrel butter; grilled portobello and roasted vegetables layered with goat cheese, baked and served with sherried red onion sauce; beef fillet sided by caramelized Walla Walla sweets and bathed in blue cheese–spiked demi-glace; or pepper-crusted duck complemented by rhubarb purée and mango salsa. Service is always sure and gracious. Next door is Shea's Lounge, a deep, narrow, sexy bistro that's wed to Chez Shea by a common door. The menu offers a dozen Mediterranean-accented dishes, superb pizzas, and a vivid salad or two. *$$$, $$; AE, MC, V; no checks; dinner Tues–Sun; full bar; reservations recommended (Chez Shea); in Pike Place Market.*

Dahlia Lounge / ★★★⯨

2001 4TH AVE, SEATTLE; 206/682-4142

Though he doesn't cook here anymore, chef/owner Tom Douglas still calls Dahlia "my baby." His chef, John Sundstrom, toils hard and succeeds in keeping Douglas's exuberant, edgy, and globally fusing approach while making creative space for himself. The result is predictably unpredictable. Start with steamed Dungeness crab *shumai* dumplings, then dive into Tuscan grilled bread salad with pesto and fresh mozzarella studded with olives and spicy cappocolla, or hardy mushroom and ham-hock soup with garlic bread crumbs. Dinner entrees include crispy skinned smoked duck nested in sautéed cabbage and chestnut tortellinis with vanilla roasted apple; or salmon rubbed with fennel, served with mint and pickled shallot rings. Douglas's restaurants all serve desserts made by pastry chef Benne Sata at his Palace Kitchen (see review). The fluffy coconut cream pie is legendary, but so is the "world famous" crème caramel. *$$; AE, DC, DIS, MC, V; local checks only; lunch Mon–Fri, dinner every day; full bar; reservations recommended; www.tomdouglas.com; downtown.* &

El Gaucho / ★★★

2505 1ST AVE, SEATTLE; 206/728-1337

El Gaucho is a retro-swank Belltown remake of the '70s-era uptown hangout with mink-lined booths, flaming shish kebabs, and blazing baked Alaskas. The current version is a huge, dark, wide-open space where cooks scurry at a wood-fired broiler and servers deliver impaled conflagrations of meat to the well-heeled. The bar crowd sips martinis as a piano bartender noodles jazz riffs on a baby grand. It's a place to see and be seen. Patrons seated at comfy banquettes in the theater-in-the-round–style dining room share chateaubriand for two or custom-aged steaks and big baked potatoes with all the trimmings. A torchlight parade of vodka-flamed lamb and beef brochettes on swords pass as diners choose from a menu that also includes an ostrich fillet, veal scaloppine, and venison chops. Seafood lovers can dredge garlic bread in buttery Wicked Shrimp, or suck saffron-scented broth from an artful bouillabaisse. The wine card is formidable, supplemented by a premium reserve list. Serious imbibers are heartened by the lengthy single-malt Scotch list and the two cigar lounges. *$$$; AE, DC, MC, V; checks OK; dinner every day; full bar; reservations recommended; www.elgaucho.com; Belltown.* &

Elliott's Oyster House / ★★★

1201 ALASKAN WY, SEATTLE; 206/623-4340

Designers envisioned a classic yacht when they spent $2 million on the remodeled setting best described as nautical but nice. Ferries pull out of the terminals next door, wowing tourists; locals know Elliott's for its slurpable oysters, outside dining, and fresh seafood. Try a rich chowder—we loved the creamy pink-tinged Dungeness crab version with a touch of cayenne. Iced shellfish extravaganzas serve two, four, or six. There's a safe but seafood-friendly wine list. Center-cut swordfish is firm yet tender with a subtle butter–macadamia nut sauce. Mesquite-grilled ahi tacos at lunch are kicked with mango, lime, and wasabi. Northwest cioppino includes cracked crab, scallops, salmon, Manila clams, Alaskan side-striped prawns, and Penn Cove mussels submerged in a dense, herby, saffron-scented tomato broth zingy with cayenne and red pepper. *$$$; AE, B, DC, DIS, E, JCB, MC, V; checks OK; lunch, dinner every day; full bar; reservations recommended; www.elliotts oysterhouse.com; Pier 56 on waterfront.* &

Etta's Seafood / ★★★

2020 WESTERN AVE, SEATTLE; 206/443-6000

The second of Tom Douglas's restaurant triumvirate, Etta's is a buoyant, hip seafood house that occupies the husk of the late Cafe Sport, where Douglas first made his mark in the '80s. The colorful, casual space features one small, conversation-friendly dining room and a larger, noisier noshery with a bar and counter seating. The freewheeling menu features starters such as fire-grilled tamales with Jack cheese and ancho chiles, and a two-bite morsel of foie gras paired with a single seared scallop in a buttery brown-pepper jus. Prepare to be wowed by whole Dungeness crab or Maine lobster, simply steamed, or wok-seared in a kick-ass chile and black bean sauce. Etta's spice-rubbed pit-roasted salmon ranks as one of Seattle's signature salmon preparations. Lush desserts won't disappoint. Start weekend brunch with a scorching Bloody Mary, and then cool your jets with a smoked salmon and goat cheese omelet or fan the flames with corned beef hash and habanero ketchup. *$$$; AE, DC, MC, V; checks OK; lunch, dinner every day, brunch Sat–Sun; full bar; reservations recommended; www.tomdouglas.com; Pike Place Market.* &

Flying Fish / ★★★★

2234 1ST AVE, SEATTLE; 206/728-8595

Flying Fish is a foodie's dream. That's because it's owned and operated by chef Christine Keff, who not only knows and digs seafood, but has created a space where everybody seems to want to be at the same time. In the well-lit, noisy rooms of this popular Belltown hangout, ultrafriendly staffers haul platters and plates to exuberant wine-imbibing diners. Two or three small starter plates can make a meal: lobster ravioli with yellow-foot mushrooms in a puddle of lobster velouté, or crispy fried calamari with hot-sweet honey jalapeño mayonnaise. Entrees include shrimp and chicken rice noodles with

Thai green curry and shiitakes, and grilled scallops with creamy herb polenta and sautéed greens. Keff encourages large parties to share platters of things like whole fried rockfish or her famous Sister-in-law Mussels. The wine list is large and accessible with lots of Northwest and California offerings. This is where Seattleites go for local seafood without the distraction of a waterfront view and all that goes with that. The mood is fun and unstuffy, and food is superlative. *$$; AE, DC, MC, V; local checks only; dinner every day; full bar; reservations recommended; www.flyingfishseattle.com; Belltown.* &

The Georgian Room / ★★★★

411 UNIVERSITY ST (FOUR SEASONS OLYMPIC HOTEL), SEATTLE; 206/621-7889

A grand space for grand occasions, the Georgian Room boasts high ceilings, ornate chandeliers, gleaming silver, and touches of gilt that transport you to a time and place that—happily—still exists. As you sink into your plush banquette-built-for-two, the tuxedoed maître d' pours your martini from an elegant shaker; an impeccably uniformed and well-trained professional waitstaff tends to your every need; and a pianist tickles the ivories. This kind of cosseting doesn't come cheap, but the inventive, seasonally changing menu—replete with luxury ingredients from truffles to foie gras—may make you forget the high tariff. Begin with the colorful vegetable cocktail—tiny baby vegetables splashed with tomato butter in a large martini glass. The intense, earthy flavors of black and white truffles, mushrooms, and goat cheese infuse almost-translucent sheets of fresh pasta, while crab cakes crowned with Alaskan spot prawns in a pungent crab broth sing of the sea. Other inspired couplings include crisp-skinned rock cod and caramelized ramps in a rich red wine sauce; nubbins of duck cracklings and foie gras in a salad of dandelion and fennel; and rosy-centered veal tenderloin slices ringed around a beehive of rich and delicious yellow Finn mashed potatoes. Private parties can arrange for seclusion in the Georgette Petite room. Afterward, step into the Georgian Terrace for a civilized Cognac and cigar. *$$$; AE, DC, MC, V; no checks; dinner Mon–Sat; full bar; reservations recommended; www.fshr.com; downtown.* &

Harvest Vine / ★★★

2701 E MADISON ST, SEATTLE; 206/320-9771

It's hard to re-create the leisurely gusto with which the Spanish eat and drink—especially in Seattle. But Joseph Jimenez de Jimenez and his crew do it every night in this rustic shoebox of a place, where it's standing room only for tapas and paella. This is a grazing place. Get a bottle of wine and start ordering *platitas* from the more than two dozen tapas that make up most of the menu. Everything is shareable, like the salad of grilled escarole and black truffles circled by a slice of delightfully subtle smoky salmon; or the gratin of cardoons with a tomato sauce and mild but rich idiazabel cheese. Skewered venison chunks, grilled rare and tender, rest in a mess of garlicky oyster mushrooms; sweet *piquillo* peppers stuffed with herbed Dungeness crab lie in a puddle of shellfish sauce. Sit at the copper-clad bar and watch as Jimenez presides with precision, humor, and charm. This is one of the most inviting and warm restaurant experiences in town. *$$; MC, V; checks OK; dinner Tues–Sat; beer and wine; reservations not accepted; Madison Valley.* &

I Love Sushi / ★★☆

1001 FAIRVIEW AVE N, SEATTLE; 206/625-9604
11818 NE 8TH ST, BELLEVUE; 425/454-5706

Don't let the have-a-nice-day name put you off. Chef Tadashi Sato has created a pair of bustling, bright, high-energy sushi bars with immaculately fresh fish, on both sides of Lake Washington. The staff at each place is friendly and helpful—a delicious place to learn for those unfamiliar with Japanese food, though Sato and his army of chefs attract many Japanese customers who know a good thing when they eat one. Sushi combinations are a bargain (particularly at lunch), while traditional Japanese specialties such as sea urchin, abalone, and fermented bean paste raise the stakes somewhat. À la carte dishes, like flame-broiled mackerel or salmon, the ubiquitous tempura, or geoduck *itame* sautéed with spinach are excellent. *$$; AE, MC, V; no checks; lunch Mon–Fri, dinner every day (Seattle); lunch Mon–Sat, dinner every day (Bellevue); full bar; reservations not necessary; www.ilovesushi.com; South Lake Union (Seattle), east of I-405 (Bellevue).* &

Il Terrazzo Carmine / ★★★

411 1ST AVE S, SEATTLE; 206/467-7797

Be prepared to spend an entire evening at Il Terrazzo, for dining at Carmine Smeraldo's restaurant is an event. Graze through the glistening array of antipasti and watch for Seattle's rich and famous, likely to be dining beside you to the strains of classical guitar in this comfortably airy restaurant. For a lusty starter try calamari in *padella*, tender squid in a heady tomato garlic sauté. Deciding among pastas is a feat, but sauces on the stunning array of meat entrees get the greatest applause. Sweetbreads with prosciutto and peas are lightly smothered in a wonderful wine sauce. Fork-tender veal has an equally good reduction sauce, slightly zingy from capers. The extensive wine list is international in scope but retains a sharp focus on premier Italian offerings. Prices are high, but you can grab a table in the bar and share antipasto with wine, and call it dinner. Either way, keep dessert simple—perhaps a silky flan, or house-made biscotti with a glass of *vin santo* for dipping. *$$$; AE, DC, DIS, MC, V; no checks; lunch Mon–Fri, dinner Mon–Sat; full bar; reservations recommended; Pioneer Square.* &

Kaspar's / ★★☆

19 W HARRISON ST, SEATTLE; 206/298-0123

Swiss-born Kaspar Donier imaginatively couples classic international cooking styles with fresh Northwest ingredients. An easy, intimate room with bamboo accents and shoji screens in shades of brown and green has a lower-level lattice-shaded solarium. Well-trained servers make you feel welcome. Some patrons stop by just to duck into the cozy wine bar for outstanding wines by the glass drawn from a broad, mostly West Coast list. Appetizers might include wonderful crispy sea bass and Dungeness wontons with little puddles of aioli and baby spinach leaves. Donier has been serving variations on his signature dish for years: Duck Prepared Two Ways—pink-fleshed roasted Muscovy duck breast, with a crispy bone-in duck leg confit, served with licorice or chanterelle sauce. One recent disappointment: the kitchen was a little heavy-handed with salt. Desserts are sublime. *$$$; AE, MC, V; no checks; dinner Tues–Sat; full bar; reservations recommended; info@kaspars.com; www.kaspars.com; near Seattle Center.* &

Kingfish Café / ★★

602 19TH AVE E, SEATTLE; 206/320-8757

In 1996, the Coaston sisters opened their dream restaurant, a stylish, casual, contemporary space with enlarged sepia-tinted family photos—including one of distant cousin Langston Hughes. Buoyed by long lines of people waiting for a taste of chef Tracey McRae's sassy Southern soul food (and maybe a glimpse of silent partner, Sonic Gary Payton), they expanded into the space next door less than a year later. People still wait, but it's worth it for the likes of Big Daddy's Pickapeppa Skirt Steak, topped with a cool peach; velvety pumpkin soup; crab and catfish cakes with green-tomato tartar sauce; seafood curry with coconut grits; and buttermilk-fried chicken. Lunch is a bargain—try the pulled-pork sandwich with peach and watermelon barbecue sauce. At Sunday brunch, crab and catfish cakes are topped with a poached egg and hollandaise. *$$; no credit cards; checks OK; lunch Mon, Wed–Fri, dinner Mon, Wed–Sat, brunch Sun; beer and wine; reservations not accepted; east Capitol Hill.* &

Lampreia / ★★★★

2400 1ST AVE, SEATTLE; 206/443-3301

He's young, he's grumpy, he's a genius. Scott Carsberg, from blue-collar West Seattle, headed east and was mentored by a master Tyrolean chef. The spare ocher dining room is like his minimalist menu creations: appetizers such as a little cloud of celery sprouts with a tiny orange herb flower dressed with fresh lemon and olive oil. The silky, sweet squash soup is just that; the Walla Walla onion tart with *osetra* caviar is sweet and salty in a thin, buttery crust. The intermezzo course might be a pile of creamy whipped potatoes set on a crispy crepe-like "tulip" of Reggiano and piled with spot prawns; Carsberg shaves over the shrimp a heap of *tartufi bianchi*, rare Piedmontese white truffles. Main courses include his famous veal chop with fonduta cheese sauce that has diners sucking the bones. The grilled swordfish and braised couscous with black truffles is simple and perfectly executed. Servers bring a selection of hand-crafted local cheeses, which make a fine end to a meal, or a better prelude to a chocolate delectable or delicate lemon tart with strawberry sauce. Service, as directed by Carsberg's wife, Hyun Joo Paek, is seamless and reverential. *$$$;*

AE, MC, V; no checks; dinner Tues–Sat; full bar; reservations recommended; Belltown. &

Macrina Bakery & Café / ★★

2408 1ST AVE, SEATTLE; 206/448-4032

Seattle was a one-bread town until Leslie Mackie, originator of the rustic bread program at Grand Central Bakery, transformed it into a bread-lover's mecca. She's gained national acclaim as a bread baker, and she and her small army of bakers can hardly keep up with the demand for gutsy, exceptional breads, which you'll find on the tables at the city's finest restaurants. Mornings, Belltown regulars show up for warm buttery things, bowls of fresh fruit, home-made granola, and creamy lattes in the sunny Euro-chic cafe setting. Others hasten out the door with a loaf of crusty whole wheat cider bread warm from the oven. Lunch brings simple, artful soups, salads, and panini, and a classy meze trio of daily-changing Mediterranean-inspired *nosherai. $; MC, V; local checks only; lunch Mon–Fri, brunch Sat–Sun; beer and wine; reservations not accepted; Belltown.* &

Marco's Supperclub / ★★★

2510 1ST AVE, SEATTLE; 206/441-7801

Ex-pat Chicagoans Marco Rulff and Donna Moodie opened their first bistro in Belltown well before the neighborhood became the hippest food corridor in Seattle. From the day they opened it, the husband and wife have had more than luck going for them. Their formula for success includes years of tableside experience, an adventurous and capable chef, and a strong staff of friendly yet sophisticated servers. Savvy diners hit their sexy, noisy, and busy restaurant for its warm, funky atmosphere and trip-around-the-world menu. Forgo pastas, but order the fried sage appetizer, subtly spiced Jamaican jerk chicken with sautéed greens and mashed sweet potatoes, or seasonal specials such as pork tenderloin marinated in juniper berries and herbs, or cumin-and-coriander-spiked Moroccan lamb. A bar runs the length of the room—great for dining alone. In summer sit on the colorful, plant-filled back deck. *$$; AE, MC, V; local checks only; dinner every day; full bar; reservations recommended; Belltown.* &

Matt's in the Market / ★★★

94 PIKE ST, 3RD FLOOR, SEATTLE; 206/467-7909

Barely two dozen seats occupy this seafood bar and restaurant that might be one of Seattle's best-kept secrets. Sit at the mosaic-tiled counter and watch chef Erik Cannella nimbly jockey sauté pans between two portable gas burners and one small oven. Owner Matt Janke does just about everything else, acting as host, waiter, busperson, dishwasher, and sommelier. The interplay of flavors in the best dishes ranges from subtle to explosive; salmon and scallop pâté is so light it's almost mousse, while sturgeon in a jacket of coriander and mustard seed holds its own under fiery lime pickle sauce. Daily specials augment the

HOW TO PASS FOR A LOCAL

Every city has its own set of idiosyncrasies. Visitors who want to mesh more naturally with the locals might benefit from these insights into Seattle's native style.

Umbrellas: Despite the city's rep, it doesn't rain buckets here daily (Miami has more rain annually). Only newcomers open umbrellas during a light shower.

Shades: Residents have to combat the sun's glare more than raindrops. As a result, sunglasses are de rigueur nearly year-round.

Attire: It varies widely by neighborhood. For example, while the Capitol Hill crowd favors black, body piercings, and Doc Martens, Green Lakers sport spandex, bare midriffs, and running shoes. The main thing is, Seattleites are flexible when it comes to degrees of formality. A night at the opera here can mean evening gowns or Gap wear.

Coolness: This isn't a climate reference but an attitudinal one. Frankly, natives aren't an effusive lot—just ask any touring actor waiting for a standing ovation. Rumor has it that it takes two years to make a real friend here. It's not that we're unfriendly—just politely reserved.

Vocabulary: "Yeah" is as common a part of Seattle speech as "Oh my gawd!" is to a suburban teenager. Not to be confused with the intimidating interrogative "Oh yeah?!" favored by East Coasters, Seattle's "Yeah" is simply a laid-back form of assent or agreement.

Jaywalking: That crowd on the corner isn't making a drug deal, they're waiting for the crosswalk sign to change. Natives are notorious sticklers for obeying these signs—and so are the police. Newcomers blithely crossing against lights may find themselves ticketed, at about $38 a pop.

Bicyclists: Some days they seem to outnumber cars. Observing the traditional politeness of the city, locals resist the urge to bump off cyclists who unconcernedly hold up traffic.

Travel espresso cups: They're everywhere. Isn't that why car cup holders were invented? Besides, a swig of caffeine takes drivers' minds off dawdling cyclists.

Cellular phones: How do you tell a California transplant from a native Seattleite? The native tries to hide that fact that he or she even owns a cell phone—making a call in public requires the secrecy of an FBI operative.

— *Shannon O'Leary*

short menu that changes every couple of months, but everything is fresh because the cooks shop the Market twice a day. For lunch, climb the stairs for a perfect oyster po'boy, a dense and satisfying filé gumbo, or steamed mussels and clams in an ouzo-infused liquor. No one will rush you if you choose to linger over silky chocolate pot de crème while enjoying live jazz (Wednesday nights), or savor a glass of wine (from a quirky and reasonably priced list) while watching the sun sink into Elliott Bay. *$$; MC, V; no checks; lunch, dinner Tues–Sat; beer and wine; reservations not accepted; Pike Place Market.*

Monsoon / ★★☆

615 19TH AVE E, SEATTLE; 206/325-2111

This little family business is a stylish and tasty Vietnamese addition to the diverse Seattle scene. Sophie and Eric Banh preside over the exotic seasonal menus in the gleamy, steamy open kitchen. Don't miss traditional tamarind soup with tiger prawns and chicken, a slightly sweet and tangy melange. Compelling appetizers include cold shrimp shiitake mushroom rolls, *la lot* beef, and five-spice baby back ribs. Entrees are ample but not large. We loved sea scallops and crispy yam with spicy chile sauce; also fresh halibut steamed with crunchy lily buds and shiitake mushrooms in a banana leaf. Vegetarians like grilled Asian eggplant with green onions in coconut sauce, or snap peas and shiitakes. By all means order a pot of chrysanthemum tea. This place is popular, and the dining room gets noisy. Expect a wait at the door and to be treated gracefully and democratically by the other Banh sister, Yen, who capably handles service. *$$; MC, V; no checks; lunch Tues–Fri, dinner Tues–Sun; beer and wine; reservations not accepted; east Capitol Hill.* &

Pagliacci Pizza / ★

426 BROADWAY E, SEATTLE (AND BRANCHES); 206/324-0730

All Pagliacci locations offer the same simple yet eternal lure: thin and tangy cheese pizzas. Their tasty crusts are the result of thorough research by the owners, who ultimately settled on Philadelphia-style. This place is about pizza, and that's it. You can take out from all Pagliacci locations, or eat in at the Capitol Hill, Lower Queen Anne, and University District branches. Comfortable, echoing, and sometimes hectic, they're fine places for a solo meal. A call to Pagliacci's central delivery service (206/726-1717) gets delivery from the closest outlet. *$; MC, V; checks OK; lunch, dinner every day; beer and wine; reservations not accepted; Capitol Hill.* &

The Painted Table / ★★★

92 MADISON ST (ALEXIS HOTEL), SEATTLE; 206/624-3646

Chef Tim Kelley has been quietly putting out some of the most inspired plates in Seattle in this newly decorated, richly appointed restaurant, with its grand piano and hushed atmosphere, in one of Seattle's best boutique hotels. His deft touch with game and fish, and relationships with regional growers, provide unusual vegetables and inventive offerings. Starters might include slow-cooked lobster with lotus root and pea shoots in a carrot-cardamom broth. The braised venison osso buco is quite good, with parsnip purée and roasted carrots, as is the three-clam linguine (Manila, razor, and geoduck clams). Kelley runs weekly and seasonal five-course tasting menus. Flavors are matched by gorgeous presentation and a mighty wine list. Chocolate lovers can count on several selections per menu: perhaps S'mores with warm chocolate ganache, homemade graham crackers, and vanilla-bean meringue. *$$$; AE, DC, DIS, MC, V; local checks only; breakfast, dinner every day, lunch Mon–Fri; full bar; reservations recommended; www.alexishotel.com; downtown.* &

Palace Kitchen / ★★★

2030 5TH AVE, SEATTLE; 206/448-2001

Tom Douglas's palatial open kitchen and lively bar scene are delightfully decadent—as casual as they are sophisticated. Beneath a huge painting of a lusty 17th-century banquet, you can sit at the enormous tile-topped bar or in a wooden booth, a storefront banquette, or the glassed-in private room. Douglas's food is robust and innovative. Reasonably priced finger foods include fat, spicy, grilled chicken wings; crispy-fried, semolina-coated anchovies; poached quail eggs Benedict; and Northwest cheeses. The duck soup with escarole and butternut squash is rich and delicious. Up the ante and order one of the night's applewood-grilled specials—spit-roasted meat, poultry, or whole grilled fish. Seafood gets special treatment here, as does dessert. You'll recognize favorites from the Dahlia Lounge and Etta's Seafood (see reviews); this is the dessert kitchen for all of Douglas's restaurants. The informative wine list is the most entertaining in town. *$$; AE, DC, DIS, MC, V; checks OK; lunch Mon–Fri, dinner every day; full bar; reservations recommended; www.tomdouglas.com; downtown.* &

The Pink Door / ★★★⯪

1919 POST ALLEY, SEATTLE; 206/443-3241

The low-profile entrance (a simple pink door) underscores the speakeasy ambience of this Italian trattoria at Pike Place Market. In winter, the dining room grows noisy around a burbling fountain. Come warmer weather, everyone vies for a spot on the trellis-covered terrace with its breathtaking view of the Sound. Inside or out, an arty, under-30 set happily noshes on garlicky black-olive tapenade and quaffs tumblers of wine from the reasonably priced, mostly Italian list. The menu features hearty, generously portioned pastas, daily risotto, excellent rack of lamb with mascarpone mashed potatoes, and lusty seafood-filled cioppino. Inventive salads are composed of mostly organic local produce. Live music (and sometimes a tarot card reader) in the evenings. *$$; AE, MC, V; no checks; lunch, dinner Tues–Sat; full bar; reservations recommended; Pike Place Market.*

Place Pigalle / ★★★⯪

81 PIKE ST, SEATTLE; 206/624-1756

This pretty little bistro offers picture-postcard views of Puget Sound; warm, professional service; and astonishingly ambitious French-Northwest-Italian cooking from a tiny kitchen. Hidden away in Pike Place Market, Place Pigalle is the perfect spot to sip an eau-de-vie, lunch with a friend, or engage in a romantic dinner à deux. Ask for a window table and order something as simple as onion soup gratiné (beefy broth, silky onions, chewy Gruyère) or as sophisticated as roulades of duck confit (preserved duck, goat cheese, and butternut squash rolled in pasta). Avoid the cassoulet with its under-cooked beans, nearly invisible lamb bits, and—emblematic of the kitchen's some-times inappropriate inventiveness—incongruous citrus-peel garnish. On sunny days, a small deck is attractive, but inside tables have the advantage of being in servers' sight lines. *$$$; AE, DC, MC, V; no checks; lunch, dinner Mon–Sat; full bar; reservations recommended; www.savvydiner.com; Pike Place Market.*

Ponti Seafood Grill / ★★★
3014 3RD AVE N, SEATTLE; 206/284-3000

Ponti, tucked almost under the Fremont Bridge, inspires dreams of the Mediterranean, with its canalside perch, stucco walls, red-tiled roof, and elegantly understated dining rooms, but executive chef Alvin Binuya borrows from an array of ethnic flavors, with more than a passing nod to Asia. Thai curry penne (with broiled scallops, Dungeness crab, spicy ginger-tomato chutney, and basil chiffonade) is a long-running favorite, but savvy diners turn to the fresh sheet for the most exciting offerings: grilled sea bass with tomatillo sauce; a stew of lobster and mussels in coconut broth flavored with cilantro pesto; or red wine risotto with halibut cheeks, artichoke, asparagus, and chard. Alvin's mom, Vic-toria, does the desserts here; her fruit pies are a joy. Dine outdoors in warm weather on balconies overlooking the Lake Washington Ship Canal. *$$$; AE, DC, MC, V; local checks only; lunch Sun–Fri, dinner every day, brunch Sun; full bar; reservations recommended; mnger@ponti.com; www.ponti.com; south side of Fremont Bridge.* &

Ray's Boathouse / ★★⯪
6049 SEAVIEW AVE NW, SEATTLE; 206/789-3770

With its peerless, unabashedly romantic view of Shilshole Bay and the Olympics beyond, Ray's is favored for waterfront dining by tourists and locals alike. Executive chef Charles Ramseyer can knock your socks off with steamed Penn Cove mussels awash in a creamy Thai-style lemongrass-curry broth, king salmon glazed with cherries and Petite Syrah, and what may be the world's best version of *kasu* black cod, marinated in sake lees. The award-win-ning wine list is strong in Northwest varietals. A moderately priced, casual menu—lingcod fish-and-chips, rock shrimp and crab cakes, silky chowder—is offered for lunch and dinner upstairs in the deck-rimmed cafe. When the sun shines, expect the restaurant to be slammed; a prime-time reservation in the dining room may take weeks to secure, and the cafe may have a wait of an hour or more. *$$$; AE, MC, V; local checks only; lunch, dinner every day; full bar; reservations recommended (dining room dinner); rays@rays.com; www.rays.com; Shilshole.* &

Rover's / ★★★★

2808 E MADISON ST, SEATTLE; 206/325-7442

Though chef/owner Thierry Rautureau has won the hearts of Seattleites, half his customers are out-of-towners making pilgrimages to this warmly decorated restaurant tucked into a garden courtyard in Madison Valley.

Choose from three prix-fixe menus de degustation (one is vegetarian) served with gorgeous presentation and a generous hand. Rautureau's forte is seafood, and he's adept at finding the best-quality ingredients. He's a master of sauces, using stocks, reductions, herb-infused oils, and purées to enhance breasts of quail, slices of sturgeon, wild mushrooms, Russian caviar, and foie gras. A knockout regular appetizer: eggs scrambled with garlic and chives, then layered with crème fraîche and lime juice in an eggshell cut into a tiny cup, topped with white sturgeon caviar. We've had venison medallions with boletes, duck breast with winter vegetables, and steamed Maine lobster with a Périgord truffle sauce. Expect professional service from Rautureau's loyal staff, and sticker shock when perusing the carefully chosen wine list. Weather permitting, dine in the enchanting courtyard. *$$$$; AE, DC, MC, V; checks OK; dinner Tues–Sat; beer and wine; reservations required; www.rovers-seattle.com; Madison Valley.* &

Sea Garden / ★★
Sea Garden of Bellevue / ★★

509 7TH AVE S, SEATTLE; 206/623-2100
200 106TH AVE NE, BELLEVUE; 425/450-8833

Live tanks with crabs and lobsters at the door are a clue to what's best in this busy Cantonese eatery in the International District. Sip Tsingtao while the waiter brings your lobster to the table for approval. It'll return soon, sliced in a black bean sauce or wearing ginger and green onion. Don't miss panfried sliced rock cod or panfried squid in shrimp paste. Meats are great too—we loved pork chops fried crispy and soaked in garlic honey sauce. We've heard glowing reports about boneless duck steamed with eight kinds of meat and vegetables. Ask for *chow-fon* noodles (thick rice noodles) when ordering the Sea Garden special chow mein.

Sea Garden branched into Bellevue a few years ago and the owners, an extended family, built from the ground up. It isn't grand, but is smart and bright. Service at both restaurants ranges from adequate to exasperating. *$, $$; AE, DC, MC, V; no checks; lunch, dinner every day; full bar; reservations for parties of 10 or more; www.chinesecuisine.com; International District (Seattle), at SE 2nd St (Bellevue).* &

Shiro's / ★★★☆

2401 2ND AVE, SEATTLE; 206/443-9844

Shiro Kashiba introduced the concept of sushi to several generations of Seattleites, and they've loved him and his seafoody perfection for 30 years. He sold his legendary Nikko restaurant in 1992, which moved to fancy digs in the

Westin Hotel; a year later, he retired. Briefly. In 1995, to the delight of legions of fans, he opened Shiro's in a Belltown storefront: an immediate hit. In the simple, immaculate dining room, a small menu offers full-course entrees like tempura, sukiyaki, and teriyaki. *Kasu*-style black cod is not to be missed. Hundreds of sushi variations are the main event; the blond hardwood sushi bar is always jammed with Japanese tourists, Belltown hipsters, business types—sushi fanatics all. *$$$; AE, MC, V; no checks; dinner every day; full bar; reservations recommended; Belltown.* ♿

Wild Ginger Asian Restaurant and Satay Bar / ★★★

1401 3RD AVE, SEATTLE; 206/623-4450

Wild Ginger is wildly popular. Basking in the glow of much national attention are owners Rick and Ann Yoder, whose culinary vision—inspired by time spent in Southeast Asia—has left a lasting impression on Seattle's restaurant scene. At the mahogany satay bar, order a wide array of sizzling skewered selections: from sweet onion and Chinese eggplant to tender Bangkok boar. Indulge in succulent Singapore-style stir-fried crab, fresh from live tanks and redolent of ginger and garlic; mildly hot, slightly sweet beef curry from Thailand; or *laksa*, a spicy Malaysian seafood soup whose soft, crunchy, and slippery textures and hot and salty flavors encompass everything good about Southeast Asian cookery. At press time, the Yoders were preparing to move to significantly larger and more luxurious digs in the Mann Building (Third Ave and Union St), which they've been restoring for several years. The move is scheduled for summer 2000. *$$; AE, DIS, MC, V; no checks; lunch Mon–Sat, dinner every day; full bar; reservations recommended; downtown.* ♿

LODGINGS

Ace Hotel / ★★

2423 1ST AVE, SEATTLE; 206/448-4721

It's just a baby (opened in early 1999), but the 32-room Ace is possibly the city's coolest hotel. Its owners are cool (three 30-somethings), its name is cool (taken from a tube of toothpaste), its location is cool (in Belltown above Cyclops Bar), even its press clippings are cool (*Wallpaper** and *Details* magazines). Patterned after an upscale European hostel with 21st-century style, its look is clean and spare, with white walls and loft ceilings. Smartly stark bedrooms are dominated by low-riding queen- or king-size beds, funky original art, lighted cube tables, and stainless-steel sinks and vanities. Austerity is mixed with humor: wool French Army blankets are paired with a copy of the *Kamasutra* and tin-foiled condoms. Amenities include small wall TVs, phones with data ports, and—in suites—CD players. Guests share a row of large bathrooms or can choose from nine master suites with private baths (shower only). The Ace's stripped-down style may not appeal to some (e.g., those looking for room service). Others will love its Euro-cool pose, mix of guests—from musicians to snowboarders—dogs (Sadie and Otis), and low prices. Kids, pets, and smoking

OK. Lot parking ($12 per day). *$$; AE, DC, JCB, MC, V; checks OK; doug@theacehotel.com; www.TheAceHotel.com; at Wall St.*

Alexis Hotel / ★★★

1007 1ST AVE, SEATTLE; 206/624-4844 OR 800/426-7033

This lovely turn-of-the-century hotel near the waterfront manages to be elegant, hedonistic, and whimsical all at once. Even at 109 rooms (including 44 spacious suites), it has an intimate, boutique-hotel feel. (Request a room facing the inner courtyard, because rooms above First Avenue can be noisy.) Some suites include Jacuzzis or wood-burning fireplaces, but for sheer indulgence book one of the spa suites with two-person tubs. An on-site Aveda spa provides services in the spa or your room (the hotel also has an on-call masseuse). Amenities range from voice mail, data ports, and complimentary morning tea and coffee to evening wine tasting, shoeshines, and a guest membership to the Seattle Club. Whimsical touches include in-line skating tours and a John Lennon suite, complete with original art. The Painted Table (see review) serves innovative Northwest cuisine; the Bookstore Bar is a cozy, though smoky, nook for libations. Pets OK. Some smoking rooms. Garage parking ($20 per night). *$$$$; AE, DC, DIS, E, JCB, MC, V; checks OK; charlottem@kimpton group.com; www.alexishotel.com; between Spring and Madison.* ⅋

The Bacon Mansion Bed & Breakfast / ★★

959 BROADWAY E, SEATTLE; 206/329-1864 OR 800/240-1864

Its 1909 Tudor-style architecture and family crest glowing from crimson stained-glass windows give the Bacon decidedly British airs. The old-world finery includes a stately dining room; an uncommon common room with marble fireplace, grand piano, and library; and an exquisite 3,000-crystal chandelier. Nine of eleven guest rooms have private baths and are appropriately appointed with antiques and brass fixtures. The sunny second-floor Capitol Room has a queen bed, fireplace, wet bar, sunroom, and tree-framed view of the Space Needle. The Carriage House, a separate two-story building, is ideal for a small family or two couples, and is wheelchair-accessible. Despite its upper-crust trappings, the Bacon has a friendly staff, from proprietor Daryl King to head housekeeper Carol (who will call you "honey" at least once). Kids welcome, not pets. Smoking outside only. As available, neighborhood permit parking. *$$; AE, DIS, MC, V; checks OK; 2–3 night min stays in summer; baconbandb@aol.com; www.baconmansion.com; between E Prospect and Aloha.*

Best Western Pioneer Square Hotel / ★★

77 YESLER WY, SEATTLE; 206/340-1234 OR 800/800-5514

Renovations have transformed this formerly seedy 1914 hotel into a handsome, comfortable, moderately priced establishment—a boon for travelers intent on staying in the heart of historic Seattle, among galleries, bookstores, boutiques, restaurants, and nightclubs. In each guest room you'll find rich cherrywood furniture and two armoires (one for a closet and one for the TV), as well as a small sitting alcove. Rooms are surprisingly quiet (the hotel is in close proximity to the busy Alaskan Way viaduct). Quibbles? Front-desk staff could use some polish, and the complimentary continental breakfast may be picked over if you sleep past 7:30am. Pioneer Square can be edgy at night, so timid travelers might opt for a more gentrified neighborhood. However, those looking for an authentic urban experience will find it here. Kids OK; no pets. One smoking floor. Self-parking ($12–$15 overnight). *$$; AE, DC, DIS, JCB, MC, V; no checks; info@pioneersquare.com; www.pioneersquare.com; between 1st Ave S and Alaskan Wy.* &

Chelsea Station on the Park / ★★

4915 LINDEN AVE N, SEATTLE; 206/547-6077 OR 800/400-6077

Charm is an overused B&B adjective, but can't be avoided when describing the Chelsea. The 1920s brick two-story is across from Woodland Park Zoo, and is decorated in antiques and paintings by local artists. Six rooms have king- or queen-size beds, private phones and baths (two are shower only); some have views of downtown, the Cascades, or Woodland's rose garden. The Sunlight Suite has an endearingly retro 1920s kitchen. Three spacious suites are housed in a companion brick building next door. Breakfasts (included) are creative affairs of coffee, fruit, and entrees, such as smoked-salmon hash or banana nut pancakes. Children over 6 welcome; no pets or smoking. Ample on-street, and some off-street, parking. *$$; AE, DC, DIS, MC, V; checks OK; 3-night min in summer; info@bandbseattle.com; www.bandbseattle.com; 1 block west of Hwy 99.*

Claremont Hotel / ★★☆

2000 4TH AVE, SEATTLE; 206/448-8600 OR 800/448-8601

No wonder the Claremont is heavily booked year-round: the location can't be beat—three blocks from Pike Place Market, and 1 ½ blocks from Westlake Center and the Monorail. Built in 1926, the hotel offers a richly elegant lobby and 121 guest rooms with understated traditional decor, and king- or queen-size beds (or two queens or doubles), as well as sitting areas and bathrooms of white tile and marble. Junior Suites are bigger, with granite wet bars; Executive Suites have separate living rooms. A few rooms have kitchens. All provide irons and ironing boards, two-line phones with data ports, and voice mail. Upper floors boast views of downtown, Puget Sound, the Space Needle, Lake Union, and Olympic Mountains. Room service includes a full breakfast and a 24-hour "snack" menu (a complete 24-hour menu is in the works). On the ground floor, Assaggio Ristorante (see review) is an excellent Northern Italian eatery. Two smoking floors. Valet parking ($14 per day). *$$$; AE, DC, DIS, JCB, MC, V; checks OK; rez@claremonthotel.com; www.claremonthotel.com; at Virginia.* &

Edmond Meany Hotel / ★★

4507 BROOKLYN AVE NE, SEATTLE; 206/634-2000 OR 800/899-0251

The refurbished 1931 Meany is once again an eye-catching presence in the University District. Its art deco detailing and elegant lobby (check out the terrazzo floors) have been revived, along with its guest rooms. Designed by renowned architect Robert C. Reamer, the Meany's distinctive 15-story octagonal tower allows each of the 155 guest rooms (about half of which contain king-size beds) a corner window with a view—some better than others. You're one block from shopping on "the Ave," and two blocks from the UW campus. Pleiades Restaurant and Lounge serves Northwest cuisine (along with billiards and cigars). Eddie's News Café, facing N 45th Street, is ideal for early risers who read with their espresso. Check for minimum-stay requirements during summer and football season. Two smoking floors. Limited complimentary parking. *$$; AE, DC, DIS, MC, V; checks OK; info@meany.com; www.meany.com; corner of NE 45th.* &

Four Seasons Olympic Hotel / ★★★★

411 UNIVERSITY ST, SEATTLE; 206/621-1700 OR 800/821-8106

Smiling maids, quick-as-a-wink bellhops, and a team of caring concierges ensure around-the-clock comfort at this posh 1920s landmark. Its reputation for service makes the Four Seasons a favorite with visiting celebs, but all revel in the old-world luxury that extends from the newly updated 450 guest rooms and suites furnished with period reproductions to the venerable Georgian Room restaurant (see review). Executive suites feature down-dressed king-size beds separated by French doors from elegant sitting rooms. The hotel even goes out of its way for kids, right down to a toy in the crib and a step stool in the bathroom. There are several refined meeting rooms and shops off the lobby. Enjoy afternoon tea in the Garden Court or relax in the solarium spa and pool (a massage therapist is on call). Four Seasons' prices are steep, especially considering few rooms have views, but this *is* Seattle's one world-class contender. Pets OK. One smoking floor. Valet parking ($20 per day). *$$$$; AE, DC, DIS, JCB, MC, V; checks OK; deposits required for cash guests; melissa.henninger@fourseasons.com; www.fshr.com; between 4th and 5th.* &

Hotel Edgewater / ★★

2411 ALASKAN WY, PIER 67, SEATTLE; 206/728-7000 OR 800/624-0670

The Edgewater edges out the competition when it comes to unusual claims to fame. It's the only Seattle hotel literally over the water (if watching whitecaps makes you dizzy, avoid first-floor rooms). And, in 1964, the Beatles checked in and dropped fishing lines out their hotel window (see the Fab Four photo in the gift shop). You can't fish from the windows anymore, but you can still breathe salty air and hear the ferries. And now the 230-room hotel has a flashy metal log-cabin exterior (aluminum shingles evoke silvery fish scales). The lobby and rooms (all with fireplaces) are still dressed in traditional

Northwest lodge: plenty of knotty pine, duck-and-fish kitsch, and antler art. The hotel's lobby, restaurant (don't miss Sunday brunch), and Mudshark Bar provide uninterrupted views of Elliott Bay, Puget Sound, and the Olympics. It's a short walk to Bell Street Pier (Pier 66), with restaurants, the Odyssey Maritime Discovery Center, and an overpass to nearby Pike Place Market. Some smoking rooms. Valet parking ($13 per day). *$$$; AE, DC, DIS, MC, V; checks OK; www.noblehousehotels.com; 1 block west of Elliott Ave.* &

Hotel Monaco / ★★★
1101 4TH AVE, SEATTLE; 206/621-1770 OR 800/945-2240

It's nearly impossible to be depressed—even on Seattle's grayest days—when confronted by the sunny Mediterranean look of Hotel Monaco. The upbeat mood is set in the lobby—with its nautical mural of dolphins—and sealed in the boldly designed rooms. All 189 are decorated in a blend of eye-popping stripes and florals that may strike some as insanely busy, and others as utterly charming. (It's hard to believe this jaunty Kimpton-owned hotel was once a stodgy telephone-company switching center.) As with many local hotels, views take a back seat to service and design (business travelers appreciate 6,000 square feet of meeting space). Monaco's campy principality extends to the Southern-inspired Sazerac restaurant. Located just off the hotel's lobby, it flaunts both snazzy surroundings—punctuated by whimsical chandeliers and plush purple booths—and cuisine. Chef Jan Birnbaum's Louisiana roots are firmly planted in dishes like the New Orleans red gravy–sauced pork porterhouse paired with "soft and sexy" grits, and Creole shrimp cakes spiked with zesty sauce meunière. The dessert de rigueur is gooey chocolate pudding cake armed with its own pitcher of cream. Pets OK (or ask for a bowl of loaner goldfish). Two smoking floors; valet parking ($20 per night). *$$$$; AE, DC, DIS, JCB, MC, V; checks OK; www.monaco-seattle.com; between Spring and Seneca.* &

Hotel Vintage Park / ★★★
1100 5TH AVE, SEATTLE; 206/624-8000 OR 800/624-4433

The Vintage Park takes its "vintage" theme to the limit: rooms are named after wineries, with updated winery-inspired decor, and fireside wine tasting is complimentary every evening. Part of the San Francisco–based Kimpton Group, the personable Park offers rooms facing inward or outward (exterior rooms have a bit more space, but forget about views) that come with fax machines, hair dryers, irons and ironing boards, and phones in the bathrooms. There's lightning-fast 24-hour room service, including lunch or dinner from the hotel's Italian restaurant Tulio, where the atmosphere is reminiscent of a Tuscan villa, and the pastas are great. Unfortunately, a nearby busy Interstate 5 entrance ramp makes lower floors a bit noisy; soundproofing helps on upper floors. Pets OK; one smoking floor. Valet parking ($18 per night). *$$$; AE, DC, DIS, JCB, MC, V; checks OK; www.hotelvintagepark.com; at Spring.* &

Inn at Harbor Steps / ★★

1221 1ST AVE, SEATTLE; 206/748-0973 OR 888/728-8910

Even first-time visitors to Seattle can pose as natives in this urban hideaway tucked inside a swanky high-rise retail-and-residential complex across from the Seattle Art Museum. The second Northwest property (after Whidbey Island's Saratoga Inn) from the California-based Four Sisters Inns, Harbor Steps offers 20 tastefully furnished rooms with garden views, fireplaces, air conditioning, king- or queen-size beds, sitting areas, wet bars, fridges, data ports, and voice mail. Deluxe rooms include spa tubs. Among the amenities are 24-hour concierge/innkeeper services, room service from Wolfgang Puck Café (4–10pm), complimentary evening hors d'oeuvres and wine, and a breakfast buffet. Guests have access to an indoor pool, sauna, Jacuzzi, exercise room, and meeting rooms. Kids and pets OK; one smoking floor. Self-parking garage ($12 per night). *$$$; AE, DC, JCB, MC, V; no checks; gregcrick@harborsteps.com; www.foursisters.com; at University St.* &

Inn at the Market / ★★★☆

86 PINE ST, SEATTLE; 206/443-3600 OR 800/446-4484

Perfectly positioned to capture all the wonders of bustling Pike Place Market, this 70-room brick inn remains unhurried and intimate. An ivy-draped courtyard wraps around its entrance and high-end retailers and restaurants, including country-French Campagne (see review). Newly updated rooms are handsomely dressed in a Biedermeier scheme of soft taupe, copper, and green (replacing Laura Ashley decor). Most rooms afford charming views, and those on the west have floor-to-ceiling windows that open to breezes off the Sound and unmatched vistas of the Market, Elliott Bay, and the Olympics. (Don't fret if the weather turns gloomy; some of the most memorable views come through rain-streaked windows.) Other amenities include in-room safes and refrigerators, and oversize bathrooms. Rise early to sample the Market's fresh pastries (try Le Panier Bakery) and fruit. Or, sleep late and indulge in room service from Bacco in the courtyard. In-room dinners come courtesy of Campagne (5–10pm). Campagne's bar is a snug, if smoky, spot for a nightcap. Kids welcome; no pets. One smoking floor. Valet parking ($17 per night). *$$$; AE, DC, DIS, MC, V; checks OK; info@innatthemarket.com; www.innatthemarket.com; between 1st Ave and Post Alley.* &

MV Challenger Bunk & Breakfast / ★

1001 FAIRVIEW AVE N, STE 1600, SEATTLE; 206/340-1201 OR 877/340-1201

Rooms with water views aren't unusual in Seattle, but most don't come through a porthole. This perky red-and-white two-level 1944 tug moored on south Lake Union offers eight rooms, five with their own bath. The top-level Admiral's Cabin features a four-poster queen, soaking bath, and spectacular view. You won't find luxury on board (for that, try the company's yacht)—some quarters are tight, ladders between floors are steep, and there's a faint musty smell. However, Rick Anderson has made the tug spit-and-polish neat since buying it in 1999. A continental breakfast is enjoyed in the cozy solarium, and there's 24-hour coffee and tea service and a 300-plus videotape library. Eateries are steps away, as is the fascinating Center for Wooden Boats. Kids OK; no smoking. Complimentary lot parking. *$$; AE, DIS, DC, MC, V; no checks; 2-night min; mvchallenger@bigfoot.com; www.challengerboat.com; Yale St landing.*

Paramount Hotel / ★★

724 PINE ST, SEATTLE; 206/292-9500 OR 800/426-0670
Ideally located for all sorts of diversions, the Paramount is kitty-corner from the lovely Paramount Theatre, in the lap of swanky midtown retailers, and near the convention center. Standard guest rooms are prettily appointed, though small, as are bathrooms. Consider splurging for an "executive" room with a Jacuzzi; corner locations mean more space. The adjoining restaurant, pan-Asian inspired Blowfish, is trendy but tasteful. One smoking floor. Valet parking ($18 per day). *$$$; AE, DC, DIS, JCB, MC, V; checks OK; www.westcoasthotels.com/ paramount; between 7th and 8th.* &

Pensione Nichols / ★

1923 1ST AVE, SEATTLE; 206/441-7125 OR 800/440-7125
Bohemian atmosphere, superb location—perched above Pike Place Market—and reasonable prices distinguish Pensione Nichols. Though some might find the furnishings too well-worn, antiques abound (the Nicholses also own the N. B. Nichols antique store in Post Alley). Ten guest rooms ($75 single, $95 double) share four baths. Some rooms face noisy First Avenue; others don't have windows, but have skylights and are quieter. Also available: two suites ($175 each) with private baths, full kitchens, and living rooms with water views. A large, appealing common room on the third floor has a gorgeous view; it's here the bountiful breakfast—including fresh treats from the Market—is served. No kids; well-behaved pets OK. Fire-escape smoking only. Self-parking lots. *$$; AE, DIS, MC, V; checks OK; 2-night min on summer weekends; www.seattle-bed-breakfast.com; between Virginia and Stewart.*

Sheraton Seattle Hotel and Towers / ★★☆

1400 6TH AVE, SEATTLE; 206/621-9000 OR 800/325-3535
Looming over the downtown convention center, the Sheraton goes all out for business travelers. While its 840 guest rooms are smallish and standard, emphasis is given to meeting rooms and restaurants. On the first floor are the lobby lounge and oyster bar, the casual Pike Street Cafe, and Schooners Sports Pub (complete with large-screen TVs, Northwest microbrews, and pub fare). The fine-dining restaurant, Fullers, is an oasis of serenity. Convention facilities are complete. Discriminating businesspeople head for the upper four VIP floors (31–34), with their own lobby, concierge, private lounge, and amenity-filled rooms. The top-floor health club (open to all guests) features a heated pool and

knockout city panorama. Four smoking floors. Self-parking garage ($15 per night) or valet ($18 per night). *$$$; AE, DC, DIS, MC, V; checks OK; www. sheraton.com; between Pike and Union.* &

Sorrento Hotel / ★★★⯪

900 MADISON ST, SEATTLE; 206/622-6400 OR 800/426-1265

The Sorrento is an Italianate masterpiece grandly holding court on its own corner east of downtown in Seattle's First Hill neighborhood. Opened in 1909, it recently completed a millennial makeover, adding impressively modern in-room touches such as PCs with high-speed Internet connections. A small exercise facility is another improvement. The 76 rooms are decorated in muted good taste, varying from old-world elegance to Northwest contemporary. We recommend the large corner suites (particularly the aptly named Vanderbilt or Carnegie suites, which are like small, stylish apartments). Top-floor suites make tony quarters for meetings or parties. The Fireside Room off the lobby is a civilized bar; the manly Hunt Club serves Mediterranean-influenced cuisine. Complimentary town-car service takes guests downtown. Some travelers consider the Sorrento's location—five blocks uphill from the heart of the city—inconvenient, but we find it quiet and removed. No pets; one smoking floor. Valet parking ($19 per night). *$$$$; AE, DC, DIS, MC, V; checks OK; mail@hotelsorrento.com; www.hotelsorrento.com; at Terry Ave.* &

W Seattle Hotel / ★★★

1112 4TH AVE, SEATTLE; 206/264-6000 OR 877/W-HOTELS

"Warm, witty, and welcoming" is the motto of this chain of boutique business hotels. Seattle's version, launched in 1999 by the Starwood group (owners of the Sheraton and Westin chains), has 426 rooms on 26 floors—and a surplus of style. The see-and-be-seen lobby alone could have a cover charge. Part modern art museum, part Pottery Barn catalog, it is swathed in floor-to-ceiling chocolate-velvet drapes and plush furnishings, and glows at night with candle- and fireplace light. Naturally, it's a magnet for black-garbed people with cell phones or frou-frou drinks (as is the adjacent bar leading to the hotel's Earth and Ocean restaurant). Rooms exhibit a simpler chic: colored in taupe and black and outfitted with stainless-and-glass-appointed bathrooms, safes, irons and ironing boards, coffeemakers, desks, and Zen-inspired water sculptures. Many rooms (particularly higher corner rooms) have impressive downtown views; all have queen- or king-size "heavenly beds" (rumored to cost about $4,000 each) sheathed in goose-down duvets and 250-thread-count linen, and covered in goose-down pillows. While bedside fortune cookies make mints passé, honor bars wittily yield Altoids, Pez, wax lips, and "intimacy kits." Room service is 24 hours, as is the fitness room; stylish meeting space totals 10,000 square feet. The W should add "wired" to its slogan: rooms come with 27-inch WebTV, CD and video player, two-line desk phone with high-speed Internet connection, conference calling, voice mail, and a cordless phone. Pets OK; three smoking floors.

Valet parking ($21.76 per overnight). *$$$$; AE, DC, DIS, JCB, MC, V; checks OK; hayley.king@whotel.com; www.whotels.com; at Seneca.* &

Westin Hotel / ★★☆

1900 5TH AVE, SEATTLE; 206/728-1000 OR 800/WESTIN-1

The Westin's twin cylindrical towers enclose big rooms with very big views, particularly above the 20th floor. Room decor is so-so (ritzy, glitzy suites are on the top floor), but beds are sumptuous, multilayered affairs dressed in white. Amenities are corporate-minded: business center, convention facilities spread over several floors, currency exchange, and multilingual staff. There's also babysitting services, a large pool and Jacuzzi with city view, and 24-hour exercise room. The size of the hotel (891 rooms) can contribute to lapses in service, such as occasionally long lines for check-in. But the location, near Westlake Center, is excellent, as are meals at Nikko, a Japanese restaurant, and Roy's Seattle, both on the premises. Many smoking rooms. Self-parking ($15 per night) or valet ($18 per night). *$$$$; AE, DC, DIS, MC, V; checks OK; www.westin.com; at Westlake.* &

The Eastside

The suburbs—and suburban cities—on the east side of Lake Washington across from Seattle are collectively known as "the Eastside." They include Bellevue, Redmond, Kirkland, Woodinville, and Issaquah. The **EAST KING COUNTY CONVENTION & VISITORS BUREAU** (425/455-1926; www.eastkingcounty.org) has the lowdown on Eastside goings-on.

Bellevue

Washington's fourth-largest city has been making noises for years about shaking its shopping-mall image. Its goal is to become a mini Silicon Valley. And, yes, it has an impressive downtown skyline—second only to Seattle's—populated by thriving high-tech firms (including Attachmate and drugstore.com). More convention facilities are in the works for the fairly new **MEYDENBAUER CENTER** (11100 NE 6th St; 425/637-1020), which also hosts myriad arts performances. Even the **BELLEVUE ART MUSEUM** (301 Bellevue Square; 425/454-3322), long kidded about its shopping-mall locale, is becoming a world-class contender with a new, boldly designed $23-million home set to open in January 2001 across from its old site.

But shopping is still the main attraction. Just consider the conglomeration of retail might: ever-expanding powerhouse **BELLEVUE SQUARE** (NE 8th St; 425/454-8096), packed with a triple-decker Nordstrom store, plus 200 shops and restaurants; kitty-corner is glitzy **BELLEVUE PLACE** (10500 NE 8th; 425/453-5634); and, farther east, family-oriented **CROSSROADS** mall (15600 NE 8th; 425/644-1111). The new **BELLEVUE GALLERIA** along 106th Street is more strip-style tacky (read: Hooter's), but pulls in plenty of traffic with its cinemas, Rock

Bottom Restaurant & Brewery, and Tower Records. The barn-size **BARNES & NOBLE** bookstore (626 106th NE; 425/644-1650) is worth a look. And, as if designed to give shoppers a breather from the spending spree, 19-acre **DOWN-TOWN PARK**, possessed of a fine waterfall and promenade, is in the southern shadow of Bellevue Square.

RESTAURANTS

Bis on Main / ★★

10213 MAIN ST, BELLEVUE; 425/455-2033

Joe Vilardi has successfully filled a gap in the Eastside dining scene. Using his knowledge and experience from Il Terrazzo Carmine, he created a serene urban dining experience in an area dominated by old-style kitsch and chain eateries. Couples and small groups create a low hum in the candlelit room that fronts Bellevue's old Main Street. The kitchen turns out consistently good bistro fare with some occasional Southern treats. Classics are executed well—crispy garlic chicken, and filet mignon paired with sides and sauces that show a restrained but deft touch. Northwest specials such as crab cakes and ahi tuna are simple but well constructed. Lunch offers large sandwiches and a view of Bellevue society lunchers. *$$$; AE, DC, DIS, V; checks OK; lunch, dinner Mon–Sat; beer and wine; reservations recommended; www.bisonmain.com; 2 blocks west of Bellevue Wy.*

Noble Court / ★

1644 140TH ST NE, BELLEVUE; 425/641-4011

 When you walk into Noble Court between 11am and 3pm on a weekend, be prepared to be transported to Hong Kong. The lines, the chaos, and the groups of Chinese celebrants give an air of authenticity to this vast restaurant on a small creek in the middle of Bellevue. The dim sum is the best in the Puget Sound area, and waitresses keep the carts rolling with both standard and unusual fare. Go with a large group and order everything that passes by; the bill will remain incredibly low and lunch can turn into midafternoon snacks. Catch the cart with the stuffed eggplant, and the shrimp dumplings with cilantro. If dim sum is not a favorite, the regular menu is extensive, ranging from basic meat and noodle dishes to full-blown Peking duck banquets. When a dish says the seafood is fresh, it is probably fished from the crowded tanks near the door. A focus on the food outweighs the diminishing atmosphere. *$–$$; AE, MC, V; no checks; lunch, dinner every day; full bar; reservations not necessary; off Bellevue-Redmond Rd.* &

22 Fountain Court / ★★★

22 103RD AVE NE, BELLEVUE; 425/451-0426

This small converted house in the heart of Old Bellevue continues to be one of the Eastside's most romantic destinations. Sit in one of the four small, intimate dining rooms, or the flower-filled fountain courtyard, and enjoy the beauty of your surroundings. The ambience is not reserved only for romance;

READ ALL ABOUT IT

Seattleites are bookworms. They spend double the national average on books every year, and are avid borrowers from the public library system. Their page-turning proclivities ensure that you don't have to go far in this town to find a store selling new or used titles, or both. Although they don't often write about the city, many well-known authors live and work in the area: Tom Robbins, Charles Johnson, Jonathan Raban, Rebecca Brown, Brenda Peterson, and Pete Dexter, to name a few. Here's a short list of works that will help you learn more about Seattle and the Puget Sound region:

In *The Forging of a Black Community* (University of Washington Press, 1994), Quintard Taylor examines the often troubled evolution of Seattle's Central District from 1870 through the civil-rights struggles of the 1960s.

In *Rains All the Time: A Connoisseur's History of Weather in the Pacific Northwest* (Sasquatch Books, 1997), David Laskin recounts the history of this region's relationship with "liquid sunshine."

Walt Crowley's *National Trust Guide Seattle* (John Wiley & Sons, 1998) gives a wonderful overview of the city's architecture and history that locals *and* visitors can enjoy.

Seattle City Walks (Sasquatch Books, 1999), by Laura Karlinsey, provides easy-to-use walking tours of various city neighborhoods, with historical and cultural details.

Skid Road (Comstock, 1978), by Murray Morgan, is a lively, irreverent look back at some of the events and eccentrics most responsible for creating the Seattle we know today.

One of our most beloved regional books, *The Egg and I* (J. R. Lippincott Co., 1945), by Betty MacDonald, is a delightfully whimsical memoir of life on a Washington chicken ranch.

In *The Natural History of Puget Sound Country* (University of Washington Press, 1991), Arthur R. Kruckeberg offers insights into the region's environment.

Northwest history is recorded by the people who lived it in *A Voyage of Discovery to the North Pacific Ocean and Round the World* (C. G. and J. Robinson, 1798), by explorer George Vancouver.

Writer Sallie Tisdale (*Stepping Westward: The Long Search for Home in the Pacific Northwest*; Henry Holt, 1991) and *New York Times* correspondent Timothy Egan (*The Good Rain: Across Time and Terrain in the Pacific Northwest*; Alfred A. Knopf, 1990) offer contemporary perspectives on the region.

For more detailed touring information, pick up *Best Places Seattle* (Sasquatch, 1999).

—*J. Kingston Pierce*

it is equally rewarding for small parties of friends or business associates. The essentially French menu changes with the seasons and offers an upscale selection of favorites that may include duck, filet mignon, or marlin. All are attractively presented in a variety of colorful serving plates and terrines. The wine list is not extensive but covers a wide price range. Beautifully handcrafted desserts, built to order by the on-site pastry chef, make a satisfying ending. *$$$; AE, DC, MC, V; local checks only; lunch Mon–Fri, dinner Mon–Sat; full bar; reservations recommended; off Main St.* &

LODGINGS

Bellevue Club Hotel / ★★★

11200 SE 6TH ST, BELLEVUE; 425/454-4424 OR 800/579-1110
A favorite among well-heeled business travelers, the Bellevue Club has 67 striking rooms, with modern furnishings and pieces by Northwest artists. Many overlook tennis courts, and garden rooms open onto private patios. There's ample opportunity to work up a sweat at the extensive athletic facilities, including an Olympic-size swimming pool; indoor tennis, racquetball, and squash courts; and aerobics classes. Oversize limestone-and-marble bathrooms—with spa-like tubs—are perfect for post-workout soaks. The club offers fine dining at Polaris restaurant and casual fare at the Sport Café. Six smoking rooms. Self-parking or valet ($5 per day). *$$$; AE, DC, MC, V; checks OK; kerrif@bellevueclub.com; www.bellevueclub.com; at 112th Ave SE.* &

Hyatt Regency at Bellevue Place / ★★

900 BELLEVUE WY NE, BELLEVUE; 425/462-1234 OR 800/233-1234
Part of the splashy, sprawling retail-office-restaurant-hotel-health-club complex called Bellevue Place, this 382-room, 24-story hotel offers many extras: pricier Regency Club rooms on the top three floors, some great views (particularly southside rooms above the seventh floor), two big ballrooms, several satellite conference rooms, use of the neighboring Bellevue Place Club (for $8), and a restaurant, Eques, serving Pacific Rim cuisine. Two smoking floors. Valet ($15 per night) or self-parking ($10 per night). *$$$$; AE, DC, DIS, MC, V; checks OK; www.hyatt.com; at NE 8th.* &

Redmond

Once a bucolic valley farming community, Redmond today is a sprawling McTown of freeway overpasses, offices (Microsoft and Nintendo are headquartered here), subdivisions, and retail, including the open-air, 100-plus-shop **REDMOND TOWN CENTER AND CINEMAS** (16495 NE 74th; 425/867-0808). Some of Redmond's pastoral past remains. It's not dubbed the bicycle capital of the Northwest for nothing: bikers can pedal the 10-mile **SAMMAMISH LAKE TRAIL** (which on the west hooks up to the Burke-Gilman Trail terminating in Seattle) or check out races on the 400-meter **MARYMOOR VELODROME** (2400 Lake Sammamish Pkwy; 206/675-1424; www.marymoor.velodrome.org). In summer, 522-acre **MARYMOOR PARK** (6046 W Lake Sammamish Pkwy NE; 206/296-2966) draws crowds for picnics, an annual horse show, and the late-summer **WORLD OF MUSIC AND DANCE** (WOMAD) festival (206/281-7788).

RESTAURANTS

Il Bacio / ★★

16564 CLEVELAND ST, REDMOND; 425/869-8815

In three neat, simple rooms that never impart the illusion you're anywhere but a Redmond strip mall, master chef Rino Baglio works his art. He's a man of impeccable credentials: helped prepare the wedding feast for Chuck and Di, cooked for Princess Caroline of Monaco and for the Pope, won numerous awards. A northern Italian, he largely forsakes tomato sauce, a southern specialty, for his own brand of home cooking. Venison-stuffed ravioli comes in a rich cream sauce, topped by shaved black truffles. White truffle oil accents a buttery white-wine sauce hosting three islands of veal scaloppine. Though the excellent pasticceria that established his and spouse/host Patsy's original foothold here is now gone, it's foolish not to leave room for beautifully baked desserts. *$$; AE, DC, DIS, JCB, MC, V; local checks only; lunch Mon–Fri, dinner every day; beer and wine; reservations recommended; across from Redmond Town Center.*

Kirkland

Sure, there's a crunch of expensive condos and rush-hour traffic, but this fetching town tucked into the eastern shore of Lake Washington has avoided the Eastside's typical strip-mall syndrome. People *stroll* here among congenially arranged eateries, galleries, and boutique retailers. In summer, sidewalks fill with locals and tourists; as do **PETER KIRK PARK** and the **KIRKLAND MARINA**, where you can catch an **ARGOSY** (206/623-1445) boat for a lake cruise April through September. Welcome downtown additions include the 402-seat **KIRKLAND PERFORMANCE CENTER** (350 Kirkland Ave; 425/893-9900); hip **MONDO SHRIMP** (166 Lake St S; 425/893-9458)—try the pepper-Jack shrimp quesadillas; and **WASHINGTON HARVEST FARMS** (170 Lake St; 425-889-0335), a cheery open-air fruit and veggie market. Even the obligatory mall, **KIRKLAND PARKPLACE** (6th and Central; 425/828-4468), doesn't spoil the townscape—it's several blocks east of the waterfront.

RESTAURANTS

Third Floor Fish Café / ★★★

205 LAKE ST S, KIRKLAND; 425/822-3553

This upstairs beauty has a drop-dead view west across Lake Washington from every table in the mahogany-accented, shades-of-pastel room. A change of chefs in late 1999 hasn't diverted the emphasis away from seafood—a dozen or so different types and preparations on the regular menu, plus daily specials. Starters such as a zingy ceviche of salmon and scallops layered between crispy tortilla squares, and a roasted-red-pepper soup, are menu highlights. Also good are Dungeness crab spring rolls with a mango-lime vinaigrette. Ambitious entrees result in unusual combinations that don't always work (seared ahi with shoestring potatoes?), but the fish is fresh and tasty. A five- or seven-course tasting menu is also available. The menu includes pan-roasted chicken, rosemary-marinated pork tenderloin, and braised lamb shank. The wine list proffers Washington and California vintages, and a lively piano bar competes for attention. *$$$; AE, DC, DIS, MC, V; local checks only; dinner every day; full bar; reservations recommended; on waterfront.* &

Yarrow Bay Grill / ★★★
Yarrow Bay Beach Café / ★★

1270 CARILLON POINT, KIRKLAND; 425/889-9052 (GRILL) OR 425/889-0303 (CAFÉ)

A pair of sibling restaurants, one stacked atop the other, boast gorgeous Lake Washington views. Upstairs, the tony grill ranks in the upper echelon of Eastside dining spots, thanks to the reliable creativity of chef Vicky McCaffree and consistent management. The attractive dining room is understated and sophisticated; deck dining affords sweeping views westward across the lake. McCaffree likes to assemble influences as diverse as Southwest, Northwest, Mediterranean, and Asian. An apple cider–Gewürztraminer sauce covers sea-fresh scallops. Risotto flavored with lobster stock holds sea bass, salmon, and prawns. Sake and ginger flavor a salmon fillet, along with shiitake–pickled ginger butter.

Downstairs, the Beach Café is a lively spot. Knock a few bucks off the upstairs prices and sample a jazzed-up, rotating, United Nations menu—now Turkey, then Chile, followed by Morocco, and so on—under the direction of chef Cameon Orel, along with a stable roster of sandwiches, nibbles, and meat or fish entrees. The bar scene is clamorous, and in warm weather the fun spills out onto a lakeside patio. *$$–$$$, $$; AE, DC, DIS, MC, V; checks OK; lunch Mon-Fri, dinner every day, brunch Sun (Grill); lunch, dinner every day (Café); full bar; reservations recommended; at Carillon Point.* &

LODGINGS

The Woodmark Hotel / ★★★

1200 CARILLON POINT, KIRKLAND; 425/822-3700 OR 800/822-3700

From the outside, it resembles nothing more remarkable than a lakefront office building. Inside, however, it's one of the finest hotels in or out of Seattle. The Woodmark's 100 plush rooms (the best have lake views) come with minibars and refrigerators, terrycloth robes, and matchless service (from laundry to valet). You'll get a complimentary newspaper and a chance to "raid the pantry" for late-night snacks and beverages. Downstairs is a comfortable living room with a grand piano and a well-tended fire. The hotel's restaurant, Waters, features Northwest cuisine; specialty shops (including a day spa) are nearby. Business travelers can request a pager or a cell phone for off-site calls. No pets. Some smoking rooms. Valet ($11 per night) or self-parking ($9 per night). *$$$; AE, DC, MC, V; checks OK; nancyd@thewoodmark.com; www.thewoodmark.com; at Lake Washington Blvd.* &

Woodinville

Oenophiles and hopheads (the microbrew kind) love this little Eastside town. **CHATEAU STE. MICHELLE** (14111 NE 145th St; 425/488-1133), the state's largest winery, offers daily tastings and tours, and popular summer concerts on its lovely 87-acre estate. Across the street, **COLUMBIA WINERY** (14030 NE 145th St; 425/488-2776) has daily tastings and weekend tours. Or wet your whistle at one of the state's first microbreweries, **REDHOOK ALE BREWERY** (14300 NE 145th St; 425-483-3232), which, along with daily $1 tours (including a souvenir glass and plenty of samples), has a pub with tasty grub and live music Fridays and Saturdays.

LODGINGS

Willows Lodge

14580 NE 145TH ST, WOODINVILLE; 425/424-3900

World-class wineries and voluptuous gardens surround this 88-room (6 of them suites) luxury boutique hotel opened in the summer of 2000. As the only upscale lodging option in the area, its mission is twofold: serve nearby high-tech firms (including Microsoft, which wanted a Northwesty place to impress recruits) and romantics. The luxe Northwest-style lodge features a two-level lobby lined with 100-year-old Douglas fir beams, a library, and an enormous stone-framed wood-burning fireplace. All rooms are replete with fireplaces, king- or queen-size beds, stereo-DVD-CD systems, high-speed Internet connections, lush bathrooms (some with jetted tubs), and balconies or patios with views of the gardens, Chateau Ste. Michelle and Columbia Wineries, Sammamish River (and its popular bike trail), or Mount Rainier. The poshest suite ($750 per night) boasts a high-end Bang & Olufsen stereo, whirlpool bath, and flat-screen TV. Other lodge amenities include a spa, 24-hour fitness room, and evening wine tastings. Guests will also have access to The Herbfarm Restaurant (206/784-2222; formerly in Fall City), which, along with its famed herb gardens, will occupy its own site on the grounds. Children welcome; call regarding pets. No smoking. Complimentary parking. *$$$–$$$$; AE, DC, DIS, MC, V; checks OK; www.willowslodge.com; next to Redhook Brewery.* &

Issaquah

Though every so often a cougar shows up in this wealthy Cascade-foothills suburb 15 miles east of Seattle, Issaquah is pleasantly mild-mannered. Historic **GILMAN VILLAGE** (317 NW Gilman Blvd; 425/392-6802), comprised of refurbished old farmhouses, offers an agreeable day of poking about in its 40 or so shops, and the **VILLAGE THEATRE** (120 Front St N and 303 Front St N; 425/392-2202) entertains with mostly original, mainly musical productions at its two downtown theaters. Seattleites cross the Interstate 90 bridge in packs during summer weekends to "scale" the **ISSAQUAH ALPS**, which have miles of trails—from easy to challenging; the **ISSAQUAH ALPS TRAILS CLUB** (425/328-0480) offers organized hikes. For the ultimate in townfolk-wildlife bonding, drop in the first weekend of October for **ISSAQUAH SALMON DAYS** (425/392-7024), a celebration—including food, crafts, music, and a parade—marking the return of the salmon that surge their way up Issaquah Creek.

RESTAURANTS

Shanghai Garden / ★★

80 FRONT ST N, ISSAQUAH; 425/313-3188

Owner/chef Hua Te Su takes his food and health very seriously, and Shanghai Garden is also one of the only places that offers authentic Chinese (loosely defined as Mandarin) food. The pink-bathed restaurant and lounge is larger than its sister in Seattle's International District and is part of a small restaurant row on Issaquah's main street. Attentive servers gauge your adventurous spirit before offering more esoteric dishes involving chewy innards. Crispy shrimp pleases any palate—the shellfish are breading-free and sautéed, ensuring a satisfying pop in your mouth. Hand-cut noodles are the star—try the barley green noodles for a healthy and slightly earthier chow mein. Don't forget the succulent pea vines coupled with shrimp or Chinese mushrooms for a fresh side dish. *$$; MC, V; no checks; lunch, dinner every day; full bar; reservations not necessary; at E Sunset Wy.* &

Bainbridge Island

Could these islanders be any friendlier? Spend a little time on Bainbridge and you'll soon understand why. They've got antiques shops, galleries, and a perplexing number of good restaurants. Not to mention stunning natural scenery: **FORT WARD STATE PARK** (2241 Pleasant Beach Dr NE; 206/842-4041) is perfect for picnics and the **BLOEDEL RESERVE** (7571 NE Dolphin Dr; 206/842-7631; open Wed–Sun by appointment) covers 150 gorgeous acres. Their commute is even stress-free: 35 minutes to Seattle on a seagull-chased ferry (see Access and Information in this chapter). And things keep improving: new temptations include the cheery **BLACKBIRD BAKERY** (210 Winslow Wy E; 206/780-1322) and secluded **MOON FISH** restaurant (4738 Lynwood Center Rd NE; 206/780-3473). Fortunately, you can play native too.

RESTAURANTS

Cafe Nola / ★★★

101 WINSLOW WY W, BAINBRIDGE; 206/842-3822

Popularized by sisters Melinda Lucas and Mary Bugarin, Cafe Nola is now run by Kevin and Whitney Warren, who bought the small, sunny corner cafe in

1999. Customers haven't suffered from the ownership change. Formerly a sous-chef at Marco's Supperclub in Seattle, Kevin creates pleasingly eclectic dishes. Popular with lunch crowds are hearty soups—from roasted eggplant to black bean portobello—and the grilled salmon sandwich dressed with seasonal greens. Dinner brings such fare as barbecued duck spring rolls with chile lime dipping sauce; pan-seared scallops over yellow corn grits cakes with roasted-pepper garlic sauce; and not-to-miss desserts, such as triple-layer chocolate hazelnut torte. No smoking. *$$; MC, V; checks OK; lunch Tues–Fri, dinner Tues–Sun, brunch Sat–Sun; beer and wine; reservations recommended; kkw4 dogs@aol.com; at Madison.* &

Ruby's on Bainbridge / ★★
4569 LYNWOOD CENTER RD, BAINBRIDGE; 206/780-9303

With casual French-country style and ruby-colored walls warmed by candles, this is the sort of place you could spend half the day nursing a glass of wine and nibbling herb focaccia bread; fortunately, the wine list is extensive. Better yet, go for the slightly warmed spinach and sorrel *torta* puff-pastry appetizer with cucumber and dill relish. Affable owners Aaron and Maura Crisp offer a full menu that segues from wild mushroom fettuccine to rosemary chicken baked with Bosc pear, Riesling cream, and grapes. If all this leaves you feeling deliciously languid, settle down for a flick at the adorably retro movie house next door. No smoking. *$$; AE, MC, V; checks OK; lunch Fri–Sat, dinner every day; beer and wine; reservations recommended; azenmama@hot mail.com; in Lynwood Center.* &

Streamliner Diner / ★
397 WINSLOW WY E, BAINBRIDGE; 206/842-8595

The island's equivalent of a whistle-stop cafe, this is where ferry commuters congregate for strong java (no espresso) and good grub. As in any self-respecting diner, breakfast—omelets, quiche, and tofu "scramble"—is served all day (7am–2:30pm). For lunch, try the fried two-egg-bacon-and-tomato sandwich or "potatoes deluxe" spiked with scallions and mushrooms and garnished with tomatoes, spinach, and Jack cheese. No smoking. *$; no credit cards; checks OK; breakfast every day, lunch Mon–Sat; no alcohol; reservations not accepted; at Bijune St.*

LODGINGS

The Buchanan Inn / ★★
8494 NE ODD FELLOWS RD, BAINBRIDGE; 206/780-9258 OR 800/598-3926

This beautifully renovated 1912 B&B (formerly an Odd Fellows Hall) is set in one of the island's most picturesque and sunny neighborhoods and run by one of the friendliest teams of innkeepers, Judy and Ron Gibbs. Four spacious suites have large private baths and king- or queen-size beds, separate sitting areas, CD players, coffeemakers, and mini-fridges; gas fireplaces are in two rooms. If you prefer to breakfast in your jammies, request a full or continental breakfast basket in your room. A short stroll away are Fort Ward State Park and the beach (ask Judy for the lowdown on other sights), and it's just steps to the inn's rustic cottage and a bubbling hot tub. Children over 16 OK (under 16 only if entire inn is reserved); no pets (though dogs are on-site). Smoking outside only. Complimentary off-street parking. *$$; AE, DC, DIS, JCB, MC, V; checks OK; jgibbs@buchananinn.com; www.buchananinn.com; at W Blakely.*

Seattle-Tacoma International Airport

LODGINGS

Hilton Seattle Airport Hotel / ★★
17620 PACIFIC HWY S, SEATAC; 206/244-4800 OR 800/HILTONS
An ongoing $53-million redevelopment, to be completed in January 2001, will add 200 rooms (for a total of 400), a health club, and a state-of-the-art conference center to this four-wing hotel. Until then, around 100 rooms, set around a landscaped courtyard with pool and indoor/outdoor Jacuzzi, are available. Inside are the expected complement of desks, computer hookups, irons and ironing boards, and coffeemakers. An exercise room and meeting rooms are available. So is a 24-hour business center. The hotel's restaurant serves all meals. No pets. Smoking rooms available. Limited free lot parking. *$$$; AE, DC, DIS, JCB, MC, V; checks OK; brad_logsdon@hilton.com; www.hilton.com; corner of 176th.* &

Seattle Marriott at Sea-Tac / ★★
3201 S 176TH ST, SEATAC; 206/241-2000 OR 800/228-9290
Those who want to get in and out of town with a minimum of stress appreciate the swift service at this 452-room megamotel about a block from the airport. Convenience doesn't come at the expense of enjoyment. The lobby, with its warm Northwest motif, opens into an enormous atrium complete with indoor pool and two Jacuzzis. Why bother with a standard room? For slightly higher rates, more spacious, handsomely appointed suites are available on the concierge floor and include amenities such as turndown service, hair dryers, irons and ironing boards, and a lounge that serves continental breakfasts and nightly nibbles. All guests have access to a sauna and well-equipped exercise room. A casual dining room offers the usual hotel fare. Pets OK; three smoking floors. Free self-parking lot. *$$$; AE, DC, DIS, JCB, MC, V; checks OK; www.marriott.com; corner of 176th.* &

PUGET SOUND

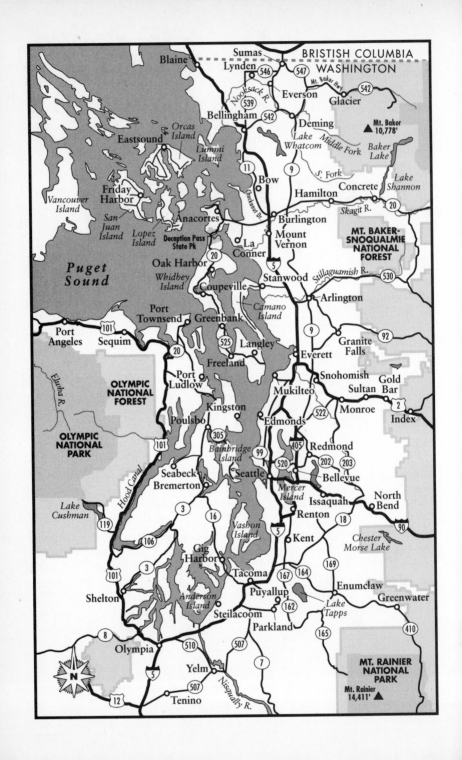

PUGET SOUND

From Olympia at the southern end of Puget Sound to Blaine at the border with Canada, Interstate 5 is flanked by a richly populated, verdantly beautiful stretch of Washington State. Waterways, islands, farmlands and forest, and stunning mountain views dominate the landscape. This region is not only the cradle of the state's port, shipping, fishing, and naval industry, it also offers some of the state's most idyllic getaways.

Driving north from Seattle, the interstate carries you to the port city of Everett, the tulip town of Mount Vernon, and the university community of Bellingham. The area is best explored by leaving the freeway and traveling back-roads, routes that lead to the state's most visited islands—including Whidbey Island and the idyllic San Juan Islands—as well as to numerous waterfront towns and villages—Langley, Coupeville, Anacortes, and La Conner—that invite travelers to linger and explore.

ACCESS AND INFORMATION

Fly into **SEATTLE-TACOMA INTERNATIONAL AIRPORT** (17801 Pacific Hwy S, SeaTac; 206/431-4444)—13 miles south of Seattle and 16 miles north of Tacoma—and you have easy access to Interstate 5. You'll need a car to best explore the region; **CAR RENTAL AGENCIES** at Sea-Tac include Alamo (800/327-9633), Avis (800/331-1212), Hertz (800/654-3131), and National (800/CAR-RENT).

Train travel offers a different view. **AMTRAK** (3035 S Jackson St, Seattle; 206/382-4125 or 800/872-7245) operates out of the King Street Station, with daily runs between Portland and Seattle, and Seattle and Bellingham.

WASHINGTON STATE FERRIES (Pier 52, Seattle; 206/464-6400 or 800/843-3779; www.wsdot.wa.gov/ferries/) provide access to the San Juan Islands, Whidbey, Vashon, and other islands in Puget Sound.

Everett Area

The Everett area extends from Edmonds on the south to Stanwood on the north. US Highway 2 heads east from Everett, and ferries head west from Mukilteo just south of Everett. Timber and fishing were once this Snohomish County seat's raisons d'etre, as were the booms and busts that followed the extraction of those natural resources. Boeing's Paine Field also contributes to the area economy. And though timber still means big business for Everett, the state-of-the-art U.S. naval base here now adds more to the area's growing economy and its ever-increasing population.

Everett

Everett is experiencing new pride, evident in its downtown revitalization. The redevelopment of the **MONTE CRISTO HOTEL**—a historic landmark boarded up for 20 years—created the **EVERETT CENTER FOR THE ARTS** (1507 Wall St; 425/257-8380), a gorgeous home for the Everett Symphony, the Arts Council, and a stunning display of Pilchuck glass. The **EVERETT PERFORMING ARTS CENTER** (2710 Wetmore Ave; 425/257-8600 box office or 888/257-3722) hosts a variety of plays, concerts, dance, and other events.

The **EVERETT AQUASOX** (3802 Broadway; 425/258-3673), the single-A short-season farm team for the Seattle Mariners, draws folks away from Seattle to enjoy baseball at the small, old-fashioned field. Don't miss the chili-dogs!

BOEING'S SOUTH EVERETT PLANT (exit 189 west from I-5 to Hwy 526, follow signs; 206/544-1264; www.boeing.com) offers 90-minute tours of the world's largest building (measured in volume), where you can watch the assembly of the aviation giant's 747s, 767s, and 777s. Tours run Monday through Friday, fill early, and have strict height requirements for children; there's a gift shop with a variety of aviation souvenirs.

RESTAURANTS

Alligator Soul / ★

2013½ HEWITT AVE, EVERETT; 425/259-6311

Casual roadhouse atmosphere—exposed brick, Mardi Gras beads hanging from artwork, hot-pepper lights—and Southern fixings of heaping portions of smoked ribs with a hot, top-rated barbecue sauce give this place its soul. The sides alone could make a meal: jalapeño cornbread, spicy corn relish, cool coleslaw, and creamy potato salad. Other dishes have even diehard Northwest-erners longing for a road trip south; try the Creole bouillabaisse, crawfish étouffée (a special order), catfish gumbo, the Tchoupitoulas Beef Napoleon—a hearty and savory blackened rib-eye steak with garlic mashed potatoes—or fried catfish with hush puppies. Great bread pudding is packed with pecans, peaches, and raisins, and served with a sweet bourbon sauce. *$$; MC, V; checks OK; lunch, dinner every day; beer and wine; reservations recommended (week-ends); alligatorsoul@aol.com; near Broadway.*

The Sisters

2804 GRAND ST, EVERETT; 425/252-0480

This place is as popular as it is funky. Soups such as mulligatawny, gazpacho, or plain old beef barley can be outstanding. Sandwiches range from average deli stuff to more healthful concoctions, including a vegetarian burger made with chopped cashews and sunflower seeds. Among the morning fare are some delights: blueberry or pecan hotcakes, or scrambled eggs with all kinds of extra goodies wrapped in flour tortillas, as well as vegetarian soups and specials. Fresh-squeezed lemonade and strawberry lemonade quench your thirst, a big slice of marionberry pie cures whatever ails you. *$; MC, V; checks OK; break-fast, lunch Mon–Fri; no alcohol; reservations not accepted; in Everett Public Market.* ♿

NORTH PUGET SOUND THREE-DAY TOUR

DAY ONE: From Interstate 5, head into **Everett** for breakfast at **The Sisters**, then go west to the **Mukilteo** ferry. A 20-minute ferry ride puts you at Clinton, on the southeast end of **Whidbey Island**. Exit off the main highway to **Langley**, a cliff-side village overlooking Saratoga Passage toward Camano Island. Between exploring in First Street galleries, antiques shops, and boutiques, head to the **Star Bistro** for lunch, then complete your tour of the town. Check in to the **Inn at Langley**, then enjoy an order of the island's own Penn Cove mussels at **Cafe Langley** (be sure to try them somewhere on the island). Enjoy a soak while watching boats in Saratoga Passage before turning in.

DAY TWO: Breakfast at the Inn gets you ready to head up the island to **Coupeville**. Drop by the **Island County Historical Museum**, tour the exhibits, and watch the video that gives you a look at island history. Get a map for exploring **Ebey's Landing**, then have lunch at **Toby's 1890 Tavern**. Go for a hike on the beach at **Fort Ebey State Park**, particularly inspiring with views west to the water and setting sun. For a rustic, historical experience, overnight at the **Captain Whidbey Inn**, where you also have dinner.

DAY THREE: Breakfast at the inn or at **Knead & Feed**. Continue north on the island, stop at **Deception Pass State Park** for a ground-level view of the furious waters in Deception Pass, then cross the **Deception Pass Bridge** and get a glimpse from above. Swing through **Anacortes** and browse at **Marine Supply and Hardware** or the **Anacortes Museum**. Grab a bite at the **Calico Cupboard**, then head south to La Conner where you can stroll through town and have an early dinner at **Kerstin's**. Take the back route out of La Conner and stop at **Snow Goose Produce**, then rejoin Interstate 5 at Conway, or continue on backroads to **Stanwood**. Check in at the **Camano Island Inn**, relaxing by the fireplace while watching the sun set behind Whidbey Island across Saratoga Passage, where you began your journey.

LODGINGS

The Inn at Port Gardner / ★★

1700 W MARINE VIEW DR, EVERETT; 425/252-6779 OR 888/252-6779
Contemporary industrial chic styling mixes with warm touches—an inviting lobby fireplace and colorful art accents—to create an up-to-the-minute getaway or stay for the corporate traveler. Overlooking the marina, the inn is set back from the Marina Village Inn, and adjacent to the new Lombardi's Italian restaurant. Sophisticated guest rooms are decorated in neutral tones. Suites have separate bedrooms and fireplaces. A continental breakfast is included. *$$–$$$; AE, DC, DIS, MC, V; no checks; inprtgrd@get.net; www.innatportgardner.com; exit 193 off I-5.* &

Marina Village Inn / ★★
1728 W MARINE VIEW DR, EVERETT; 425/259-4040 OR 800/281-7037

🌲 The Puget Sound waterfront location of this 26-room inn on Port Gardner Bay can't be beat, even if its lobby areas are looking a bit tired and dated. Rooms are contemporary with oak furnishings, satellite TV, handcrafted ceramic sinks, trouser presses, and refrigerators; many have jetted tubs. Most have telescopes for gazing out over the water. Book a room on the harbor side; sea lions might be lollygagging in the sun on the nearby jetty. *$$; AE, DC, DIS, MC, V; checks OK; mvi1728@aol.com; gtesupersite.com/marinavilinn; exit 193 off I-5.* &

Mukilteo

On the southwest edge of Everett, Mukilteo is, unfortunately, probably best known for the traffic congestion caused by folks taking the **FERRY TO CLINTON** on Whidbey Island (see Access and Information for this chapter). A block or two south of the ferry terminal (follow signs from freeway), however, are a small **WATERFRONT STATE PARK** (with picnic tables and barbecue pits) and a **HISTORIC LIGHTHOUSE** worth seeing. You can also stroll along the waterfront and fish off the docks.

RESTAURANTS

Charles at Smugglers Cove / ★★
8340 53RD AVE W, MUKILTEO; 425/347-2700

💘 Chef Claude Faure and his wife, Janet Kingma, turned this landmark building (a 1929 speakeasy and distillery set on a bluff above Possession Sound) into an elegant restaurant. The atmosphere is country French, with dining rooms upstairs and down, and a small terrace with Sound views. Such dishes as veal chop with tarragon and *poulet aux crevettes* (breast of chicken with prawns) appear on the classically French menu along with the requisite Gruyère-topped onion soup, and variations on the escargot theme. A classic and savory lunch choice is salad niçoise. Save room for a fancy dessert like crepes suzette or Grand Marnier soufflé. *$$$; AE, MC, V; local checks only; lunch Tues–Fri, dinner Tues–Sat; full bar; reservations recommended; at Hwys 525 and 526.*

Snohomish

This small community southeast of Everett, formerly an active lumber town, now bills itself as the "Antique Capital of the Northwest." Plenty of **ANTIQUE SHOPS** fill the downtown historic district; the **STAR CENTER MALL** (829 2nd; 360/568-2131) is the largest, with 175 dealers from all over the area. When you're through taking in the old, get a new perspective on Snohomish from the air: charter a **SCENIC FLIGHT AT HARVEY FIELD** (9900 Airport Wy; 360/568-1541), take a trip with **AIRIAL HOT AIR BALLOON COMPANY** (10123 Airport

Wy; 360/568-3025), or skydive with the folks at **SNOHOMISH PARACHUTE CENTER** (9912 Airport Wy; 360/568-5960; www.letsgoskydiving.com).

Stop in at **JORDAN'S** (920 1st; 360/568-2020) for lunch, popular with locals for burgers and baked goods (awesome cinnamon rolls). For a slice of something sweet, visit the **SNOHOMISH PIE COMPANY** (915 1st; 360/568-3589).

Stanwood

North of Everett, Stanwood is a sleepy little farm center with Scandinavian heritage, a Midwestern air, and one good reason for a few minutes' sightseeing. Years ago, local daughter Martha Anderson started working at **ROSEMALING** (traditional Norwegian flower painting) and teaching it to her fellow Stanwoodians. Now they've embellished many everyday businesses with charming signs decorated in this genre—not for tourist show as in Leavenworth, but out of an authentic impulse to express their heritage and make Main Street pretty.

Founded in 1971 by local glass artist Dale Chihuly and Seattle art patrons John Hauberg and Anne Gould Hauberg, **PILCHUCK SCHOOL** (206/621-8422) is an internationally renowned glass-art school. Students live and study on this campus, in the midst of a country tree farm. An open house twice each summer gives folks a chance to see craftspeople at work; call for times and directions.

Camano Island

This out-of-the-way island just west of Stanwood is only an hour from Seattle and, logically, many city folk have summer homes here. There's no ferry to catch, so this is a great spot for an easy, low-stress island getaway. **CAMANO ISLAND STATE PARK** (360/387-3031) on the southwest side of the island is a day-use park with picnic shelters and a beach to walk.

LODGINGS

Camano Island Inn / ★★

1054 W CAMANO DR, CAMANO ISLAND; 360/387-0783 OR 888/718-0783

This is a luxurious waterfront inn with spectacular water views. Cozy up in the comfy sitting room with its rustic river-rock fireplace; sink into king featherbeds. Six guest rooms (all with water views) have private bathrooms, which are large and have jetted tubs. Kayaks are available for guest use ($20 per hour); massages can be arranged. *$$; AE, DIS, MC, V; checks OK (in advance); rsvp@camanoislandinn.com; exit 212 from I-5, follow Hwy 532 onto island, then south on E Camano Dr.*

Whidbey Island

Whidbey Island has let just about everyone know that it is officially the longest island in the United States. But they haven't told too many people that Whidbey is one of only eight islands that make up Island County (with Camano, Ben Ure,

Strawberry, Minor, Baby, Smith, and Deception). Named for Capt. Joseph Whidbey, a sailing master for Capt. George Vancouver, Whidbey Island was first surveyed and mapped by the two explorers in 1792. More than 200 years later, its largest employer is the government (thanks to the Oak Harbor navy base). The island boasts pretty towns and communities, historical parks, sandy beaches, and lovely rolling farmland.

Although they have no bike lanes, Whidbey's flat, relatively traffic-free roads make for good warm-weather **BIKING**, especially if you stay off the main highway; call the South Whidbey Information Line (360/221-6765) for information on exploring. Depart from the mainland at Mukilteo (see the Everett Area section in this chapter), about 25 miles north of Seattle, for a 25-minute ferry ride (see Access and Information for this chapter) to Clinton on the south end of the island (expect long waits for cars on sunny weekends). You can also drive onto Whidbey Island at its north end, on Highway 20 just south of Anacortes. Here the island is described from south to north.

Langley

The nicest town on Whidbey carries its small-town virtues well, though it may be getting a little too spit-and-polished for some. With the addition of **LANGLEY VILLAGE**, a charming collection of old-style shops on Second Street, it has grown into a two-street town.

Swap stories with Josh Hauser at **MOONRAKER BOOKS** (209 1st St; 360/221-6962), then head to the antique- and candy-filled gift shop **WAYWARD SON** (22 1st St; 360/221-3911). For singular shopping, try **THE COTTAGE** (210 1st St; 360/221-4747) for heirloom lace and linens; **VIRGINIA'S ANTIQUES** (206 1st St; 360/221-7797), a repository of Asian and American wares; and **SISTER** (208 1st St; 360/221-5735), for unusual, attractive women's clothing. **WHY NOT WHIDBEY** (124 2nd St; 360/221-6090) displays handcrafted items including pottery, baby clothing, kitchen wares, and collectibles from more than 200 Whidbey Island artisans.

Look for original Northwest art, from paintings and pottery to sculpture and glass, at **GASKILL-OLSON GALLERY** (302 1st St; 360/221-2978). Next door at **HELLEBORE GLASS GALLERY** (360/221-2067), you can watch glassblower George Springer at work. **MUSEO** (215 1st St; 360/221-7737) gallery features glass art and handcrafts from regional and national artists.

SAPORI (197 2nd St; 360/221-3211) is a good spot for espresso and light refreshments. Head to **THE DOG HOUSE** (230 1st St; 360/221-9825) for a pitcher of microbrew (18 on tap) after a movie at **THE CLYDE** (213 1st St; 360/221-5525). The pesto pizza by the slice at **LANGLEY VILLAGE BAKERY** (221 2nd St; 360/221-3525) is a local favorite. And the **WHIDBEY ISLAND WINERY** (5237 S Langley Rd; 360/221-2040; open Wed–Sun) has a fine tasting room. Try the rhubarb wine.

RESTAURANTS

Cafe Langley / ★★

I 13 I ST ST, LANGLEY; 360/221-3090

🌲 Owners Shant and Arshavir Garibyan have maintained the sparkling consistency that established this downtown storefront cafe as the town's best bet from the moment it opened. Make a reservation (especially on weekends) and prepare for a fine Mediterranean/Greek dining experience. Don't overdo on the impossibly delicious hummus served with warm, chewy pita bread (other appetizers include Penn Cove mussels in saffron vermouth broth, and crab cakes). The Greek salad is just right before a feast of Mediterranean seafood stew, a lamb shish kebab, or one of the Land of the Sun–kissed preparations of fresh Northwest salmon or halibut, in season. Split the ever-popular Russian cream for dessert. *$$; AE, MC, V; checks OK; lunch Wed–Mon, dinner every day (closed Tues in winter); beer and wine; reservations recommended; www.langley-wa.com/cl; on main street.* &

Star Bistro / ★

201½ I ST ST, LANGLEY; 360/221-2627

An island favorite eatery, the Star (above the Star Store, a steady staple of the Langley shop scene) is a fun, color-splashed place that hops on weekends and after local events. Chef Paul Divina has put together a menu of basic, luscious vacation food—pastry-enclosed French onion soup, creamy oyster stew, spinach and caesar salads, pastas, burgers—along with fancier daily specials that often include seafood. There's a kids' menu and a breezy, sun-drenched deck, and you can pull up a stool at the red-topped bar for excellent martinis or margaritas. *$$; AE, DC, MC, V; no checks; lunch, dinner every day (dinner Tues–Sun in winter); full bar; reservations recommended (weekends); bistro@whidbey.com; www.whidbeynet.net/starbistro; on main street.*

Trattoria Giuseppe / ★

4141 E HWY 525, LANGLEY; 360/341-3454

You might not take a second look at Trattoria Giuseppe, in a little strip mall out on Highway 525—but you'd be making a mistake. Locals rave about the Italian food here. Inside, the scent of garlic and the country taverna decor are reminiscent of little places in the Tuscan countryside. Penn Cove mussels here are prepared marinara, with fresh tomatoes, garlic, and basil. We like the fusilli primavera, with vegetables, prawns, and scallops, and the *salmone con spinaci*, fresh salmon served over a bed of sautéed spinach with lemon butter sauce. Finish the meal with a traditional Italian dessert like cannoli, gelato, or tiramisù. Come Friday or Saturday night and enjoy live jazz or classical piano. *$$; AE, DIS, MC, V; checks OK; lunch Mon–Fri, dinner every day; full bar; reservations recommended (weekends); at Langley Rd.*

LODGINGS

Boatyard Inn / ★★

200 WHARF ST, LANGLEY; 360/221-5120

The industrial look of the green siding and corrugated metal roofs of this inn meshes well with Langley's still-colorful working waterfront. The place is so close to the water that the tide rises up against the first floor. Big windows, pine accents, and back-to-basics Eddie Bauer-esque Northwest furnishings characterize the Boatyard's 10 huge, breezy suites (the smallest room is 600 square feet), each endowed with a gas fireplace, galley kitchen, queen-size bed topped with cozy flannel coverlets, sofa bed, cable TV, private deck, and water view. Loft units are suitable for families or small groups. *$$$; AE, DC, DIS, MC, V; local checks only; boatyard@whidbey.com; www.boat yardinn.com; take Wharf St downhill.* &

Chauntecleer House, Dove House, and Potting Shed Cottages / ★★

5081 SARATOGA RD, LANGLEY; 360/221-5494 OR 800/637-4436

Our only quibble with these gorgeous cottages on a quiet bluff just north of downtown Langley is that it's too hard to choose one. Decorating these hideaways was a labor of love for transplanted Southerner Bunny Meals, and it shows. We prefer Chauntecleer House, but only by a nose (or should we say a beak: Chauntecleer is a Chaucerian term for "rooster," and the theme is evident throughout), for its sunny yellow walls, panoramic view of Saratoga Passage, and open-hearthed wood-burning fireplace. Upstairs in the bedroom, the theme is Northwest nautical. Dove House doesn't share the view, but it is charmingly decorated in the style of a fishing lodge, with a wonderful mixture of Northwest and Southwest art and furniture (the bronze otter was sculpted by Georgia Gerber, Seattle's Pike Place Market Rachel-the-pig artist). A wood stove adds coziness, and a second bedroom has bunks if you want to bring the kids. The newest cottage and the smallest of three, the Potting Shed has a whimsical garden theme that plays out in the hand-painted sinks and big "twig" bed. It also has a two-person jetted tub, kitchenette, and glass-front wood stove, so cozy down and enjoy the water view. A full breakfast is left in each kitchen. Chauntecleer and Dove Houses have outdoor hot tubs. *$$$; AE, MC, V; checks OK; bunny@dovehouse.com; www.dovehouse.com; follow 2nd St north from town.*

Country Cottage of Langley / ★

215 6TH ST, LANGLEY; 360/221-8709 OR 800/713-3860

Innkeepers Kathy and Bob Annecone spiffed up this collection of five cottages on 2 acres overlooking downtown Langley. Newest and largest is Cabernet Cottage with a burgundy carpet and wine-country theme; we also like the Captain's Cove with its nautical theme, and the Whidbey Rose with a pretty floral look; all have water views, gas fireplaces, and Jacuzzi tubs. All cottages have private baths, feather beds and down comforters, TVs and VCRs (with a selection of videos), refrigerators, and coffeemakers. A full breakfast is served in the muraled dining room of the main house, a restored 1920s farmhouse, or may be brought to your room on request. *$$$; AE, DIS, MC, V; checks OK; bygonera@whidbeyisland.com; www.acountrycottage.com; off Langley Rd.*

Inn at Langley / ★★★

400 1ST ST, LANGLEY; 360/221-3033

It's difficult to conceive of a more idyllic getaway, or one more evocative of the Pacific Northwest, than Paul and Pam Schell's (yes, Seattle's Mayor Schell) first private venture, built elegantly into the bluff over Saratoga Passage. Architect Alan Grainger designed the building in a marriage of three themes: Frank Lloyd Wright style, Northwest ruggedness, and Pacific Rim tranquility. Inside this rough-hewn, cedar-shingled building are 24 rooms finely decorated with an eye for pleasing detail: simple Asian-influenced furnishings, trimmings of three different woods, and quarry-tiled bathrooms with hooks made from alder twigs. Adjacent is a Jacuzzi, from which you can watch boat traffic on the passage and the flicker of your fireplace through the translucent shoji-style screen. Every room of the four-story inn views the waterfront; we prefer the upper-level rooms. Two new freestanding townhouse cottages—with an upstairs (entry-level) living room/great room, and downstairs bedroom and master bath—just east of the inn offer more expansive and expensive options in the same soothing and stylish manner. A small conference room is equipped with every business necessity. In the morning, guests gather in the dining room for a continental spread. Five-course prix-fixe dinners are served on weekends (by reservation). Diners are met at the door with glasses of sherry, which they sip while chef Steve Nogal delivers his appetite-whetting spiel. It's an evening-long celebration of Northwest foods, a delightful indulgence that can pay off in a fine—if occasionally flawed—meal. Portions are large, so pace yourself. *$$$–$$$$; AE, MC, V; local checks only; www.innatlangley.com; edge of town.* ♿

Island Tyme / ★

4940 S BAYVIEW, LANGLEY; 360/221-5078 OR 800/898-8963

Newly built Victorian-style inns seem to be all the rage these days: you get the romance of the turrets and gables without the plumbing problems and space limitations. At Island Tyme, on a quiet 10 acres about 2 miles from downtown Langley, innkeepers Cliff and Carol Wisman raise pheasants that are kept in a large aviary, as well as pygmy goats. Rooms are geared toward romance, most notably the Heirloom Suite, which has a fireplace, two-person jetted tub, and private deck. All five rooms have private baths, TVs, and VCRs, with videos for guests' use. One room allows pets. *$$; AE, MC, V; checks OK; islandty@whidbey.com; www.moriah.com/islandtyme/; 2 miles from Langley, call for directions.* ♿

Lone Lake Cottages and Breakfast / ★

5260 S BAYVIEW RD, LANGLEY; 360/321-5325

Dolores Meeks's place is still one of the most interesting B&Bs around. The rooms have an undeniable, eccentric charm and are individually decorated with Oriental antiques. One of the four is aboard the tiny *Whidbey Queen*, a beamed-ceiling stern-wheeler permanently moored on the lake. Guests staying on the *Queen* enjoy the same extras as in the other lakeside cottages: fireplace, soaking tub for two, VCR, and CD player. The one-bedroom Terrace Cottage is the nicest of the landlubber's accommodations; it looks into the domed top of a stunning aviary housing some 300 rare birds. A honeymoon suite in front of the main house is cool and comfortable, and sports a grand lake view, fireplace, kitchen, and double jetted tub. Exotic ducks, pheasant, quail, peacocks, and swans mingle in an outdoor pen. Each room has a full kitchen stocked with breakfast makings for the first two days of your stay, plus seasonings for the barbecue should you get lucky and land a trout or two. Guests are welcome to use the private beach, canoes, rowboat, and bikes. *$$$; no credit cards; checks OK; www.lonelake.com; 5½ miles from Clinton ferry.*

Saratoga Inn / ★

201 CASCADE AVE, LANGLEY; 360/221-5801

It's a two-minute walk from downtown to the Saratoga Inn, which has architectural touches reminiscent of New England. Each of 15 distinctive view rooms is festooned in warm plaids or prints and furnished with a gas fireplace, an armoire, and an entertainment center. You may choose to have breakfast delivered to your chamber. Solitude seekers opt for the separate Carriage House, with a full kitchen, stone fireplace, and king-size sleigh bed. The Saratoga Inn sometimes hosts small conferences in the richly appointed Library Boardroom. Everyone's welcome in the tearoom, where guests socialize over civilized beverages. The prestigious Four Sisters Inn group manages the property. *$$$; AE, DC, MC, V; no checks; www.foursisters.com; corner of 2nd.*

Villa Isola / ★★★

5489 S COLES RD, LANGLEY; 360/221-5052 OR 800/246-7323

Tucked into a pine-studded pastoral landscape, Gwen and Gary Galeotti's version of an Italian country villa re-creates the slow, sweet life of the Old Country. The 4 acres are landscaped with rhododendrons, flower beds, and a restful water fountain, and guests have the inspired villa space—defined by walls stenciled with grapevines, floor-to-ceiling windows, and modern European furnishings—to themselves. Six large, sumptuous suites named after legendary Italian towns continue the Mediterranean motif; each has an oversize bath (five have jetted tubs), queen-size bed, and down comforter; two suites share a deck. One of the newest suites—the largest—on the top floor, has skylights, a fireplace, and a wall of windows. Espresso and delicacies are served cafe-style in the sunny dining room or on the adjacent deck. Borrow the inn's mountain bikes or engage in a game of boccie (Italian lawn bowling) on the regulation-size court. Gwen keeps the living room flush with CDs and board games, and the kitchen stocked with Italian desserts. *$$$; MC, V; checks OK; villa@villaisola.com; www.villa isola.com; 2 miles southeast of Langley.*

Freeland

The unincorporated town of Freeland (population 1,544) is home to **NICHOLS BROTHERS BOAT BUILDERS** (5400 S Cameron Rd; 360/331-5500), manufacturers of cruise boats and stern-wheelers, and the town's largest employer. **FREELAND PARK** on Holmes Harbor has picnic tables, a play area, and a sandy beach.

LODGINGS

Cliff House / ★★★

727 WINDMILL RD, FREELAND; 360/331-1566

Seattle architect Arne Bystrom designed this dramatic house, which makes an extraordinary getaway. The striking home on a cliff above Admiralty Inlet is full of light from lofty windows, centering on a 30-foot-high atrium open to the weather and filled with native plants, and a sunken living room with a wood-burning fireplace. For a staggering $425 a night, two of you have use of the entire luxuriously furnished house and its 14 acres of woods. There are hammocks, benches, and a platform deck with a hot tub high on the cliff. The elfish Sea Cliff Cottage is a more modestly priced ($175) option that includes a queen-size feather bed, a kitchenette, and a deck overlooking the water. Peggy Moore sets the country kitchen table (in both houses) with a continental breakfast. *$$$$; no credit cards; checks OK; 2-night min; wink@whidbey.com; www. cliffhouse.net; Bush Point Rd to Windmill Rd.*

Greenbank

Here on a narrow part of the island, stop by **WHIDBEY'S GREENBANK FARM** (765 E Wonn Rd; 360/678-7700), at one time the largest loganberry farm in the country. Sample the Loganberry Liqueur or Whidbey Port, and pick a pretty picnicking spot.

LODGINGS

Guest House Log Cottages / ★★

24371 HWY 525, GREENBANK; 360/678-3115

We love this place, partly because playing house here fulfills long-lost storybook dreams. Seven varied dwellings are set in a pastoral clearing fringed with woodlands. The studio Carriage House offers a queen-size feather bed. King-size feather beds and river-rock fireplaces grace the pine-log Emma Jane Tennessee Cottage, as well as the Kentucky Pine Cottage. Comparatively modest and less expensive, but just as cozy, is the Farm Guest Cottage. The Log Cabin has stained-glass windows, and you can view the pond from the bed or deck; there's also a kitchen and a whirlpool tub for two. But everybody's favorite is the Lodge, a $310-a-night custom-built log home-for-two perched at the edge of a spring-fed wildlife pond with a broad deck and views of the Cascades and the Sound from the loft bedroom. A 24-foot-tall rugged stone fireplace plays center stage in a space that combines the old (a wood stove next to the greenhouse breakfast nook) with the new (two whirlpool tubs, a dishwasher). Breakfast makings for the first two days of your stay are left in the fully equipped kitchens. New is the Wildflower Suite with a queen-size bed, jetted tub, minikitchen, and private entrance. All accommodations have TVs and VCRs (the video library includes 400 flicks). All cottages have whirlpool spas for two. Also on the grounds are an outdoor pool and hot tub. *$$$; AE, DIS, MC, V; checks OK; guesthse@whidbey.net; www.whidbey.net/logcottages; 1 mile south of Greenbank.*

Coupeville

The second-oldest incorporated town in the state dates back to the mid-1850s; no wonder the town has a strict agenda of historic preservation. Coupeville's downtown consists of a half-dozen gift and antique shops and several restaurants. A must-see gallery is the **JAN MCGREGOR STUDIO** (19 NW Front St; 360/678-5015; open weekends year-round, every day in summer). McGregor has studied pottery around the world and specializes in rare porcelain techniques. **ISLAND COUNTY HISTORICAL MUSEUM** (NW Alexander and Front St; 360/678-3310) tells the story of Whidbey Island's early history. Annual community events include the **COUPEVILLE ARTS & CRAFTS FESTIVAL**, the second weekend in August, and March's **PENN COVE MUSSEL FESTIVAL**; for information, contact the Central Whidbey Chamber of Commerce (302 N Main St; 360/678-5434).

TOBY'S 1890 TAVERN (8 NW Front St; 360/678-4222) is a good spot for burgers, beer, and a game of pool. Homemade breads, pies, soups, and salads make a memorable meal at **KNEAD & FEED** (4 NW Front St; 360/678-5431), and real coffee lives at **GREAT TIMES ESPRESSO** (12 NW Front St; 360/678-5358) alongside New York–style pizza.

An extra bike lane follows Engle Road 3 miles south of Coupeville to **FORT CASEY STATE PARK** (360/678-4519), a decommissioned fort with splendid gun mounts, beaches, and commanding bluffs. Explore the magnificent bluff and beach at the nearby 17,000-acre **EBEY'S LANDING NATIONAL HISTORIC RESERVE** and **FORT EBEY STATE PARK** (360/678-4636). The **KEYSTONE FERRY** (360/678-6030) connecting Whidbey to Port Townsend on the Olympic Peninsula leaves from Admiralty Head, just south of Fort Casey.

LODGINGS

Anchorage Inn / ★

807 N MAIN ST, COUPEVILLE; 360/376-8282

Another "new Victorian" inn, the Anchorage offers moderately priced lodgings on Coupeville's main street. New owners have changed the style of the rooms, adding antiques to once basic rooms. Six rooms have private baths and cable

TV; we especially like the water-view room with the four-poster king bed, the room in the turret, and the Crow's Nest suite with fireplace at the top of the house. All rooms have TVs, VCRs, and cable. Full breakfast (included) is served in the antique-filled dining room. *$$; DIS, MC, V; checks OK; anchorag@ whidbey.net; www.anchorageinn.com; on Main St.*

Captain Whidbey Inn / ★

2072 W CAPTAIN WHIDBEY INN RD, COUPEVILLE; 360/678-4097

Owner John Colby Stone and innkeeper Frank J. Pustka have gone to every effort to make sure that little changes about this old Penn Cove inn, built in 1907 of sturdy and shiny-with-use madrona logs. In such a beloved place, history sometimes outranks comfort and quiet. The walls are so thin they seem to talk, sniffle, and sneeze. Upstairs, 12 smallish, almost shiplike original hotel rooms (two are suites) have marble sinks in the rooms but share two bathrooms, one for each gender. Stay clear of rooms above the bar, unless you're planning to be up until closing time. Four furnished cabins include fireplaces and baths. Best bets are 13 lagoon rooms, each with private bath and an inlet-view veranda. A particularly nice touch is the combination of feather beds and down comforters on all beds. The public rooms—a lantern-lit dining room with creaky wooden floors that seem to slope toward the sea; the deck (in warm weather); a woodsy bar; a well-stocked library; and a folksy fireplace room—are quite attractive. The restaurant continues to feature, naturally, Penn Cove mussels (you're looking at the mussel beds as you indulge), other fresh seafood, and greens from the inn's elaborate gardens. *$$; AE, MC, V; checks OK; info@captainwhidbey.com; www.captainwhidbey.com; off Madrona Wy.*

Fort Casey Inn / ★

1124 S ENGLE RD, COUPEVILLE; 360/678-8792

Built in 1909 as officers' quarters for nearby Fort Casey, this neat row of nine houses offers tidy, no-frills accommodations with a historical bent. Houses are divided into two-bedroom duplexes. Decor consists mostly of tied-rag rugs, old military photographs, and renditions of early U.S. presidents. Garrison Hall, with a small reception area and its own private bedroom and bath, can be rented for weddings or private parties. Unlike most B&Bs on Whidbey, Fort Casey Inn welcomes kids and is a fun place to explore. Ask the manager anything you need to know about Fort Casey State Park, the bird sanctuary at Crockett Lake, or nearby Ebey's Landing National Historic Reserve. Continental breakfast included. *$$; AE, MC, V; checks OK; 2 miles west of Coupeville.*

The Old Morris Farm / ★

105 W MORRIS RD, COUPEVILLE; 360/678-6586 OR 800/936-6586

Owners Mario Chodorowski and Marilyn Randock have successfully transformed their 1909 farmhouse into an elegant countryside B&B. Five guest rooms are individual in style and decor, yet reflect the home's colonial feeling.

A new offering is a Treehouse Suite with sitting room and fireplace, two queen bedrooms and one private bath, and balconies in the trees. Enjoy a grand breakfast in the red, red dining room, and evening hors d'oeuvres in the sun-washed living room. Small dinners are available by arrangement. Stroll the grounds and flower, vegetable, and herb gardens. A small gift shop includes locally made walking sticks. *$$; MC, V; checks OK; maricorp@whidbey.net; www.oldmorris farm.com; 3 miles from Coupeville overpass.*

Oak Harbor

Named for the thriving Garry oak trees, Oak Harbor is Whidbey's largest city and home to **WHIDBEY ISLAND NAVAL AIR STATION**, a large air base for tactical electronic warfare squadrons; group tours are available by advance reservation (360/257-2286). For the most part, Oak Harbor is engulfed in new and retired military folk.

An interesting stop is **LAVENDER HEART** (4233 N DeGraff Rd; 360/675-3987), which manufactures floral gifts on a 12-acre former holly farm. From the gift store, you can peek at the impressive 1,000-square-foot production facility. Kids at heart should visit **BLUE FOX DRIVE-IN THEATRE** and **BRATTLAND GO-KARTS** (1403 Monroe Landing Rd; 360/675-5667; www.bluefox drivein.com), 2 miles south of Oak Harbor. The outdoor drive-in has been a fixture on the island for years.

RESTAURANTS

Kasteel Franssen / ★

33575 HWY 20 (AULD HOLLAND INN), OAK HARBOR; 360/675-0724
A half mile north of Oak Harbor, this motel with the trademark windmill is just fine, if a shade close to the highway; the restaurant, however, is quite delightful. Kasteel Franssen, owned and operated by Joe and Elisa Franssen, has a regal, European feel and a solid reputation among locals, a big gas fireplace, and a lively piano bar. Chef and co-owner Scott Fraser of Vancouver, BC, oversees the toque, and the results are pleasing. Dinners include seafood, chicken, and beef, but Fraser also prepares game, including caribou and pheasant. Particularly good is beef tenderloin sautéed and served with a brandy Dijonnaise cream sauce. As for the inn, some upper-story rooms have antiques, and six impressive-looking rooms have hot tubs. It has a tennis court, hot tub, outdoor pool, and children's play area. Rates include continental breakfast. *$$; AE, DC, MC, V; local checks only; dinner every day (Mon–Sat in winter); full bar; reservations recommended; www.kasteel.franssen; 8 miles south of Deception Pass.*

Lucy's Mi Casita

31359 HWY 20, OAK HARBOR; 360/675-4800
It doesn't look like much, lined up along a strip of fast-food joints and automotive stores and decorated with old calendars, beer-bottle-cap curtains, and cutouts of flamenco dancers, but here Al and Lucy Enriquez keep

locals coming back with homemade Mexican food and lively atmosphere. Upstairs is a lounge with a balcony (watch out for the 27-ounce Turbo Godzilla margarita). The large menu includes shredded beef tacos, seafood burritos, and Lucy's authentic refried beans; ingredients include chile poblano imported from Mexico, tortillas shipped from California, and homemade hot sauce. Don't miss the *entomatadas*—tortillas topped with tomato sauce, cheese, and onion—a dish from Lucy's hometown of Chihuahua. *$; AE, DIS, MC, V; local checks only; lunch, dinner every day; full bar; reservations recommended (weekend); on main drag.*

Deception Pass State Park

The beautiful, treacherous gorge at Deception Pass has a lovely, if crowded— it's the state's most popular—park (41229 Hwy 20; 360/675-2417). It offers 3,600 acres of prime camping land, forests, and beach. Located at the north end of the island, the park's centerpiece—a stunning steel bridge (actually two spans) that connects Whidbey and Fidalgo Islands—is not to be missed; park in the highway pullouts at either end and walk across. **STROM'S SHRIMP/FOUNTAIN AND GRILL** (1481 Hwy 20; 360/293-2531), just north of the pass, sells fresh seafood for your cookout. They also grill up a mean oysterburger.

The Skagit Valley

To travelers on Interstate 5, the Skagit Valley is little more than a blur—except in spring, when the lush farmlands are brilliantly swathed in daffodils (mid-Mar–mid-Apr), tulips (Apr–early May), and irises (mid-May–mid-June). The pastoral countryside is flat and ideal for bicyclists, except for the gridlock that occurs on small farm lanes during the annual **TULIP FESTIVAL** (360/428-5959; usually late Mar–early Apr). Mount Vernon, the county seat, is all about fresh food and beautiful flowers, products of surrounding valley farms. For information on the many harvest festivals—June is strawberry month, September apple month, and October redleaf month—call the **MOUNT VERNON CHAMBER OF COMMERCE** (117 N 1st St, Ste 4; 360/428-8547).

Mount Vernon

Mount Vernon is the Big City to residents of surrounding Skagit and Island Counties, and a college town to a surprising number of local folk, even though Skagit Valley College is but a small school on the outskirts of town. Browse **SCOTT'S BOOKSTORE** (121 Freeway Dr; 360/336-6181) in the historic Granary Building at the north end of town, then have a pastry at the **CALICO CUPBOARD** (121-B Freeway Dr; 360/336-3107) next door. Or drop into the **SKAGIT RIVER BREWING CO.** (404 S 3rd; 360/336-2884) to sample a glass (or two) of hearty house-brewed suds, good pub grub, and weekend music. The **CHUCK WAGON**

DRIVE INN (800 N 4th; 360/336-2732) offers 50 different burgers, electric trains, and the world's largest collection of ceramic whiskey-bottle cowboys.

LITTLE MOUNTAIN PARK (exit 225/Anderson Rd off I-5, go east, then north to park entrance off Blackburn Rd) has a terrific picnic spot, plus a knockout vista of the valley—look for migratory trumpeter swans in February.

RESTAURANTS

Pacioni's Pizzeria / ★

606 S 1ST ST, MOUNT VERNON; 360/336-3314

Pizza is why you come here. And to watch new owners, husband/wife team Andrew Glocker and Glenda Downs, hand-toss the pizza dough into the air (remember the mad Italian baker in *Moonstruck?*). Vegetarian options have expanded to include the Mad Greek—feta cheese, sun-dried tomatoes, garlic, kalamata olives—and the Ala 'Biermann—roasted red peppers, sweet onions, fresh rosemary, and walnuts. Everything is made to order. *$; MC, V; checks OK; lunch Tues–Sat, dinner Mon–Sat; beer and wine; reservations not accepted; in old downtown.* &

La Conner

La Conner was founded in 1867 by John Conner, a trading-post operator, who named the town after his wife, Louisa A. Conner. Much of what you see today was built before railroads arrived in the late 1880s, when the fishing and farming communities of Puget Sound traded almost entirely by water. In an age of conformity and efficiency, the town became a literal backwater, and something of a haven for nonconformists (Wobblies, WWII COs, McCarthy-era escapees, beatniks, hippies, and bikers), always with a fair smattering of artists and writers, including Mark Tobey, Morris Graves, Guy Anderson, and Tom Robbins.

This long-standing live-and-let-live attitude has allowed the neighboring Native American Swinomish community to contribute to the exceptional cultural richness of La Conner. Even merchants here have created a unique American bazaar with shops like **COTTONS** (608 S 1st; 360/466-5825) with comfortable—what else?—cotton clothing; **NASTY JACK'S ANTIQUES** (1st and Morris Sts; 360/466-3209) with American and European treasures; **TWO MOONS** (620 S 1st; 360/466-1920) gallery of pottery, art glass, and photography; the **OLIVE SHOPPE** (101 N 1st; 360/466-4101) with olives for tasting and buying; and **O'LEARY'S BOOKS** (609 S 1st; 360/466-1305).

TILLINGHAST SEED CO. (623 Morris St; 360/466-3329) is the oldest operating retail and mail-order seed store in the Northwest (since 1885), and also has a wonderful nursery, florist shop, and general store. **GO OUTSIDE** (111 Morris; 360/466-4836) is a small but choice garden and garden-accessory store. If all this shopping leaves you in need of respite, stop by the stylish **LA CONNER BREWING CO.** (117 S 1st; 360/466-1415) for a fine selection of ales and tasty wood-fired pizzas. Kids like **WHISKER'S CAFE** (128 S 1st; 360/466-1008), a casual, easygoing burger stop; it's right on the dock.

ART'S ALIVE IN LA CONNER

Notice the quality of the light when you're in La Conner. Sometimes moody, sometimes bright, it has shaped the character of this town. In the 1940s, this picturesque waterfront village drew artists such as Mark Tobey, Kenneth Callahan, Morris Graves, and others, whose work was influenced by the Skagit Delta—its landscape, Native people, lifestyle, and especially its light. They became world famous and collectively are known as **the Northwest School**. Their work is on permanent, albeit rotating, display on the upper (second) floor of the Museum of Northwest Art (see below).

Since those days, La Conner has attracted artists, especially each November when the community hosts **"Art's Alive"** (360/466-4778 or 888/642-9284)—a weekend festival with galleries and specialty stores such as the **Wood Merchant** (709 1st St; 360/466-4741), showcasing the work of modern Northwest artists and artisans. The **Museum of Northwest Art** (121 South 1st St; 360/466-4446, www.museumof nwart.org) preserves, collects, and shows exclusively the work of Northwest artists. And while it shows work from around the country and world, the quality of the work displayed in the **La Conner Quilt Museum** (703 S 2nd St; 360/466-4288), which sometimes appear to be paintings in fabric, is in keeping with the artistic spirit of the town.

—Jena MacPherson

GACHES MANSION (703 S 2nd; 360/466-4288), home to the not-to-be-missed **QUILT MUSEUM**, is a wonderful example of American Victorian architecture, filled with period furnishings and sporting a widow's walk that looks out on the entire Skagit Valley. The **MUSEUM OF NORTHWEST ART** (121 S 1st; 360/466-4446; open Tues–Sun) is worth a visit, especially for its collection of Northwest glass art. If you come into La Conner via the Conway exit off Interstate 5, stop at **SNOW GOOSE PRODUCE** (on Fir Island Rd; 360/445-6908) for an ice cream cone in a homemade waffle cone. You can buy tulips here in the spring, as well as local produce, specialty food items, and fresh seafood (including precooked Hood Canal shrimp, a perfect snack).

RESTAURANTS

Calico Cupboard / ★

720 S 1ST, LA CONNER (AND BRANCHES); 360/466-4451

🌲 It's awfully cute—Laura Ashley meets Laura Ingalls Wilder—but the bakery is the reason to go, turning out excellent carrot muffins, pecan tarts, shortbread, raspberry bars, currant scones, apple Danishes, and more. Our advice for avoiding the weekend crowds: Buy your goodies from the bakery's takeout counter and find a sunny bench by the water. Hearty waffle and omelet breakfasts are offered, but most folks come for the pastries. Two other Calicos are in Anacortes (901 Commercial Ave; 360/293-7315) and

Mount Vernon (121-B Freeway Dr; 360/336-3107). *$; no credit cards; checks OK; breakfast, lunch every day (early dinner Thurs–Sat in Mount Vernon); beer and wine; reservations not accepted; on main drag.*

Kerstin's / ★★

505 S 1ST, LA CONNER; 360/466-9111

The former location of Andiamo and The Black Swan, with its postage-stamp lower level and upstairs dining room that views Swinomish Channel—has a new duo that's likely to stay a while—especially considering the local raves. Chef and co-owner David Poor (formerly operated La Petite in Anacortes) and his wife, Kerstin, a former ballet dancer from New York, have lightened up these charming old main street cottage-style digs. Poor grew up in Anacortes with oysters and lamb as his favorite foods. While his menu changes seasonally, count on two entrees—moist, fall-off-the-bone-tender lamb shank served with cabernet sauce over roasted-garlic risotto, and Samish Island oysters, baked in the shell with garlic cilantro butter, and a small kick of Tabasco. David is particularly proud of the vegetarian special, a savory, layered dish of roasted vegetables including portobello mushrooms, zucchini, roasted red pepper, sautéed spinach, carmelized red onions, and eggplant. *$$; AE, DC, MC, V; local checks only; dinner Thurs–Mon (lunch in spring and summer); full bar; reservations recommended (weekends); dpoor@fidalgo.net; east side of 1st.*

La Conner Seafood & Prime Rib House / ★

614 1ST ST, LA CONNER; 360/466-4014

Every weekend, those in the know drop in to get their names on the waiting list, then pop out for 20 minutes of window shopping. Their reward is excellent seafood (pasta with fresh Dungeness crab, or baby Rock Point oysters sautéed with fresh fennel), and the young are happy with fish-and-chips. Prime rib dinners come in three sizes (large, regular, and lite); or try it in a sandwich—rib dip or with blue cheese—for lunch. The Possessed by Chocolate brownie-torte dessert is a specialty. In warm weather, diners flee the split-level dining room of channel-view tables for the ample outdoor seating on the deck. *$$; AE, DC, DIS, MC, V; checks OK; lunch, dinner every day; full bar; reservations recommended (weekends); www.laconnerseafood.com; on waterfront.* ♿

Palmers Restaurant and Pub / ★★

205 WASHINGTON, LA CONNER; 360/466-4261
416 MYRTLE ST, MOUNT VERNON; 360/336-9699

Palmers continues to be La Conner's favorite restaurant. Thomas and Danielle Palmer's place is perched on a knoll just behind town at the far end of the La Conner Country Inn (see review). Locals like the hobbitlike pub with wall murals painted by La Conner artists. For a more elegant atmosphere, two rooms upstairs have lace curtains on the west-facing windows that draw in the golden evening sun, or a wood stove to take off the chill on winter evenings. The deck is pleasant too. Dinners are reliable; the pepper-crusted pork tenderloin with fresh rosemary is flavorful and delicious. A sautéed breast of duckling with fresh ginger and raspberry demi-glace shows the kitchen can work just as successfully with more exotic offerings. The new, second Palmers in Mount Vernon, is a more lively hangout than the original. *$$; AE, MC, V; checks OK; lunch, dinner every day (lunch Sat–Sun in off season); full bar; reservations recommended (weekends); at 2nd.*

LODGINGS

The Heron in La Conner / ★★

117 MAPLE ST, LA CONNER; 360/466-4626 OR 877/883-8899

The Heron is one of the prettiest hostelries in town, with 12 jewel-box rooms. Splurge on room 31, the Bridal Suite, with Jacuzzi and gas fireplace, or room 32, with gas fireplace, spacious sitting area, and a wonderful view of the Skagit Valley and Cascades. Downstairs is an elegant living room with wing chairs and a formal breakfast/dining room, where a continental breakfast is served. Out back, have a barbecue in the stone fire pit or slip into the hot tub. *$$; AE, MC, V; checks OK; heroninn@ncia.com; edge of town.*

Hotel Planter / ★

715 S 1ST ST, LA CONNER; 360/466-4710 OR 800/488-5409

A hotel since 1907, the Victorian-style brick establishment has known the most famous (and infamous) characters of La Conner's colorful past. Current owner Don Hoskins used his connoisseur's eye and artisan's care to create a style that is a tasteful blend of past (original woodwork staircase and entrance) and present (private baths and armoire-hidden TVs in every room). Four rooms face the waterfront (and the often noisy main street); four others overlook a Renaissance garden courtyard (with a hot tub guests use by reserving time); four have limited views. The staff, well versed on the Skagit Valley, is exemplary. *$$; AE, MC, V; checks OK; south end of main street.*

La Conner Channel Lodge / ★★

205 N 1ST ST, LA CONNER; 360/466-1500 OR 888/466-4113

At the edge of Swinomish Channel, the Channel Lodge is an urban version of its more casual cousin, the La Conner Country Inn, a few blocks inland (see review). It's an appealing place, due mainly to its prime waterfront location. Your fireplace (gas) is lit upon your arrival, and some rooms have jetted tubs with a channel view. (If you're not splurging for a splash, request a channel-view room away from, or at least not directly below, those with potentially noisy waterjets.) Decks are nooks just big enough for a chair while you watch the tugs work the waterway. The continental breakfast includes fresh fruit, pastries, and homemade granola. *$$$; AE, DC, MC, V; checks OK; www.laconnerlodging. com; north end of town.* ⅜

La Conner Country Inn / ★

107 S 2ND ST, LA CONNER; 360/466-3101 OR 888/466-4113

Despite its name, the La Conner Country Inn is more of a classy motel than a true country inn. All 28 rooms have gas fireplaces, and sport country pine furnishings, pretty floral bedspreads, and armchairs. The inn is especially accommodating to families; rooms with two double beds are generously sized. Complimentary breakfasts are served in the library, where an enormous fieldstone fireplace and comfy couches beckon you to read awhile. Check out the cozy Bird's Nest on the second floor, if it's not being used for a meeting. *$$; AE, DC, MC, V; checks OK; www.laconnerlodging.com; downtown off Morris.* &

Skagit Bay Hideaway / ★★

17430 GOLDENVIEW AVE, LA CONNER; 360/466-2262 OR 888/466-2262

A sybaritic and romantic spot, this Northwest shingle-style cottage, designed by architect Earlene Beckes and operated by her and partner Kevin Haberly, is a waterfront hideaway that offers privacy and luxury. From two 600-square-foot suites (with mini-kitchens and double-headed showers), you can watch the sun set over the water and island views from your own rooftop spa, or enjoy a fire in your own cozy living room. There's also a separate guest house. *$$–$$$; AE, DIS, MC, V; checks OK; hideaway@skagit bay.com; www. skagitbay.com; 1½ miles west of La Conner across Rainbow Bridge.*

White Swan Guest House / ★★

15872 MOORE RD (FIR ISLAND), LA CONNER; 360/445-6805

"It reminds guests of Grannie's farmhouse," says affable host Peter Goldfarb of his classic B&B that's been a popular fixture for over 14 years on Fir Island, halfway between the La Conner exit (at Conway) off Interstate 5 and the town itself. Poplars line the driveway, Adirondack chairs dot the garden, and the grounds are full of perennials. Tranquil farm fields stretch beyond. The house is splashed with warm yellow, salmon, evergreen, and peach wall tones and fabric accents, and seems to soak up the sunlight—even in the rain. Pamper yourself with a soak in the large claw-footed tub (three guest rooms share two baths), or curl up on the sofa in front of the wood stove. A charming guest cottage (one of the few in the valley) out back provides an especially private accommodation, great for families or romantics; it has an open first floor with living/dining room and kitchen area, and a queen-bedded room upstairs. Dog lovers enjoy meeting Goldfarb's two friendly canines. Goldfarb serves a country continental breakfast of fresh scones or muffins, fruit from his orchard, and coffee; his wonderful chocolate chip cookies are waiting in the afternoons. Bring binoculars for bird-watching and bikes for touring the island's flat farmlands. *$$; MC, V; checks OK; www.thewhiteswan.com; 6 miles southeast of La Conner, call for directions.*

The Wild Iris Inn / ★★

121 MAPLE AVE, LA CONNER; 360/466-1400 OR 800/477-1400

This 19-room inn gears itself toward romance with spacious suites, each featuring a gas fireplace, oversize Jacuzzi, and panoramic Cascades views from balcony or patio. Each is individually decorated, so specify white wicker and lace, or darker, more masculine furnishings. Most standard rooms face the parking lot and seem a bit cramped. Dinner is served Tuesday through Saturday; make reservations, because it's open to the public. The intimate dining room has country charm, but the real magic is in the seasonally changing menu, which might include fresh salmon with peppercorn butter, or grilled duckling breast with mushrooms, sun-dried cherries, and marsala. The Budda Bowl is a vegan one-bowl meal. The breakfast buffet might offer hot spiced fruit soup, vegetable quiche, imported cheeses, or "eggs en croute"—baked pastry eggs. *$$$; AE, MC, V; checks OK; www.wildiris.com; edge of town.* &

Bellingham Region

Bellingham is the hub of northwestern Washington, an area that extends from the small community of Edison in the south to Blaine at the Canadian border. It includes Lummi Island, the Dutch-style town of Lynden, and the Nooksack Valley leading to Mount Baker recreation area.

Chuckanut Drive

This famous stretch of road (Hwy 11) between Burlington or Bow and Bellingham used to be part of the Pacific Highway; now it is one of the prettiest drives in the state, curving along the Chuckanut Mountains and looking out over Samish Bay and its many islands. Unfortunately, if you're in the driver's seat you'll have to keep your eyes on the narrow and winding road. Take the Chuckanut Drive exit off Interstate 5 northbound (or follow 12th St south out of Bellingham).

As you wend your way north to Bellingham through the bucolic communities, it's hard to believe Interstate 5 is only minutes away. Removed from traffic and shopping malls, you'll discover orchards, oyster beds, slow-moving tractors, and fields of mustard. For an interesting detour, visit the **BREAZEALE–PADILLA BAY NATIONAL ESTUARINE RESEARCH RESERVE AND INTERPRETIVE CENTER** (1043 Bayview-Edison Rd; 360/428-1558; open Wed–Sun, 10am–5pm). Learn about the Padilla Bay estuary through displays, saltwater tanks, and a library. A 2-mile shoreline trail begins just a short drive south of the Center. Nearby **BAYVIEW STATE PARK** (360/757-0227; open year-round) has overnight camping and beachfront picnic sites, perfect for winter bird-watching.

Permanent and part-time residents inhabit **SAMISH ISLAND**, as do numerous oyster beds. **BLAU OYSTER COMPANY** (919 Blue Heron; 360/766-6171; open Mon–Sat; 7 miles west of Edison via Bayview-Edison Rd and Samish Island Rd) has been selling Samish Bay oysters, clams, and other seafood since 1935. Follow signs to the shucking sheds. If you're hungry or thirsty as you make your way through **EDISON**, stop at the (smoky) **LONGHORN SALOON** (5754 Cains Ct; 360/766-6330) for tasty burgers, local oysters, and a huge selection of beers.

LARRABEE STATE PARK (off Chuckanut Dr; 360/676-2093; 7 miles south of Bellingham) was Washington's first state park. Beautiful sandstone-sculpted beaches and cliffs provides a backdrop for exploration of the abundant sea life. Picnic areas and camping are good. The INTERURBAN TRAIL, once the electric rail route from Bellingham to Mount Vernon, is now a 5-mile running, walking, riding, and mountain-biking trail connecting three parks on Chuckanut Drive: Larrabee State Park to Arroyo Park to Fairhaven Park (in Bellingham).

TEDDY BEAR COVE is a lovely beach on a secluded shore along Chuckanut Drive just south of the Bellingham city limits; it's also popular with nudists. Watch for a parking lot on the left side of the road as you drive south from the city.

RESTAURANTS

The Oyster Bar on Chuckanut Drive / ★★★

2578 CHUCKANUT DR, BOW; 360/766-6185

A 1999 facelift incorporating a taller roof, lodgelike styling, and interior upgrades such as a fireplace and additional booths has improved the appearance of this famed Chuckanut Drive restaurant. But little can improve upon the spectacular view of Samish Bay and gourmet fare—they're still tops. The small menu focuses on seafood and local bounty, and changes frequently. Start with a half-dozen raw oysters fresh out of the bay. Then try the Belgian endive or watercress salad. The main course might be a generous fillet of wild salmon or a perfectly cooked filet mignon. The award-winning wine list can be overwhelming, but veteran servers steer you right. A light cheese soufflé accompanies every meal. A creamy and delicious cheesecake is almost always on the menu—try the lemon for a light finish. No young children, please. *$$$; AE, MC, V; local checks only; dinner every day; beer and wine; reservations recommended; www.chuckanutdrive.com; north of Bow.*

The Oyster Creek Inn / ★

190 CHUCKANUT DR, BOW; 360/766-6179

This well-loved creekside restaurant was rebuilt from the ground up and reopened in summer 2000. The new, larger windows open onto expanded views of lush, green trees and rippling water. Expect the same stellar offerings in the new digs. Start with a glass of house wine made by manager Doug Charles. The oyster sampler or excellent crab cakes are good choices for first-time visitors; daily specials are enticing, and desserts—such as wild blackberry pie in summer—are a must. *$$; AE, MC, V; local checks only; lunch, dinner every day; beer and wine; reservations recommended; 30 minutes south of Bellingham.* &

The Rhododendron Cafe / ★

5521 CHUCKANUT DR, BOW; 360/766-6667

The Rhododendron Cafe is the perfect starting or ending point for a scenic trek on Chuckanut Drive. It may not have the view of other Chuckanut eateries, but the commitment to making everything from scratch—including basil and shallot buns for burgers and sandwiches—makes this a delicious stop. Once the site of the Red Crown Service Station in the early 1900s, the Rhody serves homemade soup (chowder is excellent) and a tasty portobello burger. Lightly breaded and panfried Samish Bay oysters are available for lunch or dinner. The dinner menu includes grilled pork loin and chicken Parmesan with marinara. A nightly seafood stew changes with the monthly ethnic theme—Spanish, Italian, Louisianan, Middle East, Caribbean—check the blackboard for the country of the month. The Rhody Too is an art gallery and gift shop next door. *$$; AE, MC, V; checks OK; breakfast Sat–Sun, lunch, dinner every day Apr–Aug (lunch Fri–Sun, dinner every day off season, closed late Nov–Dec); beer and wine; reservations recommended (weekends); at Bow-Edison junction.*

LODGINGS

Benson Farmstead Bed & Breakfast

10113 AVON-ALLEN RD, BOW; 360/757-0578 OR 800/441-9814

Once part of a working dairy farm, this large 17-room house, surrounded by English-style gardens and fruit trees, is packed with antiques and Scandinavian memorabilia. Four upstairs guest rooms (all with private baths) are outfitted with iron beds and custom quilts. Best are the Wildflowers and the English Garden Rooms. A new family suite is in the Grainery out back. In the evening, relax in the hot tub or the parlor, sharing Sharon Benson's desserts and coffee. Jerry Benson cooks a country breakfast. Don't be surprised to hear music in the air; the Bensons are talented pianists and violinists (as are their four sons). Kids especially like the playroom and the three cats. *$$; MC, V; checks OK; bensonfarmstead@hotmail.com; www.bbhosts.com/bensonbnb; exit 232 west off I-5.*

Samish Point by the Bay / ★★

4465 SAMISH POINT RD, BOW; 360/766-6610 OR 800/916-6161

Theresa and Herb Goldston have fashioned a tranquil getaway on their estate-like property at the west end of Samish Island. Solitude and privacy are assured in their Cape Cod–style Guest House, a three-bedroom cottage with a gas fireplace in the cozy living room and a hot tub on the back deck. It accommodates two to six (rates are based on party size). The fully equipped, modern kitchen is stocked with continental breakfast fixings. An additional guest room is in the main house. The grounds have miles of wooded trails, and access to a beach with a picnic table and a great view of the Chuckanut Mountains. *$$$; AE, MC, V; checks OK; hgtg@samishpoint.com; www.samishpoint.com; end of road on Samish Island.*

Bellingham

Situated where the Nooksack River flows into Bellingham Bay, this community—full of fine old houses, award-winning architecture at the university, stately streets, and lovely parks—has been rediscovered in recent years. **LAKE WHATCOM RAILWAY** (on Hwy 9 at Wickersham; 360/595-2218) makes scenic runs on July and August Saturdays using an old Northern Pacific engine.

WESTERN WASHINGTON UNIVERSITY (on Sehome Hill south of downtown; 360/650-3000) is a fine expression of the spirit of Northwest architecture: warm materials, formal echoes of European styles, and respect for context and the natural backdrop. Stop at the visitor parking kiosk on the south side of campus for a map of the university's outdoor sculpture collection.

The Old Town around Commercial and W Holly Streets hosts **ANTIQUE AND JUNK SHOPS** and some decent eateries. **BELLINGHAM FARMERS MARKET** (downtown at Railroad Ave and Chestnut St; 360/647-2060; Sat, Apr–Oct) features produce—including the county's famed berry harvests—fresh seafood, herbs, flowers, and crafts.

FAIRHAVEN, a once-separate town that was the result of a short-lived railroad boom in 1889–93, has retained its old-time charm and is now a Bellingham neighborhood good for exploring. The **MARKETPLACE** (Harris and 12th Sts), the grand dame and central figure among the attractive old buildings, was restored in 1988 and houses a number of interesting shops and dining options. The district is rich with diversions: crafts galleries, coffeehouses, bookstores, a charming garden/nursery emporium, and a lively evening scene. **VILLAGE BOOKS** (1210 11th St; 360/671-2626) carries an eclectic mix of new and used best-selling, children's, and regional titles, and has a knowledgeable staff and an attached cafe. **TONY'S COFFEES** (1101 Harris; 360/738-4710) is the local beanmeister, and the **EUROPEAN PASTRY SHOP AND CAFE** (1307 11th; 360/671-7258) has a tantalizing array of lovely pastries, as well as salads and sandwiches. Stop in at the attractive **ARCHER ALE HOUSE** (1212 10th; 360/647-7002) for a wide selection of brews, including hard-to-find Belgian beers, and some tasty pizza and focaccia.

The **WHATCOM MUSEUM OF HISTORY AND ART** (121 Prospect St; 360/676-6981; www.cob.org/museum) is a four-building campus. The main building is a massive Romanesque structure dating from 1892 and was used as a city hall until 1940. It has permanent exhibits on historic Bellingham as well as an adventurous exhibition schedule. Check out the presentations on local wildlife and Native American culture in the Syre Education Center (201 Prospect) down the block, and the **CHILDREN'S MUSEUM NORTHWEST** (227 Prospect) a few doors farther north. Across the street, the Arco Building has changing art and history displays. One block from the main museum is **HENDERSON BOOKS** (116 Grand Ave; 360/734-6855), a 7,000-square-foot store with 250,000 volumes of used books in excellent shape (the staff is fanatical about the condition of the books), and a particularly good collection of art books.

NO EXPERIENCE NECESSARY

Sea kayaking is an elegant, delightful way to explore the waterways, bays, and islands of Puget Sound. Miles of secluded coastline and engaging wildlife—including eagles and other birds, harbor seals, river otters, minke whales, even orcas—guarantee you're never bored. A real plus is that sea kayaking is surprisingly easy for even novices. All you need is good health, an adventurous spirit, and a good teacher/guide. Half-day or shorter outings help you "get your feet wet." Ambitious overnight trips with provisions are like specialized backpacking/camping trips—by water—and become more of an adventure and an investment.

Several outfitters in Bellingham and the San Juan Islands offer short or long trips: **San Juan Safaris** (Roche Harbor Marine Activity Center, San Juan Island; 360/378-6545) trips leave from Roche Harbor Resort; ask about whale-watching trips. **Shearwater Kayak Tours** (Eastsound, Orcas Island; 360/376-4699; www.shearwaterkayaks.com) does half-day and longer trips from Eastsound and Rosario Resort. **Moon Dance** (Bellingham; 360/738-7664) offers half-day and longer outings, including exploring the petroglyphs of Bellingham Bay. With **Northern Lights Expeditions** (Fairhaven; 800/754-7402), you can take an extensive trip (with gourmet meals) up the Inside Passage and in Western Canada. —*Jena MacPherson*

The summer **BELLINGHAM MUSIC FESTIVAL** (360/676-5997; late July–mid-Aug) has quickly become an institution, featuring more than two weeks of orchestral, chamber, and jazz performances. The **MOUNT BAKER THEATER** (104 N Commercial; 360/734-6080; www.mtbakertheatre.com), built in 1927 and renovated in 1995, is home to the **WHATCOM SYMPHONY ORCHESTRA** and the site of a wide array of concerts, plays, films, and special events.

Bellingham has two attractive brewpubs: the **BOUNDARY BAY BREWERY** (1107 Railroad; 360/647-5593) downtown, and the **ORCHARD STREET BREWERY** (709 W Orchard; 360/647-1614), north of downtown in an office park. Orchard Street is popular among locals for its food and its beer; Boundary Bay serves a delicious lamb burger and other tasty pub grub. **MOUNT BAKER VINEYARDS** (11 miles east of Bellingham on Mount Baker Hwy/Hwy 542; 360/592-2300; open every day) is an attractive, cedar-sided, skylit facility that specializes in lesser-known varietals such as Müller Thurgau and Madeleine Angevine.

SEHOME HILL ARBORETUM (adjacent to WWU campus; 360/650-3000) sports over 3 miles of trails, with prime views of the city, Bellingham Bay, and the San Juans. **WHATCOM FALLS PARK** (1401 Electric Ave; 360/676-6985) has more than 5 miles of trails overlooking several scenic falls. **BIG ROCK GARDEN PARK** (2900 Sylvan, near Lake Whatcom; 360/676-6985; open daily, Apr–Oct) is a wonderful woodland site with a vast array of azaleas, rhododendrons, and Japanese maples. The **SKI-TO-SEA RACE** (360/734-1330) attracts teams from all over the world to participate in this annual seven-event relay race on Memorial Day weekend.

A handsome port facility in the historic area of Fairhaven houses the southern terminus of the **ALASKA MARINE HIGHWAY SYSTEM** (355 Harris Ave; 360/676-8445 or 800/642-0066); Bellingham is where many travelers begin the long journey up the coast and through Alaska's famed Inside Passage. Sticking closer to home, the **ISLAND SHUTTLE EXPRESS** (355 Harris Ave, Ste 105; 360/671-1137) provides passenger-only ferry service from Bellingham to the San Juans, April through September; whale-watching and overnight cruises are also offered. The **WHATCOM COUNTY FERRY** (360/676-6759 or 360/676-6730; www.co.whatcom.wa.us), which leaves Gooseberry Point north of Bellingham, services Lummi Island.

RESTAURANTS

Cafe Toulouse / ★

114 W MAGNOLIA ST, BELLINGHAM; 360/733-8996

Cafe Toulouse's claim to fame continues to be huge, well-orchestrated breakfasts and lunches for the local office crowd. The menu offers favorites familiar to cafe regulars: Greek and provençal frittatas, huevos rancheros, hefty sandwiches, soups, pastas, and espresso drinks, all served up in a basic French bistro–style atmosphere. *$; AE, DIS, MC, V; checks OK; breakfast, lunch every day; no alcohol; reservations recommended for 5 or more; downtown near Cornwall.* &

Colophon Cafe
Colophon Cafe Downtown

1208 11TH ST, BELLINGHAM; 360/647-0092
308 W CHAMPION ST, BELLINGHAM; 360/676-6257

Located in the town's best bookstore, in a 100-year-old building in Bellingham's historic Fairhaven district, the original Colophon offers table service and a summer outdoor wine garden on its lower level (and indoor seating year-round). The African peanut soup with chunky fresh tomatoes, grainy peanuts, and pungent ginger comes in vegetarian and nonvegetarian versions, and remains justly famous. Real cream pies—rich, light, and wonderful—are another specialty: Key lime, chocolate brandy, and peanut butter.

Decorated like a 1950s diner with two-toned booths and bar stools, the new Colophon Cafe Downtown opened in early 2000 and has been packed ever since. This location serves the same desserts, soups, sandwiches, and delicious quiches as the Fairhaven restaurant; the only difference is hours, which are geared to downtown workers. *$; AE, DIS, MC, V; checks OK; breakfast, lunch, dinner every day (Fairhaven), breakfast, lunch Mon–Fri (downtown); beer and wine; reservations recommended (weekends); www.colophoncafe. com; near Harris Ave (Fairhaven), downtown.*

India Grill / ★

1215½ CORNWALL AVE, BELLINGHAM; 360/714-0314

The space is commercial in style—rectangular and glass-fronted—however, music and decorating touches put you in the appropriate mood. Delicious Northern Indian cuisine, a long list of tempting vegetarian choices, and a generous and inexpensive lunch buffet are the draws here. Lamb *saag*, a spinach and lamb combo, and the Kadahi shrimp, a succulent prawn and vegetable dish served in a wok, are great choices if you're a nonvegetarian newcomer. Dinner is a deal (there's a 13-course offering for less than $15). *$; DIS, MC, V; checks OK; lunch, dinner every day; full bar; reservations not necessary; downtown between Holly and Chestnut.* &

Pacific Cafe / ★★

100 N COMMERCIAL, BELLINGHAM; 360/647-0800

The Pacific Cafe has been a leader on Bellingham's gastronomic front since 1985. Co-owner Robert Fong comes to Washington via Hawaii—supplemented with years of travel in Europe, India, China, and Malaysia—and the menu reflects that sophisticated mix. Curries and seafood dishes are specialties, but don't overlook the duck, served in two very different ways: marinated and served Chinese-style—garlic, thai chile, fresh lemons, sophisticated marinades—with hoisin ginger sauce, or Napa Valley duck, grilled and served medium rare. Expect great desserts from pastry chef Wayne Kent, who's studied in New York with Jacques Peyard, possibly America's best pastry chef. Made fresh, they include *lilikoi* (passionfruit) sorbet, butter pecan ice cream, and hand-dipped Belgian chocolate truffles. Quality vintages reflect a fine-tuned palate. Tucked into the historic Mount Baker Theater building, its ambience is civilized and modern—abstract watercolors on the walls, quiet jazz on the speakers. *$$; MC, V; local checks only; lunch Mon–Fri, dinner Mon–Sat; beer and wine; reservations recommended (weekends); near Champion.* &

Pepper Sisters / ★★

1055 N STATE ST, BELLINGHAM; 360/671-3414

Cheerful, knowledgeable service; a great location in a vintage brick commercial building; and a wide-awake kitchen have turned Pepper Sisters into an institution, known for its Southwestern fare. Daily seafood specials showcase the chefs' ability to combine local provender with what the owners call High Desert cuisine: say, grilled salmon with a cilantro, almond, and caper sauce. The kitchen shows the same verve with plainer fare: roasted potato and garlic enchilada with green chile sauce, or a spicy eggplant tostada. Their traditional flan is a standout, and the coffee, the local Tony's brand, is brewed with a dusting of cinnamon. *$; MC, V; checks OK; dinner Tues–Sun; beer and wine; reservations recommended for 5 or more; south of downtown.* &

LODGINGS

Best Western Heritage Inn / ★★

151 E MCLEOD RD, BELLINGHAM; 360/647-1912 OR 800/528-1234

Three tasteful, Wedgewood blue, shuttered and dormered structures nestle amid a small grove of trees adjacent to Interstate 5 and a conglomeration of malls. This Best Western is one of the most professionally run hotels in the area. Rooms have a classic elegance with cherrywood high- and lowboys, wing chairs in rich fabrics, and stylish desks with comfortable chairs. Other thoughtful touches include in-room coffee and tea, hair dryers, free newspapers, a guest laundry facility, an outdoor pool (in season), and indoor hot tub. Request a room away from the freeway. European-style continental breakfast—fruits, meats, cheeses, and pastries—is free. *$$; AE, DC, DIS, MC, V; checks OK; heritageinnbham@aol.com; www.bestwestern.com/ heritageinnbellingham; exit 256 off I-5.*

North Garden Inn / ★

1014 N GARDEN ST, BELLINGHAM; 360/671-7828 OR 800/922-6414

This Victorian house (on the National Register of Historic Places) is especially popular with visitors to nearby WWU. Some of the 10 guest rooms (8 with private baths) have lovely views over Bellingham Bay and the islands. Rooms are attractive and have a bit more character than usual—due partly to the antique house, partly to the influence of the energetic, talented, and well-traveled hosts. Barbara and Frank DeFreytas are both musical: a piano is in one of the parlors for guests to use. *$$; AE, DIS, MC, V; checks OK; ngi@north gardeninn.com; northgardeninn.com/ngi; at E Maple.*

Schnauzer Crossing / ★★★

4421 LAKEWAY DR, BELLINGHAM; 360/734-2808 OR 800/562-2808

Sophisticated and unique, this B&B overlooking Lake Whatcom attracts a surprising range of visitors, from newlyweds to businesspeople to discerning foreign travelers, and graciously accommodates them all. Many of Donna and Monty McAllister's guests return to this lovely contemporary home with grounds that include a meditation garden and a miniature teahouse in an idyllic glade. Three accommodations are available. The spacious and elegant Garden Suite, with fireplace, Jacuzzi, TV/VCR, and a garden view, and the separate cottage overlooking the lake are the most luxurious, but guests staying in the simpler Queen Room enjoy the surroundings without the pricey amenities. The McAllisters have a finely tuned sense of hospitality that's obvious in small details: extra-thick towels, bathrobes and slippers, and gorgeous flowers year-round. Breakfast might include homemade quiche, fresh fruit parfait, and fresh-baked lime scones. The hot tub is in a Japanese garden setting. Reserve several months in advance for summer and weekends. *$$$; AE, MC, V; checks OK; schnauzerx@aol.com; www.schnauzer crossing.com; exit 253 off I-5.*

South Bay B&B / ★★
4095 SOUTH BAY DR, BELLINGHAM; 360/595-2086 OR 877/595-2086

You'll feel as if you've somehow fallen into an eagle's nest when you arrive at the top of this winding mountain road and get the bird's-eye views of Lake Whatcom. Privacy, views, forest—all offer a real getaway. Four guest rooms have lake views, queen beds with crisply ironed sheets, down comforters and pillows, and private baths with oversize jetted tubs for two; two rooms have gas fireplaces and one is a suite with living room and fireplace. Breakfast, at 9am, is an event—homemade granola, fruit, and an entree (perhaps crab in patty shells), enjoyed from the sunroom or dining room with a lake view. Before you leave, ask owners Dan and Sally Moore to tell the story of how their house came to this spot. *$$$; MC, V; checks OK; www.southbaybb.com; 25 min south of Bellingham, exit 240.*

Stratford Manor / ★
4566 ANDERSON WY, BELLINGHAM; 360/715-8441 OR 800/240-6779

Set amid farmland northeast of Bellingham, this rambling English Tudor–style home sits on a knoll overlooking a half-acre pond, perennial garden, and the surrounding countryside. Three guest rooms occupy their own wing; all have jetted tubs and gas fireplaces. Our favorite is the downstairs Garden Room, with a spacious sitting area and double jetted tub overlooking the garden. The guest wing's common area has a TV and VCR with a selection of movies. There's an outdoor hot tub. Full breakfast is served in the dining room, after wake-up coffee is delivered to your door. *$$$; MC, V; checks OK; llohse@aol.com; www.stratfordmanor.com; Sunset Dr exit off I-5.*

Lummi Island

Located just off Gooseberry Point northwest of Bellingham, Lummi is one of the most overlooked islands of the ferry-accessible San Juans. It echoes the days when the San Juan Islands were still a hidden treasure, visited only by folks who preferred bucolic surroundings and deserted beaches to a plethora of restaurants and gift shops. Private ownership has locked up most of this pastoral isle, so you won't find state parks or resorts. To stretch your limbs, bring bikes and enjoy the quiet country roads. Plan ahead; dining options are sparse. Not far from the ferry landing, the **BEACH STORE CAFE** (2200 N Nugent; 360/758-2233; open seasonally, usually dinner Thurs–Sat, brunch Sun) is an unexpected surprise; creative offerings include produce fresh from the island.

Lummi is serviced not by Washington State Ferries, but by the tiny **WHATCOM COUNTY FERRY** (360/676-6759 or 360/676-6730; www.co.what com.wa.us), which leaves Gooseberry Point at 10 minutes past the hour from 7am until midnight (more frequently on weekdays). It's easy to find (follow signs to Lummi Island from Interstate 5, north of Bellingham), cheap ($4 round trip for a car and two passengers), and quick (6-minute crossing). The ferry returns from Lummi on the hour.

Lynden

This neat and tidy community, with immaculate yards and colorful gardens lining the shady avenue into downtown, adopted a Dutch theme in tribute to its early inhabitants. Visit the charming **PIONEER MUSEUM** (217 W Front St; 360/354-3675), full of local memorabilia, antique buggies, and motorcars.

RESTAURANTS

Hollandia

655 FRONT ST, LYNDEN; 360/354-4133

Chef Dini Mollink delivers authentic hearty fare imported from The Netherlands in a tasteful bistro setting that's a quiet oasis at the south end of Lynden's unique Dutch mini-shopping mall. A good choice is the *Toeristen* menu: *Groentesoep* (firm, tasty meatballs in a luscious vegetable broth), Schnitzel Hollandia (lightly breaded chicken breast), and dessert (little almond tarts). A small spice cookie accompanies your after-dinner coffee. *$; MC, V; local checks only; lunch Mon–Sat, dinner Thurs–Sat; beer and wine; reservations recommended (weekends); at Guide Meridian.* ৬

LODGINGS

Dutch Village Inn / ★

655 FRONT ST, LYNDEN; 360/354-4440

One might question an inn located in a windmill in a Dutch-theme village. This particular inn, however, provides six tastefully furnished and luxuriously appointed rooms to please all but the most jaded of travelers. Not surprisingly, rooms are named for Dutch provinces; the Friesland Kamer room, named after the northernmost province, occupies the top of the windmill. Views are lovely, but interrupted rhythmically as the giant blades of the windmill pass by (it turns, fully lit, until 10pm). Two rooms have extra beds fitted into curtained alcoves in true Dutch fashion; two have two-person tubs. A continental breakfast of baked goods and fruit is included. *$$; AE, DIS, MC, V; local checks only; dvinn@premier1.net; turn off Guide Meridian at Front.*

Blaine

The northernmost city along the Interstate 5 corridor, Blaine is the state's most popular border crossing into British Columbia. It's the most beautiful, as well. Home to the grand white **INTERNATIONAL PEACE ARCH MONUMENT**, which spans the U.S.–Canadian border, the park surrounding the arch borders on Boundary Bay and is filled with lovely gardens and sculptures. Each June there's a Peace Arch celebration.

LODGINGS

Resort Semiahmoo / ★★★

9565 SEMIAHMOO PKWY, BLAINE; 360/371-2000 OR 800/770-7992

Nestled on a 1,100-acre wildlife preserve, Resort Semiahmoo offers golf, waterfront, views of the San Juan Islands, and acres of wooded walking trails. The inn is on Semi-ah-moo Spit, a seemingly endless stretch of beach with views west to the sea and east to Drayton Harbor. Amenities include a 300-slip marina; a house cruise vessel for San Juan excursions or scenic fishing trips; a full-service spa and salon; and an athletic club with heated indoor/outdoor pool, racquetball, tennis, and more. Guest rooms are comfortably decorated and spacious. Ask for a water-view room, with a fireplace for added ambience; other rooms overlook the parking lot. Four restaurants provide views and a range of culinary alternatives that you'd be hard-pressed to find in Blaine—and includes Stars, an award-winning Northwest gourmet dining room. The golf course, designed by Arnold Palmer, has long, unencumbered fairways surrounded by dense woods, and lovely sculptural sand traps. Adjacent is a convention center, in revamped cannery buildings. *$$$; AE, DC, DIS, MC, V; checks OK; info@semiahmoo.com; www.semiahmoo.com; exit 270 off I-5.* &

Anacortes and the San Juan Islands

There are 743 islands at low tide and 428 at high tide; 172 have names, 60 are populated, and only 4 have major ferry service. The San Juan Islands are varied, remote, and breathtakingly beautiful. They are also located in the rain shadow of the Olympic Mountains, and most receive half the rainfall that Seattle receives. Of the main islands, three—Lopez, Orcas, and San Juan—have lodgings, eateries, and some beautiful parks.

ACCESS AND INFORMATION

The most obvious and cost-effective way to reach the San Juans is via the **WASH-INGTON STATE FERRIES** (206/464-6400), which run year-round from Anacortes (see below). Keep in mind, however, that the sparsely populated islands are overrun in the summer months, and getting your car on a ferry out of Anacortes can be a long three-hour-plus wait. Bring a good book—or park the car and board with just a bike. Money-saving tip: cars pay only westbound. If you plan to visit more than one island, arrange to go to the farthest first (San Juan) and work your way east.

In summer, options for those who don't need to bring a car include the high-speed **VICTORIA CLIPPER** (2701 Alaskan Wy, Seattle; 206/448-5000), which makes a once-a-day trip from downtown Seattle to Friday Harbor (with seasonal stops at Rosario Resort on Orcas Island). The ferry departs Pier 69 at 7:30am. Another option, in summer, is the passenger-only **SAN JUAN ISLAND SHUTTLE EXPRESS** (360/671-1137 or 888/373-8522) via Bellingham.

KENMORE AIR (425/486-1257 or 800/543-9595) schedules five floatplane flights a day during peak season. Round-trip flights start at about $112 per person and leave from Lake Union in Seattle; luggage space is limited. **HARBOR AIRLINES** (800/359-3220) has daily commuter service from Sea-Tac International Airport to San Juan, Lopez, and Orcas Islands.

Anacortes

Anacortes, the gateway to the San Juans, is itself on an island: Fidalgo Island. Though most travelers rush through here on the way to the ferry, this town adorned with colorful, life-size cutouts of early pioneers is quietly becoming a place where it's worth slowing down. For picnic or ferry food, try **GEPPETTO'S** (3320 Commercial; 360/293-5033) for Italian takeout. Those with more time head to **GERE-A-DELI** (502 Commercial; 360/293-7383), a friendly hangout with good homemade food in an airy former Bank of Commerce building. And don't forget the **CALICO CUPBOARD** (901 Commercial; 360/293-7315), offshoot of the well-known cafe and bakery in La Conner.

For ferry reading material, stop by **WATERMARK BOOK COMPANY** (612 Commercial; 360/293-4277), loaded with interesting reads. Seafaring folks should poke around **MARINE SUPPLY AND HARDWARE** (202 Commercial; 360/293-3014); established in 1913, it's packed to the rafters with basic and hard-to-find specialty marine items. For the history of Fidalgo Island, visit the **ANACORTES MUSEUM** (1305 8th; 360/293-1915).

Those who plan to kayak in the islands stop by **EDDYLINE WATERSPORTS CENTER** (1019 Q; 360/299-2300), located at the **CAP SANTE MARINA** (just before Anacortes, take a right on "R" Ave off Hwy 20; 360/293-0694). Test-paddle a kayak in the harbor, then rent one for the weekend in the San Juans; reservations are necessary.

WASHINGTON PARK is less than a mile west of the ferry terminal. Here you'll find scenic picnic areas and a paved 2½-mile trail looping through an old-growth forest with great San Juan views.

RESTAURANTS

Julianne's Grill / ★★

419 COMMERCIAL AVE (MAJESTIC HOTEL), ANACORTES; 360/299-9666

Formerly the Salmon Run, Julianne's Grill is the most elegant dining room in Anacortes. The cathedral-ceilinged room has tall windows overlooking a garden and patio—a great dining spot in summer. Jerk ribs, chicken burger, and lamb add a Caribbean flair, and curries are very well done. The house special is Roast Pork Calypso, a bone-in, center-cut pork loin rubbed with ginger, garlic, and cloves, slow roasted and basted with lime juice and rum—flavorful and tender. A separate pub, across the hall, offers the same menu along with lighter, more casual fare, and live jazz Thursday through Saturday nights. *$$; AE, DIS, MC, V; checks OK; dinner every day; full bar; reservations recommended (weekends); between 4th and 5th.* ♿

La Petite / ★★

3401 COMMERCIAL AVE, ANACORTES; 360/293-4644

Bela Berghuys, longtime owner of this restaurant at the Islands Inn motel, continues to deliver French-inspired food with a touch of Dutch. Though there are only six entrees to choose from, quality is high. Try lamb marinated in sambal, or the popular pork tenderloin with a mustard sauce. If chateaubriand is on the menu, order it; it's delicious. Soup, salad, and oven-fresh bread are included. La Petite has an interesting dessert list, with plenty of chocolate options. A fixed-price Dutch breakfast is intended for (but not exclusive to) motel guests. *$$; AE, DC, DIS, MC, V; local checks only; breakfast every day, dinner Tues–Sun; full bar; reservations recommended; www.islandsinn.com; east end of Commercial.*

LODGINGS

Channel House / ★★

2902 OAKES AVE, ANACORTES; 360/293-9382 OR 800/238-4353

Just 1½ miles from the ferry dock, Dennis and Pat McIntyre's Channel House is a 1902 Victorian home designed by an Italian count. Two of four antique-filled guest rooms have views of Guemes Channel and the San Juan Islands. A cottage contains our two favorite rooms, each with a wood-burning fireplace and private whirlpool bath; the Victorian Rose has its own deck. A large hot tub is out back. The McIntyres serve cozy candlelit breakfasts (stuffed French toast is a specialty). Fresh-baked oatmeal cookies and Irish Cream coffee await guests after dinner. The McIntyres gladly accommodate guests who need an early breakfast to catch the San Juan ferry, but the Channel House is worth a longer stay. *$$; AE, DIS, MC, V; checks OK; beds@sos.net; www.channel-house.com; at Dakota St.*

The Majestic Hotel / ★★

419 COMMERCIAL AVE, ANACORTES; 360/293-3355 OR 800/588-4780

This renovated white clapboard landmark, built in 1889, dominates Anacortes's historic old town. Every one of the 23 rooms—decorated by owner Virginia Wetmore—is unique. All have English antiques; some have oversize tubs below skylights; some have decks; others have VCRs; and a few have everything. Best are the showy corner suites. On the second floor (the only smoking level) is a small library with a chess table. Up top is a cupola with a 360-degree view of Anacortes, Mount Baker, the Olympics, and the San Juans. *$$$; AE, DIS, MC, V; checks OK with preapproval; www.majesticinn.com; between 4th and 5th.* &

Lopez Island

Lopez Island, flat and shaped like a jigsaw-puzzle piece, is a sleepy, bucolic place, famous for friendly locals (drivers always wave) and gentle inclines. The latter makes it the easiest bicycling in the islands: a relatively level 30-mile circuit suitable for the whole family. If you don't bring your own, rent bikes from **LOPEZ BICYCLE WORKS** (2847 Fisherman Bay Rd; 360/468-2847).

Two day parks—**OTIS PERKINS** and **AGATE COUNTY**—are great for exploring, with good beach access. You can camp at 80-acre **ODLIN COUNTY PARK** (on right about 1 mile south of ferry dock; 360/468-2496) or 130-acre **SPENCER SPIT STATE PARK** (on left about 5 miles south of ferry dock; 800/452-5687), both on the island's north side. Odlin has many nooks and crannies, and 30 grassy sites set among Douglas firs, shrubs, and clover. Spencer Spit has about 50 campsites, 8 of them walk-ins on the beach. Both parks have water, toilets, and fire pits. Seals and bald eagles can often be seen from the rocky promontory off Shark Reef Park, on the island's western shore.

LOPEZ VILLAGE, 4 miles south of the ferry dock on the west shore near Fisherman Bay, is basic but has a few spots worth knowing about, such as **HOLLY B'S BAKERY** (Lopez Plaza; 360/468-2133; Apr–Dec), with celebrated fresh bread and pastries, and coffee to wash them down, and **THE DELI LHAMA CAFE** (1 Village Ctr; 360/468-2150), for soups, sandwiches, and other choices.

RESTAURANTS

The Bay Cafe / ★★★

90 POST RD, LOPEZ ISLAND; 360/468-3700

For years the twinkling Bay Cafe has been reason alone to come to this serene isle. Its modern digs close to the beach (old fans remember its smaller, funkier location in the village) are spacious and retain the same rack of Fiestaware plates and rowboat suspended from the ceiling. A great sunset view of the entrance to Fisherman Bay is a bonus of the new location. It's still a come-as-you-are kind of place—and people do. The menu, which changes frequently, might include steamed mussels in a coconut saffron broth, grilled tofu with chickpea-potato cakes (vegetarians never suffer here), or a marvelous beef fillet draped in sweet caramelized onions and a roasted garlic–Roquefort sauce. Prices are reasonable, especially considering that dinners include soup and salad. There's also live jazz Sunday evenings. *$$; DIS, MC, V; checks OK; lunch, dinner every day (breakfast, lunch, dinner Wed–Sun in winter, closed Jan); full bar; reservations recommended; junction of Lopez Rd S and Lopez Rd N, Lopez Village.*

LODGINGS

Edenwild Inn / ★★

132 LOPEZ RD, LOPEZ ISLAND; 360/468-3238

 The majestic Victorian centerpiece of Lopez Village, this B&B is surrounded by a lovely garden and features eight individually decorated rooms, some with fireplaces, all with private baths and beautifully stained hardwood floors. Though the inn is not on the water, the front rooms upstairs have fine views: Room 6 features vistas of Fisherman Bay and has a fireplace and sitting area. New owners Maryanne Miller and Clark Haley serve breakfast at individual tables in the dining room. The only B&B on the island to accept children, it is also in walking distance to the restaurants and shops in town. *$$$; AE, MC, V; checks OK; edenwildinn@msn.com; www.edenwild inn. com; Lopez Village.* &

MacKaye Harbor Inn / ★
949 MACKAYE HARBOR RD, LOPEZ ISLAND; 360/468-2253

Bicyclists call this paradise after a sweaty trek from the ferry on the north end of the island to the little harbor on the south end. The tall powder-blue house, built in 1927, sits above a sandy, shell-strewn beach, perfect for sunset strolls or pushing off in a kayak. The Harbor Suite is our top choice, with fireplace, private bath, and enclosed sitting area facing the beach. Rent kayaks or borrow mountain bikes; ask the very friendly innkeepers, Mike and Robin Bergstrom, to share their island secrets; and you're off to explore. Return in the afternoon for fresh-baked cookies. If you do come by bike, be warned: the closest restaurant is 6 miles back in town. Breakfast gets you started before a long morning of paddling out to the otters. *$$$; MC, V; checks OK; 12 miles south of ferry landing.*

Orcas Island

Named not for the whales (the large cetaceans tend to congregate on the west side of San Juan Island and are rarely spotted here) but for a Spanish explorer, Orcas has a reputation as the most beautiful of the four main San Juan Islands. It's also the biggest (geographically) and the hilliest, boasting 2,407-foot **MOUNT CONSTITUTION** as the centerpiece of **MORAN STATE PARK** (800/233-0321). Drive, hike, or, if you're feeling up to it, bike to the top, but get there somehow; from the old stone tower you can see Vancouver, Mount Rainier, and everything between. The 4,800-acre state park, about 13 miles northeast of the ferry landing, also has lakes and nice campsites, obtained through a central reservation service (800/452-5687) at least two weeks ahead.

The man responsible for the park was shipbuilding tycoon Robert Moran. His old mansion is now the focal point of **ROSARIO RESORT** (see review), just west of the park. Even if you don't stay there, the mansion, decked out in period memorabilia and mahogany trim, is worth a sightseeing stop. Its enormous pipe organ is still in use for nightly performances in summer (Friday and Saturday the rest of the year).

Shaped like a pair of inflated lungs, with the cute little village of **EAST-SOUND** running up the breastbone, Orcas has its ferry landing where it's most convenient for boats to pull in, 8 miles from town. Thus, most people bring their cars to the island, especially if they want to head up the big hill, but you can walk on the ferry and rent a bicycle for the fairly level ride to town. Rent bicycles by the hour, day, or week from **DOLPHIN BAY BICYCLES** (at the Orcas ferry landing; 360/376-4157) or **WILD LIFE CYCLES** (in Eastsound; 360/376-4708). Walk-ons can also stay at the historic Orcas Hotel (see review) at the landing.

RESTAURANTS

Bilbo's Festivo / ★

NORTH BEACH RD, EASTSOUND; 360/376-4728

Orcas Islanders and visitors who have been coming here for 25 years speak of this cozy little place with reverence. Its decor and setting—mud walls, Mexican tiles, arched windows, big fireplace, handmade wooden benches and spinning fans, in a small house with a flowered courtyard—are charming, and the Navajo and Chimayo weavings on the walls are from New Mexico. The fare includes a combination of Mexican and New Mexican influences, with improvisation on enchiladas, burritos, chiles rellenos, and mesquite-grilled specials. In summer, lunch is served taqueria-style, grilled to order outdoors. *$; MC, V; local checks only; lunch, dinner every day (dinner only in off season); full bar; reservations recommended; downtown at A St.*

Cafe Olga / ★

OLGA JUNCTION, OLGA; 360/376-5098

You're likely to wait for a table at Cafe Olga, a popular midday stop for locals and visitors alike. But the cafe adjoins the Orcas Island Artworks, and browsing the sprawling cooperative crafts gallery in a picturesque renovated strawberry-packing barn helps pass the time. Wholesome international home-style entrees range from a rich Sicilian artichoke pie to a chicken enchilada with black bean sauce to a Greek salad. For dessert, try a massive piece of terrific blackberry pie. *$; MC, V; local checks only; lunch every day (closed Jan–Feb); beer and wine; reservations not necessary; at Olga Junction.* &

Christina's / ★★★

310 MAIN ST, EASTSOUND; 360/376-4904

Built above a 1930s gas station in Eastsound, Christina's offers the bewitching blend of provincial locale and urban sophistication that marks the finest rural destinations. The view of the bay and craggy islet from dining room and deck is sublime; more often than not, Christina Orchid's classic continental food is, too. Singing scallops, gathered off Guemes Island, might be gently steamed in their elegant shells with fragrant hints of thyme and garlic; king salmon might arrive adorned with tender coils of fiddlehead fern. Fillet of beef in Gorgonzola cream is a masterpiece of flavor and texture, the kind of dish that has made Christina's reputation as the finest dining room in the islands. Servings tend toward the generous, with a nice selection of appetizers sized right to split or enjoy as your own light meal. *$$$; AE, DC, MC, V; checks OK; dinner every day (Thurs–Mon in winter); full bar; reservations recommended (weekends); www.christinas.net; at N Beach Rd.*

Ship Bay Oyster House / ★★
326 OLGA RD, EASTSOUND; 360/376-5886

Ship Bay has developed a reputation as a great spot for fresh fish and local oysters: baked, stewed, panfried, or au naturel (try an oyster shooter, served up in a shot glass with Clamato and sake). The Pacific Coast locale (a comfortable old farmhouse with a view of Ship Bay) belies the Atlantic Coast ambience. The clam chowder—a New Englandy version, included with every entree—might be the best in the West, and the kitchen obviously never learned about portion control (just order a small slab of spicy-hot barbecue baby back ribs with its exceptional accompaniment of black beans and salsa, and you'll get our drift). Locals swear the best deal on the island is appetizer fare in the lounge or outdoor seating on the patio. The year 2000 brought 14 deluxe rooms (one an executive suite) with king beds, fireplaces, and whirlpool baths. *$$; AE, MC, V; checks OK; dinner every day (Tues–Sun in off season, closed Dec–Feb); full bar; reservations recommended; just east of Eastsound on Horseshoe Hwy.* &

LODGINGS

Cascade Harbor Inn / ★★
1800 ROSARIO RD, EASTSOUND; 360/376-6350 OR 800/201-2120

Forty-eight modern units—some studios with Murphy beds, some two-queen rooms, some in-between—all have decks and water views, and many configure into multi-unit suites with fully equipped kitchens. The inn shares its vistas of pristine Cascade Bay and beach access with sprawling Rosario Resort next door. Continental breakfast included. *$$$; DIS, MC, V; checks OK; cascade@rock island.com; www.cascadeharborinn.com; just east of Rosario along shore of Cascade Bay.*

Chestnut Hill Inn Bed & Breakfast / ★★★
414 JOHN JONES RD, ORCAS; 360/376-5157

Every romantic stereotype of B&B elegance is fulfilled in this renovated farmhouse, perched atop a pastoral rise not far from the ferry. Marilyn and Dan Loewke have fitted the five individually decorated guest rooms with luxurious touches large and small—feather beds, fireplaces, Egyptian-cotton linens, robes, slippers, liqueurs, loofahs. The fanciest, the Chestnut Suite, boasts a TV/VCR and stereo, chilled bottled water and champagne, and two-person Jacuzzi with a dimmer switch for the crystal chandelier above it. Even hardened chintz-haters appreciate the attention and good taste that have gone into every facet of this inn. We favor the Chapel Room, with its double shower and view of the charming steepled chapel in the pear orchard. There's also a pond (with rowboat), a stable (with horses), and a gazebo (with a full schedule of weddings)—larger weddings are held in the chapel, which holds 65. Marilyn is a gifted cook: in addition to lavish breakfasts and picnic hampers, she prepares dinners as good as anything on the island for guests in the off season (Nov–Apr). *$$$; DIS, MC, V; checks OK; chestnut@pacificrim.net; www.chestnuthillinn. com; just over a mile east of ferry landing off Laport Rd.*

Deer Harbor Inn and Restaurant / ★★

33 INN LN, DEER HARBOR; 360/376-4110

Over the last five years, Pam and Craig Carpenter have shored up this old rustic lodge, originally constructed in 1915 in an orchard of apple trees overlooking Deer Harbor. Lodge rooms are small, with peeled-log furniture, but new cabins on the property have a nice beachy feeling—knotty pine walls, log furniture, wood stoves or fireplaces, and private hot tubs on the deck. The new two-bedroom, two-bath cabin on the bluff is roomy enough to be your second home, with a fully equipped kitchen, fireplace, and deck ($269 a night during high season). Beds are heaped with comforters and quilts. Whether you stay in the cabins or lodge, breakfast is delivered to your door in a picnic basket with freshly baked goods and plenty of hot coffee. Dinners are served nightly in the old lodge's rustic dining room with a large view deck. *$$; AE, MC, V; checks OK; www.deerharborinn.com; from ferry landing, follow signs past West Sound to Deer Harbor.* &

Orcas Hotel / ★

ORCAS FERRY LANDING, EASTSOUND; 360/376-4300

This pretty 1904 Victorian, originally built as a boardinghouse just above the ferry terminal, has period pieces inside and white wicker on the deck overlooking the water. Best of the dozen accommodations are the two new, larger rooms, which have private balconies and whirlpool tubs. We've heard complaints about cleanliness and the upkeep of the gardens, but new owners Doug and Laura Tidwell are still catching up on maintenance. This small, romantic hotel is the only accommodation within walking distance of the ferry; the adjoining cafe with its grandstand deck is the place to wait with a beer or a sandwich. *$$$; AE, DIS, MC, V; checks OK; orcas@orcashotel.com; www. orcashotel.com; Orcas ferry landing.*

Outlook Inn / ★

171 MAIN ST, EASTSOUND; 360/376-2200 OR 888/688-5665

If you want to stay in Eastsound—Orcas's "big city"—you'll want to stay at the legendary Outlook Inn. The name reflects the interests of Lewis Gittner and Starr Farish, psychics to the stars who purchased the circa 1888 property more than 30 years ago. Gittner has since moved on to Thailand and, like the proverbial hippies who once flocked here, the inn has traded its countercultural spirit for luxuries money can buy. Though the old part of the inn with shared baths is still available—and affordable—newer swanky suites have bang-up views, fireplaces, decks, whirlpool baths, and heated towel racks, and they command prices a hippie would surely protest. Perhaps because we remember its humble past, the renovated Outlook Inn feels a little soulless to us. But the bar and restaurant have a loyal local clientele: always a good sign. *$$–$$$; AE, DIS, MC, V; local checks only; info@outlook-inn.com; www.outlook-inn.com; downtown.* &

Rosario Resort & Spa / ★★★

1400 ROSARIO RD, ROSARIO; 360-376-2222 OR 800-562-8820

This historic, waterfront estate built by 1900s Seattle industrialist Robert Moran was converted to a resort in the 1960s and was popular with boaters. Once infected by a dated '60s-style decor, the resort has seen expensive rebuilding and room-redecorating efforts in recent years, in an attempt to return the mansion to its former style and elegance. Teakwood floors, rich mahogany paneling, original furnishings, and Tiffany accents give you a feel for the home's past. Now the ugly, obstreperous duckling is a dazzling swan. One thing can't be overcome though: most guest rooms are perched on a hillside behind the mansion, and are a steep climb unless you take the resort's van service. The compensation is sweeping views. Other guest rooms, and a cottage, are on landscaped grounds along Cascade Bay, steps away from the water. All rooms are cheerily decorated in an upscale country style; almost all offer bay views. The Moran mansion itself houses a museum area and music room (don't miss the organ recital and presentation by historian Christopher Peacock), gift shops, lounge, veranda, and restaurants. Spa services—massages are most popular—and a swimming pool are located on the lower level. Also on the grounds are a grocery/snack shop, a kayaking concession, and new dive shop. A conference center is nearby. *$$$–$$$$; AE, DC, DIS, MC, V; checks OK; info@ rosarioresort.com; www.rosarioresort.com; from Eastsound turn east on Olga Rd and follow it 3 miles.* &

Spring Bay Inn / ★★★

464 SPRING BAY TRAIL, OLGA; 360/376-5531

It's a long dirt road getting here, but rarely is a drive so amply rewarded. Situated where 57 wooded acres meet the sea is the handsome Spring Bay Inn, as stylishly appointed inside as it is scenic outside. The interior reflects the naturalist sensibilities of innkeepers Sandy Playa and Carl Burger, an engaging and youthful pair of retired state park rangers whose crunchy-granola lifestyle sets them apart from other upscale B&B owners. The angular great room, with its fieldstone fireplace and vaulted ceiling, showcases a stunning view. Upstairs, each of four thoughtfully decorated guest rooms has its own bath and Rumford fireplace; two have balconies. Downstairs, the Ranger's Suite has 27 windows and its own hot tub. Coffee, muffins, and fresh fruit are delivered to each door— a little sustenance for the complimentary two-hour guided kayak tour around Obstruction Island. Return to the lodge for a big healthy brunch. The property is adjacent to Obstruction Pass State Park, and is laced with hiking trails and teeming with wildlife. After dark, ease tired muscles with a private soak under the stars in the bayside hot tub. *$$$; AE, DIS, MC, V; checks OK; follow Obstruction Pass Rd to Trailhead Rd, take right fork onto Spring Bay Trail.*

Turtleback Farm Inn / ★★
1981 CROW VALLEY RD, EASTSOUND; 360/376-4914 OR 800/376-4914

Located inland amid tall trees, rolling pastures, and private ponds, Turtleback offers seven spotless rooms dressed in simple sophistication and stunning antiques. It also offers efficiency: Turtleback's veteran innkeepers, Bill and Susan Fletcher, have thought of everything, from cocoa, coffee, and fresh fruit for nibbling to flashlights for evening forays. We found our room—the Nook—aptly named. It's worth the extra $50 or more to go up a notch or two: choose either of the larger upstairs rooms, or one of two downstairs rooms with private decks overlooking the meadow. Susan cooks magnificent breakfasts, and serves them on the deck in sunny weather. A new four-suite building has been added in the orchard, sided with natural cedar that will weather like a barn. Inside are spacious rooms with fir flooring, trim, and doors, each furnished with a Vermont Casting stove, king beds, bar-size refrigerator, and spacious bath with large claw-footed tub and shower; all have private decks. Children are welcome in suites by prior arrangement to ensure privacy and quiet for other guests. *$$$; AE, DIS, MC, V; checks OK; www.turtlebackinn.com; 6 miles from ferry on Crow Valley Rd.* &

Windsong Bed & Breakfast / ★
213 DEER HARBOR RD, DEER HARBOR; 360/376-2500 OR 800/669-3948

A 1917 schoolhouse-turned-B&B (the first to be registered on Orcas), the renovated Windsong is now a warmly elegant bed-and-breakfast inn. Each of four rooms is beautifully decorated and amply proportioned, with queen- or king-size bed and private bath; three have fireplaces. We favor the Rhapsody for its view through the trees to Westsound. A living room for guests offers a big TV and comfy couches; outside, a hot tub bubbles. Co-host Sam Haines serves a four-course breakfast. *$$; MC, V; checks OK; reservations@windsonginn.com; www.windsonginn.com; on Deer Harbor Rd just west of Horseshoe Hwy.*

San Juan Island

San Juan Island, the most populated in the archipelago, also supports the biggest town, **FRIDAY HARBOR**. The **SAN JUAN HISTORICAL MUSEUM** (405 Price St, Friday Harbor; 360/378-3949) is filled with memorabilia from the island's early days. Another bit of history is hidden away at the **ROCHE HARBOR RESORT** (see review). Here you'll find a mausoleum, a bizarre monument that may tell more about timber tycoon John McMillin than does all the rest of Roche Harbor. The ashes of family members are contained in a set of stone chairs that surround a concrete dining room table. They're ringed by a set of 30-foot-high columns, symbolic of McMillin's adherence to Masonic beliefs.

Other attractions on the island include the mid-19th-century sites of the **AMERICAN** and **ENGLISH CAMPS** (360/378-2240), established when ownership of the island was under dispute. The conflict led to the infamous Pig War of

1859–60, so called because the sole casualty was a pig. Americans and British shared joint occupation until 1872, when the dispute was settled in favor of the United States. The English camp, toward the island's northwest end, is wooded and secluded; the American camp at the south end consists of open, windy prairie and beach. Either makes a fine picnic spot. So does beautiful **SAN JUAN COUNTY PARK** (50 San Juan Park Rd; 360/378-2992), on the west side of the island, where it's also possible to camp on 19 sites on a pretty cove (reservations suggested). Another camping option is **LAKEDALE RESORT** (2627 Roche Harbor Rd; 360/378-2350; www.lakedale.com; reservations recommended), a private campground on 84 acres with three lakes for swimming and fishing, and six two-bedroom log cabins.

The best diving in the archipelago (some claim it's the best cold-water diving in the world) can be had here; **EMERALD SEAS AQUATICS** (180 1st St; 360/378-2772), in Friday Harbor, has rentals, charters, and classes. Several charter boats are available for whale watching (primarily Orcas) and fishing; try the **WESTERN PRINCE** (1 block from ferry landing; 360/378-5315 or 800/757-ORCA). Those distrustful of their sea legs can visit the marvelous **WHALE MUSEUM** (62 1st St; 360/378-4710), with exhibits and excursions devoted to the resident cetaceans; or go to the nation's first official whale-watching park at **LIME KILN POINT STATE PARK** on the island's west side. Bring binoculars and patience.

Oyster fans happily visit **WESTCOTT BAY SEA FARMS** (904 Westcott Dr; 360/378-2489) off Roche Harbor Road, 2 miles south of Roche Harbor Resort, where you can help yourself to oysters at bargain prices.

The island's two-decade-old **JAZZ FESTIVAL** (360/378-5509; mid-Oct in Friday Harbor) moved from summer to fall, but still features three days of jazz, blues, and Dixeland.

RESTAURANTS

Duck Soup Inn / ★★

3090 ROCHE HARBOR RD, FRIDAY HARBOR; 360/378-4878

Richard and Gretchen Allison are committed to a kitchen with an ambitious reach, using local seafoods and seasonal ingredients, and they've succeeded admirably. The wood-paneled dining room, with its stone fireplace, wooden booths, and high windows, is a charmer. The menu is limited to house specialties—succulent sautéed prawns in wild blackberry sauce, applewood-smoked Westcott Bay oysters, and grilled fresh fish. House-baked bread served with tangy anchovy paste (and butter), a small bowl of perfectly seasoned soup, and a large green salad accompany the ample portions. *$$; DIS, MC, V; checks OK; dinner Wed–Sun (closed in winter); beer and wine; reservations recommended (summer weekends); 5 miles northwest of Friday Harbor.* &

Katrina's / ★

135 2ND ST, FRIDAY HARBOR; 360/378-7290

Kate Stone runs her one-woman culinary show in this airy Victorian, where you can sit at the counter and watch her cook, or try the private and fun "mermaid" booth. Look for a rotating-menu format of simple sensations, as well as seafood, chalked on the blackboard: her signature spinach-cheese pie and green salad with toasted hazelnuts and garlicky blue cheese dressing are standouts. Breads are homemade, and so are desserts, fancy tortes or simple fruit cobblers and heaping pieces of pie. Kate's sweetest specialty: decorated birthday cakes. *$; MC, V; checks OK; lunch Mon–Fri; no alcohol; reservations not accepted; downtown.* ප්

The Place Next to the San Juan Ferry Cafe / ★

1 SPRING ST, FRIDAY HARBOR; 360/378-8707

Behind the unassuming name and the viewy waterside location that typically guarantees mediocrity is this striving concern, garnering much praise from locals. Chef/owner Steven Anderson features a rotating world of cuisines, focusing on fish and shellfish, from BC king salmon to Westcott Bay oysters. A fillet of salmon might come with gingery citrus sauce, a plate of black bean ravioli topped with tiger prawns in a buttery glaze. Servers know exactly how much time you have if your boat's in sight: with luck, enough time to savor the sumptuous crème caramel. *$$; MC, V; checks OK; dinner every day (varies in winter); beer and wine; reservations not necessary; on water, at foot of Spring St.* ප්

Springtree Cafe / ★★

310 SPRING ST, FRIDAY HARBOR; 360/378-4848

Chef/owner Steve Anderson bought the Springtree Cafe in 1999 and garners as much praise for his effort here as at The Place Next to the San Juan Ferry Cafe (see review). Decor remains simple—plain wooden tables graced by a few fresh flowers, some photographs. But the menu, emphasizing seafood, organics, and local produce, is anything but. A grilled salmon preparation is almost always on the menu, and flavors lean toward Pacific Rim rather than European. Dine outdoors under the elm tree on the patio, weather permitting. *$$; MC, V; local checks only; dinner every day (closed off season); beer and wine; reservations recommended; downtown.* ප්

LODGINGS

Duffy House / ★

760 PEAR POINT RD, FRIDAY HARBOR; 360/378-5604 OR 800/972-2089

This 1920s farmhouse looking out upon Griffin Bay and the Olympics commands a splendid, isolated site on the island's southeast side. Decorated with antiques and accented with classic mahogany trim, Duffy House offers five comfy guest rooms, all with private baths. The sunken living room sports a large fireplace and a bounty of island information. Even neophyte birdwatchers won't be able to miss the bald eagles here; they nest just across the street, near the trail to the beach. *$$; MC, V; checks OK; duffyhouse@rock island.com; www.san-juan.net/duffyhouse; take Argyle Rd south from town to Pear Point Rd.*

Friday Harbor House / ★★★

130 WEST ST, FRIDAY HARBOR; 360/378-8455

Some shudder at the sore-thumb architecture of San Juan Island's poshest inn, a sister property of the Inn at Langley on Whidbey Island. Others consider this stylish urban outpost a welcome relief from Victorian B&Bs. Regardless, the interior is a bastion of spare and soothing serenity, a mood abetted by professional management. Each of the 20 rooms is decorated in muted tones, lending a contemporary feel, with gas fireplaces and (noisy) Jacuzzis positioned to absorb both the warmth from the fireplace and the harbor view. Some rooms have tiny balconies, but not all offer a full waterfront view. Breakfast is continental, with delicious hot scones. The dining room, with its knockout harbor view, maintains the spartan cool of the rest of the inn, but warms up considerably under the influence of chef Laurie Paul's cooking. Service is efficient. *$$$; AE, MC, V; checks OK; fhhouse@rock island.com; www.fridayharborhouse.com; from ferry, left on Spring, right on 1st, right on West.* &

Friday's Historical Inn / ★

35 1ST ST, FRIDAY HARBOR; 360/378-5848 OR 800/352-2632

The former Elite Hotel is living up to its old name. Innkeepers Debbie and Steve Demarest took this longtime bunkhouse and have given it a completely new life. Eleven rooms are decorated in rich colors of wine and water. The best room is unquestionably the third-floor perch with its own deck (and water view), kitchen, double shower, and Jacuzzi. Heated bathroom floors and occasional fresh-baked cookies are just two thoughtful touches. *$$; MC, V; checks OK; fridays@friday-harbor.com; www.friday-harbor.com; 2 blocks up from ferry.*

Harrison House Suites / ★★★

235 C ST, FRIDAY HARBOR; 360/378-3587 OR 800/407-7933

This crisply renovated Craftsman inn, run by the effusive Farhad Ghatan, features five impressive suites: all with kitchens and private baths, four with decks, three with whirlpool tubs. It's modern and angular, and rooms with views overlook the whole scenic sweep of Friday Harbor. There's a pretty water garden, plus flower, fruit, and vegetable gardens for use of the guests—the only place we've seen in the islands where you can pick your own salad and toss it in your own kitchen. All this and it's underpriced, for the region—great for families and/or groups. Complimentary fresh-baked breads are served each evening; mornings, it's fresh scones. Ghatan also runs a little cafe on the premises—guests only—for private dinners, parties, and catered events. *$$; AE, DIS, MC, V; checks OK; hhsuites@rockisland.com; www.san-juan-lodging.com; 2 blocks from downtown.* &

Highland Inn / ★★★

WEST SIDE OF SAN JUAN ISLAND; 360/378-9450 OR 888/400-9850

Innkeeper of note Helen King sold her deservedly famous 12-room Babbling Brook Inn in Santa Cruz, California, packed it up, and moved to the west side of San Juan Island. There she built the inn of her dreams: just two lovely suites, one at each end of her house, both with views of the Olympic Mountains, Victoria, and Haro Strait from the 88-foot-long deck. Licensed for just two couples a night (no children), the Highland Inn is everything you could ask for in privacy and hospitality. Suites are huge, with sitting rooms, wood-burning fireplaces, and marble bathrooms—each with its own whirlpool tub for two and steam-cabinet shower. Guests may use the whirlpool bath on the deck, and share a common dining room. *$$$; AE, MC, V; checks OK; helen@highlandinn. com; www.highlandinn.com; call for directions.*

Lonesome Cove Resort / ★

416 LONESOME COVE RD, FRIDAY HARBOR; 360/378-4477

Back in 1945, Roy and Neva Durhack sailed their 35-foot yacht here from the Hawaiian Islands. They were getting ready to sail around the world, but once they saw Lonesome Cove, their wanderlust subsided. They're not here anymore; the (Cellular One) McCaw brothers of Seattle bought the place and reduced the wooded acreage from 75 to 10 acres, but the resort remains pretty. Six immaculate little cabins set among trees at the water's edge, manicured lawns, and domesticated deer that wander the woods make the place a favorite for lighthearted honeymooners. Sunsets are spectacular. No pets—too many baby ducks around. *$$; MC, V; checks OK; 2-night min, 5-night min in summer; take Roche Harbor Rd 9 miles north to Lonesome Cove Rd.* &

Roche Harbor Resort

ROCHE HARBOR; 360/378-2155 OR 800/451-8910

🌲 When you walk out of the stately old ivy-clad Hotel de Haro at Roche Harbor and gaze out at the trellised, cobblestoned waterfront and yacht-crammed bay, you might forget all about the creaky, uneven floorboards; the piecework wallpaper; the sparse furnishings. This faded gem evolved from the company town that John McMillin built a century ago for his lime quarry, once the largest west of the Mississippi. At this writing, four new luxury suites (the McMillin Suites) are opening in McM's old house, which also houses the resort's largest restaurant. Suites have killer views, large claw-footed soaking tubs, big beds, and room service. The old hotel has seen some renovation since Teddy Roosevelt visited, but not so you'd notice. Here are single rooms with shared baths and four suites with private baths. The more-than-a-century-old resort has a terrific view and pretty gardens, plus a few nicely renovated cottages and condos. Between strolling the gardens, swimming, tennis, and visiting the mausoleum (really), there's plenty to do at Roche Harbor. *$$$; AE, MC, V; checks OK; roche@rocheharbor.com; www.rocheharbor.com; on waterfront on northwest end of island.* &

Wharfside Bed & Breakfast / ★
K DOCK, FRIDAY HARBOR; 360/378-5661

If nothing lulls you to sleep like the gentle lap of the waves, the Wharfside's the B&B for you. It's this region's first realization of the European tradition of floating inns. Two guest rooms on the 60-foot sailboat *Jacquelyn* are nicely finished, with full amenities and that compact precision that only living on a boat can inspire. Both staterooms, fore and aft, have queen beds. Aft has its own bathroom; fore uses the bath in the main cabin. When the weather's good, enjoy the huge breakfast on deck and watch the boaters head to sea. *$$; AE, MC, V; checks OK; www.slowseason.com; north of ferry terminal on waterfront at marina.*

Tacoma, Olympia, and the South Sound

Going south, Interstate 5 takes you to the state's second-largest city, Tacoma, which is experiencing a renaissance, especially in the arts, making it attractive to travelers, and to the state's picturesque bayside capitol in Olympia.

Vashon Island

Faintly countercultural, this bucolic isle is a short ferry ride from downtown Seattle (foot passengers only), West Seattle (the Fauntleroy ferry), or Tacoma (the Point Defiance ferry), all via **WASHINGTON STATE FERRIES** (206/464-6400). It's a wonderful place to explore by bicycle, although the first long hill up from the north-end ferry dock is a killer. Few beaches are open to the public, but some public spots invite a stroll and offer a view.

Vashon has several island-based companies that market goods locally and nationally; many offer tours, but call ahead: **K2 SKIS, INC.** (19215 Vashon Hwy SW; 206/463-3631); **SEATTLE'S BEST COFFEE** (19529 Vashon Hwy SW; 206/463-5050); and **MAURY ISLAND FARMS** (99th and 204th on Vashon Hwy; 206/463-9659) with berries and preserves. **WAX ORCHARDS** (22744 Wax Orchards Rd; 206/463-9735) isn't open for tours, but you can stop and pick up fresh preserves, fruit syrups, and apple cider. Island arts are on display at the **BLUE HERON ART CENTER** (19704 Vashon Hwy SW; 206/463-5131). The **COUNTRY STORE AND GARDENS** (20211 Vashon Hwy SW; 206/463-3655) is an old-fashioned general store stocking many island-made products, along with natural-fiber apparel, housewares, and gardening supplies; you can tour the display gardens. **VASHON ISLAND KAYAK COMPANY** (Jensen Acres boathouse at Quartermaster Harbor; 206/463-9257) offers instruction and day trips, including one to Blake Island and Tillicum Village.

RESTAURANTS

Chui Ga Pan Asian Cuisine / ★

9924 SW BANK RD, VASHON; 206/463-2125

Just off the main drag through downtown Vashon is Chui Ga (previously Turtle Island Cafe), a small and friendly spot run by the Chee family (Chui Ga means "House of Chee"). Choose from a variety of Asian dishes—phad thai (meat or vegetarian), ahi tuna sashimi and sushi, Chinese-style Mongolian beef. The wine list offers a good selection of reasonably priced domestic and imported wines, by the bottle or glass, or try sake or Japanese beer. Desserts from Pacific Dessert Company. *$$; MC, V; checks OK; lunch Mon–Fri, dinner every day; beer and wine; reservations recommended; near Vashon Hwy.* &

Express Cuisine / ★

17629 VASHON HWY SW, VASHON; 206/463-6626

This storefront restaurant and catering company may not look like much from the outside, but locals line up for gourmet takeout dinners, or fill communal tables to enjoy dishes like tender prime rib, mouth-watering sirloin stroganoff, and smoked salmon over linguine with a mushroom alfredo sauce. Dinners include an excellent soup or salad (if seafood chowder is on the list, choose it). Service is counter-style. Come early or call ahead for takeout; otherwise, you might have to wait. *$; no credit cards; local checks only; dinner Wed–Sat; beer and wine; reservations not accepted; near Bank Rd.* &

LODGINGS

Back Bay Inn / ★

24007 VASHON HWY SW, VASHON; 206/463-5355

Although the Back Bay Inn is located on a busy, potentially noisy corner, the four antique-filled upstairs rooms are charming. Ask for one of the bigger, end-of-the-hall rooms. Overnight guests play checkers in the downstairs fireplace library. Chef/owner Robert Stowe features wild game, such as pheasant and elk, in the dining room, open to the public Tuesday through Saturday nights, as well as for breakfast on weekends (every morning for guests). The extensive breakfast menu includes omelets (smoked salmon or shiitake mushroom, for example) and other waker-uppers. *$$; AE, MC, V; checks OK; www.amazinggetaways. com; in Burton.*

Harbor Inn / ★

9118 SW HARBOR DR, VASHON; 206/463-6794

Innkeeper Kathy Casper hosts guests at her modern Tudor-style home on the waterfront near Burton Acres Park. Three antiques-accented guest rooms have water views and private baths. Best is the showstopping suite with its king-size four-poster bed, gas fireplace, and spacious bath, featuring a jetted tub for two and separate shower. Full breakfast prepared individually to order could include French toast, omelets, or fruit and cereal. There's a TV/VCR in each room and

video library with over 200 titles, and two mountain bikes for guests' use. *$$$;
no credit cards; checks OK; casperk@mindspring.com; near Burton.*

Tacoma

Flanked by Commencement Bay and the Narrows and backed by Mount
Rainier, Tacoma is no longer just a blue-collar mill town, but a growing urban
center with a thriving cultural core. The city has fervently embraced the idea of
preservation. Historic buildings in the downtown warehouse district have been
converted from industrial use to hip residential and commercial functions; the
University of Washington now has a branch campus here. Stately homes and
cobblestone streets in the north end are often used as sets by Hollywood's
moviemakers, and students still fill the turreted chateau of Stadium High School.

OLD CITY HALL (625 Commerce), with its coppered roof, Renaissance
clock, and bell tower; the Romanesque **FIRST PRESBYTERIAN CHURCH** (20
Tacoma Ave S); the rococo **PYTHIAN LODGE** (925½ Broadway); and the one-
of-a-kind coppered **UNION STATION** (17th and Pacific), built in 1911 and now
the much praised Federal Courthouse—all delight history and architecture
buffs. The old Union Station rotunda is also graced by some spectacular work
by glass artist and Tacoma native Dale Chihuly. This permanent exhibit is actu-
ally an annex of the Tacoma Art Museum, open to the public at no charge, so
do drop in for a peek.

The **TACOMA ART MUSEUM** (12th and Pacific; 253/272-4258) is housed for
the time being in a former downtown bank; watch for its grand new home in
2003. The small museum has paintings by Renoir, Degas, and Pissarro, as well
as a collection of contemporary American prints. The **WASHINGTON STATE
HISTORY MUSEUM** (1911 Pacific Ave; 888/238-4373) is housed in a handsome
building just south of Union Station. It offers a state-of-the-art museum experi-
ence, providing history and innovation under the same roof; from the outside,
however, the museum has been designed to blend into its surroundings and
complement the station. The **RUSTON WAY WATERFRONT** (between N 49th and
N 54th Sts), a 6-mile mix of parks and restaurants, is thronged with people in
any weather.

The **BROADWAY CENTER FOR THE PERFORMING ARTS** (901 Broadway
Plaza; 253/591-5894) often does shows at both the Pantages and Rialto The-
aters. The restored 1,100-seat **PANTAGES THEATER** (901 Broadway Plaza),
originally designed in 1918 by nationally known movie-theater architect B.
Marcus Priteca, is the focal point of the reviving downtown cultural life—dance,
music, and stage presentations.

POINT DEFIANCE PARK (on northwest side of Tacoma, call for directions;
253/305-1000) has 500 acres of untouched forest jutting out into Puget Sound
and is one of the most dramatically sited and creatively planned city parks in
the country. The wooded 5-mile drive and parallel hiking trails open up now
and then for sweeping views of the water, Vashon Island, Gig Harbor, and the
Olympic Mountains. There are rose, rhododendron, Japanese, and Northwest

native gardens; a railroad village with a working steam engine; a reconstruction of Fort Nisqually (originally built in 1833); a museum; a swimming beach; and the much acclaimed **POINT DEFIANCE ZOO AND AQUARIUM** (5400 N Pearl; 253/591-5335). Watching the almost continuous play of seals, sea lions, and the white beluga whale from an underwater vantage point is a rare treat.

WRIGHT PARK (Division and "I" Sts) is a serene in-city park with many trees, a duck-filled pond, and a beautifully maintained, fragrant conservatory, built of glass and steel in 1890. One of the area's largest estates is now **LAKE-WOLD GARDENS** (12317 Gravelly Lake Dr SW; exit 124 off I-5 to Gravelly Lake Dr; 253/584-3360; open Thurs–Mon, Apr–Sept, and Mon, Thurs, and Fri in winter), on a beautiful 10-acre site overlooking Gravelly Lake in Lakewood, 10 minutes south of Tacoma. Recognized nationally as one of the outstanding gardens in America, Lakewold Gardens offers guided and nonguided tours.

The **TACOMA DOME** (2727 E "D" St; 253/572-3663), the world's largest wooden dome, is the site of many entertainment and trade shows as well as a sports center. Fans who like baseball played outdoors in a first-class ballpark arrive in enthusiastic droves at Cheney Stadium to watch the **TACOMA RAINIERS** (2502 S Tyler St; 253/752-7707), the triple-A affiliate of the Seattle Mariners.

Thirsty at the end of the day? **ENGINE HOUSE NO. 9** (611 N Pine St; 253/272-3435) near the University of Puget Sound is a friendly, neighborhood beer-lover's dream of a tavern (minus the smoke). Another fun tavern to check out is **THE SPAR** (2121 N 30th; 253/627-8215) in Old Town.

RESTAURANTS

Altezzo / ★★

1320 BROADWAY PLAZA (SHERATON TACOMA HOTEL), TACOMA; 253/572-3200

This attractive restaurant is "lofty" in space and attitude. Its location at the top of the Sheraton provides a great view of downtown and the surrounding area (request a window table), and some of the best Italian cuisine in Tacoma. New chef Daniel O'Leary hails from San Francisco and does a delicious cioppino; the ravioli with asparagus and a light lemon cream sauce works well too. The tiramisù is the real McCoy. The bar is a great place to kick back with a glass of wine and a plate of antipasto and enjoy the view. *$$; AE, DC, MC, V; checks OK; dinner every day; full bar; reservations recommended; between 13th and 15th.*

Bimbo's / ★

1516 PACIFIC AVE, TACOMA; 253/383-5800

Don't be put off by the slightly disreputable name or location: here's a family Italian restaurant that's attracted regulars for 75 years. Members of the original owner's family are still cooking traditional recipes with little regard for trends. Rabbit, once the most common source of meat in their region of Tuscany, is served year-round in a hearty, full-bodied tomato sauce. Pork ribs are meaty and luscious, and aficionados of that Italian favorite, tripe, find it judiciously treated here. The hallmark tomato sauce must cook for hours to reach that thick, rich flavor and deep color; it's a perfect partner for the hearty pasta dishes. *$; AE, DIS, MC, V; local checks only; lunch Mon–Sat, dinner every day; full bar; reservations not necessary; at 15th.*

The Cliff House / ★★

6300 MARINE VIEW DR, TACOMA; 253/927-0400

Over the years, this restaurant survived on its commanding view of Commencement Bay and Tacoma's north end, and its formal, pretentious airs. Chef Jon Brzycki came on board, however, and established a menu that ensures this place will do more than survive: homemade venison sausage with a wild-rice pancake and dried-fruit chutney, a delicious smoked-duck salad with a sesame dressing, or pan-roasted pheasant with a light touch of port wine sauce accented with pears and cranberries. Desserts, less noteworthy, are a trip down memory lane, with cherries jubilee and crepes suzette flambéed tableside. Maybe finish with a brandy and enjoy the view. *$$$; AE, DC, MC, V; no checks; lunch, dinner every day; full bar; reservations recommended; follow East Side Dr to top of hill.*

East & West Cafe / ★

5319 TACOMA MALL BLVD, TACOMA; 253/475-7755

What this restaurant lacks in location, it makes up for tenfold in great food and charm. East & West Cafe is a haven of Asian delights on the busy thoroughfare south of the Tacoma Mall. Owner Vien Floyd, a Saigon native, has gained a loyal local following. Her incomparable personality helps make meals here a treat. The emphasis is on Vietnamese and Thai cuisine, a mix that invites you to experiment: the Saigon Crepe is a large curried crepe filled with bean sprouts, strips of chicken, prawns, and vegetables, with dipping sauce. Vegetables are always crisp and bright and full of fresh flavor; sauces have character; meats are tender—you really can't go wrong. For the price, it's hard to have a better meal in Tacoma. *$; AE, DIS, MC, V; local checks only; lunch, dinner Mon–Sat; beer and wine; reservations not accepted; 56th St exit off I-5.* ⅊

Fujiya / ★★

1125 COURT C, TACOMA; 253/627-5319

Absolute consistency is what attracts a loyal clientele from near and far to Masahiro Endo's stylish downtown Japanese restaurant. For years this has been a favorite spot for sushi and sashimi. Begin your meal with *gyoza* (savory pork-stuffed dumplings). The real test of a Japanese restaurant is tempura, and Endo makes certain his is feathery-crisp. For those who prefer seafood cooked, the yosenabe (seafood stew) is full of delicious things served in a small cast-iron pot. He's a generous and friendly man, Mr. Endo; seldom an evening goes by that he doesn't offer a complimentary tidbit of one kind or another. *$$; AE, MC, V; checks OK; lunch Mon–Fri, dinner Mon–Sat; beer and wine; reservations recommended (dinner); between Broadway and Market.*

Harbor Lights / ★
2761 RUSTON WY, TACOMA; 253/752-8600

Decor is circa 1950, with glass floats, stuffed prize fish, and a giant lobster, but Tacoma's pioneer Ruston Way waterfront restaurant still packs them in (reserve early). Up-to-the-minute it may not be, but that doesn't seem to bother seafood fans who regularly crowd into the noisy dining room to consume buckets of steamed clams and mounds of perfectly cooked panfried oysters. Fillet of sole is grilled to perfection; halibut-and-chips are the best around, as are crisp hash browns. The portions are so gargantuan that only an ace trencherman can dig his way to the bottom of the plate. *$$; AE, DC, DIS, MC, V; checks OK; lunch Mon–Sat, dinner every day; full bar; reservations recommended; City Center exit off I-5.*

Katie Downs / ★
3211 RUSTON WY, TACOMA; 253/756-0771

Katie Downs's Philadelphia-style deep-dish pizza is a winner. Place your order at the counter for one of the classic combinations. Especially good is the Fearless, which recklessly matches smoked bacon and provolone cheese with white onions, spicy peperoncini—and lots of fresh garlic. Since pizzas can take 30 minutes to make and bake, order steamer clams to tide you over while you wait and watch the tugs, barges, freighters, and sailboats move across Commencement Bay. This place is noisy, boisterous, and fun, but remember it is a tavern (no minors). *$; MC, V; local checks only; lunch, dinner every day; beer and wine; reservations not accepted; City Center exit off I-5.* &

Stanley and Seaforts Steak, Chop, and Fish House / ★★
115 E 34TH ST, TACOMA; 253/473-7300

Every seat in this restaurant has a panoramic view of Tacoma, its busy harbor, and, on a clear day, the Olympics. But this is one view restaurant that doesn't rest on its sunsetting laurels. The emphasis is on quality meats and seafood simply grilled over applewood with flavorings of herbs and fruits. It's the combination of interesting menu selections and dependability that has made Stanley and Seaforts a favorite for two decades. The spacious bar features distinctive Scotch whiskeys—and a great sunset. *$$; AE, DC, DIS, MC, V; local checks only; lunch Mon–Fri, dinner every day; full bar; reservations recommended; City Center exit off I-5.* &

LODGINGS

Chinaberry Hill / ★★
302 TACOMA AVE N, TACOMA; 253/272-1282

This 1889 mansion (on the National Register of Historic Places) in Tacoma's historic Stadium District has been beautifully restored by Cecil and Yarrow Wayman and turned into a charming, romantic bed-and-breakfast. Lovers of old homes delight in the attention to detail, like the pocket door between the living room and dining room, faced with two different types of wood to match the wood used in each room. Three rooms are in the main house: we prefer the Pantages Suite, with its view of Commencement Bay and a Jacuzzi, or the Manning Suite, which has bay windows overlooking the garden, a fireplace, and a Jacuzzi. Families enjoy the Catchpenny Cottage behind the main house; once the estate's carriage house, it has been made over into a lovely two-story retreat (plans are in the works to make two separate suites out of the two floors). The Waymans serve a full breakfast in the dining room or, on sunny days, on the veranda overlooking the water. *$$$; MC, V; checks OK; wayman 29@mail.idt.net; www.wa.net/chinaberry; City Center exit from I-5.*

Sheraton Tacoma Hotel / ★
1320 BROADWAY PLAZA, TACOMA; 253/572-3200 OR 800/845-9466
This is the best hotel in town. With the Tacoma Convention Center next door, it attracts a lot of conventioneers and corporate travelers. The recently updated decor includes lively red and gold fabrics that grace the lobby and guest rooms in a style that likens it to other properties managed by the highly regarded Kimpton Group (affiliated with such fine hotels as the Alexis and the Vintage Park in Seattle). Most rooms look out over Commencement Bay or have a view of Mount Rainier. For some of the best Italian food in the area, head to top-floor Altezzo (see review). *$$$; AE, DC, MC, V; checks OK; www.sheratontacoma.com; between 13th and 15th.*

The Villa Bed & Breakfast / ★★
705 N 5TH ST, TACOMA; 253/572-1157
In the heart of Tacoma's historic residential North End, this home stands out from the crowd. Built for a local businessman in 1925, it was designed with the Mediterranean in mind: open and airy, with high arched windows, tiled roof, and a palm tree out front. Becky and Greg Anglemyer transformed the spacious home into a gracious bed-and-breakfast. Our favorite room is actually the relatively small Maid's Quarters on the top floor—utterly private, with a grand view of Commencement Bay and the Olympics. Guests have more space in the Bay View Suite, with a fireplace, a sitting area, and a bay-view veranda. A CD player in every room (and a good CD collection downstairs) is music to our ears. *$$; MC, V; checks OK; villabb@aol.com; www.tribnet.com/bb/villa.htp; City Center exit from I-5.*

Puyallup
At the head of the fertile Puyallup Valley southeast of Tacoma, this frontier farm town serves as one gateway to Mount Rainier, with Highway 410 leading to Chinook Pass, and Highways 162 and 165 leading to the Carbon River and Mowich Lake. The bulb, rhubarb, and berry farmland continues to be cultivated, but much of it has been strip-malled and auto-row-ravaged around the edges. Avoid the fast-food strip on Highway 161 to the south, and head east up the valley to Sumner and the White River (Hwy 410), or Orting, Wilkeson, and Carbonado (Hwys 162 and 165).

The **EZRA MEEKER MANSION** (312 Spring St; 206/848-1770; open Wed–Sun, 1–4pm, mid-Mar–mid-Dec) is the finest original pioneer mansion left in Washington. Its builder and first occupant, Ezra Meeker, introduced hops to the Puyallup Valley. The lavish 17-room Italianate house (circa 1890) now stands beautifully restored in the rear parking lot of a Main Street furniture store.

Puyallup is big on old-time seasonal celebrations, and it's home to two of the biggest in the Northwest: the **DAFFODIL FESTIVAL AND PARADE** (253/627-6176; early Apr), and the Western Washington Fair—better known as the **PUYALLUP FAIR** (110 9th Ave SW; 253/845-1771; Sept)—one of the nation's biggest fairs, with food, games, rides, and premier touring bands. **PUYALLUP DOWNTOWN FARMERS MARKET** is held Saturdays, starting at 9am, at Pioneer Park (corner of Pioneer and Meridian Sts). It runs throughout the growing season, usually late May through September.

Parkland

RESTAURANTS

Marzano's / ★

516 GARFIELD ST, PARKLAND; 253/537-4191
The reputation of Lisa Marzano's voluptuous cooking has people arriving from miles away. In fair weather, outside seating on two deck areas is an added plus to this large space. Meals begin with fresh-baked crusty bread, ready to be topped with shredded Parmesan and herbed olive oil. For entrees, try the stubby rigatoni, perfect for capturing the extraordinary *boscaiola* sauce made with mushrooms and ham; lasagne is sumptuous, as is elegant chicken piccata pungent with capers and lemons. When all's said and done, we'd go back even if it were just for the many-layered chocolate poppyseed cake floating in whipped cream. *$$; DIS, MC, V; checks OK; lunch Tues–Fri, dinner Tues–Sat; beer and wine; reservations required; adjacent to Pacific Lutheran University, Hwy 512 exit from I-5.* &

Gig Harbor

Once an undisturbed fishing village (and still homeport to an active commercial fleet) northwest of Tacoma across the Narrows Bridge on Highway 16, Gig Harbor is now part suburbia, part weekend destination. Boating is still important, with good anchorage and various moorage docks attracting gunwale-to-gunwale pleasure craft. When the clouds break, Mount Rainier holds court for all. A variety of interesting shops and galleries line **HARBORVIEW DRIVE**, the single street that almost encircles the harbor. It's a picturesque spot for browsing and window-shopping.

Gig Harbor was planned for boat traffic, not automobiles (with resulting traffic congestion and limited parking), yet it's still a good place for celebrations. An arts festival in mid-July and a jazz festival in mid-August are two main events. The **GIG HARBOR FARMERS MARKET** (at Pierce Transit Park and Ride; Sat, May–Oct) features locally grown produce, plants, and Northwest gifts. For festival and other information, contact the **GIG HARBOR CHAMBER OF COMMERCE** (3302 Harborview Dr; 253/851-6865).

PERFORMANCE CIRCLE (6615 38th Ave NW; 253/851-7529), Gig Harbor's resident theater group, mounts enjoyable productions year-round, with summer shows staged outside in the meadow at 9916 Peacock Hill Avenue NW. Theatergoers bring picnics and blankets, and watch the shows beneath the stars. It's turned into a wonderful small-town custom.

Nearby **KOPACHUCK STATE PARK** (follow signs from Hwy 16; 253/265-3606) is a popular destination, as are **PENROSE POINT** and **JOEMMA STATE PARKS** on the Key Peninsula (south of Hwy 302, west of Hwy 16 at Purdy), all with beaches for clam digging. Purdy Spit, right on Highway 302, is most accessible.

RESTAURANTS

The Green Turtle / ★
2905 HARBORVIEW DR, GIG HARBOR; 253/851-3167

New owners Nolan and Sue Glenn, and chef Casey Aaseth, have made minor enhancements to a menu that's popular with community regulars. Panfried wontons with a vibrant dipping sauce are still a favorite. The spicy seafood sauté is a dressed-up phad thai with shrimp, scallops, and clams. Desserts are worth the extra calories here—with New York–style cheesecake, mango ice cream, a cinnamon-poached pear bathed in chocolate sauce, and a delicious chocolate macadamia nut torte. In fine weather, dine on the deck overlooking the harbor. *$$; AE, DIS, MC, V; checks OK; dinner Wed–Sun; beer and wine; reservations recommended; past Tides Tavern.* &

Marco's Ristorante Italiano / ★
7707 PIONEER WY, GIG HARBOR; 253/858-2899

Everyone in this area loves what Marco (Mark Wambold) and his wife, Mimi, have done for dining in Gig Harbor. It shows in the busy, crowded bustle of the place. Mimi's the star behind the stove, her menu ranging from traditional (spaghetti and meatballs, handmade tortellini in fresh pesto) to more original specials (a dense, tender piece of tuna sautéed in red wine). Deep-fried olives are an unusual starter. Adjacent to the restaurant is Mimi's Pantry, a retail shop featuring Italian specialty goods. *$$; AE, MC, V; checks OK; lunch, dinner Tues–Sat; beer and wine; reservations recommended; 2 blocks from harbor.*

Tides Tavern
2925 HARBORVIEW DR, GIG HARBOR; 253/858-3982

"Meet you at the Tides" has become such a universal invitation that this tavern perched over the harbor often has standing room only, especially on sunny days when the deck is open. People come by boat, seaplane, and car. Originally a general store next to the ferry landing, the Tides is a full-service tavern (no minors) with pool table, Gig Harbor memorabilia, and live music on weekends. Indulge in man-size sandwiches, huge charbroiled burgers, a gargantuan shrimp salad, and highly touted fish-and-chips (pizzas are only passable). *$; AE, MC, V; checks OK; lunch, dinner every day; beer and wine; reservations not accepted; www.tidestavern.com; downtown Gig Harbor.*

LODGINGS

The Maritime Inn
3212 HARBORVIEW DR, GIG HARBOR; 253/858-1818
The Maritime Inn is in downtown Gig Harbor, across the street from the waterfront. Fifteen rooms are comfortably appointed with queen-size beds, gas fireplaces, and TVs; several "specialty rooms" offer themed decor (the Polo Room, the Victorian Room) and a bit more space, including sundecks, at slightly higher cost. Space or no, the price is a bit high considering the lack of conversational privacy in the rooms. Avoid those on the front of the inn closest to the street. *$$; AE, DIS, MC, V; checks OK; info@maritimeinn.com; www.maritimeinn. com; downtown.* &

Steilacoom and Anderson Island

Once an Indian village and later the Washington Territory's first incorporated town (1854), Steilacoom today is a quiet community of old trees and houses, with no vestige of its heyday, when a trolley line ran from Bair's drugstore northeast to Tacoma. October's **APPLE SQUEEZE FESTIVAL** and midsummer's **SALMON BAKE**, with canoe and kayak races, are popular. The **STEILACOOM TRIBAL MUSEUM** (1515 Lafayette St; 253/584-6308) is located in a turn-of-the-century church overlooking the South Sound islands and the Olympic range. City Hall (253/581-1900) has tourist information.

PIERCE COUNTY FERRIES (253/596-2766) run from here to bucolic **ANDERSON ISLAND**, with restricted runs to McNeil Island (a state penitentiary). Anderson Island, a well-kept secret (there's one restaurant on the island that serves hamburgers and pizza), is home to a great B&B.

RESTAURANTS

Bair Drug and Hardware Store
1617 LAFAYETTE ST, STEILACOOM; 253/588-9668
Side orders of nostalgia are gratis when you step into Bair Drug. Except for the customers, little has changed since it was built in 1895. Products your grandparents might have used—cigars, washtubs, perfume, and apple peelers—are on display. Old post office boxes mask the bakery, which turns out pies and pastries, such as flaky apple dumplings. Best of all is a 1906 soda fountain, where you can still get a sarsaparilla, a Green River, or a genuine ice cream soda. On weekday afternoons, by reservation only, you can enjoy a traditional high tea, complete with tiny tea sandwiches and tartlets. Friday nights, come for a steak or crab-cake dinner. *$; MC, V; local checks only; breakfast, lunch every day, dinner Fri; beer and wine; reservations recommended (weekends); at Wilkes.* &

ER Rogers / ★

1702 COMMERCIAL ST, STEILACOOM; 253/582-0280

View restaurants on Puget Sound are not novelties, but views like this one are still exceptional, particularly when seen from a restored 100-year-old Queen Anne–style home. Much is noteworthy here, but the Steilacoom special prime rib, first roasted, then sliced and quickly seared, is tops. You can't beat the huge Sunday buffet brunch, with its selection of seafood: oysters on the half shell, cold poached salmon, flavorful smoked salmon, cracked crab, pickled herring, steamed clams, and fettuccine with shrimp. A beautiful upstairs bar has a widow's walk just wide enough for one row of tables. *$$; MC, V; checks OK; dinner every day, brunch Sun; full bar; reservations recommended; ERRogersmansion@aol.com; corner of Wilkes.* ♿

LODGINGS

Anderson House on Oro Bay / ★★

12024 ECKENSTAM-JOHNSON RD, ANDERSON ISLAND; 253/884-4088 OR 800/750-4088

A short ferry ride from Steilacoom and a few miles from the dock is a large house surrounded by 200 acres of woods. Randy and B. Anderson stay next door at grandfather's house, so guests have exclusive use of the whole house, with its four large bedrooms and antique furnishings. Full farm breakfasts feature breads hot from the oven, fruit pizzas, and other treats. Lunch and dinner are also served with advance notice. In addition, the Andersons rent a three-bedroom cedar fishing cabin (wood stove–heated, but updated with full kitchen amenities, microwave, and washer/dryer) hidden on Outer Amsterdam Bay with a sweeping view of the Olympics from the deck. A short bike ride from Anderson House brings you to a mile-long secluded beach. Arrangements can be made to pick up guests from the ferry. Boaters and those with seaplanes have their own dock, but check the tides. *$$; MC, V; checks OK; www.non.com/ anderson; call for directions.*

Olympia

The state capitol's centerpiece—immediately visible from the freeway—is the classic dome of the **WASHINGTON STATE LEGISLATIVE BUILDING** (416 14th Ave; 360/753-5000). Lavishly fitted with bronze and marble, this striking Romanesque structure houses the offices of the governor and other state executives. The State Senate and House of Representatives meet here in annual sessions that can be viewed by visitors.

Opposite the Legislative Building rises the pillared **TEMPLE OF JUSTICE**, seat of the State Supreme Court. To the west is the red brick **GOVERNOR'S MANSION** (501 13th Ave SW; 360/586-TOUR; open to visitors Wed, 1pm–2:45pm; reservations required).

The handsome **WASHINGTON STATE LIBRARY** (415 15th Ave SW; 360/753-2114), directly behind the Legislative Building, is open to the public during business hours; it boasts artifacts from the state's early history. The **STATE CAPITOL MUSEUM** (211 W 21st Ave; 360/753-2580) houses a permanent exhibit that includes an outstanding collection of Western Washington Native American baskets.

Downtown, on Seventh Avenue between Washington and Franklin, is the restored **OLD CAPITOL**, whose pointed towers and high-arched windows suggest a late-medieval chateau. The **WASHINGTON CENTER FOR THE PERFORMING ARTS** (on Washington between 5th Ave and Legion Wy; 360/753-8586) has brought new life to downtown. Across Fifth Avenue, the **CAPITOL THEATRE** (206 E 5th; 360/754-5378) provides a showcase for the offerings of the active **OLYMPIA FILM SOCIETY** as well as locally produced plays and musicals. Toward the harbor, the lively **OLYMPIA FARMERS MARKET** (near Percival Landing; 360/352-9096; open Thurs–Sun during growing season) displays produce, flowers, and crafts from all over the South Sound. Increasingly, the waterfront park of **PERCIVAL LANDING** (700 N Capitol Wy) is becoming a community focal point, the site of harbor festivals of all kinds. In another part of downtown, just off the Plum Street exit from Interstate 5 and adjacent to City Hall, is the serene **YASHIRO JAPANESE GARDEN**, which honors one of Olympia's sister cities.

The historic heart of the whole area (Olympia, Lacey, and Tumwater) is **TUMWATER FALLS** (exit 103 off I-5), where the Deschutes River flows into Capitol Lake. A nice walk along the river takes you past several waterfalls. This is the site of the chief local industry, the Tumwater Division of the **MILLER BREWING COMPANY** (exit 103 off I-5, follow signs; 360/754-5000; 9am–3:30pm, Mon–Sat), which brews Olympia beer. If you need something sweet after strolling the falls, stop at **DESSERTS BY TASHA NICOLE** (2822 Capitol Blvd SE; 360/352-3717) in Tumwater: The chocolate-dipped cheesecake on a stick is to die for.

There is also a triad of colleges here: the Evergreen State College, west of Olympia on Cooper Point; St. Martin's, a Benedictine monastery and college in adjacent Lacey; and South Puget Sound Community College, across US Highway 101. The **EVERGREEN STATE COLLEGE** (2700 Evergreen Pkwy NW; 360/866-6000) offers a regular schedule of plays, films, and experimental theater, as well as special events such as its annual February Tribute to Asia. Its library and pool are public.

The area's finest nature preserve lies well outside the city limits. This is the relatively unspoiled Nisqually Delta—outlet of the Nisqually River that forms at the foot of a Mount Rainier glacier and enters the Sound just north of Olympia. Take exit 114 off I-5 and follow signs to the **NISQUALLY NATIONAL WILDLIFE REFUGE** (360/753-9467). A 5-mile hiking trail follows an old dike around the delta, a wetland alive with bird life, and a mile-plus boardwalk through freshwater wetlands. Just south, a rookery of great blue herons occupies the treetops. Between the delta and Tacoma to the north is Fort Lewis Military Reservation, with surprisingly preserved habitat as well.

RESTAURANTS

Budd Bay Cafe / ★

525 N COLUMBIA ST, OLYMPIA; 360/357-6963

There's no doubt about it: the Budd Bay Cafe, with its long row of tables looking out across Budd Inlet, is still a preferred after-hours haunt of many of today's legislators, lobbyists, and state government movers and shakers. Restaurateur John Senner and owner Brett Hibberd are on hand most of the time, seeing that everyone is satisfied. Don't look for elaborate dishes here; the menu (steaks, sandwiches, pasta, salads, seafood) is designed for boaters and people to whom good talk matters more than haute cuisine. The bar is pleasant and lively, with long lists of wines by-the-glass and specialty beers. *$$; AE, DC, DIS, MC, V; checks OK; lunch Mon–Sat, dinner every day, brunch Sun; full bar; reservations recommended; BBcafe@olywa.net; www.olywa.net/BBayCafe; between A and B Sts.*

Capitale / ★★

609 CAPITOL WY S, OLYMPIA; 360/352-8007

In downtown Olympia, across Sylvester Square from the old courthouse, is a tiny, casual place serving up delicious food in a pleasant atmosphere. The walls are lined with the work of local artists, and jazz music often complements the meals; in good weather a few tables are added outside, giving this place a nice neighborhood feel. The menu is Italianesque, with interesting variations. Consider the oven-roasted wild mushrooms with sun-dried tomatoes and goat cheese served with pesto flatbread; the rectangular pizzas are excellent. *$$; MC, V; checks OK; lunch Mon–Fri, dinner Mon–Sat; beer and wine; reservations recommended; Fourfork@orcalink.com; at Legion St.* &

Gardner's Seafood and Pasta / ★★

111 W THURSTON ST, OLYMPIA; 360/786-8466

To loyal fans, Gardner's is the hands-down favorite in Olympia, with very good reason. This homey place with its wood floors and profusion of fresh flowers on all the tables makes you feel as though you're in the home of a good friend who cooks like a dream. Owners Leon and Jane Longan offer good, simple food that always hits the spot. During the right season, you might find the true Puget Sound delicacy of a dozen Calm Cove Olympia oysters, each the size of a quarter, served on the half shell. Pastas can be bland, but the appetizers, such as the roasted rock shrimp with garlic, never are. Connoisseurs of ice cream won't want to pass up Gardner's homemade product. *$$; AE, MC, V; checks OK; dinner Tues–Sat; beer and wine; reservations recommended; north on Capitol Wy to Thurston.* &

La Petite Maison / ★★

101 DIVISION NW, OLYMPIA; 360/943-8812

This tiny, converted 1890s farmhouse—overshadowed by a beetling office building—is a quiet, elegant refuge for Olympians seeking imaginative, skillfully prepared Northwest cuisine (the menu changes daily). Among its appetizers are steamed Kamilche clams and mussels, and delicate and flavorful Dungeness crab cakes served with dill sauce. Entrees include Muscovy duck with cherry glaze, and filet mignon with wild mushrooms. In spring or summer, it's pleasant to sit on the restaurant's glassed-in porch—though the view of overtrafficked Division Street outside may make you long for the days when this place was a farm. *$$; AE, MC, V; checks OK; dinner Mon–Sat; beer and wine; reservations recommended; 1 block south of Harrison.* ও

Louisa / ★★

205 CLEVELAND AVE SE, TUMWATER; 360/352-3732

Located just south of downtown Olympia in Tumwater, Louisa continues to generate quite a buzz. Co-owner Jeff Taylor (formerly of Capitale) and his wife, Connie, have fashioned a pleasantly stylish dining room with lots of blond wood, Oriental rugs, and a few scattered antiques. The cuisine is primarily Italian, with a few Northwest and Pacific Rim influences: main dishes like cheese tortellini and chicken piccata are supplemented by starters such as fresh spring rolls with soy and black vinegar dipping sauce, or local mussels in a coconut-lime-lemongrass sauce. Interestingly, the wine list features only a few Italian wines; most hail from the Northwest or California. *$$; MC, V; checks OK; dinner Mon–Sat; beer and wine; reservations recommended; follow Capitol Blvd south to Cleveland.*

Seven Gables / ★★

1205 WEST BAY DR NW, OLYMPIA; 360/352-2349

Visually, this dinner house is the most striking restaurant in Olympia, occupying as it does the fine old Carpenter Gothic residence built by the city's turn-of-the-century mayor, George B. Lane. The site takes full advantage of a splendid Mount Rainier view. Steven and Glenda Taylor are the owners of the delightful spot. Their elegant menu includes such items as homemade seafood sausage with lobster sauce, red snapper in walnut crust with basil cherry sauce, and beef tenderloin with white mushroom essence. Daily specials include a vegetarian feature. *$$; AE, MC, V; checks OK; dinner Tues–Sun; full bar; reservations recommended; 1 mile north of 4th Ave bridge.* ও

The Spar

114 E 4TH AVE, OLYMPIA; 360/357-6444

Above the restaurant's old-fashioned booths are blown-up Darius Kinsey photos of teams of old-time loggers beaming over unbelievably mammoth trees they've just brought to earth. Indeed, some 60-odd years ago, the Spar used to be known as a workingman's hangout. Today it's classless, with a mixture of students, attorneys, businesspeople, artists, politicians, fishermen, tourists, and leisured retirees. The Spar's robust milk shakes and homemade bread pudding are locally acclaimed, although much of the menu is purely average. Willapa Bay oysters or fresh salmon from the Farmers Market are sometimes available; the prime rib dinner is popular on weekends. And they are known for their full-service cigar counter. *$; AE, DC, MC, V; checks OK; breakfast, lunch, dinner every day; full bar; reservations not accepted; www. cigarshop.com; 1 block east of Capitol Wy.*

Sweet Oasis / ★

507 CAPITOL WY, OLYMPIA; 60/956-0470

This spot on Capitol Way is particularly informal, but offers some delicious Mediterranean foods. Among the daily specials are spanakopita and homemade soup. Friday and Saturday you can get *kibby sineeyah*, a deliciously offbeat dish combining ground lamb with bulgur, pine nuts, and spices, baked in squares. Falafel, meat pies, and other traditional Mediterranean items are available too. Dessert pastries are house-made and very good. On some Saturdays you get an artful belly-dancing performance, winding casually among the tables. *$; MC, V; local checks only; lunch Tues–Sat, dinner Thurs–Sat; beer and wine; reservations recommended for groups of 4 or more; at 5th Ave.* ⅃

LODGINGS

Cavanaughs at Capitol Lake

2300 EVERGREEN PARK DR, OLYMPIA; 360/943-4000 OR 800/325-4000

Few urban hotels around Puget Sound take such striking advantage of the Northwest's natural beauty as this one, dramatically perched on a high bluff above Capitol Lake, with the Capitol dome—illuminated at night—rising to the north against a green backdrop. Rooms are fairly large at this former Holiday Inn Select, an outdoor pool is heated (seasonal), and music occasionally plays in the lounge. Some rooms can be noisy; request one on the water side. *$$; AE, DC, DIS, MC, V; checks OK; www.cavanaughs.com; exit 104 from I-5.* ⅃

Harbinger Inn / ★★

1136 E BAY DR, OLYMPIA; 360/754-0389

Occupying a restored 1910 mansion, this B&B offers mission style furnishings, a fine outlook over Budd Inlet and the distant Olympic Mountains, and five choice guest rooms. Nicest is the Innkeeper's Suite on the top floor, with its king bed, sitting room, gas fireplace, and large bathroom with a soaking tub. Rooms on the front of the house have views, but rooms on the back side are farther from the street, with only the sound of a small artesian-fed waterfall to disturb the tranquillity. All rooms have private baths (although the bath for the Cloisonne Room is downstairs on the main floor, directly below the room). The inn is situated near excellent routes for bicycle riding, and Priest Point Park is close by. A full breakfast is served; entree varies but the inn is noted for its scones. The Harbinger is popular with lobbyists, so reserve ahead during the legislative session. *$$; AE, MC, V; checks OK; harbingerinn.uswestdex.com; 1 mile north of State St.*

Tenino

This little burg south of Olympia on Highway 507 is known for **WOLF HAVEN** (3111 Offut Lake Rd; 360/264-4695), an educational research facility that teaches wolf appreciation and studies the question of whether to reintroduce wolves into the wild. The public is invited to see the wolves or join them in a howl-in.

RESTAURANTS

Alice's Restaurant / ★

19248 JOHNSON CREEK RD SE, TENINO; 360/264-2887

In a fine turn-of-the-century farmhouse on a lively little creek, Alice's serves hearty dinners, all including cream of peanut soup, fresh greens with hot bacon dressing, trout, an entree (baked ham with pineapple glaze, fresh oysters, a selection of game dishes, perhaps ostrich, and even catfish), and choice of dessert. In conjunction with the restaurant, Vincent de Bellis operates the Johnson Creek Winery, whose wines make up the wine list. *$$; AE, DC, DIS, MC, V; no checks; dinner Fri–Sun (or by arrangement); beer and wine; reservations required; call for directions.*

Yelm

RESTAURANTS

Arnold's Country Inn / ★

717 YELM AVE E, YELM; 360/458-3977

Long known as one of Olympia's most accomplished chefs, Arnold Ball established his latest restaurant just outside Yelm on the road to Mount Rainier. Steaks and meat dishes dominate here. Besides steak Diane, familiar Arnold's specialties include chicken sautéed with raspberry brandy, roast duckling l'orange, and traditional escargots. Arnold is careful with small details: his rolls baked on the premises are warm and delicious, as are his fine pies. His wine list is adequate, but many patrons drive all the way from Olympia just for the food. *$$; AE, MC, V; local checks only; breakfast, lunch, dinner Tues–Sun; full bar; reservations recommended; Old Nisqually exit off I-5, follow Reservation Rd/Hwy 510.* &

OLYMPIC PENINSULA

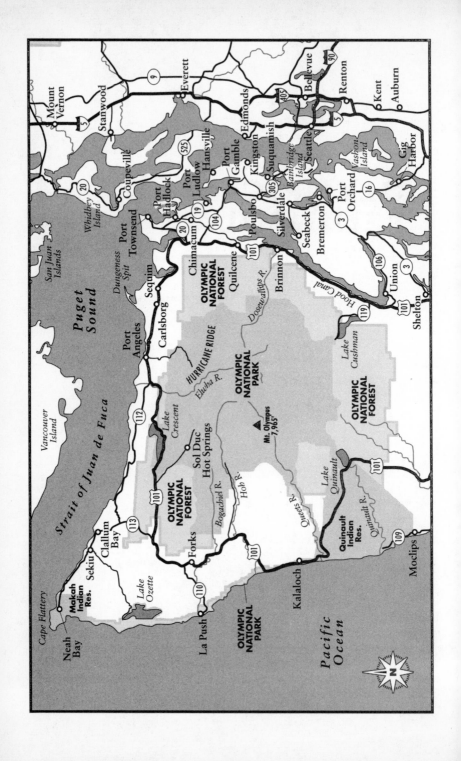

OLYMPIC PENINSULA

The scenery within the 5,000 square miles of the Kitsap and Olympic Peninsulas varies considerably. In Kitsap County, you'll see Silverdale's mall country with neon lights and fast-food joints, get caught up in Poulsbo's Scandinavian atmosphere, or ponder history through the dollhouse homes in the historic mill town of Port Gamble. Cross the Hood Canal Bridge to the Olympic Peninsula—land of emerald farmland carpets, hulking forests of cedar and fir, and crashing swells that pound the Pacific Coast—and traipse amid the Victoriana of Port Townsend.

With each change in topography comes a change in climate. You could bask in the sun in Sequim (popular with retirees, in the rain shadow of the Olympics), and two hours later find yourself pelted by hammering raindrops in Forks. The variations make planning a trip easy: bring everything. Good sturdy shoes and a water-repellent jacket are musts year-round. The only thing you probably *won't* need is formal wear—the Olympic Peninsula is fairly laid-back.

Countless opportunities exist here for picnicking, hiking, camping, photography, boating, fishing, shopping, and more. Residents are a hearty lot of artists and mill workers, loggers and entrepreneurs. They stay for tradition's sake, for the space, and for the opportunities.

And, of course, for the trees. US Highway 101 wraps snugly around an empire built and ruled by Mother Nature. In the center, Olympic National Park is home to some 1,200 plant species, 300 bird species, and 70 different kinds of mammals. More than 5 million people every year come to soak in the hot springs, wander the forest, hug the 250- to 500-year-old fir and cedar trees, and sneak a peek at teeming wildlife adept at the art of camouflage. Visitor centers at Hurricane Ridge and the Hoh Rain Forest feature helpful rangers and interpretive, hands-on learning exhibits.

Perhaps the Olympic Peninsula's rainy winter weather (rainfall ranges from 24 inches a year in Port Angeles to more than 130 in the Hoh Rain Forest) is nature's way of keeping visitors just that. If you don't mind getting wet, though, you'll learn why 200,000 people call it home.

ACCESS AND INFORMATION

You could drive around Puget Sound to reach the Olympic Peninsula, but the scenic WASHINGTON STATE FERRIES (800/84-FERRY) run regularly between downtown Seattle and Bremerton on the Kitsap Peninsula or Winslow on Bainbridge Island. Boats also dock in Port Townsend (from Keystone on Whidbey Island) and on the Kitsap Peninsula in Kingston (from Edmonds) and in Southworth, near Port Orchard (from Fauntleroy in West Seattle).

Arriving in Port Angeles by boat is a snap from Victoria, British Columbia, with the MV COHO, operated by Black Ball Transportation (360/457-4491), and, in spring and summer, via the much quicker VICTORIA EXPRESS (360/452-8088 or 800/633-1589), a foot-passenger ferry that runs two or three times daily, summer and early fall. In summer, **ROYAL VICTORIA TOURS** (888/381-1800; www.royaltours.com) offers guided bus trips to Victoria and Butchart Gardens.

PUBLIC BUS TRANSPORTATION between communities is available through Kitsap Transit (800/501-RIDE or 360/373-8277), Jefferson County Transit (360/385-4777), West Jefferson Transit (800/436-3950), Clallam Transit System (800/858-3747 or 360/452-4511), and Mason County Transit Authority (800/281-9434 or 360/426-9434). Olympic Bus Lines (360/452-3858) also make connections between Seattle and the Olympic Peninsula.

Small planes land at airports in Bremerton, Jefferson County, Shelton, Sequim, and Port Angeles. The largest airline to serve the peninsula is **HORIZON AIR** (800/547-9308), which lands at Fairchild International Airport in Port Angeles. **HARBOR AIR** (800/359-3220) also serves the Kitsap and Olympic Peninsula.

Average temperatures on the Peninsula range from 45°F in January to 72°F in August. Rainfall averages 2–3 inches per month, less in Sequim and more—up to 121 inches annually—in Forks. For information on visiting the area, contact the **PORT TOWNSEND CHAMBER OF COMMERCE VISITOR INFORMATION CENTER** (2437 E Sims Wy, Port Townsend; 360/385-2722 or 888/ENJOYPT; www.ptchamber.org) or the **NORTH OLYMPIC PENINSULA VISITOR & CONVENTION BUREAU** (360/452-8552 or 800/942-4042; travel@olypen.com) in Port Angeles.

Kitsap Peninsula

Kitsap Peninsula sits between the larger Olympic Peninsula and the mainland, roughly defined by Puget Sound (and Bainbridge and Vashon Islands) on the east and Hood Canal on the west. Connected to the Olympic Peninsula by a small stretch of land at the southern end of Hood Canal, it links to the body of Western Washington via the Tacoma Narrows Bridge. The Hood Canal Bridge connects Kitsap to the Olympic Peninsula.

Port Orchard

The center of this small town hugs the southern shoreline of one of Puget Sound's many fingers of water—Sinclair Inlet. With its boardwalk and beach access, the waterfront area is a true gathering place. The **PORT ORCHARD FARMERS MARKET** (Marina Park, one block from Bay St; Sat, late Apr–Oct) offers a tantalizing selection of cut flowers, fresh vegetables, baked goods, and crafts. Take home Hood Canal oysters or ask the oyster lady to grill a few. Antique shops abound, and the **SIDNEY ART GALLERY AND MUSEUM** (202 Sidney Ln; 360/876-3693) displays Northwest art.

HORLUCK TRANSPORTATION (360/876-2300), a privately owned foot ferry that runs every half hour, seven days a week, provides an economical means of travel between downtown Port Orchard and the main ferry terminal at Bremerton. Otherwise, drive north on Highway 3.

OLYMPIC PENINSULA THREE-DAY TOUR

DAY ONE: Starting in Edmonds, grab breakfast on the ferry as you cruise to Kingston. On your way to Port Townsend, take a detour through charming little **Port Gamble** and grab an ice cream or a coffee at the general store. Cross the Hood Canal Bridge to the Olympic Peninsula and follow signs to Port Townsend. Slow down on your way through the Chimacum Valley to drink in the bucolic splendor—this is dairy-farm country. Stop at the Harbormaster Restaurant at **Port Ludlow Resort and Conference Center** for a lunch of fish-and-chips. Once in Port Townsend, check in at the **Quimper Inn**, then wander through the Uptown district, stopping at **Aldrich's** for coffee. Go downtown via the Taylor Street steps, built to accommodate ladies who took tiny steps in their tight Victorian skirts, to the **Haller Fountain**. Window-shop downtown, finishing up with a wine-tasting at the **Wine Seller**, then take dinner at the **Silverwater Café** and perhaps a movie at the **Rose Theater**.

DAY TWO: Head out of town after the Quimper Inn's breakfast and take Highway 20 to Highway 101 west toward **Sequim**. Take the Sequim exit for a roving mural tour—the main street is peppered with trompe l'oeil works. Continue down 101—it joins up with the main street as you head west—toward Port Angeles. Pick up a sandwich and a cranberry muffin at **Sunny Farms Country Store** (261461 Hwy 101; 360/683-8003), between Sequim and Port Angeles. Follow signs to **Hurricane Ridge** in Olympic National Park, where in summer meadows are filled with wildflowers, and winter activities include free guided snowshoe tours and cross-country skiing. After playing all day, return to Port Angeles and check in to the **Tudor Inn** and soak in a nice hot bath, then head to dinner at **C'est Si Bon**.

DAY THREE: The inn's breakfast prepares you for when Mother Nature beckons again. Continue west on Highway 101 to **Forks**, stopping at **Espresso Eleganté** for coffee or the **Rain Drop Cafe** (111 S Forks Ave; 360/374-6612) for lunch. Then visit the **Timber Museum** to learn about trees and the logging industry. Head east into the **Hoh Rain Forest** to tromp rain-forest trails flanked by ancient trees dripping with lacy moss, and perhaps spy a herd of Roosevelt elk. On the way back to Forks, pick up some groceries and find your way to the **Shady Nook Cottage**, where you can cook your own dinner and relax for tomorrow's drive home. Too tired to cook? Stop in at **Si Señora** for locals' favorite Mexican food.

LODGINGS

Reflections Bed and Breakfast Inn / ★★

3878 REFLECTION LN E, PORT ORCHARD; 360/871-5582

Every cliché that's used to describe an excellent Northwest bed-and-breakfast applies to this sprawling B&B set on a hillside overlooking Sinclair Inlet, with the Olympic Mountains as backdrop. Former New Englanders Jim and Cathy Hall extend warm hospitality to their guests—and serve a hearty breakfast of regional dishes. The Halls furnish four guest rooms (two with private baths) with family antiques, including heirloom quilts. The largest has a private porch and a soaking tub. All have water views. The well-tended grounds include a hot tub, a gazebo, and birds eating and preening at various feeders. *$$; MC, V; no checks; jimreflect@hurricane.net; www.portorchard.com/reflections; east of Port Orchard off Beach Dr.* &

Bremerton

Bremerton and its naval station have been entwined since the early 1890s, when a young German, William Bremer, sold close to 200 acres of bay front to the U.S. Navy for $9,587. The naval shipyards are still downtown, and rows of moth-gray ghost ships—silent reminders of past naval battles—loom offshore. Only the destroyer USS *Turner Joy* (300 Washington Beach Ave; 360/792-2457), which saw action off Vietnam, is open for self-guided tours (daily May–Sept, Thurs–Mon Oct–Apr). Adjacent to the ferry terminal and the *Turner Joy*, the **BREMERTON NAVAL MUSEUM** (360/479-7447) depicts the region's shipbuilding history back to bowsprit-and-sail days; open daily in summer, closed Mondays, Labor Day through Memorial Day.

Farther north on the Kitsap Peninsula is the **TRIDENT NUCLEAR SUBMARINE BASE** at Bangor. Occasionally a pod of orcas can be glimpsed escorting one of the mammoth submarines through the local waters to deep-sea duty. Since 1915, Keyport has been the major U.S. site for undersea torpedo testing. Now it also is home to the extraordinary **NAVAL UNDERSEA MUSEUM** (360/396-4148; open daily, closed Tues, Oct–May), housing the first Revolutionary War submarine.

RESTAURANTS

Boat Shed / ★

101 SHORE DR, BREMERTON; 360/377-2600

This casual seafood restaurant overhanging the Port Washington Narrows is aptly named. Rough wood panels the walls inside and out, and a solitary fish tank serves as decor. Scaups and scoters patter along the water while boats of every size pass by. Local seafood is the main attraction here: rich clam chowder, popular Dungeness crab cakes, and seasonal seafood dishes adorned with a variety of homemade salsas and chutneys. Landlubbers choose the knockwurst piled with red onions and cheese on sourdough, or steak. *$; AE, MC, V; local checks only; lunch, dinner every day, brunch Sun; full bar; reservations recommended; east side of Manette Bridge.* &

Seabeck

LODGINGS

Willcox House / ★★★

2390 TEKIU RD, SEABECK; 360/830-4492 OR 800/725-2600

Col. Julian Willcox and his wife, Constance, once played host to such famous guests as Clark Gable at this copper-roofed, art-deco, 10,000-square-foot manse on the east side of Hood Canal. Oak parquet floors, walnut-paneled walls, and a copper-framed marble fireplace—one of five fireplaces in the house—grace the front rooms. All five rooms have private baths and views of Hood Canal and the Olympics. One has a fireplace; one has a double soaking tub. Downstairs are a bar, a game room, and a clubby library, where you can look out over the canal and the impressive gardens. Comb the beach for oysters, fish from the dock, or hike the hillside trails. Owner Cecilia Hughes serves a hearty breakfast, offers lunch to multinight guests, and provides a prix-fixe dinner (open to nonguests on weekends by reservation). Diners love the roasted pork tenderloin served Saturdays, and if you're lucky, you'll come on a night when Hughes has made one of her famous chocolate truffle cakes. The place is about a half-hour drive from the Bremerton ferry, though some guests arrive by boat or floatplane. $$$; DIS, MC, V; checks OK; www.willcoxhouse.com; 9 miles south of Seabeck, call for directions.

Silverdale

RESTAURANTS

Bahn Thai / ★★

9811 MICKELBERRY RD, SILVERDALE; 360/698-3663

Fifteen years of cooking at Seattle's Bahn Thai put Rattana Vilaiporn in perfect position to take over operations at the Silverdale location. She's kept the menu and the same clean, exotic look of the place, with sunken tables and lots of Thai art. Come with a group to share a variety of the brightly flavored dishes of Thailand: *tod mun*—spicy, crisp patties of minced fish, green beans, and lime leaves; *tom yum goong*, a favorite soup of prawns and lemongrass; and six exotic curries, including *mussamun*—beef and potatoes sauced with a medium curry infused with coconut milk and cloves, nutmeg, and cinnamon. $; AE, MC, V; local checks only; lunch, dinner every day; beer and wine; reservations not necessary; kbahnthai@excite.com; ½ block north of Bucklin Hill Rd. &

Yacht Club Broiler / ★

9226 BAYSHORE DR, SILVERDALE; 360/698-1601

This simple restaurant has a water view and some elegant touches: copper-covered tables, walls lined with delicate rice-paper fish prints, and bare wood floors softened by Oriental-style rugs. As you might expect from its name and location (on Dyes Inlet), seafood is big here. More unexpected is the high quality of that seafood (as the commercial fishermen who eat here will attest), be it sweet, moist Dungeness crab cakes, halibut prepared in a variety of ways, or a bucket of plump steamed clams. *$$; AE, DC, DIS, MC, V; checks OK; lunch, dinner every day, brunch Sun; full bar; reservations recommended; Silverdale exit off Hwy 3.* &

LODGINGS

Silverdale on the Bay / ★

3073 NW BUCKLIN HILL RD, SILVERDALE; 360/698-1000 OR 800/544-9799

This tastefully designed resort hotel serves equally well for a conference or a getaway, although encroaching shopping malls are a distraction. Many of the 150 rooms and suites have balconies with sweeping views over Dyes Inlet; some have fireplaces. Extras establish it as the resort it aspires to be: indoor lap pool, large brick sundeck, sauna, weight room, and video-game room. The Mariner Restaurant offers white-linened tables, professional service, and nicely prepared meals that aren't too pricey. The crab chimichanga recently took first place in a local restaurant competition. Enjoy a breakfast of boardinghouse-style biscuits and gravy, or Belgian waffles piled with strawberries and cream. *$$; AE, DC, DIS, MC, V; checks OK; sdhotel@silverlink.net; www.west coasthotels.com/silverdale; at Silverdale Wy.*

Poulsbo

Poulsbo was once a community of fishermen and loggers, primarily Scandinavian. Today it's full of gift shops, and its snug harbor is full of yachts. Scandinavian heritage, however, is still strong—**FRONT STREET** sports its "Velkommen til Poulsbo" signs, and the architecture is a dolled-up version of the fjord villages of Norway. Stroll the boardwalk along Liberty Bay, or rent a canoe or kayak from **OLYMPIC OUTDOOR CENTER** (360/697-6095).

ALLEN'S WATERFRONT DELI (360/779-2763) makes good sandwiches, soups, quiche, and desserts; or select something from the overwhelming choices at the famed **SLUY'S BAKERY** (18924 Front St NE; 360/779-2798). Too crowded? Walk south a block to **LIBERTY BAY BAKERY AND CAFÉ** (18996 Front St NE; 360/779-2828). **BOEHM'S CHOCOLATES** (18864 Front St NE; 360/697-3318) also has an outpost here.

RESTAURANTS

Benson's Restaurant / ★★★

18820 FRONT ST, POULSBO; 360/697-3449

White linen, clean lines, and walls dressed in Georgia O'Keeffe–style flower prints make an elegant first impression at Poulsbo's newest downtown neighbor. Owners Kelly and Jeffrey Benson go out of their way to charm diners with suggestions for appropriate wines and specials, while the well-mannered waitstaff is friendly and efficient. The menu offers mouth-watering selections that rate high on the good-for-you scale: puffy homemade gnocchi under a tomato-basil and grilled-vegetable sauce; grilled fresh salmon with hazelnut butter; tender lamb shish kebabs sweetened by a subtle rosemary marinade. Mushrooms stuffed with crab and artichoke hearts could use a little more of both. For dessert try chocolate mousse torte, or lovingly presented apple tart under caramel glaze, with vanilla ice cream. Wednesdays are good for wine lovers; bottles and glasses are half-price. *$$; AE, MC, V; checks OK; lunch, dinner Tues–Sat, brunch Sun; beer and wine; reservations recommended; bensons.restaurant@prodigy. net; from Lincoln St NE, head to water.* &

LODGINGS

Manor Farm Inn / ★★

26069 BIG VALLEY RD NE, POULSBO; 360/779-4628

A lavish retreat in the middle of nowhere, Manor Farm is a small gentleman's farm with horses, pigs, sheep, cows, chickens, and a trout pond—a beguiling mix of the raw and the cultivated that succeeds in spoiling even the city-bred. There are seven bright guest rooms; individual rooms might feature wood-burning fireplaces, private porches, and king-size beds. Breakfast happens twice at Manor Farm: first a tray of hot scones and orange juice at your door, then breakfast for guests and the general public—fresh fruit, apple crepes, eggs Benedict (courtesy of resident hens), and rashers of bacon, for example. New owners, the Plemmons family, have revived the restaurant and dubbed it Christopher's at the Inn. No kids under 16 at the inn or restaurant. *$$$; AE, MC, V; checks OK; information@manorfarminn.com; www.manorfarminn.com; off Hwy 305, ½ hour from Bainbridge ferry dock.*

Suquamish

In Suquamish, on the Port Madison Indian Reservation (follow signs past Agate Pass), the **SUQUAMISH MUSEUM** in the Tribal Center (15838 Sandy Hook Rd NE; 360/598-3311) is devoted to studying and displaying Puget Sound Salish Indian culture. Chief Sealth's grave is nearby, on the grounds of St. Peter's Catholic Mission Church. Twin dugout canoes rest on a log frame over the stone, which reads, "The firm friend of the whites, and for him the city of Seattle was named."

Port Gamble

Built in the mid-19th century by the Pope & Talbot timber people, who traveled here by clipper ship from Maine, this is the essence of the company town. Everything is still company-owned and -maintained—though the company is now Olympic Resource Management, not Pope & Talbot—and the dozen or so Victorian houses are beauties and in splendid repair. The town, which was modeled on a New England village, also boasts a lovely church and a vital and well-stocked company store. The historical **PORT GAMBLE MUSEUM** (on Rainier Ave; 360/297-8074) is a gem, with an ideal presentation of a community's society and industrial heritage, designed by Alec James, a designer for the displays for the Royal Provincial Museum in Victoria. The lumber mill is no longer in operation.

Hansville

Just beyond the unassuming fishing town of Hansville are a couple of the prettiest, most accessible, and least explored beaches on the peninsula. To the east is **POINT NO POINT**, marked by a lighthouse (great for families). Follow the road from Hansville to the west and you'll reach **CAPE FOULWEATHER**. The short trail through the woods is tough to find, so look for The Nature Conservancy sign on the south side of the road.

Hood Canal

Highway 101 hugs the west side of Hood Canal through tiny towns with names like Lilliwaup, Hamma Hamma, Duckabush, and Dosewallips, and vacation homes line the miles of scenic shoreline. In bays and inlets along the way, oyster and clam populations are making a comeback; stop at any roadside stand or store for fresh crab and oysters. Sample the wines at **HOODSPORT WINERY** (N 23501 Hwy 101; 360/877-9894), plus fine chocolates and gourmet treats, at the cottage tasting room.

Once serious timber country—the logging community of Shelton still sells thousands upon thousands of Christmas trees nationwide each year—this stretch of highway also serves as the jumping-off spot for many recreational areas in the Olympic National Forest, including **LAKE CUSHMAN** and its state park (7211 N Lake Cushman Rd; 360/877-5491). Numerous hiking trails lead to remote, cloud-draped alpine lakes and meadows.

Shelton

RESTAURANTS

Xinh's Clam & Oyster House / ★★

221 W RAILROAD AVE, STE D, SHELTON; 360/427-8709

Chef Xinh Dwelley knows how to choose fresh bivalves. For 20 years, she worked as the quality control manager (and did her fair share of shucking) at Taylor United Inc., a Shelton shellfish company. And there she won attention when she began cooking elaborate lunches for visiting shellfish buyers. Today, Xinh runs not only Shelton's finest seafood restaurant, but one of the best (and freshest) little clam and oyster houses on the Olympic Peninsula. Xinh herself picks out the best of each day's haul. Slide down a few Olympias or Steamboat Island Pacifics on the half shell and then see what she can do with a sauce. The menu sports an Asian twist, with a few Italian dishes. You won't find a better heaping plate of mussel meats in a Vietnamese curry sauce. *$$; MC, V;*

checks OK; dinner Tues–Sat; beer and wine; reservations recommended; www. taylorunited.com/xinhs; at 3rd St. &

Union

RESTAURANTS

Victoria's / ★★

E 6790 HWY 106, UNION; 360/898-4400

The stone-and-log structure on the east bank of Hood Canal has been a stopover since the early 1930s. Locals remember its various functions as a lively dance hall and tavern, a drugstore, and a bed-and-breakfast, but in the past decade it has evolved into one of the area's better eateries. High-beamed ceilings, a fireplace, and large windows that look out on a nearby brook and sheltering trees set the scene for equally appealing food. Seafood can be exceptional, and portions of prime rib are ample. Victoria's signatures include salmon with melted Brie, and medallions of beef. Desserts are imaginative—and rich. Try the Hood Canal Pie with a thin chocolate layer over amaretto ice cream surrounded by an Oreo crust, laced with raspberry sauce and crème fraîche. *$$; MC, V; checks OK; dinner Wed–Sun; full bar; reservations recommended; ¼ mile west of Alderbrook Inn.* &

Quilcene

Every summer weekend, concerts are given by the internationally acclaimed, Seattle-based Philadelphia String Quartet and world-class guest artists at the **OLYMPIC MUSIC FESTIVAL** (11 miles west of Hood Canal Bridge on Hwy 104, then ¼ mile south from Quilcene exit; 360/732-4000), where music lovers sit on hay bales in a century-old Dutch colonial barn or stretch out with a picnic on the gentle hillside while listening to chamber music.

RESTAURANTS

Timber House

HWY 101 S, QUILCENE; 360/765-3339

Surrounded by cedar and hemlock, the Timber House resembles nothing so much as a hunting lodge gussied up to be comfortable for womenfolk. Descriptive logging scenes are painted on hand-carved tables and counters. Local seafood is the main draw here; Quilcene oysters come from down the road, and more comes from the waters around the Sound. Dungeness crab is a winner: sautéed, as a sandwich filling, in an omelet, or in a salad. Locals swear by the roast beef dinners. *$$; MC, V; checks OK; lunch, dinner Wed–Mon; full bar; reservations recommended (weekends); ½ mile south of Quilcene.* &

Port Townsend and the Northeast Corner

During the early days of clipper ships, Port Townsend was the official point of entry to Puget Sound and it continues to be the main draw to this region.

Port Ludlow

LODGINGS

Heron Beach Inn / ★★

I HERON RD, PORT LUDLOW; 360/437-0411

The Heron Beach Inn (sister to the Inn at Langley and Friday Harbor House) guards the entry to Hood Canal. It exudes the atmosphere of a New England estate crammed onto one small point of land (near the harbor to the Port Ludlow Resort), but inside is a gorgeous, peaceful retreat with 37 big, well-appointed rooms—with fireplaces, great views, and deep tubs. Play chess in the common room, or hold a private wine-tasting in front of a blazing fire. In the restaurant overlooking the water, a refined staff serves an ambitious and elegant collection of entrees. *$$$; AE, DIS, MC, V; checks OK; www.heronbeachinn.com; next to marina.* &

Port Ludlow Resort and Conference Center

200 OLYMPIC PL, PORT LUDLOW; 360/437-2222 OR 800/732-1239

Pope & Talbot's legendary 1880s sawmill manager's "biggest damn cabin on the Sound" (actually a splendid Victorian home) once shared this site—overlooking the teardrop bay—with the busy Port Ludlow mill. It is now a popular resort facility, catering to groups, with a marina, tennis courts, 27-hole championship golf course, hiking and cycling trails, and year-round swimming pool on 1,500 developed acres. Individually decorated suites—privately owned by out-of-towners—are very livable, with fireplaces, kitchens, and private decks, many with views of the harbor. Stay away from standard rooms, which resemble budget motel rooms, complete with paper-thin walls, noisy heaters, and appliances and plumbing that just don't work quite right. The Harbormaster Restaurant has a pleasant bar and deck. *$$$; AE, MC, V; checks OK; resort@port ludlowresort.com; www.portludlowresort.com; 6 miles north of Hood Canal Bridge on west side.*

Port Hadlock

The false-front, Old West–style buildings in Port Hadlock have been painted with the same hot pinks, blues, and purples that some supermarkets use to ice cakes—a new take on "local color." South of Hadlock on Highway 19, the CHI-MACUM CAFE (2953 Rhody Dr; 360/732-4631) serves great homemade pie. A transplanted Frenchman and his American wife bake heartachingly delicious bread and pastries at THE VILLAGE BAKER (10644 Rhody Dr; 360/379-5310). Heading north, at the Shold Business Park off Highway 19, buy a bag of superb fresh bagels (baked daily) and toppings to go at **BAGEL HAVEN BAKERY & CAFE** (227 W Patison; 360/385-6788).

RESTAURANTS

Ajax Cafe / ★

271 WATER ST, PORT HADLOCK; 360/385-3450

When we first found this place more than 20 years ago on the abandoned Hadlock waterfront, a disheveled row of cabins was for rent next door, a ramshackle building and pier were for sale, and the *Comet*, a huge wooden fishing vessel, was sinking in the bay. The Ajax Cafe, in a forgotten hardware storefront, was funky and riotous fun. In those days, even the local magistrate ordered the red wine that was listed as "special coffee" on the menu (because the cafe had no liquor license). Not much has changed, except the Ajax, which has been cleaned up without losing its character (and now has a liquor license). Owners Tom and Linda Weiner serve up big plates of seafood with fresh vegetables. The signature dish is a flavorful fishermen's stew: poached fish swimming in leek and saffron broth and served with garlic aioli; locals crave Blackjack Ribs spiked with Jack Daniels that melt away from the bone. Live music (jazz, blues, folk) plays most nights. *$$; MC, V; local checks only; dinner Tues–Sun; beer and wine; reservations recommended; www.ajaxcafe.com; in lower Hadlock on waterfront, off Oak Bay Rd.* &

Marrowstone Island

Marrowstone Island faces Port Townsend across the bay. To get there from Port Ludlow or Hadlock, watch for signs directing you to Indian Island, Fort Flagler State Park, and Marrowstone from Oak Bay Road. **FORT FLAGLER STATE PARK** (10541 Flagler Rd; 360/385-1259), an old coastal fortification, has acres of trails, grassy fields, and miles of beaches to walk, as well as RV and tent camping. Seals hang out at the end of a sand spit, as do nesting gulls. Long ago, Marrowstone's enterprise was turkey farming; today, locals farm oysters and harvest clams. At the historic (oiled floors, covered porch) **NORDLAND GENERAL STORE** (5180 Flagler Rd; 360/385-0777), you can pick up a bag of oysters or, in summer, rent a small boat to paddle on Mystery Bay. In winter, locals gather around the wood stove in the back of the store with espresso.

LODGINGS

The Ecologic Place / ★

10 BEACH DR, NORDLAND; 360/385-3077 OR 800/871-3077

This gathering of eight rustic cabins in a natural setting is a great spot for families who'd rather spend more time out than in—though indoor offerings include books, puzzles, and games. The Ecologic Place borders on a tidal estuary that flows into Oak Bay and then Puget Sound, and offers a view of the Olympics and Mount Rainier. The unique cabins have never been acquainted with an interior decorator, but have everything you need—wood stoves, equipped kitchens, comfortable mattresses on queen-size beds, and fine-for-the-children bunks and twin beds—to enjoy the simple beauty of the place. Bring bikes, boats, books, bathing suits, binoculars, children, and groceries. *$$; MC, V; checks OK; www.ecologicplace.com; right at "Welcome to Marrowstone" sign.*

Port Townsend

Wealthy folk settled here and built more than 200 Victorian homes; foreign consuls off vessels from around the globe added a cosmopolitan flavor to the port town's social life. When the mineral deposits petered out, the railroad never came, and the elite investors left, Port Townsend became a land of vanished dreams and vacant mansions. The restored buildings with wraparound views, now a National Historical Landmark District, lie at the heart of the town's charm. A **HISTORIC-HOMES TOUR** (888/ENJOYPT) happens the first weekend in May, and again the third weekend in September, and the **JEFFERSON COUNTY HISTORICAL SOCIETY** (210 Madison St; 360/385-1003) has a fascinating museum in the original city hall.

Colorful shops line Water Street. **ANCESTRAL SPIRITS GALLERY** (701 Water St; 360/385-0078) has an abundant and elegant collection of sculpture, prints, paintings, jewelry, and music by Native craftspeople across the country. **NORTH-WEST NATIVE EXPRESSIONS ART GALLERY** (637 Water St; 360/385-4770), owned by the Jamestown S'Klallam tribe, holds a wide selection of Puget Sound, British Columbia, and Southeast Alaska prints, jewelry, and related books. Local bookstores include **MELVILLE AND CO.** (914 Water St; 360/385-7127) and **WILLIAM JAMES BOOKSELLER** (829 Water St; 360/835-7313). **EARTHEN WORKS** (702 Water St; 360/385-0328) specializes in high-quality Washington crafts. You'll find the best antique selection is at the **PORT TOWNSEND ANTIQUE MALL** (802 Washington St; 360/385-2590). And don't overlook the revitalization of uptown, especially **ALDRICH'S** (Lawrence and Tyler; 360/395-0500), an authentic 1890s general store with an international twist.

The best ice cream cones can be had at **ELEVATED ICE CREAM** (627 Water St; 360/385-1156); the best pastries at **BREAD AND ROSES BAKERY** (230 Quincy St; 360/385-1044); and for picnic fare, coffee, homemade chocolates, and people watching, try **MCKENZIE'S** (221 Taylor St; 360/385-3961). At the **WINE SELLER** (940 Water St; 360/385-7673), proprietor and jazz guitarist Joe Euro stocks gourmet snacks, a selection of high-end beer, and wines from around the globe.

For live music and local color, check out the historic **TOWN TAVERN** (Water and Quincy), where the enormous bar, the pool table, and the owner's great taste in music draw an eclectic crowd. **SIRENS** (823 Water St; 360/379-1100), hidden up a flight of stairs in the historic Bartlett Building, is a delightful place to enjoy a glass of wine, shoot some pool, and listen to music from the deck overlooking the bay. **ROSE THEATER** (235 Taylor; 360/385-1039), a beautifully restored arthouse, has red velvet curtains, ancient frescoed walls, and the world's best popcorn—try it with Silverwater Secret Spice and brewer's yeast.

CHETZEMOKA PARK, a memorial in the northeast corner of town to the S'Klallam Indian chief who became a friend of the first white settlers, has a charming gazebo, picnic tables, tall Douglas firs, and a grassy slope down to the beach. You can see the chief's likeness carved in the huge pillars in front of the post office, or in a bronze sculpture at the golf course. **HALLER FOUNTAIN** is where Port Townsend's brazen goddess lives. Galatea, her voluptuous body draped beneath a diaphanous swag, has graced the intersection of Washington and Tyler Streets since 1906.

The **RHODODENDRON FESTIVAL** (888/ENJOYPT) in May, with a parade and crowning of the queen, is the oldest festival in town. The Wooden Boat Foundation (360/385-3628) presents the **WOODEN BOAT FESTIVAL** (360/385-4742), at Point Hudson Marina on the weekend after Labor Day: a celebration of traditional crafts and a showcase for everything from kayaks to tugboats. The first weekend of October finds lunatic geniuses racing human-powered contraptions across town, on the water, and through a mud bog in the **KINETIC SCULPTURE RACE** (360/385-3741).

FORT WORDEN STATE PARK (200 Battery Wy; 360/385-4730), along with sister forts on Marrowstone and Whidbey Islands, was part of the defense system established to protect Puget Sound a century ago. The 433-acre complex overlooking Admiralty Inlet now incorporates turn-of-the-century officers' quarters, campgrounds, gardens, a theater, and a concert hall (see Lodgings). A huge central field, formerly the parade ground, is perfect for games or kite flying. The setting may look familiar to those who saw the movie *An Officer and a Gentleman*, most of which was filmed here. At the water's edge, an enormous pier juts into the bay—it's the summer home to the **MARINE SCIENCE CENTER** (360/385-5582), with touch tanks, displays of sea creatures, and cruises to nearby Protection Island, the region's largest seabird rookery. Also here are a safe, protected swimming beach and access to miles of beaches. On the hillside above, you can spend hours exploring deserted concrete bunkers.

Fort Worden is also home to Centrum, a sponsor of concerts, workshops, and festivals throughout the year. Many of these take place in the old balloon hangar, reborn as McCurdy Pavilion. The **CENTRUM SUMMER ARTS FESTIVAL** (360/385-3102; June–Sept) is one of the most successful cultural programs in the state, with dance, fiddle tunes, chamber music, a writers conference, jazz, blues, and theater performances.

The **PUGET SOUND EXPRESS** (431 Water St; 360/385-5288) runs a daily ferry in summer to Friday Harbor on San Juan Island.

RESTAURANTS

Fountain Cafe / ★★

920 WASHINGTON ST, PORT TOWNSEND; 360/385-1364

Each owner of the Fountain Cafe, so named because it's two doors up Washington Street from Port Townsend's one and only nude standing in a fountain, gives the place her own watermark. In the early 1980s, founder Jackie Pallister introduced tart Greek Pasta (capers, feta, lemon juice, and herbs, tossed with a heated egg-and-oil concoction—dare we say the word *mayo?*), seafood dressed in whiskey and cream, and the equally rich logan- or gooseberry fool. Another owner painted the walls (this is one of Port Townsend's oldest buildings) apple green, resulting in a rash of green walls all over town. Current owner Kris Nelson painted out the green, pumped up the menu, and improved the wine list. But we're happy to report those old faves are still on the menu. For unpretentious intimacy (there are fewer than 10 tables here), this remains our favorite place to eat lunch or dinner in town. *$$; MC, V; checks OK; lunch (summer only), dinner every day; beer and wine; reservations not accepted; one block north of Water St.*

Lanza's / ★★

1020 LAWRENCE ST, PORT TOWNSEND; 360/379-1900

Lori, the youngest Lanza sibling (of five), and her partner, Steve, reclaimed a family legacy when they took over Lanza's from outside owners. There's no mistaking the Italian in these folks, but the addition of Northwest elements makes for delightful hybrid cuisine. Start with a caesar, then move to ravioli or one of the best steaks in town. Family recipes include home-made sausage, and big calzone stuffed with smoked salmon, fat prawns, and pesto. The kitchen is stocked with organically grown local herbs and vegetables; pizza can be ordered to go. Catch live music Fridays and Saturdays. *$; MC, V; checks OK; dinner Mon–Sat; beer and wine; reservations recommended; www. olympus.net/lanzas/; uptown.* &

Lonny's / ★★★

2330 WASHINGTON ST, PORT TOWNSEND; 360/385-0700

The film *Big Night* comes to mind, not because of the decor (warmly tinted walls, arches, and 17th-century botanical prints), but because of the gregarious owner, Lonny Ritter, who has opened some of the Olympic Peninsula's best restaurants. In fact, when that movie opened at the local Rose Theater, Ritter and another chef replicated its outrageous dinner, complete with suckling pig—tickets sold out in 12 minutes. If you're used to a low-fat, salt-free diet, forget about it for one night and try the oyster stew, made with sweet cream, fennel, and diced pancetta; the chargrilled prawns with mango salsa may be easier on the arteries. Paella combines the best of earth and sea—local clams and mussels, chicken, shrimp, and sausage—in fragrant saffron rice. Waitstaff work the room nicely, filling it with self-confident chatter, as do patrons who make the trip from

Seattle just to eat here. *$$; MC, V; checks OK; dinner Wed–Mon; beer and wine; reservations recommended; lonnys@olypen.com; www.lonnys.com; adjacent to harbor.* &

Manresa Castle / ★★★

7TH AND SHERIDAN, PORT TOWNSEND; 360/385-5750 OR 800/732-1281

Yes, it's a real castle outfitted in elegant Victoriana, built in 1898 by Prussian baker and entrepreneur Charles Eisenbeis (some even swear they've seen ghosts from the place's previous incarnation as a Jesuit cloister). Rooms are furnished with antiques and have high ceilings. The Castle is now happily home to a bed-and-breakfast and the finest dining room on the Olympic Peninsula, under the exacting and creative leadership of Swiss-German chef Walter Santchi. He's cultivated an international menu of inventively prepared and artfully presented seasonal dishes. The osso buco Milanese, for example, places a tender veal shank on a bed of risotto, aromatic with parmesan and shiitakes. Other favorites include king salmon rosette or exotic curry chicken Casmir. Sunday brunch is the best deal in town. It's impossible to leave hungry after Santchi's signature Swiss *roesti*, a heap of shredded potatoes browned with bacon and ham, then topped with Swiss cheese and two fried eggs. The Castle can accommodate banquets and weddings, with reception space for 80. *$$; DIS, MC, V; checks OK; dinner every day Apr–Sept, brunch Sun (dinner Wed–Sat Oct–May); full bar; reservations recommended (weekends and summer); www.manresacastle.com; heading into town on Sims Wy, take a left onto Sheridan.*

The Public House / ★

1038 WATER ST, PORT TOWNSEND; 360/385-9708

A large space with soaring ceilings, the Public House is comfortable and casual. It features antique light fixtures, wood floors, dark green wainscoting, and a nonsmoking bar, and is a great place for a big spicy bowl of gumbo, a Vermont cheddar burger, or creamy fennel-laced seafood stew. Owner Joann Saul also owns a local sushi restaurant, Sentosa, and adds select offerings delivered from there. Down a beer from the impressive list of drafts and watch the world go by through the big front windows, or catch live music on weekends. *$; AE, DIS, MC, V; checks OK; lunch, dinner every day; full bar; reservations not necessary; www.thepublichouse.com; north side of street.* &

Silverwater Café / ★

237 TAYLOR ST, PORT TOWNSEND; 360/385-6448

Owners David and Alison Hero—he's a carpenter, potter, and baker; she's a gardener and cook—have created the restaurant of their dreams on the first floor of the town's historic Elks Club building. It's a warm, lovely gathering place combining 1800s architecture with satisfying food served on David's handmade plates with a carefully selected wine list. Start with artichoke pâté, fresh sautéed oysters, or a big spinach salad; lunches include filling salmon salad sandwiches, and hearty homemade soups. Local raves for dinner are green-peppercorn steaks, amaretto chicken in a tart and spicy lemon and curry sauce, and seafood pasta loaded with prawns and wild mushrooms and doused with brandy. You can't go wrong with seared ahi. *$$; MC, V; checks OK; lunch, dinner every day; beer and wine; reservations recommended (weekends); next to Rose Theater.* &

Wild Coho / ★★☆

1044 LAWRENCE ST, PORT TOWNSEND; 360/379-1030

This is a favorite place to wake up, and no wonder: coffee is strong and refills are free. It's a good thing, because the food takes a while. No matter; if you're going to wait, it may as well be in a place like this. Sun streams through the old storefront windows, walls are warmly painted deep orange and the ceiling dark purple, and tables are playfully set with mismatched silverware, bandana napkins, and fresh flowers. Owner Wisteria Wildwood serves healthy breakfasts all day—homemade seafood sausage or eggs cooked in a dizzying variety of ways. A salmon hash with chunky spuds and red onions leaves you wanting more salmon, but French toast comes soaked in a hazelnut egg custard and served with yogurt and bananas. Wash it down with freshly squeezed juice combos, or smoothies with a dose of spirulina, bee pollen, ginseng, ginger, or wheatgrass. Lunches bring miso-based soups, hearty salads, and lots of veggies. *$; no credit cards; checks OK; breakfast, lunch every day; beer and wine; reservations not accepted; across from Uptown Theater.* &

LODGINGS

Ann Starrett Mansion / ★★

744 CLAY ST, PORT TOWNSEND; 360/385-3205 OR 800/321-0644

The most opulent Victorian in Port Townsend, this multigabled Queen Anne hybrid was built in 1889 by a local contractor who just had to have himself a home with more of everything than his neighbors. He succeeded. The spiral stairway, octagonal tower, and "scandalous" ceiling fresco of maidens representing the four seasons are stunning. Rooms are furnished with antiques and have lovely decorative touches—hand-painted details or finely crafted ceiling moldings. The Drawing Room (with a tin claw-footed bathtub) opens to views of the Sound and Mount Baker, while the newer, romantic Gable Suite occupies the whole third floor with a skylight, a knockout view, and a spacious seating area. For a heartwarming treat, book the Master Suite with its canopy bed and antique fainting couch. Breakfasts are ample. The house is open for public tours, noon–3pm, when any unoccupied bedrooms are cordoned off for viewing. *$$; AE, DIS, MC, V; checks OK; edel@starrett mansion.com; www.starrettmansion.com; at Adams.* &

Bay Cottage / ★★

4346 S DISCOVERY RD, PORT TOWNSEND; 360/385-2035

Susan Atkins turned two cottages on the shore of Discovery Bay into a delightful retreat. The cottages have good stoves and refrigerators, a tasteful mix of antique furniture, and comfy mattresses covered with feather beds. Direct access leads to a private sandy beach—marvelous for swimming, bonfires, and beach-combing. Atkins stocks the kitchens with basic breakfast necessities, and when the mood strikes, she has been known to bake cookies for guests. Each cottage has its own picnic basket, binoculars, and library. The rose garden is an enchantment. It's an ideal retreat for romantics or—some say—a great girl getaway. No pets. *$$; no credit cards; checks OK; www.olympus.net/biz/getaways/BC/index.htm; ½ mile west of Four Corners Grocery.*

Fort Worden / ★

200 BATTERY WY, PORT TOWNSEND; 360/344-4400

Fort Worden was one of three artillery posts built at the turn of the 20th century to guard the entrances of Puget Sound. The troops are long gone, and the massive gun mounts on the bluff have been stripped of their iron, but the beautifully situated fort is now a state park, a conference center, a youth hostel (especially for teenagers biking the Peninsula), the site of the splendid Centrum Arts Festival, and an unusual place to stay. Twenty-four former officers' quarters—nobly proportioned structures dating back to 1904—front the old parade ground. These two-story houses are spacious lodgings, each with a complete kitchen, at bargain rates (great for family reunions; a few smaller homes suit couples). The most coveted of the one-bedroom lodgings is Bliss Vista, perched on the bluff, with a fireplace and plenty of romantic appeal. Alexander's Castle, a mini-monument with a three-story turret, is charming in its antiquity, sequestered away from the officer's houses on the opposite side of the Fort's grand lawn. RV sites are near the beach and tucked into the woods. Make summer reservations well in advance. *$$; DIS, MC, V; checks OK; www.olympus.net/ftworden; 1 mile north of downtown, in Fort Worden State Park.*

Hastings House/Old Consulate Inn / ★★

313 WALKER ST, PORT TOWNSEND; 360/385-6753 OR 800/300-6753

This ornately turreted red Victorian on the hill is one of the most frequently photographed of Port Townsend's "Painted Ladies." It is also one of its most comfortable. A large collection of antique dolls is displayed in the entryway, and new arrivals are often greeted by the aroma of freshly baked cookies. In the enormous Master Suite (our favorite), you can soak in a claw-footed bathtub, sip coffee in the turret alcove overlooking the water, and warm up later in front of the antique fireplace. The third-floor Tower Suite, with a sweeping bay view and swathed in lace, is the essence of a Victorian-style romantic valentine. Owners Rob and Joanna Jackson serve a mammoth seven-course breakfast—over which Joanna is more than delighted to wittily recount

FROM TIMBER TO TOURISM

Dennis Chastain passes his chain saw across a cubic yard of cedar, sawdust flying like sparks as he removes a corner. He switches to a smaller saw and gingerly shaves down rough edges with the care of a barber giving a young boy his first crew cut. After about 20 minutes, a cuddly-looking grizzly bear emerges from the block.

Chastain is a master chain-saw carver: he's won and placed in competitions all over the Northwest. People from around the world stop to admire and buy the works he creates from an outdoor shop, **Den's Wood Den**, behind his home a few miles south of Forks on Highway 101.

"When we moved here it was known as the last frontier," he says, recalling the virgin timber and big-money jobs.

That was three decades ago, when Chastain and his wife, Margaret, came from Salem, Oregon. He took a production job in a mill that eventually went belly-up. Others in the timber industry faced the same problem in the 1980s, when overlogging and new environmental rules sent a shock wave through the corridor of Highway 101: timber could no longer sustain the community.

"They wanted me to sit around on my butt and answer the telephone, and I just couldn't do that," Chastain says.

So in 1988, he turned his carving hobby into full-time work where he could gulp in the aroma of fresh cedar sawdust; Margaret takes care of sales and business. The Chastains' company is part of the Olympic Peninsula's evolution to a tourism-based economy. The towns of Port Angeles, Sequim, and Forks have stepped up efforts to bring in people to play in Olympic National Park, roam the rocky coast, and shop for antiques and local art.

The Chastains have seen some of their best friends leave town to pursue logging careers in other places, such as Alaska, Chastain says. But the Olympic Peninsula is his home.

"I have a funny feeling we may be planted here," he says.   —*Vanessa McGrady*

the inn's history. A hot tub is in the backyard gazebo. *$$$; AE, DC, MC, V; checks OK; joanna@oldconsulateinn.com; www.oldconsulateinn.com; on bluff at Washington.*

The James House / ★★★

**1238 WASHINGTON ST, PORT TOWNSEND; 360/385-1238
OR 800/385-1238**

The first bed-and-breakfast in the Northwest (1889) is still in great shape, though when a gale blows off the strait and hits the high bluff, you are glad to be in one of the three rooms that have a cozy fireplace or a wood-burning stove.

This fine B&B rests in the competent hands of Carol McGough, who continually freshens the 13 rooms and delightful garden. Rooms in front have the best water views; not all rooms have private baths, but shared facilities are spacious and well equipped. The main floor offers two comfortable parlors, each with a fireplace and plenty of reading material. Breakfast is served either at the big dining room table, or in the kitchen with its antique cookstove. Ask about the bungalow on the bluff. *$$; AE, DIS, MC, V; checks OK; innkeeper@james house.com; www.jameshouse.com; corner of Harrison.*

Lizzie's / ★
731 PIERCE ST, PORT TOWNSEND; 360/385-4168 OR 800/700-4168

Lizzie, the wife of a tugboat captain, put the deed of this model of Victorian excess in her own name, which now also graces a line of bath lotions created by owners Patti and Bill Wickline. Breakfast, served around an old oak table in the cheerful kitchen, can turn into a friendly kaffeeklatsch. Daisy's Room allows a soak in the tub in the black-and-white corner bathroom—a Victorian treat, especially if the sun is slanting in. Many of the seven bedrooms have views, and all have private baths and Victorian decor. Lizzie's Room has its own fireplace. Two parlors seem plucked from the past; in one you'll even find a vintage stereoscope. *$$; DIS, MC, V; checks OK; wickline@olympus.net; www.kolke.com/ lizzies; near corner of Lincoln.*

Quimper Inn / ★★
1306 FRANKLIN ST, PORT TOWNSEND; 360/385-1060 OR 800/557-1060

Rich earth-toned hues give the Quimper Inn's walls a mellow glow. This 1886 home has bigger windows and cleaner lines than its Victorian cousins in town, and hosts Sue and Ron Ramage have preserved the uncluttered but warm character. A first-floor bedroom resembles a library, with a comfortable bed and bath; upstairs, Harry and Gertie's Suite is a perfect escape with a separate living area, bedroom, and private bath. Michele's Room features bay windows and a brass bed, and an enormous bathroom with a 6-foot-long tub, a pedestal sink, and wicker furniture. Breakfasts are well executed. *$$; MC, V; checks OK; www.olympus.net/biz/quimper/quimper.html; corner of Harrison.*

Sequim and the Dungeness Valley

Sequim (pronounced "skwim") was once a carefully kept secret. The town sits smack in the middle of the "rain shadow" cast by the Olympic Mountains: the sun shines 306 days a year here, and annual rainfall is only 16 inches. Now Sequim has been discovered, especially by retirees, and is growing fast. Farms have become subdivisions, and golf courses sprout in what used to be pastures.

On Sequim Bay, near Blyn, the S'Klallam Indians operate the unique **NORTHWEST NATIVE EXPRESSIONS** art gallery (1033 Old Blyn Hwy; 360/681-4640). Across the highway stands the **7 CEDARS** (270756 Hwy 101; 800/4LUCKY7), a mammoth gambling casino with valet parking and good food. **CEDARBROOK HERB FARM** (1345 Sequim Ave S; 360/683-7733; daily Mar–Dec 23), Washington's oldest herb farm, has a vast range of plants—including scented geraniums—fresh-cut herbs, and a pleasant gift shop. **OLYMPIC GAME FARM** (1423 Ward Rd, 5 miles north of Sequim; 360/683-4295) is the retirement center for Hollywood animal stars and endangered species. An hour-long guided walking tour is available mid-May through Labor Day; or take a driving tour year-round.

DUNGENESS SPIT (360/457-8451), 6 miles northwest of Sequim, is a national wildlife refuge for birds (more than 275 species have been sighted) and one of the longest natural sand spits in the world. A long walk down the narrow 5½-mile beach takes you to a remote lighthouse (check a tide table before you start).

Two small but notable wineries offer tastings: **LOST MOUNTAIN WINERY** (3174 Lost Mountain Rd; 360/683-5229; tastings by arrangement or chance) and **NEUHARTH WINERY** (885 S Still Rd; 360/683-9652; daily in summer, Wed–Sun in winter).

RESTAURANTS

Khu Larb Thai II / ★

120 W BELL ST, SEQUIM; 360/681-8550

Ever since the Itti family opened their second establishment (the first is in Port Townsend), Sequim residents are thrilled that they don't have to drive so far to savor the vibrant flavors of Thailand. This gracious restaurant, prettied with a rose (the restaurant's namesake) on every table, has quickly become locals' first choice for, well, something different. Thai food stands out in the land of logger burgers, and the Ittis have perfected this aromatic cuisine. Newcomers to Thai food should request the tried-and-true *tum kah gai* (a chicken soup with a coconut milk and lime broth), the phad thai (sweet, spicy noodles stir-fried with egg, tofu, and vegetables), or the garlic pork. Aromatic curries appeal to more adventurous diners. *$; MC, V; local checks only; lunch, dinner Tues–Sun; beer and wine; reservations not necessary; at Sequim Ave.* &

Oak Table Cafe / ★

292 W BELL ST, SEQUIM; 360/683-2179

Breakfast (served until 3pm) is the thing at this cafe. It's a feast—huge omelets, fruit crepes, or legendary puffy apple pancakes. Service is friendly and efficient, and the place is noisy, boisterous, and chatty. Good, old-fashioned lunch options (turkey sandwiches, soothing—but unexciting—soups) are mixed with a few enlightened salads (such as chicken sesame). It's owned by one of the Nagler family, who also own the Chestnut Cottage and First Street Haven in Port Angeles. *$$; AE, DC, MC, V; checks OK; breakfast every day, lunch Mon–Sat; no alcohol; reservations not necessary; www.oaktablecafe.com; at 3rd.* &

LODGINGS

Groveland Cottage / ★

4861 SEQUIM-DUNGENESS WY, SEQUIM; 360/683-3565 OR 800/879-8859

At the turn of the century, this was a family home in Dungeness—a wide spot in the road, a short drive from the beach. Now the place has the comfortable salty-air feel of an old summer house, with a great room where guests convene around the fireplace. Four cheerful guest rooms have private baths, two with whirlpool tubs. A one-room cottage out back may not be as special, but has its own cooking space. The place fills up in summer with guests addicted to owner Simone Nichols' little luxuries—like coffee in your room before sitting down to her four-course breakfast. No children under 6. *$$; AE, DIS, MC, V; checks OK; simone@olypen.com; www.northolympic.com/groveland; follow signs toward Three Crabs.*

Juan de Fuca Cottages / ★

182 MARINE DR, SEQUIM; 360/683-4433

Any of these five comfortable cottages—overlooking Dungeness Spit, or with a view of the Olympics—is special, whether for a winter weekend or a longer summer sojourn. A two-bedroom suite has both views and a welcoming fireplace. All are equipped with a Jacuzzi, kitchen utensils, games, and reading material, as well as cable TV and VCR, and you can choose from a 250-video library. Outside is the spit, begging for beach walks and clam digging. *$$; DIS, MC, V; checks OK; 2-night min weekends and July–Aug; www.dungeness.com/juandefuca; 7 miles north of Sequim.*

Port Angeles and the Strait of Juan de Fuca

The north shore of the Olympic Peninsula was home to several thriving Native American tribes long before outside explorers laid claim to the area. Today this region is anchored by the blue-collar mill town known as Port Angeles—"where the Olympics greet the sea." Port Angeles Harbor, protected against wind and waves by Ediz Hook sand spit, is the largest natural deep-water harbor north of San Francisco. It is also a jumping-off point to Victoria, British Columbia, 17 miles across the Strait of Juan de Fuca on Canada's Vancouver Island.

Port Angeles

Port Angeles is primarily notable for being the northern gateway to **OLYMPIC NATIONAL PARK** (360/452-0330). The park, as big as Rhode Island, with a buffer zone of national forest surrounding it, contains the largest remaining herd of the huge Roosevelt elk, which occasionally create "elk jams" along Highway 101. Follow the signs to the park's visitor center, just south of town on Mount Angeles Road, then drive 17 miles along winding precipices to mile-high **HURRICANE RIDGE** and breathtaking views. Rest rooms and snack facilities are on the ridge, as well as plenty of hiking trails in summer, and good cross-country skiing and a weekend poma-lift downhill-skiing-and-tubing area in winter. Seasonal snowshoe rental and guided snowshoe nature walks are offered through March. Check road conditions before you go (24-hour recorded message: 360/452-0329). **OLYMPIC RAFT AND KAYAK SERVICE** (360/452-1443 or 888/452-1443) offers easy floats and kayaking ventures on the Elwha and Hoh Rivers.

In downtown Port Angeles, **PORT BOOK AND NEWS** (104 E 1st; 360/452-6367) sells a wide selection of magazines and daily newspapers like the *New York Times* and the *Wall Street Journal*. **MOMBASA COFFEE COMPANY** (113 W 1st; 360/452-3238) serves excellent fresh-roasted coffee. **GINA'S BAKERY** (710 S Lincoln; 360/457-3279), near the library, is a good place to buy picnic food, especially pastries, hulking cinnamon rolls, and freshly made sandwiches. Browse **SWAIN'S GENERAL STORE** (602 E 1st; 360/452-2357) for everything else.

RESTAURANTS

C'est Si Bon / ★★

23 CEDAR PARK DR, PORT ANGELES; 360/452-8888

Yes, it *is* good—especially if you're yearning for classic pre-nouvelle French cooking with splendid sauces. Dine leisurely in an attractive setting: the best tables are in window bays that overlook the rose garden; a new glass conservatory is a favorite for large parties. If the food is slow in coming, host Juhasz Norbert regales waiting guests with tales of his musical experiences in France and Hollywood (and others, who've heard him, beg him to bring out his violin). A big bowl of onion soup, bubbling under a brown crust of cheese, can serve as a meal in itself, particularly when followed by a refreshing salad. The most popular dish here is Tournedos Royale: filet mignon topped with sautéed crab. To assure consistency, stick to simpler preparations, such as braised lamb, classic steak au poivre, or fresh halibut and salmon in season. The chocolate mousse is wickedly rich, and the wine list has good choices. *$$$; AE, DIS, MC, V; local checks only; dinner Tues–Sun; full bar; reservations recommended; 4 miles east of Port Angeles.* &

Chestnut Cottage / ★

929 E FRONT ST, PORT ANGELES; 360/452-8344

Owners Diane Nagler and Ken Nemirow are particular when it comes to quality food and service. And it shows. Their Chestnut Cottage is the place to go for an exceptional breakfast in delightful country Victorian–style surroundings smack in the middle of downtown. A custardy apple and walnut French toast is only one of several morning treats; others include Belgian waffles, pancakes, quiches, frittatas, or lemon blintzes drizzled with raspberry purée. Children are delighted by the breakfast pizza (ham and eggs on pita). Simple porridge and berries is another kid-friendly option. Nagler and Nemirow also own First Street Haven (107 E 1st St; 360/457-0352), an equally good place for more casual breakfasts and fresh lunches, where prices are reasonable. *$$; AE, DIS, MC, V; checks OK; breakfast, lunch every day; beer and wine; reservations not necessary; east of town center.* &

Hacienda del Mar / ★

408 S LINCOLN, PORT ANGELES; 360/452-5296

This is a reincarnation of a longtime favorite Mexican restaurant, and locals say the food is better than ever. Most of the charming staff has remained, but be warned: your waiter will have you saying *si* to another margarita and dessert before you know it. Salsa gets points for being thick and zesty with a comfortable balance of cilantro and heat. The standards—fajitas, burritos, tacos—are all fine, but specialties are where the house shines. Try spinach-filled tamales with a cream cheese sauce, or seafood enchiladas. *$; AE, DIS, MC, V; checks OK; lunch, dinner every day; beer and wine; reservations not necessary; between 4th and 5th.* &

Port Angeles Brewing Company / ★★

134 W FRONT ST, PORT ANGELES; 360/417-9152

A high-ceilinged space that once served as a city-government building and food bank has been scrubbed and painted, and is now an upscale but comfortable restaurant with a bar, fine wood tables, and a sophisticated menu. Start with steamed mussels, or creamy artichoke dip punctuated with green chile, garlic, and kasseri cheese, then move to a sandwich—perhaps grilled portobello mushroom with roasted-eggplant spread, provolone, and greens—or a creative burger. Beers on tap change seasonally, but a rich stout is the perfect reason to come in from the rain. *$$; MC, V; checks OK; lunch, dinner every day; beer and wine; reservations not necessary; between N Oak and Laurel.* &

Thai Peppers / ★★

222 N LINCOLN ST, PORT ANGELES; 360/452-4995

Consider the pepper: sweetly benign, audaciously hot, or sneakily sublime. It's also a fitting name for the latest addition to Port Angeles's international dining scene. The menu offers an intriguing mix of flavors for both battle-ready and timid taste buds. Tofu nuggets, fried golden and served with a light cucumber sauce, is a shareable starter. *Po tak* soup takes a twist on *tom yum*, by adding assorted seafood to a broth enlightened with lemongrass, cilantro, kafir lime leaves, and mushrooms. Sizzling, succulent duck makes a grand appearance, basil beef combines a generous helping of both with chile-garlic sauce, and the curries (particularly red) do justice to fresh seafood. Thai Peppers comes from the same family who brought the Olympic Peninsula Khu Larb in Port Townsend and Sequim. When you're hot, you're hot. *$; MC, V; checks OK; lunch, dinner every day (Mon–Sat in off season); beer and wine; reservations not necessary; thaipep@olypen.com; between Front and Railroad.* &

LODGINGS

B. J.'s Garden Gate / ★★

397 MONTERRA DR, PORT ANGELES; 360/452-2322 OR 800/880-1332

The spanking newness of this custom-designed bed-and-breakfast is soft-
ened by rich European decor (stately antiques and down comforters), a
sweeping view across the Strait of Juan de Fuca to Victoria, and charming gardens in the enormous backyard. Each of five rooms follows a theme: the
Napoleon room has a fireplace; Victoria's Repose has flowers, a porch, and a
hot tub to satisfy the most discriminating queen; Ludvig's Chamber sports a luxurious double Jacuzzi; Marie Antoinette's Boudoir has an 1810 bedroom set;
and Marie Theresa's Suite is for honeymooners, with a king-size bed and a fireplace. The most homey touch, however, is the graceful hospitality from hosts B.
J. and Frank Paton, including home-baked treats, turndown service, and an
innovative breakfast menu. Best of all, the Patons not only know how to take
care of guests—they know when to leave them alone. No children, pets, or
smoking. *$$$; AE, MC, V; checks OK; bjgarden@olypen.com; www.bjgarden.
com; 3 miles west of Sequim, call for directions.*

Five SeaSuns / ★

1006 S LINCOLN, PORT ANGELES; 360/452-8248 OR 800/708-0777

This huge 1926 Dutch colonial house was home to only four families before
owners Bob and Jan Harbick took over and turned it into a bed-and-breakfast
in 1996. It has a well-kept interior with sunny rooms, elegantly crafted archi-
tectural details, and polished hardwood floors. A parlor outfitted with comfy
couches gives guests a homey sitting space, and rooms are decorated to evoke
the feeling of the four seasons. Pick of the lot is the Herfst (autumn) room, with
private white-tiled bath, queen-size brass bed, wicker furniture, well-placed
antiques, and hats and hatboxes of a bygone era. The Carriage House is for rent,
too, with rustic, wood-paneled decor and full kitchen. Breakfast—your choice
of two sittings—is filling and artfully presented. Why they serve orange sorbet
as a breakfast item and keep a clock that gongs throughout the night are the
only troubling mysteries of this otherwise lovely place. *$$–$$$; AE, MC, V;
checks OK; seasuns@olypen.com; www.seasuns.com; corner of E 10th.*

Tudor Inn / ★★

1108 S OAK ST, PORT ANGELES; 360/452-3138

Jane Glass is a gracious host of one of the oldest—and best looking—B&Bs
in town. This completely restored 1910 Tudor-style bed-and-breakfast is
12 blocks from the ferry terminal in a quiet residential neighborhood, and
boasts a library, a fireplace, crisp linens, and well-chosen antiques. Five rooms
are nattily decorated in turn-of-the-20th-century style; the best has a balcony
with mountain view, fireplace, claw-footed tub, and shower. Glass serves a tra-
ditional full breakfast with none of the forced conviviality around the dining
table that sometimes afflicts B&Bs; she takes a healthy approach to cooking,

using the freshest ingredients available. Well versed in Port Angeles political and cultural life, Glass will arrange fishing charters, horseback rides, winter ski packages, and scenic flights. *$$; AE, DIS, MC, V; checks OK; info@tudorinn. com; www.tudorinn.com; at 11th St.*

Lake Crescent

Highway 101 skirts the south shore of 600-foot-deep Lake Crescent with numerous scenic pullouts. The Fairholm store and boat launch are on the far west end of the lake, with East Beach 10 miles away. Lake Crescent is home to rainbow trout and steelhead, to Beardslee and the famous *crescenti* trout, which lurk in its depths. Rental boats are available. Ask about the easy 1-mile hike that takes you to 90-foot Marymere Falls.

LODGINGS

Lake Crescent Lodge / ★

416 LAKE CRESCENT RD, PORT ANGELES; 360/928-3211

Built more than 80 years ago, the well-maintained Lake Crescent Lodge has been well worn since the days when it was known as Singer's Tavern. The historic main building has a grand veranda that overlooks the deep, crystal blue waters of Lake Crescent, a so-so restaurant, and a comfortable bar. Upstairs rooms are noisy and rustic—a euphemism that means, among other things, that the bathroom is down the hall. Motel rooms are the best buy, but the clutter of tiny basic cabins, with porches and fireplaces, can be fun—though bear in mind that they were built in 1937, when President Franklin Roosevelt came to visit. Service is fine—mainly enthusiastic college kids having a nice summer. It's true this side of the lake sees less sun than the north side, but you don't come to the rain forest to see sun, do you? *$$; AE, CB, DC, DIS, MC, V; checks OK; closed Nov–Apr; www.olypen.com/lakecrescentlodge; 20 miles west of Port Angeles.* &

Sol Duc Hot Springs

Whether you arrive by car after an impressive 12½-mile drive through old-growth forests, or on foot after days of hiking mountain ridges, these hot springs are the ideal trail's end. The Quileute Indians called the area Sol Duc— "sparkling water." In the early 1900s, Sol Duc Hot Springs (28 miles west of Port Angeles; 360/327-3583; open daily mid-May–Sept; Thurs–Sun Apr–mid-May and Oct; closed Nov–Mar) became a mecca for travelers seeking relief from aches and pains. For $7.50, you can have a hot soak, followed by a swim in a cold pool. You can also opt for a lengthy massage. The hike to nearby **SOL DUC FALLS** passes through one of the loveliest stands of old-growth forest anywhere.

LODGINGS

Sol Duc Hot Springs Resort

SOL DUC RD AND HWY 101, PORT ANGELES; 360/327-3583

Surrounded by forest, 32 small cedar-roofed sleeping cabins are clustered in a grassy meadow. The favorites are those with river-facing porches. Up to four guests can share a cabin, which are carpeted and have private baths and double beds. Duplex units have kitchens, and in keeping with the natural serenity, there are no TVs anywhere (and a no-smoking policy everywhere). Camping and RV sites are available. The Springs Restaurant serves breakfast and dinner in summer, and a deli is open midday through the season. Use of the hot springs and the pool is included in the cabin rental fee. *$$; AE, DIS, MC, V; checks OK; open every day mid-May–Sept (Thurs–Sun, Apr and Oct); pamsdr@ aol.com; www.northolympic.com/solduc/index.html; turn off a few miles west of Lake Crescent, then drive 12 miles south of Hwy 101.*

Clallam Bay and Sekiu

Twenty-one miles south on Hoko-Ozette Road from Sekiu is **LAKE OZETTE**, the largest natural body of freshwater in the state. At the north end of the lake is a campground, and trails leading to several beaches where you can see the eerie, eroded coastal cliffs. It was near here that tidal erosion exposed a 500-year-old Indian village, once covered by a mud slide, with homes perfectly preserved, in the 1960s. The archaeological dig was closed in 1981 after 11 years of excavation; artifacts are on display at the Makah Museum in Neah Bay (see the Neah Bay section in this chapter).

Neah Bay

This is literally the end of the road: Highway 112 ends at this small waterside town on the northern edge of the **MAKAH INDIAN RESERVATION**. Two 8-mile-long rutted roads lead to **CAPE FLATTERY**—take the west one coming and going. The Makah allow public access across their ancestral lands—a half-mile walk on a new boardwalk to **LAND'S END**, the far northwestern corner of Washington's seacoast. From these high-cliffed headlands, cow-calf pairs of gray whales can often be seen migrating north in April and May. Salmon-fishing charters are available. Sandy **HOBUCK BEACH** is open for picnics (no fires) and surfing, and farther on, the **TSOO-YAS (SOOES) BEACH** is accessible (pay the landowners a parking fee). Call the visitors center (360/452-0330) in Port Angeles for coastal access information. The **MAKAH CULTURAL AND RESEARCH CENTER** (Front St; 360/645-2711) has a stunning exhibit of artifacts from the village discovered under Lake Ozette; it also serves as an ad hoc tourist-information center.

Forks and the Hoh River Valley

The **HOH RAIN FOREST** in Olympic National Park is the wettest location in the contiguous United States, with an average yearly rainfall of 133.58 inches. This steady moisture nurtures dense vegetation—more than 3,000 species of plant life—including the Rain Forest Monarch, a giant Sitka spruce more than 500 years old towering close to 300 feet over the moss- and fern-carpeted forest floor. Take the spur road off Highway 101, 13 miles south of Forks, to the visitors center and campground (30 miles southeast of Forks; 360/374-6925). For those with more time, one- to three-day round-trip hikes up **MOUNT OLYMPUS** provide some of the best hiking in the world. The longer trip to **GLACIER MEADOWS** is best mid-July through October. Stop in at **PEAK 6 ADVENTURE STORE** (about 5 miles up the road to the Hoh; 360/374-5254), a veritable miniature REI right where you need it most.

Forks

From this little town on the west end of the Olympic Peninsula, you can explore the wild coastal beaches, hook a steelhead, or go mountain biking, camping, or hiking. The pristine waters of the Hoh, Bogachiel, Calawah, and Sol Duc Rivers all flow near Forks, making it a key fishing destination. Ask your innkeeper, the informative **FORKS VISITORS CENTER** (1411 S Forks Ave; 360/374-2531 or 800/44-FORKS), or **OLYMPIC SPORTING GOODS** (190 N Forks Ave; 360/374-6330), next to the liquor store, for information on recommended guides, licenses, or where to land the Big One.

On the outskirts of town, the **TIMBER MUSEUM** (1421 S Forks Ave; 360/374-9663) tells the story of the West End's logging heritage. Next door at the visitors center, pick up a map for **ARTTREK**, a self-guided tour of nearly two dozen local studios and galleries; most are in artists' homes, but if the Arttrek sign is out, you're welcome. A delightful mingling of art, espresso, antiques, and books can be found where **TINKER'S TALES & ANTIQUES, ESPRESSO ELEGANTÉ**, and the **ALLEY STUDIO** share space (71 N Forks Ave; 360/374-9433).

RESTAURANTS

Si Señora / ★
90 FORKS AVE, FORKS; 360/374-5414

This casual, family-style Mexican joint sports an ambitious menu that expands from the usual cheese-and-sauce-and-meat affairs. Though it may be tempting to fill up on fresh warm tortillas and cilantro-laced salsa, save room for what will undoubtedly be a whopping entree. Selection is huge—here you can choose from inventive huevos dishes served with combinations of meat, chorizo, and cheese; specials include steak *al Mexicana* with onions, peppers, spices, and guacamole; a classic *pollo en mole*—tender strips of chicken breast in a sweet, spicy sauce—is another favorite. Pauline's Burrito features mushrooms sautéed in chunks of garlic dressed up with cheese and tangy enchilada sauce and a dollop of sour cream. A promising *chile verde* packed a nice slow heat, but would have scored higher had the plentiful pork chunks been more tender. *$; MC, V; checks OK; lunch, dinner every day (lunch Thurs–Fri in winter); beer and wine; reservations not necessary; 2 blocks south of traffic light.*

LODGINGS

Eagle Point Inn / ★★

384 STORMIN' NORMAN RD, FORKS; 360/327-3236

Cradled on 5 acres in a bend of the Sol Duc River, this spacious log lodge was designed by Chris and Dan Christensen to perfectly combine comfort and style. And it has become one of the most impressive places to stay near the rain forest. Two downstairs bedrooms, each with queen-size beds covered with thick down comforters, have commodious bathrooms. The open two-story common living quarters house Chris's collection of kerosene lamps and other interesting antiques, but leave plenty of room for guests to spread out in front of the fireplace, made of rocks from the Sol Duc River. The Christensens live nearby in what was the original lodge, leaving you just the right amount of privacy. Even if you need to get up before dawn to fish, a hearty breakfast will be ready. You can barbecue your own dinner in a covered outdoor kitchen near the river. *$$; no credit cards; checks OK; 10 miles north of Forks.*

Huckleberry Lodge

1171 BIG PINE WY, FORKS; 360/374-6008 OR 888/822-6008

Avid outdoors enthusiasts Kitty and Bill Speery own Forks's most fun adventure lodge, and go the extra mile to accommodate guests, whether it's a 4:30am breakfast, a four-course dinner, or arrangements for a full day of fly-fishing or ATV adventures. On request, the owners provide niceties (robes, slippers, toiletries, hot tub under the evergreens, sauna) and naughties (poker chips, cigars, a heated outdoor smoking canopy). You can spend the night, have breakfast, and do your own thing, but this place works best if you come with friends for a weekend. The pool table in the family room, the buffalo head (among numerous other items) in the living room, and the display of Native American artifacts reflect the spirit of this place. A cabin complete with kitchen lacks charm, but is a good choice for the more independently minded (or for longer stays). A couple of RV hookups accommodate those who want to get away from the hubbub of busy RV parks. *$$; MC, V; checks OK; hucklodg@olypen.com; www.huckleberrylodge.com; north end of Forks.*

Shady Nook Cottage / ★

81 ASH AVE, FORKS; 360/374-5497

You wouldn't expect to find an English garden tucked away only a few blocks from downtown Forks, but that's exactly the atmosphere innkeeper Deannie

Hoien has created in her two guest cottages. Hoien, an accomplished stained-glass artist, continually updates the decor with her creations. Handmade quilts lend homespun charm to spaces equipped with full kitchens, microwaves, and TVs. Hoien has a gift for coaxing bright flowers and graceful foliage from the patch of garden surrounding the cottages—a refreshing place to sit. Continental breakfast is included. *$$; no credit cards; checks OK; open Apr–Nov, other times by arrangement; shadynook@northolympic.com; www.northolympic. com/shadynook; turn west at N Forks Ave, go two blocks, and turn right onto Ash Ave.*

La Push and Pacific Ocean Beaches

The Dickey, Quillayute, Calawah, and Sol Duc Rivers merge and enter the ocean near La Push. To the north and south extend miles of wilderness coastline—the last such stretch remaining in the United States outside of Alaska, much of which is protected as part of Olympic National Park. It is home to the Quileute Indians, and today the small community still revolves around its fishing heritage. The lure of wild ocean beaches, with jagged offshore rocks and teeming tide pools, brings those seeking adventurous solitude. The only nearby lodging is **OCEAN PARK RESORT** (360/374-5267) in La Push, which is too worn to recommend, except for the two new ocean-view suites above the Lonesome Creek general store.

Several miles to the north, Mora Road leads to **RIALTO BEACH** and a three-day wilderness beach hike to **CAPE ALAVA** west of Lake Ozette. A shorter, more strenuous hike leads from **THIRD BEACH**, south of La Push, 16 miles to the Hoh River—an extraordinarily dramatic stretch. Warning: All ocean beaches can be extremely dangerous due to fluctuating tides and unfordable creeks during periods of heavy rain. Stop at the **RANGER STATION** (360/374-5460) in nearby Mora (2 miles north of Forks, take turnoff for La Push Rd; as it forks into Mora Rd, take Mora Rd about 5 miles to Mora Campground) to get information about use permits and tide tables.

Farther south along Highway 101 is the wide stretch named **RUBY BEACH** for the tiny garnet crystals that compose much of its sand, ideal for walking. A mile farther is the viewpoint for Destruction Island, a wildlife sanctuary topped by a lighthouse. Nearby, a trail leads to the world's largest western red cedar.

Several more beaches make good explorations as you continue south—particularly at **KALALOCH**, which has a campground and a fine clamming beach. **KALALOCH LODGE** (157151 Hwy 101, Forks; 360/962-2271) is one of the most isolated beachside resorts in Washington. Unfortunately, accommodations are rudimentary and the food in the restaurant standard at best. If you're looking for a view, you can't beat it, but those in the know camp.

Lake Quinault

Lake Quinault, at the inland apex of the **QUINAULT INDIAN RESERVATION**, is usually the first or the last stop on Highway 101's scenic loop around the Peninsula's Olympic National Park and Forest. The glacier-carved lake is surrounded by cathedral-like firs, the fishing is memorable, and there are several easy trails, including one to **CAMPBELL GROVE** with its enormous old-growth trees. The **RANGER STATION** (on lake's south shore; 360/288-2444) provides information on more strenuous hikes up the North Fork of the Quinault River, or to Enchanted Valley. A large 1930s log chalet at the end of the 13-mile trail can house 50–60 hikers.

LODGINGS

Lake Quinault Lodge / ★

S SHORE RD, QUINAULT; 360/288-2900 OR 800/562-6672 (WA AND OR ONLY)
A massive cedar-shingled structure, this grand old lodge was built in 1926 in a gentle arc around the sweeping lawns that descend to the lake. The rustic public rooms are done up like Grandma's sun porch in wicker and antiques, with a massive stone fireplace in the lobby; the dining room overlooks the lawns. Rooms in the main building are small but nice; half have lake views. Choice lodgings are the 36 newer lakeside rooms a short walk from the lodge. Amenities consist of a sauna, an indoor heated pool, a game room, canoes and rowboats, and well-maintained trails for hiking or running. It's a good idea to make summer reservations four to five months in advance, but winter reservations are wide-open—and a great time to experience the rain forest. The dining room puts up a classy front. Lunches are classic national park (Monte Cristos and logger burgers), but dinners are a bit more creative, with entrees such as ginger-seared halibut or blackened salmon. On occasion conventioneers abound, drawn by the spa-like features of the resort, but somehow the old place still exudes the quiet elegance of its past. *$$–$$$; AE, MC, V; checks OK; www.visitlakequinalt.com; from Hwy 101, turn east at milepost 125 onto S Shore Rd.* &

NORTH CASCADES

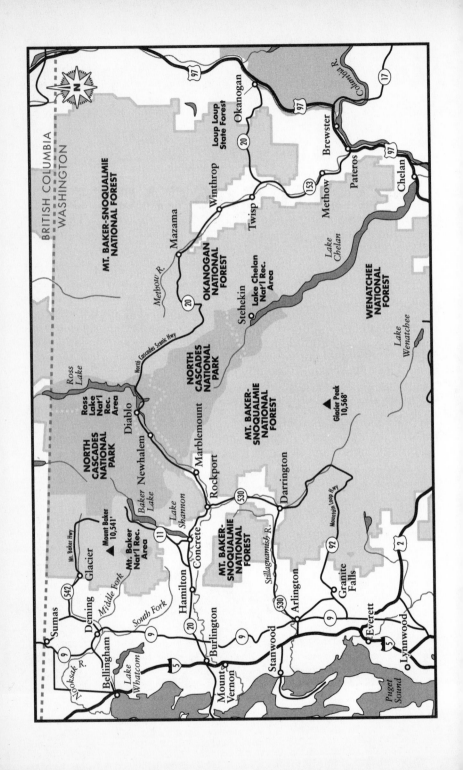

NORTH CASCADES

Few regions in Washington have the allure of the North Cascades. Settled squarely in the northwest part of the state, the mountainous area is world renowned for its ice-draped peaks, alpine meadows, and vast stands of old-growth forest. The crown jewel is North Cascades National Park, a cluster of magnificent peaks that are part of the Cascade Range. The park is surrounded by a jigsaw puzzle of federally protected wilderness areas, making the entire region nirvana for hikers and campers.

Broadly speaking, the North Cascades includes more than just the national park, encompassing Mount Baker to the north, the breathtaking North Cascades Scenic Highway that cuts across the park's center, the wide-open Methow Valley east of the Cascades, and, farther south, pristine and popular Lake Chelan.

The entire region remains relatively unscathed by development. The North Cascades contains no cities, few resorts, and little tourist-town sprawl. (Food and lodging aren't plentiful, either.) That may not last long, but for now, the towns scattered throughout the region still feel like small-town America (but with an espresso stand at every corner). These are friendly, hospitable spots, often with some interesting historical site or quirky attraction to merit a quick stop. But even locals concede the region's best feature is in their backyards. Each is a gateway to the Great Outdoors, an invitation to hiking, camping, mountain-biking, fishing, boating, and downhill and cross-country skiing. Just as nicely, there's still plenty of room for solitude.

ACCESS AND INFORMATION

Travelers tour the North Cascades via car (there are no airports or train service within this region) on the **NORTH CASCADES SCENIC HIGHWAY** (Highway 20), an east-west corridor that links Sedro Woolley near Interstate 5 (exit 230, 65 miles north of Seattle) to the town of Twisp. East of the Cascades, the Twisp-Chelan leg is connected by Highway 153 and US Highway 97.

Puget Sound visitors often tour the region by completing the **CASCADE LOOP**, which includes taking US Highway 2 across the Cascades one way and looping through the mountains on Highway 20 the other way. Many travelers prefer the counterclockwise direction, driving east on Highway 2 and returning west on Highway 20 to take advantage of superior mountain views from that direction.

Generally, the best **WEATHER** for visiting the high country is mid-June to late September. Snow closes the North Cascades Highway—typically the stretch between Mazama on the east side and Diablo on the west—from approximately mid-November to mid-April, depending on the weather. In winter, Puget Sound visitors travel to the Methow Valley by crossing the Cascades via the longer, more southerly routes of Highway 2 or Interstate 90.

For information, contact **NORTH CASCADES VISITOR CENTER** (502 Newhalem St, Newhalem, WA 98283; 206/386-4495) or **LAKE CHELAN VISITOR BUREAU** (PO Box 216, Chelan, WA 98816; 800/4-CHELAN; www.lakechelan.com).

Mount Baker

The **MOUNT BAKER HIGHWAY** (Hwy 542) rises from Bellingham, paralleling the sparkling Nooksack River and passing through little towns like Deming and Glacier, to reach two of the state's loveliest sights: 10,778-foot Mount Baker and 8,268-foot Mount Shuksan. Extreme skiers and snowboarders from all over the world journey to **MOUNT BAKER SKI AREA** (360/734-6771), 56 miles east of Bellingham. The mountain never lacks for snow—during the 1998–99 season, it set a world record for snowfall with 1,140 inches—and has the kind of steep terrain that satisfies avid boarders. The area typically is open mid-November to mid-May (the longest season in the state). In summer, enjoy beautiful vistas and exhilarating day hikes.

Deming

RESTAURANTS

Deming Steakhouse / ★

5016 DEMING RD, DEMING; 360/592-5282
Carnivores, start your molars. One of the few real steak houses in the region awaits you. You can get a tender, well-aged, 8-ounce tenderloin here for $12.95, a 12-ouncer for $16.95. The ultimate challenge is the Paul Bunyan: 72 ounces of juicy, meat-eating indulgence for $49.95—or free, if you can eat it in one hour. So far, everyone has paid. New owners have renovated the Deming, which dates back to 1922 and looked it. It's now brighter, cleaner, and more family-friendly. But this ain't the Taj Mahal; you're here for the steak, bub. Live bands play in the lounge on weekends. *$$; AE, DIS, MC, V; checks OK; lunch, dinner every day; full bar; reservations not necessary; off Hwy 542 at 1st St.* &

LODGINGS

Diamond Ridge / ★★

9216 MT BAKER HWY, DEMING; 360/599-3297 OR 800/424-1966
Set well away from the highway on an 80-foot ridge overlooking the Nooksack River, this new, luxurious B&B delivers a million-dollar view of Mount Baker. The English-style country gardens envisioned by proprietors Dawn and Dale Marr are still a work in progress, but the 400-year-old evergreens rising cathedral-like on 15 wooded acres make up for it. The 2,000-square-foot, new, log-style home aims for a lodgelike feel. The two guest rooms—both upstairs, one facing the river, the other the forest—are handsome, spacious accommodations, each offering separate balcony, private bath, and lush comforts (thick bathrobes,

NORTH CASCADES THREE-DAY TOUR

DAY ONE: Start your day in the Puget Sound area and head eastbound on the **North Cascades Highway** for a daylong scenic drive. Pack a lunch or grab a burger at a cafe in Marblemount before making your first must-stop: the **North Cascades Visitor Center** in Newhalem. Enjoy the center's exhibits, then take a short, easy hike to view the Picket Range. Back in the car, begin your drive across the mountains, allowing at least two hours for stops. **Diablo Lake** overlook and **Washington Pass** have sweeping, panoramic vistas. Continue your drive into the Methow Valley and collapse in the arms of luxurious comfort at either the **Mazama Country Inn** in Mazama or **Sun Mountain Lodge** in Winthrop, where you'll have dinner.

DAY TWO: After breakfast at the lodge, take the morning to explore the frontier atmosphere of Winthrop. Mosey around the pioneer buildings of **Shafer Museum**. Poke through the main street's Old West storefronts, antique stores, and blacksmith shop. Stop for lunch nearby at the **Duck Brand Restaurant and Hotel**, where you can nibble virtuously at healthy salads or eat yourself into a coma on Mexican food, pasta, or steak. Use the afternoon to unwind at **Pearrygin Lake State Park**. Go for a swim, rent a boat, or simply relax with a book under one of the shade trees. Wrap things up with an elegant dinner at the **Freestone Inn**, then return to your hotel.

DAY THREE: Head for Chelan, a 56-mile trip that takes about 1 ½ hours. Allow time to stop in Twisp to visit the **Confluence Gallery** and small-town shops, and have lunch at the **Methow Valley Brewing Company**. Once in Chelan, check in to **Campbell's Resort on Lake Chelan** and settle into a lakeside lawn chair on the lodge's sandy beach to soak up the sun. If you get restless, saunter out to explore town; everything is within walking distance. Enjoy dinner at **Campbell House Cafe** and wind up the day with an evening stroll through **Riverwalk Park**.

down comforter, a library of books) appreciated in these surroundings. No pets, smoking, or children under 16. $$$; MC, V; *checks OK; diamond ridge@bigplanet.com; www.diamondridgebb.com; first driveway on left following milepost 31, Hwy 542, 2 miles before Glacier.*

The Logs at Canyon Creek / ★

9002 MT BAKER HWY, DEMING; 360/599-2711

Five log cabins nestled among dense stands of alder and fir at the confluence of the Nooksack River and Canyon Creek compose this rustic retreat. Comfortable cabins sleep up to eight in bunk-bedded rooms and on pullout couches. The centerpoint of each cabin is the large fireplace (built from river cobbles and slabs of Nooksack stone), stocked with firewood. Each cabin has a fully equipped kitchen and a charcoal grill, but no phone or

TV. In summer, enjoy the small pool or mosey along the riverbed. This is a great place to bring the kids and the family dog. *$$; no credit cards; checks OK; 3-night min in summer and holidays; thelogs@telcomplus.net; www.telcom plus.net/thelogs; milepost 30.5, Hwy 542, 30 miles east of Bellingham.*

Glacier

RESTAURANTS

Milano's Restaurant and Deli / ★★

9990 MT BAKER HWY, GLACIER; 360/599-2863

🐷 This unassuming little restaurant within a market and deli doesn't initially look deserving of a stop. But slam on those brakes! To borrow the ski terminology used at nearby Mount Baker, there's black-diamond cuisine here in a blue-run atmosphere. The star offering at this informal Italian restaurant is freshly made pasta with creative fillings and sauces. The clam-packed *linguine vongole* and the chicken Gorgonzola, smothered in a rich, savory sauce, are heart-stopping *speciale della casa*. They are nearly rivaled by a slew of tasty raviolis, stuffed with spinach, porcini mushrooms, or smoked salmon. Enjoy a beer or a glass of wine from the well-priced selection, or have coffee and tiramisù. The deli does a brisk business in takeout sandwiches for those headed to the mountains. *$$; MC, V; local checks only; breakfast Sat–Sun, lunch, dinner every day; beer and wine; reservations recommended (weekends); milanodeli@ aol.com; on Hwy 542 in Glacier.* ♿

North Cascades Scenic Highway

The heart of this region is the **NORTH CASCADES SCENIC HIGHWAY** (Hwy 20), frequently heralded as one of the nation's top scenic highways. The two-lane road, completed in 1972, slices through the mountains to provide stunning roadside mountain vistas, but almost as impressive are the brilliantly hued, jade-green and turquoise **DIABLO AND ROSS LAKES** created by a hydroelectric dam project.

The highway, the most northerly cross-state route, connects the wet, west, forested side of the Cascades to the semi-arid, sunlit world east of the mountains. More than 130 miles and a half day's driving time, it climbs from peaceful farmland and lush, thick evergreens to rugged mountains and immense glaciers via **RAINY AND WASHINGTON PASSES**, then—poof!—it's a long hang-glide down into a wide-open, pastoral valley and grassy meadowlands.

Marblemount

Hundreds of bald eagles perch along the Skagit River from December through February, scavenging on spawned-out salmon. You can spy a number from the road, along Highway 20 between Rockport and Marblemount (bring binoculars). However, the best view is from the river, via a two- to three-hour float tour.

Call **CHINOOK EXPEDITIONS** (800/241-3451), **WILDWATER RIVER TOURS** (800/522-WILD), or the **MOUNT BAKER RANGER DISTRICT** (2105 Hwy 20, Sedro-Woolley; 360/856-5700) for other float-trip operators.

LODGINGS

A cab in the woods / ★

9303 DANDY PL, ROCKPORT; 360/873-4106

They're nothing fancy, but these cozy cedar log cabins tucked into quiet, secluded woods off the main highway represent one of the best values in the area. Each of the five cabins sleeps four in a bedroom and living room, and has a fully equipped kitchen and gas fireplace. Owners Dave and Andie Daniels have given the cabins a good spit 'n' polish—reroofed them, upgraded furnishings, modernized the bathrooms—and tidied up the grounds for picnicking, playing badminton, or roasting marshmallows over a campfire. The marvelous Skagit River is within walking distance. *$$; MC, V; checks OK; www.cabinwoods.com; just past milepost 103 on Hwy 20, 3 miles west of Marblemount.*

North Cascades National Park

The North Cascades are often called America's Alps, which may be travel-writing hyperbole. If not that, they're certainly Washington's Alps. Like their European counterparts, the mountains possess extraordinary grandeur and majesty, along with a wild, elusive quality that makes them a worldwide draw.

In 1968, a 505,000-acre section immediately south of the U.S.-Canada border won National Park status. The huge park contains jagged peaks draped in ice, 318 glaciers, and unspoiled wilderness hidden from everyone but the most intrepid of hikers. Part of the Cascade Range, the peaks are not especially tall—the highest hover around 9,000 feet—but their vertical rise takes them from almost sea level into the clouds, making them steep-walled, enchanting to view, and, in many places, inaccessible.

This National Park is not one you can zip into with your minivan and experience from a comfy lodge. While the North Cascades Highway bisects the wilderness area and provides dramatic views, the inner sanctum contains no network of roads, no lodges or visitor centers. No, the park will not reveal its treasures easily; you have to discover them on foot. Fortunately, the adventurous have been given 386 miles of maintained trails in the territory to explore—and the rest can take solace in a stunning scenic drive.

Access to the park, about a three-hour drive from Seattle, is via the North Cascades Highway (Highway 20). Food, lodging, and gas are minimal within the park. The main highway provides access to dozens of trails, including the **PACIFIC CREST NATIONAL SCENIC TRAIL**. Backpackers also hike into the park from Stehekin, located at the north end of Lake Chelan (see Stehekin). Hiking usually starts in June; snow commonly melts off from all but the highest trails by July. But summer storms are frequent; be prepared with rain gear. Expect four-legged company in the backcountry: black bears, elk, mountain goats, mountain lions, cougars, and a few grizzlies.

Backcountry camping requires a free permit, available at the **NORTH CAS-CADES NATIONAL PARK HEADQUARTERS** (2105 Hwy 20, Sedro-Woolley; 360/856-5700; www.nps.gov) or the **WILDERNESS INFORMATION CENTER** (7280 Ranger Station Rd, Marblemount; 360/873-4500). Both offices have park information.

Remember: Winter snow closes the park highway from approximately mid-November to mid-April, depending on the weather.

Diablo and Ross Lake

Since the only road access to Ross Lake is south from Hope, BC, the best way to get to the lake and its main attractions—campgrounds and the cabins built on log floats at **ROSS LAKE RESORT** (Rockport; 206/386-4437)—is on the **SEATTLE CITY LIGHT FERRY** (500 Newhalem St, Rockport; 206/386-4393) from Diablo. Here Seattle City Light built an outpost for crews constructing and servicing the dams on the Skagit River. The ferry leaves twice daily (8:30am and 3pm), running from mid-June through the end of October. Cost is $5 one-way; no reservations needed.

Worth visiting are the dams themselves, built by a visionary engineer named James Delmage Ross. **SKAGIT TOURS** (500 Newhalem St, Rockport; 206/233-1955) are four-hour journeys through the Skagit Project, featuring a slide presentation, a ride up an antique incline railway to Diablo Dam, and then a boat ride through the gorge of the Skagit to Ross Dam—a construction of daring engineering in its day. The tours, which cost $25, kids 6–11 half-price, include a lavish chicken dinner afterward back in Diablo. Minitours (90 minutes) are also available. Six miles down the road in Newhalem are inspirational walks to the **GRAVE OF ROSS** and to **LADDER CREEK FALLS**, with plantings gathered from around the world. Tours are arranged through Seattle City Light (206/684-3030); they run summer only, so reserve well in advance.

The Methow Valley

Just east of the Cascades, Highway 20 descends into the Methow (say "MET-how") Valley. An ideal destination for recreators and a favorite with Puget Sounders, the Methow recalls the Old West, from the faux-Western storefronts of Winthrop to the valley's working ranches and farms, to the Big Sky–and–sagebrush landscape.

Mazama

There's little to do in tiny Mazama (say "ma-ZAH-ma"), but if it's civilization you're after, head for the **MAZAMA STORE** (50 Lost River Rd; 509/996-2855). It has a sociable soup-and-espresso counter, products that range from Tim's

Potato Chips to fine wines to Patagonia shirts, a picnic area (complete with grillmeister in the summer), and the last gas pumps for more than 70 miles, if you're traveling west across the mountains. Mazama seems to be becoming a little high-end mecca for fishing; a **FLY-FISHING SHOP** next to the Mazama Store sells Sage products. In summer, the town also is home to the **METHOW MUSIC FESTIVAL** (800/340-1458), a classical-music series held in local barns and meadows.

If you've got the rig for it (high clearance is necessary; four-wheel drive is best), jump off from Mazama on the Methow Valley Road (County Road 9140) for a 19-mile, knee-buckling sojourn up a steep, rough, one-lane road, complete with hairpin curves, no guardrails, and 1,000-foot dropoffs. Your reward: **HARTS PASS** and Slate Peak, the state's highest drivable point at 7,440 feet. Open only in summer, Harts Pass delivers spectacular views of the Cascades, hiking trails, campgrounds, and fragrant meadows of wildflowers.

RESTAURANTS

Freestone Inn / ★★★

17798 HWY 20, MAZAMA; 509/996-3906 OR 800/639-3809

A floor-to-ceiling river-rock fireplace stands in the center of the Freestone Inn (see Lodgings review), separating the lobby on one side from the dining room on the other. In this intimate room, diners sit at white-clothed, candlelit tables for dinners of Northwest specialties. Chef Todd Brown uses fresh local ingredients such as wild mushrooms, game, and lake trout. A salad of baby spinach, Bartlett pears, spiced pecans, and smoked Gorgonzola is fresh and flavorful; entrees such as salmon with horseradish crust, served with French green lentils and balsamic vinaigrette, or maple-cured pork loin with sweet garlic mashed potatoes, crispy onions, and apple cider jus are sure to satisfy. Apple crisp, topped with rich vanilla ice cream, is the perfect shareable finish. The wine list offers selections from the Northwest, California, and France. $$$; AE, DC, DIS, MC, V; local checks only; breakfast every day, dinner Tues–Sun; beer and wine; reservations recommended; info@freestoneinn.com; www.freestoneinn. com; 1 ½ miles west of Mazama.

LODGINGS

Freestone Inn and Early Winters Cabins / ★★★

17798 HWY 20, MAZAMA; 509/996-3906 OR 800/639-3809

Drive up to the 12-room log lodge that is the Freestone Inn, and you'll feel you've reached *Bonanza*'s Ponderosa. The inn sets an elegant, rustic tone for the 1,200-acre Wilson Ranch. The two-story lodge blends into the landscape well, and gentle touches lend an environmental appeal. A massive river-rock fireplace centers the lobby, and there's a little library nook nearby, stocked with Northwest books. The earth-toned rooms are subdued and classy, trimmed in pine with big stone fireplaces, large bathrooms, wrought-iron fixtures, and old photographs of Wilson Ranch. The ground-floor rooms are our favorites, opening onto the lakefront lawn or snowy banks. An outdoor hot tub is just between Freestone Lake—a pond enlarged into a lake and stocked with trout—and the lodge. Although views from the inn are more territorial than grand, activities here are as vast as the Methow Valley itself; Jack's Hut serves as a base camp for virtually anything you can dream of doing—from skiing to whitewater rafting, fly-fishing to mountain biking. Additional lodging options include two luxurious Lakeside Lodges (complete with kitchens and lots of room for families or friends) and six smaller Early Winters Cabins. Continental breakfast is complimentary for guests at the inn (but not in the cabins). $$$; AE, DC, DIS, MC, V; local checks only; 1½ miles west of Mazama.

Mazama Country Inn / ★★

42 LOST RIVER RD, MAZAMA; 509/996-2681 OR 800/843-7951 (IN WA)

With a view of the North Cascades from nearly every window, this spacious 6,000-square-foot lodge makes a splendid year-round destination (especially for horseback riders and cross-country skiers), with 14 good-sized rooms of wooden construction with cedar beams. Some of the guest rooms (all fairly standard) have air-conditioning, nice on hot summer Eastern Washington nights. Each room has a private bath, quilts on the beds, and futonlike pads that can be rolled out for extra guests. Four rooms behind the sauna have individual decks, two with views of Goat Peak and two looking out into the woods. In summer, breakfast, lunch, and dinner are offered in the lodge restaurant (best are meat selections such as beef tenderloin or spicy ribs); winter brings family-style breakfasts and dinners. Six cabins with kitchen and bath are available for families or groups of up to 10. $$; DIS, MC, V; checks OK; mazama@ methow.com; www.mazamainn.com; 14 miles west of Winthrop.

Mazama Ranch House / ★

42 LOST RIVER RD, MAZAMA; 509/996-2040

Owners Steve and Kristin Devin run this ranch house (which sleeps up to 13 guests) and the eight-room motel-style addition. The main house contains five beds and a full kitchen, and is perfect for family retreats. The rooms in the addition open to a sunny deck that fronts the valley's trail system (so does the hot tub). An additional cabin, the rustic Longhorn, has its own sleeping loft and wood stove. There's no restaurant and no common lobby, but when you've got hundreds of miles of skiing, mountain-biking, and horseback-riding trails one step from your room, who needs anything but a firm bed and kitchenette? The rural ranch atmosphere is the real deal: the barn, corral, and arena are available for free to any overnighter who arrives with a horse—and in summer, many do. For the horseless, two excellent outfitters are located within a few miles: Rocking Horse Ranch (509/996-2768) and Early Winters Outfitting and Saddle Company (509/996-2659). $$; MC, V; checks OK; just south of Mazama Country Inn, same entrance. &

Winthrop

Most of the tourist activity in the Methow Valley is found in this Western-motif town where old-fashioned storefronts and boardwalks will have you looking for Gary Cooper. Stop in the **SHAFER MUSEUM** (285 Castle; 509/996-2712), housed in pioneer Guy Waring's 1897 log cabin on the hill behind the main street. Exhibits tell of the area's early history and include old cars, a stagecoach, and horse-drawn vehicles. It is said that Waring's Harvard classmate, Owen Wister, came to visit in the 1880s and found some of the material for his novel, *The Virginian*, here.

The valley offers fine whitewater rafting, spectacular hiking in the North Cascades, horseback riding, mountain biking, fishing, and cross-country or helicopter skiing. After you've had a big day outside, quaff a beer at the **WINTHROP BREWING COMPANY** (155 Riverside Ave; 509/996-3183), in an old schoolhouse

CROSS-COUNTRY SKIING THE METHOW

Bright winter sunshine, dry powder snow, jaw-dropping views of mountain peaks—add almost 200 kilometers of well-groomed trails, and you have one of the nation's premier cross-country ski destinations. The **Methow Valley Sport Trails Association (MVSTA)** maintains this vast network of trails, the second largest in the United States. The system consists of four linked sections, many of which go directly past the valley's popular accommodations, so you can literally ski from your door. (In summer, the trails are used by mountain bikers.) Ski season usually begins in early December and continues through March. For updates on snow and trail conditions, contact the MVSTA (209 Castle St, Winthrop; 509/996-3287 or 800/682-5787; www.mvsta.com).

The largest section surrounds **Sun Mountain Lodge** in Winthrop, where 70 kilometers of trail cut through rolling hills. Below it, the **Community Trail** snakes past farms and bottomland as it meanders from Winthrop to **Mazama**. Mazama's flat terrain and open meadows are ideal for novices.

The remaining section, called **Rendezvous**, is recommended for intermediate/expert skiers only. Set above the valley at 3,500–4,000 feet, the trail passes through rugged forestland, where five huts are located at strategic points for overnight stays. Each hut bunks up to eight people and has a wood stove and a propane cookstove. Huts rent for $25 per person per night (or $150 for an entire hut). **Central Reservations** (800/422-3048; www.mvcentralres.com) has maps and information and makes reservations (required) for the **hut-to-hut system**. (For $70, Rendezvous Outfitters will lighten your load by hauling your group's gear and food to the huts.) Special trails are also set aside for **snowshoers**. Skiing on MVSTA trails requires trail passes, available at ski shops in the valley: $13 daily; $10 half-day; $30 three-day pass.

—*Nick Gallo*

on the main street. **WINTHROP MOUNTAIN SPORTS** (257 Riverside Ave; 509/996-2886) sells outdoor-activity equipment and supplies, and rents bikes, skis, snowshoes, and ice skates. The **TENDERFOOT GENERAL STORE** (corner of Riverside Ave and Hwy 20; 509/996-2288) has anything else you might have forgotten. **PEARRYGIN LAKE STATE PARK** (509/996-2370), 5 miles north of town, offers good swimming and campsites.

METHOW VALLEY CENTRAL RESERVATIONS (303 Riverside Ave; 800/422-3048; www.mvcentralres.com) books lodging for the entire valley and sells tickets for major events, such as mid-July's **RHYTHM AND BLUES FESTIVAL**. For more info, contact the **METHOW VALLEY INFORMATION CENTER** (241 Riverside Ave; 888/463-8469; www.methow.com.)

RESTAURANTS

Duck Brand Restaurant and Hotel / ★
246 RIVERSIDE AVE, WINTHROP; 509/996-2192

"Meet you at the Duck" is a common refrain heard in these parts. For more than a decade, this funky, eclectic restaurant built to replicate a frontier-style hotel has been a popular gathering spot and provisioner of good, filling meals at modest prices. Originally it made its mark with mountain-sized portions of Mexican food—and today you still won't walk away hungry from one of its bulging burritos or way, way large huevos rancheros plates. The menu now includes everything from fettuccine to teriyaki chicken to Thai stir-fry. American-style breakfasts feature wonderful cheesy Spanish potatoes and billowing omelets. The in-house bakery produces delicious baked goods, including biscotti, cinnamon rolls, and fruit pies. The service can be painfully slow, giving you plenty of time to marvel at the odd, whimsical memorabilia tacked on walls. Beware, lines form in summer. Upstairs, the Duck Brand Hotel has six sparsely furnished rooms, priced right. *$$; AE, DC, MC, V; local checks only; breakfast, lunch, dinner every day; beer and wine; reservations not accepted; duckbrand@methow.com; www.methownet.com/duck; on main street in Winthrop.*

Sun Mountain Lodge / ★★
PATTERSON LAKE RD, WINTHROP; 509/996-2211 OR 800/572-0493

No question, the restaurant at Sun Mountain has long been regarded as one of the region's finest, known for featuring Northwest ingredients and locally produced foods. In recent years, however, while the emphasis on regional cuisine has remained strong, the food occasionally fails to live up to its reputation (and prices). For every misstep, however, there is usually another point that brightens the palate. For instance, a skillet-roasted pheasant breast was served with bland pappardelle and no sign of the spring peas and prosciutto wrap promised on the menu—but the meat was well prepared, deliciously tender with a mellow, smoky flavor. A potato and roasted celery ravioli sounded intriguing but arrived overcooked and accompanied by an uninteresting and watery apple salad; in contrast, a grilled rack of lamb was a model temperature and shade of pink. Whether your meal is a hit or a miss, the dining room is a lovely, open space that takes full advantage of the lodge's stunning mountain views. Lunch and breakfast are more simple, as is the menu at the adjoining Eagle's Nest Lounge. Service is friendly if not always knowledgeable; the extensive wine list focuses on Northwest varietals. A new executive chef, Kevin Kennedy, recently took over the kitchen. Let's hope he can deliver more consistency. *$$$; AE, DC, MC, V; local checks only; breakfast, lunch, dinner every day; full bar; reservations recommended; smtnsale@methow.com; www.sunmountainlodge.com; 9.6 miles southwest of Winthrop.* &

LODGINGS

Sun Mountain Lodge / ★★★

PATTERSON LAKE RD, WINTHROP; 509/996-2211 OR 800/572-0493

The location of Sun Mountain Lodge is dramatic, high on a hill above the pristine Methow Valley and facing the North Cascades. Everything's big at the massive timber-and-stone lodge, from the hewn beams and stone fireplaces to the expansive views—and every space has a view. Guest rooms offer casual ranch-style comfort, with log furniture, wrought-iron sconces, glass coffee tables, and thick, soft blankets. The newer, luxe Mount Robinson rooms are stunning, with towering views even from the whirlpool bath; more-reasonably priced Gardner rooms aren't quite as large (though plenty big), but still have fireplaces and private decks or patios; the older main lodge rooms offer many of the same amenities (robes, coffeemakers, fine toiletries, etc.). In addition, 13 appealing cabins—particularly good for families—are available just down the hill at Patterson Lake. (Children's play areas and child care/activity programs are available.) Much of the Sun Mountain experience stems from the outdoors, and a helpful activities/rental desk is waiting to get you out there. In summer, there's tennis, horseback riding, swimming (two heated, seasonal pools), fly-fishing or rafting trips, golf (nearby), mountain biking, and more. In winter, resort trails are part of the valley's 175-kilometer cross-country trail system. Or you can arrange ice skating, snowshoeing, or a sleigh ride. Soak in one of two outdoor hot tubs, or splurge on a facial and massage (construction of a full-service spa begins in 2000). Enjoy an après-ski beer in the cozy Eagle's Nest Lounge. The restaurant in the lodge offers unbeatable views, with a menu that emphasizes regional cuisine (see Restaurants review). Reserve early for summer or winter ski-season dates. *$$$–$$$$; AE, DC, MC, V; checks OK; 2-night min on weekends; smtnsale@methow.com; www.sunmountainlodge.com; 9.6 miles southwest of Winthrop.* &

Wolfridge Resort / ★★

412-B WOLF CREEK RD, WINTHROP; 509/996-2828 OR 800/237-2388

Serenity reigns at this resort, which sits—literally and metaphorically—somewhere between the home-style Mazama Country Inn and the more showy Sun Mountain Lodge. Five log buildings contain 17 units divided into two-bedroom townhouses, one-bedroom suites, hotel-style rooms, and a cabin. The lodgings are tastefully, if simply, furnished with handcrafted log furniture. But it's the 60-acre riverside setting, stolen from the set of *Bonanza*, that impresses. Lovely ponderosas blow in the wind, mountain peaks dance behind a curtain of green forest, a glorious meadow lets in the sun. For sybarites, there's an outdoor pool and a Jacuzzi in a river-rock setting. Cross-country skiers and mountain bikers, jump on the trail system that runs right outside your door. *$$–$$$; AE, MC, V; checks OK; south of Winthrop head up Twin Lakes Rd for 1½ miles, turn right on Wolf Creek Rd, and travel 4 miles to entrance on right.*

Twisp

Eight miles away from Winthrop, ordinary-looking Twisp (the name is said to come from an Indian word for the noise made by a yellowjacket) doesn't possess any of its sister city's gussied-up Western ornamentation, but it's worth a stop. On Saturday mornings, the thriving **METHOW VALLEY FARMERS MARKET** operates next to the community center April 15 through October 15. Poke around Glover Street and you'll find local arts and crafts at the **CONFLUENCE GALLERY** (104 Glover; 509/997-ARTS), theater performances during summer at the **MERC PLAYHOUSE** (101 Glover; 509/997-PLAY), and wonderful pastries and fresh bread—it's hot from 9–11am—at **CINNAMON TWISP** (116 Glover; 509/997-5030). Around the corner is the **METHOW VALLEY BREWING COMPANY** (209 2nd Ave; 509/997-6822), which delivers small-batch brews and hearty food for lunch and dinner. For more info, contact the **TWISP VISITOR INFORMATION CENTER** (509/997-2926).

Pateros

LODGINGS

Amy's Manor Inn / ★★

435 HWY 153, PATEROS; 509/923-2334

Built in 1928, this enchanting manor is dramatically situated at the foot of the Cascades overlooking the Methow River. The setting is miragelike after you've traveled through the region's arid sagebrush: an impressive stand of maples, oaks, and large pines greets you. Stone fences line the property; 6 acres of flower gardens produce bursts of color. Three guest rooms, country-French in character, have a quiet elegance. But the hidden treasures here are the culinary creations of Pamela Koehler, the owner, who has extensive training as a chef. Combine the seasonal harvest from her organic garden with her skills in the

MOUNTAIN LOOP HIGHWAY

The Mountain Loop Highway is one of Washington's less-recognized gems, over-shadowed by the spectacular North Cascades Highway to the northeast. Located east of Everett, the highway is a 78-mile scenic drive that follows three swift rivers as it swings through the foothills of the western Cascades. The prime section is a 50-mile stretch past the town of Granite Falls that makes for an ideal weekend drive (especially in fall, when the colors are out). The highway also offers access to more than 300 miles of hiking trails, ranging from baby-stroller romps to rugged climbs into remote mountains. Note: Snow closes upper elevations of the highway during winter.

The highway consists of three roads: Highway 92, Forest Road 20, and Highway 530. It starts in **Granite Falls**, 14 miles east of Everett (exit 194 off I-5), which isn't much to look at, but is the best spot to grab lunch or last-minute supplies. Choose from pizza places, diner fare, or ethnic-food restaurants. **Sally's Brown Bag** (402 E Stanley St, Granite Falls; 360/691-3268) has homemade soups, and packs sandwiches to go.

Eastbound from Granite Falls, the highway retraces an old railway bed, passing through the town of Verlot; the **Verlot Ranger Station** (33515 Mountain Loop Hwy, Granite Falls; 360/691-7791) has information on hikes and sights. During the late 1880s, prospectors discovered gold, silver, and other metals in nearby mountains. Eastern investors built a railroad to haul ore to a smelter in Everett. But after a brief flurry of activity, the endeavor was undone by high costs, constant floods, and an economic depression. The mines closed in 1907.

Outside Granite Falls, the highway plunges into thick forest as it follows the "Stilly"—the darting, fast-flowing South Fork of the Stillaguamish River. Campgrounds appear at regular intervals, offering convenient places to picnic. The following hikes make nice out-ings: **Old Robe Trail** (mile 9 from Granite Falls; easy; 3 miles round trip) leads to two former railroad tunnels; **Mount Pilchuck Lookout** (mile 11; difficult; 6 miles round trip) climbs 2,100 feet and scrambles over boulders to reach a 5,300-foot lookout tower; **Big Four Ice Caves** (mile 25; easy; 2 miles round trip), popular with families, leads to year-round ice caves. Don't go inside the caves; ice crashing down from the ceiling makes it dangerous; and **Monte Cristo** (mile 31; easy; 8.6 miles round trip) goes to a former gold-mining town, but there's little there except for a few shacks.

At **Barlow Pass**, the highway pavement ends and a 14-mile stretch of winding gravel on Forest Road 20 drops down from the mountains before it emerges in farmland near the timber town of **Darrington**. The **Country Coffee & Deli** (1180 Cascade St, Darrington; 360/436-0213) will replenish you with sandwiches, ice cream, and espresso. At Darrington, the Mountain Loop Highway swings west on Highway 530 and loops back to Arlington near Interstate 5; you can also go north 19 miles on Forest Road 20 to connect to the North Cascades Highway in Rockport. *—Nick Gallo* kitchen, and the table's bounty, be it breakfast or dinner, never disappoints. This is your best bet for miles. *$$; MC, V; checks OK; 5 miles north of Pateros.*

Lake Chelan

South of the Methow Valley, Lake Chelan sits with half a mind in the mountains and the other half in vacation playland. On one end, the 55-mile-long, fjordlike lake isolates itself in the Cascades—the remote community of Stehekin sits at this northern tip—and at the other, the lake turns sociable in the town of Chelan, happily splashing along as one of the state's most popular summer swimming, boating, and fishing destinations. The lake is never more than 2 miles wide (it's also one of the deepest in the nation), so you have a sense of slicing right into the Cascades.

Chelan

This resort area is blessed with the springtime perfume of apple blossoms, beautiful Lake Chelan thrusting into tall mountains, 300 days of sunshine a year, and good skiing, hunting, fishing, hiking, and sailing. It has been trying to live up to its touristic potential since C. C. Campbell built his hotel here in 1901, with mixed success. Now that time-share condos and B&Bs have sprouted throughout the area, the amenities have greatly improved.

The top attraction is the cruise up Lake Chelan to Stehekin (see below) on **LADY OF THE LAKE II**, an old-fashioned tour boat, or one of its faster, more modern siblings. In summer, three boats are in operation. The *Lady II*, the largest of the vessels, holds 350 and provides a leisurely four-hour trip uplake, with a 90-minute layover in Stehekin. It departs Chelan daily at 8:30am and returns around 6pm ($22 per person round trip; kids 6–11 years old travel half-price). The faster, smaller *Lady Express* shortens the trip to just over two hours one-way, with a one-hour stop in Stehekin before heading back (round-trip tickets $41). The *Lady Cat*, a catamaran that whips across the lake at 50 mph, makes the trip in 75 minutes; cost is $79 round trip. Many travelers opt for the "combination trip," traveling uplake on the *Lady Express* and returning on the *Lady II*, which allows for a three-hour, 15-minute layover in Stehekin and a return by 6pm. Reservations are not needed for the *Lady II*, but the two faster boats almost always book up; advance purchase is necessary. During off-peak season—November 1–May 1—the boat schedule cuts back drastically. For full details, contact the **LAKE CHELAN BOAT COMPANY** (1418 W Woodin Ave; 509/682-2224 or 509/ 682-4584 for reservations; www.ladyofthelake.com).

Alternatively, **CHELAN AIRWAYS** (1328 W Woodin Ave; 509/682-5065 or 509/682-5555 for reservations) offers daily seaplane service to Stehekin ($120 round trip), as well as scenic tours of the mountains. **CHELAN BUTTE LOOKOUT**, 9 miles west of Chelan, also provides a view of the lake, the Columbia River, and the orchard-blanketed countryside.

The best reason for going to Chelan is Lake Chelan itself, where some of the best accommodations are **SHORE-SIDE CONDOS**. Resort Systems, Inc. (800/356-9756; www.resortsys.com), a rental clearinghouse, has listings for condos and private homes in the area. Each condo is privately owned, so furnishings and taste vary greatly. Condos at Wapato Point (1 Wapato Point Wy, Manson; 888/768-9511 or 509/687-9511; www.wapatopoint.com), a full-fledged resort in neighboring Manson, are rented directly through its office.

Chelan's hot summer weather and the lake's clear, cool water beg you to get waterborne. Waterskiing, windsurfing, pleasure boating (personal watercraft, kayak, motorboat), and swimming—stick close to the lake's lower end for the warmest water—are popular activities. Rent boats and water-ski gear at **CHELAN BOAT RENTALS** (1210 W Woodin Ave; 509/682-4444). Popular public boat docks in the area are Don Morse Park (the city park), Riverwalk Park, Lake Chelan State Park, 25 Mile Creek State Park, and Old Mill Park (across from Mill Bay Casino just outside Manson). **SLIDEWATERS** (102 Waterslide Dr; 509/682-5751), one of the Northwest's largest waterslide parks, keeps the kids happy.

Fishing for steelhead, rainbow, cutthroat, and chinook is very good in Lake Chelan, with special emphasis on the chinook fishery. Stocked in the lake since the mid-'70s, they're the lake's prized catch. **GRAYBILL'S GUIDE SERVICE** (509/682-4292) is a reputable service; check with the **LAKE CHELAN CHAMBER OF COMMERCE** (800/FOR-CHELAN) for more guides.

RESTAURANTS

Campbell House Cafe / ★★

104 W WOODIN AVE, CHELAN; 509/682-4250

In recent years, the on-site eatery for Campbell's venerable lodge has been trying to break out of the "staid hotel restaurant" mold. Owners changed the name (adding the cafe tag), spruced up the bottom-floor setting, and added a weekly fresh sheet. Well, the decor still is somewhat dowdy and the menu sticks to safe, predictable choices, but this is where you'll find Chelan's freshest seafood, dependable steaks, and acceptable pastas. A solid wine list is a plus. Breakfast is popular, with apple pancakes, biscuits and gravy, and other standards leading the way. Upstairs, you can find casual fare—burgers, fish-and-chips, salads—at the Second Floor Pub & Veranda. The outdoor deck is a choice spot to catch a bite on a warm evening. $$$; AE, MC, V; checks OK; breakfast (cafe only), lunch, dinner every day; full bar; reservations recommended (cafe), reservations not accepted (pub); www.campbellsresort.com; downtown, facing main street near lake. &

Deepwater Brewing & Public House / ★

225 HWY 150, CHELAN; 509/682-2720

Brewmaster Scott Dietrich made an immediate splash when he opened this likable brewpub on Memorial Day 1999. It features a strong lineup of microbrews and tasty pub food to match a gregarious mood. The ribs are crowd favorites—

the lean, mean alligator ribs, started as a novelty item, are a best seller—pasta servings are generous, and the familiar appetizer fare (nachos, fried mozzarella, calamari) is good enough. Grab a seat at the outdoor terrace on a warm evening and enjoy sunset dining under a big sky. Live music on summer weekends. *$$; AE, MC, V; checks OK; lunch, dinner every day; full bar; reservations recommended (dinner); info@deepwaterbrewing.com; www.deepwaterbrewing. com; 2 miles outside Chelan on N Manson Hwy.* &

LODGINGS

Best Western Lakeside Lodge / ★

2312 W WOODIN AVE, CHELAN; 509/682-4396 OR 800/468-2781
With new owners and bigger digs, the former Westview motel has taken a definite step up. The 65-unit complex, sharp-looking in a green sage and cedar trim exterior, now includes an added wing and a complete retrofitting of the old rooms. Nice extras include spacious rooms (vaulted ceilings on the top floor), a cheerful indoor pool, and complimentary breakfast in an airy, gazebo-shaped conference room with full-length windows facing the lake. The biggest reason to stay might be the backyard. Nicely landscaped grounds slope down to a small, adjoining park fronting the water, where uplake views of the North Cascades' snowy peaks are delightful. *$$$; AE, DC, DIS, MC, V; checks OK; www.4-westview.com; 2 miles south of Chelan on Hwy 97A.* &

Campbell's Resort on Lake Chelan / ★★

104 W WOODIN AVE, CHELAN; 509/682-2561 OR 800/553-8225
Chelan's landmark resort continues to be the most popular place for visitors. Its major draw is prime lakeside property—and a sandy 1,200-foot beach. The resort's 170 rooms, many with kitchenettes, are spread out in five buildings of varying vintage. The majority are more comfortable than plush, with the most attractive in one of the new or recently remodeled buildings—Lodge 1 or 4. Amenities include two heated outdoor pools, two outdoor hot tubs, and boat moorage. With a conference center that holds 300 people, and other new additions, Campbell's today is undeniably a large-scale operation, but it still has an amiable, personable quality, thanks no doubt to the fact that the same family who built the resort still owns and operates it four generations later. Reservations are scarce in high season. *$$$; AE, MC, V; checks OK; res@campbellsresort.com; www.campbellsresort.com; on lake at end of main street near downtown.*

Kelly's Resort / ★★

12801 S LAKESHORE RD, CHELAN; 509/687-3220 OR 800/561-8978
Kelly-owned for half a century, this longtime getaway qualifies as a "find" for urban escapees. It's a peaceful retreat, though it's also like summer camp for families who return year after year to claim the same cabin. You can walk on woodland trails or take a boat out on the water, but most people seem happy to sunbathe on the sunny deck and read a hard-

cover from beginning to end. The 11 cabins set back in the woods are a bit dark, shaded by the forest, but they're fully equipped, with kitchens, fireplaces, and TVs. A great new feature is an outdoor heated pool in the woods. You can take your morning dip while deer frolic in the nearby pines. Many prefer one of the modern condo units on the lake (from the lower units, you can walk right off the deck into the water), where there's also a three-bedroom house for rent, a convenience store, and a pingpong table. The only off note: the budget prices have gone up. $$–$$$; MC, V; checks OK; 14 miles uplake on south shore.

Stehekin

A passage to Stehekin, the little community at the head of Lake Chelan, is like traveling back in time. This jumping-off point for exploring rugged and remote North Cascades National Park is reached only by a four-hour boat trip from Chelan on *Lady of the Lake II* or one of its faster counterparts (see Chelan, above), by **CHELAN AIRWAYS** floatplane (see Chelan), by hiking, or by private boat. For a shorter boat ride, catch one of the boats uplake at Field's Point. At Stehekin, you can take a bus tour, eat lunch, enjoy close-up views of the North Cascades' rugged peaks, and be back onboard the boat in time for the return voyage. The **STEHEKIN PASTRY COMPANY**, a pleasant stroll from the boat landing, fills the mountain air with fresh-from-the-oven, sugary smells of cinnamon rolls (summer only).

Exploration is the prime reason for coming here. Good day hikes include a lovely one along the lakeshore and another along a stream through the **BUCKNER ORCHARD**; numerous splendid backcountry trails attract serious backpackers. In winter, fine touring opportunities for cross-country skiers or snowshoe enthusiasts abound, though the town pretty much shuts down for the season. The **RANGER STATION** at Chelan (428 W Woodin Ave, Chelan; 509/682-2576), open year-round, is an excellent information source. A National Park Service shuttle bus (509/682-2549) provides transportation from Stehekin to trailheads, campgrounds, fishing holes, and scenic areas mid-May through mid-October.

Part of the National Park complex near the Stehekin landing, **NORTH CASCADES STEHEKIN LODGE** (at head of Lake Chelan; 509/682-4494; www. stehekin.com) is a year-round lodge featuring 28 rooms, a full-service restaurant, a general store, and a rental shop for bikes, boats, skis, and snowshoes.

The Courtney family will pick you up at Stehekin in an old bus and take you to their **STEHEKIN VALLEY RANCH** (509/682-4677; www.courtneycountry. com) at the farthest end of the valley, where you can enjoy river rafting and hiking or opt for seclusion. Open in summer, the ranch rents 12 units, 7 of which are rustic tent-cabins offering the basics (screened windows, a kerosene lamp, showers in the main building). The price is decent ($65–$75 per night per person), considering it includes three hearty, family-style meals and valley transportation. **CASCADE CORRALS** (509/682-7742), also run by the family, arranges horseback rides and mountain pack trips.

LODGINGS

Silver Bay Inn / ★★

10 SILVER BAY RD, STEHEKIN; 509/682-2212 OR 800/555-7781
(WA AND OR ONLY)

The Silver Bay Inn, at the nexus of the Stehekin River and Lake Chelan, is a gracious, memorable retreat. Friendly Kathy and Randall Dinwiddie welcome guests to this passive-solar home and spectacular setting: 700 feet of waterfront with a broad green lawn rolling down to the lake. Formerly a B&B, the inn has changed its configuration slightly. The main house now rents out as a single unit. The two-bedroom, two-bath house, decorated with antiques, has a 30-foot-long sunroom, two view decks, a soaking tub, and a faraway view. The house includes an apartment-sized unit with a private entrance, rented separately. Two lakeside cabins are remarkably convenient (dishwasher, microwave, all linens) and sleep four and six. Bicycles, canoes, croquet, and hammocks are available. The hot tub has a 360-degree view of the lake and surrounding mountains. During summer, units have a two- to five-night minimum stay and kids under 9 are not allowed (though they're welcome other months). $$–$$$; MC, V; checks OK; www.silverbayinn.com; 1½ miles up Stehekin Valley Rd from landing.

CENTRAL CASCADES

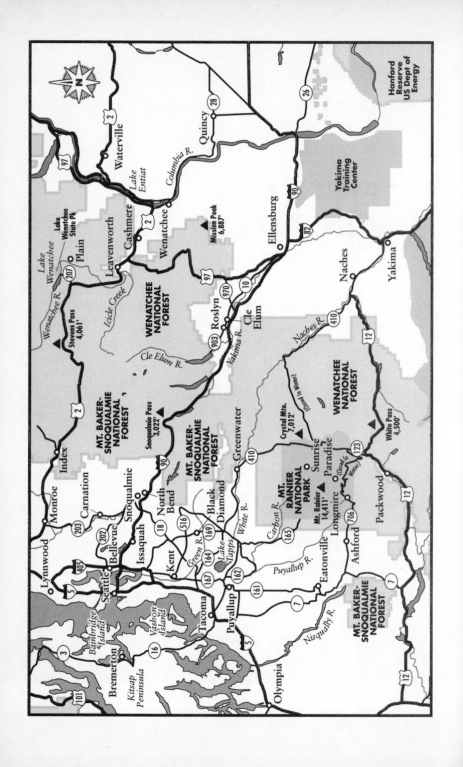

CENTRAL CASCADES

The soaring, snowcapped mountains of the Central Cascades contain not only the main arteries between Western and Eastern Washington—Interstate 90 and US Highways 2 and 12—but also the state's best recreation destinations. In summer, these thoroughfares are jammed with those seeking fir- and pine-perfumed air, pristine lakes, mountain trails, rock walls to climb, and campsites in forested glades. In winter, the routes can be choked with snow, and skiers and snowboarders flock to the summits of Snoqualmie, Stevens, and White Passes to schuss the slopes.

The mountains around the Bavarian-style village of Leavenworth, and north to the tiny village of Plain, contain countless all-season mountain get-aways. Leavenworth's many festivals draw visitors year-round. This section of the Cascades is also home to quite probably the world's most beautiful mountain—Mount Rainier. In summer, many Northwesterners make a tradition of picnicking amid wildflower meadows, an experience that on a sunny day feels like a fat slice of heaven. No wonder it's called Paradise. The mountain is an easy day trip—or overnight in one of the B&Bs or lodges nearby.

ACCESS AND INFORMATION

One of the Northwest's most beautiful drives, the 400-mile Cascade Loop, follows Highway 2 from Everett, takes in Leavenworth and Wenatchee, and heads north (see North Cascades chapter) to Lake Chelan, Winthrop, and the North Cascades Highway. The loop route can be accessed from Interstate 90 at Cle Elum by taking Highway 970 to US Highway 97 north. It joins Highway 2 just east of Leavenworth. A brochure is available from the **CASCADE LOOP ASSOCIATION** (PO Box 3245, Wenatchee, WA 98807; 509/662-3888; www.cascadeloop.com).

Interstate 90 is an elegant multilane freeway, designated a National Scenic Byway in 1998, which roughly traces the South Fork Snoqualmie River east into the Cascade foothills, cutting through the verdant Snoqualmie Valley and fir-thick hillsides like a wide boulevard. Many historic and recreational attractions flank the interstate. A map of outings and activities along the route, as well as a heritage tour map, are available from the **MOUNTAINS TO SOUND GREENWAY TRUST** (1011 Western Ave, Ste 606, Seattle; 206/382-5565; MTSGreenway@tpl.org; www.mtsgreenway.org).

Highway 2 and Stevens Pass

Highway 2 heads east-west across the state, from Interstate 5 at Everett to Spokane. The highway winds its way up to Stevens Pass along the Skykomish River, dropping down to the Wenatchee River. Along the way, towns such as Leavenworth, Cashmere, and Wenatchee give travelers reason to stop.

Index

Challenging cliffs loom just behind this tiny town, where rock climbers go to climb the Town Wall. The modest **BUSH HOUSE COUNTRY INN** (300 5th St; 360/793-2312), first established during the mining boom of 1898, now has 11 pretty (and simple) sleeping rooms; the on-site restaurant features steaks and there's a pub garden out back.

Stevens Pass

A favorite destination of Seattle area skiers, Stevens Pass (exit 194 off Hwy 2; 206/812-4510) offers downhill and cross-country. Day lodges at the summit have been spruced up, and there's the newly built, Cascadian-style **GRANITE PEAK LODGE**. The **NORDIC CENTER** is located 5 miles east of the summit.

Lake Wenatchee

Lake Wenatchee, about 5 miles north of Highway 2 on Highway 207 at Coles Corner (and the same distance northwest of Plain), has a state park at one end, with a large, sandy public swimming beach and campsites (overnight fee; reservations through Reservations Northwest, 800/452-5687) in the woods closer to the Wenatchee River and the lake. There are also lakeside campsites at the forest service's **GLACIER VIEW CAMPGROUND**, 5 miles west on Cedar Brae Road. Here you'll also find the trailhead to **HIDDEN LAKE** (a half-mile family hike to a small alpine lake). Ask at the **RANGER STATION** (22976 Hwy 207, Leavenworth; 509/763-3103) on the north side of the lake about other day hikes in the area. Play golf or tennis at **KAHLER GLEN GOLF AND SKI RESORT** (20890 Kahler Dr, Leavenworth; 509/763-2121 or 800/440-2994; www.kahlerglen.com for condo reservations).

Plain

LODGINGS

Mountain Springs Lodge / ★★

19115 CHIWAWA LOOP RD, PLAIN; 509/763-2713 OR 800/858-2276

This big mountain retreat with lots of open space lets in the sun—in any season. Check-in is at the new Beaver Creek Lodge, which houses two spacious Ralph Lauren–style suites upstairs, and a restaurant (not yet open full-time; meals available by reservation) and a full-time espresso bar on the main floor. Two 20-person-plus lodges and two smaller A-frame chalets face a sprawling lawn, good for volleyball, croquet, or cartwheels. Follow the brook to the barn, where events as special as weddings or as down-home as a family reunion chuck-wagon barbecue take place. A good place for anyone anytime, but best when you've got an energetic group and rent one of the big lodges (Pine or Ponderosa). Hot tubs and massive rock fireplaces become magnets after a

CENTRAL CASCADES THREE-DAY TOUR

DAY ONE: Head east on Interstate 90 from Seattle. Take exit 22, past Preston, a turn-of-the-century Scandinavian mill town, and Fall City, the final upstream landing for early steamboats. Highway 202 takes you to dramatic 270-foot **Snoqualmie Falls**, where you have lunch at **Salish Lodge & Spa** in fancy surroundings with views to the falls. Then tour the little town of **Snoqualmie**. At North Bend, where the rocky face of Mount Si rises to the north, return to Interstate 90 at exit 32 and continue east to **Snoqualmie Pass**. The terrain begs you to stop and enjoy a view or take a hike—such as the Wagon Road Trail. East of the summit, historic **Rosyln** is worth a detour. Grab a burger at the **Roslyn Cafe**, then on to **Cle Elum**, where you spend the night at the **Iron Horse Inn B&B**.

DAY TWO: After breakfast at your B&B, swing through town to stock up on road snacks, choosing from the goodies at the **Cle Elum Bakery** or picking up beef jerky at **Owen's Meats**. Follow signs north to Blewett/Swauk Pass (Hwy 97), a scenic drive that drops along Peshastin Creek to Highway 2; head east. Swing through **Cashmere** and visit the **Pioneer Village** and **Liberty Orchards** for fruit candy samples, then continue on to **Wenatchee**. Watch for the **Anjou Bakery** (3898 Old Monitor Rd; 509/782-4360), sign and stop for a macaroon or fudgy chocolate cookie. Your destination on a clear spring or summer day is **Ohme Gardens**, just north of Wenatchee. If you 're still hungry, grab a late lunch at **The Windmill**, then head west on Highway 2 to **Leavenworth**. Check into **Run of the River** or **Haus Lorelei Inn** and relax a bit before dinner, enjoying river and mountain views. A romantic Austrian-style dinner at **Restaurant Osterreich** ends your day perfectly.

DAY THREE: Have a leisurely breakfast, then explore Leavenworth's **Front Street** shops, but don't miss **Cabin Fever Rustics**, one of our favorite stops. Have a relaxing lunch in the calm atmosphere of **Cafe Mozart**—or, if it's sunny, eat on the patio at **Lorraine's Edel House Inn**. Of course, you may want to burn more calories, so check in at the **ranger station** for suggested hikes. Stay a second night in Leavenworth and take in a concert at the **Icicle Creek Music Center** (9286 Icicle Rd, Leavenworth; 509/548-6347; check schedule in advance). Or, if you are truly seeking simplicity off the beaten path, take Highway 2 west, enjoying the views at **Stevens Pass**, and head to Index for an overnight stay at the **Bush House Country Inn** before returning to the Puget Sound area.

day of snowmobiling (available here), in the saddle (horses for rent nearby), or on sleigh rides (on-site in winter, packages available). *$$$; AE, DIS, MC, V; checks OK; info@mtsprings.com; www.mtsprings.com; 1 mile north of Plain.*

Natapoc Lodging / ★★★

12338 BRETZ RD, LEAVENWORTH; 509/763-3313 OR 888/NATAPOC

For any city dweller who has dreamed of a weekend home on the Wenatchee River, Natapoc is the next best thing. Each log house claims 1 to 5 piney acres and at least 200 feet of riverfront. All are stocked with everything from a VCR to a microwave. And they come in all sizes, from an utterly romantic twosome to a rambling 20-something. The bigger homes are particularly good for groups (extra bedding, loads of silverware, two living areas, and a large out-of-the-way hot tub). Outdoorsy activities include fly-fishing and cross-country skiing, but frankly, all we really want to do is soak in the cabin's hot tub and make snow angels. $$$; AE, MC, V; checks OK; info@natapoc. com; www.natapoc.com; 4 miles south of Lake Wenatchee.

Leavenworth

Once a railroad yard and sawmill town, Leavenworth recast itself in the 1960s as a Bavarian-style village with tourism as its primary industry. The architecture sets the tone, and while some cringe at the dirndls-and-lederhosen decor, beyond the facade most find an appealing town suited to its stunning alpine setting. Popular festivals are the **AUTUMN LEAF FESTIVAL** during the last weekend in September and the first weekend in October, the **CHRISTMAS LIGHTING FESTIVAL** on the first two Saturdays in December, and **MAIFEST** on the second weekend in May. Call the Leavenworth Chamber (see below) for more information.

FRONT STREET is the strolling, shopping, and festival showcase street. **DIE MUSIK BOX** (837 Front St; 800/288-5883) has a dazzling—sometimes rather noisy—array of music boxes; **ALPEN HAUS MINIATURES** (807 Front St; 800/572-1559) features dollhouse furniture and miniatures; and **A COUNTRY HEART** (821 Front St; 509/548-5719) sells rustic touches for the urban home. Away from Front Street, one of our favorites is **CABIN FEVER RUSTICS** (923 Commercial St; 509/548-4238), offering accessories for the western bungalow. A good stop with kids is the **GINGERBREAD FACTORY** (828 Commercial St; 509/548-6592) for gingerbread cookies and houses.

For a respite from shopping, **CAFE MOZART** (829 Front St; 509/548-0600) offers European charm and tasteful German-style foods. The **LEAVENWORTH BREWERY** (636 Front St; 509/548-4545) makes nine seasonal beers on the premises, and offers daily tours of the small brewery. **VISCONTI'S** (636 Front St; 509/548-1213), an Italian-style restaurant adjacent to the brewery, has a tasting sampler, great with one of their savory, thin-crust pizzas.

Just southwest of town at **HOMEFIRES BAKERY** (13013 Bayne Rd; 509/548-7362), visitors can see the German-style wood-fired oven (the nine-grain bread is the best), and during fair weather can sit at the picnic table on the lawn for cinnamon rolls and coffee.

Outdoor activities abound in this area year-round; check with the **LEAVENWORTH RANGER STATION** (600 Sherbourne; 509/548-6977) on the eastern edge of town or **LEAVENWORTH CHAMBER OF COMMERCE** (894 Hwy 2, at 9th St; 509/548-5807) for maps and information on hiking, fishing, skiing, mountain biking, rafting, and horseback riding. Tour the **LEAVENWORTH NATIONAL FISH HATCHERY** (12790 Fish Hatchery Rd, off Icicle Rd; 509/548-7641) on Icicle Creek to watch the chinook salmon run in June and July—and spawn in August and September; or golf at the scenic 18-hole **LEAVENWORTH GOLF CLUB** (9101 Icicle Rd; 509/548-7267; www.leavenworthgolf.com).

SCOTTISH LAKES BACK COUNTRY CABINS (High Country Adventures; by reservation only; 425/844-2000 or 888/9-HICAMP; www.scottishlakes.com), 8 miles into the backcountry west of Leavenworth, is a cluster of eight cabins and a small day lodge at the edge of the **ALPINE LAKES WILDERNESS AREA**, one of the nation's finest such areas. Ski in, or be carted up in a heated 12-seat snowcat, and ski the 3,000-foot descent home.

RESTAURANTS

Lorraine's Edel House Inn / ★★

320 9TH ST, LEAVENWORTH; 509/548-4412

Edel House got its start as a bed-and-breakfast; today it's a pleasant restaurant with an international menu, and one of the few places in town where vegetarians find reprieve from schnitzel (though it is on the menu). Here you'll find plump portobello mushrooms with goat cheese and garlic pâté on crostini, a perfect puttanesca, or meat specials such as a grilled pork chop topped with apple and leek chutney. The ambitious menu changes frequently. Upstairs are several pretty guest rooms, and next door is a cottage suite with a large whirlpool tub and gas fireplace. Lorraine's doesn't serve breakfast, but gives overnight guests a 50 percent discount on other meals. *$$; DIS, MC, V; checks OK; lunch (summer only), dinner every day; beer and wine; reservations recommended; between Commercial and the river.* &

Restaurant Osterreich / ★★★

633 FRONT ST, LEAVENWORTH; 509/548-4031

Make your way down to the cellar of the Tyrolean Ritz Hotel, and you'll find one of Leavenworth's finest Austrian restaurants. It's dim, devoid of windows, but gently flickering candlelight warms the room. Austrian chef Leo Haas shows his talent for flavorful yet lighter-than-German fare. Come hungry. Appetizers, especially crayfish strudel with a tart sorrel salad, are outstanding. Still, many appetites have been satisfied just by an entree, such as robust braised lamb shank or duck breast with port wine–berry sauce; daily specials sometimes include foie gras. Rarely seen Austrian wines are on the list here. Desserts are excellent, but we doubt you'll have room. Upstairs, the friendly hotel offers 16 standard, streetfront rooms. *$$; AE, DIS, MC, V; local checks OK; lunch, dinner every day; beer and wine; reservations recommended; www.leavenworthdining. com; below Tyrolean Ritz Hotel.* &

LODGINGS

Abendblume Pension / ★★★

12570 RANGER RD, LEAVENWORTH; 509/548-4059 OR 800/669-7634

This is the place where you come to leave everything behind (especially the kids). It's one of the most elegant, sophisticated inns in town, run by the most gracious host. A sweeping staircase, beautifully adorned, leads upstairs. The two best rooms have wood-burning fireplaces, Italian marble bathrooms with whirlpool tubs that discreetly open to the room, and sun-drenched window seats. Every room (each with its own VCR) is an escape here, regardless of size. There's a grand piano in the parlor; a patio hot tub cascades into a garden waterfall. Breakfast is at your own table (and your own pace) in the pine-trimmed morning room. *$$$; AE, DIS, MC, V; checks OK; abendblm@rightathome.com; www.abendblume.com; north on Ski Hill Dr at west end of town.*

All Seasons River Inn / ★★

8751 ICICLE RD, LEAVENWORTH; 509/548-1425

What this modern two-story cedar house lacks in exterior charm, it makes up inside and with its relaxing riverside location. Cheery rooms (most have river views and decks; several have whirlpools), antique furnishings, amenities like chocolates in the room and evening treats, and attention to detail by owners Kathy and Jeff Falconer offer the type of comfort that soothes the spirit. *$$; MC, V; checks OK; allriver@rightathome.com; www. allseasonriverinn.com; 1 mile south of Hwy 2.*

Bosch Garten

9846 DYE RD, LEAVENWORTH; 509/548-6900 OR 800/535-0069

Friendly hosts and stylish, homey comfort make this newly built two-story home, in a residential area at the eastern outskirts of town, a good choice. Three rooms with private baths are perfect for those traveling in small groups—then the house is yours. A hot tub in a garden gazebo and a tiny orchard make this a particularly relaxing getaway on warm summer evenings. Children over 14 OK. *$$; MC, V; checks OK; popity@nwi.net; www.boschgarten.com; east of town.*

Haus Lorelei Inn / ★★

347 DIVISION ST, LEAVENWORTH; 509/548-5726 OR 800/514-8868

Here's a rarity: a bed-and-breakfast that welcomes kids. The 10 comfortable European-style rooms here are not indestructible, but not overly precious either, and each is large enough to set up a spare bed here and there. Those who don't want the kids so close by could stash them in the clubby little Hansel and Gretel Room. (Remember how you always used to make a fort in the closet? Well, here it is.) The Prinzessin, an octagonal room with a canopy bed overlooking the river on the main floor, is stunning. At the 2-acre site fronting the Wenatchee River, each of Elisabeth Saunders' rooms affords gorgeous views of the Cascades; at night you can hear the river rushing over the boulders. A tennis court and hot tub are on-site; a sandy swimming beach on the river isn't far. *$$; no credit cards; checks OK; www.hauslorelei.com; 2 blocks from downtown.*

Mountain Home Lodge / ★★★☆

8201 MOUNTAIN HOME RD, LEAVENWORTH; 509/548-7077 OR 800/414-2378

This lodge is a mile above Leavenworth in a breathtaking mountaintop setting. You reach it in summer driving 3 miles of rough dirt road; in winter, a heated snow-cat picks you up from the parking lot at the bottom of Mountain Home Road. Miles of tracked cross-country ski trails leave from the back door; you can snowshoe and sled, or try the 1,700-foot toboggan run. Complimentary cross-country ski and snowshoe equipment is available on loan. The hot tub and swimming pool overlook a broad meadow toward the mountains. Summer activities include hiking, horseshoe pitching, badminton, swimming, and tennis. Ten charming guest rooms are individually decorated with quilts and accessories in mountain or outdoor themes. Gourmet meals in the view dining area can include delicious surprises such as squash soup, pheasant, or a decadent chocolate tart; the wine list includes top Northwest offerings. Two new private pine cabins nearby offer solitude and breathtaking views. No kids. Meals included in winter. *$$$; DIS, MC, V; checks OK; mhl@televar.com; www.mthome.com; off E Leavenworth Rd and Hwy 2.*

Run of the River / ★★★★

9308 E LEAVENWORTH RD, LEAVENWORTH; 509/548-7171 OR 800/288-6491

This elegant log inn that Monty and Karen Turner created on the bank of the Icicle River just keeps getting better. It boasts such solitude, comfort, and exquisite attention to detail that you may want to spend the entire day on the deck, reading or watching the wildlife in the refuge across the river (binoculars are provided). Six rooms each have a hand-hewn log bed, private bath, cable TV, deck, complimentary robes, and even your own bubble kit, in case stargazing from the hot tub isn't enough entertainment. Best rooms face the river. Our favorite, the Aspens, warmed by a wood stove, has perhaps the best river view and is closest to the well-planned (and quiet) outdoor Jacuzzi. Others prefer upstairs rooms with reading lofts. Hearty breakfasts emphasize seasonal produce. Mountain bikes are available for off-road explorations (ask the Turners for where-to-go tips—they've printed an excellent array of area-specific activity guides). *$$; DIS, MC, V; checks OK; rofther@runoftheriver; www.runoftheriver.com; 1 mile east of Hwy 2.*

Sleeping Lady Retreat and Conference Center / ★★★

7375 ICICLE RD, LEAVENWORTH; 509/548-6344 OR 800/574-2123

This is exactly the kind of place Leavenworth needed—a quintessential Northwest retreat with an acute awareness of the environment. A former CCC camp, the place is well set up for conferences; buildings—from a dance studio to a spacious 60-person meeting house—are comfortably elegant, with touches such as Oriental rugs and wood stoves, but all spaces are high-tech-ready. The old fieldstone chapel is now a spectacular 200-seat performing arts theater (and the home of the Icicle Creek Music Center, and its own resident string ensemble; 509/548-6347). The guest rooms—with log beds and additional beds in alcoves or lofts and their own baths—are set in six different clusters. Two separate cabins include the romantic, secluded Eyrie, with its own wood stove and whirlpool bath. Two woodland-style rock pools include a large heated pool used May to September, and a small heated soaking pool used year-round. Conferences have first dibs here, yet there's flexibility for other guests on a space-available basis. Chef Damian Browne serves an excellent meal in a (slightly disconcerting) buffet-style. Watch for the outdoor glass "icicle" sculpture by Dale Chihuly, to the right of the dining room entrance. The retreat is a superb place to rest your soul and awaken your senses. *$$; AE, DIS, MC, V; checks OK; info@sleepinglady.com; www.sleepinglady.com; 2 miles southwest of Leavenworth.* &

Cashmere

This little orchard town gives cross-mountain travelers who aren't in a Bavarian mood an alternative to Leavenworth. The main street has put up Western storefronts; the town's bordered by river and railroad.

The **CHELAN COUNTY HISTORICAL SOCIETY** (600 Cottage Ave; 509/782-3230) has an extensive collection of Native artifacts and archaeological material; the adjoining **PIONEER VILLAGE** puts 19 old buildings, carefully restored and equipped, into a nostalgic grouping.

Aplets and Cotlets, confections made with local fruit and walnuts from an old Armenian recipe, have been produced in Cashmere for decades. You can tour the plant at **LIBERTY ORCHARDS** (117 Mission St; 509/782-2191)—and sample a few. In an orchard off Highway 2, 1 mile east of Cashmere, is **ANJOU BAKERY** (3898 Old Monitor Hwy; 509/782-4360), a great stop for rustic breads, streusel-topped apple pies, macaroons, chocolate cookies, and a host of other delicious baked goods.

Wenatchee

You're in the heart of apple country, with an **APPLE BLOSSOM FESTIVAL** the first part of May; call the Wenatchee Valley Convention & Visitors Bureau (116 N Wenatchee Ave; 800/572-7753). **OHME GARDENS** (3 miles north on Hwy 97A; 509/662-5785) is a 9-acre alpine retreat with cool glades and water features. It sits on a promontory 600 feet above the Columbia River, offering splendid views of the valley, river, and city. The **RIVERFRONT LOOP TRAIL** on the banks of the Columbia makes for a pleasant evening stroll—or an easy bike ride for those who want to pedal the whole 11-mile loop, which traverses both sides of the river (and crosses two bridges) from Wenatchee to East Wenatchee. Best place to hook onto the trail is at the east end of Fifth Street.

MISSION RIDGE (13 miles southwest on Squilchuck Rd; 509/663-6543; www.missionridge.com) offers some of the best powder snow in the region, served by four chairlifts; ask for ski-and-lodging package info. On the third Sunday in April, the RIDGE-TO-RIVER RELAY (509/662-8799; www.r2r.org)—participants compete in six events, including skiing, running, biking, and kayaking—is impressive.

ROCKY REACH DAM (6 miles north on Hwy 97; 509/663-7522) offers a beautiful picnic and playground area (locals marry on the well-kept grounds), plus a fish-viewing room. Inside the dam, two large galleries are devoted to the region's history. Free guided tours are offered from June 1 through early September; reservations are required.

RESTAURANTS

Garlini's Ristorante Italiano / ★

810 VALLEY MALL PKWY, EAST WENATCHEE; 509/884-1707

There's nothing fancy about the outside of this niche restaurant tucked away on one of the main streets in East Wenatchee. But inside, dim lighting, dark wood, and festive music bring Italy to the senses. Craig Still makes sure the Garlini family's old Italian favorites are cooked as expected: seafood fettuccine, chicken and veal parmigiana, and lasagne just like Mamma's. He's also added new, lighter nightly specials. Good for families and large parties. *$; AE, DIS, MC, V; checks OK; dinner Tues–Sun; beer and wine; reservations recommended; 1 block north of Wenatchee Valley Mall.*

John Horan's Steak & Seafood House / ★★

2 HORAN RD, WENATCHEE; 509/663-0018

Many of the orchards that once surrounded this 1899 Victorian farmhouse (on the National Register of Historic Places), built by Wenatchee pioneer Mike Horan, are gone. Yet the roundabout drive to the house near the confluence of the Wenatchee and Columbia Rivers sets the tone for an evening that harkens back to more gracious times. Proprietors Inga and John Peters offer country hospitality; their chef makes his mark with seasonally fresh seafood—such as roasted Dungeness crab and a marvelous Columbia River sturgeon in season—but you'll be equally impressed with the center top sirloin with garlic, basil, and feta, in a wine butter sauce. The Carriage House & Prime Rib next door—a friendly stop for a glass of wine, a Northwest microbrew, or a game of cribbage—offers casual fare such as southern barbecue. *$$$; AE, DIS, MC, V; checks OK; dinner Mon–Sat (in summer; off season, call ahead for hours); full bar; reservations recommended (weekends); johninga@johnhoranhouse.com; www.johnhoranhouse.com; just south of K-Mart plaza.* &

The Windmill / ★★

1501 N WENATCHEE AVE, WENATCHEE; 509/665-9529

A constantly changing number on a blackboard has kept track of the steaks sold at this celebrated steak house since Mary Ann and Greg

BLOOMIN' WONDERFUL FRUIT

The Wenatchee Valley is one of the state's most famous and picturesque fruit regions, with climate-perfect hot summers and cold winters to produce crisp, juicy apples. Spring and fall are the best times to visit.

Bloom time is usually around the end of April. Side roads between Leavenworth and Wenatchee offer grand blossom-touring opportunities. East from Leavenworth along Highway 2, exit at the tiny villages of Peshastin or Dryden, and meander through orchard country. Since the valley is cozy and intimate in scale—roads usually loop back to the main highway—it's hard to get lost and fun to try. Wenatchee's **Washington State Apple Blossom Festival**—the state's oldest major fest—coincides with peak bloom, normally the last week in April and first week of May, weather cooperating (see Wenatchee).

Apples ripen in September and early October, and this is a great time to travel here, stopping by a fruit stand to buy a box of apples, pears, or other tree fruits. Try **Smallwood Harvest** (1 mile east of Leavenworth on Hwy 2; 509/548-4196; Apr–Oct) for antiques, fruits, and ice cream. **Prey's Fruit**, nearby (less than 1 mile east of Leavenworth on Hwy 2; 509/548-5771), is another good stop. Top apple varieties include juicy Red and Golden Delicious, Gala, and Criterion.

The **Washington Apple Commission Visitors Center** (2900 Euclid Ave, Wenatchee; 509/663-9600; weekdays year-round, weekends May–Oct) offers bloom-time information, as well as displays, apple gift items for sale, and free juice or fruit samples.

—*Jena McPherson*

Johnson started running it in early 1997. The former roadside diner is offbeat-looking, but a better tenderloin we've never tasted in Wenatchee. Although the owners have changed once (in the past dozen years), the waitresses stay and stay. Meals are western American classics; there's seafood, but don't be a fool—stick with the meat. Ritual dictates you finish with a piece of magnificent pie made daily on premises—the fat apple double crust or coconut cream are our picks. *$$; AE, DIS, MC, V; checks OK; dinner Mon–Sat; beer and wine; reservations not accepted Fri–Sat; 1½ miles south of Hwy 2 exit.*

LODGINGS

The Warm Springs Inn / ★

1611 LOVE LN, WENATCHEE; 509/662-8365 OR 800/543-3645

The Wenatchee River is a perfect backdrop, and the pillared entrance and dark-green-and-rustic-brick exterior lend majesty to Janice and Dennis Whiting's B&B, which has five guest rooms with private baths. A new lower room with outside access is suitable for children and some pets; check first. A path behind the two-story inn (which served as a hospital in the 1920s) leads through woods to the river. Guests can relax in the sitting room or on the veranda. *$$; DIS, MC, V; checks OK; warmsi@warmspringsinn.com; www.warmspringsinn.com; turn south off Hwy 2 onto Lower Sunnyslope Rd, then right onto Love Ln.*

West Coast Wenatchee Center Hotel / ★

201 N WENATCHEE AVE, WENATCHEE; 509/662-1234 OR 800/426-0670
This is the nicest hotel on the strip (a very plain strip, mind you), with its view of the city and the Columbia River. The nine-story hotel has five nonsmoking levels. Recently renovated, the rooms are classic in style with floral accents. Rates may rise if most rooms are already booked the day you call, so make advance reservations and ask about package rates. The Wenatchee Roaster and Ale House, on the top floor, has live entertainment Tuesday through Saturday and serves breakfast, lunch, and dinner every day. The city's convention center, next door, is connected by a skybridge. Swimmers enjoy the outdoor or indoor pool. *$$; AE, DC, DIS, MC, V; checks OK; www.westcoasthotels.com; center of town.* &

Interstate 90 and Snoqualmie Pass

The most popular east-west route across Washington, Interstate 90 connects Interstate 5 at Seattle with Ellensburg, Moses Lake, and Spokane (and beyond). Highway highlights include Snoqualmie Falls, the ski areas at Snoqualmie Pass, and towns such as Cle Elum and Roslyn.

Carnation

Carnation is a lovely stretch of cow country nestled in the Snoqualmie Valley along bucolic Highway 203 (which connects Interstate 90 to Highway 2 at Monroe). At **MACDONALD MEMORIAL PARK** (Fall City Rd and NE 40th St; 425/333-4192), meandering trails and an old-fashioned suspension bridge across the Tolt River provide a great family picnic setting.

The sky's the limit for your favorite fruits and vegetables at **REMLINGER FARMS** (on NE 32nd St, off Hwy 203; 425/333-4135) U-pick farm, south of Carnation. The **STRAWBERRY FESTIVAL** in mid-June starts off the season. Throughout summer you can choose the best in raspberries, apples, corn, and grapes. In October, kids love tromping through the fields in search of the perfect jack-o'-lantern-to-be.

Snoqualmie

The lovely Snoqualmie Valley, where the mountains unfold into dairyland, is best known for its falls and its scenery, once the setting for the TV series *Twin Peaks*. The series is long gone, but *Peakers* can still purchase a T-shirt almost anywhere (even at the bank). The 268-foot **SNOQUALMIE FALLS** just up

Highway 202 from Interstate 90 (parking lot adjacent to Salish Lodge & Spa; see review) has always been a thundering spectacle. Use the observation deck or, better yet, take a picnic down the 1-mile trail to the base of the falls.

THE NORTHWEST RAILWAY MUSEUM (38625 SE King St; 425/746-4025; www.trainmuseum.org) runs a scenic tour up to Snoqualmie Falls gorge from Snoqualmie and North Bend most Saturdays and Sundays, April through October.

LODGINGS

The Salish Lodge & Spa / ★★★☆

6501 RAILROAD AVE SE, SNOQUALMIE; 425/888-2556

The falls may be the initial draw, but since you really can't see much of them from many of the rooms, it's a good thing the rooms themselves are as much a selling point as the falls. Each room offers a tempered country motif: light, clean-lined wooden furnishings, pillowed window seats (or balconies), flagstone fireplaces (with a woodbox full of split wood), and a cedar armoire. Little things are covered here: TV cleverly concealed, bathrobes, even a phone in the bathroom. Jacuzzis are separated from bedrooms by a swinging window. Tea is served to lodging guests daily, 4–6pm in the main-floor Library. On the fourth level is an extensive spa, with beautifully appointed massage and treatment rooms and hydrotherapy soaking spas. The Attic offers casual lunch and dinner options on the top floor. The excessive multicourse brunch, served family style, lives on—though we can live without it, opting instead for dinner and praying for a table with a view of the falls. Chef Stephen Janke has introduced new aspects to a menu that mixes continental touches, and an emphasis on fish and game, with Northwest-inspired produce. With more than 500 labels, the wine list is almost legendary. *$$$; AE, DC, DIS, MC, V; checks OK; www.salishlodge.com; take exit 25 off I-90, follow signs to falls.* &

Snoqualmie Pass

Four ski areas—ALPENTAL, SUMMIT WEST, SUMMIT CENTRAL, and SUMMIT EAST (52 miles east of Seattle on I-90; 425/434-7669; www.summit-at-snoqualmie.com)—offer the closest downhill and cross-country skiing for Seattle buffs (with a free shuttle that runs between them on weekends). Alpental is most challenging; Summit West, with one of the largest ski schools in the country, has excellent instruction for beginners through racers; Summit Central has some challenging bump runs; and the smallest, Summit East, is a favored spot for telemark skiers, with lighted, groomed cross-country tracks and many miles of trails.

In summer, the relatively low-lying transmountain route is a good starting point for many HIKES. Contact the North Bend Ranger Station (425/888-1421) for more information. The BEST WESTERN SUMMIT INN AT SNOQUALMIE PASS (603 Hwy 906; 425/434-6300 or 800/557-STAY), a simple hotel, tastefully done, is your only choice for year-round lodging at the pass.

Roslyn

Modest turn-of-the-century homes in this onetime coal-mining town have become weekend places for city folk, and the former mortuary is now a video store and movie theater. But the main intersection (once the stage set for the hit TV series *Northern Exposure*) still offers a cross section of the town's character.

Northern Exposure fans recognize the old stone tavern, inexplicably called **THE BRICK** (100 W Pennsylvania Ave; 509/649-2643), which has a water-fed spittoon running the length of the bar. Down the road, behind the town's junkyard, you'll find **CAREK'S MARKET** (510 S "A" St; 509/649-2930), one of the state's better purveyors of fine specialty meats and sausages.

RESTAURANTS

Roslyn Cafe

201 W PENNSYLVANIA AVE, ROSLYN; 509/649-2763

New owners Karen and Bob Hembree have turned this former funky eatery into a family stop with homestyle cooking. For lunch you'll get really good burgers, meat loaf, homemade soups, steaks, and a vegetarian menu; for dessert, cobblers and pies. Breakfast is also worth the side trip—try the Cafe Special, a grilled mix of veggies, cheese, and herbs, with a special sauce. *$; MC, V; local checks only; breakfast, lunch every day, dinner Fri–Mon; no alcohol; reservations recommended (summer weekends); khembree@ inland.net; at 1st St.* &

Cle Elum

This small mining town of about 20,000 residents parallels Interstate 90. Freeway access, from east and west of town, leads to First Street, Cle Elum's main thoroughfare, making it a handy stop when you need to grab a burger and fill your gas tank. **CLE ELUM BAKERY** (1st and Peoh; 509/674-2233; closed Sun) is a longtime local institution, doing as much business these days with travelers as with locals. From one of the last brick-hearth ovens in the Northwest come delicious *torcetti*, cinnamon rolls, and great old-fashioned cake doughnuts. **OWEN'S MEATS** (502 E 1st St; 509/674-2530), across the street, is an excellent stop for fresh meats and beef and turkey jerky.

LODGINGS

Hidden Valley Guest Ranch / ★★

3942 HIDDEN VALLEY RD, CLE ELUM; 509/857-2322 OR 800/5-COWBOY

A short hour from Seattle is the state's oldest dude ranch on 700 private and beautiful acres. Bruce and Kim Coe have spruced up some of the old cabins: the floors may still be a bit uneven, but nice touches include homemade quilts and potbelly stoves. Of the 13 cabins, our favorites are the older ones, particularly Apple Tree and Spruce number 5. The new ones, though fine, trade some charm for separate bedrooms and kitchenettes. Miles of trails, horseback riding, nearby trout fishing, a pool, a hot tub, and a basketball hoop make up for the basic accommodations. Indoor fun can be found in the ranch house (table tennis, pool table). Meals (included) are taken in the cookhouse dining room. Winters are quiet (only breakfast is served), but cross-country skiers and snowmobilers can rent the cabins; reserve one with a wood stove. *$$; MC, V; checks OK; brucecoe@televar.com; www.ranchweb.com/hidden valley; off Hwy 970 at milepost 8.*

Iron Horse Inn B&B / ★

526 MARIE ST, CLE ELUM; 509/674-5939 OR 800/2-2-TWAIN

This bed-and-breakfast (formerly The Moore House) was built in 1909 to house employees of the Chicago, Milwaukee, St. Paul & Pacific Railroad. Now on the National Register of Historic Places, the bunkhouse, with 10 guest rooms and a honeymoon suite, is pleasantly furnished with reproduction antiques. Railroad memorabilia—vintage photographs, model trains, schedules, and other artifacts—are on display. Two cabooses in the side yard are equipped with baths, fridges, queen-size beds, and private decks. New owners Mary and Doug Pittis took over in early 1999. Mary's father was a Milwaukee railroad man, and both she and Doug are railroad buffs. The proprietors will rev up the outdoor hot tub for your use. Kids OK; no pets. *$$; MC, V; checks OK; maryp@cleelum.com; ironhorseinn.uswestdex.com; adjacent to Iron Horse State Park Trail.*

Mount Rainier National Park

The majestic mountain is the abiding symbol of natural grandeur in the Northwest, and one of the most awesome mountains in the world. Its cone rises 14,411 feet above sea level, several thousand feet higher than the other peaks in the Cascade Range. The best way to appreciate the mountain is to explore its flanks: 300 miles of backcountry and self-guiding nature trails lead to ancient forests, dozens of massive glaciers, waterfalls, and alpine meadows lush with wildflowers during its short summer. Chinook and Cayuse Passes are closed in winter; you can take the loop trip or the road to Sunrise only between late May and October. The road from Longmire to Paradise remains open during daylight hours in winter; carry tire chains and a shovel and check current ROAD AND WEATHER CONDITIONS by calling a 24-hour information service (360/569-2211). Obligatory backcountry-use permits for overnight stays can be obtained from any of the ranger stations. Of the five entrance stations (entrance fee is $10 per automobile or $5 per person on foot, bicycle, or motorcycle), the three most popular are described here; the northwest entrances (Carbon River and Mowich Lake) have few visitor facilities and unpaved roads.

Highway 410 heads east from Sumner to Enumclaw, the White River entrance to the park, and Sunrise Visitors Center, continuing on to connect with Highway 12 near Naches. Note that the road beyond the Crystal Mountain spur is closed in winter, limiting access to Sunrise and Cayuse and Chinook Passes.

Highways 7 and 706 connect the main Nisqually entrance with Tacoma and Interstate 5; Nisqually is open year-round all the way to Paradise. The southeast entrance (Stevens Canyon) on Highway 123, which connects Highways 410 and 12, is closed in winter; in summer, Ohanapecosh is a favorite stop.

You can **CLIMB THE MOUNTAIN** with Rainier Mountaineering (535 Dock St, Ste 209, Tacoma; 360/569-2227), the concessionaire guide service, or in your own party. Unless you are qualified to do it on your own—and this is a big, difficult, and dangerous mountain on which many people have been killed—you must climb with the guide service. If you plan to climb with your own party, you must register and pay a fee ($15 per person) at one of the **RANGER STATIONS** in Mount Rainier National Park (Paradise Ranger Station, White River Wilderness Information Center, or Wilkeson Ranger Station; 360/569-2211). Generally, the best time to climb is late June through early September.

Black Diamond

This former coal-mining town is located on Highway 169, in Maple Valley, about 10 miles north of Enumclaw. Relatively quiet, it nonetheless comes to mind when planning a trip to Mount Rainier: **BLACK DIAMOND BAKERY** (32805 Railroad Ave; 360/886-2741) boasts the last wood-fired brick oven in the area. The bread that comes out is excellent—26 different kinds, including cinnamon, sour rye, potato, seven-grain, and garlic French—and is perfect for a Rainier excursion.

Greenwater

RESTAURANTS

Naches Tavern / ★
58411 HWY 410E, GREENWATER; 360/663-2267
Now this is the way to do a country tavern. The fireplace is as long as a wall and roars all winter to warm the Crystal Mountain après-ski crowd, hunters, loggers, and locals, who all mix peaceably. Homemade food—deep-fried mushrooms, chili, burgers, four-scoop milk shakes—is modestly priced. There's a countrified jukebox, pool tables, a lending library (take a book, leave a book) of yellowing paperbacks, and comfy furniture. Play a little cribbage, stroke the roving house pets, nod off in front of the hearth. *$; MC, V; no checks; lunch, dinner every day; beer and wine; reservations not accepted; at Greenwater.* &

Crystal Mountain

CRYSTAL MOUNTAIN SKI RESORT (off Hwy 410 just west of Chinook Pass, on northeast edge of Mount Rainier National Park; 360/663-2265), southeast of Enumclaw, is the best ski area in the state. It has runs for beginners and experts, plus fine backcountry skiing. Less well known are the summer facilities. You can ride the chairlift and catch a grand view of Mount Rainier and other peaks, and Summit House, on the mountain, is open for lunch. Rent condominiums, hotel rooms, or cabins from **CRYSTAL MOUNTAIN LODGING** (on-mountain condos; 360/663-2558; www.crystalmtlodging-wa.com), **CRYSTAL MOUNTAIN HOTELS** (360/663-2262; www.crystalhotels.com), or **ALTA CRYSTAL RESORT** (cabins; 360/663-2500; www.altacrystalresort.com). Although big plans (an almost $60-million project) are in the works to redo the resort, for now, there's just a grocery store, a sports shop, and Rafters, the bar-and-buffet restaurant atop Crystal's lodge.

LODGINGS

Silver Skis Chalet / ★★

CRYSTAL MOUNTAIN BLVD, CRYSTAL MOUNTAIN; 360/663-2558 OR 888/668-4368

These condos are your best bet if you want to stay right on the mountain. They've all got kitchens, and you can pick and choose among the 60-or-so options for details such as a fireplace. They're great for families, especially with the perk of a pool heated to 95°F, they're nonsmoking, and they have one or two bedrooms. Nonholiday midweek packages include lift tickets and are dubbed "suite deals" because they start at $65 per person, double occupancy. *$$; AE, MC, V; checks OK; crystalmtlodging@tx3.com; www.crystal mtlodging-wa.com; off Hwy 410, at end of Crystal Mountain Rd.* &

Sunrise

Open only during summer, Sunrise (6,400 feet) is the closest you can drive to Rainier's peak. The old lodge has no overnight accommodations, but it does offer a **VISITOR CENTER** (in northeast corner of park, 31 miles north of Ohanapecosh; 360/569-2177 ext 2357; www.nps.gov/mora), snack bar, and exhibits about the mountain. Dozens of trails begin here, such as the short one leading to a magnificent viewpoint of Emmons Glacier Canyon.

Eatonville

At Eatonville, just east of Highway 7, 17 miles south of Puyallup, the big draw is **NORTHWEST TREK** (on Meridian, Hwy 161; 360/832-6116; www.nwtrek. org), where animals roam free while people tour the 600-acre grounds in small open-air trams. The buffalo herd steals the show. Open daily February through October, weekends only the rest of the year; group rates available.

Ashford

If Ashford is the gateway to Paradise, then **WHITTAKER'S BUNKHOUSE** (30205 Hwy 706E; 360/569-2439) is the place to stop on the way to the very top—of Mount Rainier, that is. A good place to meet the guides, climbers, hikers, and skiers of the mountain. Rooms are basic and cheap (bunks available) but plush compared to a camping pad.

MOUNT TAHOMA SKI HUTS, run by Mount Tahoma Trails Association (360/569-2451), is Western Washington's first hut-to-hut ski trail system. It offers more than 90 miles of trails, three huts, and one yurt, in a spectacular area south and west of Mount Rainier National Park.

LODGINGS

Mountain Meadows Inn and B&B / ★★

28912 HWY 706E, ASHFORD; 360/569-2788

If seclusion near the base of one of Washington's busiest tourist destinations is what you're looking for, you'll find it here. Just off the main road, the inn is privately situated on 11 landscaped acres (with trout pond, nature trails, an outdoor fire pit, and a hot tub in a cedar grove). Three large guest rooms in the main house are filled with a hodgepodge of antiques. There's nothing kitschy here; just a tasteful home filled with some Native American baskets. A guest house has three studio apartments. *$$; MC, V; checks OK; mtmeadow@mashell.com; www.mt-rainier.net; 6 miles west of park entrance.*

Nisqually Lodge / ★

31609 HWY 706, ASHFORD; 360/569-8804

Reasonably priced and clean, this 24-room, two-story lodge just a few miles west of the Nisqually entrance to Mount Rainier National Park offers welcome respite to those willing to trade some charm for a phone, satellite TV, and air-conditioning. Returnees like the stone fireplace in the lobby and the hot tub outside—though the room walls are somewhat thin. Coffee and pastries are served for breakfast; conference and laundry facilities are available. *$$; AE, DC, MC, V; no checks; www.mtrainier-mt.com; 5 miles from park entrance.*

Wellspring / ★★

54922 KERNAHAN RD, ASHFORD; 360/569-2514

For more than a decade, Wellspring has quietly greeted outdoor enthusiasts with two spas nestled in a sylvan glade surrounded by evergreens. A soothing hour or two at Wellspring has become almost de rigueur for folks coming off Mount Rainier. Three log cabins have a very in-the-woods feel (no kitchens, no TVs, no phones—just wood stoves, refrigerators, and queen-size featherbeds with down comforters). A fourth board-and-batten building holds our two favorites: Tatoosh, with a river-stone fireplace and waterfall-like shower, and The Nest, the tiniest of rooms, with a swinging bed below a skylight that will make any bird happy. A fifth lodging, Three Bears, is a four-room cottage with full kitchen and washer and dryer; children are okay here. Pick up a basketful of breakfast when you check in, make an appointment for an hour's massage, and you'll tuck in perfectly here. *$$; MC, V; checks OK; www.info atmtrainier.com; 3 miles east of Ashford.*

Longmire

A few miles inside the southwestern border of the park, the little village of Longmire has the 25-room **NATIONAL PARK INN** (360/569-2275), rebuilt charmingly in 1990 with tasteful furnishings in an old hickory theme; open year-round. It also has a small museum with wildlife exhibits, a **HIKING INFOR-MATION CENTER** (360/569-2211 ext 3317), and a snowshoe and cross-country **SKI RENTAL OUTLET** (360/569-2411).

Paradise

At 5,400 feet, Paradise is the most popular destination on the mountain. On the way to the paved parking lot and the **HENRY M. JACKSON MEMORIAL VISITOR CENTER** (just before you reach Paradise; 360/569-2211 ext 2328), you'll catch wonderful views of Narada Falls and Nisqually Glacier. The center, housed in a flying saucer–like building, has a standard cafeteria and gift shop, extensive nature exhibits and films, and a superb view of the mountain from its observation deck. Depending on the season, you could picnic (our advice is to bring your own) among the wildflowers, explore some of the trails (rangers offer guided walks), let the kids slide on inner tubes in the snow-play area, try a little cross-country skiing, or even take a guided snowshoe tromp. And, since the 126 rooms at **PARADISE INN** (at end of Hwy 706 from the southeast/Nisqually entrance; 360/569-2275), a massive 1917 lodge with a wonderfully nostalgic feel, have recently received a much-needed refurbishing, you can comfortably spend the night in one of the most unique locations in the state.

White Pass

White Pass (509/672-3101; www.skiwhitepass.com) is an off-the-beaten-path ski destination offering downhill (with a high-speed quad lift) and cross-country skiing, located 12 miles southeast of Mount Rainier National Park at the summit of Highway 12. Its base area is the highest on the Cascade crest, at 4,500 feet. A Nordic center near the day lodge serves cross-country skiers with about 18 miles of trails. Slopeside shopping is nearby at the Village Inn (509/672-3131). Plenty of summer hiking can be found in adjacent William O. Douglas and Goat Rocks Wilderness Areas.

LODGINGS

Hotel Packwood / ★
104 MAIN ST, PACKWOOD; 360/494-5431
A couple of motels in Packwood may have more modern appliances, but this spartan lodge (open since 1912) remains a favorite. The aroma from the wood stove in the lobby makes you feel as if you're in the middle of the forest, even though you're really in downtown Packwood. A narrow staircase climbs up to the simple rooms; seven guest rooms share baths, two have private bathrooms. *$; DIS, MC, V; checks OK; just off Hwy 12 at Main St.*

SOUTHWEST WASHINGTON

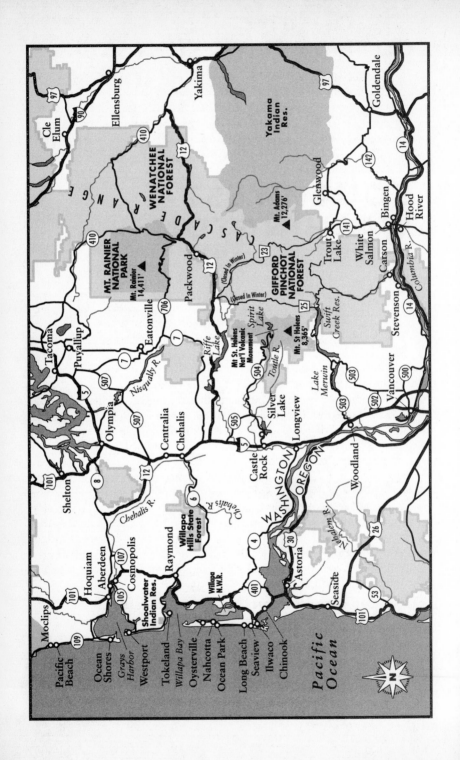

SOUTHWEST WASHINGTON

Nearly all of the varied terrain, scenery, and weather that make up the Pacific Northwest are on display in Southwest Washington. You can play on flat, sandy beaches that spread for miles along the Pacific Coast, basking in an often wet but always mild marine climate. Or trek up the slopes of geologically young mountains—including one devastated by the same volcanic forces that built its neighbors. You can also experience long, hot, arid summers by crossing those mountains, following the gorge cut by one of the country's mightiest rivers.

History looms large in Southwest Washington as well. Native Americans, in pre-Columbian times as well as today, have used the ocean to travel from what is today Pacific Beach to the mouth of Grays Harbor, and on to Willapa Bay and the Long Beach Peninsula. The natural bounty of the coast—salmon and other fish, clams and oysters, plus wild berries and mushrooms—still figure prominently in the region's economy (and diet). American sea captain Robert Gray sailed into Grays Harbor (a replica of his ship homeports at Aberdeen) in 1792, staking important claims to the region for the fledgling United States. After the United States asserted its control below the 49th parallel in 1846, loggers came to harvest timber that would supply nearly half the world, and lumber barons built mansions in places such as Hoquiam and Cosmopolis.

The great Columbia River had tempted many explorers in search of a Northwest Passage, but the then-untamed river was extremely difficult to navigate. The broad mouth where the river crashes into the Pacific became the graveyard of countless big vessels, and can still be treacherous sailing today. Still, by the 1820s the British had established in Fort Vancouver a headquarters for the Hudson's Bay Company, which would control a vast trading empire that extended up to Alaska.

American explorers Meriwether Lewis and William Clark blazed a trail overland to the region, sighting Mount St. Helens along the way. Ancestors of the natives they met had born witness to the terrible power of this seemingly serene mountain. Modern-day residents experienced this slumbering volcano's coming to life in 1980, which culminated in a massively explosive eruption on May 18.

The mouth of the Columbia marked journey's end for Lewis and Clark in 1805. The explorers' party traveled this last leg of their trek through the beautiful Columbia River Gorge, both by canoe and on foot. Today's traveler finds signs and other interpretive monuments that mark their trail.

ACCESS AND INFORMATION

Most travelers exploring Southwest Washington via car approach from Interstate 5, the multilane freeway between Seattle and Portland. Between the two metropolises, you'll find Vancouver just north of the Columbia and Longview a half-hour's drive farther north.

Other major highways that provide access in the region include US Highway 12 (travels through sleepy, tree-filled coastal mountains to Aberdeen/Hoquiam); US Highway 101 (runs south from Aberdeen to the Columbia at

Astoria); and Highway 14 (the path from Vancouver into the Columbia River Gorge), which frequently crosses over the trail of explorers Lewis and Clark and enters rugged cliffs and sloping grasslands to connect with US Highway 97, which leads north to Goldendale.

AMTRAK's (1-800-USA-RAIL) Coast Starlight route runs between Seattle and Portland, with stops at Kelso-Longview (501 S 1st Ave; 360/578-1870) and Vancouver (1301 W 11th St; 360/694-7307). **GREYHOUND BUS SERVICE** (800/231-2222) is available to Castle Rock, Kelso-Longview, Woodland, Vancouver and Goldendale.

Grays Harbor and Ocean Shores

One of the West Coast's great natural harbors, Grays Harbor has attracted folks since Captain Robert Gray first sailed in on his 1792 expedition. Generations of loggers have begun to give over to retirees drawn by bargain-priced real estate—and the natural beauty of the region. A half-million Arctic-bound shorebirds migrate to the area from as far south as Argentina, and congregate on the tidal mud flats at the wildlife refuge of **BOWERMAN BASIN** (just beyond the Hoquiam airport, Airport Wy off Hwy 109) each spring from about mid-April through the first week of May. At high tide, the birds rise in unison in thick flocks that shimmer through the air, twisting and turning, before settling back onto their feeding grounds. There are trails through the marsh, but wear boots. The **GRAYS HARBOR NATIONAL WILDLIFE REFUGE** (Hwy 109, 1½ miles west of Hoquiam; 360/753-9467) has more information.

Aberdeen and Hoquiam

Highway 12 ends in Aberdeen at Highway 101, which you take west 4 miles to Hoquiam. The timber industry brought a lot of riches to these twin towns, evidenced by such mansions as **HOQUIAM'S CASTLE** (515 Chenault; 360/533-2005), a 20-room Queen Anne house open for tours, and the splendid **7TH STREET THEATRE** (313 7th St; 360/532-0302), a restored turn-of-the-century edifice that hosts a variety of productions. Logging and sawmilling are just a shadow of their early-1900s heyday, but tourism is slowly rising to take their place. A big attraction is the **GRAYS HARBOR HISTORICAL SEAPORT** (east side of Aberdeen; 360/532-8611), home to a full-scale replica of Captain Robert Gray's *Lady Washington*, a 105-foot floating museum. The ship, available for onboard tours as well as cruises, is often at other ports of call, so phone ahead.

RESTAURANTS

Billy's Bar and Grill / ★

322 E HERON ST, ABERDEEN; 360/533-7144
The best little whorehouse in town used to be right across the street from this historic pub, and the walls at Billy's sport some original artwork that recalls Aberdeen's bawdy past. The place is named after the infamous Billy Gohl, who

SOUTHWEST WASHINGTON THREE-DAY TOUR

DAY ONE: Start the day from the Puget Sound area with a drive to **Ocean Shores**. Take lunch at the **Galway Bay Restaurant & Pub**, then spend the afternoon beachcombing, or perhaps go for a horseback ride on the beach. Check in to the **Caroline Inn** for a comfortable night in a Southern-inspired two-story suite, then head back into Ocean Shores proper for dinner at **Alec's by the Sea**. After dinner, relax in your Jacuzzi with a view.

DAY TWO: Enjoy a breakfast you make yourself in your full kitchen, then make dinner reservations at the Shoalwater in Seaview before checking out. Head south down Highway 101 about 90 miles to the **Long Beach Peninsula**. In Long Beach, make a visit to **Marsh's Free Museum** to ogle the oddities, then shop for a kite to fly on the beach. After a light lunch at the **Heron and Beaver Pub** in Seaview, fly your kite for a while and then check in at **Caswell's on the Bay Bed & Breakfast** in Ocean Park and get ready for dinner at the **Shoalwater** in Seaview.

Day Three: After a healthy breakfast at Caswell's, pack a picnic lunch and drive down to Ilwaco and Fort Canby State Park, where you can visit the Lewis and Clark Interpretive Center and the Cape Disappointment Lighthouse. Afterward, drive Highway 4 east along the Columbia River to Longview, where you can have dinner at **Henri's** (4545 Ocean Beach Hwy; 360/425-7970) if you're running late, or head north up Interstate 5 to Castle Rock, then east on Highway 503 to the **Blue Heron Inn**—make it by 7pm to enjoy the dinner included in the price of your room.

terrorized the Aberdeen waterfront in 1907. Billy shanghaied sailors and robbed loggers, consigning their bodies to the murky Wishkah River through a trapdoor in a saloon only a block away from the present-day Billy's—where you get a square-deal meal (thick burgers and seasoned fries) and an honest drink, without much damage to your pocketbook. *$; AE, DC, MC, V; local checks only; breakfast, lunch, dinner every day; full bar; reservations not accepted; corner of G St.* &

Parma / ★★★

116 W HERON ST, ABERDEEN; 360/532-3166

Adventurous, delicious cuisine—who'd expect it in Aberdeen? Parma delivers a menu of Italian and French dishes in grand style. Veal is a highlight of the regular menu—try the marsala, piccata, or a delicious cordon bleu. But nightly specials are most extravagant, including such treats as wild boar or rack of lamb with polenta, arrabbiata, spinach gnocchi with a Gorgonzola sauce, and more. Pasta is house-made, seafood couldn't be fresher, and desserts are heavenly. Finding a gem like Parma in Aberdeen is a bit like stumbling across Robert DeNiro doing dinner theater in Connecticut, but the big city hasn't lured away owner/chef

Pierre Gabelli . . . yet. *$$; AE, DIS, MC, V; checks OK; dinner Tues–Sat; beer and wine; reservations recommended, 1 block west of Broadway.* &

LODGINGS

Lytle House Bed & Breakfast / ★

509 CHENAULT, HOQUIAM; 360/533-2320 OR 800/677-2320

You can't miss the signs pointing you to Hoquiam's architectural landmark, the 1897 Hoquiam's Castle built by timber potentate Robert Lytle. Brother Joseph decided to build a smaller version next door, now known as Lytle House. The state historian describes this eight-room B&B as the county's finest example of pure Queen Anne architecture, and it retains many original fixtures, including the rose-globe crystal chandelier in the main hall, and the coal-burning fireboxes with Chinese tiles and oak mantels. If you're looking for a romantic getaway, reserve the Balcony Suite overlooking the rose garden. An excellent breakfast awaits. Though the surroundings are stately, kids are welcome. *$$; MC, V; checks OK; benchmrk@techline.com; www.lytlehouse.com; west on Emerson, right on Garfield, uphill to Chenault.*

Ocean Shores

Despite the best efforts of real estate speculators and celebrity investors in the 1960s, Ocean Shores did not develop into a Las Vegas of the North. Instead, residents managed to wrest control from the land barons, build schools, and create a real town, albeit one with strangely broad urban streets (a legacy of its pie-in-the-sky city planning).

That isn't to say building isn't booming. In addition to numerous hotels, Ocean Shores boasts a large convention center that's busy year-round. An annual June **PHOTOGRAPHY SHOW** and November **DIXIELAND JAZZ FESTIVAL** (800/762-3224) are only some of the events that draw visitors. To get out of the downtown hubbub, consider reserving one of the **PRIVATE BEACH COTTAGES** (reservations: 888/702-3224; www.oceanshores.com) that owners make available.

The long, flat beach is great for **CLAMMING**—for seasons and license requirements, check with the Department of Fish and Wildlife (48 Devonshire Rd, Montesano; 360/249-4628)—beachcombing, and even driving if you dare (remember that a lot of beach can disappear at high tide). A fun way to explore is on horseback—**NAN-SEA STABLES** (360/289-0194) brings a string of horses to the beach in front of the Shilo Inn; and **CHENOIS CREEK HORSE RENTALS** (just show up on the beach) has mounts available at the end of Damon Road, across from the Best Western Lighthouse Suites Inn (see review).

RESTAURANTS

Alec's by the Sea / ★

131 E CHANCE A LA MER BLVD NE, OCEAN SHORES; 360/289-4026

Alec's by the Sea heads a list of otherwise uninspiring dining options in Ocean Shores. Choices include fresh seafood (the oven-broiled seafood platter fills you up with salmon, scallops, prawns, crab, oysters, and more), steaks, pasta (smoked-salmon fettuccine is a winner), poultry, burgers, and sandwiches (try the Philadelphia prime sandwich with thin-sliced prime rib grilled with onions, bell peppers, and topped with Swiss cheese), as well as a thick, rich, buttery clam chowder. Alec's also has three hallmarks of the family restaurant: large portions, early-bird specials (4–6pm), and crayons for kids. *$$; AE, DC, DIS, MC, V; local checks only; lunch, dinner every day; full bar; reservations not necessary; off Point Brown Rd.* ♿

Galway Bay Restaurant & Pub

676 OCEAN SHORES BLVD NW, OCEAN SHORES; 360/289-2300

Take off the chill in the best Irish fashion in this pub with a small but tasty traditional menu. Your first course: a pint of Guinness (on tap). Main course choices include Irish stew (browned lamb, potatoes, carrots, and sautéed onions in a rich, creamy sauce), chicken and mushroom pasty, Limerick sausage roll, and Forfar bridies (chopped steak with sautéed onions, carrots, and potatoes baked in a flaky puff pastry). For dessert, perhaps a tot of 16-year-old single-malt whiskey. If you're ready to cut a reel, there's live Irish music most weekends (call for schedule). *$$; AE, DIS, MC, V; checks OK; lunch, dinner every day; full bar; reservations not accepted; www. galway-bay.com; ½ block from Shilo Inn.* ♿

LODGINGS

Best Western Lighthouse Suites Inn / ★

491 DAMON RD NW, OCEAN SHORES; 360/289-2311 OR 800/757-SURF

One of the sights you'll see as you head into Ocean Shores is a lighthouse—which turns out to be the five-story, 360-degree observation tower of the Best Western Lighthouse Suites Inn. Rooms are large and nicely decorated, and each has an ocean view as well as a fireplace, wet bar, microwave, refrigerator, coffeemaker, cable TV, and VCR. No restaurant, but a free continental breakfast. Things are a little quieter up here on the north end of town, and the hotel lights the beach at night for contemplative walks. *$$$; AE, DC, MC, V; checks OK; manager@bwlighthouse.com; www.bwlighthouse.com; at north city limits.* ♿

The Caroline Inn / ★★

1341 OCEAN SHORES BLVD SW, OCEAN SHORES; 360/289-0450

Passing several nondescript condos as you drive the long, bumpy road to the end of the peninsula, you'll know when you've reached the Caroline Inn. A gleaming white Southern gothic mini-mansion (inspired by its owners' love of *Gone with the Wind*) rises above the sea grass, its twin columns inviting you inside. Staying in one of four two-story suites, you'll find a first-floor living room with a fireplace and a balcony facing the ocean, plus a dining room and fully outfitted kitchen (you're well removed from the restaurants and entertainment in town, but that's much of the appeal). Upstairs is the bedroom, where you can relax in the Jacuzzi while gazing out at the beach, or step onto another balcony for a better view. These tastefully furnished suites are popular year-round; reserve at least a month in advance for a weekend stay. The owners plan to add a carriage house to provide a (much-requested) space for weddings; call to see if the new inn—a Southern-style mansion to be named the Judith Ann—is taking reservations. *$$$; MC, V; checks OK; oceanshores.com/lodging/caroline; toward end of peninsula, near Cutlass Ct.*

The Shilo Inn / ★★

707 OCEAN SHORES BLVD NW, OCEAN SHORES; 360/289-4600 OR 800/222-2244

Something of a crown jewel in the nation's largest privately owned hotel chain, the Shilo Inn at Ocean Shores delivers a lot for your money. For starters, every one of its 113 rooms is a junior suite: a sitting room, bedroom, and ocean-view balcony, plus a microwave, refrigerator, wet bar, four phones, more TVs with free cable than you'll know what to do with (there's even one in the bathroom), fireplace, and free newspaper. Downstairs you'll find a guest laundry, 24-hour indoor pool, spa, sauna and fitness center, a surprisingly good restaurant, and a beautiful 3,000-gallon aquarium. The Shilo is right across from the convention center, and close to all the action downtown. Our only letdown—the fireplace is electric, full of dancing colored lights and fury, but no heat. *$$$; AE, DC, MC, V; checks OK; at Chance a la Mer Blvd.*

Pacific Beach

LODGINGS

Sandpiper / ★★

4159 HWY 109, PACIFIC BEACH; 360/276-4580

The large, clean Sandpiper is a perfect place to have a family reunion, or just give the nuclear family some peaceful quality time with the ocean. Two four-story complexes have suites with amenities including sitting rooms, kitchens, baths with heated towel bars, small porches, and real log-burning fireplaces. No phones or TV (or restaurant—you'll whip up the haute cuisine in the kitchen or on the outdoor barbecue), but there's a nice kids' play area, plus a gift shop that sells board games, kites, and sand pails. Pets are welcome with advance notice and deposit. A testament to the Sandpiper's popularity: many units are reserved months in advance. *$$–$$$; MC, V; checks OK; min stays weekends, summers; oceanshores.com/lodging/sandpiper; 1½ miles south of town.*

Moclips

LODGINGS

Ocean Crest Resort / ★

HWY 109 N, MOCLIPS; 360/276-4465

The tremendous view the Ocean Crest Resort commands from its cliff-side perch among the spruce is timeless, but some of the resort's furnishings are starting to show their age. Nonetheless the inn is exceedingly popular, with minimum stays during peak periods. Rooms run from bargain studio units with no view to kitchen and fireplace units (logs provided free), to two-bedroom suites, and rates are reasonable even in summer. Best views are from the large suites in Building 5. The resort has a recreation center with an indoor pool and spa, exercise room, tanning bed, and—a real bonus—a massage therapist. The resort's somewhat pricey view restaurant, serving fresh seafood, pasta, and steaks, among other offerings, is the best dining within a half-hour's drive. Private access to the beach below is via a winding staircase that runs through a pretty wooded ravine. *$$–$$$; AE, DIS, MC, V; checks OK; oceanshores.com/lodging/oceancrest; 18 miles north of Ocean Shores.*

Westport

A spate of new oceanfront condos indicates that retirees and urban escapees have begun to flock to Westport, just as fishers have for years. **CHARTER FISHING** is still the town's lifeblood, as the cluster of motels near the docks (and the fact you can eat breakfast at just about any restaurant before 5am) attests. Changes in the salmon fishery have led to boats also offering bottom-fishing trips (for halibut and snapper, among other catches), and **WHALE-WATCHING CRUISES** are especially popular. Gray whales migrate off the coast March through May on their way toward Arctic feeding waters, where they fatten up for the trip back down to their breeding lagoons in Baja come fall.

Some of the best charters include **CACHALOT** (2511 Westhaven Dr; 360/268-0323), **NEPTUNE** (2511 Westhaven Dr; 360/268-0124), **OCEAN** (2315 W Westhaven Dr; 360/268-9144), and **WESTPORT** (2411 W Westhaven Dr; 360/268-9120 or 800/562-0157).

If you're not enthused about catching your own, Westport has plenty of seafood stores to sate your appetite. Try **BRADY'S OYSTERS** (3714 Oyster Pl, Aberdeen; 360/268-0077), just east of town on Highway 105; **MERINO SEAFOODS** (301 E Harbor St; 360/268-2510), near the docks; or **WESTPORT SEAFOOD** (609 Neddie Rose Dr; 360/268-0133).

The **WESTPORT LIGHTHOUSE** (turn left at the town's only stoplight) towers 100 feet over the dunes; call the Coast Guard (360/268-0121) for a guided tour. A scenic 2 ½-mile (round-trip) trail leads through the dunes from Westport Lighthouse State Park to **WESTHAVEN STATE PARK**; it's paved and wheelchair-accessible. In town, exhibits at the **WESTPORT MARITIME MUSEUM** (2201 Westhaven Dr; 360/268-0078) trace seafarers back to the 1700s; there are also collections of local Coast Guard, industry, and whaling artifacts. Two whale houses exhibit sea mammal skeletons and a children's Discovery Room.

LODGINGS

Chateau Westport / ★

710 W HANCOCK, WESTPORT; 360/268-9101 OR 800/255-9101

The Chateau Westport is '60s-boxy on the outside, but pretty comfy and vaguely continental on the inside. More than 100 rooms and suites are available, some with fireplaces, kitchens, and balconies. Ocean-facing views from the latter (especially on the third and fourth floors) are quite lovely. An indoor heated pool and hot tub are available, as is free continental breakfast (barely worth its price). Winter rates are a good bargain. *$$; AE, DC, MC, V; no checks; at S Forest St.* &

Long Beach Peninsula and Willapa Bay

The ocean conjures up restful visions of soothing waves lapping the shore, but too many "destination" beach areas offer a shrill edge instead—crammed, overpriced lodgings; schlock merchants hungering for tourism dollars; and cranky, overtired families hurrying to their next destination. The Long Beach Peninsula, while it has its share of bumper boats and seashell tchotchkes—and its population triples in July and August—delivers the real deal: beautiful, serene beaches blessed by a gentle marine climate. Beyond scenery and souvenirs, the peninsula offers renowned kite-flying, cranberry bogs, famous Willapa Bay oysters, rhododendrons, and some good small-town dining.

With its 37-mile-long stretch of flat beach, the Long Beach Peninsula's topography and attractions make it perfect for a lengthy exploration by bicycle, though you're allowed to drive your car on the beach as well. If you really want to get away from it all, you can visit Willapa Bay's Long Island (reachable only by boat) and its 274-acre old-growth cedar grove, part of the **WILLAPA NATIONAL WILDLIFE REFUGE** (10 miles north of Seaview on Hwy 101; 360/484-3482). Campsites are available; check at the refuge's headquarters.

Longview

Longview serves as a handy crossroads for travelers headed north to Seattle, south to Portland, or west to the Long Beach Peninsula. For a relaxing walk, stroll through the park surrounding Lake Sacajawea.

RESTAURANTS

Country Village Nutrition Shoppe and Café

711 VANDERCOOK WY, LONGVIEW; 360/425-8100

A good place to load up on organic foods before heading off to ocean beaches or Mount St. Helens, the Country Village Nutrition Shoppe and

Café is also a great stop for a tasty, filling, and inexpensive lunch. The lunch special pairs a cup of homemade soup with a tender mixed green salad or a hearty half-sandwich. Scared of "healthy" food? Opt for a baked potato stuffed with cheese and bacon. Sip a fruit smoothie with lunch, then top it off with a huge slice of delicious carrot cake. *$; DIS, MC, V; checks OK; lunch Mon–Sat; no alcohol; reservations not accepted; just off Washington Wy.* &

Chinook

Fishing has always loomed large in Chinook, located just south of the peninsula on Highway 101. Occupants of the original Chinook (a few miles away) were Natives who fished the Columbia River until European diseases decimated the population. Late in the 1800s, superefficient salmon traps made Chinook's white residents the richest per capita in the United States, until the traps were outlawed; wooden pilings still visible in Baker Bay are all that remain of this piscine strip-mining operation. Despite this worrisome past, the town is still a major Southwest Washington fishing center, and boasts thousands of feet of beautiful riverfront.

On nearby Scarborough Hill, **FORT COLUMBIA STATE PARK** (2 miles southeast of Chinook on Hwy 101; 360/777-8221; open daily, mid-May–Sept) hosts a collection of restored turn-of-the-century wooden buildings that once housed soldiers guarding the river mouth. The former commander's house is now a military museum; nearby is the youth hostel. The park also claims some of the area's largest rhododendron bushes.

Ilwaco

Despite the vagaries of the salmon fishery in recent years, Ilwaco, the first town on the Long Beach Peninsula, is still the center of charter fishing on the lower Columbia River. Two popular sport-fishing operators, both located at the port docks, are **A COHO CHARTERS** (237 Howerton Wy SE; 360/642-3333) and **SEA BREEZE CHARTERS** (185 Howerton Wy SE; 360/642-2300). Many charter operators also offer eco-tours. The **ILWACO HERITAGE MUSEUM** (115 SE Lake St; 360/642-3446) does a wonderful job illuminating the area's history, with exhibits of Native American artifacts, cranberry agriculture, logging, fishing, and more. The old **ILWACO RAILROAD DEPOT**, which linked the Long Beach Peninsula's "Clamshell Railway" with steamers out of Astoria, has been incorporated into the museum, which also houses a scale-model portrayal of the peninsula in the 1920s.

Nearby **FORT CANBY STATE PARK** (2½ miles south of Ilwaco off Hwy 101; 360/642-3078 or 800/233-0321) is a hugely popular attraction (reserve camping spots well in advance for summer stays), with 2,000 acres stretching from the picturesque lighthouse at North Head to Cape Disappointment's equally stately lighthouse at the Columbia's mouth. Hiking trails (recently linked into a large loop by hardworking Boy Scouts) take you to the shore sentinels, as well as the 2-mile-long North Jetty and Beard's Hollow beach. Open all year, the park even has yurts available for more comfortable winter stays. It's also home to the **LEWIS AND CLARK INTERPRETIVE CENTER** (360/642-3029), offering visitors a fresh and vivid retelling of the explorers' monumental journey that began in St. Louis and ended on the Pacific shore. Fascinating displays cover the history of Cape Disappointment, construction of the **CAPE DISAPPOINT-MENT LIGHTHOUSE**, local shipwrecks, and the early Coast Guard. The site boasts a stirring view of the mouth of the Columbia. High winds can occasionally close the center, which is otherwise open daily.

LODGINGS

Inn at Ilwaco / ★

120 WILLIAMS ST NE, ILWACO; 360/642-8686

Located on a quiet, dead-end street overlooking town, this bed-and-breakfast is housed in the 1928-vintage former Ilwaco Presbyterian Church. You enter through a vestibule-turned-gift-shop, and pass rows of intact pews. Full breakfast is served in the former sanctuary, transformed into a spacious dining area backed by a fireplace. All nine guest units—once Sunday-school classrooms and a nursery—have private baths, and are decorated in shades of blue and white, with plush bedding, lacy curtains, and handsome furnishings. The two-room Admiral Suite has a massive captain's bed from the Hamburg-American ship line, as well as a fireplace and a small refrigerator. A roomy parlor has myriad comfy chairs and couches, watercolor seascapes, sea charts, and a ship's binnacle. New owner Ed Bussone says "well-behaved, under-control children are OK." *$$; MC, V; checks OK; www.longbeachlodging.com; off Spruce St E.*

Seaview

Touted as an ocean retreat for Portlanders early in the 20th century, Seaview now enjoys a legacy of older, stately beach homes, a pretty beachfront, and some of the best dining and lodging on the peninsula. Nearly every road headed west reaches the ocean, and you can park your car and stroll the dunes. You can also stroll the arts scene: **CHARLES MULVEY GALLERY** (46th Pl and "L" St; 360/642-2189) is owned by the noted watercolorist; **CAMPICHE STUDIOS** (504 Pacific Ave S; 360/642-2264) features watercolors, sculptures, and photography.

RESTAURANTS

The 42nd Street Cafe / ★★☆

4201 PACIFIC HWY, SEAVIEW; 360/642-2323

Locals going out for a nice dinner usually head to the 42nd Street Cafe, saving the tonier Shoalwater (see review) down the street for special occasions. The menu is mostly Americana, with steaks, poultry, and fresh seafood predominating, but includes pastas as well, with some unusual sauces (port wine and cranberry, for example). Clam chowder is a mainstay at seaside restaurants, but the 42nd Street Cafe's variety, with heavy overtones of sherry, may not be to everyone's taste. If you opt for a salad instead, try the honey–celery seed dressing. *$$; MC, V; checks OK; breakfast, lunch, dinner every day; beer and wine; reservations not necessary; at 42nd St.* &

The Heron and Beaver Pub / ★

4415 PACIFIC HWY, SEAVIEW; 360/642-4142

The tiny Heron and Beaver Pub began in 1987 to serve as a bar to its big brother across the hall, the Shoalwater (whose kitchen it shares), while offering up simple snacks. Slowly, though, the pub (with 30 beers, a full bar, and more than 400 wines) began to poach items off the Shoalwater's menu (panfried Dungeness crab and shrimp cakes, Cajun-style "blackened" Willapa Bay oysters, to name a couple of yummy choices) until it became a dining destination for lunch or a light dinner in its own right. Recently the H&B opened a deck overlooking the Victorian gardens of the Shelburne Inn (the historic hotel whose space the pub shares), so you can enjoy your oyster shooters and wild mushroom–goat cheese lasagne outside on balmy days. *$$; AE, DC, MC, V; checks OK; lunch Mon–Sat, dinner every day, brunch Sun; full bar; reservations not accepted; www.shoalwater.com/pub.html; at N 45th.* &

My Mom's Pie Kitchen and Chowder House

4316 S PACIFIC HWY, SEAVIEW; 360/642-2342

Some time back, after the fame of the glorious pies and tasty lunches grew, My Mom's Pie Kitchen graduated from a trailer up the highway to a cute yellow house with a white picket fence at its present location in downtown Seaview. Pie varieties include banana cream, pecan, sour cream, chocolate-almond, raisin, rhubarb, and raspberry, and they sell out fast even in the off season; if you want to take one with you, call ahead. When you arrive, sit down to a nice lunch of homemade chowder, Dungeness crab quiche, sandwich, or salad. *$; MC, V; checks OK; lunch Wed–Sun; no alcohol; reservations not accepted; at 43rd.*

The Shoalwater / ★★★

4415 PACIFIC HWY, SEAVIEW; 360/642-4142

Despite garnering a slew of awards from *Bon Appetit, Saveur,* the *New York Times,* and the like, the Shoalwater may have slipped a notch—the occasional uneven meal has begun to emerge from a kitchen that otherwise is one of the splendid mainstays of Northwest cuisine. Native ingredients such as fresh Willapa Bay oysters, salmon, wild mushrooms, and Dungeness crab are employed in artful meals that fill a seafood-heavy menu. A fabulous selection of wines from the Northwest and beyond is available, pulled from a lovely antique wine closet. The Northwest bouillabaisse is heavenly, combining shellfish, crustaceans, and fresh fish in a saffron-infused fish broth and served with rouille (garlic mayonnaise) and garlic crostini. The roast herb-encrusted duck breast, served with a marionberry-cranberry and truffle butter sauce on a bed of couscous, is also excellent. A special winter treat is the Shoalwater's popular annual winemaker's dinner series, featuring seven-course meals designed around wines from a visiting winemaker; reserve well in advance. *$$$; AE, DC, MC, V; checks OK; lunch, dinner every day, brunch Sun; full bar; reservations recommended; www.shoalwater.com; at N 45th.* &

LODGINGS

The Shelburne Inn / ★★★

4415 PACIFIC HWY S, SEAVIEW; 360/642-2442

Well worn, warm, and filled with antiques and friendly charm, the Shelburne Inn is listed in the National Register of Historic Places, and in the hearts of many a romantic traveler. The 1896-vintage inn has 15 rooms filled with lovely quilt-covered four-poster beds, stained-glass windows, hand-braided rugs, and other Victorian furnishings. All have private baths, and many have decks. Owners David Campiche and Laurie Anderson prepare memorable breakfasts that take advantage of fresh seasonal ingredients (including herbs from the Victorian garden). Possible treats: razor-clam cakes, scrambled eggs with smoked salmon and Gruyère cheese, and oysters prepared any number of ways—not to mention pastries. Lunch and dinner are available downstairs at the Shoalwater restaurant or Heron and Beaver Pub (under separate ownership; see reviews). The ocean lies a few blocks away, but busy Highway 103 is right out front—request a west-facing room for maximum quiet. Best-value rooms are on the third floor, if you're up for the stairs. *$$$; AE, MC, V; checks OK; www.theshelburneinn.com; at N 45th.* &

Long Beach

Long Beach is the center of peninsula tourist activity and host to throngs of summer visitors. You'll find the largest collection of gift shops, amusement arcades, and other attractions here, as well as the beach boardwalk—a pedestrian-only half-mile stroll with night lighting (wheelchairs and baby-strollers welcome, too).

A big draw is August's **INTERNATIONAL KITE FESTIVAL**. Visit the **LONG BEACH WORLD KITE MUSEUM AND HALL OF FAME** (112 3rd St NW; 360/642-4020), or get in on the fun yourself by shopping at **LONG BEACH KITES** (104 Pacific Ave N; 360/642-2202) or **OCEAN KITES** (511 Pacific Ave S; 360/642-2229). For a tastier museum, check out the **CRANBERRY MUSEUM AND GIFT SHOP** (Pioneer Rd W and Washington St N; 360/642-3638; Wed–Sun Apr–Dec; call ahead to arrange a tour of the bogs. **ANNA LENA'S PANTRY** (111 Bolstad Ave; 360/642-8585) has more than 30 gourmet cranberry products, including cranberry fudge, but is a quilters' destination too, with a huge assortment of supplies and a schedule of quilting retreats. **MILTON YORK CANDY COMPANY** (107 S Pacific St; 360/642-2352) has been around since 1882, and offers treats and simple meals. Farther out, **CLARK'S NURSERY** (15600 Sandridge Rd; 360/642-2241) grows fields of rhododendrons.

No visit to the peninsula would be complete without a visit to **MARSH'S FREE MUSEUM** (409 S Pacific Ave; 360/642-2188). In addition to an enormous selection of knickknacks for sale, Marsh's has many antique arcade machines and music boxes (all of which take your coins, and most of which work), as well as the museum's star attraction, Jake the Alligator Man. The mummified half-man, half-alligator's image was used by the *Weekly World News* in 1993 to grace a (made-up) story about a Florida monster who ate his keeper and destroyed a laboratory.

RESTAURANTS

Las Maracas / ★

601 S PACIFIC, LONG BEACH; 360/642-8000

In the United States, you'll find that the glitzier the Mexican restaurant, the farther the food is from Mexico. The no-frills trappings of inexpensive Las Maracas is a good indicator of how authentic the food is. A huge menu offers such *platos típicos* as *pollo en adobo* (spicy chicken marinated with green peppers and onions), carne asada (slices of skirt steak braised over charcoal, served with guacamole), burritos, enchiladas, and a number of dishes that take advantage of the area's fresh seafood (the *camarones al mojo de ajo* are great—prawns sautéed with mushrooms in wine, butter, and garlic). In true Mexican style, most dishes are not *picante*—if you want the hot stuff, dab on delicious homemade salsa. In fact, almost everything at Las Maracas is made from scratch in the restaurant's kitchen—even the tortilla chips. A full bar serves potent drinks with words like *loco* in the name. *$; AE, DC, MC, V; checks OK; lunch, dinner every day; full bar; reservations not accepted; on Hwy 103.*

LODGINGS

Boreas Bed & Breakfast / ★★

607 NORTH BLVD, LONG BEACH; 360/642-8069

Since taking over in 1996, owners Susie Goldsmith and Bill Verner have been busy improving an inn that was already a romantic gem. Each of five guest rooms in the 1920s beach house now has a private bath, including the new Dunes Suite with its Impressionist wall mural and private Jacuzzi. Verner has enlarged the landscaped backyard and improved the private path to the beach. The living room, with large windows facing the ocean, is graced with a marble fireplace and baby grand piano. Masterful work is apparent in the delicious breakfasts. Possibilities include omelets filled with wild mushrooms and smoked salmon, ginger pancakes with lime sauce, French toast topped with Grand Marnier and almonds, and braised bananas, with organic coffee, hot chocolate, or one of dozens of teas. *$$; AE, DC, MC, V; checks OK; boreas@ boreasinn.com; www.boreasinn.com; 1 block west of Hwy 103.*

Ocean Park

Ocean Park was once a Methodist retreat, which offered summers free of vice. But the senses are in for a bigger shock nowadays—at least during the June **GARLIC FESTIVAL,** which features a Northwest Wine Tasting and Brew Garden, to boot. Call the Ocean Park Chamber of Commerce (800/451-2542) for current dates.

The **WIEGARDT WATERCOLORS GALLERY** (2607 Bay Ave; 360/665-5976) displays Eric Wiegardt seascapes in a restored Victorian house. Nearby, the **SHOALWATER COVE GALLERY** (25712 Sandridge Rd; 360/665-4382) exhibits nature scenes in soft pastels. **JACK'S COUNTRY STORE** (Hwy 103 and Bay Ave; 360/665-4989) is a general store dating from 1885 that can supply almost every need—even some you didn't know you had.

LODGINGS

Caswell's on the Bay Bed & Breakfast / ★★★

25204 SANDRIDGE RD, OCEAN PARK; 360/665-6535

Take the long driveway off quiet Sandridge Road and prepare to be stunned by the gleaming yellow neo-Victorian mansion that sits at its foot, surrounded by rhododendrons. Inside you'll find five spacious rooms furnished in antiques (each with private bath), a large parlor with fireplace that features an amazing panorama of Willapa Bay and distant mountains, a library with both plush carpet and hardwood floors, and a sunroom complete with spyglass, where you'll enjoy afternoon tea with cookies and sweets (feast on a full breakfast in the morning). Relax on the back veranda or stroll the ample landscaped grounds. This B&B on 3 acres next to the bay is earning a reputation as possibly the most romantic spot on the peninsula; you're close to the attractions, but far from traffic and noise. The premium Terrace Suite has a view of Willapa Bay, a balcony, and a lovely sitting room. No children. *$$$; MC, V; checks OK; www.caswellsinn.com; ½ mile south of Bay Ave–Sandridge Rd intersection.*

Shakti Cove Cottages / ★

ON 253RD PL, OCEAN PARK; 360/665-4000

Though the Shakti Cove Cottages are just off Highway 103, you'll feel miles from the outside world. Ten small cedar-shingled cabins stand in a semicircle around a gentle green, each funky-cozy, with its own carport, bath, and kitchen facilities. Amble a quarter mile down a private gravel road to the beach, likely passing black-tailed deer grabbing a meal from the Shakti's wildflower garden along the way. Shakti Cove is popular with gays and lesbians, as well as travelers with dogs (even large ones), but "covekeepers" Celia and Liz Cavalli make visitors of every kind feel at home. As one former guest wrote in the in-cabin journal: "It's so nice to feel welcomed instead of just tolerated." *$$; MC, V; checks OK; 1 block west of Pacific Hwy 103.*

Nahcotta

A healthy population of seagulls attests to Nahcotta's tenure as a center for oysters. Several stands and storefronts purvey the tasty bivalves, including **JOLLY ROGER SEAFOODS** (273rd and Sandridge Rd, on old Nahcotta dock; 360/665-

4111). On the same pier you can visit the **WILLAPA BAY INTERPRETIVE CENTER** (273rd and Sandridge Rd, next to the Ark restaurant; 360/665-4547; open weekends in summer) to learn the history of the 150-year-old oyster industry. Take advantage of the interpretive signs, info, and maps posted outside the **WILLAPA FIELD STATION** (267 Sandridge Rd), which researches shellfish management.

RESTAURANTS

The Ark / ★★

273RD AND SANDRIDGE RD, NAHCOTTA; 360/665-4133

The Ark has garnered rave reviews for years, and even got a thumbs up from the former First Diner, President Bill Clinton. Owners Nanci Main and Jimella Lucas have co-authored several cookbooks, and take advantage of the bounty of fresh ingredients nearby: oysters (lightly breaded and panfried), salmon, sturgeon, wild blackberries, Oregon blue cheese, and more. The season may determine your choices, but if possible, try calamari dijonnaise, oysters Italian, or chicken scallops and tarragon (a recipe is posted on the Web site if you're inspired). Save room for Main's dessert pastries, then stretch with a walk through the Ark's vegetable and herb gardens. *$$$; AE, MC, V; checks OK; dinner Tues–Sun (Thurs–Sun in winter), brunch Sun; full bar; reservations recommended; www.arkrestaurant.com; on old Nahcotta dock, next to oyster fleet.*

Oysterville

Oysterville is a picture postcard of a tiny 19th-century sea town, and its double row of wooden houses with picket fences is listed as a Historic District with the National Register. The photogenic 1892 Baptist church no longer holds services, but is open for visitors. Oysterville was the county seat until 1893, when a disgruntled group, tired of making the long journey to conduct official business, reportedly stole the county records and moved them to the present seat, South Bend.

OYSTERVILLE SEA FARMS (1st and Clark; 360/665-6585 or 800-CRAN-BERRY) is the sole industry here, with a retail store that sells a variety of fresh and vacuum-packed oysters in flavors ranging from smoked to habanero, as well as Anna Lena preserves, dried fruits, baking mixes, and more.

LEADBETTER POINT STATE PARK (3 miles north, on Stackpole Rd) is a large wildlife refuge that attracts thousands of birds. Miles of hiking trails lead to interpretive signs and nearly untouched beaches along Willapa Bay; no camping.

Tokeland

Isolated on the long peninsula reaching into northern Willapa Bay (on a spur road south of Highway 105, west of Highway 101 near Raymond), tiny Tokeland is all that remains of the once-bustling town named after 19th-century Chief Toke. After nearby jetties changed ocean currents and a particularly vicious storm struck in the 1930s, some 1,500 acres that once held homes, hotels, and a lighthouse are now covered with saltwater. Pick up crab meat and cocktail sauce from **NELSON CRAB** (3088 Kindred Ave; 360/ 267-2911) and picnic on the beach to enjoy the serene scenery that remains. Couples looking to really get away from it all should check out the isolated and historic **TOKE-LAND HOTEL** (100 Hotel Rd; 360/267-7006).

Mount St. Helens National Volcanic Monument

The May 18, 1980, explosion of Mount St. Helens's volcanic fury created a drastically changed landscape, as well as an attraction for the attention of hundreds of scientists and thousands of visitors from around the world. While the region can be explored via Randle in the north (on Hwy 12) or Cougar in the south (off Hwy 503), most visitors opt to travel Highway 504, also known as **SPIRIT LAKE MEMORIAL HIGHWAY**, which heads east from Interstate 5 at Castle Rock. There are five excellent visitors centers along its length, and a route that takes you to a bird's-eye view of the volcano's still-steaming crater at Johnston Ridge Observatory (mile 52; 360/274-2151). A fee ($8 per person) lets you visit the three centers run by the U.S. Forest Service (www.fs.fed.us/gpnf/mshnvm), including Johnston Ridge. The Hoffstadt Bluff Rest Area and Viewpoint (run by Cowlitz County) and the Weyerhaeuser Forest Learning Center (run by Weyerhaeuser) are free to visit.

Castle Rock

This small town is a gateway to Mount St. Helens, located at the intersection of Highway 504 and Interstate 5. **THE CINEDOME THEATER** (1238 Mount St. Helens Wy NE/Hwy 504; 360/274-9844) boasts that "Mount St. Helens erupts here every 45 minutes!" and shows the Omnimax film *The Eruption of Mount St. Helens* every day (a great introduction to your mountain tour). The theater also shows first-run theatrical movies in the evening (folks came from hours away to watch *Star Wars Episode I* on the three-story, 55-foot screen with its accompanying seat-rumbling sound system). Plenty of souvenirs—from kitschy ash creations to valuable interpretive guides—can be found in town.

LODGINGS

Blue Heron Inn / ★

2846 SPIRIT LAKE HWY, CASTLE ROCK; 360/274-9595

If you're looking for a base of operations from which to explore Mount St. Helens and you'd like a little pampering, the Blue Heron Inn is the spot. Built in 1996 by John and Jeanne Robards on property that has been in John's family for generations, the Blue Heron Inn is a lodge-style log-and-stone retreat located next to Seaquest State Park, just across from the Mount St. Helens Visitors

MOUNT ST. HELENS AND THE GORGE THREE-DAY TOUR

DAY ONE: Spend the day touring **Mount St. Helens**. You won't want to miss any of the five visitor centers spaced along the 50-mile drive, which offer various views of the landscape and pieces of the region's development since the blast more than 20 years ago. Once you've had your fill of volcanic activity, seismographs, and more, head south on Interstate 5 to **Vancouver** to check in at the **Heathman Lodge**. Enjoy dinner at the **Chart House** (make reservations in advance), then return to the Heathman to sip a glass of wine by the stone fireplace in the lobby before turning in.

DAY TWO: Have a tasty breakfast at **Hudson's Bar & Grill**, then explore historic Vancouver—visit the re-created **Fort Vancouver**, walk along the riverfront and visit **Old Apple Tree Park**, then explore **Officers Row**, where you have lunch at **Sheldon's Cafe at the Grant House**. Afterward head east on Highway 14 and take in the magnificent scenery along the **Columbia River Gorge**. Stop for an authentic Mexican dinner at **Fidel's** in Bingen, then turn north onto Highway 141 for the short drive to the **Inn of the White Salmon** for the night.

DAY THREE: After a tremendous breakfast at the inn, you're ready to enjoy the Gorge. If you're feeling adventurous, how about a rafting trip down the **White Salmon River**? If you prefer something calmer, opt for a picnic lunch at the **Wind River Cellars**. Then drive back down to Highway 14 and head east to the **Maryhill Museum**, where you spend the afternoon investigating art treasures. A little farther down the road you'll find the **Stonehenge** replica. Pack a dinner and enjoy it while you watch the sun set in the Columbia River Gorge. Continue east and then north to your night's lodging in Goldendale at **Timberframe Country Inn B&B**.

Center. Each of six rooms (as well as the Jacuzzi Suite) has a private bath, as well as a balcony with marvelous views of the volcano and Silver Lake. Included is a substantial breakfast enjoyed "family-style" with fellow guests, as well as a 7pm dinner served with local wines. *$$$$; MC, V; checks OK; www.blue heroninn.com; Hwy 504 about 5 miles east of I-5 and just west of Mount St. Helens Visitors Center.* &

Vancouver

One of the oldest white settlements in the Pacific Northwest, Vancouver is looking at a bright future, as a rapidly growing high-tech industry draws people to the area (the population grew half-again during the '90s). The British Hudson's Bay Company ensconced itself in **FORT VANCOUVER** in the early 19th century, until the territory passed to the United States, when the fort became an American military base. The stockade wall and some of the buildings of the fort have been reconstructed, and the visitors center (1501 E Evergreen Blvd; 360/696-7655) features a museum and an heirloom garden.

Another gem of Vancouver's large Central Park area is **OFFICERS ROW** (E Evergreen Blvd, between I-5 and E Reserve St), a leafy street of restored homes where officers billeted in bygone days; the Heritage Trust of Clark County (360/737-6066) gives tours. Grant House on Officers Row houses the **FOLK ART CENTER** (1101 Officers Row; 360/694-5252; Tues–Sat), a tribute to regional art. The **CLARK COUNTY HISTORICAL MUSEUM** (1511 Main St; 360/695-4681; 1–5pm Tues–Sat) reconstructs pioneer stores and businesses. **COVINGTON HOUSE** (4201 Main St; 360/695-6750) is the oldest log house (1846) in the state; call to make tour arrangements.

A lovely 4-mile waterfront walk along Columbia Way begins just under the Interstate 5 bridge (next to the Red Lion Inn at the Quay), and passes the Northwest's oldest apple tree. The **VANCOUVER FARMERS MARKET** (9am–3pm Sat, Apr–Oct) takes up several blocks at the south end of Main Street with local produce, flowers, and food vendors. The **WATER RESOURCES CENTER** (4600 SE Columbia Wy; 360/696-8478; 9am–5pm Mon–Sat) has exhibits and a superb view of the Columbia River, at the east end of Columbia Way on the edge of Marine Park.

RIDGEFIELD NATIONAL WILDLIFE REFUGE (3 miles west of I-5, exit 14; 360/887-3883) has nature trails leading to the bird refuge on the lowlands of the Columbia River. **MOULTON FALLS** (NW Lucia Falls Rd near County Rd 16; 360/696-8171) has a three-story-high arched bridge spanning the East Fork of the Lewis River, a 387-acre park, and two waterfalls. It's 2 miles south of Yacolt and 9 miles east of Battle Ground.

RESTAURANTS

Beaches Restaurant & Bar / ★

1919 SE COLUMBIA RIVER DR, VANCOUVER; 360/699-1592

A boisterous, bustling contemporary restaurant with a tremendous view of the Columbia, Beaches offers a panoply of whole-meal salads, burgers, steaks, ribs, seafood, and pastas in an effort to please the business crowd as well as families—and succeeds (a branch is set to open across the river in Beaverton at press time). Daily fresh fish specials always shine, and the cioppino is a great starter for seafood lovers. The bar keeps rollicking after the kitchen closes at 10pm (9pm Sun–Mon). *$$; AE, MC, V; local checks only; lunch, dinner every day; full bar; reservations not necessary; exit 1A off Hwy 14.* &

Chart House / ★★½

101 E COLUMBIA WY, VANCOUVER; 360/693-9211

Chart House restaurants comprise a small national chain of fine restaurants, more than half of which occupy historic sites with water views. One of three Pacific Northwest branches (with Portland and Boise), Vancouver's Chart House resides in a former Coast Guard station overhanging the Columbia.

Though the view is fantastic, the food is more than its equal. Fresh seafood and aged beef dominate the menu; the grilled ahi tuna chop with black beans and mango relish is a knockout, while the herbed prime rib with creamed horseradish and Kona onions melts in your mouth. If you think you're up for it, order dessert when you order your dinner—the Chocolate Lava Cake (with a molten center of Godiva chocolate liqueur, vanilla ice cream, and warm chocolate sauce) takes 30 minutes to prepare. *$$–$$$; AE, DC, DIS, MC, V; no checks; lunch Mon–Fri, dinner every day; full bar; reservations recommended; just south of downtown.* &

Hudson's Bar & Grill / ★★☆
7805 GREENWOOD DR (HEATHMAN LODGE), VANCOUVER; 360/816-6100
A tremendous Pacific Northwest take on American comfort food, combined with the rich woods and native basalt of its rustic decor, make Hudson's Bar & Grill a destination for a soul-warming meal. Breakfasts and lunches are excellent, but dinner is where Hudson's shines. Try the venison wrapped with apple bacon served with sweet-potato hash and candied shallots; the poached salmon fillet with acorn squash, shiitake mushrooms, and lemon chile butter; or the grilled pork medallions on black-bean cake with poblano rings and salsa verde. Fresh seasonal ingredients plus breads and pastries baked daily complement a modest selection of Northwest wines. You may want to linger with an extra glass by the large stone fireplace as you take in the piano airs wafting from the hotel lobby next door. *$$–$$$; AE, DC, DIS, MC, V; checks OK; breakfast, lunch, dinner every day; full bar; reservations not necessary; near Thurston Wy exit off Hwy 500.* &

Sheldon's Cafe at the Grant House / ★★
1101 OFFICERS ROW, VANCOUVER; 360/699-1213
In Vancouver's historic Officers Row, Sheldon's Cafe can be the culinary high point of a day's wander though the park or a summer evening stroll. Using the lower floor of a house named for Ulysses S. Grant (once a quartermaster at Fort Vancouver), Sheldon's shares space with a folk art museum. American cuisine is the emphasis, with some nice Northwest touches—Willapa Bay oysters and other fresh seafoods are especially good. The menu has plenty of other temptations among its salads, pastas, quiches, game birds, and house-smoked meats. If weather permits, dine on the Grant House's veranda, surrounded by the flower and herb garden. Save some room for apple crisp. *$$; MC, V; checks OK; lunch, dinner Tues–Sat; beer and wine; reservations recommended; midtown Vancouver, off Evergreen Blvd.*

Thai Orchid / ★★
1004 WASHINGTON ST, VANCOUVER; 360/695-7786
Using fresh, healthy ingredients (and no hydrogenated oils), the Thai Orchid has garnered a slew of awards—including the Shell Chuan Chim award from the food critic cousin of the king of Thailand. The huge selection of curried, stir-

fried, seafood, rice, and specialty dishes may require the helpful staff's assistance on choices. For both its name and its flavor, you can't go wrong with the Evil Jungle Prince curry (your choice of vegetables, beef, chicken, or pork on a bed of steamed cabbage and broccoli, all topped with curry sauce). Spicy dishes are marked on the menu and can be ordered to suit your courage. *$$; AE, DIS, MC, V; checks OK; lunch, dinner every day; full bar; reservations not necessary; www.thaiorchidrestaurant.com; at Evergreen Blvd.* &

LODGINGS

Heathman Lodge / ★★★

7801 GREENWOOD DR, VANCOUVER; 360/254-3100 OR 888/475-3100

As you walk through the massive arched timber portico of the Heathman Lodge, you'll immediately forget you're in the 'burbs, a stone's throw away from the Vancouver Mall. You might think instead—as you take in peeled-log balconies draped with Pendleton blankets, a massive basalt gas fireplace, and many other artful details—that you're in a luxurious high-mountain retreat. A wonderful blend of opposites, the Heathman Lodge features rooms that combine rustic furnishings with modern necessities—two-line phones, data ports, refrigerator, microwave, coffeemaker, and iron and ironing board, as well as an indoor pool and fitness center downstairs. Suites offer wet bars, Jacuzzis, and gas fireplaces. With a great restaurant just off the lodge's lobby (Hudson's Bar & Grill; see review), you can stay inside over a rainy weekend and never break the illusion that you're tucked away in an alpine haven. *$$–$$$; AE, DC, DIS, MC, V; checks OK; www.heathmanlodge.com; near Thurston Wy exit off Hwy 500.* &

Mount Adams
and the Columbia River Gorge

The **COLUMBIA GORGE INTERPRETIVE CENTER** (990 SW Rock Creek Dr, Stevenson; 509/427-8211 or 800/991-2338; open daily), just west of Stevenson, spins an evocative tale of the region's natural and cultural history, with a nine-projector slide show that re-creates the Gorge's cataclysmic formation; plus exhibits on timber, fur trading, hydroelectric power, and more. A working 37-foot fish wheel is an exact replica of one that once ran 24 hours a day nearby.

Mount Adams and its surrounding area, 30 miles north of the Columbia, offer natural splendor largely overlooked by visitors, who seldom venture in from the Gorge. Besides climbing to the summit of the 12,276-foot mountain—greater in mass than any of the five other major volcanic peaks in the Northwest—hikers and skiers can explore miles of wilderness trails in the **MOUNT ADAMS WILDERNESS AREA** and Gifford Pinchot National Forest. Contact the Mount Adams Ranger Station (2455 Hwy 141; 509/395-3400) in Trout Lake to register for ascents and area activities.

Stevenson

A small town blessed by scenery, Stevenson lies within the beginnings of the **GORGE SCENIC HIGHWAY** (Hwy 14), and marks the unofficial boundary of windsurfing country.

LODGINGS

Skamania Lodge / ★★

1131 SKAMANIA LODGE WY, STEVENSON; 509/427-7700 OR 800/221-7117

Skamania Lodge was designed to resemble a national park lodge, and it does, with lots of wood and stone, mission-style furniture, Native American–style rugs, and beautiful views from its perch above the Columbia River Gorge. The differences are an award-winning 18-hole golf course, an indoor fitness center, a pool, saunas, and a spa. If you don't golf, opt to use one of two tennis courts, or rent a bike and follow the map of trails. A formal dining room offers fine cuisine, and the River Rock Lounge serves lunch, appetizers, and light dinners. The lodge is huge—195 rooms, including 34 deluxe rooms with fireplaces, and 5 suites—and, with the two-state Columbia River Gorge Commission keeping a tight rein on regional construction, is likely to remain unique for the foreseeable future. *$$$; AE, DC, MC, V; checks OK; reservations@skamania.com; www. dolce.com/properties/skamania; turn north onto Rock Creek Dr just west of Stevenson.*

Carson

"Funky" is the word most often used to describe **CARSON MINERAL HOT SPRINGS** (Hot Springs and St Martin Ave; 509/427-8292). This historic resort has been around since 1897, and while the sheets have been changed since then, not much else has. You will want to reserve ahead for its renowned old-style "treatment"—a (non–co-ed) hot mineral bath, followed by a rest while swathed in towels and blankets, which you can follow with a professional massage. If you decide you want to stay at this rustic, well-worn resort, TV- and phone-free rooms and cabins are available, as well as a restaurant and 18-hole golf course.

White Salmon

Perched 700 feet above the Columbia River with lovely views of Mount Hood and Mount Adams, White Salmon is a great base of operations from which to enjoy the Gorge. The **WHITE SALMON RIVER**, with its Class II–IV rapids, serene pools, and verdant canyon, is one of the state's most popular rafting destinations and the perfect spot for beginners and intermediates, April through October. Two of the best outfitters are **PHIL'S WHITE WATER ADVENTURES** (38 Northwestern Lake; 509/493-2641 or 800/366-2004; www.gorge.net/philswwa) and **AAA RAFTING** (860 Hwy 141; 509/493-2511 or 800/866-7238). Ray Klebba's **WHITE SALMON BOAT WORKS** (105 Jewett Blvd; 509/493-4749) can teach you how to make your own woodstrip-construction sea kayak or canoe;

buy a kit to take home, or have the skilled crafters build one for you. **NORTH-WESTERN LAKE STABLES** (126 Little Buck Creek Rd; 509/493-4965) offers backcountry horseback-riding packages ranging from one-hour rides to overnight adventures.

If a less strenuous outing is in order, visit **WIND RIVER CELLARS** (196 Spring Creek Rd; 509/493-2324; open daily). Enjoy complimentary sips in a tasting room with a stunning view of Mount Hood, explore the vineyards, and bring lunch to enjoy in the pretty grape-arbor picnic area.

RESTAURANTS

Fidel's

120 E STUBEN ST, BINGEN; 509/493-1017

Lively Mexican music sets the mood at Fidel's in nearby Bingen, so why not start with an enormous margarita to go with the salsa and tortilla chips fresh out of the oven? The menu offers carne asada, chile verde, chile colorado, and omelets *machaca* (with shredded beef, chicken, or pork). Portions are generous (often big enough for two), and the chile relleno—encased in a thick layer of egg whites so that it resembles a big pillow—is good stuff. *$; MC, V; checks OK; lunch, dinner every day (call ahead in winter); full bar; reservations not accepted; 1 mile east of Hood River toll bridge.*

LODGINGS

Inn of the White Salmon / ★★

172 W JEWETT, WHITE SALMON; 509/493-2335 OR 800/972-5226

Janet Holen, who with her husband, Roger, owns the Inn of the White Salmon, rightly says their bed-and-breakfast offers the privacy of a hotel with the comfort of a B&B. This 1937-vintage jewel is a standout in both the bed *and* breakfast categories. Each room has a large, comfy antique bed, as well as private bath, phone, cable TV, and air-conditioning; several are two-room suites. Just down the hall is a relaxing parlor where you can read or listen to music, or take a dip in the hot tub at the end of the hall. Breakfast serves up a real groaning board: 20 kinds of pastries and breads, juice, tea and coffee, and your choice among entrees such as Italian or artichoke frittatas, Hungarian *flauf*, quiche, and more. You can come for breakfast only, but reservations are highly advisable. *$$; MC, V; checks OK; innkeeper@gorge.net; www.gorge.net/lodging/ iws; Hwy 141, 1½ miles north of Hwy 14.*

Trout Lake

Trout Lake, about 25 miles north of the Gorge on Highway 141, follows the White Salmon River toward its Cascades source. Volcanic activity long ago left the Mount Adams area honeycombed with caves and lava tubes, including the **ICE CAVES** near Trout Lake, with stalactites and stalagmites formed by dripping ice. Southwest of Trout Lake is **BIG LAVA BED**, a 12,500-acre lava field filled with cracks, crevasses, rock piles, and unusual lava formations.

LODGINGS
Serenity's Village / ★

MILE 23, HWY 141, TROUT LAKE; 509/395-2500 OR 800/276-7993

These four chalet-style cabins set among the firs and pines are a good base for exploring the Trout Lake Valley below Mount Adams. All are tastefully finished, warmed by gas fireplaces (or cooled by air-conditioning), and equipped with basic kitchen facilities, plus outdoor barbecues. Two larger units have lofts and Jacuzzis, but smaller units are set farther back from the highway. Serenity's has a restaurant with irregular hours; call ahead if you want food service. A TV and VCR can be requested. Kids are OK, but not pets. *$$; MC, V; checks OK; www.gorge.net/serenitys; 23 miles north of White Salmon.* &

Glenwood

LODGINGS
Flying L Ranch / ★

25 FLYING L LN, GLENWOOD; 509/364-3488 OR 888/MT-ADAMS

If you never went to camp as a kid, the 100-acre Flying L Ranch gives you the chance. Poised at the foot of Mount Adams, the ranch has trails for exploring on foot in summer or on skis in winter. You can bicycle, birdwatch in the nearby Conboy National Wildlife Refuge, or have meaningful conversations with ranch dogs Prince, Meghan, and Ellie. Accommodations are rustic—real rustic, not glossy-magazine rustic—but comfortable. You have three options: five rooms in the main lodge house (some with their own fireplaces); five rooms in the Guest House (with a small shared kitchen); and cabins nestled in the pines about 200 feet from the main buildings (each with its own kitchen, wood stove, and electric heat). Everyone has access to the spacious living room with its stone fireplace, piano, stereo, and wonderful view, as well as to the kitchen and pantry in the main house, and the hot tub in the gazebo. Full ranch breakfasts are served in the Cookhouse dining room (coffee is available for early risers); lunch and dinner you'll cook yourself, or see what you can find in tiny "downtown" Glenwood. *$$; AE, MC, V; checks OK; flyingl@mt-adams.com; www.mt-adams.com; east through Glenwood about ½ mile toward Goldendale, turn north and proceed ½ mile to driveway on right.*

Goldendale

Though Goldendale is the seat of Klickitat County, it's not a case of bright lights, big city. Which makes it the perfect location for the **GOLDENDALE OBSERVATORY STATE PARK** (602 Observatory Dr; 509/773-3141; goldobs@gorge.net; Wed–Sun in summer, weekends in winter), 1 mile north of Goldendale just off Columbus Avenue. Visitors can look through the 24 ½-inch telescope (one of the largest in the nation available to the public) or borrow a portable telescope to gaze at skies largely clear of air and light pollution. Lectures, slide shows, and films are also available. Goldendale is 10 ½ miles north of Highway 14 on Highway 97.

ART TREASURES OF THE GORGE

Wealthy eccentric Sam Hill left an indelible mark on the Columbia River Gorge. With dreams of establishing a Quaker agricultural town on the shores of the river early in the 20th century, Hill started construction on his own house, named Maryhill. After his land company failed and his visions of a utopian community died, Hill decided to make the isolated mansion perched on a lonely bluff into a museum.

Today the **Maryhill Museum of Art** (35 Maryhill Museum Dr, Goldendale; 509/773-3733; www.maryhillmuseum.org; Mar–Nov) houses an eclectic mix of collections—Native American artifacts, European paintings, American Classical Realist canvases, the royal regalia of Hill's good friend Queen Marie of Romania, the *Théâtre de la Mode* French fashion mannequins, and, perhaps the greatest treasure, a large group of watercolors and sculptures by Auguste Rodin (including the only pedestal-sized plaster version of his most famous figure, *The Thinker*). In addition to other exhibits, the museum also houses the Café Maryhill, a small deli that serves hot and cold sandwiches, desserts, espresso, and other beverages.

Hill's other monumental legacy in the region is a life-size replica of England's neolithic **Stonehenge** (about 2 miles east of the museum). Erroneously informed during World War I that the original Stonehenge was used for pagan sacrifices, Hill built his new version to honor fallen World War I soldiers from Klickitat County and as a memorial against war. Hill, who also built the Peace Arch at the U.S.-Canada border at Blaine, rests in his crypt on a river bluff not far from his replica.   —Les Campbell

LODGINGS

Timberframe Country Inn B&B

223 GOLDEN PINE, GOLDENDALE; 800/861-8408

The Timberframe is surrounded by ponderosa pines and meadows in the Simcoe Mountains. Each of the two suites has a private entrance, bath, TV, and VCR. The Tree Top room has a sundeck with a spa. B&B owner Dor Creamer provides information on local activities from windsurfing to the Goldendale Observatory, and serves a full country breakfast. She also has two RV spaces, with breakfast on request. No smoking, children, or pets. *$$; no credit cards; checks OK; Broadway/Hwy 142 exit off Hwy 97.*

SOUTHEAST
WASHINGTON

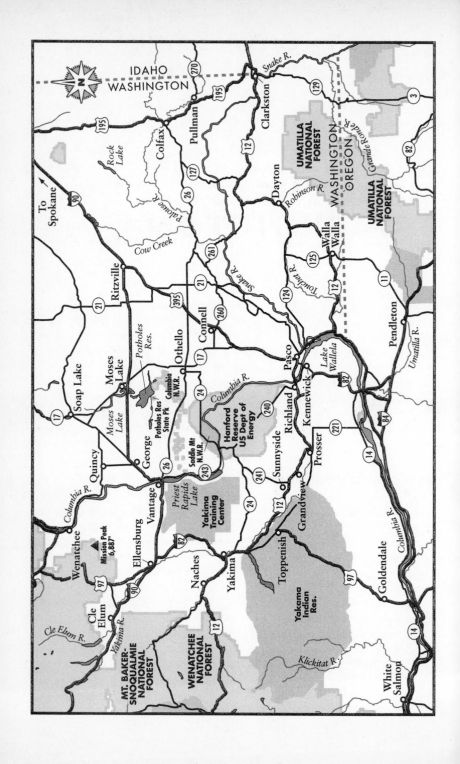

SOUTHEAST WASHINGTON

The central-to-southeast corner of the Evergreen State—from Ellensburg to Pullman—isn't very green, but it's rich in history. Here, rain is unusual, old-growth sagebrush is protected, and agriculture mixes with high-tech, making the region the heart of Washington's wine industry, and the bread basket of the Pacific Northwest.

The Southeast is its own melting pot, with strong influences from Mexican and Native American cultures. Residents are farmers, nuclear scientists, cowboys, college students, entrepreneurs, and good ol' boys. They enjoy a slower, more casual pace than in urban areas. People look at you funny if you carry an umbrella, and it's a rare restaurant that requires a jacket and tie.

Of course, each city has its bragging points. Ellensburg is famous for its lamb, chimpanzee linguistic research, and Labor Day rodeo. Yakima is known for fruit trees, wineries, and outdoor activities. The Tri-Cities claim 300 days of sunshine a year, a Lewis and Clark campsite, and discovery of the 9,200-year-old Kennewick Man bones. (He's not available for public viewing because the federal government, the tribes, and scientists are in the midst of legal wranglings, and the discovery spot is unmarked to prevent vandalism; the best way to see the bones is at the "virtual interpretive center"; www.kennewick-man.com.) Washington State University in Pullman is famous for its Cougar Gold cheese. Walla Walla's resume includes sweet onions, hot-air balloons, and pioneers.

Appreciating the shrub-steppe landscape might take a conscious effort if you're accustomed to snowcapped mountains, green hills, and humidity. But the earth-toned palette reveals its own majestic geological formations, like the Palouse Falls 198-foot waterfall and Wallula Gap basalt pillars. Out here, spaces are wide-open, the clouds—if there are any—are high above your head, and you feel like you can see a million miles in the clear, dry air.

ACCESS AND INFORMATION

Most people visiting central and Southeast Washington drive. Even if you fly, you'll want to have a car. Numerous Northwest highways lead to this dry, sunny corner. No matter what route you take, it's likely to go through some sparsely populated country. Take advantage of rest areas and be sure your gas tank is full. Bring sunblock and a light sweater (for overactive air-conditioners and cool evenings) in summer, or a turtleneck, sweater, and wind-proof jacket in winter. It can get really cold in these parts, and because it's dry, down is a good choice.

Interstate 90 is the most practical route from Puget Sound, connecting at Ellensburg with Interstate 82, which leads through the Yakima Valley to the Tri-Cities at the confluence of the Yakima, Snake, and Columbia Rivers. From there, Walla Walla is an easy trip via Interstate 82 and US Highway 12.

From Portland, Interstate 84—or the two-lane Highway 14 on the Washington side—leads to Eastern Washington. If you're heading to Ellensburg or Yakima, turn north on US Highway 97. If your destination is the Tri-Cities, take

Interstate 82/US Highway 395. Note: The Tri-Cities includes Kennewick, Richland, and Pasco, and freeway signs usually name one of those instead of the region's nickname.

The **TRI-CITIES AIRPORT** (3601 N 20th Ave, Pasco; 509/547-6352) is served by Horizon Air, Delta, United Express, and SkyWest. **HORIZON AIR** (800/547-9308; www.horizonair.com) also serves the region's smaller airports, in Walla Walla, Yakima, and Moses Lake.

Several **CAR RENTAL** companies operate out of the Tri-Cities airport, including Avis, Hertz, National, Budget, and Enterprise. The Pasco train station (535 N 1st Ave) serves **AMTRAK** (509/545-1554 or 800/872-7245) and **GREYHOUND** (800/231-2222). The local public transit company is Ben Franklin Transit (509/735-5100). The **TRI-CITIES VISITOR AND CONVENTION BUREAU** (6951 W Grandridge Blvd, Kennewick; 800/254-5824; www.visittri-cities.com) is the best source of information for Kennewick, Pasco, and Richland.

Columbia Basin

The Columbia Plateau is a vast tableland that stretches across the center of the state, much of it rich agricultural lands irrigated by the Columbia River Basin. More than 2,000 miles of canals and secondary canals water more than a million acres of fields.

Vantage and George

Situated on a splendid stretch of the Columbia just north of Interstate 90, Vantage has nothing much in the way of food and lodging—but it does have incredible scenery. **GINKGO PETRIFIED FOREST STATE PARK** (exit 136 off I-90; 509/856-2700) takes you back to the age of dinosaurs. The interpretive center is open daily 10am–6pm in summer, by appointment otherwise. It's a great spot for a picnic.

The small town of George, Washington, also just off Interstate 90, boasts the naturally terraced **GORGE AMPHITHEATER** (www.barstop.com/gorge) with a westward view over the Columbia Gorge. Big names of all musical genres play here—from Mötley Crüe and Tom Petty to Bob Dylan and the Dave Matthews Band. Arrive early to avoid country-road traffic jams. It's okay to bring food, but packs are searched and alcohol is not allowed. Rest rooms are scarce, and locals have become less tolerant of rowdy concert-goers. Ticketmaster (206/628-0888; www.ticketmaster.com) handles most concert ticket sales. George is a three-hour drive from Seattle and two hours from Spokane. Nearest accommodations are in Vantage, Ellensburg, Quincy, Ephrata, or Moses Lake. The **GORGE CAMPGROUND** (509/785-2267) charges $15 per vehicle per night.

SOUTHEAST WASHINGTON THREE-DAY TOUR

DAY ONE: Breakfast at **Ellensburg**'s **Austin's Roadside Deli**; afterward, take a quick walk to see the bull or cowboy statue nearby. Head south on Interstate 82 to **Yakima**, then stretch your legs with a nature walk on the Greenway or window-shop in the North Front Street Historical District. Sample the region's Mexican heritage with lunch at **El Pastor**. Drive to Toppenish to see the western art murals, then visit the **Yakama Nation Cultural Heritage Center**, one of the few Native American–designed and –operated museums in the state. Get back in the car and head to Sunny-side to **Darigold's Dairy Fair** for a self-guided tour of the cheese factory and a quick snack. Head south again to the **Tri-Cities**, and check in to Richland's **Red Lion Hanford House**. End the day with dinner at **Monterosso's Italian Restaurant**, in a romantically renovated railroad dining car.

DAY TWO: Dress for the outdoors, and bring sunblock, a hat, sneakers, and a bottle of water. Then grab a muffin and latte at the nearby **Taste** cafe. Spend the morning on a Columbia River Journeys **jet-boat tour** through Hanford Reach. Eat lunch and quaff a Half-life Hefeweizen back in Richland at the **Atomic Ale Brewpub & Eatery**, then hit the **Columbia River Exhibition of History Science & Technology**. Head over to **Kennewick** to the **Playground of Dreams** and Family Fishing Pond, where kids can learn how to catch-and-release, in **Columbia Park**. Have dinner at the recently rebuilt **Cedar's Pier I** on Clover Island and enjoy the view of the lighted cable bridge. Cross the bridge and end the day at Pasco's **Doubletree Hotel**.

DAY THREE: After a buffet breakfast at the Doubletree, hit the road for **Walla Walla**. Your first stop is the **Whitman Mission**, where 19th-century missionaries and Native Americans clashed. Next, visit the historic buildings of the **Fort Walla Walla Museum**. Lunch in downtown Walla Walla at **Merchants Ltd.**, then drive through rolling hills to **Dayton**, home of 88 buildings on the historic register and the region's highest-rated restaurant, **Patit Creek Restaurant**. Have dinner here, then snuggle into a room at the **Weinhard Hotel**.

Moses Lake

Moses Lake, on Interstate 90 at the northern reaches of the Potholes Reservoir, is a small town poised to grow quickly as Puget Sound manufacturing businesses look for elbow room over the mountains. The region's geography is known for its 60-million-year-old granite and 274,000 surface acres of water. Moses Lake itself has year-round fishing and boat access. The GRANT COUNTY OFF ROAD VEHICLE AREA is in the sand dunes 4 miles out of town. The FAMILY AQUATIC CENTER (401 W 4th Ave; 509/766-9246; May–Sept) has water slides, a zero-depth beach, an Olympic-size competitive pool, and handicapped access. The

MOSES LAKE CHAMBER OF COMMERCE (324 S Pioneer Wy; 509/765-7888; www.moses-lake.com) has visitor information.

RESTAURANTS

Michael's on the Lake

910 W BROADWAY AVE, MOSES LAKE; 509/765-1611

Large windows and an outdoor deck give diners a view of the second-largest freshwater lake in Washington. Entrees are fairly standard—salads and sandwiches for lunch; prime rib, chicken, and salmon for dinner. Music and entertainment keep the lounge hopping late. *$$; AE, DC, DIS, MC, V; checks OK; lunch Mon–Sat, dinner every day, brunch Sun; full bar; reservations recommended (weekends); across from Imperial Inn.*

Ellensburg and Yakima Valleys

The Ellensburg and Kittitas Valleys stretch from the eastern foothills of the Cascades toward the Columbia at Vantage. The region is a key producer of cattle and hay, and it provides a natural gateway along the Yakima River to Yakima and its upper and lower valleys, separated by Union Gap.

The Yakima Valley has more fruit trees than any other county in the United States and is first in production of apples, mint, winter pears, and hops. Not surprisingly, the importance of agriculture and the outdoors overflows into area tourist attractions, including the **AMERICAN HOP MUSEUM** (22 S "B" St; 509/865-4677) in Toppenish and the **CENTRAL WASHINGTON AGRICULTURAL MUSEUM** (4508 Main St, Fullbright Park; 509/457-8735) in Union Gap. The **YAKIMA VALLEY VISITORS AND CONVENTION BUREAU** (10 N 8th St; 800/221-0751; www.visityakima.com) has information on enjoying the region's natural beauty.

The Yakima Valley's agricultural industry has drawn migrant workers from Mexico, Texas, and California, resulting in a large Hispanic population and a culturally rich community. Over the years, many migrant families have settled in the area, bringing their native culture—and cuisine—with them.

Ellensburg

Once a contender to be Washington's state capital, Ellensburg now is a combination college-cowboy town. Its famous rodeo started in 1923 and is still a showcase for cattle-ranching skills. Because the city is at the foot of the Cascades, it's also a popular base for skiing, rafting, and hiking along the Yakima River. Outdoors aficionados enjoy canoe or raft trips through the Yakima River's deep gorges, or fly-fishing for trout. Call the **ELLENSBURG CHAMBER OF COMMERCE** (801 S Ruby St, Ste 2; 509/925-3137).

Stretch your legs to see a bit of the Far East in the Wild West at **CENTRAL WASHINGTON UNIVERSITY** (400 E 8th Ave; 509/963-2244; www.cwu.edu), and its serene **JAPANESE GARDEN**, designed by Masa Mizuno. The campus is bordered on Ninth Street by lovely tree-lined blocks of early 1900s homes. You can arrange a Saturday or Sunday workshop at the **CHIMPANZEE AND HUMAN COMMUNICATION INSTITUTE** (14th and "D" Sts, north end of campus; 509/963-2244; www.cwu.edu), where humans and chimps communicate through American Sign Language. Workshops are offered for a fee, March through November.

A surprising amount of art can be found in this small town. At the **SARAH SPURGEON GALLERY** in CWU's fine-arts complex (Randall Fine Arts Bldg; 509/963-2665), regional and national art exhibits are held weekdays year-round. The **CLYMER MUSEUM AND GALLERY** (416 N Pearl St; 509/962-6416) honors John Clymer, Ellensburg's chronicler of the western frontier whose work appeared in the *Saturday Evening Post*. **GALLERY ONE** (408½ N Pearl St; 509/925-2670) sells regional crafts and displays contemporary art. Photo opps include the **ELLENSBURG BULL STATUE** (on Pearl between 4th and 5th) in the historic downtown business district and the **COWBOY SCULPTURE** at Fifth and Pearl.

Ice cream straight from the dairy is scooped at **WINEGAR FAMILY DAIRY** (7th and Main; 509/933-1821). The nearby Kittitas Valley hills are speckled with rare blue agates, available for purchase at local gem shops such as the **ELLENSBURG AGATE SHOP** (201 S Main; 509/925-4998). West of town is **THORP MILL** (5950 Thorp Hwy S; 509/964-9640), an 1883 gristmill in mint condition and open for tours by appointment.

The community's main event is the **ELLENSBURG RODEO** (800/637-2444; www.ellensburgrodeo.com), held at the county fairgrounds on Labor Day weekend. Food, games, country-western music, and the Budweiser Clydesdales complement the three days of competition.

RESTAURANTS

Austin's Roadside Deli / ★★

311 N MAIN ST, ELLENSBURG; 509/925-3012

Chef Austin Smith uses organic and locally grown or made ingredients in menu items such as deli sandwiches, salads, pasta, seasonal soups, pizza, and Mediterranean dishes. About half the menu is vegetarian. Smith's known around town for soups, rotating through about 60 recipes. Favorites are Thai chicken and black bean. Breakfast includes an organic oats-and-molasses granola, and French toast with yogurt and huckleberry syrup. Outdoor seating is available in summer; inside is a retail area with foods and kitchen accessories, and limited seating. *$; DIS, MC, V; checks OK; breakfast, lunch Mon–Sat (every day Apr–Sept); no alcohol; reservations not necessary; downtown.*

The Valley Cafe / ★★☆
105 3RD, ELLENSBURG; 509/925-3050

Who would expect to find this gourmet gem in the cowboy town of Ellensburg? The Valley Cafe's atmosphere, cuisine, and wine selection would stand out anywhere. This decor is authentic art deco, with mahogany booths and a back bar circa 1930s. Lunch favorites are sandwiches and salads—the lemon tahini dressing is marvelous—and quiche is a specialty. Dinners are more gourmet, with fresh seafood and Ellensburg lamb. The wine list (which includes many Washington selections) has won awards from international wine publications. Yummy desserts include crème brûlée and fresh fruit pies. Top off the experience with some of the best espresso in Central Washington. A deli/wine shop next door offers breakfast pastries, box lunches, and coffee drinks. *$$; AE, DC, DIS, MC, V; checks OK; breakfast, lunch, dinner every day; beer and wine; reservations not necessary; near Main St.*

LODGINGS

The Inn at Goose Creek
1720 CANYON RD, ELLENSBURG; 800/533-0822

Ten theme rooms, all with private baths, allow you to pick your mood, from romantic to sports, to year-round Christmas. Each features a goose-down comforter, spa tub, TV, and VCR. Innkeepers Gary and Ylwa Mabee serve a continental breakfast. No smoking; no pets. *$$; AE, MC, V; checks OK; www.innatgoosecreek.com; exit 109 off I-90.* ᵹ

Yakima

This is the preeminent city of Central Washington and the seat of county government. Get beyond the resulting freeway exits and strip malls, and hit the **NORTH FRONT STREET HISTORICAL DISTRICT**, including Yakima Avenue and E "B" Street, where a 22-car train now houses shops, selling everything from women's clothing to stationery and children's toys, and restaurants. The **YAKIMA VALLEY MUSEUM** (2105 Tieton Dr; 509/248-0747; open daily) appeals to all ages with exhibits of pioneer equipment, a children's "underground" museum, a thorough display on Yakima native Supreme Court Justice William O. Douglas, and an old-fashioned soda fountain.

   THE GREENWAY (509/453-8280) is a 10-mile-long path along the Yakima and Naches Rivers for bicyclists, walkers, runners, and in-line skaters. The paved path has nature trail off-shoots—sometimes allowing a view of bald eagles or blue herons—plus a couple of playgrounds. Entrance points to the Greenway are at Sarg Hubbard Park (111 S 18th St), Sherman Park (E Nob Hill Blvd), Rotary Lake ("R" St), Harlan Landing (west side of I-82 between Selah and Yakima), and the east end of Valley Mall Boulevard.

RESTAURANTS

Birchfield Manor / ★★

2018 BIRCHFIELD RD, YAKIMA; 509/452-1960

Birchfield Manor offers French-country dining, plus lodging. Owners Wil and Sandy Masset have filled the historic home with antiques. Trained in Europe, Wil offers six entrees—perhaps double breast of chicken Florentine or an authentic bouillabaisse—and a good list of Washington wines. The restaurant features a homey atmosphere in a relaxed, pastoral setting, and has a separate cigar room. Five B&B rooms ($95–$195) are above the restaurant, with six more in a separate building. Many have fireplaces or whirlpools, and guests have access to an outdoor pool. Personalized wine tours are available. *$$$; AE, DC, DIS, MC, V; checks OK; dinner Thurs–Sat; beer and wine; reservations not necessary; 2 miles from Yakima, exit 34 off I-82 onto Hwy 24.* &

Deli De Pasta / ★

7 N FRONT ST, YAKIMA; 509/453-0571

This intimate Italian-influenced cafe is in the North Front Street Historical District. The original owners sold to their daughter and son-in-law, Melissa and Ron Richter, who haven't changed the recipes or the red-and-white classic decor. Though the menu is primarily Italian—with good pastas such as the popular smoked-salmon ravioli—it includes some international recipes. Entrees might feature steak, salmon, or duck. The wine list has many local selections. *$; AE, MC, V; checks OK; dinner Mon–Sat; beer and wine; reservations recommended; ½ block off Yakima Ave.*

El Pastor / ★★

315 W WALNUT ST, YAKIMA; 509/453-5159

The Garcia family surprises visitors with a rare and reasonably priced dining experience. Flavorful Mexican fare starts with softball-sized bowls of cilantro-laden salsa and guacamole. Selections include chicken enchiladas, taquitos rancheros, arroz con pollo, tacos *al carbon*, steak à la *chicana*, and fajitas. The family partnership creates a friendly, casual feeling, and good customer service. *$; MC, V; checks OK; lunch, dinner Mon–Sat; beer only; reservations not necessary; at 4th Ave.*

Gasperetti's Restaurant / ★☆

1013 N FIRST ST, YAKIMA; 509/248-0628

Linen tablecloths and fresh flowers accent the two dining rooms in this 35-year-old restaurant. Walls are painted in an aged stucco style, reminiscent of old Tuscany. Brad Patterson, who helped owner John Gasperetti open the place, has returned as chef, after working in Seattle's four-star Lampreia restaurant. Appetizers such as smoked-salmon cheesecake complement a range of entrees, from pastas to Washington filet mignon in a sauce of marsala wine and Gorgonzola. The award-winning wine list offers a solid selection from Washington, California, and Italy. This is the place to be seen in Yakima. *$$; AE, DIS, MC, V;*

checks OK; lunch Tues–Fri, dinner Tues–Sat; full bar; reservations recommended; N 1st St exit off I-82. &

Grant's Brewery Pub / ★

32 N FRONT ST, YAKIMA; 509/575-2922

In 1982, Bert Grant opened the first brewpub in the United States since Prohibition was repealed. Located in Yakima's old train station, the pub is rich with atmosphere and thick with memories, despite the sale to Washington wine giant Stimson Lane (owner of Chateau Ste. Michelle, Columbia Crest, and others). There's seating at the bar, booths, and a few tables. Live music, including folk, can be enjoyed most weekends. The beer runs the gamut of styles, including hefeweizen, stouts, and cask-conditioned Scottish ales; some brews change seasonally. The food is typical pub fare, with fish-and-chips a favorite. Though Grant no longer owns the pub, he can be found there when he happens to be in town. *$; AE, MC, V; checks OK; lunch, dinner every day (Mon–Sat in winter); beer and wine; reservations not necessary; in old depot building, from N 1st St head west on Yakima Ave.*

Santiago's Gourmet Mexican Cooking / ★

111 E YAKIMA AVE, YAKIMA; 509/453-1644

Dramatic brick walls, Southwestern art, and a huge mural in the bar are highlights of this downtown Yakima Mexican restaurant. In 1999, owners Jar and Deb Arcand added an outside scene of the Yakima River canyon, one of the largest murals in the state. Santiago's opened in 1980 and continues to serve popular gourmet chalupas, fish tostadas, and tacos Santiago with beef, guacamole, and two cheeses. *$; MC, V; checks OK; lunch Mon–Fri, dinner Mon–Sat; full bar; reservations not necessary; downtown near 1st.*

LODGINGS

Oxford Inn / ★

1603 TERRACE HEIGHTS DR, YAKIMA; 800/521-3050

Each of the 96 basic rooms at this chain hotel is enhanced by a small balcony overlooking the Yakima River. Moderately priced, the former Rio Mirada Motor Inn has an outdoor heated pool (open in summer), and guests have easy access to the 10-mile Greenway path along the river. Pets OK. *$; AE, DC, DIS, MC, V; checks OK; exit 33-B off I-82.* &

A Touch of Europe B&B / ★★

220 N 16TH AVE, YAKIMA; 888/438-7073

This Queen Anne Victorian house, built in 1889, wins rave reviews. Owners Jim and Erika Cenci opened in 1995 with three elegant rooms tastefully filled with antiques. All rooms have private baths and air-conditioning; the Prince Victorian Mahogany Room has a gas fireplace. Erika, the chef, was raised in Germany and has written several cookbooks. Her European-style breakfast is served in the dining room, or privately in the turret by candlelight and classical music. Gourmet lunches, afternoon high tea, and dinners for up to 20 are available by arrangement. No smoking, pets, or children. *$$; AE, MC, V; checks OK; www.winesnw.com/toucheuropeb&b.htm; exit 31 off I-82, west on Hwy 12.*

Naches

LODGINGS

Whistlin' Jack Lodge / ★★

20800 HWY 410, NACHES; 800/827-2299

 You can almost fish from the front porch of some cabins, but this 1957 mountain hideaway is also ideal for hiking, alpine and cross-country skiing, or just escaping civilization. Weekend rates vary by type of room: cottage, bungalow, or motel unit. Cottages have full kitchens and hot tubs, and are close to the river (some as little as 10–20 feet away)—and make great private retreats. Guests who come with bigger plans—and want to dine out—opt for motel rooms or bungalows. Some catch their own dinner—but Whistlin' Jack also serves panfried trout in its restaurant, with live music Thursday through Saturday nights. In summer, it's a nice drive over Chinook Pass near Mount Rainier; in other seasons, the only access is through Yakima. The lodge also has a convenience store and a 24-hour gas pump. *$$; DIS, MC, V; checks OK; www.whistlinjacklodge.com; 40 miles west of Yakima.*

Toppenish

The town's best-known son, western artist Fred Oldfield, has turned Toppenish's streets into an art gallery with more than 50 historical murals—and a new one is painted each June. Such efforts by the **TOPPENISH MURAL SOCIETY** (5A Toppenish Ave; 509/865-6516) complement stores selling Western gear, antiques, and art, making this a nice place for a walking tour—and giving an authentic feel to rodeos held here in summer.

The **YAKAMA NATION CULTURAL HERITAGE CENTER** (off Hwy 97 and Buster Rd; 509/865-2800) includes an Indian museum, reference library, gift shop, Native American restaurant, theater, and the 76-foot-tall Winter Lodge for banquets. Nearby is the tribal-run **LEGENDS CASINO** (580 Fort Rd; 509/865-8800; www.yakamalegendscasino.com). **FORT SIMCOE STATE PARK** (open May–Sept), a frontier military post built in 1865, stands in desolate grandeur 30 miles west of Toppenish on Highway 220, on the Yakama Indian Reservation.

RESTAURANTS

El Ranchito / ★★

1319 E 1ST AVE, ZILLAH; 509/829-5880

El Ranchito, just across the river from Toppenish, is the perfect midday stop for tortillas. Servings are generous and authentic, from burritos to *barbacoa*—a mild, slow-barbecued mound of beef served in a tortilla shell. Don't expect anything fancy: order cafeteria style and sit at plastic-covered tables inside or out; it's like eating in a Mexican market. Tortillas are fresh from the adjoining factory, and the mini-*mercado* sells Mexican spices and pottery. *$; no credit cards; checks OK; breakfast, lunch, dinner every day; beer only; reservations not necessary; exit 54 off I-82.*

Sunnyside and Grandview

This is true farm country, and it's famous for its wine grapes, Concords, hops, corn, apples, cherries, cucumbers, onions, peaches, pears, peppers, garlic, and dairy products—with all the accompanying aromas. If you need a snack or want to stretch your legs, stop at **DARIGOLD'S DAIRY FAIR** (400 Alexander Rd, Sunnyside; 509/837-4321). It's open daily for a sandwich, scoop of old-fashioned ice cream, a free cheese-tasting, and a self-guided tour of the factory.

RESTAURANTS

Dykstra House Restaurant

114 BIRCH AVE, GRANDVIEW; 509/882-2082

Dykstra House makes bread and rolls from hand-ground whole wheat grown in the surrounding Horse Heaven Hills. Owner Linda Hartshorn also takes advantage of local in-season produce—like asparagus—in her entrees, but her specialty is dessert. At least six homemade choices are offered each day. Favorites are apple caramel pecan torte and Dykstra House chocolate pie, served since Hartshorn opened the place in 1984. The 1914 mansion is decorated in antiques; two dealers sell items upstairs. *$$; AE, DC, DIS, MC, V; checks OK; lunch Tues–Sat, dinner Fri–Sat; beer and wine; reservations recommended (Sat dinner); exit 75 off I-82.*

Snipes Mountain Microbrewery & Restaurant / ★

905 YAKIMA VALLEY HWY, SUNNYSIDE; 509/837-2739

A huge stone fireplace and exposed rafters make Snipes feel like a mountain lodge in the center of the Yakima Valley. The tasty beer brewed on the premises, good-quality steak-house fare, and friendly service make it a good stop for lunch or dinner. Meals can be as fancy as you like, ranging from wood-fired pizza (try the Mountaineer—"beer-b-q" chicken, ale-caramelized onions, smoked Gouda, and pine nuts) to hazelnut-crusted rack of lamb with mustard demi-glace. *$; AE, DIS, MC, V; checks OK; lunch, dinner every day; beer and wine; reservations not necessary; exit 63 or 69 off I-82.* &

Taqueria la Fogata

1204 YAKIMA VALLEY HWY, SUNNYSIDE; 509/839-9019

The small, simple Mexican taqueria was remodeled in 1999, although its menu still reflects local tastes. The Michoacan specialties include posole—a stew of pork back, feet, and hominy—and menudo, a tripe and cow's-feet stew in a spicy sauce. Less adventurous diners can stick with tacos and burritos. *$; MC, V; checks OK; breakfast, lunch, dinner every day; full bar; reservations not necessary; middle of town.*

LODGINGS

Cozy Rose Inn / ★

1220 FORSELL RD, GRANDVIEW; 800/575-8381

B&B owners Mark and Jennie Jackson opened in 1995 and offer four rooms, each with a private entrance, bathroom, fireplace, cable TV, and stereo. The Country Hideaway Suite upstairs has a private view deck, living room, refrigerator, and microwave. The Rose Room has an adjoining mother-in-law bedroom. The Irish House has a full dining room, a living room, and a deck. Spendiest is the Secret Garden Suite with a two-person Jacuzzi and "king-size wonder bed." Breakfast is delivered to your room; typical fare includes French toast, omelets, and pecan pancakes. The Jacksons grow their own strawberries, herbs, and apples. They keep llamas on the property and are near a vineyard for a romantic walk. No smoking; well-behaved children over 12 OK. *$$–$$$; no credit cards; checks OK; exit 69 off I-82.*

Sunnyside Inn Bed & Breakfast / ★

804 E EDISON AVE, SUNNYSIDE; 800/221-4195

Owners Don and Karen Vlieger play host to these 13 rooms, all named after women in their family. The B&B is in two houses, one built in 1919, the other in 1925. Four rooms have outside entrances; all have phones, cable TV, air-conditioning, and Jacuzzis; and some have VCRs or fireplaces. Most popular are the Jean Room (with king-size bed), Karen (gas fireplace), Lola (sun porch), and the newest, Sherrie (a suite). If you leave the breakfast table hungry, it's your own fault for not eating enough blueberry pancakes, sausage, and fresh fruit. *$$; AE, MC, V; checks OK; exit 63 or 69 off I-82.*

Prosser

Who can resist a quick stop in Prosser, the self-purported "pleasant place with pleasant people"? Every day, the tasting room at **CHUKAR CHERRIES** (306 Wine Country Rd; 509/786-2055) gives out samples of the local Bing and Rainier cherries—especially good once they're dried and covered in chocolate.

LODGINGS

Palmer Farm Bed and Breakfast / ★

42901 N RIVER RD, BENTON CITY; 800/635-3131

This rustic farmhouse has been tastefully restored to its 1902 splendor, complete with period wallpaper and Scottish lace curtains—plus modern central air-conditioning. Trees shade the large, grassy grounds, with a view of Red Mountain vineyards. The house has a wrap-around porch and comfortable common areas, such as a glassed-in sunroom and peaceful library. It's a great base for wine-touring, because at least six wineries are within a few minutes' drive (Benton City is about 14 miles east of Prosser). Owners Virginia and Bill McKenna offer four rooms, featuring sloped ceilings and floor-length windows, and shared bathrooms (two full, two half). Breakfast might consist of lemon scones, ham,

LEWIS AND CLARK TRAIL BICENTENNIAL

Exploring the Pacific Northwest is nothing new: the concept was made famous about 200 years ago by Meriwether Lewis and William Clark.

The bicentennial celebration of Lewis and Clark's Corps of Discovery runs from 2003 to 2006. Washington, Oregon, and the nine other states along the trail are preparing for "historical tourists" following all or part of the 3,700-mile route that led to the non-Native settlement of the Northwest. The trail is clearly outlined with signs (featuring the forward-looking silhouettes of Lewis and Clark), historical markers, parks, and interpretive centers. Many sites also delve into the other side of the story: the Corps's long-term effect on the region's Native tribes. What started as friendly relations built on trading and exploring led to great tragedy for many tribal people.

Lewis and Clark started along the Missouri River from Illinois in May 1804, sent out by President Thomas Jefferson to find an overland link to the Pacific Ocean. Five months later, they entered what is now the southeast corner of Washington State on the Snake River. The Alpowai Interpretive Center in **Chief Timothy State Park** (on Silcott Rd, 8 miles west of Clarkston; 509/758-9580 or 800/233-0321) focuses on the white explorers' meeting with the Nez Perce Indians. **Lewis and Clark Trail State Park** (on Hwy 12, 4½ miles west of Dayton; 509/337-6457 or 800/233-0321) features camp sites, picnic areas, and a 1-mile interpretive trail.

The Tri-Cities is the farthest point upriver on the Columbia explored by Lewis and Clark. **Sacajawea State Park** (off Hwy 12 near Pasco; 509/545-2361), at the confluence of the Snake and Columbia Rivers, is the only park along the trail honoring the

eggs, and summer berries picked on the grounds. No smoking, no pets, no children. *$; no credit cards; checks OK; palmerfarm@bentonrea.com; palmerfarm 1902.hypermart.net/; exit 96 off I-82.*

The Tri-Cities

The Tri-Cities' main attractions are the rivers (the Yakima, Snake, and Columbia converge here), wineries (more than a dozen are scattered between Prosser and Walla Walla), and golf courses (nine public or private courses). But the area also has an intriguing history, from Lewis and Clark's stop at what is now Sacajawea State Park in Pasco to Kennewick's annual summer hydroplane races to Richland's role in ending World War II with the top-secret atomic research at Hanford. The region is made up of three cities (although Richland now sports "suburbs" of North and West Richland) and two counties (Benton and Walla Walla), but the **TRI-CITIES VISITOR AND CONVENTION BUREAU**

Indian woman guide. The 284-acre park includes the Sacajawea Interpretive Center (509/545-2361), housing a collection of Native artifacts; it is run by volunteers and open by appointment for group tours.

Paddling down the Columbia, the explorers talked with Natives near what is now **Maryhill State Park** (off Hwy 14, Goldendale; open year-round). Maryhill Museum (35 Maryhill Museum Dr, Goldendale; 509/773-3733; open Mar 15–Nov 15), on the hill across from Biggs, Oregon, has an outstanding display of Indian baskets and stone tools. **Beacon Rock State Park** (35 miles east of Vancouver on Hwy 14; 509/427-8265 or 800/233-0321) was where the explorers first noticed the effects of the Pacific Ocean's tide.

From the site of what is now **Lewis and Clark Campsite State Park** (2 miles southeast of Chinook on Hwy 101; 360/642-3078), the 33 weary travelers first saw the Pacific Ocean. Washington State's **Lewis and Clark Interpretive Center** (2½ miles southeast of Ilwaco, off Hwy 101; 360/642-3078) is on Cape Disappointment, where the explorers officially reached the Pacific.

After being pounded by cold and wet winds, they turned south to establish a winter campsite, however, at what is now **Fort Clatsop National Memorial** (92343 Fort Clatsop Rd; 503/861-2471; open daily), 5 miles southwest of Astoria, Oregon. The visitor center includes a replica of Lewis and Clark's winter quarters.

Those wanting to know more should contact the **Lewis and Clark National Historic Trail** (402/221-3471; www.nps.gov/lecl) or the nonprofit **National Lewis and Clark Bicentennial Council** (888/999-1803). —*Melissa O'Neil*

(6951 W Grandridge Blvd, Vista Field Airport, Kennewick; 800/254-5824; www.visittri-cities.com) pulls them together to provide a seamless visit for tourists.

Richland

Richland was once a secret city, hidden away while the atomic bomb workers did research in the 1940s. As nuclear reactors close and the controversy over hazardous waste continues, civic leaders are working hard on industrial diversification. But the "Atomic City" is still weaning itself from dependence on the federal Hanford Nuclear Reservation, where workers are finding ways to clean up radioactive waste left over from World War II. The town, with a highly educated population, is proud of its nuclear past—the local high school, nicknamed Atomic High, features a mushroom cloud in its school sign—and you'll see other similar symbols of Hanford's presence here. The **COLUMBIA RIVER EXHIBITION OF HISTORY SCIENCE & TECHNOLOGY** (95 Lee Blvd; 509/943-9000; www.crehst.org) displays the region's history from ice age through nuclear age. Hands-on exhibits explain how the Tri-Cities area sprang up during World War II, when the federal government created Hanford.

COLUMBIA RIVER JOURNEYS (1229 Columbia Park Trail; 509/734-9941 or 509/943-0231; May–Oct 15) offers jet-boat tours through HANFORD REACH, an ecologically preserved section of the Columbia River. Beautiful HOWARD AMON PARK (509/942-7529) lies along the Columbia River, with a paved path for bicycling, walking, or in-line skating.

ALLIED ARTS GALLERY (89 Lee Blvd; 509/943-9815) displays the work of local artists and sponsors the annual art festival in late July with a sidewalk show and handmade arts and crafts for sale. For a quick bite there's the TASTE cafe (701 George Washington Wy; 509/946-4142), which serves delicious creative pasta salads, gourmet sandwiches, muffins, homemade soups, and large cookies.

RESTAURANTS

Atomic Ale Brewpub & Eatery / ★

1015 LEE BLVD, RICHLAND; 509/946-5465

The microbrews are too good for Homer Simpson's taste in beer, but he'd appreciate their names: Half-life Hefeweizen and Plutonium Porter, for example. The standard pub food—pizza, salads, and soups—is good and the house specialty is wood-fired gourmet pizzas made with garlic, basil, shrimp, and other flavorful morsels. Finish with a B Reactor brownie. *$; AE, DIS, MC, V; checks OK; lunch, dinner Mon–Sat; beer and wine; reservations not necessary; take George Washington Wy exit off I-82.*

The Emerald of Siam / ★

1314 JADWIN AVE, RICHLAND; 509/946-9328

Thai-born Ravadi Quinn is known for sharing her native culture, through community school classes and in a cookbook. Her authentic recipes include curries, satays, noodles, and black-rice pudding. Lunch is a buffet. Dinner includes a full vegetarian menu—most popular is the sweet-and-sour tofu. *$; AE, DIS, MC, V; local checks only; lunch, dinner Mon–Sat; beer and wine; reservations not necessary; Uptown Shopping Center.*

Monterosso's Italian Restaurant / ★★

1026 LEE BLVD, RICHLAND; 509/946-4525

Formerly Vannini's, this gourmet experience is largely inspired by owners Aaron and Devin Burks's honeymoon to the Italian Riviera town of Monterosso. Coincidentally, Monterosso is Italian for "Red Mountain," which is the name of an area just west of Richland now gaining international fame for its red wines. The restaurant is in a 1947 Northern Pacific Pullman dining car restored to create an intimate atmosphere—one of the most romantic found in the Tri-Cities. Entrees include seafood, chicken, steak, veal, and about 15 kinds of pasta. Try the *tortellini oreste*—tortellini stuffed with ricotta, mozzarella, and Parmesan, then sautéed in creamy pesto sauce with sun-dried tomatoes and walnuts. Those in the know recognize Monterosso's food as authentic Italian cuisine; those who aren't just think it's delicious. The wine list is limited but high in quality, featuring such local wineries as Balcom & Moe and Hedges Cellars. If you don't see a particular wine on the list, ask if it's in the wine cellar. *$; AE, DIS, MC, V; checks OK; dinner Mon–Sat; beer and wine; reservations recommended; off George Washington Wy.*

LODGINGS

Red Lion Hanford House / ★

802 GEORGE WASHINGTON WY, RICHLAND; 509/946-7611 OR 800/733-5466
With its 150 rooms remodeled in 1999, Hanford House remains one of the most popular places to stay—although the Tri-Cities area has no shortage of hotels. What makes this one special is its prime location on the Columbia River, select view rooms, and easy access to riverfront Howard Amon Park. If you can't get a room on the river, ask for one facing the grassy courtyard and swimming pool (unless a concert there is planned). Visit the new fitness center if it's too hot to exert yourself outside. The casual-dining restaurant—serving steaks, hamburgers, and the like—also has a great view. *$$; AE, DC, DIS, MC, V; checks OK; Hwy 240 to George Washington Wy.* &

Kennewick

Kennewick is the largest of the Tri-Cities, sharing a border with Richland and an architecturally magnificent **CABLE BRIDGE** (lighted at night) with Pasco. The city is known as Southeast Washington's retail center and has several malls, including Columbia Center, but the place to visit is **COLUMBIA PARK** (between Hwy 240 and Columbia River; 509/585-4293). At the park's east end, near the Highway 395 blue bridge, volunteers in 1999 built the wooden castle–like **PLAYGROUND OF DREAMS** with climbing structures and twisty slides. It's next to the **FAMILY FISHING POND** (509/585-4293), where adults can teach children under 15 to catch and release fish. Both are handicapped accessible. The park also has a Frisbee golf course and is the site of the annual **COLUMBIA CUP UNLIMITED HYDROPLANE RACES** (509/547-2203; www.hydroracing.com) in late July. Winter sports fans here focus on the **TRI-CITY AMERICANS** hockey team (509/736-0606), which plays at the Coliseum (7100 W Quinault Ave; 509/736-2354).

RESTAURANTS

Casa Chapala / ★

107 E COLUMBIA DR, KENNEWICK; 509/586-4224
29 E BELFAIR PL, KENNEWICK; 509/783-8080
Owners Lupe and Lucina Barragan are known throughout the community for their friendly smiles, and for organizing Tri-Citians in 1999 to make the world's largest burrito. Mexican food here is reasonably authentic and quite filling. The menu has kid-size choices and several low-fat options. Beware: "Large" margaritas are huge. *$; AE, DIS, MC, V; checks OK; lunch, dinner*

every day; full bar; reservations not necessary; www.casachapala.com; east end of Kennewick, beside Hwy 240 on-ramp (Columbia Dr), at Hwy 12 and Columbia Center Blvd (Belfair Pl).

Cedars Pier I / ★★

355 CLOVER ISLAND DR, KENNEWICK; 509/582-2143

Rebuilt after a 1998 fire, the restaurant is a step above "Tri-Cities casual." Cedars is frequented by boaters who dock here after a jaunt on the Columbia River, however, so don't get too dressed up. The cuisine is high-quality surf-and-turf, with various delicious cuts of meat including sirloin and T-bone. The seafood menu might include grilled ahi with a variety of sauces, salmon, and crab—both Dungeness and Alaskan king. The clam chowder is better than average, and appetizers range from heaping plates of nachos to breaded oysters to chicken satay in peanut sauce. The wine list is good, with many excellent regional choices, including the Hogue Genesis series and Glen Fiona syrahs. If it's warm, sit on the patio. No matter the weather, ask for a table with a view of the cable bridge. *$$; AE, DC, DIS, MC, V; checks OK; dinner every day; full bar; reservations recommended; follow signs to Clover Island.*

Chez Chaz Bistro / ★

5011 W CLEARWATER AVE, KENNEWICK; 509/735-2138

Don't let the building's outward appearance make you hesitate; inside the decor is tasteful, if whimsical, and the food is good. The owners' large collection of salt-and-pepper shakers adorn tables and cover the top of the dessert display, and food- and wine-related artwork hangs on the walls. Chez Chaz offers continental cuisine and several styles of chicken sauté, which might include French, Thai, Alsatian, Turkish, and Italian. The sun bread appetizer (a delectable combination of French bread, melted cheese, and sun-dried tomatoes drizzled in olive oil) alone is worth the trip, but don't leave without at least sharing a piece of chocolate cabernet torte with French-press coffee. The Washington wine list is solid. Box lunches are available with advance notice. *$$; DIS, MC, V; checks OK; lunch Mon–Sat, dinner Tues–Sat; beer and wine; reservations recommended (dinner); between Union and Edison Sts.*

Sundance Grill / ★

413 N KELLOGG ST, STE B, KENNEWICK; 509/783-6505

The casual, business-lunch atmosphere here segues into dinner with tablecloths and live music Tuesdays through Saturdays. Chef Jim McBryar changes the menu every three months, and features seasonal fish and produce, such as Copper River salmon, stuffed portobellos, lamb chops, and panfried oysters. Standing specialties include seafood chowder, prime beef, and crème brûlée. The wine list has more than 100 choices, most from Washington. *$$; AE, DIS, MC, V; checks OK; lunch, dinner Mon–Sat, brunch Sun; full bar; reservations recommended (dinner); between Clearwater Ave and Canal Dr.*

LODGINGS

Casablanca B&B / ★

94806 E GRANADA CT, KENNEWICK; 888/627-0676

Owners Candace and Dave Dillman run a country-style B&B in a desert canyon five minutes east of Kennewick. Three comfortable rooms have private baths and French doors leading to the garden, terrace, and a vineyard view. Rooms have king- or queen-size beds, reading chairs, and desks. The guest sitting room has a big-screen TV and VCR. Breakfast is self-serve continental, although you can arrange to join the owners on the deck to plan your day of wine touring, golfing, sightseeing, or a sunset carriage ride. No smoking. *$$; MC, V; checks OK; www.casablancabb.com; exit 109 off I-82, call for directions.*

Pasco

Pasco has the most diverse population of the three cities—about half the residents are Hispanic—and an economy based on light manufacturing and food processing. Historically a railroad town, Pasco is home to the **WASHINGTON STATE RAILROADS HISTORICAL SOCIETY MUSEUM** (122 N Tacoma St; 509/543-4159; Apr–autumn), which features old motorcars, railcars, and steam locomotives, including the state's oldest—the Blue Mountain, circa 1977.

The local minor league professional baseball team plays at **POSSE BASEBALL STADIUM** (6200 Burden Rd; 509/547-6773) next to soccer and softball fields and the Tri-Cities Youth Soccer Complex. Downtown is the **PASCO FARMERS MARKET** (4th and Lewis; 509/545-0738; weekends May–Nov), one of the state's largest open-air produce markets. Farmers bring truckloads of asparagus, corn, and other vegetables at dawn—and sell out by noon. **SACAJAWEA STATE PARK** honors the remarkable Indian woman; see "Lewis and Clark Trail Bicentennial" in this chapter.

Several dams in Washington State were targeted in the late 1990s for possible removal. The goal is to increase the water supply for salmon, but flip-side concerns include possible effects on power generation and water levels for barges. **ICE HARBOR DAM** (east of Pasco on Hwy 124E; 509/547-7781) along the Snake River near Burbank is one of those slated for removal. The visitor center (open daily, Apr–Oct) features a self-guided tour showing an operating turbine, an indoor viewing area of the fish ladder, and the locks.

LODGINGS

Doubletree Hotel / ★★

2525 N 20TH AVE, PASCO; 509/547-0701 OR 800/222-8733

The Doubletree is the Tri-Cities' largest hotel, with 279 rooms, and its huge ballroom is popular for conventions and festivals. It's conveniently located next to the Tri-Cities Airport, as well as Sun Willows Golf Course and Columbia Basin College. The hotel, formerly a Red Lion, has two outdoor pools and an exercise facility. The restaurant was upgraded in 1999 to the Vineyards Steak House, featuring vintages from Tri-Cities wineries; the Grizzly Bar

SOUTHEAST WASHINGTON THREE-DAY WINE TOUR

Washington is the second-largest wine-producing state in the nation (behind California), and more than half of its wineries are in Eastern Washington, where 99 percent of the grapes are grown. The state's wine industry saw incredible growth in the late 1990s—with nearly 50 new wineries opening in 1999 alone—bringing the total to about 140. Most, though not all, of these have tasting rooms open for visits year-round.

DAY ONE: Start in Yakima and drive to Zillah and the **Wine Glass Cellars** (260 N Bonair Rd, Zillah; 509/829-3011) tasting room. Next sample a few wines at **Portteus** (5201 Highland Dr, Zillah; 509/829-6970). Take a break with an authentic Mexican lunch at **El Ranchito** before heading south on Interstate 82 to the Outlook exit, where you follow the signs to **Tefft Cellars** (1320 Independence Rd, Outlook; 509/837-7651). Then drive to Prosser for tasting at **Hogue Cellars** (Wine Country Rd, Prosser; 509/786-4557). Take an afternoon drive to the Red Mountain growing area near Benton City. Taste at **Kiona** (44612 N Sunset Rd NE, Benton City; 509/588-3219), then see the underground barrel-storage tunnels at **Terra Blanca** (34715 DeMoss Rd, Benton City; 509/588-6082). In Prosser, check in at the **Palmer Farm B&B**, then head for Richland's **Atomic Ale Brewpub & Eatery** for a casual meal.

DAY TWO: After a delightful breakfast at the B&B, stop in Prosser for fixings for a picnic lunch and take Highway 221 south to the Northwest's largest winery, **Columbia Crest** (Columbia Crest Dr, Patterson; 509/875-2061), right on the Columbia. Taste the wine, take the tour, then eat your lunch on the grounds by the fountain. Return to the Tri-Cities on a loop route east on Highway 14 and north on Interstate 82, and visit

is one of the town's hottest nightspots. *$$; AE, DC, DIS, MC, V; checks OK; exit 12 off I-82/Hwy 395.* &

Walla Walla and the Blue Mountains

The Walla Walla Valley is an important historical area: the Lewis and Clark expedition passed through in 1805, fur trappers began traveling up the Columbia River from Fort Astoria in 1811 and set up a fort in 1818, and in 1836 missionary Marcus Whitman built a medical mission west of the present town. But when a virulent attack of measles hit area tribes in November 1847, a group of enraged Cayuse men killed the missionaries. The incident came to be called the Whitman Massacre. The excellent interpretive center at the **WHITMAN MISSION NATIONAL HISTORIC SITE** (7 miles west of Walla Walla along Hwy 12; 509/529-2761; open daily) sketches out the story of the mission and the massacre; there aren't any historic buildings, but the simple outline of

Pasco's **Gordon Brothers Cellars** (5960 Burden Blvd, Pasco; 509/547-6331), off Road 68. Next stop is back across the Columbia River in south Richland, to neighboring **Bookwalter Winery** (894 Tulip Ln, Richland; 509/627-5000) and **Barnard Griffin Winery** (878 Tulip Ln, Richland; 509/627-0266). Not far away, on the west end of Kennewick, is **Powers Winery/Badger Mountain Vineyard** (1106 Jurupa St, Kennewick; 800/643-9463). Check in at Kennewick's **Casablanca B&B**, then dine at **Sundance Grill**.

DAY THREE: Fortified by breakfast on the deck of Casablanca, leave Kennewick by about 9am on your way east on Highway 12 to Walla Walla area wineries. Slow down in the tiny town of Lowden to taste award-winning wines at **Woodward Canyon Winery** (11920 W Hwy 12, Touchet; 509/525-4129) and **L'Ecole No. 41** (41 Lowden School Rd, Lowden; 509/525-0940). When you reach downtown Walla Walla, stop at the bright-yellow storefront of **Cayuse Vineyards** (17 E Main St, Walla Walla; 509/526-0686), then eat a simple lunch next door at **Merchants Ltd.** Three doors down is **Waterbrook Winery**'s (31 E Main St, Walla Walla; 509/522-1262) tasting room. It's a short hop to **Canoe Ridge Vineyard** (1102 W Cherry St, Walla Walla; 509/527-0885), then head to **Walla Walla Vintners** (Mill Creek Rd, Walla Walla; 509/525-4724) for the tasting appointment you made two weeks ago. Finish the wine tour in Dayton with a swim in the pool at your night's lodging, the **Purple House B&B Inn**, followed by a gourmet dinner at **Patit Creek Restaurant**—it's best to make reservations well in advance.

the mission in the ground is strangely affecting. A hike up an adjacent hill to an overlook offers the best impression of what the area looked like to the Whitmans and their fellow settlers. The mission became an important station on the Oregon Trail, and Narcissa Whitman's arrival was notable in that she and Eliza Spalding, also with the Whitman party, were the first white women to cross the continent overland.

Agriculture is important to the namesake county, known worldwide for its sweet onions and fine wines (see "Southeast Washington Three-day Wine Tour" in this chapter). The WALLA WALLA VALLEY CHAMBER OF COMMERCE (29 E Sumac St; 877/998-4748; www.wwchamber.com) has information on how to buy Walla Walla sweet onions, usually in season mid-June through mid-July.

Walla Walla

Downtown Walla Walla—one street, circa 1870—is considered one of the nation's best examples of a restored downtown. The community is strong on the arts, and the WALLA WALLA SYMPHONY (509/529-8020; www.wwsymphony.com) is the oldest symphony orchestra west of the Mississippi. Performances are held in Cordiner Hall (345 Boyer Ave) on the grounds of private **WHITMAN COLLEGE** (509/527-5176), which anchors the town and has a lovely campus. **FORT WALLA WALLA** (The Dalles Military Rd; 509/525-7703) has a museum featuring 14 historic buildings and a collection of pioneer artifacts. The adjacent city park allows summer camping.

RESTAURANTS

Merchants Ltd. / ★★

21 E MAIN ST, WALLA WALLA; 509/525-0900
Brothers Bob and Mike Austin traded in their upstairs dining room for more ground-level space, now seating 300 people across three storefronts downtown and serving healthy morning and midday meals. Live music plays at least once a month. A full, in-house bakery joins imported cheeses and meats for simple yet tasty breakfasts and lunches. A corner is dedicated to international groceries, another to wines. Merchants has been a mainstay—especially for upscale liberal-arts college students who thrive on Wednesday-only spaghetti dinners—since 1976. *$; AE, DIS, MC, V; checks OK; breakfast, lunch Mon–Sat, dinner Wed; beer and wine; reservations not necessary; 2nd St exit off Hwy 12.* &

Paisano's Italian Restaurant & Catering / ★★

26 E MAIN ST, STE 1, WALLA WALLA; 509/527-3511
Paisano's serves tasty, generous portions in a sophisticated setting. Chef Jennifer Parent teams with Mom and Dad—Judy and Lewis Parent—in the downtown restaurant that opened in 1996. Creative sandwiches—pesto chicken or Italian burger with prosciutto, mozzarella, and sun-dried tomatoes—come with pasta salad and fresh bread to dip in herb-infused olive oil. It's more than enough to prepare for an afternoon of wine tasting. Dinner creations might include smoked-duck capellini, scampi Paisanos, and angel hair pasta tossed with fresh herbs and olive oil. *$$; MC, V; checks OK; lunch, dinner Mon–Sat; beer and wine; reservations not necessary; 2nd St exit off Hwy 12, across from Merchants.* &

LODGINGS

Green Gables Inn / ★★

922 BONSELLA ST, WALLA WALLA; 888/525-5501
The title character from L. M. Montgomery's *Anne of Green Gables* series loved staying in guest rooms. Margaret and Jim Buchan incorporate that spirit in five rooms named for topics in the popular book, like Idlewild, with a fireplace and Jacuzzi, and Dryad's Bubble, with a small balcony. The Carriage House is good for families because it is separate from the main house and gives kids more room to run around. Full breakfast is served on fine china by candlelight. A wraparound porch and air-conditioning make for pleasant summer evenings. *$$; AE, DIS, MC, V; checks OK; greengables@hscis.net; www.greengablesinn.com; Clinton St exit off Hwy 12.*

Dayton

Dayton is a small farming town northeast of Walla Walla and one of the first communities established in Washington State. Small wonder it's chock full of historic buildings—almost 90 Victorian-era structures. The **DAYTON CHAMBER OF COMMERCE** (166 E Main St; 800/882-6299; www.historicdayton.com) offers information for a self-guided walking tour. The **DAYTON HISTORICAL DEPOT** (222 E Commercial St; 509/382-2026; tours Tues–Sat), built in 1881, is the state's oldest remaining railroad station and now a museum. The **COLUMBIA COUNTY COURTHOUSE** (341 E Main St; 509/382-4542), circa 1887, still holds government offices.

Besides old buildings, Dayton is known for easy access to skiing at **BLUE-WOOD SKI RESORT** (22 miles south of Dayton via Hwy 12; 509/382-4725; www.bluewood.com), in Umatilla National Forest in the Blue Mountains. It has clear skies, dry powder, and the second-highest base elevation (4,545 feet) in the state.

RESTAURANTS

Patit Creek Restaurant / ★★★

725 E DAYTON AVE, DAYTON; 509/382-2625

This small-town restaurant is known regionwide for its consistent continental cuisine and is one of the most highly rated restaurants this side of the mountains. Though the atmosphere is casual, the food is sophisticated and nicely presented. Bruce and Heather Hiebert turned a 1920s service station into a 10-table restaurant famous for fillet steaks in green peppercorn sauce, chèvre-stuffed dates wrapped in bacon, fresh vegetables, and huckleberry pie. The wine list is strong on Walla Walla selections. Patit Creek is a classic off-the-beaten-path discovery and the perfect, classy place to end a day of winery touring in the Walla Walla Valley or skiing at Bluewood. Just don't plan to drop in and expect a table; reservations are recommended at least two weeks in advance. *$$; MC, V; local checks only; lunch Wed–Fri, dinner Wed–Sat; beer and wine; reservations recommended; north end of town.* &

LODGINGS

The Purple House B&B Inn

415 E CLAY ST, DAYTON; 800/486-2574

This 1882 house really is purple, a B&B since the late 1980s. Four rooms have modern amenities, including air-conditioning. Two have private baths, while the others share one large bathroom. Innkeeper Christine D. Williscroft is a native of southern Germany, which shows in the inn's decor, as does her passion for Chinese antiques and Oriental rugs. Williscroft has two small dogs and welcomes other small pets—or children—if given advance warning. Full breakfast, which might include strudel or crepes, is served in a walled-in courtyard next to the private swimming pool. Lunch and dinner can be arranged for in-house guests and groups of six or more. *$$–$$$; MC, V; checks OK; 1 block off Hwy 12.* &

The Weinhard Hotel / ★

235 E MAIN ST, DAYTON; 509/382-4032

Fresh flowers and fruit in each room greet guests—a pleasant surprise for those skeptical of finding uptown style in tiny Dayton. Owners Dan and Ginny Butler restored the old Weinhard building (built as a saloon and lodge hall in the late 1800s) and filled it with elegant Victorian antiques that they collected from across the country. The 15 rooms are furnished with antique dressers, desks, and canopied beds. (Tall people, however, should ask for one of the longer beds.) All rooms have private baths, and the Signature Room has a Jacuzzi spa. Inquire about packages for romance, skiing, and wine-tasting. Inside the hotel is The Weinhard Cafe (lunch and dinner Wed–Sun), serving tasty fare in a casual bistro setting. Entrees range from homemade tamales to sockeye salmon with shiitake mushrooms and roasted garlic sauce. The wine list includes hard-to-find Leonetti Cellars offerings. No smoking. *$$–$$$; AE, MC, V; checks OK; www.weinhard.com; downtown.* &

Pullman and the Palouse

Washington's golden Palouse region, next to Idaho and north of the Blue Mountains, is made up of seemingly endless, rolling hills covered with wheat, lentils, and other crops. The area also boasts rivers, including the Snake, and several geological wonders, all of which make good day trips.

KAMIAK BUTTE COUNTY PARK (13 miles north of Pullman on Hwy 27) is a good place for a picnic with a view of the undulating hills. **STEPTOE BUTTE STATE PARK** (about 30 miles north of Pullman on Hwy 195) is great for a panoramic view or stargazing, but bring a windbreaker.

At **PALOUSE FALLS STATE PARK** (2 miles off Hwy 261 between Washtucna and Tucannon; 509/549-3551 or 800/233-0321), the Palouse River roars over a basalt cliff higher than Niagara Falls, dropping 198 feet into a steep-walled basin on its way to the Snake. A hiking trail leads to an overlook above the falls, most spectacular during spring runoff. Downstream is the **MARMES ROCK SHELTER**, where archaeologists found 10,000-year-old relics of North American inhabitants. Camping and canoeing are allowed in **LYONS FERRY STATE PARK** (on Hwy 261, 7 miles north of Starbuck; 509/646-3252 or 800/233-0321), at the confluence of the Palouse and Snake Rivers; it also has a public boat launch.

Pullman

The heart of the Palouse beats in Pullman, at the junction of Highways 195 and 27 near the Idaho border, and the heart of Pullman is **WASHINGTON STATE UNIVERSITY** (visitor center: 225 N Grand; 509/335-8633; www.wsu.edu). WSU started in 1892 and is where 17,000 die-hard Cougars live during the academic year. Campus tours are available weekdays year-round. A trip through town wouldn't be complete without sampling the ice cream or Cougar Gold cheese made at the WSU creamery, **FERDINAND'S** (inside Agriculture Science Bldg on WSU campus; 509/335-2141; open weekdays).

The town of Pullman also is known for its historic buildings, with brick masonry and early 1900s classical and Georgian architecture. Find more information at the **PULLMAN CHAMBER OF COMMERCE** (415 N Grand Ave; 800/365-6948; www.pullman.com).

RESTAURANTS

Hilltop Restaurant

920 OLSON ST, PULLMAN; 509/334-2555

This steak house has an incredible view of the university and surrounding hills, a romantic vista complemented by linens and attentive service. Red meat is the specialty, from prime rib and steaks to Sunday's midday roast beef family dinner. Homemade desserts include cheesecakes, mud pie, and chocolate truffles. Hilltop is connected to the three-story, 59-room Hawthorne Inn & Suites, where it offers room service. *$$; AE, DIS, MC, V; checks OK; lunch Sun–Fri, dinner every day; full bar; reservations not necessary; hilltop@completebbs. com; on Davis Wy.*

Swilly's Cafe & Catering / ★★

200 NE KAMIAKEN ST, PULLMAN; 509/334-3395

The renovated historic Hutchison Photography studio maintains its dedication to art, with local artwork displayed on the dining room's exposed-brick walls. Opened in 1986 by Jill Aesoph, Swilly's overlooks Paradise Creek in downtown Pullman. Casual warmth translates into homemade soups, salads, sandwiches, and burgers, plus more sophisticated dinner entrees such as Moroccan lamb, Thai shrimp, grilled tenderloin, and various pastas. Microbrews are on tap, and a moderately priced wine list is strong on Washington choices. *$; AE, DC, DIS, MC, V; checks OK; lunch, dinner Mon–Sat; beer and wine; reservations not necessary; at Olson.* &

LODGINGS

The Churchyard Inn B&B / ★

206 ST. BONIFACE ST, UNIONTOWN; 509/229-3200

The Churchyard Inn is next door to the historic St. Boniface Catholic Church in tiny Uniontown, 16 miles south of Pullman on Highway 195. The three-story house was built as a parish in 1905, converted to a convent in 1913, then turned into a B&B by Linda and Marvin Entel in 1995. Each of seven uniquely decorated rooms has a private bath. On the top floor is the 1,200-square-foot Palouse Suite, with a great room big enough for seminars or wedding receptions, a kitchen, dining area, gas fireplace, views from every window, two queen hide-abeds, and a separate room with a king bed. Breakfast and beverages are served in the dining room with a view of the Palouse farmlands. Catering is available by arrangement for groups of six or more. No pets; no children under 14.

$$–$$$; DIS, MC, V; checks OK; pullman-wa.com/housing/chrchbb.htm; 2 blocks west of Hwy 195. &

Paradise Creek Quality Inn

1050 SE BISHOP BLVD, PULLMAN; 800/669-3212

Within walking distance of WSU, this motel is just far enough off Highway 270 (the route to Moscow, Idaho) to avoid traffic noise. The 66 rooms are standard, but convenient. It's situated literally over the meandering creek for which it's named. *$; AE, DIS, MC, V; checks OK; www.qualityinn.com; ¼ mile east of campus.*

SPOKANE AND NORTHEASTERN WASHINGTON

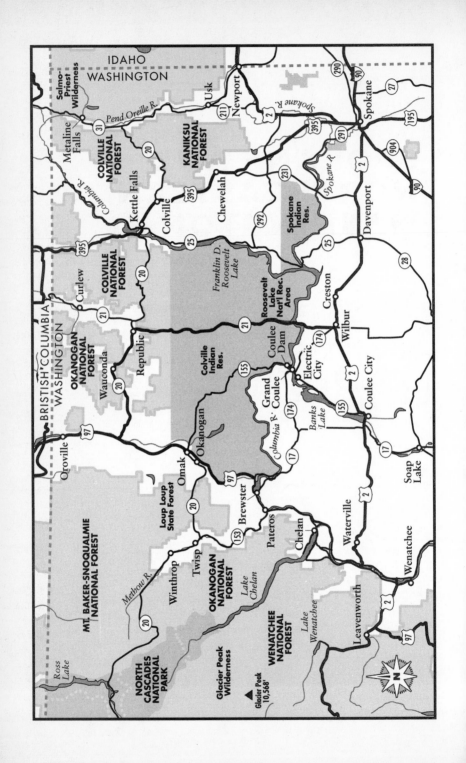

SPOKANE AND
NORTHEASTERN WASHINGTON

It's natural to think of Washington State as equal parts yin and yang: the lush, green west side of the Cascades and the arid, desertlike landscape of Eastern Washington. But that image isn't exactly accurate. The state more accurately divides into neat quarters—with the northeastern quadrant a study in contrasts. The upper-right corner of Washington starts in the sleepy spa town of Soap Lake and runs north to the Canadian border near Oroville; along this imaginary north-south line lie the towns of Grand Coulee, Okanogan, and Omak. To the east are the vast Channeled Scablands—the most visible reminder of the great floods that poured from glacial Lake Missoula thousands of years ago. That flat, featureless terrain bumps up against the gorgeous and little-explored Kettle River Range to the north, and near Colville you'll find the spectacular Selkirks, an outlying range of the Canadian Rockies.

The image of everything east of the Cascades being dry couldn't be farther from reality when you consider that one of the nation's most powerful rivers—the Columbia—runs through here, though it is much dammed and sedated now. Its tributaries in the area include the Pend Oreille, Colville, Spokane, and Okanogan, all of which create riparian areas in an otherwise sere shrub-steppe environment.

Spokane, in the far eastern reaches of the state near Idaho, is famous for its tree-lined neighborhoods. The city is forested as well, with the spiky ponderosa pines of drier climes rather than the fir-dominated forests of Western Washington. Northeastern Washington years ago was dubbed the Inland Empire, and Spokane is its largest city, some 300 miles from the burgeoning Puget Sound region.

ACCESS AND INFORMATION

The fastest, most direct route to Spokane from the Seattle area is Interstate 90; US Highway 2 is another fairly direct east-west route through Northeastern Washington. North-south routes include US Highway 97 on the eastern slope of the Cascades and US Highway 395, which runs from Spokane through Colville. The **SPOKANE AREA VISITOR INFORMATION CENTER** (201 W Main; 509/747-3230) can provide details about special events in the area, as well as a list of accommodations and restaurants in the city.

Nine airlines—Alaska, America West, Big Sky, Canadian, Delta, Horizon, Northwest, Southwest, and United—serve **SPOKANE INTERNATIONAL AIRPORT** (W 9000 Airport Dr; 509/455-6455), a 10-minute drive west of downtown.

AMTRAK's Empire Builder (509/624-5144) between Seattle and Chicago rumbles through the city, stopping in the middle of the night at Spokane's **INTERMODAL CENTER** (221 W 1st). The **TRAILWAYS** bus system (509/838-5262) also uses that depot; buses also serve Cheney.

Spokane

Water is the reason for Spokane's existence. Native American tribes gathered at the massive, thundering falls of the Spokane River every August to harvest salmon. The city was founded in 1879 because of the mill-power provided by the falls, which today are the centerpiece of a spacious downtown oasis, Riverfront Park, built on the site of Expo '74. The river is home to rainbow trout and osprey, including birds that nest within the city limits. It also provides a scenic backdrop for horseback riding, hiking, and golf.

After more than a decade of decline, Spokane's urban core shows new signs of life with the opening of a stylish mall that houses upscale retailers. **RIVER-PARK SQUARE** (808 W Main; 509/363-0304) is home to a state-of-the-art multiplex, Nordstrom, Williams-Sonoma, and the Gap, among many others.

On the South Hill, the stylish **ROCKWOOD BAKERY** (315 E 18th; 509/747-8691) is a favorite sweet spot. In summer, breakfast and lunch (sandwiches, pastries, and espresso) are offered under towering trees at **THE PARK BENCH** (1928 S Tekoa; 509/456-8066). Along the Spokane River, **FORT SPOKANE BREWING COMPANY** (401 W Spokane Falls Blvd; 509/838-3809), a popular brewpub, features occasional appearances of big-name blues performers.

Museum goers can duck inside to view Bing Crosby memorabilia, housed at the **CROSBY LIBRARY** (Gonzaga University campus, 502 E Boone; 509/484-2831), the singer's gift to his alma mater. The city's notable **CHENEY COWLES MUSEUM** (2316 W 1st; 509/456-3931), which features pioneer and mining relics as well as an art gallery, is scheduled to reopen in late 2001 after a $19-million expansion that includes a new 43,000-square-foot building.

PERFORMING ARTS

Brazilian-born **SPOKANE SYMPHONY ORCHESTRA** conductor Fabio Machetti directs diverse programs such as a pops series—impressive guest artists including native son and internationally known baritone Thomas Hampson—and the free Labor Day concert at Comstock Park (800 W 29th; 509/624-1200). The **SPOKANE CIVIC THEATRE** (1020 N Howard; 509/325-2507) offers a mixed bag of amateur performances including productions geared for kids; **INTERPLAYERS ENSEMBLE THEATRE** (174 S Howard; 509/455-7529) is a professional company with a full season featuring well-known works. The 12,000-seat **SPOKANE VETERANS ARENA** (720 W Mallon) occasionally attracts major entertainers and bands; most tickets are sold through a local agency, **G&B SELECT-A-SEAT** (509/325-7328 or 800/325-7328; www.ticketswest.com).

PARKS AND RECREATION

Civic leaders still point to the development of **RIVERFRONT PARK** as one of the turning points in the city's history. Formerly railroad yards, this expansive space is full of meandering paved paths and attractions such as an IMAX theater and a mint-condition carousel built in 1909 by Charles Looff. From here you can

NORTHEASTERN WASHINGTON THREE-DAY TOUR

DAY ONE: Wake up in Spokane with Torrefazione coffee and stellar cranberry-orange scones at **Rockwood Bakery**. Afterward, explore nearby **Manito Park**. After admiring the park's greens, lunch on the exotic salad bar at **Niko's II Greek and Middle East Restaurant** or the innovative vegetarian fare at **Mizuna**. Then check out the shopping at the spiffy new **RiverPark Square**. Later, rent in-line skates or a bike at **Riverfront Park** and head out on the **Centennial Trail**, which runs along the Spokane River. After a dinner of innovative fare at **Paprika**, take in a performance at the **Spokane Symphony Orchestra** or a local theater, or catch some tunes at **Spokane Brewing Company**. Return to your room at the **Kempis Hotel Suites** to rest up for tomorrow.

DAY TWO: For a fine eye-opener, try the veggie frittata at **Cannon Street Grill**, then head north on Highway 395 toward Colville. Golfers can stop in **Chewelah** to play a round at the **Golf and Country Club**; skiers can hit the ski slopes at **49 Degrees North**. In **Colville**, explore Main Street shops and stop in for a velvety cappuccino and a snack at the **Talk and Coffee**. Check in to **My Parent's Estate**; then drive about 10 miles back to Colville to have dinner at **Café Italiano**.

DAY THREE: Enjoy breakfast at the B&B, then head west on **Highway 20** through the Okanogan over Sherman Pass to **Republic**. On the scenic drive between Kettle Falls and Grand Coulee, stop at the area's most adventurous eatery, the **Loose Blue Moose**. From here head south on Highway 21 to cross **Lake Roosevelt** on the **Keller Ferry**, then drive northwest on Highway 174 to **Grand Coulee** and its famous dam. Tour the mammoth structure FDR built, walk in the historic town of **Coulee Dam**, or try your luck at the casino. For dinner, go Mexican at **La Presa**, then check in at the luxurious **Victoria's Cottage** and watch the summer laser light show at the dam from the B&B's garden gazebo.

also access the wonderful CENTENNIAL TRAIL, which runs from downtown Spokane through the park to Coeur d'Alene, Idaho. (A 2-mile loop passes near the pretty campus of Spokane's Gonzaga University.)

On the city's South Hill, MANITO PARK (at Grand and 18th) has a busy duck pond—where so many people feed the birds that they might turn their beaks up at your crusts. This jewel of green space also has a lovely rose garden filled with heirloom varieties, a peaceful Japanese Garden, and the ever-changing GAISER CONSERVATORY—with displays that include coffee plants, exotic orchids, and prickly cactus.

Two natural areas just a short drive from Spokane offer fine places to hike and see wildlife. The LITTLE SPOKANE NATURAL AREA (509/456-3964) is a calm, meandering 6-mile stretch of the Little Spokane River—one of the area's premiere paddling spots. It can be accessed off Waikiki Road near St. George's School in North Spokane; a well-marked parking lot is at the canoe launch, a half mile past the school. The area offers prime bird-watching, and has one of the nation's highest diversities of nesting songbirds, as well as great blue heron, wood ducks, and widgeons. **RIVERSIDE STATE PARK** (509/456-3964) extends from residential northwest Spokane to the Little Spokane River, and is a good in-city park, offering hiking and picnicking as well as the interesting Bowl and Pitcher basalt formations.

Each spring, the city hosts one of the country's largest road races. More than 60,000 runners (including a handful of world-class athletes) and walkers turn out on the first Sunday in May for 7.46-mile **LILAC BLOOMSDAY RUN** (509/838-1579). The Arena is home to the Western Hockey League **SPOKANE CHIEFS** (509/328-0450). Skiing can be sublime: **MOUNT SPOKANE** (509/443-1397), 31 miles north of the city on Highway 206, is upgrading its terrain under new ownership. There are also 17 kilometers of groomed cross-country trails with two warming huts (a Sno-Park pass is required).

RESTAURANTS

Café 5-Ten / ★★

2727 S MOUNT VERNON ST, SPOKANE; 509/533-0064

The short menu at this intimate spot focuses on inventive pasta dishes. Fettuccine comes tangled with Norwegian smoked salmon, prosciutto, sweet red onions, and crumbles of Gorgonzola. Linguine might be topped with spicy marinara and sautéed calamari or tossed with baby artichokes, roasted red peppers, garlic, and fresh mint. The house steak—a center-cut sirloin—is cut into wedges and arranged around a pile of mashed Yukon golds. Pay close attention when the server describes the seafood specials. Chef/owner Michael Waliser gets adventurous with exotics such as Hawaiian ono. *$$$; MC, V; checks OK; lunch Mon–Fri, dinner Mon–Sat; no alcohol; reservations recommended; in Lincoln Heights Shopping Center.* &

Chicken-n-More / ★

502 W SPRAGUE AVE, SPOKANE; 509/838-5071

 Spokane's sole soul-food joint is located in a small storefront shop on a downtown corner. Owner Bob Hemphill is a Texas native who slow-cooks brisket and ribs in a smoker and tops them with his signature sauce. The deep-fried catfish sandwich—slathered with red pepper sauce and ketchup—takes 15 minutes, but is worth the wait. Southern-style fried chicken is digit-licking good, especially alongside an order of jo-jos. Or try a side of red beans and rice; the coleslaw and baked beans are nothing special. The tiny dining room has a half dozen tables and some counter space. *$; no credit cards; checks OK; lunch, dinner Mon–Fri; no alcohol; reservations not accepted; across from Ridpath Hotel.*

Cannon Street Grill / ★
144 S CANNON ST, SPOKANE; 509/456-8660
There are plenty of good greasy spoons in Spokane, but this cozy little spot in the Browne's Addition neighborhood is a cut above the average breakfast place. The coffee is from Craven's, a local roaster. Morning meals include a stellar frittata made with sautéed mushrooms, red peppers, and sweet onions; plate-filling pancakes; and thick French toast. On Sundays, not-to-be missed brunch fare includes huevos rancheros with black beans, and house-smoked lox with bagels. Lunch—simple sandwiches and salads—is served weekdays. *$; MC, V; checks OK; breakfast, lunch Mon–Fri, brunch Sun; beer and wine; reservations not accepted; from Maple St exit, north to 2nd Ave, west on Cannon St.* ⅋

The Elk Public House / ★
1931 W PACIFIC AVE, SPOKANE; 509/363-1973
This lively neighborhood watering hole has an ever-changing selection of microbrews on tap and a menu designed to complement those suds. The Wisconsin bratwurst is slow-simmered in beer. A grilled lamb sandwich, slathered with tzatziki, is a three-napkin meal. And the 74th Street gumbo (inspired by a Seattle alehouse) is wickedly hot. The weekly fresh sheet offers global fare such as Spanish-style cod, Asian-inspired pork chops topped with gingery apricot chutney, or Southern-fried catfish with spicy grits. Vegetarians appreciate the option of subbing grilled Small Planet tofu in any of the entrees or salads. Be patient; service can be slow. *$; MC, V; checks OK; lunch, dinner every day; beer and wine; reservations not accepted; at Cannon St.* ⅋

Hill's Someplace Else / ★★
518 W SPRAGUE AVE, SPOKANE; 509/747-3946
Walk in the front door of this dark, smoky spot and it feels more like a bar than a restaurant, but chef/owner Dave Hill cranks out topnotch food in this casual atmosphere. Everything on the menu is made in-house, from the too-good-to-eat-just-one potato chips and spicy beef jerky to the ice cream that is the basis for the sinful Bananas Foster. The lengthy menu includes sandwiches (house-smoked-salmon panini and the Reuben are standouts), meal-sized salads, and an eclectic lineup of house favorites: duck breast with green peppercorn sauce, chicken satay, beer-batter fish-and-chips, fiery shrimp creole, pork tenderloin with sun-dried-cherry chutney. Specials change twice daily (lunch and dinner), and the Culinary Institute of America–trained Hill has a way with seafood. Just leave room for that incredible Bananas Foster. *$$; AE, MC, V; checks OK; lunch, dinner Tues–Sat; full bar; reservations recommended (dinner); across from Ridpath Hotel.* ⅋

The Italian Kitchen / ★
113 N BERNARD ST, SPOKANE; 509/363-1210
Italian is the cuisine du jour for many restaurants, but this trattoria turns out the most authentic fare in Spokane. The ravioli—filled with spinach and ricotta

or Italian sausage—is handmade, so it's tender. Try it with the rich Gorgonzola cream sauce. The lasagne is also built on a foundation of hand-rolled pasta, layered with beef and veal, bechamel and marinara. Veal piccata is nicely done, as is the scaloppine—pan-seared with prosciutto and sage. The history of the stylish dining room, done up in warm wood accents and big windows on the street side, dates back to the 1900s. In the lounge, a late-night menu is served until 11:30pm. *$$; AE, DIS, MC, V; checks OK; lunch Mon–Sat, dinner daily; full bar; reservations not accepted; 2 blocks south of Opera House.* &

Luna / ★★★

5620 S PERRY ST, SPOKANE; 509/448-2383

If this classy neighborhood spot reminds you of a sun-drenched dining room in California, that's no happy accident. Owners Marcia and William Bond solicited advice from Alice Waters, the queen of nouvelle California cuisine, before they launched their restaurant in 1994. It shows—from the warm welcome to the ever-evolving menu that focuses on fresh ingredients, including herbs and vegetables harvested from a garden just outside the kitchen. First plates might include beef carpaccio with shaved Quillisascut Cheese Company *manchego* and a *chimichurri* sauce, or coconut-crusted Small Planet tofu with a spicy Thai sauce. Main plates offer contemporary takes on classics. The tenderloin is paired with garlicky mashed potatoes and a balsamic-cabernet sauce. Seared duck breast is served with oven-roasted yams and pear confit. Goat cheese ravioli gets tossed with butternut squash, sage, and Swiss chard. Light eaters appreciate plate-size pizzas from the wood-fired oven. Luna has one of the region's best wine lists, with extensive and affordable selections from around the world. For Sunday brunch, indulge in rich smoked-salmon hash or French toast with caramelized bananas and pecans. *$$$; AE, DIS, MC, V; checks OK; lunch Mon–Sat, dinner every day, brunch Sun; full bar; reservations recommended; corner of 56th St.* &

Mizuna / ★★

214 N HOWARD ST, SPOKANE; 509/747-2004

Spokane's only upscale vegetarian restaurant revamps its offerings to reflect the change of seasons. In fall, it could mean pumpkin-filled ravioli served with sautéed apples, toasted hazelnuts and a smoky Chilean pie with ancho chile sauce, or forest mushroom croquettes paired with braised grapes. Don't miss the Asian lettuce wrap starter, with crunchy iceberg leaves enveloping a savory sauté of shiitakes, *seitan*, ginger, and garlic. At lunch, Cajun caesar, tofu-stuffed salad rolls with a peanut dipping sauce, and meatless Reuben—made with marinated, grilled *seitan*—are favorites. A cozy wine bar adds to this inviting venue's appeal. *$$$; AE, DIS, MC, V; checks OK; lunch Mon–Fri, dinner Tues–Sat, brunch Sat; wine only; reservations not necessary; just south of Riverfront Park.* &

Moxie / ★★

1332 N LIBERTY LAKE RD, SPOKANE; 509/892-5901

This gem is in an unlikely location, at one end of a busy suburban strip mall. But step inside the cozy space with an ever-changing selection of art on the walls, and you'll find some of the prettiest plates around. Chef/owner Ian Wingate—a graduate of the California Culinary Institute—is a whiz with intensely flavored sauces. The chipotle-glazed meat loaf is a house favorite, as is his Asian treatment of ahi, crusted with black sesame seeds and drizzled with ginger sauce. The fine, sherry-infused French onion soup is garnished with grilled scallion. House greens (from a local farm) are exceptional, and dressed with a spicy pumpkin vinaigrette. Desserts and breads are also made on-site. *$$$; AE, MC, V; checks OK; lunch Tues–Fri, dinner Mon–Sat; beer and wine; reservations recommended; Liberty Lake exit off I-90.* &

Niko's II Greek and Middle East Restaurant / ★★

725 W RIVERSIDE AVE, SPOKANE; 509/624-7444

The addition of a cozy wine bar and a renovated dining room have given this popular downtown eatery a fresh, lively vibe. In the bar, take a tasting tour—several samples of one varietal or a famous wine region—and order the appetizer combo (hummus, tzatziki, baba ghanouj) while studying the extensive Mediterranean menu. Solid bets are lamb souvlaki, beef kebabs, tomato chutney–topped calamari steak, and chicken curry. Steer clear of dishes with pasta, which tend to be overcooked. House-made desserts include traditional baklava, velvety chocolate decadence, and elegant crème brûlée. The kitchen stays open until 11pm, with a late-night menu on weekends. *$$; AE, DIS, MC, V; checks OK; lunch Mon–Fri, dinner Mon–Sat; beer and wine; reservations not necessary; downtown, at Post St.* &

Paprika / ★★★

1228 S GRAND BLVD, SPOKANE; 509/455-7545

In the shadow of the gothic spires of St. John's Cathedral on Spokane's South Hill, this little dining room has the most imaginative food in town. Offerings change seasonally: fall brings warming fare such as braised rabbit with chestnuts and hand-cut rosemary noodles, grilled duck breast nestled up to savory bread pudding and cranberry chutney, and rack of pork swimming in a puddle of hard cider sauce. Spring and summer dishes focus on tender greens from local growers and whimsical presentations such as Bloody Mary gazpacho served in a martini glass with a plump prawn. For variety, try chef/owner Karla Graves's seven-course tasting menu, served weeknights. The walls at this cozy spot are bathed in the warm tones of the spice for which the restaurant takes its name. Striking art on the walls is painted by the restaurant's sous-chef, who also prepares some of the in-house desserts. Seasonal creations include updated classics such as a baked Alaska with a creamy Italian meringue. *$$$; AE, MC, V; checks OK; dinner Tues–Sat; beer and wine; reservations recommended; on South Hill, across from St. John's Cathedral.* &

SPOKANE VALLEY WINE TOURING

While few grapes grow in Spokane itself, the area has a healthy wine industry. Six wineries welcome visitors, especially during the annual spring barrel-tasting (usually the first weekend in May) and holiday open house (the weekend before Thanksgiving).

Mountain Dome (16315 Temple Rd; 509/928-2788; www.mountaindome. com)—largely recognized as Washington's finest producer of sparkling wine—is a family-run operation in the foothills of Mount Spokane.

There's no nicer spot for a picnic than **Arbor Crest Cliff House** (4705 Fruithill Rd; 509/927-9894), a historic home that sits high above the Spokane Valley. The winery has a reputation for fine merlot and sauvignon blanc.

At **Latah Creek** (13030 E Indiana Ave; 509/926-0164), winemaker Mike Conway is almost always on the premises to answer questions about his merlots, cabernets, chardonnay, or the popular huckleberry riesling. **Knipprath Cellars** (5634 E Commerce; 509/534-5121), now in the former headquarters of Hale's Ale, specializes in varietals crafted in a European style, including pinot noir, chardonnay, and lemberger. Knipprath also produces a port. Tasting room hours are limited.

In an odd juxtaposition, **Caterina Winery** (905 N Washington St; 509/328-5069) sits on the ground floor of the Broadview Dairy. Gregarious vintner Mike Scott jokes that's what makes his chardonnays so rich and creamy. At **Worden's Winery** (7217 W 45th; 509/455-7835), west of downtown, the friendly tasting-room staff is glad to pour from an extensive lineup that ranges from riesling to merlot.   —Leslie Kelley

LODGINGS

Angelica's Bed & Breakfast

1321 W 9TH AVE, SPOKANE; 509/624-5598 OR 800/987-0053

Renowned architect Kirtland Cutter designed this 1907 Arts and Crafts mansion with a European sensibility in the lower South Hill neighborhood, a mix of older homes and apartments. The dramatic entryway draws guests into the inviting living room or dining room, or up the stately wooden staircase. Past the cozy sunroom on the mezzanine, all four guests rooms (with private baths) are on the second level and are named for family members. Yvonne is a standout with a four-poster bed, a gas fireplace, a walk-in closet, and spiffy wood floors. Nice touches throughout include quality linens, guest robes, reading lamps, and early morning coffee in the sunroom. *$; AE, DIS, MC, V; no checks; info@angelicasbb.com; www.angelicasbb.com; just south of downtown, off Cedar St.*

Cavanaugh's Inn at the Park / ★

303 W NORTH RIVER DR, SPOKANE; 509/326-8000 OR 800/843-4667

This hotel makes a fine base for exploring downtown Spokane and Riverfront Park on foot. It sits on the bank of the Spokane River, and runners appreciate its proximity to the scenic Centennial Trail. The big draw at Cavanaugh's is the large outdoor swimming pool, complete with a couple of water slides. Request a room—decorated in standard motel motif—with a city view. The hotel has more than 300 rooms and conference facilities, including 17 conference rooms and exhibit halls, the largest of which is 9,800 square feet. A business center is available for guests; the airport shuttle is free. *$$; AE, DC, DIS, MC, V; checks OK; just north of downtown, off Washington.*

Fotheringham House / ★★

2128 W 2ND, SPOKANE; 509/838-1891

From the first cup of fresh-ground coffee in the morning to the hazelnut truffle treats at night, pampering of guests is a hallmark of owners Graham and Jackie Johnson. The couple lovingly restored this historic Queen Anne–style mansion in the Browne's Addition neighborhood, starting in 1983, and recently added another room. The entire house is tastefully appointed with period antiques. You don't have to be a politician to enjoy the Mayor's Room, adorned with a four-poster bed draped in delicate lace, a piano desk, and a love seat; it also has a private bath. The Garden Room overlooks an urban bird sanctuary and is bathed in shades of yellow and green. It shares a bath with the Museum Room and the Mansion Room, named for the venerable restaurant across the street. Jackie's summer garden bursts with color and fragrance, especially the lovely lavender display that lines the front walkway. *$$; MC, V; checks OK; innkeeper@ fotheringham.net; www.fotheringham.net; just across from Cowley Park.*

The Kempis Hotel Suites / ★★★

326 W 6TH AVE, SPOKANE; 509/747-4321 OR 888/236-4321

A vintage Rolls Royce picks up guests at the airport, setting the tone for Spokane's 14-unit boutique hotel, seven blocks from the city center. This old apartment building has been carefully restored and beautifully updated. The lobby is bathed in natural light pouring from the ornate skylight three stories up. Each suite has a fully stocked kitchen, a tastefully appointed sitting room with cable TV, and sleeping quarters with an antique bedframe the owners acquired in Europe. The complimentary continental breakfast includes goodies from the pastry chef of the on-premise restaurant, The Winged Lion. There's a meeting room available, as well as a business center with access to computers and a fax machine. *$$$; AE, MC, V; checks OK; www.thekempis.com; near Sacred Heart Hospital.*

Marianna Stoltz House / ★
427 E INDIANA AVE, SPOKANE; 509/483-4316 OR 800/978-6587

This 1908 foursquare home is on a tree-lined street near Gonzaga University, a five-minute drive from downtown. The inviting parlor and living room are filled with elegant velvet couches and brocade armchairs. Three of the four rooms (two with private baths) are named for color schemes. The Blue Room is lit with an ornate chandelier that dates back to when the house was first built, and the Green Room has an antique settee. Or try the Ivy Suite, one of our favorites. All have cable TV and air-conditioning. Hostess Phyllis Maguire's attention to detail includes robes, free local calls on the guest phone, a fridge where you can stash beverages, and a ready supply of coffee, tea, and cookies. Breakfast is served in courses: peach-melba parfait, homemade granola, and Dutch Baby pancakes or scrambled eggs tucked into a croissant. *$$; AE, DIS, MC, V; checks OK; mstoltz@aimcomm.com; www.mariannastoltzhouse.com; Hamilton St exit off I-90.*

Waverly Place Bed & Breakfast / ★★
709 W WAVERLY PL, SPOKANE; 509/328-1856

Marge Ardnt is the gracious hostess at this pretty 1902 Victorian located in a neighborhood just north of downtown. In the summer, guests are invited to linger over afternoon lemonade on the expansive veranda that has a view of nearby Corbin Park, or take a dip in the pool. The four rooms are on three levels, the grandest quarters being the two-story master suite, with its own sitting room and claw-footed tub in the luxurious bath. Of the two rooms that share a bath, Anna's Room has a window seat that overlooks the park. Breakfast specialties include Swedish pancakes with Idaho huckleberries. *$$; MC, V; checks OK; waverly@waverlyplace.com; www.waverlyplace.com; Division St exit off I-90.*

Pend Oreille and Colville River Valleys

The wild terrain, the wildlife, and the region's wide river, the Pend Oreille (pronounced "pon-der-RAY"), which flows north to Canada where it dumps into the Columbia just north of the border, deserve more attention than they get, while the sparsely populated Colville River valley is home to tiny farming communities. But outdoor recreation, from fishing and boating to cross-country skiing and hunting, draws many to this pristine region.

The Pend Oreille

This northernmost corner of the state is generally considered a place to drive through on the way to Canada. In fact it's nicknamed "the forgotten corner." (Although movie buffs might remember the scenery around Metaline Falls from *The Postman*, Kevin Costner's 1997 post-apocalyptic box-office bomb. Film crews invaded Metaline Falls one summer and gave the town a new "old" look.)

INLAND NORTHWEST GOLF

When *Golf Digest* named Spokane one of the best places in the country to play on public links, some of the city's duffers were perturbed. It wasn't that they disagreed; they simply didn't want to share their secret.

The good news is, with so many courses in the area—40 within a half-day drive of Spokane—no one should have trouble getting a tee time. And most of those courses are still reasonably priced, averaging less than $30 for 18 holes.

The venerable **Indian Canyon** (Assembly and W West Dr; 509/747-5353) is considered the most beautiful links around—its sweeping fairways are lined with majestic evergreens. The 19th hole is especially appealing (sit on the deck and enjoy the view) after uphill jaunts on the 17th and 18th holes.

The newest city course, **The Creek at Qualchan** (301 E Meadowland Rd; 509/448-9317), is rife with water hazards. **Esmeralda** (3933 E Courtland Ave; 509/448-9317) is one of the oldest courses and is known for being fairly easygoing.

County and municipal courses include a couple of beauties that sit side-by-side east of Spokane. **Liberty Lake** (24403 E Sprague, Liberty Lake; 509/255-6233) nestles up against a wooded hillside, which comes into play on several holes. Golfers are rewarded for their efforts with a fine view of the lake on the 18th green. The neighboring **MeadowWood** (24501 E Valleyview Ave, Liberty Lake; 509/255-9539) is long and rambling with open fairways lined with tricky roughs.

Another county course, **Hangman Valley** (2210 E Hangman Valley Rd; 509/448-1212), was nearly destroyed by a fast-moving wildfire several years ago. Some players had to hurry off the course so quickly they left their balls behind and later found them melted on the greens. The desertlike landscape has since recovered, and the fringe of the course is now home to an expensive housing development.   —*Leslie Kelly*

Highway 20 heads north from Highway 2 at Newport, following the Pend Oreille River. The surrounding **SALMO-PRIEST WILDERNESS AREA** is home to grizzly, caribou, and bald eagles, among other elusive wildlife. Its 38 miles of hiking trails traverse the 7,300-foot Gypsy Peak. To the west of Metaline Falls, which is north of Highway 20 on Highway 31, hikers can trek to **THE KETTLE CREST**. Considered one of the best hikes in the region, this 42-mile trek offers opportunities to view wildlife such as black bear, deer, coyotes, and a variety of birds. The Colville Forest Service (765 S Main, Colville; 509/684-7000) has also developed some shorter loop trails that access the Kettle Crest. Summer guided wildflower tours offered in that area have become so popular that advance reservations are essential.

RESTAURANTS

Katie's Oven / ★

225 E 5TH, METALINE FALLS; 509/446-4806

They've been baking breads and pastries in the historic Washington Hotel since 1987, but it's open only a few days a week. Indulge in the gooey-good sticky buns or one of the oversize cookies. At lunch, Katie's serves a variety of sandwiches and soups, along with savory lunch buns—rolls stuffed with feta and spinach or seasoned beef and green chile. Specials change daily, but pizza is a fixture on Saturday. Espresso drinks are skillfully turned out using beans from a Spokane roaster, 4 Seasons Coffee. *$; no credit cards; checks OK; breakfast, lunch Wed–Sat in summer; no alcohol; reservations not accepted; north end of Main St.*

Colville and Kettle Falls Area

This area has the working-class feel of a lumber town. Colville and Kettle Falls are tight-knit working-class communities, where you're likely to see "Cream of Spotted Owl" bumper stickers on the logging trucks that barrel down the road. Kettle Falls is a jumping-off spot for exploring Lake Roosevelt to the south and the Okanogan to the west.

CHEWELAH, 52 miles north of Spokane on Highway 395, is home to the 18-hole challenging (and inexpensive) **GOLF AND COUNTRY CLUB** (Sand Canyon Rd; 509/935-6807). To the east is tiny but friendly **49 DEGREES NORTH** ski area (3311 Flowery Trail Rd; 509/935-6649), 58 miles northeast of Spokane, which offers free lessons for beginners.

Continuing north on Highway 395 is Colville, with a quaint Main Street of antique shops and the friendly **TALK AND COFFEE** (119 E Astor; 509/684-2373).

CHINA BEND WINERY (3596 Northport-Flatcreek Rd; 509/732-6123), north of Kettle Falls, grows only organic grapes and has the northernmost vineyards in the state. Catered lunches can be arranged (48-hour advance notice; around $10 per person); the menu focuses on the freshest ingredients from the winery's half-acre organic pea-patch.

West from Kettle Falls, Highway 20 is a little-traveled two-lane road that is one of the finest spots for fall foliage, lined with birch and maple trees. Near **SHERMAN PASS** are dramatic remnants of a 1988 forest fire. Beyond is the mountain town of **REPUBLIC**.

From Republic, Highway 21 heads south to Lake Roosevelt in the Grand Coulee area. If you're hankering to get out and explore the pretty landscape, head to **K-DIAMOND-K GUEST RANCH** (15661 Hwy 21 S; 509/775-3536 or 888/345-5355; www.kdiamondk.com). A working dude ranch, it specializes in guided mountain trail rides and down-home hospitality (everyone eats at the family's kitchen table).

RESTAURANTS
Cafe Italiano
153 W 2ND, COLVILLE; 509/684-5957

This inviting restaurant, with several dining rooms and an outdoor courtyard for summer seating, is run by the Karatzas family. Their Greek heritage shows up on the expansive menu with dishes such as sautéed scampi finished with feta cheese, and filet mignon sautéed with Greek peppers. But the fare is mostly traditional Italian: pastas, pizzas, antipasto, and spumoni. Signature dishes include veal marsala, chicken sautéed with spicy cappocolla ham, and eggplant Parmesan. The house cheesecake is made fresh daily, featuring different toppings. *$$; AE, MC, V; checks OK; lunch Mon–Fri (summer), dinner Tues–Sat; beer and wine; reservations recommended; 2 blocks west of Hwy 395.*

The Loose Blue Moose / ★
1015 S CLARK, REPUBLIC; 509/775-0441

Hummus might be a household word in many parts of the world, but it's still exotic in Northeastern Washington. That garbanzo bean dip is one of the made-from-scratch specialties at this funky coffee house that seems slightly out of place in downtown Republic. Still, locals and road-weary travelers alike have embraced a menu mix that includes a corn tortilla torta layered with tomatillo sauce, Jack cheese, and soy sausage (from the local co-op). Dinners include pesto-drenched fettucine (for under $8) and an entree-size steak salad garnished with fennel-lavender goat cheese from nearby Quillasascut Cheese Company. It might influence your travel plans to learn that every Friday is "Fondue Night." Live music can be heard on the weekends. *$; MC, V; checks OK; breakfast, lunch, dinner Wed–Sat; beer and wine; reservations recommended; loosebluemoose@hotmail.com; downtown.*

LODGINGS
My Parent's Estate / ★
HWY 395, COLVILLE; 509/738-6220

Pull into the rambling driveway and say hello to the resident llamas, which hostess Bev Parent keeps as pets. This 43-acre historic spot was the St. Francis–Regis Mission in 1869, then a Dominican convent in the early '30s. Since 1989, it's been a bed-and-breakfast. Recently, Parent closed off the guest quarters in the main house and opened a large suite in a separate building. From the tiny deck, guests might spot an amazing array of wildlife—from resident deer to the occasional barn owl. Or they might just have to settle for seeing a herd of cows grazing (and mooing) nearby. Inside there's a fireplace, a pretty bathroom with a claw-footed tub, and a tiny kitchen area where guests can eat the breakfast Parent delivers each morning. There's also a two-bedroom caretaker's cottage, which is available only for weekly or monthly rental. *$$; MC, V; checks OK; closed Oct–May; 7 miles north of downtown Colville.*

Grand Coulee Area

Grand, yes—this is a wonderful area from which to appreciate the outsize dimensions of the landscape and the geological forces that made it. The **COLUMBIA RIVER** slices through Northeastern Washington with a quiet power, as the water rushes by in silky strength through enormous chasms. In prehistoric times, glacier-fed water created a river with the largest flow of water ever known. Today it's the second-largest river in the nation, traversing a plateau of equally staggering scale.

Some 15 miles upstream of Grand Coulee Dam, the tiny **KELLER FERRY** (on Hwy 21; 509/324-6015) shuttles across the Columbia River dozens of times a day at no charge. The *Martha S.*, operated by the state Department of Transportation, holds just a dozen cars. The crossing—which lasts only 15 minutes—is the waterborne section of Highway 21, between the Colville Indian Reservation to the north of the river and the Columbia Plateau on the south. On the Grand Coulee side is a small store run by the Colville Tribe that sells fishing licenses and some groceries, and rents boats.

For many years **LAKE ROOSEVELT**, the massive 150-mile-long reservoir created by Grand Coulee Dam, was untapped by the RV-on-pontoon fleets. Now several companies offer weekly (or weekend, for a hefty price) **HOUSEBOAT RENTALS**. Some of these vessels have deluxe features such as on-deck hot tubs, stereo systems, gourmet kitchens, and outdoor rinse-off showers. For rates and reservations, contact Roosevelt Recreational Enterprises (PO Box 5, Coulee Dam; 800/648-LAKE).

Grand Coulee Dam

Clustered around Grand Coulee Dam are the towns of Grand Coulee, Coulee Dam, and Electric City. The **GRAND COULEE DAM AREA CHAMBER OF COMMERCE** (319 Midway Ave; 800/268-5332; www.infoatgrandcouleedam.org) has information. Take a self-guided historic walking tour in Coulee Dam or try your luck at the **COULEE DAM CASINO** (515 Birch St; 509/633-0766). But the biggest attraction here, of course, is the dam itself. Grand Coulee Dam—sometimes referred to as the seventh wonder of the world—was conceived as an irrigation project, and now supplies water to more than 500,000 acres of farmland. World War II gave it a new purpose, producing power for the production of plutonium at Hanford and aluminum for aircraft. As tall as a 46-story building and the length of a dozen city blocks, the dam was completed in 1942, nearly 10 years after construction began.

Since the April 19, 1995, bombing in Oklahoma City, security has been tightened at the dam. Tours are now guided, and take visitors into the bowels of this mammoth structure, past the whirring turbines and through some of the tunnels still used by engineers. A summer laser light show illuminates a portion of the 12-million cubic yards of concrete used to build the dam. For tour and light show times, call the U.S. Bureau of Reclamation **VISITORS ARRIVAL CENTER** (Hwy 155, Grand Coulee; 509/633-9265; light show Memorial Day–Sept).

RESTAURANTS

La Presa / ★

515 E GRAND COULEE AVE, GRAND COULEE; 509/633-3173

The Hernandez family doesn't make a big deal about calling its food "authentic Mexican," but it is. At least if you order the carne asada (cooked over charcoal fire), the chorizo with eggs, or the dark, cinnamon-scented chicken mole. The menu here is huge, with all sorts of steaks and seafood dishes. There's even (oddly enough) chicken teriyaki. But stick with traditional favorites such as the enchilada verde, made with fresh tomatillos. The decor is strictly velvet paintings and wool blankets, but the welcome is warm and the margaritas are icy cold. *$; MC, V; checks OK; lunch, dinner every day; beer, wine, and tequila; reservations recommended; on Hwy 21, just up from dam.* &

LODGINGS

Victoria's Cottage / ★★

209 COLUMBIA AVE, COULEE DAM; 509/633-2908

This isn't your average B&B. It's more like your own wing of one of the most impressive homes in Coulee Dam, where hosts Dave and Bonnie Schmidt respect their guests' privacy. This cottage includes a large living room with skylights over an oversize Jacuzzi tub. There's a sound system, two TVs with VCRs (one is in the bedroom), along with a sizable selection of CDs and movies. In the well-equipped pantry are drinks and everything you need to make s'mores over the portable gas "campfire" outside. A gas barbecue and a dining table are on the deck. The one-unit cottage can sleep four, with a pullout sleeper in the living room. Guests can help themselves to veggies from the owners' garden. Other thoughtful details include a well-stocked medicine cabinet (Tums, aspirin, etc., along with lotion and shampoo), plush Calvin Klein robes, a supply of board games, and mountain bikes to borrow. Fresh-baked scones and fruit are delivered to your door each morning with the newspaper. *$$; MC, V; checks OK; dschmidt@televar.com; www.reitpro.com/victoriascottage; next to tiny Douglas Park.*

Soap Lake

Soap Lake earned its name on a windy day, when frothy whitecaps dotted the surface of this lake. Many believe the lake, known for its high content of soft minerals (which also give it a soapy feel), has healing properties. Call the **SOAP LAKE CHAMBER OF COMMERCE** (300 N Daisy; 509/246-1821; www.soaplakecoc.org) for information on renting canoes and sailboats.

DRY FALLS, off Highway 17 north of town, is an example of the power of ice. When glacial Lake Missoula overflowed its ice-age dam some 12,000 years ago, torrential floods headed west to the Pacific. The force of the water carved out what is now this ancient waterfall, 3½ miles wide and 400 feet high (by comparison, Niagara Falls is 1 mile wide and 165 feet high). The **DRY FALLS INTER-PRETIVE CENTER** (inside Sun Lakes State Park, 4 miles southwest of Coulee City on Hwy 17; 509/632-5583), at the top of the canyon a half mile from the scenic overlook, is open May through September, 10am–6pm daily.

SUN LAKES STATE PARK (800/233-0321; www.parks.wa.gov), downstream from the falls, offers all kinds of outdoor activities: hiking, canoeing, camping, swimming, boating, fishing, golf, horseback riding, and simple picnicking.

LODGINGS

Notaras Lodge

236 E MAIN ST, SOAP LAKE; 509/246-0462

Soap Lake's renowned mineral waters are on tap in the bathrooms, several of which have Jacuzzis. Though the lodge was rebuilt after a 1998 fire, and the 14 rooms are still decorated with western history, some of the most popular—and quirkiest (such as the Norma Zimmer Room, named after the bubble lady on the Lawrence Welk Show)—didn't make the transition. All four lodge buildings are log cabin style and are right on the lake; six of the rooms have lake views. Owner Marina Romary also runs Don's Restaurant (14 Canna St; 509/246-1217; lunch, dinner every day), which specializes in steak, seafood, and Greek entrees. *$$; MC, V; checks OK; notaras@televar.com; www.notaraslodge.com; Soap Lake exit off Hwy 28, at Canna St.* &

Omak

Omak is a town of 4,000, located 50 miles north of Grand Coulee on Highway 155. The famous—and controversial—Suicide Race is the climax of the **OMAK STAMPEDE** (509/826-1002 or 800/933-6625; stampede@televar.com; www.omak stampede.org), the popular rodeo held here the second weekend of August on the banks of the Okanogan River. During the Stampede, Omak's population swells to 30,000.

LODGINGS

The Rodeway Inn

122 N MAIN, OMAK; 509/826-0400 OR 888/700-6625

This basic hotel has the distinction of being the closest lodgings to the Stampede grounds. Its 61 rooms include remote-control satellite TV, several Jacuzzi suites, and a few units with kitchens. There are smoking and nonsmoking rooms and an outdoor swimming pool; pets are allowed. *$; AE, DIS, MC, V; checks OK; next to movie theater.*

VANCOUVER
AND ENVIRONS

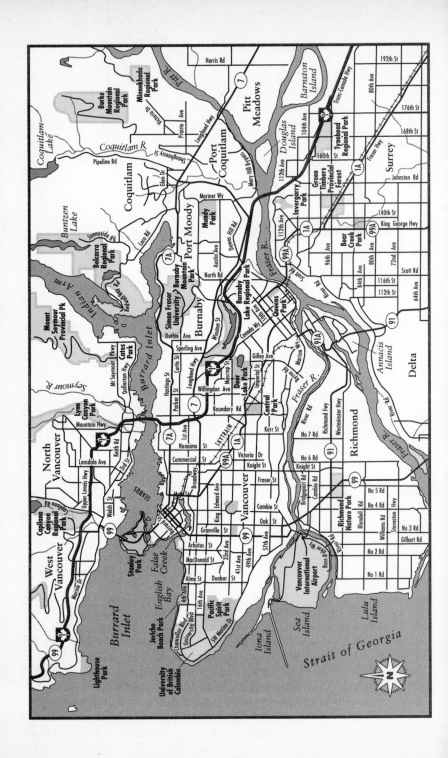

VANCOUVER AND ENVIRONS

The Vancouver area is Canada's fastest-growing metropolis and a city of magical contradictions—from rough-and-tumble Hastings Street, where timeworn brickwork still exudes a wild, seaport-town atmosphere, to trendy Robson Street, with its futuristic Japanese noodle houses and haute couture. This city nestled between mountains and ocean has long touted itself as Canada's gateway to the Pacific Rim, and British Columbia is fortunate to be plugged in to the world's fastest-growing economy. In fact, Vancouver has always accepted the waves of immigrants that have landed on its shore. The city seems living proof that a benign environment will produce an easygoing disposition.

ACCESS AND INFORMATION

VANCOUVER INTERNATIONAL AIRPORT (9 miles/15 km south of downtown on Sea Island; 604/276-6101; www.yvr.ca) is a major international airport with flights daily to every continent. An extensive renovation, completed in 1996, added a terminal dedicated to international flights. Several **CAR RENTAL** agencies, including Avis (604/606-2847), Budget (604/668-7000), and Enterprise (604/231-9222), are on the ground floor of a new three-level parkade.

Weathered but still-graceful, **PACIFIC CENTRAL STATION** (1150 Station St) is the local terminus of several regional, national, and international bus and rail services. **GREYHOUND** (604/662-3222 or 800/661-8747; www.greyhound.ca) operates five buses daily between Vancouver and Seattle, with connections in Seattle to other U.S. points. **PACIFIC COACH LINES** (604/662-8074; www.pacific coach.com) operates a modern bus service between Vancouver and Victoria via **BC FERRIES** (250/386-3431 or 888/223-3779; www.bcferries.bc.ca). **VIA RAIL** (800/561-8630; www.viarail.ca/en.trai.oues.html) is Canada's national passenger rail service. **AMTRAK** (800/872-7245; www.amtrak.com/trip/cascadacordor. html) trains make daily runs between Seattle and Vancouver. **BC RAIL** (1311 W 1st St, North Vancouver; 800/339-8752 or 800/663-8238 outside BC; www. bcrail.com/bcrpass), the provincial railway service, provides comfortable passenger transportation between North Vancouver and the central interior city of Prince George, as well as popular summer Royal Hudson turn-of-the-century-style steam train excursions to Squamish along scenic Howe Sound.

Travelers by car choose between two major highways. Highway 99, the main north-south highway connecting Vancouver to Seattle, leads south from the city across the fertile delta at the mouth of the Fraser River and connects with Washington State's Interstate 5. Highway 99 also connects Vancouver to the ski resort town of Whistler, about two hours north, and is known as the **SEA-TO-SKY HIGHWAY**. Transcontinental Highway 1, the main east-west highway, arrives from the east through lower BC mainland and terminates in Vancouver; it runs along the south shore of the Fraser River. Another alternate route is Highway 7, which runs east-west along the north shore.

Western British Columbia is blessed by a temperate maritime climate, and Vancouver's **WEATHER** is the mildest in Canada, thanks to ocean currents and major weather patterns that bring warm, moist air in waves from the Pacific year-round. Spring comes early (by mid-Mar, usually); July and August are warmest; late-summer and autumn days—through October—tend to be warm and sunny, with the occasional shower. Winter is rainy season—roughly November through March—but rain usually falls as showers or drizzle. Heavy continuous downpours are rare, as are thunderstorms and strong winds.

Vancouver

Vancouver, its residents are fond of saying, is one of the few cities in the world where you can go skiing and sailing on the same day. How remarkable, then, that it should also be one of the few where, sitting outside a Neapolitan cafe, you can eavesdrop on an impassioned argument in Hungarian and see graffiti in Khmer. It's also a festive city, with art everywhere, and a fashionable shopping strip—Robson Street—often compared to the Beverly Hills posh Rodeo Drive. Yet glance away from the opulence of the shops as you saunter along Robson and at the end of a side street the peaceful waters of Burrard Inlet lap at the shore. Beyond, the mountains on the North Shore glitter with snow for half the year.

No city is homogenous, particularly Vancouver. It's really an amalgam of 23 neighborhoods, each with its own unique character and stories. **YALETOWN**, a whirling high-tech zone that's a case of gentrification gone right, looks across to the glittering condos on the south shore of False Creek. Home to one of the largest urban redevelopment projects ever attempted in North America, the **FALSE CREEK BASIN** has its natural center in the bustling market area and arts community on Granville Island. Equally dynamic alternative cultures of different sorts flourish in **KITSILANO** (a funky, former low-rent haven for hippies that has been yuppified by baby boomers and young families) and the **WEST END** (home to Canada's most densely populated neighborhood and western Canada's largest gay and lesbian community). The West End is just south of Stanley Park; Kits is west across False Creek. The cultural mix along **COMMERCIAL DRIVE** is the contemporary home of bohemian subculture, where members of Vancouver's lesbian community can be seen alongside the graying curmudgeons of an older generation sipping espresso outside one of the many cafes. If the High Street style of British society is more to your liking, amble over to **AMBLESIDE** and rub shoulders with the sensible-shoe set browsing the private art galleries and lunching on pork pies.

The city's public transit system is an efficient way to get around town; **COAST MOUNTAIN TRANSLINK** (604/521-0400; www.bctransit.com or www.translink.bc.ca) covers more than 695 square miles (1,800 square km) with three forms of transit: bus, SeaBus, and Sky Train.

More information is available from the **VANCOUVER TOURIST INFO-CENTRE** (200 Burrard St; 604/683-2000).

VANCOUVER THREE-DAY TOUR

DAY ONE: Start your day at Granville Island. The **Public Market** opens at 9am and it's a good place to turn breakfast into a progressive meal: cappuccino at the **Blue Parrot Espresso Bar**, grape focaccia from **Terra Bread**, candied salmon from **Seafood City**. After exploring the shops, studios, and galleries, head to the **Waterfront** hotel to check in to your room before a short walk to **Gastown**. If you're ready for lunch, stop in at **Borgo Antico** for good Italian food and wine. Behind all the bric-a-brac in Gastown are some of the city's oldest buildings, as well as interesting Native art galleries. Next stop: Chinatown, for a guided tour through the **Chinese Classical Garden**, before walking the frenzied streets looking for jade treasures or tasting steamed buns from one of Chinatown's many bakeries. Return to your room and change for a run along the **Stanley Park** seawall before heading to dinner (with a sunset) at the **Raincity Grill**.

DAY TWO: After your first cup of strong coffee at the hotel, head west to the **Kitsilano** neighborhood for breakfast—big portions of eggs, pancakes, and waffles are on deck at **Sophie's Cosmic Cafe**. Next, head to the University of British Columbia and the **Museum of Anthropology** to see its jaw-droppingly impressive First Nations artifacts, and the **UBC Botanical Garden**, the oldest and one of the finest gardens in Canada. Leave time to freshen up at your hotel before you walk over to the **Hotel Vancouver** for afternoon tea (make a lunch of it) with all the trimmings in the **900 West Restaurant & Wine Bar**. Then stroll **Robson Street**, a trendy boulevard of pret-a-porter boutiques and swank eateries. If you'd like to see a live show—pop, jazz, or an evening at the symphony—ask a cab driver to take you to **Granville Street**, where the Commodore Ballroom, Orpheum Theatre, and Vogue Theatre sometimes have last-minute tickets available before 8pm. Afterward, treat yourself to a late-night snack of "tapatizers" at **Bin 941 Tapas Parlour**.

DAY THREE: Start the morning in West Vancouver with raspberry scones and coffee at the **Savary Island Pie Company**. After breakfast, leisurely browse the shops in Ambleside and Dundarave. Then it's off to **Lighthouse Park**'s 1914 lighthouse (Marine Dr at Beaton Ln, West Vancouver) and the rocky outcrop of Point Atkinson—and its stunning city view. Back in Vancouver, grab lunch at **Phnom Penh Restaurant** before heading to **Yaletown** to browse upscale boutiques and galleries. For dinner, go all out with a four-star meal at **Lumière**.

MUSEUMS

Francis Rattenbury's elegant old courthouse downtown is now the **VANCOUVER ART GALLERY** (750 Hornby St; 604/662-4719), holding more than 20 major exhibitions a year. Its permanent collection includes works by Goya, Emily Carr,

Gainsborough, and Picasso. Many of the city's commercial galleries are located on the dozen blocks just south of the Granville Bridge; art galleries here represent internationally renowned painters and photographers. Granville Island, site of the **EMILY CARR INSTITUTE OF ART AND DESIGN** (1399 Johnston St; 604/844-3800), has a number of potteries and craft studios. The avant-garde is most often at spaces such as the **MONTE CLARK GALLERY** (2339 Granville St; 604/730-5000).

The **MUSEUM OF ANTHROPOLOGY** at the University of British Columbia (6393 NW Marine Dr; 604/822-3825) has an extensive collection of artifacts from Native American cultures of coastal British Columbia (including an impressive display of totem poles), as well as artifacts from Africa and the Orient. Tucked behind the imposing facade of Cathedral Place is the **CANADIAN CRAFT MUSEUM** (639 Hornby St; 604/687-8266), Canada's first national museum devoted to crafts.

PARKS AND GARDENS

The city is blessed with a climate—similar to Britain's—well suited for flowers and greenery. Take a walk through the quiet rain forest in the heart of **STANLEY PARK** (west end of Beach and W Georgia Sts to Lions Gate Bridge; 604/257-8400). This 1,000-acre in-city park is within walking distance of the trendy shops of Robson Street, but feels worlds away; its appeal includes the seawall, formal rose gardens, Vancouver Rowing Club, Vancouver Aquarium, restaurants, painters, Totem poles, horse-drawn tours, and numerous wilderness trails. At **QUEEN ELIZABETH PARK,** dramatic winding paths, sunken gardens, and waterfalls skirt the **BLOEDEL CONSERVATORY** (Cambie St and 33rd Ave; 604/872-5513). Near Queen Elizabeth Park, **VANDUSEN BOTANICAL GARDEN** (5251 Oak St; 604/878-9274; www.vandusengarden.org) stretches over 55 acres.

The **UNIVERSITY OF BRITISH COLUMBIA** (UBC campus, SW Marine Dr; 604/822-9666; www.hedgerows.com/ubcbotgdn/index.htm) boasts superb gardens—the Botanical Garden, Nitobe Memorial Gardens, and Totem Park—along with the Physick Garden, which re-creates a 16th-century monastic herb garden. The **CHINESE CLASSICAL GARDEN** (578 Carrall St; 604/662-3207; www.discovervancouver.com/sun) within Dr. Sun Yat-Sen Park is a spectacular reconstruction of a Chinese scholar's garden, complete with pavilions and water-walkways. **KITSILANO BEACH** (Cornwall Ave and Arbutus St, bordering English Bay) is a year-round haven for joggers, dog-walkers, and evening strollers.

SHOPPING

Vancouver has always been bursting with storefronts. In **YALETOWN** (bordered by Pacific Blvd and Nelson, Cambie, and Seymour Sts), brick warehouses have been transformed into loft apartments, offices, bars, restaurants, and chic shops housing ultrahip clothing stores, and high-end home furnishings. **ROBSON STREET** (between Beatty St and Stanley Park) is the meeting place of cultures and couture, as *tout le monde* strolls among its many boutiques and restaurants.

Weekends are crowded, but there's lots to see, from art books, jewelry, and gifts by local artists at the **GALLERY SHOP** in the Vancouver Art Gallery to fashions in stores such as Nike, Guess, and Swatch.

Downtown is full of outstanding shops. In poor weather, head underground to **PACIFIC CENTRE** (700 W Georgia St to 777 Dunsmuir St; 604/688-7236), downtown's biggest and busiest mall, with 200 outlets, which connects to **VANCOUVER CENTRE** (604/688-5658). Also downtown is **SINCLAIR CENTRE** (757 W Hastings St; 604/659-1009), a striking example of the reclaimed-heritage school of architecture. At Robson and Homer, you'll find the main branch of the **VANCOUVER PUBLIC LIBRARY**, designed by world-renowned architect Moshe Safdie and inspired by the Roman Coliseum. Its store, **BOOK-MARK**, has gifts for literary folk.

South Granville, from Granville Bridge toward 16th Avenue, borders on the prestigious **SHAUGHNESSY NEIGHBOURHOOD** and caters to the carriage trade. Impressive is a new crop of Occidental antique stores—to supplement the existing British ones—that import treasures from Japan, Indonesia, and India. At **GRANVILLE ISLAND PUBLIC MARKET** (1689 Johnston St; 604/666-5784) on the south shore of False Creek, you can get everything from just-caught salmon to packages of fresh herbs to a wonderful array of fresh produce.

GASTOWN (Hastings and Water Sts between Homer and Columbia Sts) is a restored 1890s precinct, a quaint and cobbled tourist destination that specializes in everything from cookbooks to radical politics to science fiction. The old warehouses and office buildings have been refurbished, and summer and weekends find the streets bursting with visitors.

The oldest and biggest of Vancouver's ethnic communities is **CHINATOWN** (off Main St, on Pender and Keefer Sts). The Chinese groceries and apothecaries have been there for generations, and many display remnants of Vancouver's recent-past status as a neon mecca. Many of the buildings in this area were built by Chinese artisans in a style not found outside China.

Vancouver's 60,000 East Indian immigrants have established their own shopping area, called the **PUNJABI MARKET** (in south Vancouver at 49th and Main Sts), where you can bargain for spices, chutney, and sweets. One of Vancouver's longest-established groups of ethnic inhabitants, the Greeks, live and shop west of the intersection of **MACDONALD AND W BROADWAY**.

PERFORMING ARTS

THEATER. The **VANCOUVER PLAYHOUSE THEATRE COMPANY** (Hamilton and Dunsmuir; 604/873-3311; www.vancouverplayhouse.com; season Oct–May) explores contemporary and classical theater. In the heart of lively Granville Island, the **ARTS CLUB THEATRE** (1585 Johnston St; 604/687-1644) and neighboring **ARTS CLUB NEW REVUE STAGE** (604/687-1644) have become local institutions. Contemporary theater in Vancouver is largely centered in the **VAN-COUVER EAST CULTURAL CENTRE** (1895 E Venables St; 604/254-9578; www.vecc.bc.ca), known to locals as the Cultch.

MUSIC. Over the past decade, the city has witnessed a renaissance in the proliferation of classical, jazz, and world music. Under the leadership of new music director Bramwell Tovey, the 74-member **VANCOUVER SYMPHONY ORCHESTRA** (884 Granville St; 604/876-3434; www.culturenet.ca/vso) should continue to pursue artistic heights. The **VANCOUVER OPERA** (Hamilton at W Georgia; 604/683-0222; www.vanopera.bc.ca) presents four to five productions a year at the Queen Elizabeth Theatre. The **DU MAURIER INTERNATIONAL JAZZ FESTIVAL** (888/GET-JAZZ) attracts crowds of more than 250,000 jazz lovers each June, and the annual **VANCOUVER FOLK MUSIC FESTIVAL** (604/602-9798) is extremely popular too. Ticketmaster (604/280-4444) has more information about musical events and venues.

NIGHTLIFE

On an evening out in Vancouver, you can enjoy just about every clubbing experience imaginable, from an old-time rock 'n' roll bender to a no-holds-barred striptease show, to a till-dawn rave in a factory warehouse.

A piano player rules the roost weekdays and a combo sets up on weekends at the tony **BACCHUS LOUNGE** (845 Hornby St; 604/689-7777) to serenade imbibers with everything from soft rock to old standards. Live pop, jazz, and electronica are the lures that attract schools of new-music aficionados to the **STARFISH** (1055 Homer St; 604/682-4171). For live jazz, funk, blues, and hip-hop, head to the **CELLAR JAZZ CAFÉ** (3611 W Broadway; 604/738-1959).

To find out who's playing where, the best sources for up-to-date listings are the *Georgia Straight* (www.straight.com) and the Thursday entertainment section of the *Vancouver Sun* (www.vancouversun.com). For daily updates of concert announcements, contact Ticketmaster via phone or on-line (604/280-4444; www.ticket master.ca).

SPORTS AND RECREATION

Cycling, running, hiking, and water sports are all popular here. A good in-city route for runners or in-line skaters is along the 6½-mile (10.5 km) **STANLEY PARK SEAWALL**. A good one-stop source for bicycling information, including maps and guidebooks, is **CYCLING BRITISH COLUMBIA** (332–1367 W Broadway; 604/737-3034; www.cycling.bc.ca). Contact the **OUTDOOR RECREATION COUNCIL OF BRITISH COLUMBIA** (1367 W Broadway; 604/737-3058) to reach the Canoeing Association, Whitewater Kayaking Association, or Sea Kayaking Association of British Columbia, or for more information on other sports.

For fans of spectator sports, your best bet is the NHL's **VANCOUVER CANUCKS**, playing at General Motors Place (800 Griffiths Wy; 604/899-4667; www.orcabay.com). The faithful stick with the team through good times and bad, and that makes getting tickets a challenge. GM Place is also home to the National Basketball Association's **VANCOUVER GRIZZLIES**. Closer to downtown, the Canadian Football League's **BC LIONS** play at BC Place Stadium (777 Pacific Blvd; 604/589-7627; www.bclions.com). Vancouver's diverse ethnicity has created a ready-made audience for soccer, especially among homesick Brits,

Portuguese, and Italians. Swangard Stadium (intersection of Boundary Rd and Kingsway; 604/589-7627) hosts the **VANCOUVER 86ERS**. Tickets for most sporting events are available at the gates or through Ticketmaster (604/280-4444). Thoroughbreds race at **HASTINGS PARK** (Hastings St and Renfrew St; 604/254-1631; www.hastingspark.com; mid-Apr–Nov) on the grounds of the Pacific National Exhibition.

RESTAURANTS

Aqua Riva / ★★

30–200 GRANVILLE ST, VANCOUVER; 604/683-5599
Like its siblings Salmon House on the Hill and Horizons on Burnaby Mountain, Aqua Riva boasts an outstanding view of the harbor and North Shore mountains. Executive chef Deb Connors tends the wood-fired oven and rotisserie in this sparkling restaurant near Canada Place. Prices are reasonable for alderwood-grilled salmon, oven-baked pizzas, and slow-smoked barbecued ribs. Service is unfailingly friendly, and the stunning decor is especially soothing in a booth with Dana Irving's art deco wraparound mural above you. Aqua Riva is popular with the lunch crowd, who inhabit the office tower atop the restaurant, and tourists in the area. *$$; AE, DC, E, MC, V; no checks; lunch, dinner every day, brunch Sat–Sun (May–Oct); full bar; reservations not necessary; www. aquariva.com; at Howe.*

Bacchus Ristorante / ★★★

845 HORNBY ST (THE WEDGEWOOD HOTEL), VANCOUVER; 604/608-5319
Wonderfully romantic, this richly decorated room is a triumph for Wedgewood Hotel owner Eleni Skalbania and chef Robert Sulatacky, whose contemporary French cooking is spectacular. Dark wood paneling and deep burgundy velvet couches are accented by huge bouquets of flowers, creating private niches. Booths along the wall are separated by upholstered floor-to-ceiling dividers. At lunch, Bacchus attracts legal beagles from the neighboring courthouse for an ever-changing roast of the day, pizza Bacchus, or superb tortellini of sweet white corn. Afternoon tea (2–4pm) in front of the fireplace hits the spot, with finger sandwiches followed by fresh scones with dollops of Devon clotted cream, and tea pastries. The changing dinner menu might include terrine of Quebec foie gras, caramelized sea scallops, truffle and pistachio roasted breast of squab, or *daube de boeuf bourguignonne*. Hope that apple tarte Tatin happens to be on the menu, or surrender to dark-chocolate hazelnut torte served with a milk-chocolate mousse and brandied cherries. Best, Bacchus offers good French cheese, fine wines, and servers who cater to your every whim. Nightly except Sunday, a pianist tickles the ivories. Stogie aficionados have free rein in the cigar room. *$$$; AE, DC, MC, V; no checks; breakfast, lunch, dinner every day, brunch Sat–Sun; full bar; reservations required; info@wedgewoodhotel. com; www.wedgewoodhotel.com; between Robson and Smithe.* &

Bin 941 Tapas Parlour / ★★★
Bin 942 / ★

941 DAVIE ST, VANCOUVER; 604/683-1246
1521 W BROADWAY, VANCOUVER; 604/734-9421

The fact that this place is constantly packed attests to its popularity. It lures an attractive crowd, all in deep conversation that at first seems unlikely beneath the muscular yet unoppressive music. The setting is funky: a madcap mix of chrome-and-Naugahyde furniture, mismatched stools, and wild art, crammed into a shoebox of a restaurant. The food of chef/owner Gordon Martin is both dazzling and an outrageously good value. Order a pound of Prince Edward Island mussels done (superbly) any of four ways, or two fat crab cakes served with a burnt-orange-and-chipotle sauce and charred baby bok choy. Beef and fowl appear as well, in imaginative presentations; shoestring french fries—a haystack of Yukon Golds hand-cut and hand-seasoned—are the best-tasting in town. Martin headlines his menu "tapatizers" because everything can be shared or enjoyed solo while you rub shoulders, unavoidably, with those at the next table. Seven white wines and seven reds are offered by the bottle and the glass. A seat at the longer of the two bars gets you barlike conversation, but the three perches facing the open kitchen add a free lesson in exquisite plate presentation. The action continues late; Martin's second location, Bin 942, opened in August 1999 with a similar menu and is open for lunch and dinner. *$$; MC, V; no checks; dinner every day (Bin 941), lunch, dinner every day (Bin 942); beer, wine, and liqueurs; reservations recommended; www.bin941.com; between Burrard and Howe (Bin 941), between Granville and Fir (Bin 942).* &

Bishop's / ★★★★

2183 W 4TH AVE, VANCOUVER; 604/738-2025

There's no better place to eat than in this simple two-level restaurant, long a fixture on busy W Fourth Avenue, and John Bishop is the reason. Bishop warmly greets his guests (celebrity and otherwise) and, assisted by a professionally polished young staff, hovers over each table, serving, pouring, discussing. Chef Dennis Green's entrees are uncomplicated. Dungeness crab is bathed in saffron tomato broth, and wild salmon is grilled and brushed with sesame ginger glaze. Rack of lamb with truffle and goat cheese–mashed potatoes, and pan-roasted halibut (in season) on a warm new-potato salad are standouts. Everything bears the Bishop trademark of light, subtly complex flavors and bright, graphic color. Desserts such as toasted almond cake with poached apricots and homemade apricot ice cream, and moist ginger cake pooled in toffee sauce are legendary. Manager Abel Jacinto oversees an eclectic list of fine wines, including a selection of 50 half-bottles. *$$$; AE, DC, MC, V; no checks; dinner every day (closed for two weeks in Jan); full bar; reservations required; inquire@bishops.net; www.bishops.net; between Arbutus and Yew.*

Borgo Antico / ★★

321 WATER ST, VANCOUVER; 604/683-8376

It's like stepping back in time, walking on cobbled sidewalks to the iron-gated entrance of Borgo Antico ("old quarter"), Umberto Menghi's Gastown ristorante. Inside, the dining room is divided by a series of arches and has a lively, color-splashed decor. You'll find many of the same well-prepared dishes that Umberto has on the menu at Il Giardino (see review), but lower prices. We recommend the antipasto plate or the razor-thin carpaccio with arugula as a starter. Go with the chef's suggestions—swordfish simply grilled or oven roasted, risotto of the day, or tagliarini with half a fresh lobster. Serious grape nuts are drawn to the basement of this former Gastown warehouse to choose from an estimable wine list or to attend private wine functions. *$$; AE, DC, MC, V; no checks; lunch Mon–Fri, dinner Mon–Sat; full bar; reservations not necessary; inquiries@umberto.com; www.umberto.com; between Cambie and Cordova.*

Bridges / ★★

1696 DURANLEAU ST, VANCOUVER; 604/687-4400

One of the city's most popular hangouts has a superb setting on Granville Island. Seats on the outdoor deck, with sweeping views of downtown and the mountains, are at a premium on warm days. Bridges is actually three separate entities: a casual bistro, a pub, and a more formal second-story dining room. The bistro's casual offerings are the best bet; upstairs, the kitchen takes its seafood seriously, but you'll pay top dollar for it. *$$; AE, DC, MC, V; no checks; lunch, dinner every day, brunch Sun; full bar; reservations not necessary; www.bridgesrestaurant.com; Granville Island.* &

C / ★★★

2-1600 HOWE ST, VANCOUVER; 604/681-1164

Be prepared to spend an entire afternoon or evening on the patio at C, because lunch or dinner is always an event at Harry Kambolis's restaurant. C offers contemporary and exotic seafood in Zen-like surroundings with an unbeatable view. Executive chef Robert Clark creates dishes as dramatic on the palate as on the plate. Start with a taster box filled with grilled Monterey Bay squid, halibut sashimi, ahi tuna tartare, and crisp soft-shelled crab. And don't miss C's signature starters: caviar in a gold-leaf pouch, lobster tail sashimi bathed in Cognac, or octopus-wrapped scallops. A dim sum–style menu is served at lunch, featuring spicy crab dumplings, subtle steamed lobster, and macadamia nut miso buns, as well as crisp scallop and ahi tuna spring rolls. Whatever the special is, order it. You can also expect the unexpected from C's eclectic wine list. *$$$; AE, DC, E, MC, V; no checks; lunch, dinner every day; full bar; reservations recommended; www.crestaurant.com; at Beach Ave.*

The Cannery Seafood House / ★★★

2205 COMMISSIONER ST, VANCOUVER; 604/254-9606

Chef Frederic Couton has been winning awards since his arrival at the Cannery in 1996. His culinary artistry makes the trek out to this relatively remote east-end dockside location unquestionably worthwhile. Serving "salmon by the sea" for more than 25 years, the Cannery resides in a cleverly refurbished building. You'll find a baker's dozen of honestly prepared, high-quality seafood choices on the fresh sheet, including delicate arctic char, juicy grilled swordfish, and meaty tuna. Salmon Wellington has been a house specialty here since 1971 and is still a winner, recently rematched with a pinot noir sauce. Our favorite is buttery steamed Alaskan black cod. Nonfish entrees include herb-crusted rack of lamb, crispy seared duck breast, or simple grilled beef tenderloin. Wine enthusiast Michael Mameli presides over the solid cellar, and his award-winning list is one of the city's best. *$$$; AE, DC, MC, V; no checks; lunch Mon–Fri, dinner every day; full bar; reservations recommended; www.canneryseafood.com; at Victoria Dr.*

Chartwell / ★★★★

791 W GEORGIA ST (THE FOUR SEASONS), VANCOUVER; 604/689-9333

Chartwell remains in the forefront of excellent hotel dining, evoking an upper-class English men's club atmosphere with wood-paneled walls and classic furnishings. Executive chef Douglas Anderson offers a fresh take on local ingredients, with direct flavors and a keen edge. His lemon-scented cauliflower custard with a lobster salad is very fine, as are his giant Vancouver Island scallops with roe, complemented by chopped apple and smoked bacon. A sirloin, juicy and tender, served with a vegetable pie and avocado, was marvelous. Finish with goat cheese from David Wood on Saltspring Island. Master host Angelo Cecconi and his talented staff give Chartwell its distinctive stamp of personal service—warm, discreet, and attentive. A pretheater dinner menu with valet parking is an outstanding value. The wine list is an award winner, and winemaker dinners are popular. *$$$; AE, DC, DIS, JCB, MC, V; no checks; breakfast, dinner every day, lunch Sun–Fri; full bar; reservations recommended; www.fourseasons.com; at Howe St.* &

CinCin Restaurant & Bar / ★★★

1154 ROBSON ST, VANCOUVER; 604/688-7338

CinCin is a hearty Italian toast, a wish of health and good cheer, all implied in this sunny Mediterranean space. The Italian- and French-inspired dishes are boldly flavored by talented chef Romy Prasad. Launch your meal with his appetizer platter, which might include house-smoked trout, Prince Edward Island mussels, or tomato and bocconcini crostini draped with Parma prosciutto. For entrees, savvy diners order veal osso buco with fresh sage gnocchi or 42-ounce T-bone Steak for Two sided with roasted vegetables. Wine takes center stage with sommelier Michael Dinn orchestrating the 10,000-bottle cellar (a good value with reduced markup). Linger at the bar over a Mandorla

Martini or sip wine in the lounge (food's served until 11:30pm). Dine outdoors on the heated terrace overlooking Robson. *$$$; AE, DC, MC, V; no checks; lunch Mon–Fri, dinner every day; full bar; reservations recommended; cincin@ direct.ca; www.cincin.net; between Bute and Thurlow.*

Cioppino's Mediterranean Grill / ★★★☆

1133 HAMILTON ST, VANCOUVER; 604/688-7466

The name is a pun on the name of San Francisco's delicious seafood stew, and that of the very talented Pino Posteraro, who moved to this warm Yaletown room from Umberto Menghi's many restaurants. Posteraro's French-inspired Mediterranean signature dishes—foie gras and sea-bass casserole, sautéed wild chanterelles and morels, spaghettini with truffles—have earned him a loyal following. Stick to a tasting menu at lunch or dinner and you'll have one of the most brilliant meals in town for the price. No matter what Posteraro cooks from the open kitchen, it's luxurious and minimalistic at the same time. Celestino Posteraro and Massimo Piscopo preside over a friendly bar and a serious wine list. A wonderful private dining room seats up to 24. Check out the patio in the summer. *$$$; AE, DC, MC, V; no checks; lunch Mon–Fri, dinner Mon–Sat; full bar; reservations recommended; pino@cioppinosyaletown.com; between Helmcken and Davie.*

Diva at the Met / ★★★

645 HOWE ST (METROPOLITAN HOTEL), VANCOUVER; 604/602-7788

Diva is an airy, multitiered space with an exhibition kitchen that fires off daring West Coast fare. Whatever chef Michael Noble serves can be ranked with the best in town. Alaskan black cod with a mussel, leek, and saffron soup is a standout; Noble adds a braised shank to his rack of lamb and complements it with an organic-barley and mushroom salad. For a zingy, refreshing dessert, try citrus parfait in a cool tangerine soup. Brunchers swoon over smoked Alaskan black cod hash topped with poached eggs. All desserts are winners, but Stilton cheesecake is a must. Hotel manager Jeremy Roncoroni stocks a deep cellar and delights in rarities (Venturi-Schultz from Vancouver Island among them). *$$; AE, DC, JCB, MC, V; no checks; breakfast, lunch, dinner every day; full bar; reservations recommended; reservations@divamet.com; www.metropolitan. com; between Dunsmuir and W Georgia.* &

Ezogiku Noodle Cafe / ★

1329 ROBSON ST, VANCOUVER; 604/685-8608

A small gem of a place operated for the benefit of Oriental food lovers who don't want to spend a lot of money, this tiny place (70 seats, and they're close together) displays only a modest awning saying "noodle cafe." But regulars would say that doesn't start to describe it. Several varieties of ramen noodle dishes make up most of the menu, many representing a clever combination of Japanese and Chinese cuisines, and all come in huge, filling quantities. There's also fried rice, fried noodles, and tasty *gyoza*. Be prepared for a wait.

Other branches are in Honolulu and Tokyo. *$; cash only; lunch, dinner every day; no alcohol; reservations not accepted; between Bute and Jervis.*

The Fish House at Stanley Park / ★★★
2099 BEACH AVE, VANCOUVER; 604/681-7275
Take your pick—the Garden Room surrounded by large trees, the intimate Club Room overlooking the tennis courts, or the formal Fireplace Room. Count on an ardent serving staff, and chef Karen Barnaby to cook seafood the way you like it. Share prawns flambéed with ouzo or wood oven–roasted calamari with smoked-tomato vinaigrette. An ahi tuna entree comes as two-fisted loins (a pair), barely grilled through and fork-tender in a green-pepper sauce. The whole plate impresses; each of Barnaby's vegetables is a discovery in itself. Red cabbage with fennel-and-buttermilk mashed potatoes? Save room for comforting desserts—coconut cream pie or lethal chocolate lava cake. For recipes, pick up a copy of Barnaby's cookbook, *Screamingly Good Food*. *$$; AE, DC, E, JCB, MC, V; no checks; lunch Mon–Sat, dinner every day, brunch Sun; full bar; reservations recommended; info@fishhousestanleypark.com; www.fishhousestanleypark.com; entrance to Stanley Park.* &

Gotham / ★
615 SEYMOUR ST, VANCOUVER; 604/605-8282
The newest buzz in Vancouver is Gotham, with a flashy interior built to the tune of $3 million; it's no wonder most people who dine here look as if they share an equally high tax bracket. Steakhouse king David Aisenstat has turned his attention to creating a hipper Hy's. The result is a downtown dining experience as alluring as its 22-foot ceilings. To capture an intimate atmosphere in such a large space, he's used dark woods, muted lighting, and a postmodern medieval touch that broadcasts subdued bacchanalia. Meat is the main course here—USDA prime, to be precise. Stand-alone steaks (vegetables are à la carte) are even more beautiful than the people. From the New York strip to the splendid 24-ounce porterhouse, it's a cattle drive for the taste buds. It remains to be seen how the cholesterol-eschewing populace of Vancouver take to this red-meat renaissance. *$$$; AE, DC, MC, V; no checks; lunch, dinner every day; full bar; reservations recommended; www.gothamsteakhouse.com; at Dunsmuir St.* &

Habibi's / ★★
7-1128 W BROADWAY, VANCOUVER; 604/732-7487
Richard Zeinoun cooks from the heart at this casual Middle Eastern spot on W Broadway. Surprises start with the complimentary meze of olives, nuts, cucumbers, and onions. These refreshing tapas whet the appetite for *shinkleesh*, an aged goat cheese from the mountains of Lebanon; *balila*, warmed chickpeas in garlic-infused oil; or *warak anab*, grape leaves stuffed with mildly spiced rice and marinated in lemon juice. There are falafels, Lebanese- and Israeli-style hummus, fresh pita bread, and wines chosen to go with the food. Prices are downright cheap; service is friendly and enthusiastic.

Live entertainment on weekends. *$; no credit cards; checks OK; lunch, dinner Mon–Sat; beer and wine; reservations not necessary; gibzeinoun@direct.ca; www.habibis.com; between Oak and Spruce.*

Hon's Wun Tun House / ★

108–268 KEEFER ST, VANCOUVER (AND BRANCHES); 604/688-0871

By serving just-plain-good, basic Chinese specialties you'd find in hundreds of Hong Kong restaurants, and keeping prices to a minimum, what was once a small, steamy Chinatown noodle house is now something of a restaurant empire, with seven branches in the Lower Mainland. One of the keys to Hon's success is that all locations are unpretentious and comfortable. Dishes are prepared in open kitchens. Wonton is just one of the more than 90 varieties of soup available, and there's a seemingly endless list of noodle dishes. Trademark pot sticker dumplings, fried or steamed, are justly famous. Hon's also offers takeout and a full line of frozen dim sum. *$; cash only (except Robson St location); lunch, dinner every day; no alcohol; reservations not necessary; between Gore and Main.*

Liliget Feast House / ★

1724 DAVIE ST, VANCOUVER; 604/681-7044

One culinary category that Vancouver has often lacked is the authentic food of the local aboriginal population. However, for more than 20 years at least one downtown location has served nothing else, and it's a gourmet adventure. Under three different names (Muckamuck and Quilicum, and now Liliget), this restaurant provides as close as most people will ever get to dining in a real Native longhouse, even though it was designed by famed local architect Arthur Erickson. The menu includes salmon, of course, but also eulachon, toasted seaweed, wild blackberry pie, and truly impressive bannock bread. *$$; AE, DIS, MC, V; no checks; dinner every day; full bar; reservations not necessary; between Bidwell and Denman.*

Lumière / ★★★★

2551 W BROADWAY, VANCOUVER; 604/739-8185

Rob Feenie serves some of the best food in the city. The minimalistic elegance of this room showcases the chef's exquisite creations and the Armani-clad clientele. Decor was a tad austere when Feenie first opened, but tilted mirrors and wooden blinds have warmed the room. Food luxuriates in the skill of his contemporary French kitchen. Whether it's a tasting menu of potato blini, grilled yellowfin tuna, five-spice duck consommé, braised short ribs, and desserts, or something lighter, Feenie achieves a perfect balance of flavors and textures. Try a tasting menu of warm Atlantic lobster salad; fricassee of BC mussels, clams, and scallops; seared monkfish; baked pear; and passionfruit tart. The vegetarian tasting menu is filling and virtuous and might feature wild mushroom torte with leeks, fontina, and herbs; raw-milk ricotta ravioli with lemon-thyme butter and shaved white truffles; and celery-root velouté. In fact, the prix-fixe menus are so popular that Feenie plans to eliminate the à la carte menu altogether. Pastry chef Rhonda Viani's brûlées (coconut and Kaffir lime leaf), mousses (hazelnut mocha with double-milk ice cream), and *panna cottas* (light sour cream and cinnamon) will make you moan. The adequate wine list is improving. Service is informed, attentive, and helpful. *$$$; AE, DC, MC, V; no checks; dinner Tues–Sun; full bar; reservations required; between Balsam and Trafalgar.* &

Montri's Thai Restaurant / ★★★

3629 W BROADWAY, VANCOUVER; 604/738-9888

Why go anywhere else for Thai food? When Montri Rattanaraj took a mid-'90s sabbatical, fans wept at losing the best Thai food in town. But when he reopened (in contemporary wicker-accented digs), they flocked to his door: the food is better than ever. *Tom yum goong* is Thailand's national soup, a lemony prawn broth. *Tod mun* fish cakes blended with prawns and chile curry are excellent, as is salmon simmered in red-curry-and-coconut sauce. Rattanaraj's Thai *gai-yang*, chicken marinated in coconut milk and broiled, is a close cousin to the chicken sold on the beach at Phuket. Have it with *som tum*, a green papaya salad served with sticky rice and wedges of raw cabbage; the cabbage and the rice are coolants, and you will need them (Singha beer also helps). For a group of six or more, splurge for the *pla lard prig*, a whole rockfish or red snapper slashed to allow flavorings to penetrate, then quickly deep-fried. *$$; MC, V; no checks; dinner every day; full bar; reservations recommended; near Alma.* &

Nat's New York Pizzeria / ★★

2684 W BROADWAY, VANCOUVER; 604/737-0707
1080 DENMAN ST, VANCOUVER; 604/642-0777

Cousins Nat and Franco Bastone learned how to create Naples-style pizza at their uncle's pizza parlor in Yonkers. Then they opened Nat's on Broadway's busy retail strip and now serve some of the best thin-crust pizza around. Take out, or pull up a chair under the Big Apple memorabilia and sink your teeth into pie loaded with chorizo and mushrooms, or artichokes and pesto, or cappocolla and hot peppers. Or try the 5th Avenue (sweet onion, spinach, tomato, and feta) or the Hot Veg (sun-dried tomatoes, hot peppers, and mushrooms). Top it off with oven-baked garlic shavings or a selection of other condiments. Avoid Nat's Broadway location on weekdays between 11:30am and 12:15pm during the local Kits high school student rush. *$; cash only; lunch, dinner Mon–Sat; no alcohol; reservations not accepted; between Stephens and Trafalgar (Broadway), at Helmcken St (Denman St).*

900 West Restaurant & Wine Bar / ★★★

900 W GEORGIA ST (HOTEL VANCOUVER), VANCOUVER; 604/669-9378

Reminiscent of a cruise-ship dining room, this restaurant recalls the era of great luxury liners. The lovely, refurbished dining room's current chef is Dino Renaerts (from CP's Waterfront Centre Hotel), who is creating several not-to-be-missed signatures: smoked black cod with braised greens and a crisp-fried noodle cake; seared prosciutto atop a tiny ball of mozzarella, served with zucchini and tomato dressed with basil oil and balsamic vinegar; mussel and clam hot pot in a ginger miso broth. Alongside the dining room is the chic Wine Bar, offering a well-chosen 350-plus international list. 900 West has assembled the most comprehensive cellar of Canada's best Vintners Quality Alliance (VQA) wines in the country. More than 75 wines are often available by the glass, and ever-changing flights include BC's renowned ice wine. Choose from traditional, Asian, or West Coast afternoon tea in the lounge. *$$$; AE, DC, E, JCB, MC, V; no checks; lunch Mon–Sat, dinner every day; full bar; reservations recommended; ysimovic@hvc.mhs.compuserve.com; www.fairmont.com; at Burrard St.* &

Pastis / ★★★

2153 W 4TH AVE, VANCOUVER; 604/731-5020

An energetic duo—chef Frank Pabst (ex-Lumière) and attentive front man John Blakeley (ex-Diva)—in summer 1999 opened Pastis, a modern high-energy French bistro in Kitsilano. It's buzzing as West Siders and the men of the hot-stove league check out this Gallic guy on the block where Bishop's lives. You'll feel like you're in Paris sipping pastis, sharing an escargot-and-oyster-mushroom casserole and a tomato-and-tapenade tart. Also good: fig and Belgian endive salad, steak tartare, duck breast with Quebec foie gras, and thyme- and lemon-roasted free-range chicken. The Alice and Alison cheese plate is a fine finale. *$$$; AE, MC, V; no checks; dinner every day; full bar; reservations recommended; pastis@telus.net; between Maple and Cypress.*

Phnom Penh Restaurant / ★★★

244 E GEORGIA ST, VANCOUVER; 604/682-5777
955 W BROADWAY, VANCOUVER; 604/734-8898

Phnom Penh was once a Vancouverites' secret, but it now wins a steady stream of accolades from sources as diverse as local magazine polls and *The New York Times*. Decor is still basic, but the menu has expanded to include cuisines of China, Vietnam, and Cambodia. Pineapple-spiked hot and sour soup, with chicken, fish, or prawns, is richly flavored and redolent with lemongrass and purple basil. An excellent appetizer of marinated beef sliced carpaccio-thin is seared rare and dressed with nuoc cham (spicy, fishy sauce—a Vietnamese staple). Sautéed baby shrimp in prawn roe and tender slivers of salted pork cover hot, velvety steamed rice cakes. Grandma's recipe of garlic chile squid, prawns, or crab with lemon pepper dip has been uniformly declared "unbeatable." Chicken salad with cabbage is a refreshing twist, and the oyster omelet is a dream. If it's good enough for Julia Child, it should be for you. Service is knowledgeable and friendly. *$; AE, MC; no checks; lunch, dinner Wed–Mon; full bar; reservations not necessary; between Gore and Main (Georgia St), between Laurel and Oak (Broadway).*

Quattro on Fourth / ★★★

2611 W 4TH AVE, VANCOUVER; 604/734-4444

Antonio Corsi and son Patrick run one of Vancouver's most comfortable Italian restaurants. An impressive selection of antipasto includes no less than eight different carpaccios. Razor-thin-sliced raw swordfish is superb; so, too, grilled radicchio bocconcini and portobello mushrooms. Kudos for grilled beef tenderloin cloaked in aged balsamic syrup, pistachio-crusted sea bass, and spicy deboned Cornish game hen. Spaghetti Quattro ("for Italians only") rewards with a well-spiced sauce of chicken, chiles, black beans, and garlic. The mostly Italian wine list is stellar, from a rustic Montepulciano D'Abruzzo (Illuminati Riparosso) to a 1990 Masseto Tenuta dell'Ornellaia (Marchesi Lodovico A.). The Corsis have the largest grappa selection in Vancouver; the heated patio seats 35. *$$$; AE, DC, MC, V; no checks; dinner every day; full bar; reservations recommended; at Trafalgar St.* &

Raincity Grill / ★★★

1193 DENMAN ST, VANCOUVER; 604/685-7337

Grape nuts love the extensive Pacific Northwest wine list (more than 100 by the glass), but that's only one reason to visit this bright, contemporary restaurant. Fantastically situated at a happening intersection, Raincity provides excellent views of English Bay year-round through tall windows. Now that Scott Kidd is in the kitchen, dazzled fans insist the food is better than ever. At lunch, skip the turkey burger and order grilled caesar, duck confit with macaroni and cheese, or soothing shrimp risotto. At dinner, choose seared veal liver, or the crispy Dungeness crab roll. A glass of dessert wine and caramel nut torte or blueberry pie make a perfect finish. Expect ever-professional service. *$$; AE, DC, MC, V; no checks; lunch, dinner every day, brunch Sat–Sun; full bar; reservations recommended; www.raincitygrill.com; at Morton.* &

Rodney's Oyster House / ★★

1228 HAMILTON ST, VANCOUVER; 604/609-0080

It's hard to find a spot at the bar at this nautical Toronto transplant in Yaletown. A team of experts carefully check the temperature, freshness, and quality of more than a dozen briny bivalves (many from the East Coast). While the slogan here is "The lemon, the oyster, and your lips are all that's required," you'll be catered to, nonetheless. Rodney's makes four sauces—you'll want the seawich if you grew up with cocktail sauce on your shrimp. There's a choice of creamy chowders, steamed mussels and clams, local Dungeness crab, and East Coast lobsters. *$$–$$$; AE, E, MC, V; no checks; lunch, dinner Mon–Sat; beer, wine, and Scotch; reservations not necessary; between Davie and Drake.*

Sami's / ★

986 W BROADWAY, VANCOUVER; 604/736-8330
1795 PENDRELL ST, VANCOUVER; 604/915-7264

Bicycles hanging from the ceiling and engaging art are part of the casual intimacy of Sami's dining room. This Indo-American bistro sets the trend for some of the city's best fusion food. East and West meet in a harmony of spices and fresh local ingredients that dazzle with their creative pairings. BBQ Crab and Shrimp Masala Cakes baked in naan, tandoori chicken and caramelized shallot-stuffed dumpling with cilantro-cashew pesto, and melt-in-your-mouth beef short ribs braised in cumin and ginger fill the room with an exotic/erotic aroma. Specials change daily, and recently included an incredible appetizer of smoked salmon, capers, and red onion with a curry salsa, baked on a flatbed of naan. Spiced corn mulligatawny soup is a refreshing starter; a selection of BC and California wines, and local and imported beers are on hand. Sandwiched between a 7-Eleven and a Pizza Hut, Sami's door hides a laid-back elegance, like a jewel in a sea of convenience food. *$$; DC, MC, V; no checks; lunch, dinner every day; beer and wine; reservations not necessary; at Oak St (Broadway), at Denman St (Pendrell St).*

Savary Island Pie Company

1533 MARINE DR, WEST VANCOUVER; 604/926-4021

It's always worth crossing the Lions Gate Bridge to sit in the homey and hip Savary Island Pie Company. It opens at 6:30am and during the day it's a hangout for West Van moms and their preppie pups. Most evenings it turns into a house party with Adam Woodall's Savary Island Pie Company Band. Everything is good here, but the Savary is famous for strawberry rhubarb and lemon buttermilk pies, raspberry scones, cranberry-pecan muffins, vegetarian pizza foccacia, and multigrain bread. They also serve homemade soups (tomato Parmesan is a must), sandwiches, chicken potpie, and shepherd's pie. Eat in or take out. *$; cash only; breakfast, lunch, dinner every day; beer and wine; reservations not accepted; between 15th and 16th Sts.*

Seasons in the Park / ★★★

CAMBIE ST AT W 33RD AVE, VANCOUVER; 604/874-8008

Considerable attention in the kitchen has contributed to Seasons in the Park's rapidly rising reputation. Although the Queen Elizabeth Park setting and stunning view of downtown and the North Shore mountains still guarantee a line of tour buses outside, today's visitors to Seasons come as much for the food as the view. Diners are treated to chef Pierre Delacorte's menu of just-picked produce, succulent seafood, and local wines. Popular dishes include a sun-dried tomato tart baked with Stilton, seared prawns and scallops sauced with Pernod and green peppercorns, and constantly changing wild or farmed Pacific or Atlantic salmon entrees. For dessert, sun-burned lemon pie with fresh fruit coulis ends on a high note. Seasons is also a good place to get hitched—on the patio or in the 60-seat gazebo. *$$$; AE, MC, V; no checks;*

lunch Mon–Fri, dinner every day, brunch Sat–Sun; full bar; reservations recommended; seasons@settingsun.com; www.settingsun.com/seasons; Queen Elizabeth Park. &

Shanghai Chinese Bistro / ★★

1128 ALBERNI ST, VANCOUVER; 604/683-8222
Consistently good food and cheerful servers have made this tasteful, airy, L-shaped "bistro moderne" a popular haunt for downtown Chinese-food cognoscenti. The unique and magical nightly noodle show provides another excuse to bring visitors for a good nosh before heading next door for karaoke. Hand-pulled noodles Shanghai-style are a must, and so are chile wontons. Panfried live spot prawns with chile paste and soy, and salt-and-chile crab are finger-licking good. Try a plate of pea shoots lightly touched with garlic, or come for a late-night snack of dim sum (from 10:30pm). *$$; AE, JCB, MC, V; no checks; lunch, dinner every day; full bar; reservations not necessary; between Bute and Thurlow.*

Sophie's Cosmic Cafe / ★★

2095 W 4TH AVE, VANCOUVER; 604/732-6810
The walls of this funky Kitsilano diner are a kitsch collector's dream. Old felt pennants, prehistoric 7-Up bottles, toys—you name it. Don't worry about the wait—there's plenty to look at, including Sophie's collection of colorful lunch boxes and hats once stashed in her attic. Evenings, people are drawn by burger platters, pastas, and boffo spicy mussels (arrive early—they sell out), as well as chocolate shakes. On weekends, fans queue in the rain for stick-to-ribs breakfasts, especially Mexican eggs (with sausage, peppers, and onions, spiced with potent hot-pepper sauce). There are plenty of vegetarian choices all day. Sophie's is a Kits institution, with the mood of a mellow fiesta. A covered deck accommodates all-weather puffers. *$–$$; MC, V; no checks; breakfast, lunch, dinner every day, brunch Sat–Sun; full bar; reservations not accepted; at Arbutus St.* &

Stepho's Souvlakia / ★

1124 DAVIE ST, VANCOUVER; 604/683-2555
Known as much for its lines as for cheap and delicious Greek food, Stepho's remains a fixture in Vancouver's West End. Pungent tzatziki and travel-agency images of Greece set the mood in this newly renovated and expanded space. White stucco walls and arched doorways give the room a light, airy feel. Even with added tables, lines persist—for good reason. Huge portions of chicken, lamb, or beef brochettes fight for space on plates loaded with rice pilaf, buttery roast potatoes, and Greek salad, all served with tzatziki and hot pita. The hummus is outstanding. Check the specials for tender and toothsome baby back ribs. All this, plus prompt, polite service and a well-priced wine list have made Stepho's the budget eater's mecca for Mediterranean meals. *$; AE, MC, V; no checks; lunch, dinner every day; full bar; reservations not accepted; between Bute and Thurlow.* &

The Teahouse at Ferguson Point / ★★

7501 STANLEY PARK DR, VANCOUVER; 604/669-3281

This stunning location in Stanley Park is a tourist magnet, with its series of light, airy dining rooms, park setting, and spectacular view of English Bay, but a faithful following of locals attests to consistent fare and warm, professional service. Appetizers range from Teahouse stuffed mushrooms (crab, shrimp, and Emmentaler) to steamed mussels in a saffron-anchovy broth. Salmon is always a good bet, served with seasonal sauces, and rack of lamb in a fresh-herb crust is a perennial favorite. Desserts include dark- and milk-chocolate *torta milano* with mascarpone mousse and lemon *chiboust*. For summer weddings, check out the sunset patio overlooking the bay. *$$$; AE, MC, V; no checks; lunch Mon–Fri, dinner every day, brunch Sat–Sun; full bar; reservations recommended; info@sequoiarestaurants.com; www.sequoiarestaurants.com; Ferguson Point.* &

Tojo's / ★★★★

202–777 W BROADWAY, VANCOUVER; 604/872-8050

Tojo Hidekazu is Tojo's. One of the best-known sushi maestros in Vancouver, he has a loyal clientele that regularly fills his spacious upstairs restaurant, though most want to sit at the 10-seat sushi bar. He's endlessly innovative, surgically precise, and committed to fresh ingredients. Show an interest in the food, and he might offer you tastes from the kitchen: Tojo tuna or "special beef" (very thin beef wrapped around asparagus and shrimp) or shrimp dumplings with hot mustard sauce. Tojo-san created the BC roll (barbecued salmon skin, green onions, cucumber, and daikon) now found in almost every Vancouver Japanese restaurant. The dining room has a stunning view of the North Shore mountains. Japanese-menu standards like tempura and teriyaki are reliable, and specials are usually superb: pine mushroom soup in the fall, steamed monkfish liver October through May, and cherry blossoms with scallops and sautéed halibut cheeks with shiitake in spring. Cold Masukagami sake is hot at Tojo's. *$$$; AE, DC, JCB, MC, V; no checks; dinner Mon–Sat; full bar; reservations recommended; between Heather and Willow.* &

Vij's / ★★★

1480 W 11TH AVE, VANCOUVER; 604/736-6664

This is where food writers impress informed eaters from out of town. Bombay native Vikram Vij dishes up imaginative home-cooked Indian fare. His seasonal menu changes every three months but almost always includes a mean curry (lamb chops in a fenugreek-and-cream curry with turmeric potatoes) or a killer *saag* (pan-seared squab breast with rapini-and-cumin rice). Decor is minimalist, casual, and modern; black walls and East Indian ornaments allow food to take the spotlight. Start with a glass of Vij's fresh-ginger-and-lemon libation, and *samosa* appetizers filled with ricotta and served with Bengali sauce containing five spices called *panchpooran*. Courtesy and simplicity rule as Vij waits carefully on all who arrive early enough to get in. The wine list is small but excellent; prices are civilized, too. *$$; AE, DC, MC, V; no checks; dinner every day; beer and wine; reservations not accepted; between Granville St and Hemlock.* &

Villa del Lupo / ★★★

869 HAMILTON ST, VANCOUVER; 604/688-7436

Chef Julio Gonzalez Perini's dazzling experiments with flavor bring off-duty local chefs to this elegant Victorian townhouse. Order the veal steak, and marvel at the delicate blending of tastes and textures found in a sautéed morel stuffed with rich foie gras. Prices tend to be high, but so is quality, and portions are generous. Almost everything on the northern Italian menu is wonderful. Roasted sea bass wrapped with Parma ham, prosciutto, and sage is remarkable. Osso buco is a hearty house specialty and a consistent favorite. The wine list goes far beyond the Italian border. Grappa and eaux-de-vie are available as well. Service is amiable and correct. *$$$; AE, DC, MC, V; no checks; dinner every day; full bar; reservations recommended; between Robson and Smithe.*

LODGINGS

The Four Seasons / ★★★★

**791 W GEORGIA ST, VANCOUVER; 604/689-9333
OR 800/332-3442 (US ONLY)**

Guests wallow in luxury at this upscale Four Seasons hotel. It's a modern tower that's connected to 165 shops in the Pacific Centre mall below. Although the hotel is in the middle of the high-rise downtown core, many guest rooms and suites offer surprising city views and peeks at the harbor. Meticulous attention to detail means bathrobes, hair dryers, VCRs, shoe shines, 24-hour valet and room service, twice-daily housekeeping, and complimentary morning coffee and tea in the lobby. Facilities include an indoor/outdoor pool, health club (with iced towels), and rooftop garden. Kids are welcomed with milk and cookies on arrival, teddy bears in cribs, step stools in the bathroom, and child-sized plush robes. Business travelers appreciate phones with voice mail in English, French, or Japanese; modular phone jacks for computer hookup; and full business services. Chartwell (see review) is the city's best hotel dining room. The Garden Terrace, just off the lobby, is a place to see and be seen. *$$$; AE, DC, JCB, MC, V; no checks; www.fourseasons.com; at Howe St.* &

Hotel Vancouver / ★★★

900 W GEORGIA ST, VANCOUVER; 604/684-3131 OR 800/441-1414

One of the grand French château–style hotels owned by the Canadian Pacific Railway, the Hotel Vancouver dates back to 1887. The steeply pitched, green-patina copper roof has dominated the city's skyline since 1939. A recent overhaul was more restoration than renovation, and the hotel is again appropriately opulent. Stone arches, friezes, and other design elements hidden by earlier remodeling have been restored or re-created. A new Lobby Bar and the elegantly casual 900 West restaurant (see review) replaced the original main-floor lobby and Timber Club. A shopping arcade includes 11 high-end stores. The 508 spacious, elegant guest rooms feature dark wood furnishings, comfortable seating, and welcome touches, such as real cream for coffee, thick terry cloth robes, duvets, and a morning newspaper. There is a health club with a lap pool beneath skylights. Ask for a room high above the street noise. *$$$; AE, DC, DIS, E, JCB, MC, V; checks OK; reserve@hvc. cphotels.ca; www.fairmont.com; at Burrard St.* &

Hyatt Regency / ★★
655 BURRARD ST, VANCOUVER; 604/683-1234 OR 800/233-1234
No surprises here. This is a good Hyatt Regency, like others around the world. A modern white downtown tower, it's popular with conventions and tour groups yet offers personalized service. Adjacent to the Royal Centre shopping mall and two blocks from Pacific Centre mall, it has good harbor and mountain views from north-facing upper floors. Try for a corner room with a balcony. The Regency Club floor, with keyed access, has its own concierge, complimentary breakfast, midday cookies, and late-afternoon hors d'oeuvres. Use of the health club and pool are complimentary for all guests. Even standard rooms are among the largest in the city. *$$$; AE, DC, DIS, E, JCB, MC, V; checks OK; www.hyatt.com; at W Georgia.* &

Johnson Heritage House / ★★★
2278 W 34TH AVE, VANCOUVER; 604/266-4175
To say that owners Ron and Sandy Johnson are fond of antiques is an understatement. They have restored a 1920s Craftsman-style home on a quiet street in the city's Kerrisdale neighborhood and turned it into one of Vancouver's most intriguing bed-and-breakfasts. Everywhere in the three-story house are relics of the past: coffee grinders, gramophones—even carousel horses. Above the front door, the porch light is a genuine old Vancouver street lamp. Top-floor and basement rooms are cozy; the Carousel Suite, with its mermaid-theme bath and antique slate fireplace, is grandest. Each room has a separate guest telephone line, guidebook, and map to Vancouver. Breakfast is served in a bright, airy, cottage-style room. Children 12 and over OK; no pets. *$$; no credit cards; checks OK; www.johnsons-inn-vancouver.com; at Vine, in Kerrisdale.*

Kingston Hotel / ★★
757 RICHARDS ST, VANCOUVER; 604/684-9024
Guests often say this centrally located inn reminds them of a European bed-and-breakfast, especially its facade of cut granite, heavy wood, and Tudor-style windows. Rooms with private baths have color TVs; others have hand basins and share bath and TV facilities. All rooms have phones. Continental breakfast is served in the small lounge downstairs. Facilities include a sauna and coin-op laundry. A neighborhood pub, the Rose and Thorn, popular with a young crowd, is on the main floor. This three-story bed-and-breakfast inn—no elevator—is a great downtown value, and offers senior discounts. *$; AE, MC, V; no checks; www.vancouver-bc.com/kingstonhotel; at Robson St.*

Metropolitan Hotel / ★★★

645 HOWE ST, VANCOUVER; 604/687-1122 OR 800/667-2300

The Met has been a hit since owner Henry Wu began to woo Vancouverites and cosmopolitan travelers in 1995. Mandarin International built this richly appointed, 197-room hotel in time for Expo 86; Metropolitan Hotels brought back the sparkle, attention to detail, and personal around-the-clock service. Located in the heart of downtown's business and financial district, this red-brick tower offers outstanding concierge service, private Jaguar limousine service, nightly turndown service on request, 24-hour room service, a full-scale business center, and one of the finest hotel health clubs in the city. All rooms are deluxe, with balconies and city views, elegant contemporary appointments, European duvets, and Frette bathrobes; 18 suites are palatial. Technologically enhanced business guest rooms include laser printers and in-room faxes. Diva at the Met is the hotel's storefront bar and restaurant (see review). *$$$; AE, DC, MC, V; no checks; reservations@metropolitan.com; www.metropolitan. com; between Dunsmuir and W Georgia.* ᵫ

"O Canada" House / ★★

1114 BARCLAY ST, VANCOUVER; 604/688-0555

On a quiet street where the West End meets downtown, this beautifully restored 1897 Victorian home is where the national anthem, "O Canada," was written in 1909. Potted palms nestled in Oriental urns; a welcoming fireplace; large, comfy chairs; and soft lights greet you at every turn. Sherry is served in the evenings. A wraparound porch looks onto the surrounding English-style garden. Late-Victorian decor continues into six guest rooms with private baths and modern conveniences such as TVs, VCRs, fridges, and telephones. The South Suite has an adjoining sitting room. The Penthouse Suite offers two gabled sitting areas, skylights, and a view of downtown. The separate, diminutive guest cottage, a new addition, also has a gas fireplace and private patio. *$$$; MC, V; no checks; www.vancouver-bc.com/OCanada House; at Thurlow St, 1½ blocks south of Robson St.*

Pan Pacific Hotel / ★★★

300–999 CANADA PL, VANCOUVER; 604/662-8111 OR 800/663-1515, 800/937-1515 (US ONLY)

No hotel in Vancouver has a more stunning location, a better health club, or a more remarkable architectural presence. As part of Canada Place, the Pan Pacific juts out into Vancouver's inner harbor with its five giant white sails— actually the roof of a huge convention center. It's a little confusing when you first enter the hotel. Check-in is up the escalator to the third floor; guest rooms start on the eighth floor. Standard guest rooms are small, but suites are spacious. Decor is flawlessly understated and intentionally muted, in tones of cream and beige. Nothing deters from the views. The best face west, but you can't beat a corner room (with views from your tub). Watching floatplanes come and go against the backdrop of Stanley Park, Lions Gate Bridge, and the North

Shore mountains is hypnotizing. A complete range of guest services is offered. The fine-dining restaurant, the Five Sails, has received well-deserved recognition. *$$$; AE, DC, E, JCB, MC, V; no checks; reservations@panpacific-hotel. com; www.panpac.com; at foot of Burrard St.* ⅻ

Sheraton Suites le Soleil / ★★★

567 HORNBY ST, VANCOUVER; 604/632-3000
It's easy to walk right by the bland exterior facade of Sheraton Suites le Soleil ("the sun"). But inside, the decor demands attention. The opulent high-ceilinged lobby features original oil paintings, a grand fireplace, and a cozy sitting area. Like the lobby, 112 guest suites are a little small, but efficient layouts make the loss of space less noticeable. Besides, suites are beautifully decorated and furnished in tones of regal red and gold, focusing on le Soleil's solar theme. Some have floor-to-ceiling windows and large balconies. Amenities include bathrobes, Aveda toiletries, and coffeemakers. Guests have access to the state-of-the-art YWCA fitness center next door. *$$$; AE, DC, MC, V; no checks; www.lesoleilhotel.com; near Dunsmuir St.*

The Sutton Place Hotel / ★★★★

845 BURRARD ST, VANCOUVER; 604/682-5511 OR 800/543-4300
With its elegant interior and understated beige facade, Sutton Place would rank as a top hotel in any European capital. Each of 397 sound-proofed rooms and suites in this sumptuous residential-style hotel has all possible amenities, including newspapers (on request), umbrellas, shoe shines, and twice-daily housekeeping. Beds are king-size; furnishings are museum-quality reproductions of European antiques. There are 11 nonsmoking floors, the fastest elevators in town, a concierge, and bellhops who snap to attention when you arrive, whether you are wearing blue jeans or black tie. Sutton Place's Fleuri restaurant and its lounges are popular with locals. The richly paneled Gerard Lounge is ranked as one of the Northwest's best watering holes. Le Spa is replete with swimming pool, fitness room, and beauty salons. Sutton Place also provides the best wheelchair-accessible rooms in the city. *$$$; AE, DC, DIS, E, JCB, MC, V; no checks; info@vcr.suttonplace.com; www.suttonplace.com; between Robson and Smithe.* ⅻ

The Waterfront / ★★★

900 CANADA PLACE WY, VANCOUVER; 604/691-1991 OR 800/441-1414
The large and tastefully appointed rooms in the Canadian Pacific Hotel's 23-story Waterfront are among the city's best. Underground walkways connect the hotel to Canada Place and to the Vancouver Convention and Exhibition Centre. Expect wonderful surprises, such as third-floor guest rooms with private terraces and herb gardens that supply Herons Restaurant. Two Entree Gold Club floors offer a private concierge, continental breakfast, nightly hors d'oeuvres, and private conference room. Of 489 guest rooms, 29 are suites—one fit for royalty. The two-level, 2,000-plus-square-foot Royal Suite has a private balcony, full

kitchen, dining room, and living room on the main floor, and a master bedroom with Jacuzzi upstairs, as well as a second bedroom with two double beds and a private bath. Works of Canadian artists are prominently displayed. Amenities include a health club, outdoor pool with a view, nightly turndown service, nonsmoking floors, and rooms for people with disabilities. Harborside rooms have upgraded amenities and data ports for business travelers. *$$$; AE, DC, DIS, E, JCB, MC, V; no checks; www.cphotels.com; at Howe and Cordova Sts.* &

The Wedgewood Hotel / ★★★
845 HORNBY ST, VANCOUVER; 604/689-7777 OR 800/663-0666

Owner and manager Eleni Skalbania takes great pride in the Wedgewood—for good reason. It is ideally nestled in the heart of Vancouver's finest shopping district and across the street from the art gallery, the gardens of Robson Square, and the courthouse. The Wedgewood offers old-world charm and scrupulous attention to detail. From its location to the renowned Bacchus Ristorante (see review), this 93-room hotel is all a small urban luxury hotel should be. It's also the only upscale hotel in the city where you'll almost never find tour buses. Finely appointed rooms, surprisingly large and decorated with vibrant colors and genuine English antiques, feel like a grand home. Nightly turndown service, a bare-essentials fitness room, and 24-hour room service are offered. This is a place to spend your honeymoon—and many do. *$$$; AE, DC, DIS, E, JCB, MC, V; no checks; info@wedgewoodhotel.com; www.wedgewoodhotel.com; between Robson and Smithe.* &

West End Guest House / ★★
1362 HARO ST, VANCOUVER; 604/681-2889

Don't be put off by the blazing-pink exterior of this early-1900s Victorian home, on a residential street close to Stanley Park and a block off Robson in the busy West End. Owner Evan Penner runs a fine eight-room inn (each with private bath)—summer vacancies are rare. Rooms are small but nicely furnished; staff have worked in major hotels and know hospitality. Afternoon sherry or iced tea is served on the covered back deck overlooking the English-style garden. Nightly turndown service, feather beds and lambskin mattress covers, robes, telephones—even teddy bears—are provided. Breakfast is a bountiful cooked meal served family-style or delivered to your room. There is guest parking—a rarity in the West End. Families with children are accepted, but be careful with the antiques. *$$$; AE, DIS, MC, V; checks OK; info@westendguesthouse.com; www.westendguesthouse.com; at Broughton St, 1 block off Robson.*

The Westin Grand Vancouver / ★★★
433 ROBSON ST, VANCOUVER; 604/684-9393 OR 888/680-9393

The Westin's exquisite new 31-story, piano-shaped—hence the name—boutique hotel on the east end of Robson opened for business in spring 1999. A semicircular marble staircase rises from the dark-wood-paneled street-level entrance to the second-floor lobby, bar, and restaurant. (An elevator is behind the stairs.) The modern elegance is carried over into 207 guest suites featuring blond-wood furnishings, gray fabrics, and spacious marble bathrooms. Picture windows highlight city views. Each suite has two TVs, a kitchenette, large soaker tub, bathrobes, cordless phones, two phone lines, data port, large desk, and high-speed Internet access. Two suites per floor are outfitted for business travelers, with fax machines, office chairs, desk lamps—even staplers. The outdoor pool and Jacuzzi on the second-floor sundeck seem a world away from the street below. There's also a fitness center, as well as a business center with secretarial services. Vodka is a popular upscale nightclub at street level. *$$$; AE, DC, E, MC, V; checks OK; www.westin.com; next to Library Square.*

Around Vancouver

Richmond

This Vancouver suburb is south of the city, between the North Arm and the main Fraser River. The airport is between Richmond and Vancouver. Many Asians have moved into Richmond, as evidenced by the increasing number of out-standing **CHINESE RESTAURANTS** and the **ASIAN MALLS**.

RESTAURANTS

Sun Sui Wah Seafood Restaurant / ★★★

4940 NO. 3 RD, RICHMOND; 604/273-8208
3888 MAIN ST, VANCOUVER; 604/872-8822

The splashy Sun Sui Wah in Richmond, with its sail-like sculpture stretching across the glass-domed roof designed by Bing Thom, is fast becoming the talk of the town. Simon Chan brought the proven track record and signature dishes of this successful Hong Kong group to Vancouver a decade ago, and his team has been playing to packed houses ever since in Vancouver and Richmond. Reasons are legion: crispy, tender roasted squabs and sculpted Cantonese masterpieces such as luscious broccoli-skirted steamed chicken interwoven with black mushrooms and Chinese ham; deftly steamed scallops on silky bean curd topped with creamy-crunchy *tobikko* (flying-fish roe) sauce; Alaskan king crab in wine and garlic; lobster hot pot with egg noodles; giant beach oysters steamed in black-bean sauce; and lightly sautéed geoduck paired with deep-fried "milk"—fragrant with sweet coconut in a fluffy crust. Reserve early; these are wedding hot spots. *$$; AE, MC, V; no checks; lunch, dinner every day; full bar; reservations recommended; www.sunsuiwah.com; Alderbridge Plaza (Richmond), and at E 23rd Ave (Vancouver).* &

VANCOUVER HERITAGE WALK

Once visitors get over gawking at Vancouver's dramatic natural setting, they start noticing the richness and depth of its architectural landscape. Because Vancouver is a young and rapidly changing city, buildings constructed in the 1950s and 1960s are as vital to its architectural heritage as those from the late 1800s. Getting a sense of all this history is as easy as taking a walk.

A good place to start is Vancouver's oldest standing church, **Christ Church Cathedral** (690 Burrard St), completed in 1895 and now an island of antiquity amid a sea of traffic and glass high-rises. Christ Church is worth a visit for its beautiful stained-glass windows and the recent renovations to its exposed-beam, Gothic Revival structure. Just across the street, **Hotel Vancouver** (900 W Georgia St) opened for business in 1939: its richly detailed, chateau-style exterior (complete with verdigris roof) is matched by an equally lavish interior restoration. Also nearby is the old **Vancouver Public Library** (corner of Burrard and Robson). Although it hasn't vanished like so many of the city's other modernist landmarks, this clean-lined 1957 building has had a recent makeover as a Virgin Megastore, the studios of local station VTV, and a Planet Hollywood location. For comparison's sake, it's worth a look at the new **Library Square** (350 W Georgia St), which—no matter what anyone says—bears a strong resemblance to the Roman Colosseum.

LODGINGS

Fairmont Vancouver Airport Place / ★★★

**VANCOUVER INTERNATIONAL AIRPORT, RICHMOND; 604/207-5200
OR 800/676-8922**

While most airport hotels simply cater to harried business travelers, here is an oasis of tranquility. Rising above Vancouver's international terminal, it is the closest hotel to the airport. (Check in at satellite counters situated in baggage claim areas, and check your bags on to certain flights from your room.) A waterfall in the lobby and floor-to-ceiling Vision Wall soundproof glass on all floors eliminate outside noise. The Globe, with its subtle aeronautical motif, is a reasonably priced restaurant with a full menu, plus gourmet pasta and pizza bars at lunch. Even if you're not a guest, it's the perfect spot to while away spare boarding time, in front of large fireplaces or at the bar. Nonguests can use workout facilities—weights, treadmills, stationary bikes, rowing machines, a lap pool, saunas, hot tub, plus workout clothes and robes—for $15. From poolside picture windows, you can muse on the bustle in the terminal below. This might be Canada's most technologically advanced and environmentally sound hotel. The room heat turns on when you check in; lights turn on when you insert your key in the door—and turn off when you leave; the "do not disturb" sign

From the corner of Georgia and Burrard Streets, head south to the **Marine Building** (355 Burrard). From a distance, this 21-story art deco treasure, built in 1929–30, looks like something out of Gotham City. But comic-book analogies fail when you examine the exterior, inlaid with richly detailed terra-cotta friezes, and the opulent green- and blue-tiled foyer. Several blocks east on Hastings Street, the **General Post Office** building (757 W Hastings St), completed in 1910, is now part of the Sinclair Centre retail complex; its corner clock tower makes dramatic use of double columns and arcades, finishing with a dome and weather vane. Close by, the colonnaded former **Canadian Pacific Railway station** (601 W Cordova St), whose airy 1914 hall houses shops, offices, and the entrance to the Waterfront Sky Train and SeaBus stations. From here it's a short walk east to **Gastown**. Along Water Street you'll find some of the city's oldest hotels and warehouses, many of them refurbished as lofts and offices. Another promising route lies south on **Granville Mall**, home to numerous heritage buildings, including the **Orpheum Theatre** (884 Granville St). Finished in 1927—and rescued from demolition during the 1970s—this onetime vaudeville theater has a low-key facade but houses a spectacular mix of baroque styles.

If you want an expert guide, July through September the **Architectural Institute of BC** offers six rotating walking tours of Vancouver neighborhoods, including downtown, Chinatown, the West End, and Strathcona. Tours depart from the institute's offices (101–440 Cambie St; 604/685-8588; www.aibc.bc.ca).   —*Nick Rockel*

illuminates from a central control panel on the nightstand (which also shuts off the doorbell and routes calls to voice mail). Entree Gold rooms feature automated curtains, plus phones have keyboards and LCD screens for sending faxes and checking e-mail. *$$; AE, DC, E, MC, V; checks OK; www.cphotels.com; on departure level of Vancouver International Airport.*

North Vancouver

Across Burrard Inlet at Second Narrows, North Vancouver is backed by mountains that are Vancouver's playground. Grouse Mountain, the Capilano Suspension Bridge, Capilano Regional Park, and the Capilano salmon hatchery are popular. The public market at LONSDALE QUAY (123 Carrie Cates Ct; 604/985-6261), lesser-known than the one at Granville Island, boasts two levels of shops and produce, its open stalls filled with everything from toys and crafts to produce and smoked salmon. A large Iranian population has settled in North Vancouver, as the many IRANIAN MARKETS and saffron-scented restaurants attest.

RESTAURANTS

The Tomahawk / ★

1550 PHILIP AVE, NORTH VANCOUVER; 604/988-2612

Step inside the Tomahawk and be greeted by garden gnomes in a fountain—a prelude to the deeper level of kitsch that awaits. Fake native carvings and souvenir-variety paintings fill every conceivable space. It's the Louvre of tacky art. Menu names are a match for the decor. Legendary is the Yukon Breakfast, piled with five rashers of bacon, two eggs, hash browns, and toast, served all day. For lunch try the Big Chief Skookum Burger, if you can say it with a straight face, and chow down on a double beef-patty burger topped with a hot dog plus all the fixings, and a mountainous side order of fries, pickle, and slaw. For something smaller, try one of a slew of sandwiches. Cap your feast with baked-on-the-premises pie (lemon meringue, Dutch apple, or banana cream). The Tomahawk has been a Vancouver institution for more than 70 years. *$; AE, DC, MC, V; no checks; breakfast, lunch, dinner every day; no alcohol; reservations not accepted; at Marine Dr.* &

LODGINGS

Thistledown House / ★★★

3910 CAPILANO RD, NORTH VANCOUVER; 604/986-7173

This gorgeous Craftsman-style home was built in 1920 from timber cut on the nearby mountain, and has been completely restored and luxuriously furnished. Antiques and period pieces intermingle with eclectic international art. Six guest rooms have private baths, soundproofed walls, thick terry cloth robes, and down or silk duvets. Two rooms have gas fireplaces and separate sitting areas. Our favorite, Under the Apple Tree, has a two-person Jacuzzi and a private patio. One room even has a private porch. Ideal innkeepers, owners Rex Davidson and Ruth Crameri are a genial former restaurateur and an expert on Scottish history, and a professional interior designer from five generations of Swiss hoteliers, respectively. Afternoon tea, with complimentary sherry and fresh pastries, is served on the porch overlooking the flower garden or in the living room by the fireplace. Guests linger to exchange travel stories over sumptuous four-course breakfasts. The menu might include homemade granola with mulled milk or stirred yogurt, a selection of breads and jams, sherried grapefruit, alder-smoked Pacific salmon, and fresh fruits. Service is so flawless, it's hard to believe this B&B opened just a few years ago. It's not so hard to believe that most guests are return visitors. *$$$; AE, DC, E, MC, V; no checks; davidson@helix.net; www.thistle-down.com; across from Capilano Suspension Bridge.* &

LOWER MAINLAND
BRITISH COLUMBIA

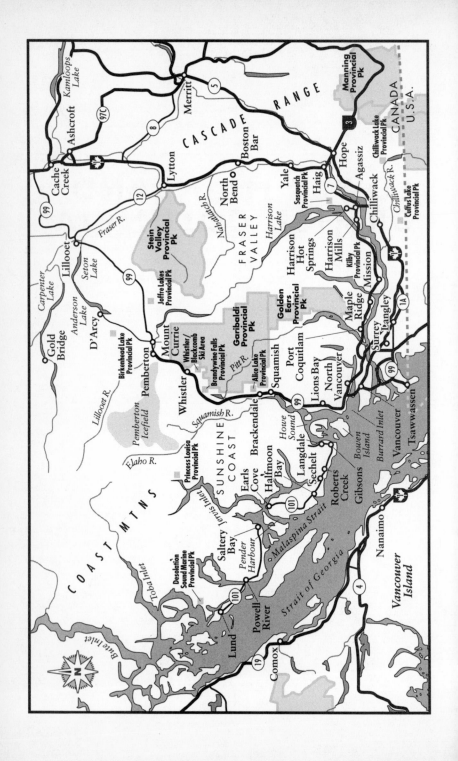

LOWER MAINLAND
BRITISH COLUMBIA

The term "Lower Mainland" came into currency among Vancouver Island settlers in the 19th century. Early immigration into the Crown Colony of British Columbia spilled over from Vancouver Island into the lush farmland of the Fraser River estuary and Fraser Valley. Vancouver Islanders used the term "mainlanders" to emphasize the separation between the two. The Strait of Georgia that divides the island from the Lower Mainland represents as much a psychological schism as it does a physical split. It didn't help when, by the end of the 1800s, Vancouver and the Lower Mainland had stolen the limelight from Victoria.

The Lower Mainland has grown well beyond the Fraser River basin to encompass Greater Vancouver, the Sunshine Coast, the Sea to Sky corridor, as well as the Fraser Valley regions. The success of Vancouver's International Exposition in 1986, and Whistler's ascendancy as one of the world's hippest resorts, have thrown a halo around the hinterland. Visitors come for a look around, and keep coming back—or stay. Who wouldn't want to live where eagles drop by at supper? Drawn by such a magnetic landscape, a new breed of entrepreneurs have set out to offer food and lodging in the midst of it all. In many cases the neighbors, if not the world, beat a path to their doors.

ACCESS AND INFORMATION

Border crossings (and customs) link Washington State and the Lower Mainland at four locations. The busiest are the crossings at Blaine, Washington, where Interstate 5 links with Highway 99 at the Peace Arch, and at Douglas, linking with Canada's Highway 15. The others are located just south of Aldergrove and at Sumas just south of Abbotsford. The nearest major airport is **VANCOUVER INTERNATIONAL AIRPORT** (3211 Grant McConachie Wy, Richmond; 604/276-6101).

Highway 1 (Trans-Canada Hwy) runs east-west and links the South Fraser Valley with Vancouver. Highway 17 links the BC Ferries' Tsawwassen terminal with Highway 99. The North Shore is reached by traveling west on Highway 1 across the Ironworkers Memorial Second Narrows Bridge. Highway 1 (or the Upper Levels Hwy, as it is called on the North Shore) crosses North and West Vancouver to Horseshoe Bay, site of the BC Ferries terminal that connects the North Shore with Nanaimo on Vancouver Island, Langdale (and Highway 101) on the Sunshine Coast, and nearby Bowen Island. From Horseshoe Bay, Highway 99 (the Sea to Sky Highway) links the North Shore with the upcountry communities of Squamish, Whistler, Pemberton, and Lillooet.

Sea to Sky Highway (Highway 99)

The scenic Sea to Sky Highway crosses paths with two historic routes—the Pemberton Trail and the Gold Rush Heritage Trail—that linked the coast with the interior in the days before automobiles. Along these ancient pathways, generations of Coast Salish people traded with their relations in the Fraser Canyon, and in the 1850s, prospectors stampeded north toward the Cariboo gold fields. In 1915, the Pacific Great Eastern railway began service between Squamish and the Cariboo, proving an ideal way to reach trailheads in **GARIBALDI PROVINCIAL PARK** (604/898-3678) and fishing camps such as Alta Lake's Rainbow Lodge, at the foot of London Mountain.

By the mid-1960s, the prospect of skiers heading from Vancouver to the fledgling trails on London Mountain—by this time renamed Whistler—prompted the provincial government to open a road north from Horseshoe Bay to Whistler. Space being at a premium along steep-sided Howe Sound (North America's southernmost fjord), road and railway parallel each other for much of the 28 miles (45 km) between Horseshoe Bay and Squamish, at the head of the sound. By 1975, the highway was pushed through to Pemberton, and by 1995 the last stretch was paved between Pemberton and Lillooet. Today, vehicles breeze along the entire route in five hours.

The railway (which now departs from its southern depot in North Vancouver) and Highway 99 helped introduce visitors to the region's backcountry. (The 12-hour train trip between North Vancouver and Prince George in the Central Interior is one of Canada's most scenic.) Certainly, Whistler's success has propelled development, both commercial and recreational, in other parts of the region, particularly Squamish and Pemberton. So too has the popularity of the mountain bike and the sport-utility vehicle—both of which make the backcountry more accessible.

Along the Sea to Sky Highway, at the **TANTALUS RANGE VIEWPOINT** (15½ miles/25 km north of Squamish), you can see a dozen or more peaks. **BRANDYWINE FALLS PROVINCIAL PARK** (21 miles/34 km north of Squamish) south of Whistler features Brandywine Falls, Daisy Lake, and the Black Tusk's volcanic snaggletooth. **NAIRN FALLS PROVINCIAL PARK** (2 miles/1.2 km south of Pemberton) north of Whistler also features waterfalls.

ACCESS AND INFORMATION

GREYHOUND/MAVERICK COACH lines (604/898-3914 in Squamish, 604/932-5031 in Whistler) offers frequent daily service between Squamish and Mount Currie just east of Pemberton. **BC RAIL** (604/631-3500, 800/339-8752 in BC only, or 800/663-8238) offers regular passenger service between Squamish and Lillooet on the *Cariboo Prospector* day liner. In summer, BC Rail operates excursions between North Vancouver and Squamish aboard the *Royal Hudson* steam train, and a boat/train excursion between the two (water travel is via the MV *Britannia*). Call BC Rail or **FIRST TOURS** (604/688-7246) for information.

SEA TO SKY THREE-DAY TOUR

DAY ONE: After breakfast head north on Highway 99, pausing at **Shannon Falls Provincial Park** to see the falls. Lunch at the nearby **Roadhouse Diner at Klahanie,** then continue on to Squamish. Stroll the hour-long **Squamish Estuary Trail,** then visit **Raven Sun Gallery** and **Brackendale Art Gallery.** Check in at the **Howe Sound Inn & Brewing Company** in downtown Squamish; in the pub, admire the view of Stawamus Chief Mountain, and quench your thirst from an arm's-long list of microbrews. Time to freshen up before dinner at the inn's **Red Heather Grill.** Get an early night.

DAY TWO: Have breakfast at the inn, and make sure there's film in your camera for the breathtaking drive to **Whistler.** Nonstop, the drive is only 45 minutes, but take your time. Pause at the **Tantalus Range Viewpoint** to see a dozen or more peaks, and at **Brandywine Falls Provincial Park** to see the falls and the Black Tusk. Lunch in Whistler at **Hoz's Pub,** where insiders have been heading for the past 20 years. Just outside is the beginning of the 10-mile (16-km) **Valley Trail.** Check in to your room at the **Edgewater Lodge** on Green Lake before heading into Whistler Village, where you can catch happy hour at the **Dubh Linn Gate Irish Pub** (604/905-4047) in the Pan Pacific Lodge. Head back to the lodge for the sunset on Blackcomb and Whistler Mountains and dinner at the Edgewater; otherwise, treat yourself to dinner at **Araxi Restaurant and Bar.**

DAY THREE: Up early for a quick breakfast delivered to your room before heading north. Stop at **Nairn Falls Provincial Park** for a quick jaunt to the falls, then into **Pemberton** and to **Grimm's Gourmet & Deli** to pick up picnic supplies. Poke your head in the **Pemberton Pioneer Museum** before beginning the two-hour drive to Lillooet; pause at the top of Cayoosh Pass in **Joffre Lakes Provincial Park** to enjoy your picnic. Just before Lillooet, stop at the BC Hydro recreation area on **Seton Lake** to walk the beach, then climb to the viewpoint. In Lillooet check in to your room at the **Tyax Mountain Lake Resort,** then stroll over to **Dina's Place** for dinner. Catch the sunset from the patio as the smell of sagebrush rises in the air.

The **SQUAMISH CHAMBER OF COMMERCE AND VISITOR INFO CENTRE** (37950 Cleveland Ave, Squamish; 604/892-2034; info@squamishchamber.bc. ca; www.squamishchamber.bc.ca) and **TOURISM WHISTLER** (4010 Whistler Wy, Whistler; 604/932-3928 in Whistler, 604/664-5625 in Vancouver, or 800/944-7853; www.tourismwhistler.com) are good resources for the area.

Squamish

Squamish (population 16,000), or "Squish," as it's affectionately known, is a relief. Far smaller than Vancouver, larger than Whistler, and equidistant from both, Squamish is the envy of the south coast. It has so many things going for it—location, geography, wildlife, weather—that as forestry declines as the town's major employer, tourism and outdoor recreation have taken on greater importance. Travelers have *always* been drawn to Squamish, from the days of the Coast Squamish people, who journeyed between Burrard Inlet and Stawamus (pronounced STA-a-mus) at the mouth of the Squamish River, to more recent times when steamships began ferrying anglers, climbers, and picnickers here over a century ago. Things have only intensified since then.

Today, the **GARIBALDI ECOADVENTURE CENTRE** (Shannon Falls, Hwy 99; 888/684-8828; info@toursquamish.com; www.toursquamish.com) coordinates and promotes the wide variety of offerings available. It's located in the **ROADHOUSE DINER** at Klahanie (604/892-5312), opposite **SHANNON FALLS PROVINCIAL PARK** (604/898-3678), site of BC's third-highest waterfall, at 1,105 feet (335 m). Two blocks west of downtown Squamish is the hour-long **SQUAMISH ESTUARY TRAIL** (west end of Vancouver St). Bring binoculars; this is bald eagle country. If you want to take one home with you, you might find an authentic carved replica at **RAVEN SUN GALLERY** (101 Baker Rd; 604/892-3820) or **BRACKENDALE ART GALLERY** (41950 Government Rd, Brackendale; 604/898-3333).

RESTAURANTS

Red Heather Grill / ★

37801 CLEVELAND AVE (HOWE SOUND INN), SQUAMISH; 604/892-2603 OR 800/919-2537

The most elegant dining room in Squamish features tastefully understated decor that matches the indoor-outdoor feel of the inn. Pull up a Craftsman chair to a sturdy wooden table, or plunk down in an oversize couch beside the fireplace next to the bar. Artwork by local painters fairly leaps off the walls, but the dining experience doesn't always live up to the ambience. Some entrees suffer from an over-the-top blend of ingredients. But you can't go wrong with the appetizers, often a meal in themselves. Try Cajun Fanny Bay oysters or peppered, seared yellow fin tuna. The Salmon Sampler—smoked, candied, barbecued tips with mango salsa, red pepper mayonnaise, and assorted relishes—is good with house bread, such as whole wheat focaccia or herb-and-cheese. (Loaves are available for purchase.) The grill has its own wood-fired pizza oven from which inventive creations emerge. *$$; AE, MC, V; no checks; lunch, dinner every day, brunch Sun; full bar; reservations recommended; hsibrew@howesound.com; www.howesound.com; downtown Squamish.* &

LODGINGS

Howe Sound Inn & Brewing Company / ★

37801 CLEVELAND AVE, SQUAMISH; 604/892-2603 OR 800/919-2537

This 20-room inn with its massive fieldstone chimney is part brew pub, part restaurant, and part roadhouse. Owners Dave Fenn and Stephan Shard not only fashioned a two-story traveler's hotel, they also created a meeting place for local outdoor enthusiasts. Guests can pick up information on climbing and kayaking routes, or get the latest road report. Simply appointed rooms are modestly sized. The upstairs reading lounge is perfect for planning the next day's outing. Other amenities include a sauna and climbing wall. Breakfast orders are taken the previous evening and it's delivered to your door. In the 1990s, pioneering BC brewmaster John Mitchell, who opened the province's first microbrewery at Horseshoe Bay in 1982, set up shop here. His creations include Baldwin and Cooper Best Bitter, named for the climbers who first successfully scaled Stawamus Chief Mountain opposite the inn in the 1960s. *$$; AE, MC, V; no checks; hsibrew@howesound.com; www.howesound.com; downtown Squamish.* &

Whistler

The summit of the small Whistler Valley contains the resort municipality of Whistler (population 7,500), above which world-class ski runs crisscross Blackcomb and Whistler Mountains. At the heart of Whistler lies Alta Lake, from which water flows south to the Pacific via the Cheakamus and Squamish Rivers, and north via the River of Golden Dreams through the Harrison watershed and the Fraser River. No other valley in the Sea to Sky region has such a wealth of small and medium-sized lakes. And no other lakes have quite the scenery to mirror. Above the tree line, you can still see remnants of the most recent ice age in glaciers on the highest peaks of surrounding Garibaldi Provincial Park.

Whistler's layout is a complex collection of "villages" that are best traversed on foot. Roads surround these pedestrian-friendly plazas and link them to the large hotels and restaurants. Hop one of the Whistler Wave buses to the lifts; it's easier than trying to park in Whistler Village, and it only takes a few minutes.

WHISTLER MOUNTAIN (elevation 7,160 feet/2,182 m) and **BLACKCOMB** (elevation 7,494 feet/2,284 m) were rivals for two decades before merging in 1997. Separately or together, they comprise what many skiers and snowboarders consider the premier North American winter resort. You can just as easily explore one as the other; each offers a complimentary perspective on its companion and has a loyal following of ski and snowboard devotees. They have been around long enough (Whistler since 1965, Blackcomb since 1980) to have developed trails over a total of 7,071 acres that have been shaped, groomed, and gladed to hold snow and reduce obstacles. For information on **LESSONS AND RENTALS** at either mountains, as well as ticket prices, contact guest relations (800/766-0449, 604/932-3434 in Whistler, 604/664-5614 in Vancouver; www. whistler-blackcomb.com). Call for current **SNOW CONDITIONS** (604/932-4211 in Whistler, 604/687-7507 in Vancouver).

Whistler Village's **LOST LAKE** features an 18-mile (29-km) network of packed and tracked trails for **CROSS-COUNTRY SKIERS**. At the log chalet near the start (on Valley Trail north of Lorimer Rd; 604/932-6436), pay your fee (about $12 during the day, $4 in the evening, no charge after 9pm) for use of the trails. Skiing around the lake takes 60–90 minutes. Trails are marked for beginners to experts; the 2 ½-mile (4-km) Lost Lake Loop Trail is lit for night skiing. A designated cross-country ski trail in winter and a hiking loop in summer, the **VALLEY TRAIL**'s access points include the Whistler Golf Course (on Hwy 99 in Whistler Village), the Meadow Park Sports Centre (on Hwy 99 in Alpine Meadows), and Rainbow Park (on Alta Lake Rd).

SNOWMOBILING is big at Whistler. For years the Showh Lakes Forestry Road has been the winter location for Whistler Snowmobile Guided Tours (36–4314 Main St; 604/932-4086; www.snowmobiles-bc.com). **HELI-SKIING/BOARDING** in Whistler can be arranged with Whistler Heli-Skiing (3-4241 Village Stroll; 604/932-4105) and Blackcomb Helicopters (9990 Heliport; 604/938-1700). **SNOWCAT SKIING/SNOWBOARDING** can also get you into Whistler's untracked backcountry; vendors include West Coast Cat Skiing (9615 Emerald Pl; 888/246-1111 or 604/932-2166).

SLEIGH RIDES put the jingle bells into outdoor winter fun. To hitch a ride, call Blackcomb Horse-Drawn Sleigh Rides (604/932-7631) in Whistler. If you'd rather mush, call Husky Kennels (8046 Parkwood; 604/932-5732) to go **DOGSLEDDING**.

If you can walk, you can **SNOWSHOE**. Some of the most inviting trails in Whistler are those in the forest surrounding Olympic Station on Whistler Mountain. Canadian Snowshoe Adventures (604/932-0647; www.iias.com/outdoors) offers rentals and guided tours, including evening outings on Blackcomb.

Although diehards can ski Horstman Glacier until mid-August, come summer, do what the locals do. Turn your back on the Village square and head for the hills (many consider the area to be the best **MOUNTAIN BIKING** terrain in the world), the lakes (this is where **BOARD-SAILING** started in Canada), or the rivers (by **RAFT, CANOE,** or **KAYAK**). The **VALLEY TRAIL**, a mostly level loop of almost 10 miles (16 km) that passes many of Whistler's neighborhoods and Lost Lake, takes you through cool forest to Alpha, Nita, and Alta Lakes. The tourism and activity offices noted under Access and Information below can provide any info you need.

GOLFERS can try the scenic Arnold Palmer–designed Whistler Golf Club (4001 Whistler Wy; 604/932-3280), rated one of the best courses in the world by *Golf* magazine, or the equally esteemed Robert Trent Jones Jr. link course at Chateau Whistler (4599 Chateau Blvd; 604/938-2092). Another possibility is Nicklaus North (8080 Nicklaus N Blvd; 604/938-9898), a Jack Nicklaus–designed course in the Green Lake area.

Tourism Whistler's **ACTIVITY AND INFORMATION CENTRE** (4010 Whistler Wy; 604/932-2394) can offer advice and arrangements for any winter or summer recreation you desire. Whistler has achieved such a high level of international popularity that on some weekends, rooms cannot be had for love or money. With more than 2 million ski visits alone each winter, in Whistler advance reservations are recommended for all lodging and restaurants. Many

EAGLE EYES

The largest gathering of bald eagles in southwestern British Columbia occurs along the banks of the Squamish River as it flows past Brackendale. Each year, from November until mid-February, thousands of these majestic avian specimens come from points north and east to feast on a late-fall coho salmon run. Biologists aren't quite sure why the Squamish (and its tributary, the Mamquam River) is so popular—one theory holds that the depletion of salmon runs in other parts of the province is to blame—but there's no denying the vast number of birds that roost along these rivers during the winter.

In 1996, the BC government created the **Brackendale Bald Eagle Sanctuary** (an hour's drive north of Vancouver, along Hwy 99), an act that recognized the importance of this area. (But for the eagle population to sustain itself, the riparian habitat of the life-giving salmon runs will have to be preserved—a critical component not guaranteed by legislating a piece of ground a "sanctuary.") It's a bit surprising to find a bird recently taken off the endangered species list in such abundance. Indeed, if you walk the trails or riverbanks here in the predawn darkness and wait for the first rays of sunlight, you'll be rewarded by the sight of 70–80 eagles in a single tree. (As crowds of bird-watchers and sightseers gather later in the day, the eagles start roosting farther away.) Because the peak viewing period is in the dead of winter, the cottonwood trees are bare of leaves, making for easy viewing. Additionally, a flock of trumpeter swans can often be seen near the mouth of the Squamish.

The Sunwolf Outdoor Centre (604/898-1537) offers naturalist-guided raft tours of the Squamish River during winter. The Brackendale Art Gallery (604/898-3333) pays homage to the eagles by hosting an official eagle count in January each year (dates vary from one year to the next). In 1994, a record 3,769 eagles were counted.

—Steven Threndyle

rooms in the area, as well as condos, are owned by different management companies. All may be reached through Tourism Whistler's **CENTRAL RESERVATIONS** (604/932-4222 in Whistler, 604/664-5625 in Vancouver, or 800/944-7853 from the United States and Canada, except BC).

RESTAURANTS

Araxi Restaurant & Bar / ★★★

4222 WHISTLER VILLAGE SQUARE, WHISTLER; 604/932-4540

A cousin to Vancouver's CinCin, the newly renovated and perennially trendy Araxi attracts a young, beautiful, and well-dressed crowd, and is one of Whistler's culinary cornerstones. In a town with so many restaurants per square foot, that means something. Araxi is located in the center of "action central"—Whistler Village Square—with sought-after summer patio dining. The softly illuminated interior features rich earth tones and dark wood accents. Chef James Walt's surprising starters include blue-shell mussels steamed in a curry-scented broth accented with clover honey and basil, or spring rolls stuffed with homemade sausage, prawns, and vegetables, served with a ginger-and-cilantro sauce. Juicy slow-roasted venison strip loin is served with woodland mushroom and provolone ravioli, spaghetti squash seasoned with a warming touch of nutmeg, and a bright cranberry–blood orange chutney. Walt's version of paella combines local fish, shellfish, chorizo, and chicken in a saffron-laced risotto. Two sommeliers ensure Araxi's big, changeable, and impressive wine cellar is yours to explore every night. Dessert? Share rich chocolate espresso mousse served with mascarpone cream and delicate butter biscuits, or ginger-scented crème brûlée. *$$$; AE, DC, MC, V; no checks; lunch, dinner every day (dinner only Dec–Apr); full bar; reservations recommended; heart of Whistler Village.* &

Caramba! / ★★

12–4314 MAIN ST, WHISTLER; 604/938-1879

 This fun, boisterous, Mediterranean-influenced restaurant reflects owner Mario Enero's ability to wow even those on a modest budget. He's combined high-energy service with big, soul-satisfying portions of pasta, pizza, and roasts. Start with savory baked goat cheese served with a tomato coulis and garlic toast points. Then delve into Fettuccine Natasha, accented with chunks of fresh salmon and a peppery vodka-and-tomato cream sauce. Munch on a melanzane pizza heaped with roasted eggplant, roma tomatoes, and goat cheese. Or try mouth-watering grilled bay trout with bacon-and-onion mashed potatoes. The open kitchen, earthen hues, and alderwood-burning pizza ovens lend a warm, casual tone to the room. *$; AE, MC, V; no checks; lunch, dinner every day; full bar; reservations recommended; Village North, at Town Plaza Square.* &

Chef Bernard's / ★★

1–4573 CHATEAU BLVD, WHISTLER; 604/932-7051

Chateau Whistler's former executive chef, Bernard Casavant, is now Whistler's foremost caterer. When you walk into Chef Bernard's, you enter Casavant's kitchen. Fortunately, he included a few wooden tables and a takeout counter. The lights are a little bright, and '80s rock wafts from a portable radio, but the food is outstanding. With an emphasis on farm-fresh local produce, Casavant creates a flawless fusion of classic French and Pacific Northwest cuisines. Start with Brie-and-carrot soup, or organic field lettuce salad with herb-crusted chicken breast. Try pan-seared wild salmon fillet in a lemongrass and star anise marinade served with basmati rice and a spicy orange-ginger sauce. Chef Bernard keeps locals coming back for his fried free-range egg sandwich made with aged cheddar and bacon on a toasted granola bun. Fresh pies are a dessert treat. BC wines and beers dominate the beverage list. *$; AE, MC, V; no checks; breakfast, lunch, dinner every day; beer* *and wine; reservations not accepted; chefbernards@cyberlink.bc.ca; www. cyberlink.bc.ca/~chefbernards/; Upper Village, at Blackcomb Wy.* &

Hoz's Pub & Creekside Grillroom / ★

2129 LAKE PLACID RD, WHISTLER; 604/932-4424

Good basic fare in a down-to-earth atmosphere might seem hard to find in Whistler, but the locals know a spot that pleases almost every palate. From deluxe burgers, barbecued chicken, and ribs (served with beans, hand-cut fries, and slaw) to cod or salmon fish-and-chips, Hoz's satisfies. Surprises include Rahm Schnitzel (pork cutlet topped with mushroom and port sauce) and New York Neptune (charboiled strip steak topped with white asparagus, baby shrimp, and hollandaise). Wear your best flannel shirt, and check pretensions at the door. If you're in the mood for steak, check out the Creekside Grillroom; Ron "Hoz" Hosner has spiffed up his eatery next to the pub and is serving up first-rate boneless prime rib and pepper steak. The wine list offers a good West Coast selection. A beer-and-wine store (11am–11pm) is on-site. *$; AE, DC, MC, V; no checks; breakfast, lunch, dinner every day; full bar; reservations recommended; hoz@whistlerweb.com; www.whistleronline.com/grillroom; 1½ blocks west of Hwy 99, Creekside area.*

La Rua / ★★★

4557 BLACKCOMB WY (LE CHAMOIS), WHISTLER; 604/932-5011

Mario Enero runs a stylish but comfortable restaurant in Le Chamois hotel that prides itself on snap-of-the-finger service and a great wine list. Chef Tim Muehlbauer has devised some superb dishes served in ample portions. Start with duck breast served on truffle potatoes topped with raspberry jus and hazelnut oil; or savor the port-marinated ostrich carpaccio with capers and shallots. No one makes better lamb, serving a Washington State rack with mint pesto or a shank set atop a mound of root vegetables and lentils; venison medallions aren't bad either. Toothsome pastas, such as butternut squash agnolotti with smoked duck in a curry cream sauce, are sure to win your heart. Save room for homemade biscotti and chocolate truffles. In warm weather, cigar aficionados leave the deep-red dining room (filled with bold works of art) and hit the deck for a smoke and a glass of ice wine or port. *$$$; AE, DC, MC, V; no checks; lunch, dinner every day; full bar; reservations recommended; www.whistler.net/larua; Upper Village, Lorimer Rd and Blackcomb Wy.* &

Las Margaritas Restaurante y Cantina / ★★

2021 KAREN CRES (WHISTLER CREEK LODGE), WHISTLER; 604/938-6274

Tucked away on the edge of the road at Creekside Village, Las Margaritas, a big open room filled with sturdy oak tables and chairs, has a classic cantina atmosphere. It gets crowded, but who cares? Locals flock here for its namesake cocktails, among them the Rosarita Margarita (with a splash of cranberry juice). Start with the Fiesta Platter—samplings of guacamole, chicken wings, cheese quesadillas, chicken taquitos, and mini chimichangas, along with sweet jalapeño salsa, sour cream, and *salsa de agua-cate*. Besides some unique twists on tacos, enchiladas, chimichangas, and que-sadillas, the cantina offers good sirloin steak or chicken breast fajitas. The grilled-salmon burrito is served with black beans and house salad. Service is as warm and friendly as the cuisine and the atmosphere. *$$; AE, DC, MC, V; no checks; dinner every day; full bar; reservations recommended (weekends); Creekside Village at Hwy 99.* &

Quattro at Whistler / ★★★

4319 MAIN ST (PINNACLE INTERNATIONAL HOTEL), WHISTLER; 604/905-4844

Right from the start, carbo-loading skiers loved to slide into Antonio Corsi's restaurant at the Pinnacle International Hotel. Quattro at Whistler is upbeat, vibrant, and innovative. La Cucina Leggera, or "the healthy kitchen," is the motto of Quattro, a concept that fits West Coast sensibilities like a good set of ski boots. Funghi fanciers love carpaccio featuring sliced portobello mush-rooms topped with flavorful white truffle oil and shaved Asiago. Kudos also for prawns sautéed with thyme, garlic, and a sprinkle of fresh lemon, served with a painstakingly prepared creamy herb risotto. Try gnocchi al Gorgonzola, an idyllic marriage of tender potato and semolina dumplings and sharp Gor-gonzola topped with roasted pecans. Entrees of braised lamb shank simmered with root vegetables and porcini mushrooms served over a creamy polenta, or roasted lean duck breast accompanied by sun-dried cherry and grappa syrup, are irresistible. Portions are generous. The mainly Italian wine list is stellar. The staff is knowledgeable, friendly, and attentive. Stunning desserts change daily. *$$$; MC, V; no checks; dinner every day; full bar; reservations recommended; Village North, at Library Square.* &

Rim Rock Cafe and Oyster Bar / ★★★

2101 WHISTLER RD (HIGHLAND LODGE), WHISTLER; 604/932-5565

Filled to the rafters with a hip local crowd, this cozy cafe with a stone fireplace has been dishing out great food for years. Split into two levels (smokers downstairs), the Rim Rock is housed in the unprepossessing High-land Lodge. Bob Dawson and Rolf Gunther's restaurant is remarkable proof that fresh seafood and wondrous cuisine are not anomalies in the mountains. The fresh sheet features starters such as raw Fanny Bay oysters topped with vodka, crème fraîche, and caviar. Main events range from herb-infused salmon to panfried mahimahi in an almond-ginger crust to a mouth-watering grilled filet mignon topped with fresh herb butter or creamy tricolored peppercorn sauce. The Death by Chocolate dessert can make grown men cry. In summer, book a table on the cozy back patio and dine amid fresh herbs in the chef's garden. Service is top-drawer—knowledgeable but not arrogant. *$$$; AE, MC, V; no checks; dinner every day; full bar; reservations recommended; 3 miles (4.8 km) south of Whistler Village, at Creekside.*

Splitz Grill / ★★

4369 MAIN ST (ALPENGLOW), WHISTLER; 604/938-9300

It's been a long time since a hamburger (or any of its '90s-style chicken, salmon, or lentil cousins) has been this thick, juicy, and tantalizing. Chef Trevor Jackson struck the right chord in the hearts of locals and visitors by offering a not-so-humble grilled sandwich on a crusty bun with your choice of toppings—from chili, garlic mayo, ketchup, tahini, sauerkraut, and hummus to fresh tomato, sprouts, avocado, salsa, and kosher pickles. A satisfying meal is less than $10, including thick, house-cut fries and a soft drink. Maybe that's why more than 44,000 burgers were sold from this tiny spot (only eight counter seats) in its first year. Sweet temptations include ice cream sundaes, floats, shakes, cones, and a caramelized banana split. *$; AE, MC, V; no checks; lunch, dinner every day; no alcohol; reservations not accepted; Village North, across from 7-11.*

Sushi Village / ★★

4272 MOUNTAIN SQUARE (WESTBROOK HOTEL), WHISTLER; 604/932-3330

To satisfy an appetite for healthy portions of Japanese cuisine, locals head to Sushi Village. You can't miss it, even though it's perched on the second floor of the Westbrook Hotel; ravenous young skiers and snowboarders patiently wait in line with upscale sophisticates. It's worth it. The simple Japanese-style decor allows for privacy even with large parties. The staff is knowledgeable, gracious, and consistent. Delicious and extremely fresh sushi, sashimi, and *maki* platters, as well as abundant combinations served in wooden sushi boats, are prepared by animated experts at the counter. Tempura, gyoza, yakitori, teriyaki, and satisfying meal-sized noodle soups are just a few hot dishes. Food is straightforward, dependable, and a good deal. Semiprivate tatami rooms and takeout are available. *$$; AE, DC, MC, V; no checks; lunch Wed–Sun, dinner every day (weekends only off season); full bar; reservations recommended for 4 or more; sushivil@direct.ca; Whistler Village, at Sundial Cres.* &

Trattoria di Umberto / ★★★

4417 SUNDIAL CRES (MOUNTAINSIDE LODGE), WHISTLER; 604/932-5858

Two large, romantically lit dining rooms separated by a massive open kitchen welcome you to this busy, lively, very northern Italian establishment. Animated conversation is as much a part of the atmosphere as the potted plants and sculptures, the poolside view, and the rustic Italian decor. Service is fast and friendly. Classic Tuscan starters include beef carpaccio topped with shaved Parmesan, accompanied by a mélange of aromatic vegetables, and hearty Tuscan bean soup. But it's entrees like the grilled quail with sage, or the cioppino (a saffron- and fennel-laced stew combining crab, prawns, mussels, and a variety of fish in a rich tomato broth) that will leave you singing the kitchen's praises. No trattoria can exist without pasta and risotto dishes:

smoked-duck-and-portobello risotto, and penne with pesto and smoked salmon, are just two examples at Umberto's. A respectable wine list, desserts large enough to share, cappuccino, and espresso complete the experience. *$$$; AE, DC, MC, V; no checks; lunch, dinner every day; full bar; reservations recommended; inquire@umberto.com; www.umberto.com; Whistler Village, at Blackcomb Wy.* &

Val d'Isère / ★★★

4314 MAIN ST (BEAR LODGE), WHISTLER; 604/932-4666

Val d'Isère offers a grand combination: fine dining and people-watching. Nearly every seat has a street-level view of the plaza. The interior is intimate: a provençal motif tastefully executed in muted tones of blue and gold, illuminated by table lamps. Superchef Roland Pfaff still presides over this French kitchen with overtones of Alsace, offering palate-pleasing delicacies. His starter of Queen Charlottes smoked herring and Granny Smith apple salad served in a buttery potato mille-feuille with smoked-mussel vinaigrette is heartwarming. For entrees, we couldn't resist the delicately seared Alaskan scallops, served with champagne sauce and Israeli couscous, or the richly flavored braised duck legs, enhanced by duck stock and rosebud reduction, paired with bulgur risotto. Wines from France, the United States, and Canada grace the impressive cellar list. Pfaff's signature dessert is a chocolate cream–centered chocolate cake presented on a custardy crème anglaise. *$$$; AE, DC, MC, V; no checks; dinner every day (closed Canadian Thanksgiving–American Thanksgiving); full bar; reservations recommended; valdiser@direct.ca; www.valdisere-restaurant.com; Village North, at Town Plaza Square.* &

LODGINGS

Brew Creek Lodge / ★★

1 BREW CREEK RD, WHISTLER; 604/932-7210

 Originally built as a private home in the 1970s, Brew Creek Lodge became a quiet hideaway bed-and-breakfast on the road to Whistler in the 1980s. Brew Creek itself flows down the steep, rugged slopes of Mount Brew. The creek charges through the lodge's 12 acres to nearby Daisy Lake. The massive post-and-beam main lodge features six spacious rooms on its top floor, all with bathrooms en suite. Elsewhere on the property, accommodations include two family-size suites that adjoin the Guest House (sleeps eight), the Trappers Cabin (sleeps four), and the Treehouse (sleeps two); rooms have no TVs or phones. Fanciful architectural flourishes attest to the original owner's enthusiasm, though it would be hard to improve on the site's natural beauty. Instead, everything blends harmoniously, right down to the wine cellar hollowed in the volcanic bedrock of the Brew Creek Lodge basement. Cross-country trails lead from the lodge, and Whistler is 20 minutes north. The lodge has its own creekside hot tub and swimming pond. *$$–$$$; AE, MC, V; no checks; www.brewcreek.com; 12 miles (16 km) south of Whistler.* &

Chateau Whistler Resort / ★★★★

4599 CHATEAU BLVD, WHISTLER; 604/938-8000 OR 800/606-8244

Many of Canada's classic resort hotels have been built under the Canadian Pacific Hotels banner. The 12-story, 563-room Chateau Whistler is no exception. The largest resort hotel built in Canada in the past century, this is arguably *the* place to experience Whistler, a pleasant five-minute walk from the buzz of the village, at the base of Blackcomb. Its sun-drenched east side takes in sweeping views of the mountains from slopeside suites, the hotel's main dining room and lounge, or the indoor/outdoor pool and spa complex. West-facing accommodations are priced slightly lower, and offer views of Rainbow Mountain. All the pampering touches one would expect are provided. Given the grand impression of the chateau's foyer, however, standard rooms—particularly junior suites—are only adequately sized, but public areas are some of the nicest in Whistler. Hooked rugs soften the slate slab floor, and two mammoth limestone fireplaces are accented by folk-art and twig furniture. The privately owned spa on-site is a stylish addition. *$$$$; AE, DC, DIS, JCB, MC, V; checks OK; cwres@cphotels.ca; www.chateauwhistlerresort.com; at foot of Blackcomb.* &

Delta Whistler Resort / ★★

4050 WHISTLER WY, WHISTLER; 604/932-1982 OR 800/268-1133

As the first major hotel to open in Whistler Village at the base of the dual mountain operations in the 1980s, the Delta Whistler Resort nabbed a prime location. Gradual redevelopment has added a dome-covered year-round tennis facility, a heated outdoor lap pool, as well as a spa and fitness center with steam rooms, hot tubs, and saunas. The resort's standard rooms are surprisingly ordinary. Deluxe studios are worth the extra expense, equipped with balconies and fireplaces, full kitchens, Jacuzzis or soaking tubs, and clothes dryers. Also convenient are bike and ski rental shops in the 300-room, pet-friendly hotel. The Delta's West Coast cuisine–themed Evergreen restaurant was one of the first in Whistler to use local organic produce. *$$$$; AE, DC, DIS, JCB, MC, V; checks OK; reservations@delta-whistler.com; www.delta-whistler.com; Whistler Village.* &

Durlacher Hof Alpine Country Inn / ★★★

7055 NESTERS RD, WHISTLER; 604/932-1924

Erika and Peter Durlacher have a reputation as Whistler's most welcoming and generous innkeepers. Their Austrian pension commands a view of both Blackcomb and Whistler and is minutes from the slopes. Erika's painstaking attention to detail is evident in the cozy après-ski area (where complimentary afternoon tea is served) and immaculate rooms (some suites feature whirlpools) with hand-carved pine furniture, comfortable beds, and goose-down duvets. A groaning sideboard holds lavish breakfasts, and Erika prepares special dishes for each guest—perhaps *Kaiserschmarren* (pancakes with stewed plums) or *Afpfelschmarren* (fresh apple pancakes). From the moment you get up to the last cup of *Glüwein* late at night (the guest lounge is also a licensed bar), sharing the Hof with the Durlachers is a joy. They also rent out a studio in Whistler Village. *$$$–$$$$; MC, V; checks OK; peterika@ direct.ca; www.durlacherhof.com; Nesters neighborhood.* ♿

Edelweiss Pension Inn B&B / ★★

7162 NANCY GREENE DR, WHISTLER; 604/932-3641 OR 800/665-2003

One of the drawbacks of success is that it can lead to exclusiveness. Edelweiss Pension is a perennial favorite among Whistler regulars, so it's hard to get a reservation at Ursula and Jacques Morel's Bavarian-style guest house. Run in a European (*gemütlichkeit*) fashion, the pension has eight spotlessly clean rooms with eiderdown comforters and private baths. (The honeymoon suite features a Jacuzzi and gas fireplace.) Jacques, a former competitive skier, and Ursula cook ample breakfasts with international flair in their sunny breakfast room. Twice a week, the Morels prepare a *raclette* (melted cheese over ham, baby potatoes, bread, or vegetables) and serve it with French or German wine and espresso. Regardless of how brisk, friendly, and accommodating the hosts are, downstairs rooms get noisy early during ski season, when guests clomp around in their boots. *$$; AE, MC, V; checks OK; seasonal closings; ursula@whistleronline.com; www.whistleronline.com/ursula/edelweiss; 1 mile (1.6 km) north of Whistler Village in White Gold estates.*

Edgewater Lodge / ★★

8841 HWY 99, WHISTLER; 604/932-0688 OR 888/870-9065

The 12-room Edgewater Lodge sits in solitude on its sylvan 45-acre Green Lake estate. For all its potential, owner Jay Simmons keeps the place low-key. It has no lobby; rooms are small, with picture-windows featuring great views. Half of the rooms have dens with pullout beds. As well as a lakeside Jacuzzi, guests can use a small beach area with summer canoe and kayak rentals. Immediate access to the outdoors is what sets the lodge apart—at the confluence of the River of Golden Dreams and aptly named Green Lake. Whistler's 17-km-long recreational Valley Trail connects the property with the rest of Whistler. Meadow Park Sports Arena—complete with indoor skating rink, fitness center, and swimming pool—is adjacent, as is the Nicklaus North golf course. Pets are welcome. Whistler insiders laud the lodge's 45-seat lakefront restaurant for its service, fine food, and stellar location. *$$–$$$; AE, DC, MC, V; local checks only; jays@direct.ca; www.edgewater.lodge.com; across from Meadow Park Arena.*

Pan Pacific Lodge / ★★★★

4320 SUNDIAL CRES, WHISTLER; 604/905-2999 OR 888/905-9995

"Lodge" is not the word that first springs to mind when you arrive at Pan Pacific Hotels' Whistler property. Its modest lobby shares an entrance with an Irish pub. Only a deer-antler chandelier and Morris chairs arranged beside a riverstone fireplace evoke the spirit of classic mountain lodges. But on the eight floors above, 121 studio, 1-bedroom suites, and 2-bedroom suites with floor-to-ceiling windows give the impression you're floating among the peaks. All have fireplaces, soaker tubs, plush robes, Internet hookups, full kitchens, and private balconies. Pan Pacific Hotels are renown for their subtle blend of Japanese and western interior designs; fin de siècle touches abound. Whistler Mountain dominates the southeastern skyline, while Sproat and Rainbow Mountains provide the panorama to the northwest. A heated outdoor pool and hot tubs grace the lodge's second-floor terrace, with a spa, fitness center, and steam room tucked inside. In spring, après-ski action on the adjacent plaza heats up; during April's annual 10-day Whistler Ski and Snowboard Festival, those seeking tranquillity should request a northwestern room (slightly less expensive too). *$$$$; AE, DC, MC, V; no checks; whistler@ panpacific-hotel.com; www.panpac.com; off Blackcomb Wy.* &

Whistler Village Inn & Suites / ★★

4429 SUNDIAL PL, WHISTLER; 604/932-4004 OR 800/663-6418

With the opening of Blackcomb Mountain for skiing in 1980, Whistler Village began to take shape. It was as much a joy to stay at the Whistler Village Inn then as it is today, especially because it has been completely renovated for 2000. Just around the corner from the base of the lifts for both mountains, the inn's view suites, with full kitchens, wood-burning fireplaces, patios, and cozy sleeping lofts provide a comfortable experience. There's also a heated outdoor pool, a steaming hot tub, and a sauna. Complimentary continental breakfast is served in the lobby under the baleful gaze of a regal moose head. The Whistler Village Inn sits in the heart of the village, so you can walk everywhere. *$$–$$$$; AE, DC, DIS, MC, V; no checks; wvi@direct.ca; www. whistlervillageinn.bc.ca; heart of Whistler Village.* &

Pemberton and Mount Currie

For over a century, Pemberton was isolated from the rest of the Lower Mainland, because travel in and out of the valley was regulated by the railway. When a highway was finally punched through from Whistler in 1975, the long period of separation ended. At first, there was only a trickle of traffic along this stretch of Highway 99—logging trucks southbound for Squamish, and the occasional carload of climbers headed north to what is now **JOFFRE LAKES PROVINCIAL PARK**, with its turquoise jewel of an alpine lake and an ice- and rock-encrusted skyline. In the past decade, the pace of tourism has accelerated. The 1986 World Exposition in Vancouver kick-started bus tours to Whistler and beyond; and paving the highway between Pemberton and Lillooet made exploring the corridor a breeze.

Today, this agriculturally and recreationally rich valley is experiencing growth in visitors and new residents. Quick access to hiking, climbing, mountain biking, and backcountry ski touring is one reason for the surge. It's also the traditional territory of the Lil'wat Nation, who today are headquartered in the towns of Mount Currie and D'Arcy. Everyone is welcome at events such as the

LILLOOET LAKE RODEO, held each May in Mount Currie, and the August **SALMON FESTIVAL** in D'Arcy. The quaint **PEMBERTON PIONEER MUSEUM** (Camus and Prospect, Pemberton; 604/894-6135) offers a glimpse of pioneer life. **PEMBERTON TOURISM** (604/894-6175 or 604/894-6984) can provide info on all activities, and a Pemberton visitor info booth is open May 15 through September 30 on Highway 99 and Portage Road.

In Pemberton, seek out small cafes such as **PONY ESPRESSO** (1426 Portage Rd; 604/894-5700) and **GRIMM'S GOURMET & DELI** (7433 Frontier Ave; 604/894-5303). **WICKED WHEEL PIZZA** (2021 Portage Rd; 604/894-6622), in nearby Mount Currie, is packed on all-you-can-eat nights.

Lillooet

As the Sea to Sky Highway winds between Pemberton, Lillooet, and Hat Creek, it passes through the most notably varied terrain of its entire length. Here the coastal temperate zone changes rapidly to aridity. Much of this area lies in the rain shadow of the Coast and Cascade mountains. By the time the last moisture in the clouds has been raked off by the peaks around Cayoosh Pass, there's little left to water the countryside to the east. Ponderosa pine and sage take over from western hemlock and devils club. This section of Highway 99 is also called the Duffey Lake Road. Cayoosh Creek runs east from Duffey Lake and accompanies the highway for most of its 62 miles (100 km). Just before Lillooet, BC Hydro's recreation area at **SETON LAKE** has a viewpoint where *kikulis*, or pit homes, once housed a First Nation community.

Lillooet (population 2,060), first known as Cayoosh Flats, was the staging ground for the Cariboo Gold Rush of the late 1850s. Summer temperatures here are routinely among the hottest in the province. From May to October, the **LILLOOET INFOCENTRE** (790 Main St; 250/256-4308 or 250/256-4556 off season) is located in an A-frame former Anglican church, which it shares with the town museum. While in town, check out the **LILLOOET BAKERY** (719 Main St; 250/256-4889); the **4 PINES MOTEL** (108 8th Ave; 250/256-4247 or 800/753-2576) is a good place to rest your head.

RESTAURANTS

Dina's Place / ★

690 MAIN ST, LILLOOET; 250/256-4264

A whitewashed Greek restaurant suits Lillooet's often scorchy summer days. Until the Pololos family arrived in 1999, no place in town had a 40-seat patio like Dina's. This is the place to be in early evening, as long shadows begin to overtake the sun-drenched hillside above the mighty, muddy Fraser River. Zesty panfried *saganaki* made with Kefalotiri goat cheese neatly sums up the Pololos's northern Greek roots. Plenty of fresh oregano in the *keft-edhes scharas* (spicy meatballs) suits Lillooet's sagebrush environment. Twenty-six kinds of pizza keep one oven going, while creamy moussaka and *paithakia* lamb chops and other entrees keep another busy. Aside from halibut steaks and calamari (a must-try recommendation), it's probably best to pass on pricier seafood dishes. Besides, real stampeders don't eat surf-and-turf. (For late risers, the lunch menu offers omelets.) *$$; MC, V; no checks; lunch, dinner every day; full bar; reservations not necessary; on east side of Main St.* &

LODGINGS

Tyax Mountain Lake Resort / ★

TYAUGHTON LAKE RD, GOLD BRIDGE; 250/238-2221

Billed as the largest log structure on the West Coast, Tyax Mountain Lake Resort is set beside Tyaughton Lake in the wilderness of the Chilcotin Range, about 100 miles (160 km) north of Vancouver. In summer, floatplanes are an accepted mode of reaching the resort. Tyax also operates a shuttle service that picks up guests at the Lillooet train station—a 90-minute scenic drive to the resort via Highway 20. Floatplanes take anglers up to Trophy Lakes; a helicopter lifts thrill-seekers to enjoy heli-anything (skiing, hiking, and even fossil hunting). But it's not all a high-tech adventure; you can simply canoe, gold pan, ice-skate, or ride horses. Twenty-nine suites in the spruce-log lodge have beamed ceilings, balconies, and down-filled quilts. Six chalets each have kitchen, loft, and balcony overlooking Tyaughton Lake and the mountains. Lodge guests take all meals in the dining room. Other amenities include a sauna, outdoor Jacuzzi, game room, aerobics classes, and workout rooms. *$$$; AE, MC, V; no checks; fun@tyax.bc.ca; www.tyax.bc.ca; 56 miles (90 km) west of Lillooet on Hwy 40, then 3 miles (5 km) north on Tyaughton Lake Rd.* &

Fraser Valley

Yet another aspect of the Lower Mainland's landscape is the wide, fertile Fraser Valley, which runs 93 miles (150 km) inland from the Pacific east to the small town of Hope. Half the population of British Columbia lives in or within easy driving distance of the valley. The Fraser River—broad, deep, and muddy—flows down the middle of the Fraser Valley. River crossings are limited, forcing travelers to choose the north (Hwy 7) or south (Hwy 1) side. Except for the cities of Maple Ridge and Mission on the north, and Abbotsford and Chilliwack south of the Fraser River, this is a prairie, where cowboy boots and Stetsons aren't out of place. The mostly rural fertile land supports a blend of farming, forestry, and outdoor recreation.

Fort Langley

Several historic 19th-century forts in British Columbia have been preserved as reminders of the West's original European settlers. In Fort Langley (population 2,600), on the south side of the Fraser off Highway 1, **FORT LANGLEY NATIONAL HISTORIC SITE** (23433 Mavis St; 604/888-4424) is a preserved and restored Hudson's Bay Company post. The **LANGLEY CENTENNIAL MUSEUM** (across from fort; 604/888-3922) houses a permanent collection of memorabilia, as well as rotating displays of contemporary arts and crafts. **GLOVER ROAD**, Fort Langley's main street, features shops, cafes, and restaurants, many in heritage buildings. The large community hall has been lovingly preserved.

Chilliwack

The name's not the only thing that's curious about the prosperous farming and dairy center of Chilliwack (population 62,500): speakers set in downtown blare easy-listening music, and antique cars seem plentiful. Reasons to stop include the 10 large theme gardens at **MINTER GARDENS** (8½ miles/14 km east of Hwy 1/Hwy 9 junction; 604/794-7191) and **BRIDAL VEIL FALLS PROVINCIAL PARK**, a day-use-only picnic site (9 miles/15 km east on Hwy 1; 604/463-3513).

RESTAURANTS

La Mansione Ristorante / ★

46290 YALE RD E, CHILLIWACK; 604/792-8910

In 1978, La Mansione Ristorante opened in one of Chilliwack's most important heritage houses, a handsome mock-Tudor mansion with leaded-glass windows. A loyal following (plus recent arrivals) come to sample delicious seafood chowder, brimming with shrimp, crab, and clams in a saffron-scented tomato fumet, or veal panfried in butter with lemon and capers. Specialties include chateaubriand, rack of lamb, and veal scaloppine Sergio (stuffed with Dungeness crab). For local flavor, try seared Northern Velvet venison in peppery cherry brandy glaze, or grilled Fraser River salmon on a sea of lemon pepper and basil pesto. The emphasis is Italian, down to the *piatto del giorno*, a three-course, fixed-price dinner special. There's only a vague nod to vegetarian palates. The fireplace warms winter evenings. Owner Peter Graham carries an extensive selection of wines by the glass. *$$$; AE, MC, V; no checks; dinner Tues–Sun; full bar; reservations recommended; lemans@dowco.com; www.clw.diz.com/ lamansioneristorante; near Williams St.*&

Harrison Lake

All of 12 miles (18 km) long, the Harrison River, which drains south from Harrison Lake into the Fraser River, is among BC's shortest yet most significant waterways. Throughout fall, major runs of spawning salmon make their way upstream into numerous tributaries of the Harrison watershed. This quiet backwater is anchored by **KILBY PROVINCIAL PARK** (604/824-2300) at the crossroads community of Harrison Mills on Highway 7, on the north side of the Fraser. The beach at Kilby Provincial Park is popular with water-skiers with wet suits; water temperatures in Harrison Bay are influenced by outflow from chilly Harrison Lake, and rarely rise above 70°F (20°C). The beach is also popular with anglers, trumpeter swans, and a thousand or more bald eagles, which come in late autumn to feast on the annual salmon run.

KILBY HISTORIC STORE (604/796-9576; open May–Oct, and at Christmas), adjacent to Kilby Provincial Park, has a wonderful pioneer history. The restored boardinghouse, post office, and general store give a feel for life on the Fraser River at the turn of the 20th century, when stern-wheelers linked small towns with the docks downstream at Mission and New Westminster.

Bigfoot (Sasquatch, locally) is said to frequent the southern end of Harrison Lake—perhaps itching for a soak in **HARRISON HOT SPRINGS** fabled waters. The indoor public bathing pool (224 Esplanade Ave; 604/796-2244 or 800/663-2266) is one of the most inviting places in this lakefront town (population 1,060). **HARRISON LAKE** is the world's southernmost fjord, and is too cold for most swimmers, but a constructed lagoon at the south end of the lake is rimmed by a wide swath of sand, and a small, quiet row of low buildings. In summer, rent sailboats or bikes, hike nearby trails, ride a helicopter, or tip a few at a pub or two.

Annual events include June's long-running **HARRISON FESTIVAL OF THE ARTS**, focusing on arts and cultures of the Third World, especially Africa and Latin America, and the **WORLD CHAMPIONSHIP SAND SCULPTURE** competition, on the second weekend in September. Contact the **HARRISON HOT SPRINGS VISITOR INFO CENTRE** (499 Hot Springs Rd; 604/796-3425; harrison@uniserve.com; May–Oct) for details.

LODGINGS

Fenn Lodge Bed & Breakfast Retreat / ★

15500 MORRIS VALLEY RD, HARRISON MILLS; 604/796-9798 OR 888/990-3399

Built in 1905, Fenn Lodge was once the home of a local lumber baron. The Victorian classic now has seven guest rooms on the upper floor, two of which share bathrooms. Decor is understated and bright: creamy wallpaper, brass beds, overstuffed duvets. Owners Diane Brady and Gary Bruce are world travelers and art collectors. It shows in touches such as the harem bed in the bridal suite, and Chinese artwork displayed throughout the rambling main floor. Two life-size herons preside over the sitting room with its granite fireplace. In the formal dining room, Chinese bamboo instruments are arranged around a grand piano. Breakfast is served at a large kitchen table and features tasty French toast, pancakes, fresh fruit, jams, muffins, eggs—whatever suits you. The estate grounds contain a heated spring-fed swimming pool, a maze based on that of San Francisco's Grace Cathedral, and a children's playground. Kayaks are available for guest use. In autumn, the Chehalis River on the north side of the 90-acre property runs red with spawning salmon. Dinner is offered by prior arrangement. *$$–$$$; MC, V; checks OK; info@fennlodge.com; www. fennlodge.com; 2½ miles (4 km) northeast of Hwy 7 on Morris Valley Rd.*

The Harrison Hot Springs Hotel / ★★

100 ESPLANADE AVE, HARRISON HOT SPRINGS; 604/796-2244

OR 800/663-2266

This legendary hotel on the south shore of beautiful Harrison Lake was originally built in 1885. The current establishment has two wings, an older one from the 1950s and a more recent addition from the 1990s. Avoid the old wing, where noise seeps between the walls. A maze of hot-spring pools are steps away from the new wing; ask for a pool walk-out room. Two indoor pools are available only for use by hotel guests. Spacious grounds that surround the hotel are lovingly landscaped, with tennis courts and an exercise circuit. In addition, there is a full spa. Clearly, the best thing about the hotel is the hot-spring water. Food and service at two hotel restaurants, the Lakeside Terrace and Copper Room, and bar are excellent. In the off season, a roaring hearth in the large foyer takes the chill from the damp air. Children are made welcome with a water park and special menus. *$$–$$$; AE, DC, DIS, MC, V; checks OK; hhsph@uniserve.com; www.tourbc.com/travel/ harrison; west end of Esplanade Ave on lake.* &

Hope

Hope (population 7,100) is a pretty little Fraser River town with a pioneer past. Hope's two main streets are lined with service centers, because it's an important highway junction, but the heart of town is frequently overlooked. Make a point of spending a few minutes here, if for no other reason than to breathe the incredibly fresh air that characterizes Hope. The **HOPE VISITOR INFO CENTRE** (919 Water Ave; 604/869-2021)—and the **HOPE MUSEUM**—at the south end of Water Street that fronts the Fraser River is a font of up-to-date news and directions to other sights within the Hope area, including popular **MANNING PROVINCIAL PARK** (16 miles/26 km east of Hope on Hwy 3; 250/840-8836), with its basic but classic, family-fun **MANNING PARK LODGE** (Hwy 3, Manning Provincial Park; 250/840-8822 or 800/330-3321).

RESTAURANTS

Pinewoods Dining Room / ★

HWY 3 (MANNING PARK LODGE), HOPE; 250/840-8822

Pinewoods Dining Room—with porch posts carved with likenesses of black bears—offers three happily coexisting dining choices beneath its cedar roof: the Bear's Den Pub, the Cascade Cafe, and the Pinewoods dining room. The time of day, your culinary inclination, and your appearance (i.e., how recently you've been camping) will determine your choice. Pinewoods' log-and-pine-paneled interior makes this the cheeriest building at the resort. Walls are covered (but not cluttered) with prints and photographs of wildlife and adorned with vintage snowshoes, skis, toboggans, and oars, brightly lit by windows that look out on a range of Cascade peaks. Specials include vintage skier's breakfasts such as "3-2-1-Call Bob" (three sausages, two eggs, and one pancake), Daralyn's homemade jumbo cinnamon buns, burgers and fresh salads, personal pizzas and pastas, wraps and wings. Entrees in the Pinewood dining room range from salads to schnitzels, steaks to stir-fries. The daily soups always please. *$–$$; AE, MC, V; checks OK; breakfast, lunch, dinner every day; full bar; reservations not necessary; info@manningparkresort.com; www. manningparkresort.com; adjacent to lodge on Hwy 3.* &

The Sunshine Coast

The world's longest highway, the Pan-American (Hwy 1 and 101 in parts of the United States and Canada) stretches 9,312 miles (15,020 km) from Castro, on Chile's *Cona Sur*, to Lund on BC's Sunshine Coast. The 87-mile (140-km) stretch of Highway 101 between Langdale and Lund leads to dozens of parks with biking, hiking, and ski trails; canoe and kayak routes; beaches; and coastal viewpoints.

Much of the Sunshine Coast is naturally hidden. Side roads with colorful names like **RED ROOF** and **PORPOISE BAY** lead to places that don't announce themselves until you all but stumble upon them, such as **SMUGGLER COVE PROVINCIAL MARINE PARK** near Sechelt and **PALM BEACH PARK** south of the town of Powell River.

The Sunshine Coast lives up to its name. With an annual total of between 1,400 and 2,400 hours of sunshine—that's an average of four to six hours per day, depending on where the measurements are taken—bright days outnumber gloomy ones by a wide margin. The area benefits from a rain shadow cast by the Vancouver Island mountains, which catch most of the moisture coming off the Pacific (though clouds regroup in the Coast Mountains to the east and provide sufficient winter snow to coat trails for cross-country skiing).

The region is split into two portions, on either side of Jervis Inlet. Roughly speaking, the southern half between the ferry slips at Langdale and Earls Cove occupies the **SECHELT PENINSULA**, while the northern half between the ferry slip at Saltery Bay and Lund sits on the **MALASPINA PENINSULA**. The coastline is deeply indented by the Pacific at Howe Sound, Jervis Inlet, and Desolation Sound. Jervis and Desolation attract a steady stream of marine traffic in summer. Come moodier months, clouds become ensnared in snaggle-toothed peaks.

ACCESS AND INFORMATION

The Sunshine Coast is only accessible from the rest of the Lower Mainland by boat or airplane. Travelers aboard **BC FERRIES** (604/669-1211 in Vancouver, 604/487-9333 in Saltery Bay, or 604/485-2943 in Powell River; www.bcferries. bc.ca/ferries) leave Horseshoe Bay in West Vancouver for a 9 ½-mile (15.5-km), 45-minute ride to Langdale on the Sechelt Peninsula. Highway 101 links Langdale with Earls Cove, 50 miles (80 km) north. Another ferry crosses Jervis Inlet to Saltery Bay, a 60-minute ride. Highway 101 makes the second leg of this journey 37 miles (60 km) north to Lund. BC Ferries also connects

Powell River on the Malaspina Peninsula with Comox on the east side of central Vancouver Island.

One of the best parts about enjoying the northern Sunshine Coast in the off season (Sept–May)—particularly midweek—is being able to catch ferries without experiencing interminable lineups. You'll still have to allow six hours to reach the Malaspina Peninsula from Horseshoe Bay, but you can do it without hurrying, enjoying the travel time just as much as the play time once you arrive. Ferry connections are scheduled to allow adequate time to make the drive from one dock to the next. Those traveling up the entire coast or returning via Vancouver Island should ask at the Horseshoe Bay terminal about special fares (saving up to 30 percent) for the circle tour (four ferry rides).

Gibsons

Gibsons (population 3,900) is a small waterfront community 2½ miles (4 km) west of the BC Ferries dock in Langdale. Stop at the **GIBSONS VISITOR INFO CENTRE** (668 Sunnycrest Rd; 604/886-2325; gibsons-chamber@sunshine.net) to stock up on maps and brochures. Check out the nearby federal wharf where the **BELDIS FISH COMPANY** (at end of C dock) often has fresh tuna, shrimp, and salmon for sale. A short walk along the harbor seawall leads past a plaque commemorating the arrival of George Gibson and his two sons in May 1886. The trio came ashore from the family boat, the *Swamp Angel*, and promptly took up residence. A cairn at **CHASTER REGIONAL PARK** (on Gower Point Rd; 604/886-2325) honors an even earlier arrival: Capt. George Vancouver camped here in June 1792.

RESTAURANTS

Chez Philippe / ★★

1532 OCEAN BEACH ESPLANADE (BONNIEBROOK LODGE), GIBSONS; 604/886-2188

Parisian Philippe Lacoste trained in Normandy before coming to Vancouver, where he worked at the prestigious Le Crocodile and Le Gavroche restaurants, then moved to Gibsons in the early 1990s. French-inspired with Northwestern influences, the menu features chilled scallop and salmon medallions, and escargot fricassee with wild mushrooms in red wine sauce. The fixed-price table d'hôte offers a four-course meal with entrees ranging from trout, red snapper, grilled prawns, and scallops in polenta shells to seafood ragout in Natua sauce, New York steak, chicken with wild mushrooms, rack of lamb, and duck à l'orange. Though limited, the wine list offers reasonably priced selections. In winter, a crackling fireplace lights up the dining room with the old-country ambience of a French *relais*. In summer, catch the sunset while finishing with profiteroles, filled with ice cream and topped with hot chocolate sauce. *$$$; AE, DC, MC, V; no checks; dinner every day (Fri–Mon in winter); full bar; reservations recommended; info@bonniebrook.com; www.bonniebrook. com; follow Gower Point Rd from downtown.*

LODGINGS

Bonniebrook Lodge / ★

1532 OCEAN BEACH ESPLANADE, GIBSONS; 604/886-2188

As of 2000, upstairs rooms in this popular bed-and-breakfast have been completely renovated and now have en suite baths. In addition to four rooms in the yellow clapboard house on the water (a guest house since 1922), two "romance" suites have been added. These are equipped with gas fireplaces, Jacuzzi tubs, overstuffed couches, wrought-iron queen bed frames, terry cloth robes, and wooden armoires. Breakfast (perhaps a pesto omelet, fresh strawberry jam, and muffins) is served in the lodge's Chez Philippe restaurant or delivered to suites—following an early thermos of coffee. Explore the lodge's private beach, as well as nearby Chaster Regional Park. *$$; AE, MC, V; no checks; closed Jan; info@bonniebrook.com; www.bonniebrook.com; follow Gower Point Rd from downtown.* &

Rosewood Country House Bed and Breakfast / ★★

575 PINE ST, GIBSONS; 604/886-4714

In 1990, owner Frank Tonne felled and milled the timber growing on his steep slope overlooking the Strait of Georgia and built a Craftsman-style mansion, using classic doors and windows rescued from older Vancouver houses. The result harkens back to the spacious elegance of earlier times. White walls and blond wood give the house a warm, honeyed glow, a perfect setting for Oriental rugs and period furniture. Rosewood features two self-contained ground-floor suites with fridges, wet bars, entertainment systems, fireplaces, stained-glass windows, and French doors that open onto the garden. One has an antique bath by an ocean-view bay window. Co-owner Susan Tonne handles details such as menu planning. Wake up to champagne and orange juice in the airy sunroom. Guests can request breakfast in bed, rolled in on a silver tea service. Breakfast can be pretty much whatever guests would like; romantic dinners (book in advance) are a specialty, served in a private dining room. Book several months in advance for weekends, May through October. *$$–$$$; MC, V; checks OK; rosewood@uniserve.com; www.rosewoodcountryhouse.com; 4 miles (6.4 km) west of Gibsons.* &

Roberts Creek

Follow Highway 101 north from Gibsons 4 miles (7 km) to the artistic community of Roberts Creek. Your first stop in Roberts Creek (population 2,250) should be **MCFARLANE'S BEACH**, a sandy crescent where the creek meets the ocean. Early in the 19th century, Harry Roberts, son of the patriarch who established the town, operated a freight shed here. On its side he painted "Sunshine Belt"—and visitors ever since have been referring to Sechelt Peninsula as the Sunshine Coast.

REACHING THE PEAKS

The Coast Mountains, which begin in Vancouver and sweep north along the BC coast and through Alaska, are the tallest range in North America and among the most heavily glaciated. An imposing palisade of these peaks defines much of BC's Lower Mainland region. Some of the most rugged terrain in the province was uplifted here by a combination of glacial and volcanic activity about 12,000 years ago. Reaching the tallest peaks, such as **Wedge Mountain** in Garibaldi Provincial Park near Whistler, requires advanced mountaineering skills. At 9,527 feet (2,904 m), Wedge is the highest peak in a park that is characterized by massive expanses of rock and ice.

If you're willing to settle for something less than the view from the loftiest pinnacles, there are less challenging approaches that still provide breathtaking panoramas. On a clear day, few skylines can compete with the six peaks—Black, Strachan, Hollyburn, Grouse, Fromme, and Seymour mountains—on Vancouver's North Shore. Roadways climb from sea level to viewpoints in **Cypress Provincial Park** and **Mount Seymour Provincial Park**. For more information and to request maps of Cypress Provincial Park and Mount Seymour Provincial Park, contact **BC Parks Zone Office** at Mount Seymour Provincial Park (604/929-4818 or 604/924-2200).

If you don't have a vehicle, leave the driving to someone else and ride the Grouse Mountain Skyride gondola up **Grouse Mountain** (604/980-9311 or 604/986-6262), at the north end of Capilano Road in North Vancouver. It's readily accessible by public transit via TransLink (604/521-0400; www.coastmountainbus.com). The gondola takes visitors on a thrilling ascent up the slopes of Grouse Mountain and deposits them at

Today, a wide path leads from a parking area on Roberts Creek Road out onto a breakwater and boardwalk, and to a municipal park. From the breakwater, look north toward the sandy beaches at **ROBERTS CREEK PROVINCIAL PARK** (Hwy 101, 9 miles/14 km north of Gibsons; 604/898-3678), popular for summer picnics. On **BC DAY** (604/886-2325; first weekend in Aug), the community hosts an annual Gumboot parade and Mr. Roberts Creek contest.

RESTAURANTS

The Creek House / ★★

1041 ROBERTS CREEK RD, ROBERTS CREEK; 604/885-9321

Yvan Citerneschi's restaurant, in a house with a view of a tree-filled garden, is decorated simply with white walls, light wood floors, flowers on tables, and original contemporary art. He's the former chef at Vancouver's Le Bistro, and on any given night you may choose from 10 seasonal entrees, such as wild boar, rack of lamb provençal, sautéed prawns, or locally caught rabbit. Mango mousse lights up the evening. Afterward, walk down to the beach to see the twinkle of distant lights on the mainland and Vancouver Island. $$; MC, V;

4,100 feet (1,250 m). From there, moderate hiking trails lead off from Grouse Mountain Chalet to a variety of viewpoints.

No matter which approach you choose, the views will all be dominated by the local landscape's most impressive feature: snow-covered **Mount Baker** (12,906 feet/3,279 m). Though this semidormant volcano is in the Cascade Mountains of nearby Washington State, its skyraking presence rears up above the Lower Mainland like none other. Just as sensational are sweeping views of Greater Vancouver, the Strait of Georgia, and Vancouver Island.

Farther inland, gondolas and chairlifts at Whistler take visitors to lofty heights on **Whistler Mountain** (7,160 feet/2182 m) and **Blackcomb Peak** (7,494 feet/2,284 m). These are the same lifts that deposit skiers, snowboarders, snowshoers, and sightseers at the Rendezvous Lodge on Blackcomb and the Roundhouse Lodge on Whistler in winter. Come summer, once the snow has melted, an extensive network of moderate-to-challenging walking and hiking trails leads off from each lodge into the surrounding landscape that borders on Garibaldi Provincial Park. Here, the surrounding peaks stand out in such sharp relief that they seem to be papercut against the backdrop of a Pacific blue sky. Chubby hoary marmots (whose distinctive whistle provided the inspiration for the mountain's name) sun themselves on warm rocks while ravens and eagles circle overhead. For more information and maps of sightseeing trails on Blackcomb and Whistler Mountains, contact guest relations (800/766-0449 toll free, 604/932-3434 in Whistler, 604/664-5614 in Vancouver; www.whistler-blackcomb.com). —*Jack Christie*

local checks only; dinner Wed–Sun; full bar; reservations recommended; creekhouse@uniserve.com; www.creekhouse.com; at Beach Ave. ♿

Gumboot Garden Café

1057 ROBERTS CREEK RD, ROBERTS CREEK; 604/885-4216

Just around the corner from the Creek House is an old maroon house with a simple sign: Café. Inside, a terra-cotta sun on the yellow-painted wall radiates warmth, as do painted linoleum "tablecloths." The menu shines with a strong Mexican influence. Try the Huevos Gumboot, a hearty breakfast dish available all day: eggs and black beans on a tortilla with Monterey Jack, green onions, and homemade salsa. Breads and cheesecakes are baked daily, and produce is often organic. Locals come to hang out and listen to music Friday nights. In keeping with the community and clientele, service is laid back. Check out the garden around back. The building that houses the cafe shares quarters with a juice bar, bookstore, hair salon, and clothing store. *$; MC, V; checks OK; breakfast, lunch every day, dinner Thurs–Sat; beer and wine; reservations recommended; www.heartofthecreek.com/gumboot; junction of Lower Rd.* ♿

LODGINGS

Country Cottage B&B / ★★

1183 ROBERTS CREEK RD, ROBERTS CREEK; 604/885-7448

🌲 Philip and Loragene Gaulin's 2-acre farm includes the vintage Rose Cottage tucked inside the front gate, and the more recently constructed Cedar Lodge next to the sheep pasture. The first is a one-room fantasy, complete with fireplace, small kitchen, and quilt-covered bed. Farther back on the property is Cedar Cottage, a tree house for grownups. Wood and stonework set the tone, as does a chandelier fashioned from deer antlers and a loft bed. Pendleton blankets drape the hearthside couch. Skylights brighten the interior on even the gloomiest days. A wood-burning river-rock fireplace occupies one corner. On Sundays, guests are welcome to accompany Philip on his weekly backcountry ski outing in nearby Tetrahedron Provincial Park. Get ready with a breakfast of fresh eggs scrambled with smoked salmon, or Belgian waffles that Loragene cooks up on her wood-burning stove. Reserve well in advance. *$$–$$$; no credit cards; checks OK; 9 miles (14 km) from Langdale ferry, off Hwy 101.*

Sechelt

If it weren't for a small neck of land less than a half mile wide, a large portion of the peninsula north of Sechelt would be an island. This wedge of sand backs ocean water, which flows in from the northwestern entrance to the Sechelt Inlet near Egmont, into three inlets. Sechelt Inlet is the largest. Nestled on the wedge is Sechelt (population 7,750), one of the fastest-growing towns in Canada, and home to the Sechelt First Nation. Visit the Nation's cultural center, **HOUSE OF HEWHIWUS** (5555 Hwy 101; 604/885-8991)—House of the Chiefs—which houses an art center and the Raven's Cry theater, and offers tours. **SECHELT VISITOR INFO CENTRE** (5755 Cowrie St; 604/885-0662; sechelt_chamber@sunshine.net) fills you in on the rest.

RESTAURANTS

Blue Heron Inn / ★★

5521 DELTA RD, SECHELT; 604/885-3847 OR 800/818-8977

🌲 One of the most consistently pleasant places to dine on the Sunshine Coast is the Blue Heron. Partly for the waterfront views of the Sechelt Inlet (complete with blue herons, of course), partly for the food (fresh clams, a carpaccio-style roast loin of veal, grilled wild salmon with fennel, smoked black cod with hollandaise, halibut fillet with red onion and strawberry salsa, creamy caesar salad, bouillabaisse), and partly for the relaxed vacationlike atmosphere (fresh flowers, local art). Gail Madeiros makes sure you're comfortable while her husband, Manuel, makes sure you're well fed. Presentations are stunning, and food rolls out of the kitchen like clockwork, a boon if you're trying to catch a ferry. In winter, a fieldstone hearth warms the solid wood–beam interior. *$$; AE, MC, V; local checks only; dinner Wed–Sun; full bar; reservations recommended; blueheron@uniserve.com; www.ewest.com4/blueheron; west of*

Hwy 101 on Wharf St, right along Porpoise Bay Rd for 1 mile (1.6 km), watch for sign on left side. &

Halfmoon Bay

The scenery gets wilder as you proceed north. **SMUGGLERS COVE PROVINCIAL MARINE PARK** (just west of Halfmoon Bay; 604/898-4678) is a wonderful way to experience the coastal wilderness firsthand. Trails lead through an enchanting stand of old-growth forest and around the cove's indented shoreline.

LODGINGS

Lord Jim's Resort Hotel / ★
5356 OLE'S COVE RD, HALFMOON BAY; 604/885-7038 OR 877/296-4593
This is a resort in transition, from big-game sports lodge to wellness retreat spa. Owner Hugh Gatsby's nest of simple cottages clings to the sun-splashed slopes above Ole's Cove. The location is prime, and the best place to enjoy it in summer is from the resort's freshwater pool. Rooms are attractive, with handsome furnishings and colorful bedspreads. Motel-style cabins are simply appointed and harken back to the 1970s, when Lord Jim's aspired to be *the* resort on the Sunshine Coast. Cabin 11 (Maple) enjoys the most secluded (and sunny) location. Its veranda is overhung by smooth-skinned madrona (arbutus) trees. Views stretch west to Thormanby Island and south to Smugglers Cove. Great paddling is to be had from the resort's wharf and small pebble beach. The restaurant's menu is appetizing, but the bar has a tiki-tiki ambience—complete with stuffed lynx, cougar, and chinook salmon. *$$$; AE, MC, V; no checks; lordjims_resorthotel@sunshine.net; www.lordjims.com; west on Mercer Rd off Hwy 101.*

Pender Harbour

It's hard to tell where freshwater lakes end and saltwater coves begin at the north end of the Sechelt Peninsula, a confused, puzzle-shaped piece of geography. Narrow fingers of land separate the waters around Agamemnon Channel from a marvelous patchwork of small and medium-sized lakes. Three oceanside communities comprise Pender Harbour: **MADIERA PARK**, **GARDEN BAY**, and **IRVINES LANDING**.

On Highway 101, two unique **CEREMONIAL POLES** are mounted in front of Pender Harbour Secondary School. One is in the traditional West Coast style of the Sechelt Nation; the other incorporates local symbols such as a logging truck and a floatplane. As you head north of Pender Harbour, the highway winds around Ruby Lake and climbs above it, allowing a good view of the jewel-like setting.

An impressive natural show occurs twice daily in **SKOOKUMCHUK NARROWS PROVINCIAL PARK** (Hwy 101; 604/898-3678) in Egmont, about 7 miles (12 km) north of Ruby Lake: one of the largest saltwater rapids on Canada's West Coast boils as tons of water force their way through Skookumchuk

Narrows at the north end of Sechelt Inlet. A 2 ½-mile (4-km) walking/cycling trail leads from the outskirts of Egmont to viewing sites at North Point and nearby Roland Point. At low tide, the bays around both points display astonishingly colorful and varied forms of marine life: giant barnacles, colonies of sea stars, sea urchins, and sea anemones.

LODGINGS

Ruby Lake Resort / ★

RUBY LAKE, MADIERA PARK; 604/883-2269 OR 800/717-6611

Ruby Lake Resort is a collection of 10 units facing a private lagoon just across the highway from the lake. An engaging family from Milan—the Cogrossis—bought the resort and rebuilt the cedar cottages, now nicely furnished with full kitchens and TVs. It's a great place to bring the kids; paddleboats are available, and you can rent canoes. The resort's restaurant draws accolades for its Northern Italian cuisine and fresh seafood. Waterfowl by the hundreds flock to the lagoon. Come in time for the daily eagle feeding at 6pm. In his spare time, chef Aldo Cogrossi builds birdhouses, more than 40 of which adorn the sides of cabins, telephone poles, rooftops, and the neighboring Suncoaster Trail, an ambitious mountain bike and hiking trail project that will eventually extend from Langdale to Egmont. *$$; MC, V; no checks; talk2us@rubylakeresort.com; www.rubylakeresort.com; 6 miles (10 km) south of Earls Cove.*

Powell River

Travelers looking to experience the smooth, sedate pace of ferry sailings enjoy the journey between Earls Cove and Saltery Bay. Pack binoculars: the hour-long sailing is a mini–Inside Passage experience. Powell River (population 14,150) is a pleasant drive 19 miles (31 km) north of the ferry terminal at Saltery Bay. Look for the **VISITOR INFO CENTRE** (4690 Marine Ave; 604/485-4701; prub@prcn.org) located in a storefront downtown. Just down the street is the **ROCKY MOUNTAIN PIZZA & BAKERY** (4471 Marine Ave; 604/485-9111), where you can perch on a stool and people-watch while enjoying organic coffees, chunky soups, pizza-size cinnamon buns, salads, wraps, pizza by the slice, and deli sandwiches. You'll find fresh seafood at **PORTUGUESE JOE'S FISH MARKET** (beside Comox–Texada Island dock; 604/485-5991).

RESTAURANTS

jitterbug café / ★

4643 MARINE DR, POWELL RIVER; 604/485-7797

Walk through Haida-born landscape artist April White's Wind Spirit Gallery, and you'll find one of Powell River's most enduring eateries: the jitterbug café. It's a stylish little place, a renovated 1920s West Coast–style home, with solid oak tables in a sunny room. Gallery art adorns the walls, and sweeping views of islands in the Strait of Georgia open up to the west from the back deck. Simple meals are based on local ingredients—and some wonderful homemade breads. Shrimp season begins in April; blackberries appear on the menu in August. The extensive offerings include salads, burgers, and ribs, and fresh seafood is a specialty. At lunch, try a chicken sandwich on warm cheese bread, or smoked-salmon pasta. Dinners offer sautéed chicken breast with an Asiago cheese sauce, and a delightful and delicious lemon linguine. Try one of the house crepes for dessert. True to its name, the cafe features live music on Friday and Saturday evenings. Ask about the rustic guest cottage, which predates the main house. *$$; AE, MC, V; no checks; lunch, dinner Tues–Sat; full bar; reservations recommended; jitterbug@windspirit. com; www.windspirit.com; downtown.* ঙ

LODGINGS

Beach Gardens Resort & Marina / ★★
7074 WESTMINSTER AVE, POWELL RIVER; 604/485-6267 OR 800/663-7070
Sitting on a protected section of Malaspina Strait, the Beach Gardens Resort is a Mecca for divers, who come for the near-tropical clarity of the water and the abundant marine life (a dive shop is on-site). Off season, the resort is often booked with conventions and seminars. There are tennis courts and a fitness center with steam rooms, saunas, and large indoor pool. A lawn slopes down to a sizable marina that accommodates boaters. Rooms are pleasantly comfortable, bright, clean, and painted with soft marine hues. Tiled bathrooms with full tubs are their crowning feature. Request a room in the new wing; from the balconies are views of Texada Island to the west. Divers prefer the less expensive, viewless cabins. The dining room offers reliable seafood entrees—and a fantastic caesar. Upstairs, the rocking pub enjoys one of the best views. *$$–$$$; AE, MC, V; no checks; bgradens@prcn.org; www.beachgardens.com; off Marine Ave.* ঙ

Lund

You can't get more well hidden than in the little port of Lund at the north end of the Sunshine Coast, especially in May and September, at the beginning and end of high season. The Malaspina Peninsula narrows to a thin finger of land here, wedged between Malaspina Strait on the west and Okeover Arm to the east. Lund retains much of the wilderness charm that drew a family of settlers from Finland here a century ago. In the intervening years, the settler's original **LUND HOTEL** (1436 Hwy 101; 604/414-0474) has undergone a modest facelift or two and is now owned by the Sliammon First Nation. Flowers cascade from hanging baskets and carpet the hotel's garden. **NANCY'S BAKERY** (on wharf; 604/483-4180) is loaded with goodies like blackberry cinnamon rolls, and the **STARBOARD CAFÉ** (on Lund harbor) serves espresso in a breezy little bistro. A jolly-looking red **WATER TAXI** (604/483-9749), the *Raggedy Anne*, ferries passengers and supplies to nearby Savary Island. **OKEOVER ARM PROVINCIAL PARK** (off Hwy 101, 3 miles/5 km east of Lund; 604/898-3678) is the choice of kayakers exploring Desolation Sound.

RESTAURANTS

The Laughing Oyster Restaurant / ★★

10052 MALASPINA RD, POWELL RIVER; 604/483-9775

Seek out the Laughing Oyster Restaurant. Its waterfront location, coupled with a split-level design, means everyone has a good view of Okeover Arm, particularly from the large patio. On dark and stormy evenings, you may prefer a corner table beside the fireplace. Start with a microbrew and smoked salmon–and–spinach caesar or BC mussels, cooked to perfection. Large portions reflect Powell River's mill town influence. Even those who aren't big oyster fans rave about the flavor of these—fresh off the restaurant dock to the table. A signature plate of Laughing Oysters is prepared with sun-dried tomatoes and red peppers under a drift of feta cheese. The staff is unwaveringly friendly, with the right degree of attentiveness. The reasonably priced wine list isn't deep but is thoughtfully chosen. *$$$; AE, MC, V; no checks; lunch, dinner every day, brunch Sun; full bar; reservations recommended; falk@prcn.org; www.laughing-oyster.bc.ca; 20 minutes north of Powell River.* &

LODGINGS

Desolation Resort / ★★

MALASPINA RD, POWELL RIVER; 604/483-3592

Desolation Resort opened on the steep hillside above Okeover Arm in 1998. Six uniquely designed wooden chalets perch on pilings. Fir floors flow into patterned pine walls and ceilings below steep-pitched cedar-shake roofs. Wide verandas offer sweeping views, and stairs lead to a floating dock. Carved figures of herons, gulls, and an ancient mariner sit on pilings. The quiet is broken only by the lapping of waves on the shore or the *awk* of a raven as it swoops among ramrod-straight firs flanking the cabins. Rental canoes and kayaks are available at the resort. Cabins are simply furnished; duvets spread atop flannel sheets provide the coziness you'd expect of a warm bed, but bedside lighting is inadequate. Chalets feature full kitchens. *$$; AE, MC, V; no checks; desolres@prcn.org; www.desolationresort.com; 20 minutes north of Powell River.* &

VICTORIA AND VANCOUVER ISLAND

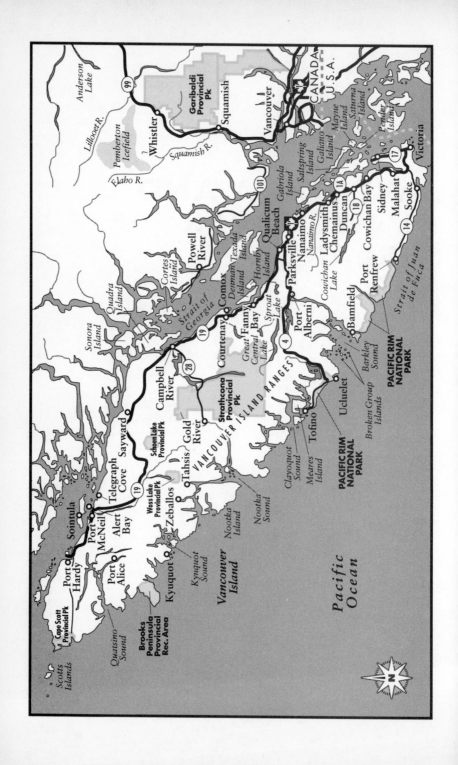

VICTORIA AND VANCOUVER ISLAND

Canadians throng to Vancouver Island because the Pacific Ocean moderates the climate to the mildest in the country: in winter, rain substitutes for snow. Wilder and less inhabited than other parts of the Pacific Northwest, this is a utopia of outdoor pursuits, from sea kayaking to mountain biking. All's not empty wilderness, of course. The island's east coast is booming with tourists and snow-weary retirees—and plenty of golf courses, marinas, restaurants, and good hotels. Victoria, a city of gardens subscribing to a whimsical "more English than the English" character, is the capital of British Columbia and most visitors' first taste of Vancouver Island.

ACCESS AND INFORMATION

It's an island, so most people get there by boat. From Seattle, the **VICTORIA CLIPPER** (206/443-5000 in Seattle, 250/382-8100 in Victoria, or 800/888-2535 elsewhere) zips to downtown Victoria via a high-speed passenger-only cata-maran in two or three hours. In summer, you can choose a five-hour Seattle-to-Victoria passenger-only cruise via the scenic San Juans on **WASHINGTON STATE FERRIES** (206/464-6400 or 250/381-1551); a three-hour trip runs year-round, once or twice daily, from Anacortes to Sidney, BC, 17 miles (27 km) north of Victoria by highway. Reserve at least one day prior to departure; cars should arrive one hour early. **BLACK BALL TRANSPORT** (360/457-4491 in Port Angeles, 206/622-2222 in Bellingham, or 250/386-2202 in Victoria; www. northolympic.com/coho) operates the serviceable MV *Coho* car-and-passenger ferry from Port Angeles on the Olympic Peninsula to Victoria, a frequently choppy 1½-hour trip across the exposed Strait of Juan de Fuca. Two to four sail-ings daily; reservations not accepted, but call ahead for wait times. From Bellingham, **VICTORIA SAN JUAN CRUISES** (206/738-8099 or 800/443-4552) makes a three-hour round-trip cruise—including whale-watching and salmon dinner—May 13 through October 8.

    BC FERRIES (250/386-3431 24-hour automated line, 888/724-5223 car reservations in BC, or 604/444-2890 car reservations outside BC) runs car fer-ries from British Columbia mainland (Tsawwassen terminal) into Swartz Bay, 20 miles (32 km) north of Victoria. Car reservations are an additional $15. Staterooms are available on the new "super ferries."

    The fastest way to travel is straight to Victoria's Inner Harbour **BY AIR**. Kenmore Air (425/486-1257 or 800/543-9595; www.kenmoreair.com) makes regular daily flights from downtown Seattle. From Sea-Tac International Airport, Alaska Airlines (800/252-7522; www.alaskaair.com) flies into **VICTORIA INTER-NATIONAL AIRPORT** (1640 Electra Blvd; 250-953-7533 or 250-953-7500), 11 miles (18 km) north of the city. From downtown Vancouver, Helijet Airways (604/273-1414) gets you to Victoria by helicopter in 35 minutes. Seaplanes for

Harbour Air (604/688-1277 or 800/665-0212; www.harbour-air.com) carry passengers from Vancouver. From the Vancouver airport, fly with Air BC (604/688-5515 or 888/247-2262) or Canadian Regional (800/665-1177).

In peak season, May through August, crowds are thickest, prices are highest, and tourist services are at their best. Gardens and greenery are freshest in May and June; days are sunniest July and August, when summer in Victoria can be desert-dry. April and September are pleasant months for quieter, reduced-rate travel (note that some hotel rates do not drop until mid-Oct); December through February are rainy, but rates are often quite low, especially for U.S. travelers who have enjoyed a favorable exchange rate in recent years. The **VANCOUVER ISLAND VISITOR INFOCENTRE** (250/382-3551) and the **VICTORIA VISITOR INFOCENTRE** (800/663-3883) have more information.

Victoria

Ever since Rudyard Kipling's hallowed turn-of-the-century visit, Victoria has been selling itself as a wee bit of Olde England. The fancy is an appealing one, conjuring red double-decker buses and high tea as keynote themes in the Garden City. Kilted bagpipers rub shoulders with Victoria's annual 3.65 million tourists, who come from America and Japan—and elsewhere in Asia and Latin America—to walk along the waterside Causeway, sit for caricatures, marvel at jugglers, and tap their feet to the one-man blues band of Slim Chance. In the harbor, Barbara Streisand's sleek, modern yacht may rest within hailing distance of an antique three-masted sailing ship.

The great thing about Victoria—rated among the world's top 10 cities by numerous upscale travel magazines—is that in the historic downtown, everything from the elegant Parliament buildings to old Chinatown are within walking distance. In recent years Victoria has seen an explosion of whale-watching tours, and outdoor enthusiasts can sea kayak or mountain bike from the city's doorsteps. Minutes from downtown, seaside Dallas Road and Beach Drive meander through the city's finest old residential districts, offering a view of the spectacular Olympic Mountains of Washington State to the south across the Strait of Juan de Fuca.

ACCESS AND INFORMATION

A horse-drawn carriage ride is a romantic favorite: catch **VICTORIA CARRIAGE TOURS** (251 Superior St; 250/383-2207) at the corner of Belleville and Menzies; the larger **TALLY HO** carts (8615 Eber Terrace; 250/383-5067) at the same corner offer rides at a family rate. The Inner Harbour is the locus of numerous popular maritime excursions. **VICTORIA HARBOUR FERRIES** (250/708-0201) offer tours of local waterways. The **ESQUIMALT AND NANAIMO (E & N) RAILWAY** (888/VIA-RAIL) takes you back to the days of scenic rail travel from a 19th century–style station near the Johnson Street Bridge, through the gorgeous heights of the Malahat Mountain area and up past the scenic beaches of the

VICTORIA THREE-DAY TOUR

DAY ONE: Breakfast at the **Boardwalk** restaurant, the casual sister to the Victorian Restaurant at **Ocean Pointe Resort**, with window and patio seating overlooking the attractive **Inner Harbour**. Proceed on a walking and shopping tour of downtown. Lunch at the exquisitely vegetarian **Re-bar** restaurant. Reaching the Inner Harbour, flag down a **horse-drawn carriage** for a tour of **Beacon Hill Park**. Leave the meter running at the **Beacon Drive In Restaurant** to grab an ice cream, and then swing by the gracious **Carr House**. After the tour, check in to the view-blessed Windsor Suite at the swish **Prior House Bed & Breakfast Inn**. Return to the Inner Harbour to catch a pint-sized **Victoria Harbour Ferry** to the dock at the **Ocean Pointe Resort**, a five-minute meander along the waterfront to **Spinnakers** brewpub. Spend the afternoon quaffing Mount Tolmie Darks, and laze into a casual pub dinner with a view.

DAY TWO: Take out bagels and cream cheese from **Mount Royal Bagel Factory**, then drive to **Mile Zero** and follow Dallas Road to Clover Point. Fly your kite on the windy embankment, as the locals do, and enjoy bagels by the sea. Continue along Beach Drive, stop at Willows Beach, and pass through the Uplands to gaze at million-dollar heritage homes. Lunch at the outdoor tables of **Olive Olio's** (3840 Cadboro Bay Rd; 250/477-6618), then drive out to view **Butchart Gardens**, deservedly world famous for its more than 1 million blooms. Continue your drive north to the end of the Saanich Peninsula to dine at **Deep Cove Chalet**; return leisurely along semirural W Saanich Road, stopping at the vintage 1920s **Dominion Astrophysical Observatory** to gaze at the stars.

DAY THREE: Savor hot coffee, croissants, and fruit salad at **Demitasse Coffee Bar** for breakfast. Visit **Craigdarroch Castle**, and see the stately signature manor of a Scottish coal baron. Back downtown, people-watch at **Torrefazione Italia** and grab a wrap to go from **Electric Juice Bar** (Government St between Yates and View; 250/380-0009). Then stroll to the **Royal British Columbia Museum** to examine the fine First Nations arts. Take in the turn-of-the-century grandeur of the **Empress Hotel**, and sip high tea. Relax, perhaps in the quiet orchard of **St. Ann's Academy**. Later, dine on fine West Coast cuisine at **Cafe Brio**. Have a change of scenery by staying the night at the **Magnolia Hotel & Suites** to conclude your tour of Victoria.

Qualicum area. Perched on the Inner Harbour in a converted art deco garage, **TOURISM VICTORIA** (812 Wharf St; 250/953-2033; www.tourismvictoria.com) is brimful of brochures and helpful staff.

MAJOR ATTRACTIONS

Stroll through the main-floor hallways and shops of the venerable **EMPRESS HOTEL** (721 Government St; 250/384-8111 or 800/441-1414), a postcard doyen since 1907. The elegant Rattenbury-designed 1893 provincial **PARLIA-MENT BUILDINGS** (501 Belleville; 250/387-3046) has, in summer, frequent historical tours. **VICTORIA BUG ZOO** (1107 Wharf St; 250/384-2847) fascinates children and adults, with features such as a surprisingly cute miniature apartment, scaled to its cockroach denizens.

CRAIGDARROCH CASTLE (1050 Joan Cres; 250/592-5323), once visited only by 19th-century socialites, is now open to the public to take in the ballroom, grand foyer, and parlors of Victoria's richest resident, coal baron Robert Dunsmuir. Inside, fine wood banisters and paneling glow still with old money, while the quaint turret sunroom reveals the fine views the elderly Mrs. Dunsmuir enjoyed while doing needlework or plotting advantageous marriages for her 10 children. Heritage home connoisseurs enjoy **POINT ELLICE HOUSE** (2616 Pleasant St; 250/380-6506), an early Victoria residence in tasteful Italianate style, and **CARR HOUSE** (207 Government St; 250/383-5843), the substantial birth home of admired West Coast artist and eccentric Emily Carr.

MUSEUMS AND GALLERIES

Across the street from the Empress Hotel, the **ROYAL BRITISH COLUMBIA MUSEUM** (675 Belleville; 250/387-3014; www.rbcm.gov.bc.ca) delights with its extensive collection of coastal Canadian indigenous art—from Nuu-chah-nulth whaling hats to Haida masks—and the Old Town display, a reconstructed 19th-century streetscape. Kids are drawn to Open Ocean, a simulated submarine ride, and the new Imax theatre. The **ART GALLERY OF GREATER VICTORIA** (1040 Moss St; 250/384-4101) is notable as a small but cozy repository for a select collection of Asian art; the calming courtyard garden is home to North America's only Shinto shrine.

PARKS AND GARDENS

On the southern edge of downtown, the city's beloved **BEACON HILL PARK** boasts 184 acres of manicured gardens interspersed with some natural forest and meadows. The rightfully renowned **BUTCHART GARDENS** (800 Benvenuto Ave; 250/652-5256) are 13 miles (21 km) north. This 1904 country estate is crowded with blossoms, in the manicured precincts of the Italian Garden, Rose Garden, and the delicate Japanese Garden. For nondrivers, take city bus No. 75 Central Saanich; it stops on Douglas Street in front of Crystal Gardens.

SHOPPING

For those seeking English goods, Government Street north to Yates Street offers the best selection of tweeds and china. For men's suits, **BRITISH IMPORTERS** (138 Victoria Eaton Centre; 250/386-1496) will please, as will upscale **W & J WILSON** (1221 Government St; 250/383-7177), a local institution also featuring fine, understated women's wear. The Irish have a strong shopping contingent in **AVOCA HANDWEAVERS** (1009 Government St; 250/383-0433) and **IRISH LINEN STORES** (1019 Government St; 250/383-6812). **MURCHIE'S TEA & COFFEE** (1110 Government St; 250/381-5451) has the finest teas, from green

Chinese Gunpowder to the classic Empress blend. The **ENGLISH SWEET SHOP** (738 Yates St; 250/382-3325) offers British treats like Scotch tablet and acid drops. Chocolate lovers head to historic **ROGERS' CHOCOLATES** (913 Government St; 250/384-7021) and **CHOCOLATERIE BERNARD CALLEBAUT** (623 Broughton St; 250/380-1515), which sells exquisite Belgian-styled chocolates. Shops such as **SASQUATCH TRADING** (1233 Government St; 250/386-9033) and **COWICHAN TRADING** (1328 Government St; 250/383-0321) offer hand-knit Cowichan sweaters, a specialty of Vancouver Island First Nations peoples. **EA MORRIS TOBACCONISTS** (1116 Government St; 250/382-4811) sells pipes, Cuban cigars, and flasks in an authentic 19th-century shop, and stately **MUNRO'S BOOKS** (1108 Government St; 250/382-2464) offers discerning reading pleasures. In summer, buy a kite for tomorrow at **KABOODLES TOY STORE** (1320 Government St; 250/383-0931).

BEACON DRIVE IN RESTAURANT (126 Douglas St; 250/385-7521) has the city's best soft ice cream. Fresh Montreal-style bagels and cream cheese are found at **MOUNT ROYAL BAGEL FACTORY** (6-1115 N Park St; 250/380-3588). At **DEMITASSE COFFEE BAR** (1320 Blanshard St; 250/386-4442) breakfast is the thing. Outdoor seating, along with espresso, is popular at **TORREFAZIONE ITALIA** (1234 Government St; 250/920-7203).

A section of Government Street (between View and Johnson Sts) has become in recent years a posh mecca of trendy stores; Johnson Street (between Government and Wharf Sts) has quirky independent shops, highlighted by the welcoming enclosure of historic **MARKET SQUARE** (Johnson St, between Government and Store Sts). Victoria's **CHINATOWN** (Fisgard St between Government and Store Sts), the oldest in Canada, is becoming something of a memory as the last Chinese grocers on the remaining block of Fisgard are transformed to other businesses, but it is still worth visiting, especially to see narrow, shop-lined Fan Tan Alley. Outside of Old Town, **ANTIQUE ROW** (Fort St east of downtown from Blanshard to Cook) beckons connoisseurs of 18th- to 20th-century goods; there's a sprinkling of Persian rug shops as well.

PERFORMING ARTS

The **MACPHERSON PLAYHOUSE** (3 Centennial Square; 250/386-6121), a former vaudeville theater, features British sex farces through the summer and soul-stirring operas come fall. **THE ROYAL THEATRE** (805 Broughton St; 250/386-6121) is home to a range of performances, from the **VICTORIA SYMPHONY ORCHESTRA** (846 Broughton St; 250/385-9771) to the jazz croonings of Island-born Diana Krall. The most-anticipated public event of the year is the sunset **SYMPHONY SPLASH**, an Inner Harbour concert held the first Sunday of August. The free weekly *Monday Magazine*, available in yellow boxes throughout downtown, has the best entertainment listings.

SPORTS AND RECREATION

The wittily named **PRINCE OF WHALES** (812 Wharf St; 250/383-4884) outfits participants in orange survival suits for a three-hour Zodiac-boat tour of local sea life; chances of killer whale sightings are best May through September. Launch a self-propelled ocean adventure from the Gorge Waterway, an inlet off the Inner Harbour: **GORGE KAYAKING CENTRE** (2940 Jutland Rd; 250/380-4668 or 877/380-4668) and **OCEAN RIVER SPORTS** (1437 Store St; 250/381-4233) rent kayaks and canoes.

RESTAURANTS

Cafe Brio / ★★★

944 FORT ST, VICTORIA; 250/383-0009
Owners Greg Hays and Silvia Marcolini literally invite you into their home at this lively Antique Row restaurant, serving *cucina domestica* (Italian cuisine focusing on seasonal regional foods). Chef Sean Brennan mirrors the change of seasons in his West Coast menu with Tuscan touches. Appetizers include smoked ivory salmon, seared Alaskan scallops, and crispy quail. Local organic grower Tina Frazer supplies specialty produce for Brennan's entrees, from rack of lamb served with a caramelized onion and goat cheese tart and olive vinaigrette, to delightful and affordable dinner selections like the spaghettini with fried bread crumbs, anchovy, chiles, and olives. The wine list is well chosen, with a good selection of West Coast wines and minimal markups. *$$–$$$; AE, MC, V; no checks; lunch Tues–Fri, dinner Mon–Sat; full bar; reservations recommended; www.cafe-brio.com; downtown.* &

Herald Street Caffe / ★★★

546 HERALD ST, VICTORIA; 250/381-1441
This lively Old Town restaurant has served fine, innovative West Coast cuisine for more than a decade. The interior is filled with grand floral arrangements and eclectic local art. Appetizers such as Dungeness crab cakes with cilantro-lime pesto and tomato salsa, and alder-smoked salmon on apple potato latkes, are delicious. The caesar is probably the best in town. Longtime favorites on chef Mark Finnigan's menu include his signature bouillabaisse, cashew-crusted chicken, rack of lamb with mint and whole-grain mustard, and beef tenderloin stuffed with pâté. For dessert: Shaker lemon pie or homemade ice creams and sorbets. An excellent wine list is combined with knowledgeable, courteous service. Tables may be a little close together, but on busy nights the atmosphere is quite electric. Late hours (till 1:30–2am) make this an ideal post-theater venue. *$$–$$$; AE, DC, E, MC, V; no checks; lunch Wed–Sun, dinner every day; full bar; reservations recommended; heraldstcaffe@pacificcoast. net; www.cafe-brio.com/dining/HeraldStreetCaffe.htm; at Government St.* &

Il Terrazzo Ristorante / ★★★

555 JOHNSON ST, VICTORIA; 250/361-0028
You'll find a true taste of Italy in this beautiful restaurant tucked away on Waddington Alley. Surrounded by five outdoor fireplaces and an abundance of plants and flowers, Il Terrazzo offers a haven of privacy in busy Old Town. (Alfresco dining on the covered, heated terrace is possible

nearly year-round.) The chefs exude tremendous passion, creating northern Italian cuisine that bursts with flavor. Classic minestrone, char-grilled baby squid, creamy risotto Milanese with seafood, wood-oven pizzas, marvelous pastas, and exquisite meat dishes such as veal marsala attest to the menu's diversity. Service is not always swift; patience is sometimes needed for pasta dishes. An extensive wine list showcases a range of fine Italian wines. *$$–$$$; AE, MC, V; no checks; lunch Mon–Sat, dinner every day; full bar; reservations recommended; terrazzo@pacificcoast.net; www.ilterrazzo.com; near Market Square.* &

J & J Wonton Noodle House / ★★
1012 FORT ST, VICTORIA; 250/383-0680

You might easily bypass this popular Chinese restaurant with its unassuming facade. But when the door opens and you catch the tantalizing aroma of ginger, garlic, and black beans, you won't. This busy, modest, spotlessly clean restaurant treats you to the flavors of Hong Kong, Singapore, Sichuan cooking, and northern China. A large kitchen window lets you watch chefs busily prepare wonton soup, imperial prawn with spicy garlic wine sauce, spicy ginger fried chicken, or Sichuan braised beef hot pot. Noodles are a specialty and are made fresh daily. Service is friendly, efficient, and knowledgeable. *$; MC, V; no checks; lunch, dinner Tues–Sat; beer and wine; reservations not necessary; jwong6@sprint.ca; between Vancouver and Cook Sts.* &

Kaz Japanese / ★★
1619 STORE ST, VICTORIA; 250/386-9121

The center of attention in this small, understated restaurant is its soft-spoken, humble owner, Kaz Motohashi. The Japanese community rank his sushi among the city's best. A traditionalist, Motohashi has nonetheless adapted his menu to western tastes. Along with fine nigiri-sushi such as *sake* (salmon), *tako* (octopus), and ahi (Hawaiian tuna), you'll find a range of North American–style rolls, such as prawn tempura roll and California Roll (with real crab). The menu offers other delicacies, such as noodle soup, curry rice, and teriyaki. Start with the addictive chicken *karaage* (deep-fried marinated chicken wings) or the light and crispy tempura. *$–$$; AE, MC, V; no checks; lunch, dinner Mon–Sat; beer and wine; reservations not necessary; at Fisgard St.* &

Med Grill / ★★
1010 YATES ST, VICTORIA; 250/360-1660
4512 W SAANICH RD, VICTORIA; 250/727-3444

Owner Paul Simpson transformed a defunct carpet store into a Mediterranean paradise. Skylights and massive windows illuminate the terra-cotta floor, rich wood trim, and lively yellow walls. Have a cocktail at the black marble horseshoe-shaped bar before being seated. A statue of the wine god Bacchus greets diners ascending to the cozy upstairs room that overlooks the main dining area. The menu offers moderately priced Mediterranean dishes, from pizza to pasta to spit-roasted meats. (A side order of Med bread is a must.) From martinis to wines by the glass, drinks are attractively priced. Service sometimes slows when the place is packed, and can be a bit too familiar for some. The large outdoor patio is open in summer. $–$$; AE, MC, V; no checks; lunch, dinner every day; full bar; reservations recommended; medgrill@yahoo.com; www. medgrillfood.com; at Vancouver St (Yates St), at Viewmont (Saanich Rd). &

Re-Bar Modern Foods / ★★

50 BASTION SQUARE, VICTORIA; 250/361-9223

Victoria's original vegetarian, health-food, smoke-free restaurant is packed with lunchtime crowds. Sip one of the refreshing fresh fruit drinks, such as the Atomic Glow (apple, strawberry, and ginger juices) or the Soul Charge (carrot, apple, celery, ginger, and Siberian ginseng) while perusing the menu. Delicious pizzas topped with oyster mushrooms, Anaheim chiles, tomatillo salsa, Asiago, and Monterey Jack are house specialties, along with pastas, Oriental salads, and black bean chili. Breads are all homemade. Lemon tahini dressing and basil vinaigrette are delicious salad-toppers. Friendly, helpful service exemplifies the Re-Bar's philosophy. $; AE, MC, V; no checks; breakfast, lunch, dinner every day, brunch Sat–Sun; beer and wine; reservations recommended (weekend brunch); at Langley St. &

Sam's Deli / ★

805 GOVERNMENT ST, VICTORIA; 250/382-8424

As many downtown office workers can attest, this 20-year-old restaurant offers the most bang for your buck. Located a stone's throw from the Empress Hotel and the Inner Harbour, this busy deli offers cafeteria-style service. The shrimp-and-avocado sandwich is an all-time favorite, as are large tureens of daily soup. The ploughman's lunch—a selection of meat or pâté, two different cheeses, kosher dill pickles, fresh fruit, and sourdough—is also popular. Spinach salads, pastrami or roast beef on dark rye, desserts, and a range of local draft beers and natural fruit juices are also available. Large windows and a sizable patio provide great people-watching, or get takeout and picnic at the Inner Harbour. $; MC, V; no checks; lunch, dinner every day; beer and wine; reservations not accepted; www.samsdeli.com; at Humboldt St. &

Spice Jammer Restaurant / ★★

852 FORT ST, VICTORIA; 250/480-1055

This pretty little Indian restaurant, with western decor, is overseen with effervescent charm and good humor by manager Amin Essa. His wife, Billie, is the chef, who makes excellent curries. A window onto the kitchen provides a behind-the-scenes look at the cooks busily preparing East Indian and East African dishes, with an emphasis on tandoori-style cooking (naan, chicken tikka, spicy prawns). Appetizers range from vegetable, chicken, or beef samosas to fried *mogos* (an East African dish of fried cassava-root wedges served with tamarind chutney). The curries come as you like: mild, medium, hot, and—if you dare—extra hot. Wake up your senses with vindaloos and masalas, as well as bhuna beef, *palak* lamb, *aloo gobi*, and rice pilaf, cooked with cardamom, cumin, saffron, and cinnamon. Token alternatives to curries are offered, but don't give them a second glance. *$–$$; AE, MC, V; no checks; lunch Tues–Sat, dinner Tues–Sun; full bar; reservations not necessary; spicejammer@aol.com; downtown.* &

Spinnakers / ★

308 CATHERINE ST, VICTORIA; 250/386-2739

One of the first brewpubs on the Island, Spinnakers has been around since 1984. On the Inner Harbour, it has the best view of any pub in Victoria. In the Tap Room upstairs, traditional pub fare is the order of the day, with rather ho-hum fish-and-chips, burgers, pastas, and curries, but good salads. Noggins chowder is fresh and consistently tasty. (You'll also find pub games here.) Downstairs in the dining room (where you can bring minors), you'll find a similar menu, plus potpies, stir-fries, and the inevitable ploughman's lunch. Both levels serve beers brewed on-site, including raspberry ale, oatmeal stout, and Scottish ale. A gift/bake shop at the entrance sells baked goods created in-house, Spinnaker's bottled beer and malt vinegar, and pub memorabilia. *$; AE, DC, DIS, MC, V; no checks; breakfast, lunch, dinner every day; full bar; reservations not necessary; spinnakers@spinnakers.com; www.spinnakers.com; near Chinatown.* &

Victorian Restaurant at Ocean Pointe Resort / ★★★

45 SONGHEES RD, VICTORIA; 250/360-2999

Here's an elegant space with an unsurpassed view, in one of Victoria's finest hotels (see review). Unquestionably one of the best chefs in Victoria, Craig Stoneman has created a superb menu, from maple-glazed caribou steak and game sausage, to baked macadamia nut–crusted salmon and lobster in a Pernod lime cream. His fruit salad, of sautéed jumbo prawns in a citrus curry dressing, prepared tableside, is magical. Or opt for the reasonably priced—and creative—three-, four-, or five-course table d'hôtel menu. Desserts (rhubarb and blackberry frozen parfait and sour cherry consommé, white chocolate raspberry torte with a saffron crème anglaise) are well crafted and artistically presented. Jacques Forest, the charming maître d'hôtel, does a remarkable job of pairing food and wine, and his servers are among the most polished in town. *$$$; AE, DC, JCB, MC, V; no checks; dinner Mon–Sun in high season (winter hours vary); full bar; reservations recommended; reservations@oprhotel.com; www.oprhotel.com; across Johnson St Bridge from downtown.*

LODGINGS

Abigail's Hotel / ★★

906 MCCLURE ST, VICTORIA; 250/388-5363 OR 800/561-6565

This elegant 22-room heritage manor overlooking busy Quadra Street was joined in recent years by a carriage house with additional suites. Abigail's is within walking distance of Beacon Hill Park and Inner Harbour attractions. The substantial, four-story Tudor facade and monumental tiled entrance promise grandeur. Basic rooms, thoroughly modernized and furnished with a mix of new and antique furniture, are a bit like standard hotel rooms, but all is in good taste, and the high-ceilinged lobby is hung with a fine antique brass and crystal chandelier. Dormer attic rooms display more elaborate furnishings and fixtures, such as a wrought-iron bedstead nestled in a canopied niche. The third-floor "Celebration Rooms" feature a luxurious double-sided wood-burning fireplace, facing both the bedroom and the deep tub. Rooms in the carriage house have an equally antique feel, and come at the top end of the hotel's price range. Down duvets and fireplaces in select rooms promise cozy nights, and mornings bring a three-course breakfast in the country-style dining room. Children over 10 are accepted, but better for families is Abigail's two-bedroom beachhouse, 10 minutes from downtown. *$$$–$$$$; AE, MC, V; no checks; innkeeper@abigailshotel.com; www.abigailshotel.com; at Vancouver St.*

Andersen House Bed & Breakfast / ★★
301 KINGSTON ST, VICTORIA; 250/388-4565

An exceptionally ornate and well-preserved home built in 1891 for a prosperous sea captain, Andersen House has four pleasing rooms. Inside the Queen Anne–style structure, furnishings are a mix of antiques, Persian rugs, and tribal artifacts. The spacious Captain's Apartment has a large bath with colorful art deco–inspired stained glass, a main room with evening views of the Parliament Buildings, and a separate bedroom with space for little ones. The Casablanca Room has a private balcony with steps to the lush garden, whose fruit harvests go into jams served at breakfast. Downstairs, the Garden Suite has its own private entrance, champagne goblets, and a CD collection, including Louis Armstrong, Frank Sinatra, and Diana Krall. The dining room's 12-foot ceilings and dramatic antique chandelier are rendered homey by a communal table where guests enjoy breakfast. For a storied stay in Victoria, spend the night in the *Mamita* 1927 motoryacht, built in Vancouver for a coast rum-runner; it is an easy 5-minute walk from the main house. *$$$–$$$$; MC, V; checks OK; andersen@islandnet.com; www.islandnet.com/~andersen; at Pendray.*

Beaconsfield Inn / ★★★
998 HUMBOLDT ST, VICTORIA; 250-384-4044

This nine-room Edwardian manor, built by businessman R. P. Rithet as a wedding gift for his daughter, is tastefully furnished in Arts and Crafts antiques. In downstairs rooms, swirling art nouveau designs glimmer in rows of stained-glass windows. The Emily Carr and Duchess Suites display understated, pin-striped elegance. Others are bright, airy retreats with flowered bedspreads. Most rooms have fireplaces and many have whirlpool tubs for two. Common rooms are the true wonders here: the library harkens back to the days of men's smoking jackets, with wood paneling and dark brown leather couches. The dining room has large leaded-glass windows and intimate tables.

Complimentary full breakfast is served here, or in the adjacent wicker-furnished sunroom. Owners Judi and Con Sollid now also offer self-catering accommodations in their 1,600-square-foot Beach Cottage, a more modern structure nestled up to the sands at Cadboro Bay and furnished in country pine antiques, with a natural stone fireplace and beachfront hot tub for two. *$$$$; MC, V; checks OK; beaconsfield@islandnet.com; www.islandnet.com/ beaconsfield/; at Vancouver St.*

Empress Hotel / ★★★

721 GOVERNMENT ST, VICTORIA; 250/384-8111 OR 800/441-1414

This dowager landmark, built in 1908 by Canadian Pacific Rail in the style of a French chateau, was part of a nationwide chain of luxury destination hotels. Though the national rail system is a thing of the past, the Empress remains a darling. The main-floor lobby is a public gallery, with tourists gathering to admire the rich wood paneling and antique chandeliers, and sip afternoon tea. Standard rooms are small and expensive for what you get (the privilege of the Empress name); a newer 21-room Entrée Gold section has its own check-in area and gilded Victorian salon. Satisfyingly luxurious rooms can be had, with stellar views to match. The Empress Room is the most visually impressive dining room in Victoria. The grand space retains the original carved beams in the ceiling, spacious tables, and comfortable chairs. Entrees such as smoked duck with a sour cherry sauce and rosemary biscotti, or sensational seared tuna with a wasabi-ginger sauce and grilled veggies, are original and well executed. *$$$–$$$$; AE, DC, MC, V; checks OK; www.cphotels.ca/; between Humboldt and Belleville.* &

Haterleigh Bed & Breakfast / ★★

243 KINGSTON ST, VICTORIA; 250/384-9995

This turn-of-the-century heritage home, which popular upper-crust architect Thomas Hooper built for himself in 1901, bills itself as "Victoria's most romantic inn." The honeymoon suite is a floral confection—with a wedding cake–style archway between rooms and a Jacuzzi tub. Stained-glass windows are large and exceptional, particularly the curved set in the period Morning Parlor. At the back, the Secret Garden Room has a view of the Olympic Mountains. Everything antique in the six-room inn is in mint condition. Proprietors Paul and Elizabeth Kelly treat guests to three-course breakfasts, and sherry and chocolates on arrival. Located in the James Bay hotel district, the Haterleigh is close to Inner Harbour action. *$$$$; MC, V; no checks; paulk @tnet.net; www.haterleigh.com; at Pendray.*

Joan Brown's Bed & Breakfast / ★★

729 PEMBERTON RD, VICTORIA; 250/592-5929

Joan Brown is a gregarious B&B proprietor, and she'll welcome you warmly into her turn-of-the-century mansion built for a former provincial lieutenant governor. Although the Rocklands neighborhood home has long lost its wood siding for stucco, all the ornate wooden fretwork and classical columns are in place. Stained glass and chandeliers are fit for a king's representative, and the sitting room is over-the-top Victorian—all floral swags and bric-a-brac. Upstairs rooms, some with fireplaces and garden views, are decorated with Laura Ashley prints; furnishings are a homey mix of antique and modern. The well-stocked library will keep you occupied on a rainy afternoon; when the clouds part, walk a few blocks to the groomed gardens of the present lieutenant governor's mansion, and the grandiose halls of Craigdarroch Castle (see Major Attractions in this chapter). *$$–$$$; no credit cards; checks OK; off Fort St.*

Laurel Point Inn / ★★★
680 MONTREAL ST, VICTORIA; 250/386-8721 OR 800/663-7667
With its lush garden setting on an oceanfront peninsula with sweeping views, the modern Laurel Point Inn is popular with chic wedding parties. For guests, the angular, set-back design means all of the more than 200 suites have ocean views. The lobby is small but tasteful, with a wood Northwest Coast indigenous sculpture, and monumentally sized, contemporary lighting. Art is a hallmark here: hallways and best rooms feature fine Asian and indigenous pieces. The nicest rooms are in the newer South Wing; junior suites offer the most "bang for the buck": sliding tatami-style doors lead into a vast bathroom with Jacuzzi, while the moderate-sized room feels spacious with pale wood paneling and a cream-colored bedspread. (For the price, however, it was distressing to see hand-sewn mending in the cover.) The hotel's exclusive gift shop prepares you for all occasions. *$$$–$$$$; AE, DC, JCB, MC, V; no checks; reservations@ laurelpoint.com; www.laurelpoint.com; follow Douglas south, turn east on Belleville.* &

Magnolia Hotel & Suites / ★★★
623 COURTNEY ST, VICTORIA; 250/381-0999 OR 877/624-6654
Opened in October 1998, the 66-room Magnolia styles itself after European boutique hotels. Service is attentive and accommodating, and suites are tastefully luxurious. First impressions count here: the lobby is paneled in rich mahogany, and underfoot are limestone tiles. Many rooms have gas fireplaces, such as our favored seventh-floor "diamond level" corner suite, with reasonably good harbor views. Striped upholstery imparts a baronial welcome to armchairs placed by the floor-to-ceiling windows. Bathrooms are sumptuous, with marble counters and Jacuzzi baths; robes and even umbrellas are thoughtfully provided. For business travelers, rooms have desks with data ports and multi-line speaker phones; a discreet conference room is available. Downstairs, Hugo's Grill is all dark wood and artful metal trellising; the long curved bar is a notable feature. The Magnolia is well placed downtown, just off Government Street's shopping attractions and a block from the Empress. The new low-rise building is refreshingly free of Victoria's usual faux-Tudor or peach-colored California-modern touches; the glass and sandstone-toned building, ornamented with green tilework, fits in well with its surroundings. *$$$$; AE, D, E,*

MC, V; *no checks; magnoliahotel@bc.sympatico.ca; www.magnoliahotel. com; at Gordon St.*

Ocean Pointe Resort / ★★★

45 SONGHEES RD, VICTORIA; 250/360-2999 OR 800/667-4677
Dominating the Inner Harbour along with the great monuments of the Empress and the Parliament Buildings, the Ocean Pointe's exterior doesn't share their built-for-the-ages demeanor. Its interior, however, is luxurious, with sweeping views from the spacious lobby on up. Standard rooms, while well kept, are small and basic: one pays for what is *outside* the window. During low season (mid-Oct–mid-Apr), upgrade to a "Specialty Room" at little additional cost. These huge affairs feature a bedroom, two bathrooms, a living and dining area, a small kitchen, and miles of window views. In the hotel's Victorian Restaurant (see review), you'll be among high rollers: the sommelier has seen foreign executives blow thousands on a single bottle of wine. The Ocean Pointe is making a name for itself with its spa, where services range from a rosemary pine pedicure to ayurvedic aromatherapy to shiatsu massage. *$$$–$$$$; AE, DC, JCB, MC, V; no checks; reservations@oprhotel.com; www.oprhotel.com; across Johnson St Bridge.* &

Prior House Bed & Breakfast Inn / ★★★

620 ST. CHARLES ST, VICTORIA; 250/592-8847
Truly a queen among B&Bs, this large 1912 manor is sure to impress with its dramatic stonework lower levels and Tudor styling above. Gardens are splendid, and visible from numerous rooms, some with balconies. Most luxurious is the Lieutenant Governor's Suite: the bath is glamorous with mirrored walls and ceilings, green marble whirlpool tub and long vanity counter, gold swan fixtures, and crystal chandeliers. The bedroom has a more traditional antique feel. On the third floor, the Windsor Suite's French doors lead to a private balcony with a sweeping view; in the bath, a whirlpool tub sits under a skylight. Best value at this elegant establishment is the Boudoir, a cozy suite with a fireplace, and a private, vintage 1912 bathroom across the hall. For more privacy, ground-level garden suites have separate entrances, patio space, and one or two bedrooms, but lack the aged patina of upstairs rooms. The Prior House is located in the established residential Rockland neighborhood, close to the Lieutenant Governor's Mansion. *$$$–$$$$; MC, V; checks OK; innkeeper@ priorhouse.com; www.priorhouse.com; at Rockland.*

Around Victoria

Sooke to Port Renfrew

Forty minutes west of Victoria on the West Island Highway (Hwy 14), Sooke is a quiet town worth visiting; residents are committed to retaining the natural beauty and rural character of the area, dotted with old farmsteads, beaches, and contemplative forests and park reserves. Boat enthusiasts enjoy a stroll through the town's marina. Beyond Sooke, the road continues past stellar beach parks and, unfortunately, clear-cuts, to Port Renfrew.

ROYAL ROADS UNIVERSITY (2005 Sooke Rd, Victoria; 250/391-2511), on the road to Sooke, is a grand former Dunsmuir family castle in medieval style; the beautiful grounds are open to the public, 10am–4pm. Also on the way to Sooke is the old farmstead town of **METCHOSIN**; a drive along back ways like Happy Valley Road is a pastoral pleasure, with small farms set in rolling valleys and hills. In this area, the shallow, relatively warm waters of **WITTY'S LAGOON REGIONAL PARK** (west of Victoria via Hwy 14 and Metchosin Rd) are popular with local families.

For local crafts, organic vegetables, and children's activities, stop by the **SOOKE COUNTRY MARKET** (at Sooke Elementary School; 250/642-7528; Sat, May–Sept).

The entire coast between Sooke and Port Renfrew has excellent parks with trails down to ocean beaches; French Beach (7 miles/11 km east of Jordan River) is the start of the rigorous **JUAN DE FUCA MARINE TRAIL** (250/391-2300), the more accessible younger sister to the West Coast Trail. Zip down to the beach for a picnic or spend a few days hiking the length of the coastal park to **SOMBRIO BEACH** (21 miles/34 km east of Jordan River), popular with local surfers in fall and spring. **BOTANICAL BEACH** (follow signs at end of paved road just west of Port Renfrew) has exceptionally low tides in early summer that expose miles of sea life in sheltering pools.

RESTAURANTS

Country Cupboard Café / ★★

402 SHERINGHAM POINT RD, SOOKE; 250/646-2323

Proprietor Jennie Vivian knows three words to keep them coming: mile-high cheesecakes. Regulars include chocolate amaretto and caramel pecan, while vanilla white chocolate makes an occasional appearance. Pies, too, are fantastic creations, changing daily: perhaps walnut raisin coconut? Hearty main-course standards include pork baby back ribs and grilled spring salmon. Huge burgers satisfy local loggers and those fresh off nearby French Beach; oyster burgers, steamed Sooke clams, and locally smoked salmon do too. A small wine list features BC vintages. Patio dining makes room for summer crowds. *$$; MC, V; no checks; lunch, dinner every day; beer and wine; reservations recommended; at West Coast Rd, 15 minutes west of Sooke.*

Good Life Bookstore Café / ★

2113 OTTER POINT RD, SOOKE; 250/642-6821

After browsing the selection of books—Good Life specializes in BC, gardening, children's, and cooking—move over to the funky cafe in this converted old house. The cuisine is an eclectic collection of Pacific Rim tastes.

VANCOUVER ISLAND THREE-DAY TOUR

DAY ONE: From Victoria, get a charging start with a healthful breakfast at **Re-Bar Modern Foods**, then head north and hop aboard one of the many Swartz Bay ferries plying the island-bejeweled waters, to **Saltspring Island**. Browse the crafts and organic produce of the popular **Saturday Market** in the heart of Ganges, the largest village in the Gulf Islands. Have a casual lunch at **Alfresco**'s downstairs cafe, then drive up Cranberry Road to the top of **Mount Maxwell** for a panorama of the archipelago, from Saltspring to the U.S. mainland. Check in to a room at the splendid **Hastings House**, exuding the gentility of an English manor-farm. Have an exquisite dinner here in the highly rated dining room, perhaps at a table by the stone fireplace.

DAY TWO: After a delicious full breakfast at Hastings House, zip out to **Vesuvius Harbour** on the island's northern end and catch the ferry to Crofton on Vancouver Island just south of Chemainus. From there, drive north on the Trans-Canada Highway to **Nanaimo** to lunch at the **Wesley Street Cafe**. Continue north on the faster inland Highway 19 to Parksville, and take Highway 4 west. Take a little detour on Highway 4A to visit the whimsical village of **Coombs**; ponder the goats grazing on the grass roof of the **Old Country Market** and browse some shops. Continue west, pausing briefly on the road to **Port Alberni** to admire the towering old-growth trees of Cathedral Grove in **MacMillan Provincial Park**. The long drive across the island takes you past lakes and along rivers to the Pacific, where you turn north toward **Tofino**. Check in to a waterfront room at the **Wickaninnish Inn** just outside of Tofino, and dine in the exquisite **Pointe Restaurant** there.

DAY THREE: Grab an organic coffee and muffin at the earthy **Common Loaf Bake Shop** in Tofino. Wander the small downtown strip, poking around in the shops there for First Nations art and hemp clothing and body products. Lunch at the casual, eclectic **RainCoast Café** before driving to the inimitable **Long Beach** to soak in the natural splendor (or, if bold, the icy waters). Pack your memories into the car and head back the way you came, pausing to dine at the **Mahle House** in Nanaimo and stay over at the **Dream Weaver B&B** in **Cowichan Bay** a bit north of Victoria.

Tasty soups include bouillabaisse and jambalaya; dinner includes comfort food such as grilled rib-eye steak with mushrooms and pearl onions, and the more adventurous chicken breast stuffed with smoked salmon, Brie, and cream cheese. Lemon sour cream pie or a maple crème caramel round out the experience. *$$; MC, V; no checks; lunch, dinner every day (lunch Tues–Sat, dinner Fri–Sat in winter); beer and wine; reservations recommended; downtown.*

Sooke Harbour House / ★★★★

1528 WHIFFEN SPIT RD, SOOKE; 250/642-3421 OR 800/889-9688

Owners Frederique and Sinclair Philip, and their team of chefs, have garnered international attention for their rare dedication to the freshest local ingredients blended with a good deal of energy and flashes of innovation. Organically grown edible plants from the inn's own gardens complement what dedicated island farmers, fishermen, and the wilderness provide. Entrees range from cold-cured sockeye salmon tartare with zucchini blossoms stuffed with goat cheese polenta, to pan-seared Qualicum Beach scallops, to roast sirloin of Cedar Glen Farm veal. Sooke Harbour House's award-winning wine list features excellent French vintages and an impressive array from BC. You'll pay dearly for all this attention to detail, but the commitment to flavors may make you forget the high tariff. *$$$; JCB, MC, V; checks OK for House guests; dinner every day; full bar; reservations required; info@sookeharbourhouse. com; www.sookeharbourhouse.com; off Hwy 14.* &

LODGINGS

Fossil Bay Resort / ★★

1603 WEST COAST RD, SOOKE; 250/646-2073

This one wins raves from even fussy, seasoned travelers; private hot tubs with views of the Strait of Juan de Fuca and the Olympic Mountains linger foremost in their minds. Cliffside cottages, featuring simple basics and full kitchens plus cozy fires, are islands of solitude. The modern design is reminiscent of a subdivision, but the joy of doing nothing is delightfully old-fashioned. Pets are accepted in two of six cottages. *$$$–$$$$; MC, V; checks OK; 2-night min, 3-night min on holiday weekends; wild@fossilbay.com; www.fossilbay. com; 3¾ miles (6 km) east of Sooke.*

Hartmann House / ★★★

5262 SOOKE RD, SOOKE; 250/642-3761

This exquisite three-room B&B exudes old English charm. Outside and in, the Tudor-inspired home is alive with blossoms: The bay-windowed exterior is draped with pink flowers in season; an old-fashioned porch with white wicker chairs overlooks well-groomed gardens. The Honeymoon Suite is the largest and most luxurious, with a four-poster canopy bed, a whirlpool tub, fireplace, and hardwood flooring; French doors lead to a private courtyard. Expect to see garden herbs, fruits, and flowers gracing the well-supplied breakfast table. *$$–$$$; MC, V; no checks; 2-night min; info@hartmannhouse. bc.ca; www.sookenet.com/hartmann; 3¾ miles (6 km) east of Sooke.*

Markham House / ★★

1853 CONNIE RD, SOOKE; 250/642-7542 OR 888/256-6888

For an English country–garden setting, book into Markham House. Virgil the chocolate Lab is as welcoming as innkeepers Lyall and Sally Markham, who know when to leave you alone and when to invite you to chat on the veranda of their Tudor-style B&B. People choose Markham House for gentle pleasures: fireside port before turning in, feather beds, and country hospitality. Immaculately groomed grounds include a small river, a trout pond, a putting green, and glorious iris gardens with more than 100 species. Two bedrooms have private baths; the Garden Suite has a double Jacuzzi overlooking the pond. The self-contained Honeysuckle Cottage is spotlessly clean and filled with antiques. *$$–$$$; AE, DC, JCB, MC, V; no checks; mail@markhamhouse.com; www.markhamhouse.com; turn south off W Island Hwy before Sooke Harbour.*

Ocean Wilderness Inn & Spa Retreat / ★

109 WEST COAST RD, SOOKE; 250/646-2116 OR 800/323-2116

A groomed English garden, popular with wedding parties, surrounds this weathered wood-sided homestead-style inn, set in 5 acres of old-growth rain forest. Nine rooms—some with ocean views—are done in antique style, featuring fanciful, fabric-canopied beds. A log-constructed living room has a natural stone fireplace; in the dining room, country breakfasts are made with farm-fresh produce. Reserve a soak in the hot tub, enclosed in a Japanese gazebo for privacy. The Rainforest Rejuvenation Spa is a recent addition: mud and seaweed treatments, body wraps, and massages are available; guided meditation, tai chi, and *qi gong* are other soul-cleansing options. *$$–$$$; MC, V; checks OK; ocean@sookenet.com; www.sookenet.com/ocean; 10 minutes west of Sooke.* &

Point No Point Resort / ★

1505 WEST COAST RD, SOOKE; 250/646-2020

The Soderberg family owns a mile of beach and 40 acres of undeveloped Northwest coastline facing the Strait of Juan de Fuca and the Pacific. They rent 22 reasonably rustic cabins among the trees near the cliff (newest are the Blue Jay and Otter duplex cabin), catering to those who eschew TV and phones in favor of remote beauty. Four pricier cabins have hot tubs; four hang right over the water; some allow pets. The only distractions are the crash of rolling swells, and the crackle of the fire. Wood is supplied, but bring your own food, though the dining room serves lunch, afternoon tea, and dinner in summer. Guests have praised meals—entrees include grilled swordfish with an orange beurre blanc, or pan-seared pork medallions with apples and pears in a brandy cream reduction. *$$–$$$; AE, MC, V; checks OK; Hwy 14, 15 miles (24 km) west of Sooke.* &

Sooke Harbour House / ★★★★

1528 WHIFFEN SPIT RD, SOOKE; 250/642-3421 OR 800/889-9688

This bucolic establishment is widely considered one of British Columbia's finest inns, located at water's edge, on the end of a quiet neighborhood road. A sensitive addition to the original 1931 white clapboard farmhouse accommodates the inn's popularity. All rooms have views of the Strait of Juan de Fuca and the Olympic Mountains, as well as decks and fireplaces. Distinctive theme rooms delight the curious and the refined: the Mermaid Room is lavished with suitably fabled art, and the Ichthyologist's Study features a stunning salmon carving and line drawings of fish. The Victor Newman Longhouse Room features museum-quality First Nations art. Expect extras such as fresh-cut flowers, robes, and a decanter of fine port. The lavish complimentary breakfast—hazelnut-maple syrup waffles with loganberry purée, or fresh garden vegetable quiche with scones and preserves, for example—is delivered to your room. Also included is a light lunch in season (lower off-season rates include a continental breakfast). An in-house masseuse and reflexologist are on call; should you wish to venture out, perhaps to the acclaimed Sooke Harbour House restaurant (see review), a beauty consultant is available. A conference facility was added in 1999. *$$$$; AE, DC, E, JCB, MC, V; checks OK; info@sookeharbourhouse.com; www.sookeharbourhouse. com; end of Whiffen Spit Rd.* &

Sidney and the Saanich Peninsula

This pretty rural area, although increasingly encroached on by development, holds some bucolic corners, particularly off W Saanich Road. While waiting in the ferry lineup to Vancouver, duck into the nearby **STONEHOUSE PUB** (2215 Canoe Cove Rd, Sidney; 250/656-3498) for a snack or a beer.

RESTAURANTS

Blue Peter Pub and Restaurant

2270 HARBOUR RD, SIDNEY; 250/656-4551

The "blue peter" is the international flag yachtsmen use to signal that their ship is about to sail. Sailors are often found moored to the deck of this pub, where requisite burgers, club sandwiches, and fish-and-chips are a cut above average. The more formal dining room doesn't always meet expectations; however, the promise of sunsets in summer fills the restaurant inside and out. *$; MC, V; no checks; lunch, dinner Mon–Sun (Tues–Sun in winter); full bar; reservations not necessary; 2 miles (3 km) north of Sidney.*

Carden Street West / ★★★

1164 STELLYS CROSS RD, BRENTWOOD BAY; 250/544-1475

 The name of this rural restaurant doesn't relate to its current address, but instead to its original site, the still-popular Carden Street Cafe in Guelph, Ontario. When owners Paulette Jolley and Michael Mino decided to move to Vancouver Island, they brought with them philosophies that made their first effort so successful: personalized service and delicious food. Area residents are frequent visitors to this charming, almost farmhouse-looking structure (once a fruit stand). The 40-seat dining room is gardenlike and full of rich, tropical colors. Connie O'Brien's main menu is "spicy international"— inspired by the owners' many travels—and includes outstanding West African– and Southeast Asian–style curries. A special sheet offers a range of less spicy, but full-flavored tastes. The wine list is limited, but a good choice of beer and fruity drinks goes well with spicier flavors. Desserts include cheesecake, chocolate mousse, and light-as-air pavlovas. *$$$; AE, MC, V; local checks only; dinner Tues–Sat; beer and wine; reservations recommended; at W Saanich Rd.* ⅚

Deep Cove Chalet / ★★★

11190 CHALET RD, SIDNEY; 250/656-3541

Chef/owner Peter Koffel brings European opulence to this stunning, rural seaside setting in Sidney. The large windows of this chaletlike structure overlook meticulously kept lawns and a splendid view of Saanich Inlet. Guests can stroll the manicured lawns between courses, wineglasses in hand. Lobster bisque, cheese soufflé, scrambled eggs and caviar, sautéed oysters with béarnaise sauce, and beef Wellington are just a few classics. Finish with crepes suzette or cherries jubilee. The extensive wine list offers fine vintages from Burgundy, Bordeaux, and California. Groups can book a private dining suite upstairs. *$$$–$$$$; AE, MC, V; local checks only; lunch Wed–Sun, dinner Tues–Sun; full bar; reservations recommended; deep.cove.chalet@home.com; www.deep-cove-chalet.sidney.bc.ca; northwest of Sidney, call for directions.* ⅚

The Latch Country Inn / ★★

2328 HARBOUR RD, SIDNEY; 250/656-6622

The old Latch Restaurant used to intimidate locals with its über-class attitude, but in recent years the tone has come down a notch to a welcome casual-elegant, which seems better suited to its 1925 heritage home, designed by noted Victoria architect Samuel Maclure for the lieutenant governor of British Columbia. The restaurant focuses on fresh Pacific Northwest flavors in European-style cooking. The daily-changing menu might feature appetizers such as steamed Saltspring Island mussels, and strudel with chicken, hickory-smoked apple, and goat cheese. Entrees range from New York steak with roasted-garlic mashed potatoes to a vegetarian baked pumpkin and goat cheese gâteau, to a leg of venison with a chipotle thyme jus. Desserts tantalize with offerings such as Kahlua crème caramel, and the triple chocolate *bacio nero*. Five guest suites take advantage of antique rich wood paneling hewn from local Douglas fir. In fall 2000, a new 20-suite hotel opened on the property; the Shoal Harbour Inn, done in country style, features Tsehum Harbour vistas, fireplaces, a spa, and a health club. *$$–$$$$; AE, MC, V; checks OK; dinner every day (varies in winter); full bar; reservations required; latch@latchinn.com; www.latchinn. com; 2 miles (3 km) north of Sidney.*

Malahat

The Malahat is a talismanic word among local drivers: it signals steep roads with few passing lanes, and obscuring winter fogs. But for leisurely drives, the Malahat (Trans-Canada Hwy/Hwy 1, from Victoria to Mill Bay) is the prettiest on the island. Lush Douglas fir forests hug the narrow-laned highway, past beloved **GOLDSTREAM PROVINCIAL PARK** (3400 Trans-Canada Hwy/Hwy 1;

250/391-2300 or 250/478-9414)—where you can view the salmon run in November—and at the summit, northbound pullouts offer breathtaking views over Saanich Inlet and the surrounding undeveloped hills.

RESTAURANTS

Malahat Mountain Inn / ★★

265 TRANS-CANADA HWY, VICTORIA; 250/478-1944

Funky, casual, and imaginative best describe the cuisine at this view-blessed restaurant on the Malahat drive (Hwy 1). Large wrought-iron candlesticks and greenery punctuate the dramatic color scheme, and booths offer cozy intimacy. Even on a foggy winter's day, cars jam the parking lot, and inside, patrons chatter happily. The menu is big on seafood and pastas; produce is organic, and meat is free-range. At lunch, soup specials change daily—perhaps tasty beef barley with caramelized onion. At dinner, vegetarians dig into the mixed vegetable capellini; meatier fare includes a pan-roasted lamb sirloin, and a lamb osso buco. Finish with a creamy lemon pie. *$$; AE, MC, V; no checks; lunch, dinner every day; full bar; reservations recommended; at top of the Malahat drive (Hwy 1).*

LODGINGS

The Aerie Resort / ★★★★

600 EBEDORA LN, MALAHAT; 250/743-7115

Celebrities in search of discreet luxury seek out the Aerie Resort, while regular folk prefer it for festive grandeur: the Aerie has hosted more than 500 weddings since it opened in 1991. Accolades are invariably heaped upon this modern view resort in the lush hillsides of the Malahat region, a half-hour's drive from downtown Victoria. Gleaming white, terraced units were designed as a modern take on Mediterranean villages. Set in 10 acres of meticulously kept gardens, it achieves an idyllic Isle-of-Capri mood. Most rooms feature whirlpool tubs, dramatic fireplaces, private decks, Persian and Chinese silk carpets, and plush modern furnishings. Resort amenities such as an indoor pool, indoor and outdoor hot tubs, tennis courts, and a Beauty & Wellness Centre—offering massage, aromatherapy, and other services—ensure a relaxing stay. Rates include a full breakfast in the spectacular and fêted Dining Room, which features imaginative seasonal cuisine. *$$$$; AE, MC, V; no checks; aerie@relaischateaux.fr; www.aerie.bc.ca; take Spectacle Lake turnoff from Trans-Canada Hwy.*

The Gulf Islands

Stretching for 149 miles (240 km) up the broad expanse of the Strait of Georgia are clusters of lushly forested islands, Canada's more remote version of the U.S. San Juan Islands. From the air or by boat, these islands appear positively Edenic.

Well-stocked stores, bank machines, and even restaurants are scarce to nonexistent on many of the islands, so plan accordingly. But natural beauty and recreational opportunities abound—all in the rain shadow of Vancouver Island's mountains. Like Victoria, the Gulf Islands are considerably less rainy than Vancouver, though rain gear is still advised in winter. The Gulf Islands are harmoniously inhabited by artisans and small-scale organic farmers.

The Gulf Islands fall into three groups. The best known and most populous are the **SOUTHERN ISLANDS**: of these, Saltspring, Galiano, Mayne, Saturna, and Pender are accessible via the ferry terminal at Swartz Bay outside Victoria (or from Tsawwassen outside Vancouver), while Gabriola is reached from Nanaimo. Visited several times a day by ferry, the southern Gulf Islands—particularly Saltspring and Galiano—offer the widest selection of inns, eateries, shopping, and services. Farther north, laid-back **DENMAN AND HORNBY ISLANDS**, with trails beloved by mountain bikers, are a short hop from Buckley Bay, 12½ miles (20 km) south of Courtenay. Quadra, Cortes, and Sonora make up the closely linked **DISCOVERY ISLANDS**—fishing and boating meccas east of Campbell River.

ACCESS AND INFORMATION

BC FERRIES (250/386-3431 or 888/223-3779; www.bcferries.bc.ca) offer many trips daily, but plan ahead in summer for car traffic, because popular runs fill up fast. Island hopping is possible, but schedules are complex and times do not always mesh; see specific islands below for additional detail. Advance reservations are possible on southern Gulf Islands routes for an extra fee (reservations: 604/444-2890 or 888/724-5223). Less stressful—and less expensive—is leaving the car at home; most inns and B&Bs offer ferry pickup. Bring your own bike or rent one; the islands are wonderful for cycling. **TOURISM VANCOUVER ISLAND** (335 Wesley St, Ste 203, Nanaimo; www.islands.bc.ca) has information on touring the Gulf Islands.

Saltspring Island

Saltspring is the largest and most populous of the southern Gulf Islands (with 9,200 residents), and is packed densely with artisans' studios and pastoral farms. Original First Nations inhabitants called the island Klaathem for the salt springs on the island's north end. Non-native settlement here dates back to the mid-19th century, and early settlers included African-Americans from San Francisco in the decades after the Civil War. The "Kanakas," as the indigenous people of Hawaii were then called, also played an important role.

Today, the pioneer landscape has left an imprint of postcard farms and three sweet stone-and-wood churches on Fulford-Ganges Road. Ancient Douglas fir forests cloak small mountains, interspersed with sparkling lakes. **MOUNT MAXWELL PROVINCIAL PARK** (6 miles/11 km southwest of Ganges via Fulford-Ganges Rd and Cranberry Rd; 250/537-5252), on the west side of the island 2,000 feet above sea level, has a hearty hike with a rewarding view. For camping, the sandy beach at **RUCKLE PROVINCIAL PARK** (10 minutes from Fulford Harbour ferry dock, take left onto Beaver Rd; 250/653-4115) on the island's east side is good, and fishing enthusiasts head to **ST. MARY LAKE** (north of Ganges on North End Rd) seeking cutthroat and rainbow. Warm ocean currents allow pleasant summer swimming in the clear ocean waters.

The big draw for locals and tourists is Ganges's **SATURDAY MARKET IN THE PARK** (Centennial Square, on Fulford-Ganges Rd; 250/537-5252; Apr–Oct): local goat cheeses pressed with violets, organic produce, pottery, hand-smoothed wooden bowls, and more. Similarly fine wares can be found at the much-praised **ARTCRAFT** (250/537-5252) sale in Ganges's Mahon Hall, daily June through mid-September. The annual (since 1896) September **SALTSPRING FALL FAIR** (Farmer's Institute, Rainbow Rd) is a family favorite, with sheep shearing, crafts, animals, games for kids, baked goods, and more. Enjoy a snack and organic coffee at the vegetarian bakery and cafe **BARB'S BUNS** (1–121 McPhillips Ave, Ganges; 250/537-4491).

Three BC Ferries routes serve Saltspring. The shortest leaves Swartz Bay, outside Victoria, and lands 35 minutes later at Saltspring's **FULFORD HARBOUR**, a small artists' village at the island's south end. Ferries leave less frequently from Tsawwassen on the mainland for the 1½-hour trip to **LONG HARBOUR** on the island's northeast shore. A short hop from the Vancouver Island logging town of Crofton takes you to Saltspring's **VESUVIUS HARBOUR**, on the island's northwest side, notable for the congenial waterfront pub at the Vesuvius Inn, where you'll fare better with beer than food. Ganges is located between Long Harbour and Vesuvius Harbour.

RESTAURANTS

Alfresco Waterfront Restaurant / ★

GRACE POINT SQUARE, GANGES; 250/537-5979

Best for family lunches, Alfresco's downstairs cafe shines with a large selection of daily soups, from a hearty European garlic and sausage to vegetarian mulligatawny (a spicy Indian concoction). Assorted wraps are menu staples, while specials might include seafood enchiladas. The downstairs cafe has a homey country atmosphere. Dinner upstairs is more upscale, with prices set mainly by the ocean-view patio; entrees include the ubiquitous Saltspring lamb, and steak. *$$–$$$; MC, V; local checks only; lunch, dinner every day (Fri–Sat in winter); full bar; reservations recommended; turn east before Thrifty's Foods.*

Restaurant House Piccolo / ★★

108 HEREFORD AVE, GANGES; 250/537-1844

The chef is "Piccolo" himself, and he brings upscale Scandinavian cuisine to this cozy environment in the heart of Ganges. Start with a fillet of marinated herring with new potatoes and dill—paired with ice-cold aquavit or beer. For an extra dash, throw in an order of Russian caviar on ice. Main dishes range from classic wiener schnitzel to West Coast salmon specialties; for those who prefer

French cuisine to German, breast of Muscovy duck mandarin Napoléon doesn't disappoint. Vegetarians enjoy gently sautéed BC forest mushrooms with tagliatelle pasta. Try the Finnish-style dessert of "frosty" cranberries with a warm caramel sauce. *$$$; AE, DIS, MC, V; local checks only; dinner every day; full bar; reservations recommended; downtown.*

LODGINGS

Anne's Oceanfront Hideaway / ★★

168 SIMSON RD, SALTSPRING ISLAND; 250/537-0851 OR 888/474-2663

In this immaculate home with views of Stuart Channel and Vancouver Island, sign in to the Garry Oak Room and rest placidly on the four-poster bed. On quiet island evenings, contemplate the sunset from the wraparound veranda, and anticipate the smell of morning baking. The inn's four rooms are decorated in country floral style. Wheelchair users praise accessibility here, and others applaud the hospitality of proprietors Rick and Ruth-Anne Broad. A four-course breakfast might include eggs in phyllo pastry with lamb patties and chutney. Take advantage of the hot tub, exercise room, canoes, and bikes. Hummingbirds are frequent visitors to the patio. *$$$–$$$$; AE, MC, V; local checks only; annes@saltspring.com; www.bbcanada.com/939.html; north of Vesuvius ferry terminal.* &

Beddis House Bed and Breakfast / ★

131 MILES AVE, SALTSPRING ISLAND; 250/537-1028

Charming Beddis House, a white clapboard farmhouse built in 1900, is close to a private beach on Ganges Harbour. Hidden at the end of a country road, it's far enough from town that you can see the stars at night and the seals and otters during the day. Guests make themselves at home in the modern coach house. It contains three very private rooms with claw-footed tubs, country-style furniture, wood stoves, and decks or balconies that look toward the water. Breakfast and afternoon tea are served in the old house, where there is also a guest lounge. *$$$; MC, V; no checks; beddis@saltspring.com; www.saltspring.com/beddishouse; follow Beddis Rd from Fulford-Ganges Rd, turn left onto Miles Rd.*

Bold Bluff Retreat / ★★

1 BOLD BLUFF, SALTSPRING ISLAND; 250/653-4377

Bold Bluff's two private cabins are on a secluded peninsula overlooking Sansum Narrows, between Saltspring and Vancouver Islands, where marine wildlife abounds. Simple but bright, the two-bedroom Salty's Cabin sits on a rocky outcropping; the tide rushes in and out right under the deck. Solar power, a composting toilet, and a propane stove ensure a self-sufficient and eco-friendly holiday with no disturbances and time to relax. The kids will be thrilled if they catch sight of nearby resident killer whale pods. The three-bedroom Garden Cottage is nestled in an old orchard, accented by a luxuriant rose arbor. Antique furnishings and a piano lend a warm glow inside the rustic shingled cottage. A French door leads onto a porch with Adirondack chairs; a trampoline, swing, and private beach make this an excellent family spot. Amenities include a full kitchen and bath. Owner Tamar Griggs will gladly pick up guests for the 5-minute boat ride to the roadless peninsula on the island's southwest quadrant. Hike up the hill to view the eagles' nests with Griggs's powerful scope, then warm up by the fire. *$$$; no credit cards; checks OK; boldbluff@ saltspring.com; www.salt-spring.bc.ca/boldbluff; accessible by boat from Burgoyne Bay, 10 minutes northwest of Fulford Harbour ferry.*

Hastings House / ★★★★

160 UPPER GANGES RD, GANGES; 250/537-2362 OR 800/661-9255

This 30-acre seaside estate is the most exquisite getaway on the southern Gulf Islands. Pass the bucolic pasture of frolicking lambs and, as the weathered barn and old farmhouse come into view, it feels as stately as England, circa 1820. Varied accommodations are individually decorated with Persian rugs, first-class antiques, and modern country plaids and florals. The Farmhouse has two two-level suites overlooking the water. In the Manor House, two upstairs suites feature the same lovely views from casement windows, warmed by substantial stone fireplaces. The Post is a secluded, compact cabin popular with honeymooners; French doors open to a garden patio. The current refined decor belies this structure's history as a Hudson's Bay trading post. The wood-sided barn is richly weathered, and divided into smaller suites overlooking the garden and pasture. Fireplaces or wood stoves are a given throughout; double whirlpool tubs are in select rooms. Opened in July 1999, seven new Hillside Suites offer ocean views from all rooms, even bedrooms, in a modern West Coast–style wood building. The formal dining room and more intimate Snug offer cuisine among the most refined on the BC coast. The prix-fixe menu changes daily and features fresh, local ingredients. *$$$$; AE, MC, V; local checks only; 2-night min on weekends and holidays; hasthouse@ saltspring.com; www.hastingshouse.com; just north of Ganges.* &

The Old Farmhouse / ★★★

1077 N END RD, SALTSPRING ISLAND; 250/537-4113

On this island boasting more than 100 B&Bs, the Old Farmhouse stands out. Hosts Gertie and Karl Fuss transformed their two-story white clapboard heritage home into a picture-perfect inn. Four guest rooms, each with private bath and patio or balcony, are charmingly decorated: brilliant white wainscoting, floral wallpaper, French doors, polished pine floors, sparkling stained-glass windows, feather beds and starched duvets, fresh roses. It's all maintained by professional hosts, who know everything about the island down to ferry times. A gazebo, hammock, and two porch swings assist in relaxation. Morning coffee is delivered to your room, followed by an elegant and copious breakfast at the country dining room table. *$$$; MC, V; checks OK; farmhouse@saltspring. com; 2½ miles (4 km) north of Ganges.*

Weston Lake Inn / ★★
813 BEAVER POINT RD, SALTSPRING ISLAND; 250/653-4311

Owners Susan Evans and Ted Harrison have become experts at fading into the background and letting guests enjoy their comfortable, contemporary farmhouse. Harrison's framed, petit-point embroideries hang in the three guest bedrooms; paintings by local artists, including Evans's mother, are carefully chosen; and the bounty of their organic garden appears in your hearty breakfast at the antique dining room table. Along with homemade granola, fresh fruit, and baked goodies, look for eggs Benedict, waffles, or toasted bagels with smoked salmon. Two living rooms are open for guest use, one with a TV and VCR, the other for quiet reading. Stroll the lovingly developed gardens, or laze in the hot tub overlooking the lake. Need more? Charter Harrison's 36-foot sailing sloop *Malaika*. *$$–$$$; MC, V; no checks; 2 miles (3.5 km) east of Fulford Harbour.*

North and South Pender Islands

Much of these two islands, united by a small bridge, is green and rural, but a massive subdivision on North Pender was one of the catalysts for the creation of the watchdog Islands Trust in the 1970s. Thank this group for helping the Penders, along with other southern Gulf Islands, retain their charm. The population here is decidedly residential, so don't expect many restaurants, lodgings, or shops. Beaches, however, abound: **MORTIMER SPIT** (at western tip of South Pender) and **GOWLLAND POINT BEACH** (at end of Gowlland Point Rd on South Pender) are among 20 public ocean-access points. Maps are available at the **PENDER ISLAND VISITOR INFORMATION CENTRE** (2332 Otter Bay Rd; 250/629-6541).

To take advantage of the fabled Gulf Island viewscape, **MOUNT ELIZABETH** (off Clam Bay Rd on North Pender) and **MOUNT NORMAN** (accessible from Ainsley Rd or Canal Rd on South Pender) have established trail systems. The gentle terrain of South Pender is particularly appealing for cyclists; rent bikes at **OTTER BAY MARINA** (2311 MacKinnon Rd; 250/629-3579) on North Pender. Those with a nautical eye enjoy watching the yachts and cruisers pull in at **BEDWELL HARBOUR**'s Canada Customs office on South Pender. (Public ferries dock at Otter Bay on North Pender.) While waiting for the ferry, grab an excellent burger (try a venison or oyster variation) at the humble trailer **THE STAND** (Otter Bay Ferry Terminal; 250/629-3292).

LODGINGS

Bedwell Harbour Resort
9801 SPALDING RD, SOUTH PENDER ISLAND; 250/629-3212 OR 800/663-2899

This sprawling resort complex, in operation for decades, includes a marina, cabins, villas in a condo building, hotel rooms, a pub, restaurant—you name it. The location is ideal on South Pender: a sheltered cove and marina, backed by a gentle, wooded hillside, with stunning sunset views. Newer, more luxurious accommodations are available in the condominiums—two-bedroom villas done in broad pine, with fully equipped kitchens, fireplaces, and decks. A breakfast package (served in the dining room) is available with rooms that lack kitchens. A restaurant, waterfront pub, and general store are on-site. A pool and daycare are also available. *$$–$$$; AE, MC, V; no checks; closed Oct–Mar; bedwell@ islandnet.com; www.islandnet.com/~bedwell; follow Canal Rd from bridge to Spalding, Spalding to Bedwell Harbour.*

Saturna Island

The second-largest of the southern Gulf Islands, Saturna has a scant 315 residents: no traffic jams, no village center, but two general stores, a bakery, and a pub overlooking the **LYALL HARBOUR** ferry stop. No camping is available on the island, but hiking abounds: climb **MOUNT WARBURTON**, the second-highest peak in the southern Gulf Islands. **WINTER COVE MARINE PROVINCIAL PARK** (1 mile/1.6 km from ferry dock, at Saturna Point) is an inviting place to beachcomb or picnic above the Strait of Georgia, or drive to the tidal pools and sculpted sandstone of remote **EAST POINT**. **SATURNA VINEYARD**, attached to its namesake lodge and restaurant (see review) is a new attraction: planted with pinot noir, merlot, chardonnay, and Gewürztraminer, its first wines were released in 1999.

LODGINGS

Saturna Lodge / ★

130 PAYNE RD, SATURNA ISLAND; 250/539-2254

This lovely frame lodge sits high on a hill overlooking Boot Cove and an oyster farm. Windows wrap around the simple dining room, where a crackling fire beckons on cool evenings. Seven bright and sunny B&B rooms upstairs are contemporary in feel, with pleasant sitting areas and views. All have private baths; the honeymoon suite has a soaker tub and private balcony. Guests are picked up from Winter Cove anchorage and the Saturna ferry dock. The lodge restaurant has seen high turnover in the kitchen and management in recent years, making it difficult to rely on. *$$–$$$; MC, V; checks OK; www.saturna-island.bc.ca/lodge.htm; follow signs from ferry.*

Mayne Island

During the Cariboo Gold Rush of the mid-1800s, Mayne was the southern Gulf Islands' commercial and social hub, a way station between Victoria and Vancouver. Today, the pace of life is more serene. Rolling orchards and warm rock-strewn beaches dominate this pocket-sized island of 5 square miles (13 square km). Hike up **MOUNT PARKE** to reach Mayne's highest point, with an excellent view of ferries plying Active Pass between the Gulf Islands and the mainland at Tsawwassen. A complete tour of the island by bicycle takes five hours—longer if you stop for a pint at the well-worn **SPRINGWATER LODGE** (400 Fernhill Dr; 250/539-5521).

RESTAURANTS

Oceanwood Country Inn / ★★★

630 DINNER BAY RD, MAYNE ISLAND; 250/539-5074

Four-course dinners in the dining room overlooking Navy Channel are exquisitely prepared by chef Paul McKinnon. He carries on the tradition of the restaurant's Pacific Northwest cuisine, a gold medalist in the Vancouver Food and Restaurant Show. Two entrees are offered daily, perhaps braised local lamb with herb risotto, or Sooke rainbow trout with brown basmati rice and steamed vegetables. Appetizers are strikingly unique: Oceanwood's own daylilies stuffed with smoked-salmon mousse, for example. At dessert a fragrant lavender broth might make an appearance on a rhubarb and blueberry strudel. The careful wine list has been decorated at the Vancouver International Wine Festival. *$$$; MC, V; Canadian checks only; dinner every day (closed Dec–Feb); full bar; reservations required; oceanwood@gulfislands.com; www.oceanwood.com; right on Dalton Dr, right on Mariners, immediate left onto Dinner Bay Rd, look for signs.*

LODGINGS

A Coach House on Oyster Bay / ★★

511 BAYVIEW DR, MAYNE ISLAND; 250/539-3368

Snuggle by the fire in one of three spacious rooms here, or sit awhile by the window gazing at the expansive view over the Strait of Georgia to the mainland's monumental Coast Mountains. Select rooms have four-poster beds, private hot tubs, or oceanview decks. Get closer to the view in the outdoor hot tub just inches from the high tide line. The stone-paved drive lends a touch of elegance, as does the garden gazebo. The satisfying four-course breakfast often includes cereal, blueberry muffins, fresh fruit, and hot peach crepes. Avid scuba divers, hosts Heather and Brian Johnston can recommend the best dive sites around the island; they also charter boat cruises or arrange kayak rentals. *$$$; MC, V; checks OK; just east of Georgina Point Lighthouse.*

Oceanwood Country Inn / ★★★

630 DINNER BAY RD, MAYNE ISLAND; 250/539-5074

The split-level, high-ceilinged Wisteria Room is the largest of the 12 rooms at the Oceanwood Country Inn, and features a country gingham theme and a view over Navy Channel from the deck's soaking tub. Fireplaces and double Japanese-style tubs are features of many rooms. Some, like the Lilac Room, are done in a floral theme with hand-stenciling; others, like the blue-hued Heron Room, come in more soothing masculine tones. Rooms overlook either ocean or garden, replete with roses, daffodils, tulips, dahlias, and lavender. Mingle with other guests in the games room or library, and walk down the path to the rocky beach after dinner. Complimentary breakfasts are substantial: look for fresh-squeezed fruit and vegetable juices, croissants or coffee cake, and poached eggs with hash browns and sausage. After a day of kayaking or bird-watching, settle into a meal at the excellent dining room (see review). Note: Readers have suggested that some guest rooms could be more carefully maintained. *$$$–$$$$; MC, V; Canadian checks only; closed Dec–Feb; right on Dalton Dr, right on Mariners, immediate left onto Dinner Bay Rd, look for signs.*

Galiano Island

Residents here dismiss bustling Saltspring as "towny," as well they might on their undeveloped, secluded island. Dedicated locals work hard to protect the natural features extending along the island's narrow 19 miles (30 km): densely forested cliffs, towering bluffs, wildflower meadows, and sheltered harbors.

On **BODEGA RIDGE**, trails wind through old-growth forests and skirt flower-studded fields; views stretch to the Olympic Mountains in Washington State. From **BLUFFS PARK** and **MOUNT GALIANO**, you can watch eagles, ferries, and sweeping tides on Active Pass. Most Galiano roads—especially the partially paved eastern route—allow you to pedal a bicycle untroubled by traffic, but there's some steep going here. **GULF ISLANDS KAYAKING** (250/539-2442) lets you see the islands by water. **MONTAGUE HARBOUR** (5 miles/8 km north of ferry dock at Sturdies Bay; 800/689-9025 camping reservations), on the west side of the island, is a lovely, sheltered bay with beaches, picnic and camping areas, boat launch, and stunning sunset views.

Despite being the closest of the southern Gulf Islands from the Tsawwassen ferry (one hour), Galiano has a sparse 1,200 residents and only a few services and shops, clustered at the south end. Eateries are scarce, though you'll find hearty pub food and local color at the **HUMMINGBIRD INN** (Sturdies Bay and Georgeson Rds; 250/539-5472). Have lunch in the new-age ambience of vegetarian-friendly **DAYSTAR MARKET CAFÉ** (on Sturdies Bay Rd; 250/539-2800). While away time in the Sturdies Bay ferry lineup at Village Bay at **TRINCOMALI BAKERY AND DELI** (2540 Sturdies Bay Rd; 250/539-2004); elbow up to the locals at the few shared tables and munch on a sausage roll.

RESTAURANTS

Woodstone Country Inn / ★★☆

743 GEORGESON BAY RD, GALIANO ISLAND; 250/539-2022 OR 888/339-2022
The dining room at this inn (see review) ranks high: co-innkeeper/chef Gail Nielson-Pich serves a fine four-course table d'hôte dinner, which might include a cioppino of fresh mussels, shrimp, and seafood in a spicy tomato ragout, or vegetarian spinach and ricotta pie with a roasted-garlic and tomato sauce. Desserts are outstanding; Galiano residents are fiercely loyal to the bread pudding with rum sauce. Enjoy the feast in a neoclassical room (think Italianate columns) overlooking serene fields. *$$$; AE, MC, V; checks OK; dinner every day (closed Dec–Jan); full bar; reservations required; woodstone@gulfislands.com; www.gulfislands.com/woodstone; head left off Sturdies Bay Rd, follow signs.* &

LODGINGS

The Bellhouse Inn / ★★

29 FARMHOUSE RD, GALIANO ISLAND; 250/539-5667 OR 800/970-7464

 Andrea Porter and David Birchall are consummate gentlefolk farmers, conversing with guests and feeding sheep with equal aplomb. This historic American wood-shingle-style farmhouse, painted soothing barn red, contains three lovely upstairs guest rooms with small balconies. The largest boasts picture windows, allowing an expansive view of Bellhouse Bay from bed, and an en suite Jacuzzi. Guests can play croquet on the grounds, or laze in a hammock. The yard is punctuated with iron farming relics; a stone pathway loops from drive to doorstep; and fruit trees blossom in spring. A popular wedding location, the Bellhouse is our favorite Galiano spot. The interior is graced with heritage touches, from antique opera glasses to a delicate feather duster. The comfortable guest lounge is lined with books. Large breakfasts consist of fruit, granola, and hearty egg dishes such as seafood eggs Benedict. The hosts will pick up guests at the ferry terminal or their boat moorage. Meander the inn's 6 pleasant acres and into nearby Bellhouse Park, or make your way to the sandy beach, a rare treat on Galiano. Larger groups can spread out in the duplex cabin; each side has two bedrooms, a kitchen, and private patio. *$$–$$$; MC, V; checks OK; bellhouse@gulfislands.com; www.bellhouseinn. com; uphill from ferry terminal, left on Burrill, left on Jack.*

Woodstone Country Inn / ★★☆

743 GEORGESON BAY RD, GALIANO ISLAND; 250/539-2022

This modern, executive-style manor house overlooks field and forest, and is a choice stopover for large cycling tours and business retreats. Best rooms are on the lower level, and feature private patios. The tone of the refined decor is set by classic English print fabrics in florals and stripes; Persian rugs warm the floors in some rooms; wicker furniture adds country charm, as does hand stenciling on the walls. However, the flat gray carpeting underfoot in the rooms, darkened with traffic marks, has a substandard air, as do white faux-wood doors on some bathrooms. All but two rooms have fireplaces, while upper-end rooms have Jacuzzis. Reports on service have been mixed, from particularly considerate to cool—with some suggestion that lower-priced rooms have received similarly lower service. Breakfast and afternoon tea, the latter in the cozy book-stocked common room, are included. Locals recommend the upscale dining room (see review). *$$–$$$; AE, MC, V; checks OK; closed Dec–Jan; woodstone@gulfislands.com; www.gulfislands.com/woodstone; bear left off Sturdies Bay Rd, follow signs to turnoff.* ♿

Gabriola Island

Although this most accessible island has become a bedroom community for nearby Nanaimo (20 minutes by ferry), it remains fairly rustic. The highlight of the fine seaside walks along the west shore is the **MALASPINA GALLERY** (take

Taylor Bay Rd to Malaspina Dr and park at end of road), fanciful rock formations and caves carved by the sea. (Bring good shoes; it's rocky.) You'll have to
look elsewhere, however, for recommended accommodations.

Denman and Hornby Islands

Tranquil and bucolic, the sister islands of Denman and Hornby sit just off the
east coast of central Vancouver Island. The larger, Denman—10 minutes by
ferry from Buckley Bay, 12½ miles (20 km) south of Courtenay—is known for
pastoral farmlands and talented artisans. The relatively flat landscape and
untraveled byways make it a natural for cyclists. Work up an appetite and stop
for a pizza and espresso at the **DENMAN ISLAND BAKERY** (3646-A Denman
Island Rd, Denman Island; 250/335-0444).

Ten minutes from Denman by ferry, Hornby is a dream for mountain bikers
seeking idyllic, or hair-raising, forest trails; ask at **HORNBY ISLAND BIKE SHOP**
(5875 Central Rd, Union Bay, Hornby Island; 250/335-0444). Locals favor the
burgers and caesar salads of the **THATCH PUB** (4305 Shingle Spit Rd, Hornby
Island; 250/335-2833). Hornby's **HELLIWELL PROVINCIAL PARK** (far northern
tip of island) impresses with dramatic seaside cliffs and lush forest, while beach
lovers seek out **TRIBUNE BAY PROVINCIAL PARK** (east shore of northern
isthmus). Especially in summer, reserve island accommodations before venturing onto the ferry.

LODGINGS

Sea Breeze Lodge

5205 FOWLER RD, HORNBY ISLAND; 250/335-2321

Owned for decades by the Bishop family, Sea Breeze has evolved into a
comfortable family retreat with a loyal following. Thirteen well-used
beachside cottages have been joined by another, spiffier cabin. Best is the view;
enjoy it from the hot tub. Cabin rates include three home-cooked meals, June
through September. Comfort foods such as wholesome soups from the lodge's
own cookbook often appear. The Bishops happily accommodate dietary needs,
from vegetarian to vegan. The dining room is open only on weekends in fall,
and is closed in winter; cabins with kitchens are available year-round. *$$$$;
MC, V; checks OK; on Tralee Point.*

Discovery Islands

QUADRA, **CORTES**, and **SONORA** make up the closely linked Discovery
Islands—fishing and boating meccas east of Campbell River. To visit the more
accessible of the Discovery Islands, take the 10-minute ferry ride from Campbell River to Quadra Island; from Quadra's Heriot Bay dock, another 45-minute
ferry trip takes you to Cortes Island. To reach Sonora Island, try the regularly
scheduled floatplane service from Campbell River offered by **AIR RAINBOW**
(3050 Spit Rd; 250/287-8371) or go leisurely by private boat.

LODGINGS

April Point Lodge / ★★★

APRIL POINT RD, QUADRA ISLAND; 250/285-2222 OR 800/663-7090

Between April and October this famous resort—newly acquired by the esteemed Oak Bay Marine Group of Victoria—draws serious fisherfolk and celebrities from all over the world for the salmon fishing: bluebacks in April and May, chinook from April through early September, coho through summer. The staff expertly matches guides with guests. Fishing is the primary activity, but April Point also offers family-oriented activities, such as bicycle and kayak rentals, and lovely beach walks. A lighthouse is to the south; east is Rebecca Spit Provincial Marine Park. The resort's spacious and beautifully appointed accommodations range from large guest houses to lodge rooms and comfortable cabins; some have fireplaces, hot tubs or Jacuzzis, living rooms, kitchens, sundecks, and water views. The main lodge is sunny and cheerful, and the food (including fresh sushi) is very good—many vegetables and herbs come from the lodge's island farm. Meals are served April through October. *$$$; AE, DC, MC, V; checks OK; www.aprilpoint.com; 10 minutes north of ferry dock.* &

Sonora Resort and Conference Centre / ★★

SONORA ISLAND; 604/341-4995 OR 888/576-6672

Sonora Resort is big and it's posh—a multimillion-dollar resort for those who want to fish from the lap of luxury. You'll pay about $1,000 per night, but everything (well, except the professional massage) is included: airfare from Vancouver, guided fishing, rods and tackle, rain gear, gourmet meals, drinks, and more. Luxurious suites with Jacuzzis are grouped in six lodges; each has a common room with hot tub, steam bath, and complimentary bar. Other amenities include billiards tables, a small convention center, a lap pool, and tennis courts. The kitchen is competent and serves a well-selected variety of fresh seafood. At lunch, the chef boats out to guests and barbecues their catch; dinners may be prepared on a Japanese teppanyaki grill on the shore. *$$$$; MC, V; checks OK; open June–Sept; www.sonoraresort.com; 30 miles (48 km) north of Campbell River, accessible by private boat or regular floatplane service only.*

Tsa-Kwa-Luten Lodge / ★★

1 LIGHTHOUSE RD, QUADRA ISLAND; 250/285-2042 OR 800/665-7745

Built on an 1,100-acre forest by the Laichwiltach First Nation, this oceanview lodge was inspired by traditional longhouse design. Native art is featured throughout the lodge and its 34 units, which include four self-contained cottages. The star attraction here, as elsewhere in the salmon-rich Campbell River area, is fishing; guided packages are available. Co-stars include the great outdoors and good views, mountain biking (rent at the lodge), or the outstanding Kwagiulth Museum (a 45-minute forest walk away from the lodge). Alternately, stroll beaches to ponder ancient Native petroglyphs, or trek to nearby

Cape Mudge Lighthouse. Lodge staff can arrange boat cruises, scuba diving, or kayaking. The lodge hosts Kwagiulth dances four Fridays each summer. The Big House dining room serves breakfast, lunch, and dinner every day—New York steak, vegetarian pasta, cedar-baked salmon, clams, and other fresh seafood; seasonal pies—try blackberry or sour cream and peach—make welcome appearances. *$$–$$$; AE, DC, E, MC, V; no checks; open May–Sept; tkllodge@connected.bc.ca; www.capemudgeresort.bc.ca; 10 minutes south of ferry dock.*

The Cowichan Valley and Southeast Shore

The Cowichan Valley is a gentle stretch of farmland and forest from the town of Shawnigan Lake north to Chemainus; the microclimate of this pleasant area lends itself to grape-growing, making it the only vineyard region on the island. While generally not up to the standards of interior BC vineyards, some worthy vintages are produced here. Try a pinot noir at **BLUE GROUSE VINEYARDS** (Blue Grouse Rd, off Lakeside Rd, Cowichan Valley; 250/743-3834); and make the tasting rounds also to **CHERRY POINT VINEYARDS** (840 Cherry Point Rd, Cobble Hill; 250/743-1272) and **VIGNETI ZANATTA** (5039 Marshall Rd, Glenora; 250/748-2338). At **MERRIDALE CIDER WORKS** (1230 Merridale Rd, Cobble Hill; 250/743-4293), cider is made in the English tradition. Best time to visit is mid-September to mid-October, when apples, grown on the premises, are run through the presses. The rolling, pastoral landscape continues through the Chemainus Valley north to the hub towns of Nanaimo and Parksville.

Cowichan Bay

This is a sweet little seaside town off Highway 1 with a few restaurants, craft stores, and marinas. The Wooden Boat Society display and the hands-on exhibits at the **MARITIME CENTRE** (1751 Cowichan Bay Rd; 250/746-4955) are worth a visit.

LODGINGS

Dream Weaver B&B / ★★

1682 BOTWOOD LN, COWICHAN BAY; 250/748-7688 OR 888/748-7689

This modern wood-shake home has plenty of character, modeled on gabled, multistoried Victorian-era construction. Rooms range from feminine florals to gentlemanly and distinguished. The large Magnolia Suite, nestled in the top-floor gables, is done in traditional white cottons and flower prints, with a double Jacuzzi tub opposite the gas fireplace. A small balcony offers views of picturesque Cowichan Bay. The Primrose Suite evokes the mood of an old-style smoking room, with deep hues and salon armchairs, but features contemporary clean lines; fully modern amenities include Jacuzzi, gas fireplace,

TV, VCR, and CD player. Hosts Cathy and Ken McAllister serve guests a full breakfast. *$$–$$$; MC, V; local checks only; dreamwvr@islandnet.com; www.vancouverisland-bc.com/dreamweaver; in village center.*

Duncan

Forty-five minutes north of Victoria on the Trans-Canada Highway, the City of Totems is designated by little totem poles sprinkled along the roadside—some more artistic than others. Another claim to fame (for those with a Guinness World Records bent) is the world's largest hockey stick, notably affixed to a community arena on the west side of the highway. In the old downtown, a good lunch can be had at the popular **ISLAND BAGEL COMPANY** (48 Station St; 250/748-1988). The **NATIVE HERITAGE CENTRE** (200 Cowichan Wy; 250/746-8119) on Duncan's southern edge is a must-see for admirers of First Nations arts and crafts. Watch as the region's renowned Cowichan sweaters—handmade of thick wool with indigenous designs in cream and browns or grays—are knit in summer. The center also features an open-air carving shed, where First Nations carvers craft 12- to 20-foot totem poles with handmade tools. An excellent gallery and gift shop has many Native prints and wares for sale.

RESTAURANTS

The Quamichan Inn / ★★

1487 MAPLE BAY RD, DUNCAN; 250/746-7028

Chef Martin Hewitt turns out fresh seafood dishes and steak and rib favorites to satisfied diners at this dependable establishment, owned by Pam and Clive Cunningham for the past 20 years. Look for English meals with Yorkshire pudding and classic West Coast salmon. Dessert touches include fresh cream; look also for seasonal pies and homemade ice cream in summer. Take your after-dinner coffee in the garden of this restored turn-of-the-century home, profuse with fragrant wisteria, blooming fuchsias, and colorful dahlias. The proprietors gladly pick up yachties and drop them off after dinner. Inn accommodations consist of three guest rooms, and rates include an English hunt breakfast: eggs, bacon, sausage, and fried tomato. *$$$; AE, MC, V; checks OK; dinner Tues–Sun; full bar; reservations recommended; just east of Duncan, take exit at Duncan, turn right at Chevron, left onto Maple Bay Rd.*

LODGINGS

Fairburn Farm Country Manor / ★★

3310 JACKSON RD, DUNCAN; 250/746-4637

This lovingly restored 1884 manor house is today a 130-acre organic sheep farm where part of the charm, especially for animal-loving kids, is the chance to pitch in with chores. Host Anthea Archer handles most culinary and conversational responsibilities with aplomb, while Darrel Archer keeps the farm humming. Together they ensure that guests enjoy the freshest of breakfasts: freshly churned butter on homemade bread, local preserves, and frittatas of free-range eggs and organic yellow tomatoes. Furnishings are antique throughout the stately home; some of the six large rooms have fireplaces and the largest has a whirlpool tub. Two rooms have en suite baths; the others have private baths. A self-contained two-bedroom cottage overlooks the fields. *$$–$$$; MC, V; checks OK; open Apr–mid-Oct; 7 miles (11 km) south of Duncan.*

Chemainus

Heralded as "the little town that did," seaside Chemainus bounced back from the closure of its logging mill, and turned to tourism with flair. Buildings are painted with **MURALS** depicting the town's colorful history, making Chemainus a noted tourist attraction on Highway 1A.

RESTAURANTS

The Waterford Restaurant / ★★
9875 MAPLE ST, CHEMAINUS; 250/246-1046
The Waterford, ensconced in a heritage building in the old town, features Victorian-inspired, floral-swag decor that speaks to the heart of an older clientele. Lunch prices are reasonable for upscale cuisine offered by chef Dwayne Maslen: sole amandine, filling mushroom or seafood crepes, or prawns, all $10 or less. Dinner is pricier: choices can include rack of lamb dijon, chicken breast filled with chorizo and blue cheese, or classic filet mignon. *$$; AE, MC, V; local checks only; lunch, dinner Tues–Sun; full bar; reservations recommended; a few blocks from downtown.* &

Ladysmith

RESTAURANTS

Crow and Gate Neighbourhood Pub / ★★
2313 YELLOW POINT RD, LADYSMITH; 250/722-3731
The Crow and Gate was one of the first neighborhood pubs in British Columbia, and retains pride of place as the nicest pub we have seen in this region. English fowl stroll the pastoral grounds, and quaint buildings give the feel of a gentleman's farm. Inside this popular watering hole, light from the flames of a substantial fire glint off diamond-pane windows, while long plank tables invite conversation. Traditional English pub fare includes steak and kidney pie, ploughman's lunch, beef dip, and—in a nod to local conditions—panfried oysters. All come highly praised. *$; MC, V; no checks; lunch, dinner every day; full bar; reservations not necessary; 8 miles (13 km) south of Nanaimo.*

LODGINGS

Yellow Point Lodge / ★★☆

3700 YELLOW POINT RD, LADYSMITH; 250/245-7422

This well-loved oceanfront lodge draws guests back every year, from honeymoon to anniversary—even in winter (summer weekends are often booked months in advance). The plush log-and-timber lodge has rooms within hearing range of the crashing surf; closest are the White Beach cabins on the waterfront. Cabin 2 features one room with a tall, log-constructed bed with a view, and a fireplace nestled in a rustic beamed interior, though its frowsy pea-green velour couch has seen better days (as have a number of cabin furnishings and carpets). The Madrona cabin is large enough for modest entertaining. The water on the private 1½ miles (2.4 km) of coastline is exceptionally clear. Daily rates include three meals served at group tables in the lodge: comfort foods like beef and mashed potatoes, or classic BC salmon. Recreational facilities include tennis courts and jogging trails, as well as a sauna and hot tub in a wooded copse. $$$; MC, V; checks OK; 2-night min on weekends, 3-night min on holidays; 9 miles (14.5) km east of Ladysmith.

Nanaimo

Nanaimo is more than the strip mall it appears to be from Highway 19. The early island settlement of Nanaimo began as a coal mining hub. The **HUDSON'S BAY COMPANY BASTION** (at Bastion and Front Sts), built in 1853, is one of few left standing in North America. It's part of the **NANAIMO DISTRICT MUSEUM** (100 Cameron Rd; 250/753-1821), which also has a replica of a Chinatown street (the original Chinatown burned in 1960).

In Nanaimo's old town, near the old train station, cafes mix with vintage shops and houseware boutiques. Lunch at **DELICADO'S** (358 Wesley St; 250/753-6524) on wraps fired up with chipotle sauce and black bean–and-corn salsa, or at **GINA'S** (47 Skinner St; 250/753-5411), an ever-popular Mexican restaurant with a view.

Not only is Nanaimo a transportation hub, with frequent ferries to Vancouver, it's also a good place to launch a **SCUBA DIVING** holiday. Numerous companies offer equipment rentals and guided tours. Those who prefer their thrills out of the water head for the **BUNGY ZONE** (15 minutes south of Nanaimo; 250/753-5867 or 800/668-7771) to experience North America's only bungy jumping bridge, over the Nanaimo River. Or check out the **BATHTUB RACE** on the last weekend of July, a tradition since 1967. **BIKE TRAILS**—meandering lanes and wilderness single-tracks—snake around the city's edge.

The spit at **PIPERS LAGOON** (northeast of downtown) extends into the Strait of Georgia, backed by sheer bluffs that are great for bird-watching. **NEWCASTLE ISLAND PROVINCIAL MARINE PARK** is an auto-free wilderness reached by a foot-passenger ferry from Nanaimo's inner harbor (summer only); it has a long shoreline trail, a wheelchair-accessible trail, and a fine old-growth forest.

MILE ZERO

Along waterfront Dallas Road in Victoria, tour buses flock to the simple wooden sign put up by the Canadian Automobile Association in the 1950s to mark the beginning, or end, of the Trans-Canada highway. (Overlook the fact that you must complete the last stretch of highway by getting on a ferry and crossing the Strait of Georgia.) It's symbolic of the great 19th-century dreams Victoria once had to be the jumping-off point for the wealth of the Canadian nation.

The highway marker provides a link to a time when Victoria was a busier port than Vancouver. When the politicians of Victoria voted to join the Canadian confederation in 1871, it was only on the promise of a railway link extending to the capital. When Ottawa was slow to complete even the mainland route, politicians in Victoria began to threaten separation. But local citizens didn't sit back and wait. The promise of black gold—in those days, coal—became the impetus for a privately developed rail line from Victoria to Nanaimo, finished in 1886, at great personal gain to coal magnate Robert Dunsmuir. The government not only gave him an efficient means to ship his coal to port, it compensated his work with 2 million acres of prime Vancouver Island land and $750,000 in cold cash. Dunsmuir's empire was assured. See the more visible signs of his wealth in his two Victoria-area mansions, Craigdarroch Castle, now a museum, and Hatley Park, now Royal Roads University.

While Dunsmuir's wealth flourished, the fortunes of Victoria were on the wane: the large port of Vancouver was far outstripping the business and population of colonial Victoria. But big dreams die hard. By the 1950s, age of the automobile, Victoria clung to its right as Mile Zero of any transcontinental project. When, in 1954, the BC government made a go of reviving its lagging section of the Trans-Canada Highway, Victoria made sure it was at the front of the line.

—*Alisa Smith*

Golf courses with views proliferate from Nanaimo northward. Most noteworthy is the **NANAIMO GOLF CLUB** (2800 Highland Blvd; 250/758-6332), a demanding 18-hole course 3 miles (5 km) north of the city. Others include **PRYDE VISTA GOLF CLUB** (155 Pryde Ave; 250/753-6188), in Nanaimo, and **FAIRWINDS** (3730 Fairwinds Dr; 250/468-7766), at Nanoose Bay.

RESTAURANTS

The Mahle House / ★★

2104 HEMER RD, NANAIMO; 250/722-3621

Find this cozy 1904 home-turned-restaurant in Cedar, just minutes southeast of Nanaimo, and sample the inventive cuisine of chef/co-owner Maureen Loucks. Begin with "porcupine" prawns, quickly deep-fried in shredded phyllo; then taste chicken stuffed with crab and drizzled with saffron sauce. The vegetarian platter includes roasted-garlic-and-goat-cheese mashed potatoes. The mixed grill is for adventurous meat eaters, highlighting Jamaican jerk pork and local Selby Street sausage. Mahle House has a 1-acre vegetable garden and a smaller herb garden; the rabbit comes from down the road, the salmon from Yellow Island, the mussels from Saltspring Island, and scallops from Qualicum Beach. Desserts are exquisite: Harlequin Mousse with white and dark chocolate sauce and a swirl of chocolate and caramel, crème brûlée napoleon with layered phyllo and custard, and peanut butter pie. Co-owner Delbert Horrocks takes justifiable pride in his extensive wine list, a medallist at the International Wine Festival in Vancouver. *$$$; MC, V; local checks only; dinner Wed–Sun; full bar; reservations recommended; at Cedar.* &

The Wesley Street Cafe / ★★
321 WESLEY ST, NANAIMO; 250/753-4004
Seasoned owner Jennifer Rollison still heads up her tight ship in person, and selected chef Ian Ter Veer for his imaginative handling of Pacific Northwest cuisine, emphasizing local seafood, and fresh organic produce; herbs come from Rollison's gardens. The wide-ranging wine list comes highly praised. Ever-popular Fanny Bay oysters come house-smoked, peppercorn-crusted, and cornmeal-crusted. Regulars clamor for Dungeness crab cakes with chipotle mayonnaise, or Moroccan spice-crusted ahi; veteran diners also order the mixed grill, featuring caribou in a thyme reduction. In summer, homemade lavender ice cream is a cool way to finish a meal. Although dinners are predominately meat-oriented, a vegetarian torte or risotto is available, and the chef will modify any dish. *$$$; AE, MC, V; checks OK; lunch, dinner every day; full bar; reservations recommended; uphill from downtown on Bastion, left on Wesley.*

LODGINGS

Coast Bastion Inn / ★
11 BASTION ST, NANAIMO; 250/753-6601 OR 800/663-1144
The reputable regional chain of Coast Hotels put its stamp on this downtown landmark. The high-rise tower with harbor views offers 179 rooms and is a perennial favorite for conferences. Rooms are clean and furnishings new, though decor is typically bland. A trio of formula eateries on the premises hope to satisfy guests' dining moods: family-style Cutters Café, the adult-oriented Offshore Lounge, and the Sgt. O'Flaherty deli. Relax in the sauna or hot tub. *$$$; AE, DC, MC, V; no checks; cbastion@nanaimo.ark.com; www. coasthotels.com; at Front St.*

Parksville

Parksville and the surrounding area are renowned for sandy beaches, especially in lovely **RATHTREVOR BEACH PROVINCIAL PARK** (a short drive east of Hwy 19; 250/954-4600), the province's most-visited park. Families love its lengthy shallows and relatively warm water temperatures, camping, and annual July's sandcastle competition. **MORNING STAR** (525 Lowry's Rd; 250/248-2244) offers golfing.

A little farther afield, picnic at thunderous **ENGLISHMAN RIVER FALLS PROVINCIAL PARK** (8 miles/12.8 km southwest of town; 250/954-4600 or 250/248-3931), and mosey along to **COOMBS**, a tiny town on Highway 4A that hovers between cute and kitsch with its overblown pioneer theme, based on a small core of true old-time buildings. Shop for produce and gifts at the popular **OLD COUNTRY MARKET** (mid-Mar–Nov), where goats graze on the grassy roof. **MACMILLAN PROVINCIAL PARK** (20 miles/32 km west of Parksville on Hwy 4) contains Cathedral Grove, a sky-high old-growth forest of Douglas firs and cedars up to 800 years old.

RESTAURANTS

Red Pepper Grill / ★

193 MEMORIAL AVE, PARKSVILLE; 250/248-2364

This turn-of-the century home set in an established garden has a cheery yellow exterior, and a cozy, intimate interior layout. Dine in the former living room or bedroom on pasta dishes, or highly praised steak and prawns. The Italian and California-style cuisine is designed to please, not surprise. For a delicious take on the West Coast standard, try chef Owen Castaris's alder-grilled salmon fillet rubbed with brown sugar, sea salt, and sweet butter. Finish with a "tuxedo" brownie, layered with dark and light chocolate and a raspberry filling. *$$; AE, MC, V; local checks only; lunch Mon–Fri, dinner every day; full bar; reservations recommended; at McMillan St.*

Tigh-Na-Mara Resort Hotel / ★

1095 E ISLAND HWY, PARKSVILLE; 250/248-2072

In keeping with the seaside hotel's theme (see review), the restaurant features a log-house look, with large windows that slide open in summer. Try a fresh catch at dinner—perhaps herb-crusted halibut, or steamed natural-smoked black cod. Rack of lamb or prawn curry are sure crowd-pleasers, as are a prawn, scallop, and ginger stir-fry, or fettuccine with tomato and pine nuts. Desserts are prepared by a resident baker and change daily—perhaps Grand Marnier crème caramel. We found service somewhat abrupt, but others report pleasant experiences. *$$–$$$; AE, DC, MC, V; local checks only; lunch, dinner daily; full bar; reservations recommended; 1¼ miles (2 km) south of Parksville on Hwy 19A.*

LODGINGS

Tigh-Na-Mara Resort Hotel / ★★

1095 E ISLAND HWY, PARKSVILLE; 250/248-2072 OR 800/663-7373

Of the resorts that sprawl the length of beloved Rathtrevor Beach, Tigh-Na-Mara stands out. The mini-village of log cabins are spread throughout 22 acres of wooded grounds. Cabin furnishings are rather worn, and bathroom fixtures are dated, but the cabins offer privacy, full kitchens, front porches and barbecues, as well as fireplaces (standard in all rooms here). Ocean-front condominium accommodations are newer and spiffier, with a few log-beam details. Some rooms have Jacuzzi tubs and kitchens. Guests can use an exercise room, indoor pool and hot tub, steam room, or tennis courts—and 700 feet of beachfront. The on-site restaurant (see review) is popular. Except for con-ferences, maid service is not included and fresh linens are self-serve. Pets are allowed in some cottages in the off season. Kids are welcome, as evidenced by on-site playgrounds. *$$–$$$; AE, DC, MC, V; local checks only; 3- to 7-night min in summer, 2-night min on winter weekends; 1¼ miles (2 km) south of Parksville on Hwy 19A.*

Qualicum Beach

This little town 20 minutes north of Parksville on Highway 19 has a pleasant beachfront promenade and a growing downtown shopping district. For its size, it has a good selection of cafes, from the Euro-swank **HAVANA CAFÉ** (673 Memorial Ave; 250/752-6414) to the earthy lunch favorite **HARVEST MOON CAFÉ** (133 2nd Ave; 250/752-2068). Sit yourself on a vintage chrome barstool at the **BLACK SLACKS SODA SHOPPE** (208 W 1st Ave; 250/752-1411) near the old railway station. For more retro character (and greasier food), drive 10 min-utes north for coffee at the **COLA DINER** (6060 W Island Hwy; 250/757-2029), a joyful ode to a 1950s burger joint in sparkly red vinyl and chrome. Then get some exercise golfing at **EAGLECREST** (2035 Island Hwy W; 250/752-9744).

RESTAURANTS

Lefty's / ★
710 MEMORIAL AVE, QUALICUM BEACH; 250/752-7530
The bright, funky ambience and art-filled walls here rival casual cafe experi-ences of Vancouver or Victoria, and food is priced accordingly. Baked-on-the-premises coconut cream pie is superior. Specialties include wraps stuffed with fresh West Coast fusions like Cajun chicken; flavorful chorizo sausage pizza; or cheddar corn pie, a quiche-like creation. At dinner, Lefty's transitions to pastas, and steak and prawns. Organic coffees are a bonus. *$$; MC, V; local checks only; lunch, dinner every day; full bar; reservations not necessary; corner of W 2nd.*

Old Dutch Inn / ★
2690 W ISLAND HWY, QUALICUM BEACH; 250/752-6914
This place has dreamy breakfasts—and waitresses in triple-peaked, starched lace caps. The Dutch theme is taken seriously here, with turned oak chairs and delft tiles. The menu includes the Dutchie, a delicious sort of French toast sand-wich filled with homemade blueberry preserves; classic *pannekoeken;* and the Eggs Benedict Dutchie, with fine smoked salmon and a shaved potato cake with green onions, perfectly done and greaseless, on the side instead of hash browns. Join retirees and travelers at lunch, for a *uitsmyter,* an open-face sandwich with

Dutch smoked ham and cheese, or Indonesian-inspired *loempia*, a 10-spice spring roll with pork and roast peanuts. (Vegetarians are happiest here at breakfast.) The chef is a cut above, having cooked for Queen Elizabeth when she stayed in private homes nearby. Expansive windows take in all of Qualicum Bay. *$$; MC, V; no checks; breakfast, lunch, dinner every day; full bar; reservations recommended; center of town.*

LODGINGS

Bahari Bed & Breakfast / ★★

5101 W ISLAND HWY, QUALICUM BEACH; 250/752-9278 OR 877/752-9278
Enter through the modern gray-toned exterior via auto-open, double carved doors dominated by a large seashell handle. Inside, glimmering hammered copper forms part of an Asian-inspired tree design. The look of Bahari is modern and adventurous—the epitome of Pacific Rim style. The two-story foyer, hung with a dramatic Japanese kimono, feels like a modern museum. Art and materials are first class, such as a vivid green raw-silk bedspread in the garden-view room. In the kitchen, Japanese design principles are exercised when a window artfully frames the boughs of an exquisitely gnarled fruit tree. Some of the five rooms have fireplaces, and one has an ocean view. A private hot tub in the woods overlooks Georgia Strait and the northern Gulf Islands. Service is personable, but uneven. Children are welcome in the two-bedroom, 1,200-square-foot self-catering suite. *$$$; AE, MC, V; no checks; 2-night min for suite; lhooper@macn.bc.ca; www.baharibandb.com; 10 minutes north of town.*

Hollyford Guest Cottage Bed & Breakfast / ★★

106 HOYLAKE RD E, QUALICUM BEACH; 250/752-8101 OR 877/224-6559
These newcomers are quickly gaining a reputation for their fine hospitality, lovely antiques, and every-detail service. The original small English cottage surrounded by holly hedges and laurels has been thoughtfully renovated to add three guest rooms. In the entrance, slate tiles and a tea board speak of upscale comforts, as do tempting sherry and truffles. Heated floors make for a cozy stay. The antique ambience is made more unique with the addition of host Jim Ford's collection of western and RCMP memorabilia, inspired by his prairie upbringing. Breakfasts often feature gourmet takes on Irish cuisine, influenced by Marjorie Ford's Irish heritage. Lazy afternoons call for tea on the little deck surveying the snug garden. *$$$; MC, V; no checks; south off Memorial Ave.*

Barkley Sound and Tofino

Most visitors pass through Port Alberni on the way to Tofino via Highway 4, or wait to take the scenic boat trip on the **LADY ROSE** or **FRANCES BARKLEY** (250/723-8313 or 800/663-7192) to Barkley Sound and Bamfield, Ucluelet, or the Broken Islands Group. The boats offer passenger day trips as well as freight service. Bring warm clothes, a rain jacket, binoculars, and plenty of film.

Port Alberni

Shops, galleries, and restaurants cluster at the **ALBERNI HARBOUR QUAY**, where boats to Barkley Sound dock in this industrial logging and fishing town. On Highway 4 to Tofino, the favored nosh stop is the **CLAM BUCKET** (4833 Johnston Rd; 250/723-1315).

LODGINGS

Eagle Nook Resort / ★★
BARKLEY SOUND; 250/723-1000 OR 800/760-2777

No roads lead to the wilderness oasis of Eagle Nook, and that's what makes it special. It caters to the outdoors lover who revels in luxury at the end of a rugged day. Kayaking, fishing, and scuba-diving top most guests' lists. Many enjoy hiking the trails interlacing the resort's 70 forested acres. Owner Roger Francoeur offers daylong nature cruises to see harbor seals, cormorants, and bald eagles in the Broken Islands, a remote part of Pacific Rim National Park. Back at the resort, guests enjoy satisfying meals from comfortable window seats. Fare might be Continental-influenced cuisine, or West Coast fusion with a Thai twist (chefs change yearly). All 23 rooms have ocean views; the deck features a hot tub, and the lounge, a roaring fire. Most visitors arrive via the resort water taxi service from Port Alberni's Harbour Quay; direct flights can be booked from Seattle via local floatplane operators. The resort is 20 minutes from Tofino by boat. Packages include all meals and use of kayaks. *$$$$; AE, MC, V; checks OK; open June–Sept; 2-night min; eaglenk@cedar.alberni.net; www.alberni. net/~eaglenk/eaglenk.htm; accessible by boat or floatplane only.*

Bamfield

This tiny fishing village of 500, home to a marine biology research station, is reached by boat (see the introduction to this section), or via a logging road from Port Alberni or Lake Cowichan. However you get here, you'll feel you've hit the end of the line. Bamfield bustles when the **WEST COAST TRAIL** summer season hits—it's the end of the line for the world-famous, five-day, mettle-testing wilderness trail that's so popular, BC Parks must take reservations to protect it. For reservations, maps, and complete information on this spectacular, coast-hugging trek, contact **BC PARKS** (250/726-7721 information or 800/663-6000 reservations). For a West Coast Trail sampler, do a day hike and camp within earshot of the pounding surf of Bamfield. The Chamber of Commerce (250/728-3006) has more information.

LODGINGS

Wood's End Landing Cottages / ★
168 WILD DUCK RD, BAMFIELD; 250/728-3383

These cute cedar-shake-and-driftwood cabins have a craftsman's touch. Proprietor Terry Giddens built them out of materials he beachcombed and recycled from tumble-down Bamfield buildings. Four cottages and two suites, set among 50-year-old perennial gardens, overlook Bamfield Inlet. The hilltop Woodsman cabin and the Angler suite have the best views. Each cabin has two loft bedrooms and cooking facilities. Bring your own food (though the town's cafes offer meals in season) and be prepared to entertain yourself in this remote area. A rowboat is available for guest use, and Giddens also runs nature tours and fishing trips. *$$$; MC, V; no checks; woodsend@island.net; www.woodsend.travel.bc.ca; across inlet from government docks.*

Ucluelet

"Ukie" is still a little rough around the edges, as the economic staples of fishing and logging only recently began to wane here. Resident enthusiasm for industrial logging perhaps faltered when the hills facing the harbor were clear-cut. This ugly duckling is making a go at becoming a tourism swan like sister town Tofino. With the development of view-rich **AMPHITRITE POINT**, including Roots Lodge at Reef Point (see review), condominiums, and shopping, it's making a good start.

Budget B&B accommodations line the road into town, and offer easy access to **PACIFIC RIM NATIONAL PARK** (250/726-4212); stop by the visitor center just inside the park entrance, off Highway 4. Three separate areas of the park allow visitors to appreciate the abundant wildlife and grand vistas of the Pacific Ocean. For hikers from as far away as Germany, the West Coast Trail reigns supreme (see Bamfield section in this chapter). The **BROKEN ISLANDS GROUP**, accessible only by boat, attracts intrepid kayakers, scuba divers, and fishing folk. Visitors to Ucluelet have come to enjoy the expanse of awe-inspiring **LONG BEACH**. The park's lone campground, Greenpoint (at park's midway point, well marked by signs; 800/689-9025), is often full during peak times and is closed in winter.

Six miles (10 km) north of Ucluelet, the **WICKANINNISH INTERPRETIVE CENTRE** (1 Wickaninnish Rd; 250/726-4701; 10:30am–6pm daily) has oceanic exhibits and an expansive view, shared by the on-site Wickaninnish Restaurant, a popular eatery with somewhat slow service (and not to be confused with the Wickaninnish Inn; see review in Tofino section of this chapter).

During March and April, 19,000 gray whales migrate past the West Coast on their way to the Bering Sea, and can often be seen from shore; orcas and humpbacks cruise the waters much of the year. For close-up views, many companies run whale-watching tours from both Ucluelet and Tofino; tours are easy to arrange once you arrive. The **PACIFIC RIM WHALE FESTIVAL** (250/726-4641; mid-Mar–mid-Apr) hosts events here and in Tofino; contact the festival office for information and schedules.

RESTAURANTS

Matterson House / ★

1682 PENINSULA RD, UCLUELET; 250/726-2200

Tofino residents happily make the half-hour drive to Ucluelet for a filling, satisfying breakfast or dinner (generous helpings at reasonable prices) at casual Matterson House. Breakfast standards such as eggs Benedict and huevos rancheros make way for lunch's Matterson Monster Burger, fully loaded with bacon, cheese, mushrooms, and more. Look also for caesar salads, chicken burgers, and homemade bread—and nothing deep-fried. Dinner sees hungry hikers and residents dig into prime rib, a mixed seafood platter, or veggie lasagne. Desserts often feature fruit crumbles and cheesecakes such as Kahlúa espresso. *$$; MC, V; local checks only; breakfast, lunch, dinner every day; full bar; reservations not necessary; near harbor.*

LODGINGS

Roots Lodge at Reef Point / ★

310 SEABRIDGE WY, UCLUELET; 250/726-2700 OR 888-594-7333

The Roots Lodge complex—owned by and named for the Canadian retailer—is not yet complete, but its shape is well under way. It clearly aims to be a player in the Long Beach area's highly competitive luxury class. Part of an ambitious development plan for pretty Amphitrite Point, the lodge will adjoin condominiums, shops, restaurants, and a cinema, connected by boardwalks and referencing traditional West Coast functional architecture. The Roots Lodge is done in nouveau cannery style: natural wood and chic corrugated aluminum, and ten beach-hugging rustic cabins. (There are also eight suites.) Breakfast is included in the price. A restaurant, bookstore, gallery, and forthcoming spa are resort highlights, and custom Roots Home furnishings set the tone. A Roots outlet on-site completes the brand-name experience. *$$$$; AE, MC, V; no checks; www.roots.com; follow highway through town and continue toward lighthouse.*

A Snug Harbour Inn / ★★

460 MARINE DR, UCLUELET; 250/726-2686 OR 888/936-5222

The million-dollar view here encompasses the rugged coast and islands where harbor seals and killer whales play. Through powerful binoculars in the main sitting room, guests can get close enough to feel they've already taken a whale-watching tour. On the main floor, a nautical theme centers on a model of the ship belonging to proprietors Skip and Denise Rowland. Expect a luxurious stay. Room decor is modern, especially in the dramatic black-carpeted Atlantis Room, popular with honeymooners, featuring a black whirlpool tub. Others favor the more exotic Sawadee ("Welcome" in Thai) Room, which reflects the Rowlands' five years in Thailand with rich woods, fabrics, and carvings, and an elegant double-sided fireplace facing both bedroom and bath. The split-level Lighthouse Room has the best view and is ornamented with round brass ships'

SURF'S UP, EH?

Ever thought to hang ten in the Great White North? Canadian and California surfers alike get hyped on the excellent breaks and pristine beaches around Tofino. Legendary **Long Beach**, an 11-mile (17-km) crescent backed by Douglas fir forests, was first surfed by American draft dodgers who came to live rent-free on the then-isolated beach. In Canada, surfing is a winter sport: that's when tsunamis off Japan bring the year's best waves. As other tourists cuddle up to cozy fires to watch the storms, committed surfers hit the beach in thick hooded wet suits. With proper gear, the cold is kept at bay.

Winter waves are a little too wild for beginners, but sunny days after May 1 bring throngs of boys and girls of summer with their flowered shorts and surfboards to catch more mellow waves. A number of options exist for seasoned surfers or newbies wanting to give it a try:

Surf Sister (250/725-4456) offers supportive women-only weekend clinics or individual lessons. "A girl's thing is where it's at," enthuses Jenny Hudnall, the school's bubbly founder. Take her word for it: she's among the best surfers, male or female, in Tofino. Taking a clinic gives newbies the pointers they need to get up on the board and stay safe in the water.

Live to Surf (1180 Pacific Rim Hwy; 250/725-4464), run by longtime local surfer gal Liz Zed, offers lessons to men and women, and rents wet suits and boards. Beginners should request a longboard, more stable and easier to stand up on than modern-day shortboards.

Inner Rhythm Surf Camps (250/726-2211) organizes surfing safaris: let them pack the gear, and all you have to do is hop in the van and chat with the wave-loving *wahine* beside you.

For those not venturing as far as Tofino, good winter surfing can also be had at **Jordan River** and **Sombrio Beach**, on the West Coast Highway a couple of hours from Victoria; rent your gear in town before heading out in the obligatory VW van.

—*Alisa Smith*

portholes and picture windows. A helicopter pad on the property serves as the departure point for trips to a deserted island or secluded glacier—or high-style arrivals. *$$$$; MC, V; no checks; asnughbr@island.net; www.ucluelet.com/asnugharbourinn; through village and right on Marine Dr.*

Tofino

At the end of the road is the wild West Coast, drawing surfers, kayakers, and nature lovers from throughout the Pacific Northwest, Europe, Japan, and elsewhere. On summer weekends, it's a grown-up playland: SUV racks haul mountain bikes and other outdoor paraphernalia. Tofino has been called "the next Whistler," as condo and hotel developments burgeon between town and Pacific Rim National Park: we only hope careful planning keeps the spirit of this special place intact. A large number of international visitors has resulted in more excellent hotels, B&Bs, and restaurants than one would expect from a town of less than 2,000.

People arrive at Tofino primarily by car, via the winding mountainous route of Highway 4 (5 hours from Victoria). **NORTH VANCOUVER AIR** (604/278-1608 or 800/228-6608) flies from Seattle, Vancouver, or Victoria—but you'll want a vehicle once you get here. You can rent a car from **BUDGET** (250/725-2060) or **TOFINO KITE AND BIKE SHOP** (250/725-1221).

TOFINO SEA KAYAKING COMPANY (320 Main; 250/725-4222) offers kayak rentals, or guided tours with experienced boaters and naturalists. You can also explore the coast with one of numerous water taxi companies. The float-planes of **TOFINO AIR LINES** (50 1st St; 250/725-4454) take guests to remote sea lion caves and beaches. **REMOTE PASSAGES** (71 Wharf St; 250/725-3330 or 800/666-9833) offers half- or full-day Zodiac boat tours of Clayoquot Sound. Whale-watching companies also abound. The **PACIFIC RIM WHALE FESTIVAL** (250/725-3414; mid-Mar–mid-Apr) hosts events here and in Ucluelet; contact the festival office for information and schedules.

The **NUU-CHAH-NULTH BOOKING AND INFO CENTRE** (250/725-2888) is operated by knowledgeable First Nations people and offers water taxi service, Meares Island interpretive tours, eco-tours of Pacific Rim National Park, and wilderness adventures. A number of boat and floatplane companies offer day trips to the calming pools of Hot Springs Cove; overnight at the six-room **HOT SPRINGS COVE LODGE** (250/670-1100), operated by the Hesquiaht First Nation.

Gift shops and galleries are sprinkled throughout town. The longhouse of the **EAGLE AERIE GALLERY** (350 Campbell St; 250/725-3235 or 800/663-0669) features art by Tsimshian Roy Henry Vickers, known internationally for prints that cross traditional indigenous motifs with contemporary, stylized landscapes in bold colors. **HOUSE OF HIMWITSA** (300 Main St; 250/725-2017 or 800-899-1947) features First Nations masks, jewelry, and gifts. **FIBER OPTIONS** (120 4th St, Ste 5; 250/725-2192) displays hemp products—from linenlike dresses to natural soaps. Get organic coffee and baked treats at **COMMON LOAF BAKE SHOP** (180 1st St; 250/725-3915).

RESTAURANTS

The Pointe Restaurant / ★★★★

OSPREY LN AT CHESTERMAN BEACH (WICKANINNISH INN), TOFINO; 250/725-3100 OR 800/333-4604

A truly outstanding environment—natural cedar posts and beams soar to a 20-foot ceiling, centered around a circular wood-burning stove with a hammered-copper hood and chimney. Elegance is achieved without stuffiness: gleaming wood table tops are not concealed by starchy linens, but service is white glove. The restaurant is perched over a rocky headland and waves crash just outside the 240-degree panoramic windows, making a meal here an event of Wagnerian grandeur. Chef Jim Garraway carries on the innovative West Coast style and many favored dishes established by previous award-winning chef Rodney Butters. Seafoods are highlighted, as are island-fresh and organic produce. The wine list features many deserving BC vintages. A breakfast specialty is the torte, topped off with exquisite Ucluelet goat cheese; sample the fresh daily juice special, perhaps a refreshing organic pear and melon. Even the presentation of tea is an art: an embossed iron teapot on a glass tray, loose Earl Grey leaves in a sieve, and a tiny granite vase with a single salal leaf. *$$$$; AE, MC, V; checks OK; breakfast, lunch, dinner every day; full bar; reservations recommended (dinner); wick@wickinn.com; www.wickinn.com; off Hwy 4, north of Long Beach.* &

RainCoast Café / ★★

120 4TH ST, TOFINO; 250/725-2215

Though they acknowledge that the atmosphere is lacking, locals embrace the RainCoast as having the best food in town—and they'll fight you for the last slice of chocolate peanut butter pie. An ever-changing soup and sandwich special comes highly recommended. Food here, often featuring a Thai twist, is more adventurous than at most local establishments. Vegetarians, look for a polenta torte with Parmesan cheese, roma tomatoes, and white wine ragout; wild rice cakes with roasted-garlic mashed potatoes; and even a stuffed marinated tofu. Even vegans can sink their teeth into the verde pasta. Seafood stew showcases the region's bounty, while free-range chicken is stuffed with roasted garlic, chèvre, and more. *$$; AE, MC, V; local checks only; dinner every day; beer and wine; reservations recommended; near Fisherman's Wharf.* &

Schooner Restaurant / ★★

331 CAMPBELL ST, TOFINO; 250/725-3444

In a town where the crab dock and wharf are as well-known landmarks as compass points, it's no surprise that seafood is the specialty here. Enjoy the captain's platter for two—a bounty of "all the seafood in the house," from mussels to salmon—on the sunny veranda as you take in the view. The highly recommended halibut Bawden Bay comes stuffed with crab and Brie, complemented by an apply brandy sauce. If ambitious, top the feast with the supreme chocolate overload cake; modest sorts may refresh their palates with sorbet. *$$$; AE, MC, V; no checks; lunch in summer, dinner every day; full bar; reservations recommended; downtown, near corner of 2nd.*

Sea Shanty Restaurant / ★★

300 MAIN ST, TOFINO; 250/725-2902

Part of the House of Himwitsa—with an attached Native-run gallery and lodge—this log building occupies a prime waterfront spot. The casual pine and country-furniture atmosphere complements Northwest Coast–French fusion food. Fresh steamed crab is a favorite. Some locals find prices a bit high for what you get. The five rooms of the Himwitsa Lodge (250/725-3319 or 800/899-1947) upstairs are clean, new, and modestly appointed—except for those with a deck hot tub. *$$$; MC, V; no checks; breakfast, lunch, dinner every day; full bar; reservations not accepted; himwitsa@island.net; across from main dock.* &

Surfside Café / ★

120 1ST ST, TOFINO; 250/725-2882

This popular delivery-only pizza company set down roots and expanded its menu—and stays open till midnight on weekends. Thick-crust Sicilian pizza is a favorite, with a pesto or tomato base, stacked with your choice of toppings. Pub-style options include chicken burgers, steak sandwiches, caesar salads, and veggies with dip. The Surfside delivers almost anywhere, to feed surfers at Long Beach, for example, or boaters at the dock. *$; MC, V; checks OK; breakfast, lunch, dinner every day; full bar; reservations not accepted; off main intersection.*

LODGINGS

Cable Cove Inn / ★

201 MAIN ST, TOFINO; 250/725-4236 OR 800/663-6449

Tucked at the edge of Tofino's town center, Cable Cove Inn has all possible views: past the wharves to Meares Island, and out to the open sea. Six rooms exude a distinguished air, with mahogany-toned furniture and green marble whirlpool tubs; all have fireplaces and private, ocean-facing decks, while the best (corner) room has a wraparound balcony. Steps lead to the sheltered cove below the inn. The upstairs lounge centers around a cozy wood-burning stove surrounded by cushy leather couches; continental breakfast is served, and a full kitchen is available for guests. Northwest Coast Native prints liberally grace the walls. *$$–$$$; AE, MC, V; checks OK; cablecin@island.net; www.cablecoveinn.com; at north end of Main St.*

InnChanter / ★★★

HOTSPRINGS COVE; 250/670-1149

Locals recommend this unique, luxuriously refitted 1920s boat moored in Hotsprings Cove. The elegant floating B&B done in velvet and chandeliers features five staterooms, a salon with wood-burning stove, and a 700-square-foot sundeck. Host Shawn Shelongosky is a brilliant and quirky conversationalist, and an excellent chef who attends to all guest meals (included). He specializes in sumptuous vegetarian fare, but uses a lot of fresh seafood—look for a salmon barbecue on deck—and for meat eaters prepares such dishes as whiskey-stuffed chicken marinated in honey and garlic. Best of all, when the hot springs day tours leave, you can take a rowboat ashore and have them to yourself. Reach the InnChanter by plane or water taxi, booked at the government dock in Tofino. Hosts recommend guests bring rain gear and an extra set of warm clothes; be prepared to stay an extra day if weather won't allow travel. *$$$; MC, V; no checks; innchanter@uniserve.com; www. innchanter.com; take water taxi to Hotsprings Cove.*

Middle Beach Lodge / ★★★

400 MACKENZIE BEACH RD, TOFINO; 250/725-2900

These wonderful rooms are spacious, and decor is tasteful and homey: wicker chairs, crisp natural-toned bedding and curtains, cheery colors. The long, narrow lodge lobby is graced with weathered antiques, while the centerpiece of the comfortable lounge is a massive stone fireplace. Service is friendly and casual. Lodge rooms offer cozy balconies, writing desks, and premier views. The Beach Lodge is kept romantic and quiet with an adults-only policy; the newer Headlands Lodge welcomes families. Palatial, two-level oceanfront cabins have large waterside patios, but are kept down to earth with plank flooring recovered from historic Victoria warehouses. Immense windows let in the light, and kitchenettes allow full independence. The hotel serves a continental breakfast of home-baked goods and jams, and high season brings fresh fish barbecues and nightly dinners in the restaurant. *$$$–$$$$; AE, MC, V; no checks; 2-night min in high season; lodge@middlebeach.com; www.middlebeach.com; south of Tofino off Hwy 4.*

Paddler's Inn Bed and Breakfast / ★

320 MAIN ST, TOFINO; 250/725-4222

This simple white wood-sided establishment—Tofino's original hotel—has been brightened with red-and-blue window boxes and trim, and turned into a kayaking mecca. The on-site headquarters of the Tofino Sea Kayaking Company allows guests to arrange guided tours landing at the Vargas Island Inn (see review) and other coastal pitstops. In the convivial bookstore and coffee bar, owner Dorothy Baertt dispenses useful information along with espresso. Upstairs, five simple rooms (with shared bath) are appointed with Scandinavian-style furniture and overlook the waterfront. Guests serve themselves from a continental breakfast bar in the kitchen; those in the Paddler's Suite (with private bath) may opt to cook their own. *$; MC, V; checks OK; paddlers@island.net; www.island.net/~paddlers; just above 1st St dock.*

Vargas Island Inn

ON VARGAS ISLAND; 250/725-3309

Kayakers—especially those on guided tours, who are served fresh crab, salmon, or cod—are keen on the Vargas Island Inn. After a couple of hours' paddling from Tofino, twin gables on a venerable Tudor-style home prompt cries of "Land ho!" Accommodation choices are rooms in the inn, a dormitory-style hostel, or camping in the cedar woods above the beach. It's best described as rustic, with no phones, and propane or solar-generated power. Take the 2-mile (3.2-km) hike to the pretty beach at Ahous Bay, a provincial park, then enter the soothing sauna. The hosts have a long history with the area: Neil Buckle's grandfather was a lighthouse keeper on a nearby island at the beginning of the 20th century, and settled here in 1910. *$; AE, MC, V; checks OK; accessible by water taxi or private boat from Tofino.*

Wickaninnish Inn / ★★★★

OSPREY LN AT CHESTERMAN BEACH, TOFINO; 250/725-3100 OR 800/333-4604

Dare we say that everything here is perfect? Certainly, guests believe so: it is one of a few places on Vancouver Island booked full even in winter. Service is impeccable: desk clerks listen attentively to guests' stories and laugh at their jokes. The artful environment includes architectural details by master carver Henry Nolla, natural bent-wood chairs, and black-and-white nature photographs. All rooms feature ocean views, fireplaces, private balconies, and down duvets; extra-large, deluxe corner suites are available. The soothing, full-service Ancient Cedars Spa downstairs offers aromatherapy, hydrotherapy, massage, manicures, and other pamperings. The crowning glory is The Pointe Restaurant (see review). The Wickaninnish, known for pioneering the dramatic concept of winter storm-watching, has been touted from the time it opened in 1996. Some rooms allow pets. *$$$$; AE, MC, V; checks OK; wick@wickinn.com; www.wickinn.com; off Hwy 4 north of Long Beach.* &

The Comox Valley

The Comox Valley on the island's middle east coast, has skiing in winter, water sports in summer, a quaint shopping district in the town of Courtenay on Highway 19, and scenic access to Powell River on Highway 101 on the mainland Sunshine Coast by BC Ferries (250/339-3310). Skiers flock to **MOUNT WASHINGTON** (250/338-1386), where four chairlifts operate for more than 140 days of the year, and there are 29 kilometers (17.9 miles) of cross-country track.

Fanny Bay

Blink and you'll miss this tiny hamlet. For a true roadhouse experience, stop at the **FANNY BAY INN** (7480 Island Hwy; 250/335/2323)—or the FBI, as it is more familiarly known. Considering its famed oyster region locale, we were disappointed to see only one oyster option (batter-fried with toast and french fries) on the standard-fare menu. But we bought the T-shirt anyway.

LODGINGS

Long House Inn at Ships Point / ★★

7588 SHIPS POINT RD, FANNY BAY; 250/335-2200 OR 800/925-1595

Seasoned B&B hosts Lorinda and Dave Rawlings expanded their waterfront home and enlarged the rooms, leaving two spacious guest suites with views of Baynes Sound and the Vancouver Island mountains. The Eagles Nest is named for the dramatic mural that serves as its focal point; the Hummingbird Room is done in bold blues and sunny yellows. Both have double soaker tubs and fireplaces. Lorinda's four-course breakfasts are tasty and elaborate. Start with fresh juice—look for the house specialty of orange, grapefruit, and cranberry—and home baking, maybe a poached pear. The hot entree might be a Hangtown Fry (Fanny Bay oyster omelet) or an orange soufflé. Walk 30 feet down to the beach, and visit the bird sanctuary or an artist's gallery. *$$$$; AE, MC, V; checks OK; innkeeper@shipspoint.com; www.shipspoint.com; 5 miles (8 km) north of Deep Bay.*

Courtenay and Comox

These adjacent towns are the hub of the valley. Courtenay's in-town browsing ranges from antique, kitchenware, and retro clothing shops to the thought-of-everything **TRAVELLER'S TALE SHOP** (526 Cliffe Ave, Courtenay; 250/703-0168). Break for a delectable treat at **HOT CHOCOLATES** (238 5th St, Courtenay; 250/338-8211). Ask at local bike shops for directions to mountain bike trails. The ferry to Denman Island leaves from Buckley Bay, about 10 minutes south of Courtenay.

RESTAURANTS

The Old House Restaurant / ★★

1760 RIVERSIDE LN, COURTENAY; 250/338-5406

This carefully restored, rambling pioneer home rests amid colorful flower gardens and verdant trees—though the trees may be thinned considerably if a neighboring development is approved. Across the river, a working sawmill sets the tone of old Courtenay. Inside, a roaring stone fireplace beckons on cool days, while porcelain and copper wares create a charming ambience. Start dinner at this white tablecloth establishment with seafood mushroom caps, stuffed with shrimp, crab, and spinach cream cheese. Next, many opt for a fresh BC salmon fillet baked on a cedar plank and sparked with homemade fruit salsa; or panfried maple rye pork medallions. The "chocolate wedge" is a rich dessert paté; also good is butter pecan bread pudding with warm caramel rum sauce. *$$; AE, DC, MC, V; no checks; lunch, dinner every day; full bar; reservations recommended; just before 17th St Bridge to Comox.* &

LODGINGS

Greystone Manor

4014 HAAS RD, COURTENAY; 250/338-1422

Extensive English flower gardens are the jewel of this establishment; enjoy the vibrant colors out your window and contemplate views of the Strait of Georgia and the Coast Mountains beyond. Greystone Manor is a welcome alternative to a night in a featureless highway hotel. Three guest rooms with private baths give you all the basics—though ours was fairly small. Decor of this 1914 home is highlighted with antiques; the common parlor has a cozy fire but could do with new carpeting. *$$; MC, V; no checks; www.bbcanada.com/1334.html; 3 miles (5 km) south of Courtenay.*

Campbell River and North Vancouver Island

The north end of Vancouver Island sees raw industrial towns abutting unpopulated wilderness featuring plenty of outdoor pursuits, from Hemingway-worthy fishing expeditions to spectacular hiking.

Campbell River

If you're here, you're probably fishing: Campbell River is known as the "salmon capital of the world." Bag your limit of Tyee, chinook, spring, pink, or chum salmon pretty much year-round on one of many **FISHING CHARTERS** located on the waterfront. Fly-fishing the river for pinks is gaining popularity. **CHARTER FLIGHTS** are available from Seattle via Kenmore Air (800/543-9595) and Vancouver via Air BC (604/688-5515) or Canadian Regional (800/665-1177); they land at the airport 20 minutes from downtown.

During July's **SALMON FESTIVAL**, this mall-rich town of 20,000 is abuzz with famous and ordinary fisherfolk. The **CHAMBER OF COMMERCE** (1235 Shoppers Wy; 250/287-4636) can provide info on the festival, as well as on the region's trails and dive sites. Locals like the **IDEAL CAFÉ** (2263 Island Hwy; 250/287-9155), a truck stop serving hearty diner fare.

STRATHCONA PROVINCIAL PARK (about 30 miles/48 km west of town on Hwy 28; 250/337-5121) is a place of superlatives. It contains Canada's highest waterfall as well as Vancouver Island's tallest mountain, and offers a wide range of landscapes, including a glacier, alpine meadows and lakes, and large stands of virgin cedar and Douglas fir. Mountaineers and rock-climbers get their thrills here. Easily accessible by road, the park has campgrounds and boat-launching facilities at Buttle Lake. The park also has fine trout lakes and an extensive trail system for backpacking. An information kiosk is open year-round; the ranger station is open in summer.

RESTAURANTS

Koto / ★★

80 10TH AVE, CAMPBELL RIVER; 250/286-1422

It makes sense: a very fresh sushi bar in the middle of fishing country. Chef Takeo (Tony) Maeda has single-handedly developed the locals' taste for *nigiri*. Teriyaki is a big seller too—beef, chicken, or salmon—but look for more exotic food from the deep, such as sea eel, sea urchin roe, and octopus. It's a nice meal, especially if you pull into town late. Only one sushi chef does it all, so when it's busy, service can be slow. *$$; AE, MC, V; no checks; lunch Tues–Fri, dinner Tues–Sat; full bar; reservations recommended; behind Bank of BC building.*

LODGINGS

Painter's Lodge / ★

1625 MCDONALD RD, CAMPBELL RIVER; 250/286-1102 OR 800/663-7090

Fishing is the raison d'être of this lodge run by the reputable Oak Bay Marine Group of Victoria, but you couldn't ask for a prettier location. Prime suites in the main lodge overlook Discovery Passage and Quadra Island. At 4am, the hotel is abustle with eager anglers, and the sounds of seaplanes and a fleet of Boston whalers can be heard (nonanglers may find it a bit too active). On occasion, the lodge has been known to put up large groups of loggers, making for a rowdy time, particularly in the pub. Strive to catch the big one here, and maybe your photo will join the historic row of big-time anglers in the plush lobby. Relax in the Fireside Lounge or pub to hear stories of the one that got away. Fare in the Legends dining room is not especially inspired, but the guarantee of fresh-caught fish and seafood staples helps compensate. Ask about fishing packages. *$$$–$$$$; AE, DC, E, MC, V; no checks; open Apr–Oct; obmg@pinc. com; www.obmg.com; 2½ miles (4 km) north of Campbell River.*

Strathcona Park Lodge

EDGE OF STRATHCONA PARK, CAMPBELL RIVER; 250/286-3122

This is a mecca for those who enjoy healthful, active living. Accommodations in the log-and-timber lodge and self-contained lakefront cabins with kitchens are modest but adequate. Outdoors packages range from a hike on Mount Albert Edward, the island's fourth-highest peak, to rock climbing and rope courses for families (cliffs in Strathcona Park are beloved by Island climbers); paddle a canoe on Upper Campbell Lake. Arrive punctually for buffet meals in the Whale Room, because guests here pack big appetites. Organic produce from nearby gardens makes seasonal appearances. *$$; MC, V; checks OK; limited facilities Dec–Feb; 28 miles (45 km) west of Campbell River.*

Gold River

With the recent closure of the mill in this pretty town, many inhabitants of Gold River are moving on (though retirees are moving in). From here, the utilitarian **UCHUK III** (on Government Dock off Mill Rd; 250/283-2325; reservations required) embarks on a 10-hour cruise along the largely uninhabited western coast of Vancouver Island, a breathtaking stretch of rugged inlets and islands. On the way to the remote settlement of **KYUQUOT**, the boat stops at logging camps, fish farms, and settlers' cabins; you spend the night in a bed-and-breakfast and return the next day.

Port McNeill and Telegraph Cove

The major asset of this remote area is its proximity to all things wild and wonderful—boating, diving, whale-watching, salmon fishing, and tide pooling. The inspiring **UMISTA CULTURAL CENTRE** (Front St; 250/974-5403) in the nearby town of Alert Bay is only a short ferry ride away from the Port McNeill waterfront (schedules are available there); learn about potlatch traditions of the local Kwakwaka'wakw people. **STUBBS ISLAND CHARTERS** (24 Boardwalk, Telegraph Cove; 250/928-3185) offers morning and afternoon cruises to view killer whales in Johnstone Strait; groups of five or more can spend the night in modest harborfront cabins, managed by **TELEGRAPH COVE RESORT** (250/928-3131); call for reservations. For a satisfying basic meal, stop in at **BB'S COOKHOUSE** (9–1705 Campbell Wy, Port McNeill; 250/956-4117).

July through October, **WHALE-WATCHING** is superior from the town of Telegraph Cove, 10 miles (16 km) south of Port McNeill. Old homes in Telegraph Cove have been gaily painted and revived as overnight lodgings. Kayak outfitters operate out of Port McNeill and Telegraph Cove.

LODGINGS

Hidden Cove Lodge / ★★
PORT MCNEILL; 250/956-3916
Sandra and Dan Kirby's waterfront retreat on 9½ acres is interspersed with walking trails and offers back-to-basics relaxation. Eight rooms with private baths are furnished in pine, and rates include home-cooked breakfasts such as eggs Benedict or pancakes. By arrangement, Sandra and the lodge staff cook up lunches and dinners of Dungeness crab, baby back spareribs, or other hearty favorites. Two two-bedroom cottages with full kitchens allow families to cook their own. The Kirbys can sign you up with local companies for anything from whale-watching to heli-fishing. A wraparound, window-lined lounge allows for quiet contemplation of herons, eagles, and whales, or a chance to mix with other guests. *$$$; MC, V; checks OK; take Beaver Cove/Telegraph Cove cutoff from Hwy 19.*

Port Hardy

A harborfront promenade sweetens the stay in this gritty town at the end of the road. Loggers, fishermen, and miners have long made up much of the population here, though these industries are fading. Travelers stop to catch the acclaimed 15-hour **BC FERRIES CRUISE** north to Prince Rupert on the mainland or to Bella Coola and Bella Bella on the midcoast. Reservations are required

(250/949-6722 or 888/223-3779). Book summer accommodations here well in advance, because ferry passengers tend to fill the hotels.

The famous Edward S. Curtis silent film *In the Land of the War Canoes*— part anthropology, part fanciful pot-boiler—was filmed in nearby **FORT RUPERT** (250/949-6012), a good place to purchase authentic First Nations art.

Some well-traveled islanders call **CAPE SCOTT PROVINCIAL PARK** (37 miles/60 km west of Port Hardy; 250/949-2816) the most beautiful place on earth. A 1½-hour drive over gravel roads west of Port Hardy, and a 20-minute boardwalk hike take you to spectacular San Josef Bay; camping is permitted. A longer, more grueling hike leads to the island's northern tip; the **CHAMBER OF COMMERCE** (7250 Market St; 250/949-7622) provides information and directions.

LODGINGS

Oceanview B&B / ★

7735 CEDAR PL, PORT HARDY; 250/949-8302

This well-appointed executive-style home boasts sweeping ocean vistas from three guest rooms, which locals judge to be the area's best. The shore is a 10-minute walk, and hosts Bob and Chantal Charlie will arrange for pickup from the nearby Prince Rupert ferry dock. Down duvets, TVs, VCRs, and fireplaces are features here. In the country-style kitchen, enjoy a breakfast of home-baked bread, muffins, bagels, cold meats and cheeses, fruit, yogurt, and more. Homey room touches include substantial bedsteads in brass or wrought iron, pine armoires, and wall stenciling. Guests are greeted with homemade chocolate chip cookies. *$$; cash only; oceanvue@island.net; www.island.net/~oceanvue; follow Hwy 19 through town, left on Market, left on Cedar.*

SOUTHERN INTERIOR AND THE KOOTENAYS

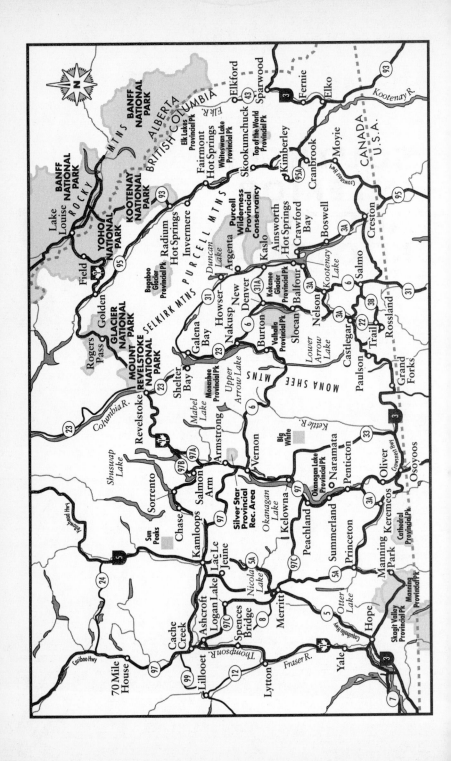

SOUTHERN INTERIOR
AND THE KOOTENAYS

This corner of Canada is vertically defined. Draw away from the West Coast's ocean beaches, and you run smack up against range upon range of mountains: the Coast Mountains, the Cascades, the Monashees, the Selkirks, the Purcells, and the Rockies.

Which isn't to say there aren't open spaces among the peaks. In the Okanagan region, for example, gently undulating benchland is intensely planted with vineyards above broad, blue lakes. Wilder corners of the Okanagan's semi-desert burn with yellow sagebrush blossoms.

Traversing the Kootenays—that land where the peace-and-love generation abides—the going gets extreme. Many valleys in this cedar-and-pine-carpeted wilderness receive only a shaft or two of sunlight in winter months—too many pinnacles get in the way. To make sense of the Kootenays, imagine four mountain ranges puckered together like an accordion's bellows. No wonder roads in this part of BC scatter off in more directions than windblown fireweed seeds. When the Rockies finally present themselves, they project a stateliness that makes the rest of the pack look like peaks in training.

ACCESS AND INFORMATION

Almost every main road or highway in BC intersects with the Trans-Canada Highway (Hwy 1) at some point. In this region, Highway 1 covers more than 372 miles (600 km) between Hope and the BC-Alberta border. Other major highways here include Highway 3 (Crowsnest Hwy); Highway 97, linking Highway 1 to the Okanagan Valley; Highway 5 (Coquihalla Hwy); and Highway 95.

The major urban area, Kamloops, is served by **AIR BC** (800/663-3721), **CANADIAN AIRLINES INTERNATIONAL** (800/665-1177) and **VIA RAIL** (800/561-8630). **GREYHOUND BUS LINES** (800/663-8868) offers daily service to all towns along the Trans-Canada Highway. The **KELOWNA INTERNATIONAL AIRPORT** (1–5533 Kelowna International Airport; 250/765-5125) is served by Air BC, Canadian Regional Airlines, Central Mountain Air, Horizon Air, and Westjet. Twice-daily Canadian Regional and Westjet flights from Vancouver and Calgary arrive at **PENTICTON AIRPORT** (Lancaster Rd and Hwy 97; 250/492-6042).

Kamloops and the Thompson River

As the Coquihalla Highway (Hwy 5) winds north from Hope to Kamloops, it passes through semi-arid desert and gently rolling highlands, paralleling the Fraser and Thomson Rivers. Wide-open views of sagebrush-covered mountainsides shaped by eons of weathering and lonesome beauty prevail here, as do famous fly-fishing waters.

Merritt

The waters around Merritt (population 7,000) are famous for producing fighting rainbow trout. **FLY-FISHING** is the style of choice, and "A lake a day as long as you stay" is no idle boast for the Nicola Valley. Close to 50 percent of BC's total freshwater sport fishing occurs in the Thompson-Nicola region: the Thompson and Nicola Rivers are historic salmon-spawning tributaries of the Fraser River, and the smaller tributary streams are where rainbow trout, Dolly Varden char, and kokanee lay their eggs.

It's the lakes, however, that attract anglers. Chapperon, Douglas, and Nicola Lakes have long been noted for ample fish stocks. **NICOLA LAKE**, renowned for its depth, is said to harbor 26 varieties of fish, some weighing up to 20 pounds. The easiest to reach, it's located about 4 miles (7 km) east of Merritt on Highway 5A. Use the boat launch at **MONCK PROVINCIAL PARK** (off Hwy 5A, 13 ½ miles/22 km north of Merritt; 250/851-3000) for access. Ice fishing, spear fishing, and set line fishing are also done in the Nicola area lakes. Licenses, tackle, and sound advice are available at **MCLEOD'S DEPARTMENT STORE** (2088 Quichena Ave; 250/378-5191).

LODGINGS

Sundance Ranch / ★★

KIRKLAND RANCH RD, ASHCROFT; 250/453-2422

At this dude ranch set in high plateau country, east of the Thompson River, low ranch buildings of dark-stained wood contain handsome pine-paneled rooms. The outdoor pool is grand, and there's a tennis court, but the real attraction is the corral. A large herd of good horses is available for two daily rides—morning and late afternoon. More than a dozen buffalo live in adjacent fields. Excellent evening meals are often served on the patio; Saturday nights there's a dance. Rustic public rooms set the scene for drinks, parties, and games. You'll sleep well, breathing the cool, sage-scented air. Sundance operates on the American Plan, with everything included: accommodations, meals, horses, and the use of all ranch facilities. Children can stay in their own wing or with their parents. Note: On long weekends in May (Victoria Day), September (Labor Day), and October (Canadian Thanksgiving), the ranch is booked several months in advance. Weekends in May, June, September, and October are increasingly popular; reserve several weeks in advance. *$$$$; MC, V; no checks; open Mar–Oct; sundance@wkpowerlink.com; www.sundance-ranch. com; 5 miles (8 km) south of Ashcroft.* &

Kamloops

Kamloops (population 77,500) is by far the largest of the major urban areas in the region. It sprawls across the weathered slopes of the Thompson Plateau through which runs the mighty Thompson River, whose north and south arms converge here. With the forest industry waning, Kamloops (a Shuswap First

SOUTHERN INTERIOR THREE-DAY TOUR

DAY ONE: Start your day with breakfast at the **Kootenay Baker**, followed by an architectural tour of more than 350 heritage sites in downtown **Nelson**. Then stroll Baker Street and look for bargains at the **Patagonia** factory outlet. Grab some lunch down the street at the **Rice Bowl Restaurant** (301 Baker St; 250/354-4129). Walk it off afterward with an energetic march to **Gyro Park**, pausing to enjoy art on display at a gallery or two along the way. Once at the park, head to the lookout for a panoramic vista. Drive over to **Willow Point Lodge**, where you'll be spending the evening, having first made dinner reservations at the **All Seasons Cafe**. Make it as late a night as you want. You'll soak off any cobwebs at a hot spring in the morning.

DAY TWO: After breakfast at Willow Point, drive north on Highways 3A and 31 to **Ainsworth Hot Springs**. Trade your clothes for a bathing suit and relax in the resort's public soaking pools. When you're ready for lunch, drive the short distance along Kootenay Lake to **Kaslo**. Find a table on the patio at the **Rosewood Cafe**, and revel in your newfound sense of well-being. Afterward, stroll down to the waterfront for a tour of the lovingly restored **S.S. Moyie**. Enjoy the scenic drive on Highway 31A between Kaslo and New Denver, and let your eyes do the work as you sightsee along Slocan and Upper Arrow Lakes. Beware neck strain from trying to take in all the **Valhalla Range**. On Highway 23, catch the free, 30-minute ferry across Upper Arrow Lake from Galena Bay to Shelter Bay. It's only a short drive from Shelter Bay to **Mulvehill Creek Wilderness Inn** south of Revelstoke. Walk through the surrounding forest to enjoy the extraordinary stillness. By prior arrangement, dinner is served at the inn.

DAY THREE: After a leisurely breakfast in the dining room, head for the inn's beach on **Upper Arrow Lake**. When you're ready, drive into **Revelstoke** and stop at **the 112** for a weekday lunch. Point your car's nose up the **Meadows in the Sky Parkway** in nearby **Mount Revelstoke National Park**. Have plenty of film ready to record the profusion of wildflowers. Look east toward Rogers Pass and the massive Illecillewaet Glacier. That's where you're headed once you return to Highway 1. Pull over at the top of the pass for a visit to the sod-roofed information center. Primed by your crash course here in the century of mountaineering tradition in **Glacier National Park**, enjoy the drive past the peaks to **Golden**. Drive on to **Emerald Lake Lodge** in Field, where you have dinner and spend the night.

Nations term for "meeting of the waters") is turning its attention to tourism. Fly-in fishing lodges are located on many of the 700 lakes in the region, where anglers cast for trophy-sized **KAMLOOPS TROUT**, a unique strain that puts on an eye-popping, acrobatic performance when hooked. These wild rainbows are native to central and south-central Interior regions of the province. The

KAMLOOPS INFOCENTRE (1290 W Trans-Canada Hwy; 250/372-7722 or 800/662-1994; www.kamloopsbc.com) can provide a list of lodges.

RESTAURANTS

Peter's Pasta / ★

149 VICTORIA ST, KAMLOOPS; 250/372-8514

 What Peter's Pasta lacks in ambience, it makes up for in sauces. It's easy to overlook this narrow cafe in downtown Kamloops, but the locals rave about the homemade pasta that Peter puts on your plate. Given that its popularity outweighs its modest size, you may encounter a short wait. Diners choose from four pastas and a generous range of sauces, including clam, tomato, and alfredo. Small and large portions are offered; all come with tasty garlic bread. Salads are extra, but you may not need one. The dessert menu includes several Italian ices, but look for the chocolate mousse. *$; MC, V; no checks; lunch Tues–Fri, dinner Tues–Sat; beer and wine; reservations recommended; downtown.*

LODGINGS

Riverland Motel / ★

1530 RIVER ST, KAMLOOPS; 250/374-1530 OR 800/663-1530

 When visiting Kamloops, you'll want to stay beside the banks of the South Thompson River. Not just because rivers have a soothing quality to them, but also because the centrally located Riverland Motel is a traveler's dream. It offers quick access to major highways, and is within walking distance of dining, shopping, and scenic attractions. Request a riverside room for a view of the weathered palisades that rise above the Thompson's north shore. Opened in 1991, the motel's 58 standard rooms are clean and pleasantly furnished, with fridges in all rooms. Other soothing amenities include an indoor pool and whirlpool, laundry facilities, and complimentary continental breakfast. For a few dollars more, choose a kitchen unit or an executive suite, complete with Jacuzzi tub. Let the kids loose on the broad lawn between the hotel and the river. The adjacent Storms Restaurant features a full lunch and dinner menu of creative pastas, seafood, ribs, and racks, best enjoyed on the sheltered patio overlooking the river. *$–$$; AE, MC, V; no checks; riverlandmotel@kamloops.com; www.kamloops.com/riverlandmotel; from Hwy 1 or Hwy 5, take Jasper exit.* &

Sun Peaks

Sun Peaks Resort truly arrived as a four-season mountain resort when Canada Post officially awarded it with a postal code of its own in 1998. Now *that's* recognition. (Originally known as Tod Mountain, major investor Nippon Cable chose the name to reflect a change in image, from regional ski hill to international year-round recreation destination.) The finishing touches have since been put on six artfully configured slopeside hotels that anchor the village. Decidedly

European, the atmosphere feels like a neighborhood, and nothing seems out-of-place. From November to April, Sun Peaks hosts skiers and snowboarders who come for the crisp, dry powder snow on **MOUNT TOD**. Another part of the draw is world champion—and Canada's woman athlete of the century—Nancy Greene Raine, who serves as director of skiing at Sun Peaks. Dogsledding or snowshoeing with a naturalist are other options. In summer, hikers and cyclists traverse meadows displaying a rainbow of wildflowers.

Thirty miles (50 km) northeast of Kamloops on Highway 5 and Tod Mountain Road, Sun Peaks takes about 45 minutes to reach from Highway 1, but it's a pleasant drive along the North Thompson River. The resort, operated by the **SUN PEAKS MOUNTAIN RESORT ASSOCIATION** (Ste 50, 3150 Creekside Wy; 250/578-7842 or 800/807-3257; info@sunpeaksresort.com; www.sunpeaksresort.com) is self-contained, so you won't need your car once you get here. It features 3,100 feet of vertical drop, 1,000 acres of marked skiable terrain (and 10,227 skiable acres total), and five lifts.

LODGINGS

Father's Country Inn / ★

TOD MOUNTAIN RD, HEFFLEY CREEK; 250/578-7308

A stay at Father's Country Inn, a bed-and-breakfast hideaway 5 miles (8 km) west of Sun Peaks Resort, confirms that no matter how far you roam, you'll still find surprises. Proprietor David Conover Jr. comes by his profession honestly. For decades, his parents ran a popular resort on one of BC's southern Gulf Islands. There Conover learned the art of making serious coffee and killer pancakes (by prior arrangement, he also prepares dinners). Conover fills plates and cups to the brim for guests who anticipate long days in the outdoors. Chances are, the conversation may turn to the photographic print business he runs from his rambling six-room inn. Conover markets not only his resort legacy but the images his father took of Marilyn Monroe, whom Conover Sr. befriended while on a photo shoot for the U.S. Army in Los Angeles during World War II. Her young face is displayed throughout the inn. Father's Country Inn's plain exterior masks the richness of its interior, which includes a large swimming pool. Rooms, each named for a season and decorated accordingly, are equipped with fireplaces and sumptuous tubs. Snow trekkers appreciate the inn's fully equipped ski room complete with drying racks, lockers, and a waxing bench. *$; MC, V; checks OK; info@dconover.com; www.dconover.com; from Hwy 5 follow Tod Mountain Rd 14 miles (23 km) toward Sun Peaks.* &

Nancy Greene's Cahilty Lodge / ★★

3220 VILLAGE WY, SUN PEAKS RESORT; 250/578-7454 OR 800/244-8424
Having perfected their hostelry skills at Whistler in the 1980s, Nancy Greene Raine and her husband, Al, migrated east across the Coast Mountains to Sun Peaks and opened the Cahilty Lodge, named for a pioneer ranching family. It's a condominium hotel, and room amenities

SKIING THE SOUTHERN INTERIOR

In the United States, Colorado alone has more ski resorts than all of Canada. "We have to be *clever*," asserts Olympic gold medalist Nancy Greene Raine, with the kind of determined edge in her voice that implies she's won before, and can win some more. Greene Raine's strategy of cleverness for **Sun Peaks Resort** near Kamloops, where she first skied in 1964, when the Canadian Alpine Championships were held there, involves positioning the resort for the long haul. "We see ourselves as the second step on a two-step holiday—mega and mellow. More visitors are coming to Canada on a two-week ski holiday. They take a week at Whistler-Blackcomb for the big hit, then they want to come to a resort where they can get the feeling for small-town Canada. We're a small resort where you actually *meet* people."

Internationally, the word is out that Canada is *the* place to learn to ski and snowboard. According to Greene Raine, who hosts clinics for intermediate and advanced skiers, quality of teaching accounts for much of the world's reawakened interest in BC skiing. More people learned to ski and snowboard in 1999 at Whistler-Blackcomb than at any other resort in North America. Acknowledged as the premier winter destination on the continent, Whistler-Blackcomb also brings attention to smaller BC resorts, such as Sun Peaks Resort.

"In the past," Greene Raine recalls, "this was perceived as a place where a small group of rugged, wild, and woolly skiers went to enjoy some of the best powder skiing in the province. Sun Peaks has finally brought the mountain to the attention of a wider group, something that's been promised here for the past three decades. We're finally helping deliver the goods." For other BC resorts, see various sections in this chapter.

—*Jack Christie*

range from those with modest cooking facilities (coffeemaker and microwave) to fully equipped suites that sleep eight. A hot tub and an exercise room are downstairs, plus a ski and mountain bike room. Also downstairs is Macker's Bistro, arguably the most consistent restaurant at Sun Peaks. Laidback and mellow in tone, the menu is imaginative, if limited, and skewed toward families and fun. Adjacent to the lodge is the resort's sports center with swimming pool and weight room, outdoor skating rink, and tennis courts. The lodge's centerpiece is Greene Raine's trophy cabinet in the entranceway. If the sociable hostess takes a shine to you, she might let you try on her Olympic gold medal. *$$$–$$$$; AE, DC, JTB, MC, V; no checks; info@cahiltylodge.com; www.cahiltylodge.com; east on Creekside Wy to Village Wy.* &

Sun Peaks Lodge / ★★★

**3185 CREEKSIDE WY, SUN PEAKS RESORT; 250/578-7878
OR 800/333-9112**

Some lodgings are so special that, once in your room, you simply want to throw yourself into a comfy chair and revel in your good fortune. Such is the ambience at Sun Peaks Lodge. Built by Germany's Stumbock Club, the trappings are worthy of those in a quality European hotel, from harmonious decor to comfy terry cloth robes. Wrap yourself in one and head for the sauna, steam room, and hot tub. Many of the 44 rooms feature windowed breakfast nooks. Step from the lodge to the high-speed quad chairlifts that—winter and summer—ascend Mount Tod. Also here is the Val Senales fine dining room, where a buffet breakfast (included) and multicourse dinners are prepared. Tucked into the ground floor is the resort's best-kept secret: the Stube, a traditional European wine cellar where lunch, après-ski, and late-evening fare is served amid cozy wood paneling. *$$$–$$$$; MC, V; no checks; info@ sunpeakslodge; www.sunpeakslodge; in the heart of Sun Peaks Resort.* &

The Okanagan Valley

The Okanagan Valley is almost arid enough to be a desert. Beloved for the unparalleled variety of its climate and landscape, the Okanagan has something for everyone: hoodoos, orchards, vineyards, mountains, valleys, lakes, highlands, ski slopes, and trails.

From Highway 1 east of Kamloops, at Monte Creek, Highway 97 runs south to the head of Okanagan Lake at Vernon. As you head down the valley, you'll encounter orchards and vineyards, testimony to the presence of some of the best fruit- and vegetable-growing land in the world, while dozens of parks surround 79-mile (128-km) Okanagan Lake. As you pass through the lush Oliver and Osoyoos regions, near the Canada-U.S. border, you'll find spectacular backcountry, with the remains of old mining settlements dotting the highway.

Vernon and Silver Star

The Okanagan, as it appears today, began developing over a century ago in Vernon (population 33,100). For decades this was one of the largest fruit-producing towns in the British Empire, thanks to the abundance of freshwater for irrigation—also great for swimming on those *hot* days. The creation of **SILVER STAR PROVINCIAL PARK** (Silver Star Rd, east of Hwy 97; 250/494-6500) in 1940 drew visitors away from the three surrounding lakes (Okanagan, Swan, and Kalamalka) into the Monashee Mountains. By the 1980s, **SILVER STAR MOUNTAIN RESORTS**, adjacent to the park, emerged as the main drawing card for winter recreation in the north Okanagan, offering 2,500 feet of vertical drop, 1,440 acres of skiable terrain, and 8 lifts. With its Victorian-style mining-town atmosphere, Silver Star cemented Vernon's reputation as a four-season destination. Downhill skiers, snowboarders, and mountain bikers use the resort's runs while cross-country skiers and snowshoers head out along the provincial park's 30 miles (50 km) of forested routes. In the 1990s, the establishment of the National Altitude Training Centre added status to the resort. For information, contact **VERNON TOURISM** (6326 Hwy 97 N; 250/542-1415 or 800/665-0795; verntour@junction.net; www.vernontourism.com), or **SILVER STAR MOUNTAIN RESORTS** (250/542-0224 or 800/663-4431; reserve@junction.net; www.silverstarmtn.com).

RESTAURANTS

The Eclectic Med Restaurant / ★★

3117 32ND ST, VERNON; 250/558-4646

Since May 1996, British-import Andrew Fradley's Eclectic Med Restaurant has been winning the hearts (and palates) of epicureans in Vernon. Mediterranean as much in style and attitude as menu influence, EM was voted "best romantic dinner" in the north Okanagan in 1999. Small wonder. One look at its Mexican clay tile flooring, butter-colored walls, wooden shutters, heavy jute sailcloth curtains, wovenback beechwood chairs, and birch tables, and you know you've entered another realm. Be transported by Caribbean, Thai, East Indian, and other cross-pollinating influences. Chilean sea bass, Moroccan lamb, salmon Tropicana, and Calypso pork top the extensive menu. These pairings harken back to North African–born Fradley's dozen years in Portugal before arriving in Canada. Cocktails are served casually in heavy-based tumblers, as are hefty 7-ounce portions of wine. Try the hand-mixed sangría, fresh-squeezed margaritas, or traditional martinis. The wine list is notable for a selection of reserve wines from Okanagan estate wineries, not generally available. *$$; AE, MC, V; no checks; lunch Mon–Fri, dinner every day; full bar; reservations recommended; at 32nd Ave in central Vernon.* &

LODGINGS

The Kickwillie Inn / ★★

SILVER STAR RESORT; 250/542-4548 OR 800/663-4431

Before the Kickwillie Inn, poised on the open slopes above Silver Star's mountain village, was converted to seven suites in the 1980s, this was Silver Star's day lodge. Today, it's still the best seat in town. Guests ski, snowboard, mountain bike, or walk from their door onto the slopes. Come and go as you please: each suite has its own private entrance, a spacious living area, full bath, and kitchen, plus outside ski lockers. Suites 1 and 2 enjoy mountain views and, along with Suite 3, boast fireplaces. In this sublime setting, the absence of television is a blessing, particularly for those who treasure time together. If you really can't unplug, a TV room is located beside the ski waxing room. The Kickwillie shares rooftop hot tubs next door at the Pinnacles. *$$$–$$$$; AE, MC, V; checks OK; reserve@junction.net; www.silverstarmtn.com; 14 miles (22 km) northeast of Vernon.*

Kelowna

Sprawled on the sides of Okanagan Lake's hourglass waist, Kelowna ("grizzly bear" in the native Okanagan dialect) is the largest (population 100,000)—and liveliest—city in the valley. **CALONA WINES** (1125 Richter St; 250/762-3332) became the Okanagan's first wine producer here in the 1930s; now more than 40 wineries operate here. Kelowna is a jumping-off point for outdoor fun, whether at the lakeside beach or exploring the nearby **MONASHEE MOUNTAINS**. The area also boasts 15 of the 37 **GOLF COURSES** between Vernon and Osoyoos. Most open in March, and some years golfers play into November. **T TIMES CENTRAL BOOKING SERVICE** (250/762-7844 or 800/689-4653) books tee times at most area courses. Kelowna even has its own version of the Loch Ness monster: Ogopogo. For more information on wineries and other activities, contact **KELOWNA VISITORS AND CONVENTION BUREAU** (544 Harvey Ave; 250/861-1515 or 800/663-4345; kvb@kelownachamber.org; www.kelownachamber.org).

RESTAURANTS

de Montreuil Restaurant / ★★★

368 BERNARD AVE, KELOWNA; 250/860-5508

Okanagan-born brothers Grant and Michael de Montreuil have introduced more than just original cooking to Kelowna's restaurant scene; they offer a fixed-price menu of "Cascadian cuisine" with a twist. Guests can choose two to four courses from appetizers (perhaps wild boar pâté with plum chutney), salads (sautéed hot and cold spinach with chorizo), soups (halibut broth with wild mushrooms), and entrees (wild sockeye glazed with lavender jelly or roasted free-range chicken infused with tarragon and lime on a bed of quartered potato, whole carrots, and snow peas). The kitchen favors locally grown organic ingredients. Everything on the menu (which can change overnight) bursts with just the right flavors and seasonings. Never expect the same thing twice at this 80-seat gallery restaurant. Diners can opt to order à la carte, but shouldn't. At lunch, things are more casual: sandwiches, burgers, and pizzas. Bottled microbrews only, and a wide representation of local estate, cottage, and farmgate wines. $$$–$$$$; AE, MC, V; no checks; lunch Mon–Fri, dinner every day; full bar; reservations recommended; demontreuil@home. com; corner of Pandosy. &

Doc Willoughby's Downtown Grill / ★

353 BERNARD, KELOWNA; 250/868-8288

New to Kelowna (and a hit from the moment it opened), Doc Willoughby's has a pub atmosphere, but isn't a pub. Darren Nicoll and Dave Willoughby (the restaurant is named for his grandfather) stripped this 1908 landmark in downtown Kelowna to the walls, then rebuilt it with wood salvaged from a century-old site in Vancouver's Gastown. Hardwood floors, solid maple tables, and a prominent bar (featuring nine custom-brewed draft beers) provide the atmosphere; upscale pub fare and regular live-music define the flavor. Shepherd's pie shares the billing with Arizona egg rolls. Cedar plank salmon is the priciest item on an affordable menu. Pizza, pasta, stir-fry, and hot-baked chocolate chip cookies with two scoops of vanilla ice cream and fudge sauce are other highlights. The wine bar features 14 of BC's Vintners Quality Alliance (VQA) wines. Triple your fun with a flight of three 2-ounce samples. Whatever your choice, you'll enjoy yourself. *$$; AE, MC, V; no checks; lunch Mon–Sat, dinner every day; full bar; reservations not necessary; docwilloughby@home.com; near Pandosy St.* &

Vintage Room / ★★★

1171 HARVEY AVE (COAST CAPRI HOTEL), KELOWNA; 250/860-6185

Arguably the best restaurant in the Okanagan, the elegant, pricey Vintage Room garners awards for the quality of its food, the depth of its wine list, and impeccable service. That it does so with stunning regularity is probably because the Vintage bends over backward to accommodate your every whim. Since it opened its doors in 1960, the Vintage Room has offered some of the most sophisticated food in the Okanagan Valley: classic fare such as escargot, chateaubriand, and lobster. Much of the restaurant's success is due to longtime maitre d' (and local boy) Bart Dorssers and Austrian-trained executive chef Herbert Ferner. Ferner originally trained as a *chef de patissier*. His sure touch with desserts is one of the Vintage's signatures. Monthly fresh sheets for food and wine ensure that presentations remain progressive and flamboyant. If you're planning a wine tour, ask Dorssers for some pointers (he has extensive firsthand knowledge of the local wine scene), and say we sent you. *$$; AE, DC, MC, V; no checks; lunch Mon–Fri, dinner every day, brunch Sun; full bar; reservations recommended; ground floor Coast Capri Hotel.* &

LODGINGS

The Grand Okanagan Resort / ★★★

1310 WATER ST, KELOWNA; 250/763-4500 OR 800/465-4651

"The Grand," as the staff of the red-roofed resort refer to it, could as easily be in San Diego as on the east side of Okanagan Lake. Its modernist design presents a dignified profile that harkens back to Kelowna's Mission past and proclaims the city's triumphant emergence from the desert. Rooms in the 10-story main tower have panoramic views—all are decorated in soft pastel shades. Suites on the 9th (smoking) and 10th (nonsmoking) floors enjoy their own lounge, where complimentary continental breakfast is served. Robes, newspapers delivered to the door, and underground parking are other perks. By far the best rooms, however, are the standards: floor-to-ceiling windows open onto French balconies, and coziness abides. Brew some in-room coffee while you plan your excursions to the nearby wine country, ski hills, bike trails, or golf courses. Or use the resort's fitness facility, complete with spa, hot tubs, saunas, and indoor/outdoor pool. Three restaurants, a pub, and an Internet cafe complement the resorts's big drawing card, the Lake City Casino. Beware the masked one-arm bandits. *$$$$; AE, DC, DIS, MC, V; business checks OK; reserve@grandokanagan.com; www.grandokanagan.com; ½ mile (1 km) west of Harvey.* &

Hotel Eldorado / ★★★

500 COOK RD, KELOWNA; 250/763-7500

Modeled after the Eldorado Arms Inn built in 1926 for an emigre Austrian countess, the current hotel was rebuilt in 1990 after a fire. Owner Jim Nixon meticulously restored the grand dame with hardwood floors, a stone fireplace, antique furnishings, and a great collection of Okanagan memorabilia. Make May and September reservations at least three months in advance; that's when national champion Gary Athans runs the hotel's water-ski school. But you don't have to attend class to rent a boat and equipment (wakeboards, skis, ropes, PFDs) from the Eldorado's marina. Winter rates include breakfast and lift tickets to nearby Big White Mountain (see below). Each of the 20 rooms features elegant touches such as antique armoires; most have private balconies, some even sport Jacuzzis. The hotel's restaurant fare is consistently excellent. Breakfast in its sunroom is an extremely pleasant way to wake up, particularly when a soft breeze wafts in off the lake. The local vineyards are well represented on the Eldorado's dining and bar menus. *$$–$$$; AE, DC, MC, V; no checks; jim@eldoradokelowna.com; www.sunnyokanagan/el; 4 miles (6.5 km) south of Okanagan Floating Bridge.* &

Lake Okanagan Resort / ★★

2751 WESTSIDE RD, KELOWNA; 250/769-3511 OR 800/ 663-3273

When Lake Okanagan Resort appeared on the scene in the 1980s, it had a dynamic impact on valley standards. For many years—and for many families—this was *the* place to stay, particularly in summer. Since then, it's been renovated throughout, and chef Dave Ryan has worked wonders with the menu at Chateau, the resort dinner restaurant. Dining out is a pleasant option here, though all accommodations come with kitchens. Most sought-after are Jacuzzi suites on the top floor of the Kingfisher, the resort's central facility. Each includes a living room, entertainment center, kitchenette, dining area, full bath with separate bedroom and king bed, a Jacuzzi tub, and private balcony. At the north end of the property are 13 three-bedroom condos and chalets in a parklike setting. Getting around the 300-acre property can be a challenge; the hillside rises steeply above the private beach and though chalets and condos have a gentler incline, they're farther from the beach. The resort boasts some of the finest tennis courts in the Okanagan, and a nine-hole, par-3 golf course. This is the perfect place to turn your kids loose and let everyone do their own thing. *$$–$$$; AE, MC, V; checks OK; info@lakeokanagan.com; www.lakeokanagan.com; 10½ miles (17 km) north of Kelowna.* &

Big White

BIG WHITE SKI RESORT (Big White Rd, 14 miles/23 km east of Hwy 33; 800/663-2772; bigwhite@silk.net or cenres@bigwhite.com; www.bigwhite. com) is an easy hour southeast of Kelowna on the western perimeter of the Monashees. This mountain village boasts the highest elevation of any winter resort in BC, offering 2,500 feet of vertical drop, 2,075 acres of skiable terrain, and seven lifts. In winter, you can ski from the door of your condominium, lodge, or vehicle. But once you arrive at Big White, you have to leave your wheels behind. As the horse-drawn wagon that serves as local transportation trots by, hop on; park yourself on a hay bale and let the team of vapor-snorting Percherons do the rest.

A variety of on-hill accommodations can be arranged through **BIG WHITE CENTRAL RESERVATIONS** (800/663-2772). Restaurants—**RAAKEL'S, SNOW-SHOE SAMS,** and **THE LOOSE MOOSE TAP & GRILLE** are best bets—dot the village, as well as a small grocery and liquor store.

LODGINGS

White Crystal Inn / ★★

BIG WHITE RD, KELOWNA; 800/663-2772
What was considered one of the best small resort hotels in Canada has grown. With the addition of a new wing, this classic four-story chalet went from 20 rooms to 50. So successful was the original design that Big White Resort copied it for the new Chateau Big White nearby. But they couldn't replicate the White Crystal's impeccable location adjacent to Bullet Alley, a run that leads directly to the resort's high-speed quad chairlifts. The White Crystal retains its intimacy. All rooms are outfitted in cedar and slate; each comes with a fireplace, two queen-size beds, and a small kitchen. For larger groups, some rooms feature lofts with three single beds. Downstairs you'll find a sauna, ski and snowboard lockers, plus heated parking. On the lodge's main floor are the Grizzly Bear Restaurant and Fireside Bistro. A generous buffet breakfast is included, served in the brightly lit bistro with woody Canadiana accents. Room service is also available. *$$$; AE, MC, V; checks OK; cenres@bigwhite.com; www.bigwhite.com; on right as you enter resort.*

Naramata

From Kelowna heading south on rugged Naramata Road you'll find **OKANAGAN LAKE PROVINCIAL PARK** (west side of Okanagan Lake on Hwy 97, 15 miles/24 km north of Penticton; 250/494-6500) with dramatic prospects. Sage-covered slopes and bleached headlands jut out into the broad lake. On the southeast side of Okanagan Lake, 10 miles (16 km) north of Penticton, Naramata is surrounded by vineyards and orchards.

RESTAURANTS
The Country Squire / ★★★

3950 1ST ST, NARAMATA; 250/496-5416

On the eve of their third decade, chef Patt Dyck and her husband (and maitre d'), Ron, show no sign of flagging. They've found a winning—and unique—formula. Be prepared to order your entree when you make a reservation. From there, Patt designs a five-course meal to complement your selection. Choices include beef tenderloin robed in pâté de fois gras and mushroom duxelle, then wrapped in puff pastry and served with brown and béarnaise sauces. The dish is "celebrated" tableside—a German term for carved and flambéed. Other options are Madagascar-style pork tenderloin, steak Diane, rack of lamb, boneless breast of French guinea fowl, Pacific prawns shelled and broiled in seasoned butter and fresh shallot sauce, and fillet of sea bass baked in edible parchment paper. An outstanding tenderloin of locally raised venison is marinated in red wine, fresh herbs, and juniper berries, then roasted and served with a black muscat, red currant, and black currant sauce. The wine list is as deep as Okanagan Lake. *$$; MC, V; local checks only; dinner Wed–Sun; full bar; reservations required; csquire@vip.net; www.country-squire.com; follow 1st St north along lake.* &

LODGINGS
Sandy Beach Lodge & Resort / ★★★

4275 MILL RD, NARAMATA; 250/496-5765

The resort's cabins are completely booked two years in advance for July and August (priority is given to returning guests). That said, six bed-and-breakfast rooms in the log lodge are still up for grabs—and are a real bargain at this retreat on Okanagan Lake. Each has its own private, covered veranda overlooking the lake. Lighted tennis courts, a swimming pool, and hot tub bookend the lodge, which also houses a restaurant and a bright sitting room dominated by a fieldstone hearth. Half of the 13 two-bedroom cabins sit on the wide swath of private beach, while the rest are nestled just a stone's throw behind; each accommodates up to six. Green lawns between them are perfect for croquet. Everything is immaculate and looks as if it just opened yesterday. May and September are pleasant months to visit, when competition for the resort's rowboats and canoes is less fierce. Cabins are closed November through February, but the lodge remains open. Ask about special cabin rates September and October, and March through June (two-day minimum stay). *$$$–$$$$; MC, V; no checks; mlnewton@vip.net; www.sandybeachresort.com; end of Mill Rd off Robson.* &

Penticton

Penticton, the "Peach City" (population 32,000), might just as easily be called Festival City. It always has some serious fun going on, including the rockin'-good-time **AUGUST PEACH FESTIVAL** (250/493-4055 or 800/663-5052), now in its sixth decade; weeklong wine festivals in May and October; a three-day microbrewery festival in April; the May **MEADOWLARK FESTIVAL** (250/492-5275; www.meadowlarkfestival.bc.ca), a nature festival in Penticton and nearby Okanagan Mountain Provincial Park celebrating the return of the meadowlark, a barometer species; a campy **BEACH BLANKET FILM FESTIVAL** (250/493-4055 or 800/663-5052) in July; and a jazz festival in September. **TOURISM PENTICTON** (185 Lakeshore Dr; 250/493-4055 or 800/663-5052; tourism@img.net; www.penticton.org) has more information on all festivals.

Oenophiles who want to plot a **WINE TOUR** itinerary (and those who simply aspire to informed conversation on the 300-plus varieties of wine produced in the region) should visit the **BC WINE INFORMATION CENTRE** (888 Westminster Ave W; 250/490-2006; www.bcwineinfo.com).

APEX MOUNTAIN RESORT is 21 miles (33 km) west of town (on Green Mountain Rd; 250/292-8222 or 877/777-2739; info@apexresort.com; www. apexresort.com). With more than 60 runs, including an amazing series of black-diamond powder chutes on the slopes below Beaconsfield Mountain (elevation 7,187 feet/2,178 m), Apex more than holds its own. It has 2,000 feet of vertical drop, 550 acres of skiable terrain, and four lifts. Most visitors eschew the on-hill accommodations and stay in Penticton, a 30-minute drive to the lifts.

RESTAURANTS

Granny Bogner's Restaurant / ★★★

320 ECKHARDT AVE, PENTICTON; 250/493-2711

One of the Okanagan's best restaurants is also one of the most consistent: great food, great location, great building, and desserts that alone make the trip worthwhile. Diners relax in front of the fireplace in the rambling Arts and Crafts–style house with a glass of wine or after-dinner coffee. The menu covers a broad spectrum, but it's presentation that sets Granny Bogner's apart. Entrees arrive garnished with an eye for color and shape; vegetables are artfully arranged. Chef Peter Hebel loves to play with shrimp, crab, or smoked salmon. Start with the baked oysters casino, or perhaps the bouillabaisse (a real bargain). Fillets of halibut, red snapper, or salmon Courtenay poached in white wine and glazed with hollandaise sauce comes next. Hebel's Swiss background shines in beef rouladen with red cabbage and spaetzle; also good is the chateaubriand bouquetière in béarnaise sauce. Dessert specials often use fresh local fruit. The wine list represents the best local estate wineries, including highly vaunted Okanagan ice wines. *$$$$; AE, MC, V; no checks; dinner Tues–Sat; full bar; reservations recommended; 2 blocks south of Main.* &

LODGINGS

God's Mountain Crest Chalet / ★★★

4898 LAKESHORE RD, PENTICTON; 250/490-4800

At God's Mountain Crest Chalet, Martha Stewart might meet her match in owner Ulric Lejeune. Interior-designer Lejeune and his wife, Ghitta, have created the Club Med of bed-and-breakfasts. The rambling Mediterranean-style mansion overlooks the broad Skaha Lake, and the rolling hills beyond. Step inside to find an eclectic blend of curios, antiques, and subtle religious iconography. Scarves drape the length of the 60-foot grand salon. Quiet pervades, even at breakfast, when guests gather for a sumptuous epicurean buffet. Sit in the shrouded intimacy of an opium bed or at the glass-topped table where conversation swirls around Lejeune's Teutonic presence. (On request, breakfasts are served to guest rooms on silver trays.) Guests are quartered in nine rooms and suites spread over three floors. Request Suite 5: tastefully appointed, it features a raised tub with lake views. All suites open onto verandas or private balconies, and are fitted with reflective glass for privacy and temperature control. A large swimming pool and hot tub (for late-night stargazing) are surrounded by gardens and orderly rows of grapevines. *$$; MC, V; checks OK; www.godsmountain.com; 3 miles (5 km) south of Penticton.*

Oliver and Osoyoos

The 12-mile (20-km) stretch of Highway 97 between Oliver (population 4,500) and Osoyoos (population 4,000) boasts the most vibrant agricultural land in the valley. Over the past three decades, this has become the preferred grape-growing region: one-quarter of the 40-plus wineries in the Okanagan are located near Oliver. Despite Osoyoos's Spanish decor, a close inspection of names on roadside fruit stands and orchards demonstrates a Portuguese leaning. Immigration from the Azores intensified in the 1950s along with arrivals from Germany, Hungary, and more recently India. And an influx of retirees spurred the construction of golf courses, pubs, and hotels; fixed incomes help keep prices moderate. **OSOYOOS CHAMBER OF COMMERCE** (Hwys 3 and 97; 250/495-6161 or 888/676-9667; tourism@osoyooschamber.ca; www.town.osoyoos.bc.ca; www.oliverchronicle.com) has information.

RESTAURANTS

Jacques' Neighbourhood Grill / ★★

34646 HWY 97, OLIVER; 250/498-4418

Jacques' Neighbourhood Grill is the place to taste the region's natural abundance. Chef Jacques Guerin and his wife (and manager), Suzi, have been serving it right since 1977. Seasonal vegetables grace dishes such as roast garlic and potato soup; fresh salads include sautéed apple wrapped in phyllo with goat cheese on mixed greens with balsamic vinaigrette and roasted walnuts; and inspired entrees such as medallions of pork slowly grilled with maple syrup and garnished with gingered pear compote and port demi-glace tempt the palate. Chicken and seafood are other routes to follow. *Specialite de la maison* is Jacques' pepper steak. Guerin's classical touch betrays his Parisian roots. The wine-cellar atmosphere is completed by a wood-beamed ceiling, built by legendary Okanagan wine pioneer Joe Busnardo. Jacques' features an extensive list of local wines. For privacy, request seating in Jacques' intimate grotto. *$$$; AE, MC, V; no checks; dinner Tues–Sun (closed Oct and Jan); full bar; reservations recommended; miro58@hotmail.com; downtown at 346th St.*

LODGINGS

Vaseux Lake Lodge / ★☆

9710 SUNDIAL RD, OLIVER; 250/498-0516

Billed as the smallest resort in the Okanagan, Vaseux Lake Lodge consists of four townhomes. The two-story lodge's hidden beauty is revealed once you step inside and view the lake. Sunlight floods through skylights in the vaulted ceiling, as well as through floor-to-ceiling windows on the main floor. Scandinavian furnishings and down duvets provide understated warmth. Each unit has its own library with books on the region's natural history. Since 1922, Vaseux Lake has been a designated wildlife sanctuary. Each season has its own attractions. In spring and fall, birdwatchers flock here. No powerboats are allowed on the shallow 2½-mile (4-km) lake. Paddle with turtles and beavers, and watch as eagles and osprey practice fishing skills while bighorn sheep frolic on the slopes of McIntyre Bluff. Bring your binoculars as well as your beach toys. The one-bedroom, one-bath townhomes are self-contained and completely outfitted, including full kitchens (groceries are available in nearby Oliver) and barbecues, but guests should arrange their own boats and bikes. *$$–$$$; MC, V; checks OK; vaseux@tnet.net; vvv.com/~vaseux; south end of Vaseux Lake, one block west of Hwy 97.*

Keremeos

LODGINGS

Cathedral Lakes Lodge / ★★

CATHEDRAL PROVINCIAL PARK; 250/226-7560 (SEASONAL) OR 888/255-4453

Cathedral Lakes Resort is tucked deep in the heart of the Cascades, so getting here is half the adventure. Set below a stunning catalog of peaks, the rustic lodge may inspire you to try backcountry camping here on the Canada-U.S. border. Ridge rambling is made significantly easier for guests (and campers by prior arrangement) courtesy of the lodge's 4x4 pickup service. They do the driving on the 13-mile (21-km) fire road that climbs to 6,798 feet (2,072 m). Hiking trails lead from the lodge to the craggy peaks above, where you'll get views of the Cascade Range's Mount Baker and Mount Rainier, and the volcanic tableau visible from Lakeview Mountain. Or launch a canoe on Lake Quiniscoe, one of four trout-stocked lakes close to the lodge.

If you're a duo, reserve Herb Clark's circa 1930s cabin; *amore rustica* never looked so good. Ten other cabins offer a variety of room configurations. The lodge's all-inclusive American Plan comes with pack lunches for summiteers. Book well ahead. *$$–$$$; no credit cards; checks OK; open Jun–Oct, 2-night min; info@cathedral-lakes-lodge.com; www.cathedral-lakes-lodge.com; turn south on Ashnola River Rd, 3 miles (5 km) west of Keremeos, then 13 miles (21 km) to lodge base camp.*

The Kootenays

The Kootenays, east of the Okanagan on Highway 3, are a world of two minds. Yahk, a small town on Highway 3 between Creston and Cranbrook, marks the great divide between the western and eastern hemispheres of this cranial conundrum. It's hard to finger what exactly characterizes the difference between the west and east Kootenays. Winter sunlight barely brushes the steep-sided valleys of the west Kootenays, but residents can escape cabin fever in several lively towns, such as Castlegar, Nelson, or Trail. In contrast, a brilliant winter sun splashes cheerily down on the broad slopes of the Columbia and Elk Valleys in the east Kootenays. Out here there are far fewer signs of human habitation. Open grasslands stretch out on all sides while the Rockies preside sedately above. Yet those who know this region well refer to all of it simply as "deep country."

Throughout both the east and west Kootenay regions winds the majestic **COLUMBIA RIVER**, with its source in Columbia Lake near the town of Fairmont Hot Springs on the Rockies' western slopes. The river flows north for over 186 miles (300 km) before hooking west and south to begin its long journey—over 250 miles (400 km)—to the U.S. border. For nearly half this length, it widens to form **UPPER AND LOWER ARROW LAKES**, vast reservoirs of water that moderate winter temperatures and help retain moisture in the local atmosphere, thus greatly influencing the types of vegetation found there.

Transportation in the Kootenays is primarily by road, which might involve changing between Pacific and Mountain time zones from one town to the next, because only part of the east Kootenays (mainly from Creston to Yahk) remains on Mountain Standard Time year-round. Another time zone transition point is on the Trans-Canada Highway (Hwy 1) between Revelstoke and Golden in BC's Glacier National Park.

Rossland

In the years before multimillion-dollar high-speed quad chairlifts, it was possible to make your own ski lift for less than $1,000. All it took was a length of sturdy rope, a few wooden towers, some pulleys, and an engine with adequate horsepower. One such rig was erected on Rossland's Red Mountain. As time went on, a progressive group of local skiers installed western Canada's first chairlift here in 1947. Of course, if you had powder skiing at your door the way the folks in Rossland do, you'd want the newest-fangled technology too. So fabled are the snow conditions in this tucked-away town that a century ago Red Mountain hosted the first Canadian Ski Jumping and Ski Racing Championships. That was in the early days of mining in the region, an industry that still stokes the local economy. One of the Scandinavian miners, Olaus Jeldness, not only organized the championships but won the event. The mountain has produced two of the best women skiers to ever represent Canada, Olympic gold medal winners Nancy Greene Raine and Kerrin Lee-Gartner.

At 3,356 feet (1,023 m) elevation, Rossland (population 3,500) is snugly perched close to **RED MOUNTAIN SKI AREA** (3 miles/5 km north of Rossland on Hwy 3B; 250/362-7700, 250/362-7384, or 800/663-0105; redmtn@ski-red. com or redmtn@wkpowerlink.com; www.ski-red.com), which offers 2,900 feet of vertical drop, 1,200 acres of skiable terrain, and six lifts. The **BLACK JACK CROSS-COUNTRY SKI CLUB** (Hwy 3B; 250/362-5811; www.rossland.com/blackjack) lies next to Red Mountain. More than 50 kilometers of packed and tracked trails lead from here through evergreen forests, across frozen lakes, and past abandoned homesteads.

Rossland, once called the Golden City, now bills itself as Canada's "Alpine City," with popular annual festivals like January's **WINTER CARNIVAL**, first held in 1897, and the **RUBBERHEAD MOUNTAIN BIKE FESTIVAL** (near Labor Day). The **CHAMBER OF COMMERCE** (2185 Columbia Ave, Le Roi Mall; 250/362-5666, or 250/362-7722 mid-May–mid-Sept; www.rossland.com) has information.

Stroll the town's steep streets to admire the solid construction of the **MINERS' UNION HALL** (1895) on Columbia Street, the **FLYING STEAMSHOVEL INN** (1898) and the **ROSSLAND LIGHT OPERA BUILDING** (1911) on Washington Street, and **ST. ANDREW'S UNITED CHURCH** (1898) on Queen Street. The scale of the heritage buildings that line many of Rossland's streets indicate the boom times and glory years of a century ago.

RESTAURANTS

Sunshine Cafe / ★

2116 COLUMBIA AVE, ROSSLAND; 250/362-7630

Virtually anyone feels a bit of shine in Rossland's favorite little cafe, which features a range of internationally inspired foods. The food doesn't try to be fancy, just good, and there's lots of it. Start with the Malaysian egg rolls (ground beef, coconut, and spices) dipped in a plum sauce, then go on to one of the Mexican dishes, the Budgie Burger (boneless chicken breast with ham or Swiss), or curried chicken. Huevos rancheros are a breakfast favorite. Mealtimes are crowded, especially during ski season. *$; MC, V; local checks only; breakfast, lunch, dinner every day; beer and wine; reservations recommended; sunshine@netidea.com; www.rossland.com/sunshine; just east of Queen St.*

LODGINGS

Angela's Bed & Breakfast / ★★

1540 SPOKANE ST, ROSSLAND; 250/362-7790

 It's one thing to stay with a knowledgeable host—that's what makes bed-and-breakfasts special—but quite another to find your host might be your ski guide. That's part of the charm of staying at Angela Price's creekside home. Price has spent a lifetime pursuing her passion for powder, both here at Red Mountain and elsewhere in Canada and Colorado. That quest is what draws guests here. The comfort provided at Angela's is as attractive as the quality (and quantity) of Kootenay snow. Guests choose between a pair of two-bedroom suites with separate entrances. One has a fireplace in the master bedroom, an ancient carved church window, and a redwood hot tub just outside the door. The other has a full kitchen. Beds are draped with comfy down duvets, and all guests feel spoiled by Price's attention to detail. Breakfasts are guaranteed to fortify you for a day in the steeps: oatmeal, eggs Benedict, organic jams, and serious coffee. If you time it right, you might also get an invite to Angela's annual February oyster bash. *$$; MC; checks OK; closed summers; 4 blocks from Uplander Hotel.*

Ram's Head Inn / ★★

RED MOUNTAIN RD, ROSSLAND; 250/362-9577 OR 877/267-4323

The Ram's Head Inn has been singled out by more than one travel guide as *the* place to stay in the Kootenays, despite the competition for that honor. What sets the Ram's Head apart is its cozy size—34 guests maximum—and little touches, such as a pair of slippers waiting for you at the door. The inn's mountain setting also works in its favor. Conversation comes easily among guests as they gather for an early morning breakfast or relax on an overstuffed couch beside the towering granite fireplace after a day exploring nearby trails. Guests have a choice of 13 rooms with private baths; the larger ones have balconies. All are furnished with hand-hewn timber beds, wicker chairs, maple armoires, eiderdown comforters, TVs, and telephones. The ground floor (hidden from view by snowbanks in winter) is taken up with ski lockers, a waxing room, a games room with pool table, and a sauna. A barrel-shaped hot tub steams outside. Ask about the reasonably priced ski packages. *$$–$$$; AE, DC, DIS, MC, V; checks OK; theinn@ramshead.bc.ca; www.ramshead.bc.ca; off Hwy 3B at Red Mountain.*

Slocan Lake

A century ago, **NEW DENVER** was a mining town; today it's the modest commercial hub of the Slocan Valley. Visit the town's **SILVERY SLOCAN MUSEUM** (202 6th Ave, New Denver; 250/358-2201) to get the complete picture on its pioneer past. During World War II, an internment camp at New Denver housed some 2,000 Japanese-Canadians displaced from their West Coast homes. A replica of the 1945 Peace Arch, symbolizing harmony and peace between all peoples, commemorates the memory of this painful time, at the **NIKKEI INTERNMENT MEMORIAL CENTRE** (306 Josephine St, New Denver; 250/358-2663; June–Sept, 9:30am–5pm).

VALHALLA PROVINCIAL PARK (west side of Slocan Lake off Hwy 6; 250/825-3500) is a magnificent world-class wilderness area including nearly 20 miles (30 km) of the pristine wilderness shoreline of Slocan Lake. According to Norse mythology, Valhalla was a palace roofed with shields wherein lived the bravest of the slain Norse warriors. There, under the god Odin, they lived a happy life waiting for the day they would march out of the palace and do battle with the giants. The spirit of Valhalla lives on in the splendor of this portion of southeastern BC, where great palaces of rock call forth majestic images with names such as Asgard, Gimli, and Thor.

The Valhalla Range is a dramatically diverse area in the Selkirks. Deep river valleys, large subalpine lakes and magnificent granite peaks to 9,275 feet (2,827 m) grace this park. In the northwest, New Denver Glacier (9,049 feet/ 2,758 m) dominates the landscape. Boat across Slocan Lake to the park from Highway 6 between Slocan and New Denver to reach most of this wilderness. Slocan, Silverton, and New Denver, the closest communities, all have boat launches.

LODGINGS

Silverton Resort / ★

LAKE AVE, SILVERTON; 250/358-7157

You'll be pleased with this little resort in the heart of Hidden Valley. Bill Lander's cabins on the shores of Slocan Lake are a great place for water play; bring your own canoe, kayak, or rowboat, or rent one. Mountain bikes are available too. One of the under-reported stories of the resort is that it's a great place to do nothing—just sit on the sundeck and enjoy the view. The lake is so large that it remains ice free year-round. Guest stay in one of six hemlock-log cabins—all spotlessly clean and named after mythological heroes. Four have sleeping lofts; all have kitchens and south-facing decks and are at the water's edge (though not far from the road). In winter, the fireplace in cabin 4 (Thor) adds a special touch to its charm, while cabin 1 doubles as a sauna. Also available is the 1,200-square-foot main lodge, with a washer and dryer, large country-style kitchen, living/dining area on the main floor, and two large bedrooms upstairs. It accommodates up to eight. The lakefront resort backed by a glacier in Valhalla Provincial Park is pure heaven—but plenty of others feel the same, so make July and August reservations no later than March. $$–$$$; MC, V; checks OK; www. silvertonresort.com; on lakeshore beside Hwy 6. &

Nakusp

Nakusp occupies a crook in the arm of Upper Arrow Lake and is set squarely between the Monashee and Selkirk Mountains. This is hot spring country. Along Highway 23 between Nakusp and Galena Bay at the northern end of Upper Arrow Lake are two commercial and four wilderness springs. You can't drive to the wilderness springs in winter (backroads aren't plowed), although you can reach them on snowshoes or skis.

LODGINGS

Halcyon Hot Springs Resort

HWY 23, NAKUSP; 250/265-3554 OR 888/689-4699

Like the proverbial phoenix, Halcyon Hot Springs Resort rose from the ashes of its long-defunct predecessor, which operated here between the 1890s and the 1950s. (In between, visitors climbed the hillside above Arrow Lake to soak in a remnant rustic timber pool.) Opened in 1999, the new resort sits on the shore of Arrow Lake. Mount Thor dominates the skyline to the west. One- and two-bedroom chalets sleep up to six and are equipped with en suite bathrooms, kitchenettes, TVs, phones, and sundecks. Nearby, in the sheltering forest, are four cabins that each sleep six on twin bunks and a double futon. Cabin guests share a communal bathroom. A licensed restaurant is located in the main building. Halcyon in Greek means "calm, serene," and that's how one feels after bathing in the two hottest pools, kept at 95°F (35°C) and 107°F (42°C). The cold plunge pool is a bracing 55°F (13°C). An outdoor swimming pool (83°F/28°C) is open in summer. Mineral analysis of the water reveals a higher quantity of lithia, a natural relaxant, than any spring in this thermally active region. *$$–$$$; AE, MC, V; no checks; halcyon@cancom.net; www. halcyon-hotspings.com; 20 miles (32 km) north of Nakusp.* &

Kaslo

New Denver anchors scenic Highway 31A as it snakes east for 29 miles (47 km) through mining country to Kaslo. Along the way, it follows the railbed of the Kaslo & Slocan Railway, and passes the ghost towns of Zincton, Retallack, Three Forks, and Sandon. Don't expect to make time on this exciting, rock-and-rolling road, but it's a picturesque alternate route to Nelson.

Much like the beached stern-wheeler **S.S. MOYIE** (324 Front St; 250/353-2525; ssmoyie@pop.kin.bc.ca; www.kin.bc.ca/moyie/moyiehome1; open daily, 9:30am–5pm, mid-May–mid-Sept), this former mining hub on **KOOTENAY LAKE** retains the flavor of its glory years. The steamer was affectionately known as "the sweetheart of the lake" in her heyday.

RESTAURANTS

The Rosewood Cafe / ★★

1435 FRONT ST, KASLO; 250/353-7673

The Rosewood has a loyal clientele of grown-ups (and kids) who visit from as far afield as Spokane, Washington. Reservations are a must in summer, when tourists flock to Kaslo. The fact that chef Grant Mackenzie does much of his cooking outdoors on an 8-foot barbecue helps. You'll smell the Rosewood long before you reach its white picket fence. Since it opened in 1994, the capacity has expanded to 125 seats, 55 of which are on a spacious patio overlooking Kootenay Lake. Each year the menu is completely revised. Many dishes are available in both half- and full-size, because portions are typically large in this part of the world. Everything on the menu is made fresh daily and tastes like it, from mayonnaise to bread to sauces. Alberta prime rib, local venison, blackened BC red snapper, and jambalaya are specialties. Numerous vegetarian selections, such as tortellini with curried tomato sauce, reflect chef Mackenzie's multicultural influences. Principal dishes are available all day, and a fresh sheet of 8 to 10 daily specials provides even more choice. The Rosewood prides itself on the depth (and breadth) of its wine and cocktail menu. *$$$; MC, V; local checks only; lunch, dinner every day, brunch Sun (closed Jan); full bar; reservations recommended; rosewood@netidea.com; at east end of Front St.* &

Ainsworth Hot Springs

Ainsworth Hot Springs is a sleepy spot on Highway 31, about 30 miles (50 km) north of Nelson, that was a boomtown during the heyday of silver, zinc, and galena (lead ore) mining in the Kootenays a century ago. Today, if it weren't for the hot springs, it's likely that few travelers would slow down through the small community perched above **KOOTENAY LAKE**—almost 99 miles (160 km) long, it's one of BC's largest freshwater lakes.

AINSWORTH HOT SPRINGS RESORT (10 miles/16 km north of Balfour on Hwy 31; 250/825-3500, 250/229-4212, or 800/668-1171; www.hotnaturally. com) boasts a most unusual setting, a former mine shaft entrance into which several steamy springs vent. Hot water drips from the rough-hewn granite ceiling and flows waist-deep through a narrow, horseshoe-shaped tunnel into the resort's large outdoor pool. Mist trapped in the tunnel thickens the air, further augmenting the subterranean experience. Mineral deposits left by hot springs that seep down the sides of the tunnel have coated the walls with a smooth, ceramiclike glaze in shades of white, red, and green. The overall effect is mind bending. Water inside the caves reaches 111°F (44°C) or hotter; in the nearby glacier-fed plunge pool it's a frigid 39°F (4°C). Water in the swimming pool is a calming 95°F (35°C). Lodgings and a restaurant are available.

Crawford Bay

The tiny community of Crawford Bay, accessible via an hour's ferry ride across Kootenay Lake from Balfour on Highway 3A, is home to one of BC's finest golf courses, **KOKANEE SPRINGS GOLF COURSE** (16082 Woolgar Rd; 250/227-9226). Just up from the ferry dock is **LA CHANCE SWISS RESTAURANT** (16818 Hwy 3A; 250/227-9477; Apr–Oct) a local hangout with a menu that leans toward Swiss and German fare.

LODGINGS
Wedgwood Manor / ★★

16002 CRAWFORD CREEK RD, CRAWFORD BAY; 250/227-9233
OR 800/862-0022

On 50 acres that tilt west toward the Selkirks, this lovely 1910 board-and-batten house is one of the finest lodgings in southeastern British Columbia. Downstairs are a dining room and a parlor with a fireplace (where afternoon tea is served). Six rooms have private baths. The four spacious upstairs rooms open onto a quiet, comfortable reading room; the Charles Darwin Room and the Commander's Room get most afternoon sun. The room off the parlor is tiny, but has a big garden view from the double bed. In summer, the large front porch is a pleasant spot from which to gaze out over the lawn and flower gardens to Kokanee Glacier across the lake. The owners have taken over the former servants' quarters next door. *$$; MC, V; checks OK; open Apr–mid-Oct; wedgwood@lightwave.bc.ca; www.bctravel.net/wedgwood; east of Nelson on Hwy 3A, take Balfour ferry to Kootenay Bay.* &

Nelson

Nestled in a valley on the shore of Kootenay Lake south of Balfour, Nelson (population 9,200) sprang up with the silver and gold mining boom in the late 1890s, and has retained its Victorian character. Its main streets have changed little in a century, luring more than one filmmaker here. More than 350 heritage homes and commercial buildings are listed in this picturesque city. Pick up a map (or join a free guided tour in summer) at the TOURIST INFORMATION BUREAU (225 Hall St; 250/352-3433). Built on a hillside above the Kootenay River, Nelson's steep stretches are best scaled in sturdy shoes. For the grandest overall view of Nelson, stroll to the vista point in GYRO PARK (corner of Park and Morgan Sts; 250/352-5511), on a hillside just north of the town center. The park has picturesque gardens and a wading pool. The lookout has a panoramic vista of the town, Kootenay Lake, and the rock and ice formations that rise above.

An interesting pictorial exhibit of the region's history is at the NELSON MUSEUM (402 Anderson St; 250/352-9813; open year-round). From theatrical productions to wildlife lectures to classical guitarists to nationally known folk-rock groups, something is almost always going on at the CAPITOL THEATRE (421 Victoria St; 250/352-6363). The entire town turns into an art gallery, with artists' work exhibited in almost 20 shops, restaurants, and galleries during the ARTWALK GALLERY TOURS (250/352-2402; June–Aug); pick up a map at the Tourist Information Bureau. For a calendar of weekly events, pick up a free copy of the *Kootenay Weekly Express*, at local businesses around town.

Nelson has raised afternoon browsing to a fine art. In addition to the many galleries, there are a plethora of other interesting shops in the downtown area. Outdoor enthusiasts stop at SNOWPACK OUTDOOR EXPERIENCES, together with Canada's only PATAGONIA factory outlet (333 Baker St; 250/352-6411), in the basement of Snowpack. For art and crafts by regional artists, visit the

CRAFT CONNECTION (441 Baker St; 250/352-3006). The KOOTENAY BAKER (295 Baker St; 250/352-2274) boasts one of the best selections of health foods in the region, including organic baked goods.

The mountains surrounding Nelson are a Mecca for hikers, backcountry skiers, and sightseers; a popular destination is KOKANEE GLACIER PROVINCIAL PARK (18 miles/29 km northeast of Nelson off Hwy 3A; 250/825-3500). South of town on Highway 6 toward Salmo are the CLEARWATER CREEK CROSS-COUNTRY SKI TRAILS, also called the Apex-Bush Cross-Country Ski Area (7 miles/11 km south of Nelson; 250/352-6411), an extensive system of groomed trails maintained by the Nelson Nordic Ski Club. Your initial reaction to WHITEWATER SKI AREA (about 12 miles/19 km south of Nelson on Hwy 6; 250/352-4944 or 800/666-9420; 250/352-7669 snow report; info@ skiwhitewater.com; www.skiwhitewater.com) in the Selkirk Range ultimately depends on what's important to you in a downhill skiing/snowboarding vacation. In an age of on-slope sushi bars and handcrafted microbreweries at the base of the lifts, Whitewater represents a Zen approach to ski development; it's basically four ski lifts strung up in the wilderness. Or you might see it as big peaks; a ton of light, dry powder; and some rudimentary, no-nonsense lifts to get you to the top. Whitewater's high base elevation of 5,400 feet (1,640 m) ensures plentiful snow, few midseason thaws, 1,300 feet of vertical drop, and 2,000 acres of skiable terrain.

RESTAURANTS

All Seasons Cafe / ★★

620 HERRIDGE LN, NELSON; 250/352-0101

In business since 1995, All Seasons Cafe is downtown, but on a narrow lane that takes a while to find. A storybook ambience envelops those who finally reach its doors. For a quick meal, ask for a seat near the bar. Sip a microbrew while you marvel at the smooth texture of the gravlax appetizer. Otherwise, ask for a table in the garden; overhead heaters ensure warmth even on cool spring or fall evenings. Art in the main dining room prompts an opinion should conversation lag. All Seasons' professed style of "Left Coast Inland Cuisine" leads to seriously scented dishes, such as halibut or prawns, prepared by chefs Gordon Rothenberg and Derek Laframboise. A steady stream of fresh sage-and-oregano bread arrives by the basket (ask to take a loaf home). Try the venison sausage in tomato sauce, followed by warm peach and polenta upside-down cake. Sunday brunch features delicacies such as an asparagus and Brie flan with Italian figs and warm honey. *$$$; MC, V; local checks only; dinner every day, brunch Sun; full bar; reservations recommended; allseas@netidea.com; between Hall and Josephine.* ✆

Fiddler's Green / ★★

2710 LOWER 6 MILE RD, NELSON; 250/825-4466

Summer dining is best, but regardless of the season, this is Nelson's favorite spot for a special-occasion dinner. Locals may quibble over whether the food is the best in town, but they agree unanimously that this old estate house has the best atmosphere and garden dining. Choose from three intimate dining rooms and one larger area (if the season calls for inside dining, ask to sit next to the fireplace). As the seasons change, chef Mark Giffin ushers in new menu offerings such as a warm roasted winter vegetable and goat cheese tart. Though it serves many reliable chicken, beef, pork, and lamb entrees, Fiddler's Green caters to a growing local fondness for vegetarian and seafood dishes. Try crisp artichoke and chickpea falafel on a bed of steamed spinach with quinoa tabbouleh and lemon parsley yogurt. The delicious house salad is a blend of locally grown mixed greens tossed with pumpkin seeds and slices of poached pear, drizzled with a Gorgonzola and cranberry vinaigrette. After savoring the salmon and prawn cakes accompanied by watercress mayo and crispy leeks, who needs dessert? As overseen by hosts Harald and Lynda Manson, service here is understated and cheerily attentive. *$$; MC, V; checks only; dinner every day, brunch Sun; full bar; reservations recommended; lmanson@netidea.com; north lakeshore.*

LODGINGS

Emory House / ★

811 VERNON ST, NELSON; 250/352-7007

A pretty cottage at the north edge of downtown, the Emory House is perfectly situated for those who want to explore Nelson on foot. Arts and Crafts fans appreciate the beautifully preserved hardwood floors, woodwork, and built-in dining buffet. Opt for rooms that overlook the lake. (Two rooms have private baths; two rooms share one.) Because owner Mark Giffin (who shares responsibility with co-owner Janeen Mather) is a chef, breakfast is an event that might include a banana-walnut Belgian waffle, or an omelet with Gouda, sun-dried tomatoes, and herbs and edible flowers from the garden. *$$; MC, V; checks OK; emorybnb@kootenay.net; www.bbcanada.com/189.html; north end of Vernon St.*

Inn the Garden / ★

408 VICTORIA ST, NELSON; 250/352-3226 OR 800/596-2337

This bed-and-breakfast is where many Nelson residents book their out-of-town guests: high praise indeed. Toronto ex-pats Lynda Stevens and Jerry Van Veen bought this Victorian home, only a block from Main Street, and decorated it in a garden theme. Each room is named for a tree. Fir is the smallest and the only one with a private bath (the downside is that it adjoins the noisy bathroom shared by the other four rooms on the second floor). North-facing rooms enjoy views of Nelson's waterfront. Upstairs, the Tamarack Suite occupies the third floor. Complete with a small kitchen, sitting room, and bath, it's roomy enough for two couples to share. The best deal is the adjacent three-bedroom bungalow. Although the terraced grounds are landscaped, the bungalow's flower-festooned backyard is tops. Stevens stocks the bungalow kitchen for breakfasts but leaves the rest of the meals for guests to arrange. If you run low on her homemade granola or fresh-baked muffins, hop next door to the main house to replenish the larder. Ask about special rates on Whitewater lift tickets. *$$–$$$; AE, MC, V; checks OK; www.innthegarden.com; 1 block south of Baker St.*

Willow Point Lodge / ★★

2211 TAYLOR DR, NELSON; 250/825-9411 OR 800/949-2211

You'll feel quite welcome in Anni Muhlegg's rambling, three-story 1920 Edwardian home perched on a hill amid 3 ½ spacious acres. The living room features a large stone fireplace; breakfast is served in the sumptuous dining room or on the open deck in summer. Of the six guest rooms, the spacious Green Room is tops: it sports a large, private, covered balcony looking out toward the Selkirk Mountains and Kootenay Lake. All rooms feature private baths. Over the past several years the already parklike setting has been further enhanced with the planting of hundreds of perennials. Enjoy the garden from the cool of a newly built gazebo. A walking trail leads from the house to three nearby waterfalls, the farthest being a pleasant 30-minute stroll. In winter, Whitewater ski packages are available. After a day in the powder, a soak in Willow Point's large outdoor spa is guaranteed to soothe aches and pains. Note: The lodge fills quickly in summer; reserve well in advance. *$$–$$$; MC, V; local checks only; willowpl@uniserve.com; www.pixsell.bc.ca/bcbbd/4/4000193. htm; 2 ½ miles (4 km) north of Nelson.* &

Kimberley

On the west side of the broad Columbia Valley in the Selkirk Mountains lies the mining town of Kimberley. Like many foundering mining towns in the 1970s, Kimberley looked to tourism and—like Leavenworth, Washington—chose a Bavarian theme to bolster its economy. Accordion music is played on loudspeakers at the center of the Bavarian Platzl (the town's three-block walking street). For a quarter, a yodeling puppet pops out of the upper window of Canada's largest cuckoo clock. With so many Bavarian-themed restaurants in one place, competition among chefs is of Wagnerian proportions. If you're shopping for some goodies for your picnic lunch (or dinner at your condo), head for **KIMBERLEY SAUSAGE AND MEATS** (360 Wallinger Ave; 250/427-7766); they also sell fish.

With the town's largest employer, Cominco, set to close its zinc mine here, Kimberley will become an increasingly attractive place to play. **KIMBERLEY ALPINE RESORT** (Gerry Sorenson Wy; 250/427-4881, 250/427-7332 ski info, or 800/258-7669; kimberley@skilouise.com; www.skikimberley.com) west of town has nearly 50 downhill runs and features some of the longest night-lit runs in North America, with 2,300 feet of vertical drop, 1,750 acres of skiable terrain, and seven lifts. There are 18 miles (30 km) of Nordic trails, some of which are also lighted at night. A frenzy of nonstop construction currently characterizes the resort, where a Marriot hotel anchors the new resort base.

At 3,650 feet (1,113 m), Kimberley is the highest incorporated city in Canada. From this height, views of the snowcapped Rockies are stunning. The **HERITAGE MUSEUM** (105 Spokane St; 250/427-7510) has an excellent display of the town's mining history and memorabilia. Gardeners shouldn't miss the teahouse, greenhouse, and immaculately kept **COMINCO GARDENS** (306 3rd Ave; 250/427-2293), once maintained by Cominco and now by the city, on the grounds of the Kimberley District Hospital. A footpath leads from the Platzl to the gardens.

RESTAURANTS

The Old Bauernhaus Bavarian Restaurant / ★
289 NORTON AVE, KIMBERLEY; 250/427-5133
Tony and Ingrid Schwarzenberger, who built the House Alpenglow (see review), brought a 360-year-old Bavarian farmhouse to Kimberley and reassembled it. As in the Alpenglow, wood is *everywhere*. In a town where Bavarian flavor is as heavy as Sacher torte, this is the genuine article. You'll feel as if you've stepped through a time warp. Heidi and her grandfather might just as easily be sitting at one of the hand-carved tables. The menu reflects the Schwarzenbergers' Swiss-German background: wiener schnitzel, raclette, *maultaschen* (ravioli stuffed with spinach and ricotta), spicy Debracziner sausage, apfelstrudel, and homemade ice cream. In winter, the rough-hewn but artfully arranged wood-plank walls ooze warmth. In summer, mountain breezes whisper among the tall sunflowers in the brightly hued garden, where patio tables are set. *$$–$$$; MC, V; local checks only; dinner every day (closed 2 weeks Nov and Apr); full bar; reservations recommended; luis@ cyberlink.bc.ca; left off Gerry Sorenson Wy.* &

LODGINGS

House Alpenglow / ★
3 ALPENGLOW CT, KIMBERLEY; 250/427-0273 OR 877/257-3645

 Do yourself a favor: book one of the four rooms at House Alpenglow. Rooms at this bed-and-breakfast are spacious, quiet, and lovingly furnished. The wooden ambience is everywhere, even the ceilings. All rooms feature king-size beds; two have en suite baths. Room 3 has a private entrance to the outdoor hot tub and yard. (In this forested setting, guests are apt to find themselves sharing the yard with foraging wildlife, such as deer or bears.) Breakfast is included, and shows that Merna Abel loves to cook. Smells of fresh croissants and muffins fill the morning air, enticing guests from bed. Abel's jams and jellies sweeten the feast. After a plateful of bratwurst and cheese on homemade pumpernickel or rye bread, you may not need to eat again until supper.

Halfway between downtown Kimberley and Kimberley Alpine Resort, Alpenglow is several minutes downhill from the ski and hiking trails. If you're not inclined to drive to town for dinner, the Old Bauernhaus Bavarian Restaurant (see review) is across the street. *$–$$; no credit cards; checks OK; alpenglo@rockies.net; www.kimberleybc.net/alpenglow; west side of Gerry Sorenson Wy, near Trickle Creek Golf Course.* & *(summer only)*

Inn West/Kirkwood Inn / ★

840 NORTH STAR DR, KIMBERLEY; 250/427-7616 OR 800/663-4755

 Three miles (5 km) uphill from Kimberley, adjacent to the ski and summer resort, is the Inn West/Kirkwood Inn. Guests can choose one- or two-bedroom hotel rooms (Inn West) or condominium suites (Kirkwood Inn). The fully equipped condos have full kitchens, gas fireplaces, and Jacuzzi tubs, as well as access to laundry facilities and sauna, hot tub, and heated swimming pool (seasonal). Skylights ensure that high-ceiling condos are brightly lit. Each has a balcony with barbecue. Hotel rooms are smaller versions of the condos and include similar amenities, such as gas fireplaces, balconies, and barbecues. The newly renovated facility is clean and quiet. In winter, guests can step out of their rooms onto the Kimberley Nordic Club trails, or walk a short block to the lifts. Either way, ski to your door. Specially priced ski packages are available. Note: Reserve well in advance for early July, when the annual International Old-time Accordion Festival is in full swing, and for the last two weeks in February, when university students from BC and Alberta flock to Kimberley during their "reading week" break. *$$–$$$; AE, MC, V; no checks; inn@cyberlink.bc.ca; www.innwestkirkwood.com; next to lodge at Kimberley Alpine Resort.* &

Fernie

The craggy cleft of the Lizard Range above **FERNIE ALPINE RESORT** (Ski Area Rd; 250/423-4655, 250/423-3555 snow report, or 800/258-7669; info@skifernie.com; www.skifernie.com) is often likened to an open catcher's mitt. Sheer limestone faces tower above the ski lifts, trapping snow-laden storms and making Fernie, along with Whitewater and Powder King near Prince George, a must-ski on BC's powder circuit. The ski area rises visibly about 3 miles (5 km) from Main Street, where you can see the massive bowls. Trails on the lower mountain cut through dense forest.

In the late 1990s, the resort underwent the largest expansion of any winter resort in North America. It doubled the size of its terrain with the addition of two new lifts for a total of eight and, in 1999, the finishing touches were put on seven new lodges. It has 2,800 feet of vertical drop and 2,500 acres of skiable terrain. Then again, prime parking at the bottom of the slopes is reserved for people who arrive in RVs from small towns across the prairies, the backbone of the resort's clientele. With them in mind, Fernie provides a spiffy changing room, complete with showers. And don't be intimidated by the size of the parking lot or the distance to the lifts; visitors and equipment are transported in horsedrawn sleighs, exactly the special touch that defines BC's small-town winter resorts.

An elegant stone courthouse presides over the major changes occurring here, though Fernie (population 5,000) is more a rough-and-tumble mining and logging town than a ski resort. Après-ski action gets pretty wild at the **GRIZZLY BAR** in the day lodge (Ski Area Rd; 250/423-4655), especially when the powder hounds start howling. The 1992 Olympic gold medalist Kerrin Lee-Gartner brings respectability to Fernie, where she relocated in 1999 from Calgary to construct Snowcreek Lodge. Visitors are as likely to cross paths with the downhiller and her young family at the local coffee shop, **OUR CAPPUCCINO CORNER** (502 2nd Ave; 250/423-4224), as they are on the slopes.

LODGINGS

Griz Inn / ★

SKI AREA RD, FERNIE; 250/423-9221 OR 800/661-0118

 When the Griz Inn opened in 1983, it signaled the beginning of a new era in tourism at Fernie Snow Valley, which had been primarily the preserve of locals. For the next 15 years, the Griz and the lodge across the way, the Wolf Den, provided the only overnight accommodations at the base of the lifts. Beginning in 2000, visitors can consider a sweeping list of new lodges and condos, though none outperforms the Griz's prime location. Guests enjoy second-to-none views of the mountains and trails from private balconies. Built with families in mind, the largest suites sleep 12-16 in a combination of bedrooms, lofts, and pullout couches. All suites have full kitchens, and are clean and bright. The Griz features a large indoor pool and two outdoor hot tubs. The inn's Powder Horn Restaurant serves early morning breakfasts through late-night snacks. *$$; AE, MC, V; checks OK; closed briefly in late spring, early fall; reservations@grizinn.com; www.grizzinn.com; off Hwy 3 west of Fernie.* &

Fairmont Hot Springs

Fernie is not the only winter destination in the BC Rockies. North of Fernie and Kimberley on Highway 95, Fairmont Hot Springs Resort has quietly accommodated both soakers and skiers since the 1920s with what is arguably the biggest outdoor thermal pool and one of the chilliest ski hills in the province. Be sure not to miss the view from the switchback road above the resort of the Columbia Valley to the Selkirk and Bugaboo Mountains, including the beginning of the 1,200-mile (2,000-km) Columbia River. Viewpoints in the east Kootenays don't come any better than this.

LODGINGS

Fairmont Hot Springs Resort / ★★★

FAIRMONT HOT SPRINGS; 250/345-6311 OR 800/663-4979

Even without the hot springs, Fairmont Hot Springs Resort would smell like a rose. (In contrast to many other thermal springs, Fairmont's are odorless and sulphur-free.) In summer, wild perfumes from the pine forest intermingle with those from beds of marigolds and petunias lining the walkways. Attention to detail is astonishing, and it shows in the frequent use of blond wood. All appointments have been thoughtfully chosen and blended to harmonious perfection. Archival photographs adorn the walls, reminding guests that they are partaking in a centuries-old tradition; it just wasn't this comfortable back then. Many rooms come with kitchens that, when not in use, are hidden from view by folding wooden doors. A dining area adjoins twin queen beds. Each room has a private balcony or patio with cottage-era lounge chairs, perfect for relaxing after a long soak. The Olympic-size hot-springs pool lies below. Rooms 492, 494, and 496 are the most private of the ground-floor rooms. The resort has a full-service dining room, coffee shop, and lounge. *$$$–$$$$; AE, DC, DIS, MC, V; no checks; info@fairmontresort.com; www.fairmontresort.com; turn east off Hwy 93/95.* &

Radium Hot Springs

Radium Hot Springs (Hwy 93, 2 miles/3 km from Radium Junction; 250/347-9485) makes an ideal soaking stop at the base of the Kootenay Range. The hot springs, open to the public year-round, are equipped with two pools: one heated, the other cooler for swimming. Unlike some hot springs, these waters are free of odorous sulphur. Water temperatures vary with the seasons; in spring the snowmelt cools the thermal springs. Those staying in Kootenay or Banff National Parks overnight must stop at the park entrance and pay a fee. (Bring the receipt to the hot springs; a fee is charged in addition to the entrance fee for those not staying in the park.) Nearby is golfing, lodging, tennis, and camping.

For an added experience, explore the section of Highway 93 that runs northeast from Radium Hot Springs into KOOTENAY NATIONAL PARK (250/347-9505). Some of the best viewpoints in the East Kootenays are dotted along here. Standouts include Kootenay Valley Viewpoint, about 9 miles (15 km) east of Radium Hot Springs; Hector Gorge Viewpoint, at 29 miles (46 km); and the Continental Divide, about 60 miles (95 km) away at the Alberta border.

PANORAMA RESORT (250/342-6941 or 800/663-2929; info@panorama resort.com; www.panoramaresort.com), west of Invermere and north of Fairmont Hot Springs, has 4,000 feet of vertical drop, 2,000 acres of skiable terrain, and 10 lifts.

LODGINGS

Radium Resort / ★★

**8100 GOLF COURSE RD, RADIUM HOT SPRINGS; 250/347-9311
OR 800/667-6444**

Golf is the show at this resort: nearly all rooms look onto fairways or greens of two 18-hole golf courses. Nongolfers can play tennis, squash, or racquetball—or relax on balconies or the patio outside the indoor swimming pool. Some of the 118 guest rooms are two-bedroom condominiums. Standard rooms are in separate buildings connected by covered walkways. The best lodgings of the lot—condos or "villas"—are a vigorous walk from the full-service dining room; the resort also offers a bed-and-breakfast package in winter, when many restaurants in nearby Radium are closed. Golf and ski packages are also available. *$$$; AE, DC, E, JCB, MC, V; checks OK; sales@springsresort.bc.ca; www.springsresort.bc.ca; south of Radium on Hwy 93.* &

Trans-Canada Highway and the National Parks

Field

You can't go much farther east of Field and still be in British Columbia. Field is the modest commercial hub, as it were, of **YOHO NATIONAL PARK**. Auberges and hostels, popular with hikers set to explore the backcountry, line the town's main street. With adjacent **BANFF, JASPER,** and **KOOTENAY NATIONAL PARKS,** Yoho is part of a vast Rocky Mountain wilderness. Field is also where Canadian Pacific Railway trains pause on their journey through the mountains. There's extensive hiking along almost 250 miles (400 km) of trails in Yoho, a park characterized by rock walls and waterfalls. Many trails begin beside or near Highway 1—it runs for 30 miles (48 km) through the park. The highway parallels the Kicking Horse River as it winds through a beautiful, broad valley, but by the time Highway 1 reaches the park's headquarters in Field, about 18.5 miles (30 km) from its west gate, the tone of the landscape shifts to one of glaciated peaks. For more information, call the **YOHO INFORMATION CENTRE** (250/343-6783) or **PARK ADMINISTRATION** (311 Stephen Ave; 250/343-6324). A park pass (800/748-7275; $25 annual, $9 for four days, or $4 daily) is required for all visitors to national parks, and is available at the gates or by phone with a credit card. Permits are good in national parks throughout Canada.

LODGINGS

Emerald Lake Lodge / ★★★

BOX 10, FIELD; 250/343-6321 OR 800/663-6336

Emerald Lake Lodge was one of a string of hotels built by the Canadian Pacific Railway 100 years ago. When it opened in 1902, it was considered the CPR's crowning jewel. After falling on hard times, the lodge was restored to elegance in 1986 by the owners of Deer Lodge in Lake Louise, and Buffalo Mountain Lodge in Banff, Alberta. On a 13-acre peninsula that overlooks aptly named Emerald Lake, the lodge features 85 spacious rooms spread among 24 chalet-style buildings. Rooms feature twig chairs and duvet-covered beds in front of fieldstone fireplaces. Private decks open onto the lake and Presidential Range peaks. Note, however, that some cabins are less than soundproof. Built of massive hand-hewn timbers and birch, the main lodge houses a grand salon with two towering fireplaces, a formal glassed-off dining room, and the Kicking Horse Bar, furnished with 1890 oak saloon fixtures brought from Canada's Yukon Territory. Upstairs, a majestic, green-felt billiards table occupies center stage in the games room. Guests gather year-round for meals in the formal Mount Burgess dining room. In summer, casual fare is served at Cilantro on the Lake, an airy bistro adjacent to the boathouse. Stop for afternoon tea on the main lodge's veranda. *$$$–$$$$; AE, DC, MC, V; no checks; info@crmr.com; www.crmr.com; 6 miles (10 km) south of Hwy 1.* &

Golden

LODGINGS

Hillside Lodge and Chalets / ★★

1740 SEWARD FRONTAGE RD, GOLDEN; 250/344-7281

A century ago, the Canadian Pacific Railway constructed several Alps-style chalets in Golden to house Swiss mountain guides, who escorted CPR lodge guests into Glacier National Park to the west. More recently, Hubert and Sonja Baier built similar cabins for guests in search of a tranquil Rocky Mountain retreat. Five cabins (a two-bedroom and four one-bedrooms) and a main lodge with four en suite rooms are nestled beside the Blaeberry River on a benchland above the Columbia River Valley. Each brightly lit, fresh-smelling cabin is furnished with a wood-burning fireplace and hand-crafted Bavarian furniture. Views stretch out to forever on all sides. Guests share the 60-acre property with both wildlife and the docile llamas that the Baiers raise. Breakfast is included, and is served in the main lodge beside a cheery hearth in winter, and on the sun porch in summer. Fresh-baked goodies with homemade jams, muesli (Alpine granola), cold cuts, and cheese fortify guests for exploring. Dinner is available by prior arrangement. The charming Baiers are willing to make arrangements for horseback riding, snowshoeing, tobogganing, or cross-country skiing. *$$; MC, V; no checks; hillside@rockies.net; www.mistaya.com/hillside; 8 miles (13 km) west of Golden.*

Revelstoke

Revelstoke, 350 miles (565 km) east of Vancouver, and nestled beside **MOUNT REVELSTOKE NATIONAL PARK** (250/837-7500), is a railway town with a blend of Anglo, Italian, and Dutch residents. It's a great place to break up a trip, taking time to unwind beside the Columbia River, or make it your base for exploring Mount Revelstoke, Glacier, and Yoho National Parks to the east. The town is also just the right size for a stroll through well-tended neighborhood streets; pick up a self-guided heritage walking-and-driving tour brochure from the **REVELSTOKE CHAMBER OF COMMERCE** (204 Campbell Ave; 250/837-5345; corev@ junction.net; www.revelstokecc.bc.ca). Steep-pitched metal roofs confirm the area's heavy snowfall, as does the **CANADIAN AVALANCHE CENTRE** (300 1st St W; 250/837-2435 or 800/667-1105; www.avalanche.ca) downtown, a font of information and a "must-see" for backcountry snow trekkers.

In summer, drive the 15 ½-mile (25-km) **MEADOW IN THE SKY PARKWAY** to the highest elevation of any road in Canada and a view of surrounding ice-fields: nothing beats the scenic drive from Revelstoke east to the information center at the top of Rogers Pass in **GLACIER NATIONAL PARK** (250/837-7500). As the road climbs toward Rogers Pass, a series of roadside pullouts lead to viewpoints. Short interpretive trails, such as the Skunk Cabbage and the Giant Cedars, are sheltered by thick forest. A constant roar rises from the Illecillewaet River. At the information center, a unique sod-roofed building features a fascinating pictorial display that documents the history of mountaineering at Glacier Lodge. Tucked between the Monashee and Selkirk Mountains, this is one of the most scenic locales in the province.

RESTAURANTS

The 112 / ★★

112 1ST ST E, REVELSTOKE; 250/837-2107 OR 888/245-5523

Located in historic downtown Revelstoke's Regent Inn, built in 1931, the 112 is a unanimous favorite among locals. The dining room's cedar-paneled interior and historic ambience would be the pride of any town, but the great food is its biggest drawing card. Chef Peter Mueller specializes in veal dishes, but seafood appetizers such as clams béarnaise, or entrees such as lasagne Florentine with Dungeness crab, seafood cioppino, lamb provençal, or veal Oscar are also highly recommended. The wine list includes some French and Australian labels but emphasizes BC vintners. On Sundays, when the 112 is closed, the Regent Inn's pub menu proffers a mild sampling of the 112's delights. It's solid pub fare—zesty caesar salads, zingy wings, burgers, and a trendy selection of wraps—with a chatty neighborhood flavor. $$$; AE, MC, V; local checks only; lunch Mon–Fri, dinner Mon–Sat; full bar; reservations not necessary; regent@ regentinn.com; at Mackenzie. &

LODGINGS

Four Seasons Manor Bed and Breakfast / ★★

815 MACKENZIE AVE, REVELSTOKE; 250/837-2616 OR 877/837-2616

This imposing 17-room Victorian is easily the grandest residence in Revelstoke, and proprietors Susan Akhurst and Bob Restal opened it as a bed-and-breakfast in June 1999. A low granite stone wall surrounds the mansion's spacious lawns, bordered by a formal garden. An ornately carved wooden staircase, affixed with art nouveau lamp standards, leads guests upstairs. Quiet prevails. Two of the three spacious guest rooms are fitted with classic claw-footed iron tubs the size of subcompact cars (the third suite has a modern bath). Each room is appropriately named for its view. The Mackenzie overlooks the nearby ski hill on that mountain, while the prospect from the Begbie's leaded-glass windows is of a nearby glacier. Four tiled and mantled fireplaces impart a cozy air to high-ceilinged rooms on the first two floors, including the dining room, where a large gourmet breakfast is served. Expect fresh fruit, muffins, and scones, followed by a choice of eggs Benedict, sausages with baked apple croissant, Belgian waffles, or blueberry-banana pancakes. If this doesn't suit you, make a request. *$$; MC, V; checks OK; fourseasonsmanor@cablelan.net; www.revelstokecc.bc.ca/vacation/4seasonsbb; 6 blocks south of 1st.* ♿

Mulvehill Creek Wilderness Inn / ★★★

4200 HWY 23 S, REVELSTOKE; 250/837-8649 OR 877/837-8649

Revelstoke has dubbed Connie and René Hueppi "the happy Hueppis." This dynamic Swiss couple have created a remarkable wilderness inn, a 20-minute drive south of Revelstoke. The inn, with batten-and-board construction and a small tower room, is nestled in a tranquil, brightly lit clearing. The rambling ranch house structure holds eight suites (a half-suite is available for children), each painstakingly furnished with original wildlife artwork and painted in soft shades. The Otter's Burrow is the largest, with private deck and Jacuzzi, perfect for honeymooners. An extensively planted garden contains a large heated outdoor pool, hot tub, trampoline, and playground. A buffet breakfast offers homemade jams and jellies, fresh bread and muffins, fruit salad, egg dishes courtesy of the inn's chickens, and fresh cheese and local produce from Salmon Arm to the west. In winter, guests can snowshoe, toboggan, or cross-country ski an extensive trail network on nearby Mount McPherson. In summer, two donkeys (Simba and Daisy) stand by to carry picnics to a nearby lake, where guests can canoe and fish. By arrangement, Connie will prepare your catch. Otherwise, dinner in the inn's spacious dining room includes raclette, fondue, and other Swiss specialties. (Breakfast is included, but dinner is extra and requires a day's notice.) Reservations are a must, June through August. *$$–$$$; AE, MC, V; checks OK; mulvehil@junction.net; www.mulvehillcreek.com; 12 miles (19 km) south of Revelstoke.*

NORTHERN
MAINLAND
BRITISH
COLUMBIA

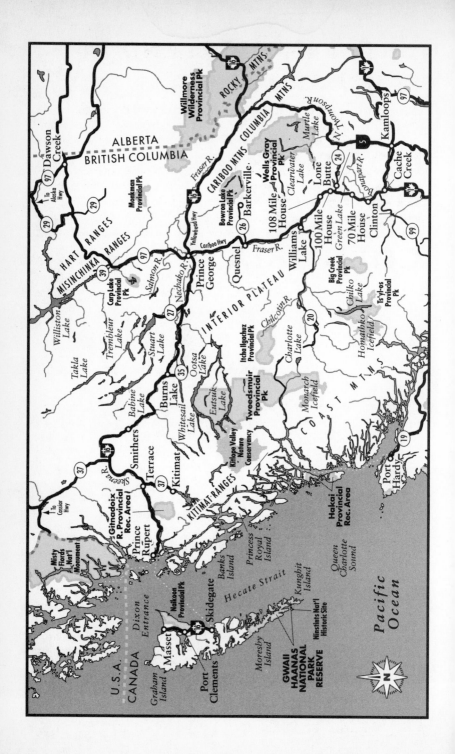

NORTHERN MAINLAND BRITISH COLUMBIA

From the rain-forested Central Coast to the northeastern Rockies, northern British Columbia is a vast swath of underpopulated wilderness. Like most Canadian provinces, BC is bottom heavy, with much of its population tucked away in the southwest corner of the province.

Northern BC is a land steeped in history. Legendary explorer Alexander Mackenzie walked this way in 1793, becoming the first European to cross North America by land. Routes through the region follow centuries-old Native trading trails, or those of more recent Gold Rush and Telegraph Trails. Evidence from the days of the stampeders persists in places such as the roadhouses at Hat Creek, 108 Mile House, and Cottonwood Creek.

The heart of central BC is the vast Interior Plateau, a land of lakes of all sizes. This is fishing country, but also a land of long, cold winters and short, hot summers. In winter, the temperature can drop below minus 20°F (-30°C) for weeks on end. In summer, clouds of insects swarm in early evening. If you plan to travel in this area, know your enemies and come prepared.

Finding the best restaurant or lodging in the most northerly parts of BC is a simple task: if they're open, they must be doing something right. This is particularly true along the Alaska Highway (Hwy 97) and the Stewart-Cassiar Highway (Hwy 37).

ACCESS AND INFORMATION

The highways that run through northern BC, which remains for the most part undeveloped and sparsely populated, are Highways 16, 37, and 97. The latter is the main access road to the region from southern BC. Many towns along Highway 97 are helpfully referred to by distance from Lillooet (mile 0) north along the Gold Rush Trail that preceded construction of the Cariboo Highway. Thus 70-Mile House, for example, marks the distance between Lillooet and this point, the original site of a pioneer roadhouse. From Dawson Creek—mile 0 on the Alaska Highway—Highway 97 winds north and northwest to Watson Lake on the BC-Yukon border, via Fort St. John and Fort Nelson (just over 700 miles/1,140 km).

PRINCE GEORGE AIRPORT (4141 Airport Rd, Prince George; 250/963-2400; www.airport.pg.bc.ca) is home base to NT Air (800/963-9611), Westjet (800/538-5696), Central Mountain Air (800/663-3721), Canadian Regional Airlines (250/963-8481 or 800/665-1177), and Air BC/Air Canada (250/561-2905 or 888/247-2262). Canadian Regional Airlines also takes passengers from Vancouver to Sandspit on Moresby Island in the Queen Charlottes. **HARBOUR AIR SEAPLANES** (604/278-9897) flies from Prince Rupert to Moresby. Air BC, Central Mountain Air, and Canadian Regional Airlines link southern BC with Terrace and Smithers, on Highway 16 near Kitwanga.

BC RAIL'S CARIBOO PROSPECTOR (604/984-5246 in Vancouver or 800/339-8752 provincewide) makes three north-south runs weekly between North Vancouver and Prince George. **VIA RAIL'S SKEENA** (800/561-8630) provides east-west service from Jasper, Alberta, to Smithers and Prince Rupert.

BC FERRIES (250/669-1211; www.bcferries.bc.ca) takes travelers from Prince Rupert to Skidegate Landing on Graham Island in the Queen Charlotte Islands and to Port Hardy on Vancouver Island to the south. The **ALASKA MARINE HIGHWAY** (800/642-0066; www.dot.state.ak.us) links Prince Rupert with Skagway in Alaska to the north and Bellingham, Washington, to the south.

The Cariboo Highway

Clinton

Clinton (population 900) anchors the exotically colored Bonaparte River Valley at mile 47 on the historic Gold Rush Trail, 270 miles (450 km) north of Vancouver. From here north, the route leads out of the Coast Mountains and onto the open Fraser Plateau. History is the frontier trading post's strong suit. Framed by wrought iron and pine, the **PIONEER MEMORIAL CEMETERY** (east side of Hwy 97) at the north end of town presents an apt gateway to northern BC. Times were a lot rougher in years past, as a quick scan of old photos mounted in the **CARIBOO LODGE RESORT** (250/459-7992) attests.

At the town's annual **MAY BALL RODEO** (250/459-2261), raffia-festooned horses and floats parade along the Cariboo Highway to the Clinton fairground, where chuckwagon drivers and saddle bronc riders hold sway. Rodeo time kicks off with the Ball and Tea, the longest continually held event in British Columbia (more than 130 years). For more information on Clinton, self-styled "guest ranch capital of BC," contact the mayor's office (306 Lebourdais Ave; 250/459-2261); it's that kind of place.

LODGINGS

Echo Valley Ranch Resort / ★★★☆

BOX 16, JESMOND; 250/459-2386 OR 800/253-8831

Falcons and eagles soar at Echo Valley, the Cariboo's premier guest ranch. After vacationing at nearby Big Bar Ranch, Norm and Nan Dove raised the bar when they bought the adjacent property. In 2000, construction of a new East-meets-West wellness center completed a complex of six imposing peeled-log cabins and lodges artfully positioned on an open shoulder of land above Cripple Creek. The Marble Range mountains spread off to the north. A hay barn shelters mountain bike and tack rooms, a greenhouse, a handful of pioneer chinked-log Chilcotin outbuildings, a horse paddock and cattle pen, plus an aviary with resident peregrine and gyrfalcons. A black-topped runway parallels the entrance road, an in-line skater's dream.

NORTHERN MAINLAND BC THREE-DAY TOUR

DAY ONE: Start your day in **Prince Rupert** with a walk through downtown. Begin at the Visitor Information Centre, where a **ceremonial (or totem) pole** featuring an eagle sets the tone. At the **Museum of Northern British Columbia**, learn about interpretations of carving styles throughout the Northwest Coast, then visit the **Kwinitsa Station Railway Museum**. Have lunch at the **Cow Bay Café**, then tour the harbor and nearby **Dodge Cove** with the Prince Rupert Water Taxi, or rent a kayak or canoe at Sea Sport and go for a paddle. Don't miss the **North Pacific Cannery Village National Historic Site** in nearby Port Edward. In the afternoon, check into **Eagle Bluff Bed & Breakfast** and relax to the sound of the ocean lapping against the wharf. Then it's off to dinner at nearby **Smile's Seafood Cafe**.

DAY TWO: After breakfast at Eagle Bluff, head for the BC Ferry terminal for the crossing to the **Queen Charlotte Islands** (Haida Gwaii). Grab a quick bite for lunch on the ferry, then at Skidegate stop at the **Haida Gwaii Museum**, and look for whales. Head north to Massett. Check in at **Copper Beech House**, where dinner is waiting.

DAY THREE: Breakfast at the Copper Beech House fortifies you for the trip out to nearby Rose Spit in **Naikoon Provincial Park**. Spend the morning exploring its beach and digging for razor clams. After lunch (also at Copper Beech House), drive south to **Tlell**. Spend the afternoon beachcombing in the park before heading to **Queen Charlotte City** for dinner, where you'll have to choose between **Howler's Bistro** or **Oceania**. Afterward, stroll the town's waterfront, then it's off to Skidegate to catch the overnight ferry sailing back to the mainland at Prince Rupert.

Guests stay in the central six-bedroom Dove Lodge, the nine-bedroom Lookout Lodge, two private cabins (with private bedrooms, bathrooms, sitting areas, fireplaces, lofts, and private decks), or one special cabin set aside in a refuge of its own with a four-poster bed, fireplace, romantically furnished sitting area, and private deck with outdoor Jacuzzi under the stars. One caveat: in winter, light sleepers should request rooms elsewhere than Dove Lodge's main floor, where a heating system proves bothersomely loud. Otherwise, it's all here: welcoming ambience, pampering amenities (including full spa and swimming pool), and warm family atmosphere—as well as sumptuous gourmet meals. Dove or one of his pilots fly guests in from Kamloops or pick them up at the BC Rail stop at nearby Kelly Lake. *$$$$; MC, V; no checks; 3-night min Wed–Sun; evranch@uniserve.com; www.evranch.com; on unpaved Big Bar Rd 30 miles (50 km) west of Clinton on Hwy 97.* &

Interlakes District

Detour east off the Cariboo Highway at either 70 Mile or 93 Mile House and you'll be in the Interlakes micro-region. **GREEN LAKE** is the first of hundreds, large and larger, strung between here and the upper Thompson River. For a quick sample, drive the Green Lake scenic loop north from Green Lake to Lone Butte on Highway 24. Each lake boasts at least one guest ranch or fishing camp.

LODGINGS

Crystal Waters Guest Ranch / ★★

HWY 24, BRIDGE LAKE; 250/593-4252

Saddle up with rodeo man Gary Cleveland and spend a day in the saddle roaming 640 acres. Chow down on hearty ranch-raised repast. Budget 2½ hours for dinner, at least. Soak in the unique wood-fired, lakeside hot tub. Cleveland and his wife, Marisa Peters, perfected the art of guest ranching while working at several nearby spreads, including his dad's fishing camp. Here at Crystal Waters, they've distilled the appealing essence of a small guest ranch experience: intimacy and spontaneity. Demonstrate that you can handle a horse, and you're free to roam. (Few guest ranches in the Cariboo offer this alternative to guided rides.) Canoes are available to explore the clear, almost-private Crystal Lake. Five quiet, honey-hued log cabins, two at lakeside, accommodate two to eight guests each (request the Loon's Nest, one of our favorites). Sweet, homey touches abound, such as the omnipresent use of horseshoes for doorhandles and coat hangers, and towel racks shaped from polished tree roots. A firelit guest lodge rebuilt from the old homestead and relocated near lakeside provides a quiet retreat. *$$–$$$; MC, V; checks OK; open Dec–Oct; cwranch@bcadventure.com; www.bcadventure.com/crystal; 3 miles (5 km) southwest of Hwy 24 at Bridge Lake on North Bonaparte Rd.* &

100 Mile House

100 Mile House (population 1,900) is home to February's 50-km, "classic technique" **CARIBOO CROSS-COUNTRY SKI MARATHON**. Arguably the best track-set, cross-country skiing in BC is found on the 120 miles (200 km) of community trails that loop between here and 108 Mile House. For information on cross-country skiing in the Cariboo, contact **GUNNER'S CYCLE & SKI SHOP** (250/791-6212) next to the Best Western in 108 Mile Ranch.

RESTAURANTS

Trails End Restaurant/1871 Lodge / ★★

HWY 97 (THE HILLS HEALTH AND GUEST RANCH), 108 MILE HOUSE; 250/791-5225

You don't have to stay at The Hills to enjoy its two dining facilities. Trails End is located in the main lodge; a more informal dinner is served on weekends in the ranch's new 1871 Lodge. Both dining rooms feature cozy corners with fireplaces. In keeping with the ranch's healthful theme, the Trails End menu includes both generous Cariboo-country selections or lighter spa fare, with the emphasis on seafood, meat, and vegetarian dishes, prepared with a sure and understated hand. Patrons are encouraged to help themselves from baskets of fresh fruit to sustain themselves on outdoor excursions. A Swiss-inspired dinner menu in the 1871 Lodge includes all-you-can-eat fondue, hot-rock steaks cooked at your table, or a nightly chef's special. BC microbrews and wines are highlighted. *$$–$$$; AE, MC, V; checks OK; breakfast, lunch, dinner Mon–Sun, brunch Sun; full bar; reservations required (dinner); the-hills@bcinternet.com; www.spabbc.com; east side of Hwy 97 just north of main intersection.* &

LODGINGS

The Hills Health and Guest Ranch / ★★★

HWY 97, 108 MILE HOUSE; 250/791-5225

Since 1985, Pat and Juanita Corbett's Hills Health and Guest Ranch has epitomized the essence of the Cariboo region: hardworking, free-spirited, family-centered, health-oriented. Recipients of three International Specialty Spa of the Year Awards, the Hills shows the Corbetts' personal touch, including Juanita's fondness for images of roosters, apparent everywhere. Guests can choose hotel-style rooms in either the Ranch House or Manor House Lodge (breakfast included), or private self-contained chalets that sleep six. Lodge rooms are outfitted with twin beds, rocking chairs, and floral touches. Best views are from Manor House rooms (odd-numbered 31–47) that overlook the ranch's private ski and snowboard hill. Chalets 1–4 also overlook the hill with ski-in/ski-out potential. Caution: A rope tow, which operates until 9pm, deposits skiers beside chalet 5. The faux-log chalets are more simply furnished than lodge rooms and have complete kitchens and large decks with gas barbecues, and are pet friendly. Main attractions are the large spa and fitness center, including heated swimming pool, saunas, and hydrotherapy pools. Hundreds of kilometers of cross-country ski trails lace the woods. Tie on your skates on the pond beside Willy's Wigwam, a cozy environment for warming hands and feet. In summer, twice-daily guided hikes are offered, and a rack of mountain bikes is at guests' disposal, as well as a corral of patient horses. *$$–$$$; AE, MC, V; checks OK; thehills@bcinternet.com; www.spabbc.com; east side of Hwy 97 just north of main intersection.* &

The Wolf Den Country Inn / ★

CANIM LAKE RD, FOREST GROVE; 250/397-2108 OR 877/397-2108

After stints in Banff, Alberta, and eastern BC's Columbia Valley, Chantelle and Jamie Ross retreated to Forest Grove in 1992 to establish a country inn and outdoor adventure center. Their rambling log rancher on 160 acres has four guest rooms, each with its own floor-to-ceiling window that overlooks Bridge Creek. Snuggle on the Pendleton blanket–draped couches; a stone fireplace blazes in the private guest living room. An outdoor hot tub on the broad deck is open to the stars. Purebred Siberian huskies sit kenneled in the 20-acre pasture below the inn. Exceptionally quiet, the dogs are clean and great with children. The Rosses offer intimate (six-person max) dogsledding adventures in winter, or guided horseback and canoe outings in summer. The Wolf Den specializes in women's and kids' groups. Stay the night just to wake up to one of Chantelle's farm-fresh breakfasts. She also takes requests for gourmet lunches or dinners. *$–$$; MC, V; checks OK; wolfden@ bcinternet.net; www.dogsled-canada.com; 19 miles (30 km) east of Hwy 97 at 100 Mile House.*

Barkerville Historic Town

Historic Barkerville is a satisfying blend of authentic, well-preserved heritage storefronts and restored homes in a wilderness setting tucked high in the Cariboo Mountains. At the height of the Cariboo Gold Rush, it was the largest city west of Chicago and north of San Francisco. As testament to this, nearly 100 of the homes, stores, and workshops that remain are open for viewing—14 of them, such as the post office, are still operational. More than 40 pre–1900 buildings line the streets, most mounted on raised foundations to dodge the annual spring flooding of nearby Williams Creek.

Barkerville is located east of Quesnel and Highway 97 at the northern terminus of the Gold Rush Trail. Highway 26 winds and climbs past viewpoints with historical connections to the Gold Rush of the 1860s. The **QUESNEL VISITOR INFO CENTRE** (Le Bourdais Park, 705 Carson Ave, Quesnel; 250/992-8716 or 800/992-4922) stocks brochures on various points of interest.

Prince George

The largest city in the BC interior, Prince George (population 78,000), "City of Bridges," is the crossroad of rivers, railroads, and highways. The mighty Fraser and Nechako Rivers blend near old **FORT GEORGE** (south end of 20th Ave), now a municipal park; get information from **FRASER–FORT GEORGE REGIONAL MUSEUM** (333 Gorse St; 250/562-1612). Walk or bike the park's riverside pathways to sense the site's importance in the destiny of the region. The Lheit-Lit'en Nation knew this place as Thle-et-leh, meaning "the confluence." Highway 16 leads east to the Rockies and west to Prince Rupert; Highway 97 leads north to Dawson Creek and the Alaska Highway. Whichever direction you're headed, there's not much to keep you in this mill town: a municipal pool, art gallery, and park are downtown.

LODGINGS

Coast Inn of the North

770 BRUNSWICK ST, PRINCE GEORGE; 250/563-0121 OR 800/663-1144

 Generally speaking, Coast Hotels throughout the province set an admirable standard for comfort. The Inn of the North is a case in point. No matter where you've come from, you've most likely spent more than a few hours getting here. By now, you're ready for a rewarding evening where you can do as little or as much as you like. The 150-room inn is a refuge where you can walk around in your slippers while you decide which of three in-house restaurants—Irish, English, or Japanese—to favor. Best bets are the corner rooms, spacious premium suites that are a touch roomier than the standard quaint but well-appointed rooms. The sauna and heated pool are especially welcome in winter, a long season in the Cariboo. (With this in mind, plug-in heaters are provided in the secured parking area; your car's engine will thank you.) The Coast's pet program provides a bed and groceries for Fido, considered "one of the family" by staff. When it comes time to walk the dog, Fort George Park is only a five-minute drive away. *$$$; MC, V; checks OK; j.douglas@coasthotels.com; www.coasthotels.com; Hwy 97 north to 15th Ave, east on 15th to Victoria, north on Victoria to 10th Ave, east on 10th Ave to Brunswick.* &

The Northwest Coast

Prince Rupert

Most days in Prince Rupert, BC's northernmost port, if you can see the ocean, it's going to rain; if you can't see it, it's raining. On the upside, there are lots of interesting things to do *indoors* in Prince Rupert. Don't miss the **MUSEUM OF NORTHERN BRITISH COLUMBIA** (1st Ave E and McBride; 250/624-3207). Under its cedar-shaked, copper-flashed roof sits one of the province's finest collections of Native art. A local artist may be creating a piece while you're here, such as a ceremonial apron woven from mountain-goat hair. From the museum, an elevated walkway leads to the waterfront and the **KWINITSA STATION RAILWAY MUSEUM** (north end of Bill Murray Dr in Waterfront Park; 250/627-0938).

Prince Rupert is home to one of the best collections of **CEREMONIAL (TOTEM) POLES** on the West Coast, and you'll find more of the traditionally carved poles (in Tsimshian or Haida style) at City Hall (424 3rd Ave W), the Civic Centre (1000 McBride St), Moose Tot Park (6th and McBride), and Totem Park (Summit Ave). If it's not raining, walk up to Roosevelt Park (Summit Ave) for one of the best views of downtown and the inner harbor. You can tour the harbor and nearby **DODGE COVE** with the **PRINCE RUPERT WATER TAXI** (Cow Bay; 250/624-3337), or rent a kayak or canoe at **SEA SPORT** (295 1st Ave E; 250/624-5337) or **ECOTREK KAYAKS** (203 Cow Bay Rd; 250/624-8311), in a boathouse on the wharf. A good spot to warm up afterward is the **COW BAY CAFÉ** (205 Cow Bay Rd; 250/624-1212). Or try the **SHRIMP GUY**, a town fixture (on 3rd Ave) who sells fresh seafood right off the back of his truck.

Just south of town in Port Edward is the **NORTH PACIFIC CANNERY VILLAGE NATIONAL HISTORIC SITE** (1889 Skeena Dr, 7 miles/11 km southwest of

Hwy 16; 250/628-3538; open May 15–Sept 15). Until the 1970s, it employed as many as 1,500 workers. Boardwalks link offices, stores, cafes, and homes with the West Coast's oldest standing cannery, perched on the banks at the mouth of the mighty Skeena River.

RESTAURANTS

Smile's Seafood Cafe / ★

131 COW BAY RD, PRINCE RUPERT; 250/624-3072

Most days, the fish-packing plant at Cow Bay may be idle, but the spirit of the 1920s lives on at Smile's. Tucked demurely beside the railway, Smile's and the neighboring electrical supply store, Love Electric, set the mood here. Fresh shrimp, Dungeness crab, halibut, and black cod are often accompanied by home-cut french fries in jackets. Ask your server for tips on picking up fresh seafood for a picnic. *$$; MC, V; no checks; breakfast, lunch, dinner every day (open Feb–Dec); full bar; reservations not necessary; 2 blocks east of McBride on 3rd Ave to Cow Bay Rd.*

LODGINGS

Eagle Bluff Bed & Breakfast / ★

201 COW BAY RD, PRINCE RUPERT; 250/627-4955 OR 800/833-1550

The ocean laps beneath the pilings at Eagle Bluff, a gem of a place to stay on Cow Bay. Five of six rustically elegant rooms are in a restored former marine store. Fireplaces in two of the rooms (Captain's Quarters and the Heron Room) impart warmth and a feeling of well-being, no matter what's brewing outdoors. Atop the main house, also home to owners Mary Allen and Brian Cox, is a two-bedroom suite, ideal for families. Breakfast specialties include smoked salmon, eggs Benedict, fresh fruit salad, and Mary's own muffins—or just about anything else you request. Rent a kayak and paddle off for the day, then tuck in with a hot cup of tea while eagles, osprey, herons, and gulls swirl overhead. *$–$$; MC, V; no checks; eaglebed@citytel.net; www.citytel.net/ eaglebluff; 1 block west of Hwy 16 on the harbor.* &

Queen Charlotte Islands/Haida Gwaii

These islands are arguably one of the most beautiful and diverse landscapes in the world. Sometimes called Canada's Galapagos, they are home to a distinctive ecosystem and people, the Haida First Nation. The older, Haida name for this place comes from the mists of time and seems to be most appropriate: Xhaaidlagha Gwaayaai, "Islands at the Boundary of the World."

The Charlottes sit about 60 miles (100 km) off the mainland, and are made up of about 150 islands. Two large islands, Graham to the north and Moresby to the south, comprise the majority of the land mass. Most of **MORESBY ISLAND** is inaccessible except via logging road, chartered boat, sea kayak, floatplane, or on foot. Many visitors come to see the abandoned villages on Moresby in **SOUTH MORESBY/GWAII HAANAS NATIONAL PARK RESERVE** (250/559-8188).

TOUR OF THE TOTEMS

One of the most unique scenic drives in BC leads around a well-marked circuit in the Hazelton Valley called the **Trail of the Totems.** The **Hazelton InfoCentre** (on Hwy 16; 250/842-6071) has information on the self-guided Tour of the Totems as well as the Hands of History Tour.

First stop is just north of Highway 16 on Highway 37 in the village of **Kitwanga**, one of several locations in the Hazelton region where ceremonial poles are situated. A dozen poles face the Skeena River beside a century-old wooden bell tower and church. The weathered poles are carved with an array of animal and humanlike images.

The more than 20 poles in the small village of **Kitwancool**, about 12 miles (20 km) north along Highway 37, are reputed to be the oldest and finest examples of such poles. These include a trio of newly fashioned ones. All 20 are intricately carved and thought provoking. Little people crowd together on some poles like townsfolk on the exterior of a medieval European cathedral. Some of the tallest poles have been left uncarved on top and are surmounted by figures of raven, bear, eagle, wolf, or humans. Nearby, a shed houses some of the oldest poles, weathered almost beyond recognition, with just an eye or a beak to suggest the original design. A freshly cut log often lies beside the shed, awaiting its turn. (Note: The Gitanyow have placed a ban on taking photographs or video recording of their poles. Please respect their wishes.)

Return to Highway 16 and travel east, to stop next at **Kitseguecla**, a small Skeena River settlement near Hazelton. There are two wonderfully unique poles here; large sculptures grace the front yards of several homes in the community.

Just north of Hazelton on a paved side road, pull into the **ëKsan Historical Village** (Box 326, Hazelton; 250/842-5544) to see its rich display of totems, jewelry, and clothing. A museum in one of the longhouses honors the Gitksan ancestors who beautified the items they carved for everyday use. Seven lovingly decorated longhouses are grouped at the confluence of the Skeena and Bulkley Rivers, and several are open to visitors at no charge. Guided tours are offered of the Fireweed, Wolf, and Frog Clan houses for a small fee.

Continuing north, the **Kispiox** ceremonial poles are the most animated, with carved tears dripping from eyes of inlaid abalone. The 18 poles here have the appearance of being held in the palm of the Creator. The views of the Skeena River from here are staggering. Kispiox is built on high ground, about 18 miles (30 km) north of Hazelton on the side road.

—Jack Christie

GRAHAM ISLAND is served by BC Ferries; the ferry terminal is at **SKIDE-GATE**. Just north of the terminal is the **HAIDA GWAII MUSEUM** (at Qay'llnagaay, east of Hwy 16 at Second Beach; 250/559-4643); whale spotting is almost guaranteed here. Just west of Skidegate is **QUEEN CHARLOTTE CITY,** with a serene waterfront; take it all in at **HOWLER'S BISTRO** (2600 3rd Ave; 250/559-8602), where lunch draws a cheerful crowd and dinners are candlelit and cozy, accented by strains from a jukebox, and **OCEANA CHINESE & CONTINENTAL RESTAURANT** (3119 3rd Ave; 250/559-8683), where the name says it all.

From Skidegate, Highway 16 goes north to **TLELL** and **MASSET**, at the southern and northern ends, respectively, of **NAIKOON PROVINCIAL PARK** (250/557-4390), which lies to the east of the highway on the shores of Hecate Strait. At the long, hard-packed beach at Rose Spit, you can dig for razor clams; from the top of Tow Hill, you can look north through the ocean mist toward Southeast Alaska.

For information on all aspects of a visit to the Queen Charlottes, contact the **VISITOR INFORMATION CENTRE** (3220 Wharf St; 250/559-8316). Though there are few roads on the islands and distances are not great, consider taking your vehicle, particularly in the off season (Oct–May). Otherwise, travel as a foot passenger on BC Ferries to Skidegate on Graham Island, or arrive by plane at nearby Sandspit on Moresby Island. A small ferry based in Queen Charlotte City connects the two.

LODGINGS

Copper Beech House / ★★★

1590 DELKATLAH ST, MASSET; 250/626-5441

Situated above the beach at Masset Inlet, this 1914 red-shingled gem has been stewarded by proprietor David Phillips's steady hand since 1986. Much like the surrounding rain forest, the garden is as tangled as the web of memorabilia and rare collectibles that Phillips has amassed under his roof. Guests can choose from a spacious upstairs suite with private bath, two suites on the main floor with a shared bath, or two suites on the garden level, including the intimate Harbour Master's Keep. Meals are included in the remarkably reasonable room rates at this full-service inn. Phillips's menus take full advantage of the fresh fare offered up by the North Pacific waters (crab and eulachon pâté, for example), the surrounding forests (wild venison), and his own rambling garden (peach and tomato soup). Copper Beech's sensual ambience is abetted by the host's penchant for candlelit dinners. Phillip's connections within the Haida community garner introductions to artists and guides for guests. Bicycles are provided, and Phillips can always rustle up a couple of kayaks. *$$–$$$; MC, V; checks OK; info@copperbeechhouse.com; www.copperbeechhouse.com; beside federal dock in Masset harbor.* &

Index

We Stand By Our Reviews

Sasquatch Books is proud of *Best Places Northwest*. Our editors and contributors go to great lengths and expense to see that all of the restaurant and lodging reviews are as accurate, up-to-date, and honest as possible. If we have disappointed you, please accept our apologies; however, if a recommendation in this 13th edition of *Best Places Northwest* has seriously misled you, Sasquatch Books would like to refund your purchase price. To receive your refund:

1. Tell us where and when you purchased your book and return the book and the book-purchase receipt to the address below.
2. Enclose the original restaurant or lodging receipt from the establishment in question, including date of visit.
3. Write a full explanation of your stay or meal and how *Best Places Northwest* misled you.
4. Include your name, address, and phone number.

Refund is valid only while this 13th edition of *Best Places Northwest* is in print. If the ownership, management, or chef has changed since publication, Sasquatch Books cannot be held responsible. Tax and postage on the returned book is your responsibility. Please allow six to eight weeks for processing.

Please address to Satisfaction Guaranteed, *Best Places Northwest*, and send to:
Sasquatch Books
615 Second Avenue, Suite 260
Seattle, WA 98104

Best Places Northwest Report Form

Based on my personal experience, I wish to nominate the following restaurant, place of lodging, shop, nightclub, sight, or other as a "Best Place"; or confirm/correct/disagree with the current review.

_____

_____

_____

_____

(Please include address and telephone number of establishment, if convenient.)

REPORT

Please describe food, service, style, comfort, value, date of visit, and other aspects of your experience; continue on another piece of paper if necessary.

_____

_____

_____

_____

_____

_____

_____

I am not concerned, directly or indirectly, with the management or ownership of this establishment.

_____

SIGNED

_____

ADDRESS

_____

_____

PHONE   **DATE**

Please address to Best Places Northwest and send to:
SASQUATCH BOOKS
615 SECOND AVENUE, SUITE 260
SEATTLE, WA 98104
Feel free to email feedback as well: **BOOKS@SASQUATCHBOOKS.COM**